EYEWITNESS HISTORY

The 1990s

Richard A. Schwartz

Facts On File
An imprint of Infobase Publishing

To Ileana, whose love and support have
nurtured me throughout this project.
And to Arielle,
whose youthful enthusiasm is an inspiration.

The 1990s

Copyright © 2006 by Richard A. Schwartz
Maps and graphs copyright © 2006 by Infobase Publishing

Facts On File, Inc.
An imprint of Infobase Publishing
132 West 31st Street
New York NY 10001

Library of Congress Cataloging-in-Publication Data
Schwartz, Richard Alan, 1951–
       The 1990s / Richard A. Schwartz.
         p. cm.
       Includes bibliographical references and index.
       ISBN 0-8160-5696-X (alk. paper)
       1. United States—History—1969—Juvenile literature. 2. United States—Politics and government—1993–2001—Juvenile literature. 3. United States—Politics and government—1989–1993—Juvenile literature. 4. Nineteen nineties—Juvenile literature. I. Title. II. Series.
      E885.S38 2006
      900.82'9—dc22   2004028884

You can find Facts On File on the World Wide Web at
http://www.factsonfile.com

Text design by Joan M. Toro
Cover design by Cathy Rincon
Maps and graphs by Dale Williams

Printed in the United States of America

VB JT 10 9 8 7 6 5 4 3 2 1

This book is printed on acid-free paper.

CONTENTS

INTRODUCTION

The first decade since the end of World War II to be dominated by a single superpower—the United States—instead of by cold war rivalry between heavily armed, ideologically hostile nuclear powers, the 1990s introduced a still-evolving new world order in which America's major political goals, alliances, and principles were redefined in many important arenas. Internationally, the abrupt resolution of the cold war coincided with a rise in factionalism, as the Soviet Union splintered into separate, competing republics; Serbs, Croats, and Bosnians fought over portions of Yugoslavia; civil war broke out in Somalia and continued in Angola and Afghanistan; racial violence surged in Germany; Jews faced increasing anti-Semitism in France; Hindus and Muslims fought in India; Hutu and Tutsi slaughtered one another in Rwanda; the Irish Republican Army and Basque separatists exploded bombs in urban centers in Northern Ireland, England, and Spain; and religious fundamentalists denounced Western-style secularism throughout the globe, especially in the Islamic-dominated countries in Asia and the Middle East, but also in the Jewish state of Israel, predominantly Hindu India, and even the Christianity-dominated United States.

These and other conflicts resulted in deadly violence that cumulatively drove tens of millions of people from their home and killed millions more. Many were slaughtered outright in the fighting, but many others died of starvation, exposure, disease, and other conditions that emanated from warfare. According to studies by the United Nations, some 90 percent of the wars' casualties were civilians, the majority of whom were women and children. During the 1990s, more than 2 million children were killed, 4 million were physically mutilated, and another million were orphaned or separated from their families.[1]

Despite this general tendency toward fragmentation and divisiveness, when Iraq, a former Soviet client state, invaded and annexed oil-rich Kuwait and thereby asserted its claim to be taken seriously as a world superpower, the United States assembled an international coalition that, under U.S. military and political leadership, crushed the highly touted Iraqi army. The 1991 Persian Gulf War, which demonstrated the efficiency, effectiveness, and overwhelming power of America's high-tech, professional military services, made clear to the world that the United States would not tolerate challenges to the status quo that might undermine its national security, whether by military or economic means. It further demonstrated the extent to which technological advances achieved during the 1980s had overwhelmingly made the United States the premier military power in the world. In particular, new stealth technology enabled U.S. bombers to approach their targets undetected; precision-guided munitions allowed them to strike the targets with unprecedented accuracy; and global-reach capabilities enabled planes to depart from and return to bases in the United States while flying missions anywhere in the world. The only nation to enjoy all of these capabilities, the United States, which spent more money on defense than all other nations combined, remained the dominant military power throughout the decade.

America's essential identity nonetheless transformed throughout the 1990s, as it has done throughout the country's history. In particular, the decade saw significant changes not only in the nation's demographic makeup, but also in mainstream values and generally accepted practices and beliefs. This evolution led both to greater institutional tolerance of cultural diversity and to increased friction caused by competing ways of life. That friction often provoked expressions of outrage—some of them violent—by those whose demographic advantages were diminishing or whose values and belief systems were threatened by changes in the evolving cultural climate.

The 2000 census showed that during the 1990s the U.S. population grew by the largest amount ever measured. Reversing a three-decade decline in the rate of growth, the total population grew by 13.2 percent, to more than 281,000,000—an increase of 32.7 million from the population counted in 1990. Much of the growth was attributed to new births; during the 1990s, the birth rate averaged two children per adult woman, which was higher than the national death rate. Immigration, especially from Asia, the Caribbean, Central America, and South America, also contributed to the increase. Within America, the existing trend of migration to the South and West continued. Led by Nevada and other so-called Sun Belt regions, all 50 states experienced population growth. At the end of the decade metropolitan New York City, with almost 21.2 million inhabitants, remained the largest urban center, as it had been in 1990. It was followed by Los Angeles (16.4 million), Chicago (9.2 million), Washington, D.C. (7.6 million), and San Francisco (7 million). But a decades-long trend of "white flight" from the inner cities continued, as, by 2000, non-Hispanic whites accounted for less than 50 percent of the inhabitants in 48 of the 100 largest cities, and, overall, the white population grew by only 5 percent in the fastest-growing cities, compared to 23 percent for African Americans, 69 percent for Asians, and 72 percent for Hispanics. Overall, the Hispanic population grew by some 58 percent to 35.3 million, an increase of almost 13 million from the beginning of the decade. As a result, for the first time ever Hispanics were more numerous than black Americans (34.7 million), who previously had constituted the nation's most populous minority. Although the population of white non-Hispanics grew by 5.9 percent to 211 million and they still constituted a large majority of the overall population, by the end of the decade they accounted for only 75 percent of the nation's inhabitants, compared to 76 percent in 1990 and 80 percent in 1980. The number of multiracial inhabitants also grew, as people who identified themselves as white and "other" represented the largest combination. The census also showed an increase of illegal aliens living in the United States, possibly as many as 11 million, or one of every 25 residents.[2]

The clashing of cultures in a changing population, along with the persistence of other long-standing social and political divisions, fueled the fires of factionalism in North American society. Separatists gained power in Quebec by demanding withdrawal from the Commonwealth after the failure of more moderate factions to amend Canada's constitution in order to create a separate status for the French-speaking province. Existing rivalries likewise intensified within the United States, including conflicts between political liberals and conservatives, the wealthy and the nonwealthy, labor and management, antiabortion and pro-choice activists, gun-control advocates and the National Rifle Association, religious fundamentalists and secular hedonists, environmentalists and industrialists, and proponents and opponents of expanded rights for—or diminished restrictions upon—women, homosexuals, African Americans, Hispanics, and other ethnic minorities. Even the heartwarming story of the rescue at sea of Elián Gonzales, a little Cuban boy whose mother drowned in November 1999 trying to take him to the United States, became a controversy of international proportions when federal agents raided the home of Elián's Miami relatives in order to return him to his father in Cuba—and to life under a totalitarian Communist regime. Devastating race riots broke out in Los Angeles and elsewhere in response to apparently egregious acts of racism, while, on the other hand, vocal neo-Nazi separatist groups such as the Aryan Nations declared the formation of new, independent countries within U.S. territory, to be governed by principles of white supremacy. White supremacists were also responsible for bombing a federal building in Oklahoma City; and Eric Robert Rudolph, an outspoken opponent of abortion with ties to white supremacist groups, was charged with bombing abortion clinics and a gay nightclub and with detonating a bomb in Atlanta during the 1996 Summer Olympics. Islamic fundamentalists bombed, but failed to destroy, New York's World Trade Center and plotted unsuccessfully to destroy other public targets in the New York City region.

In response partly to the nation's changing demographic characteristics and partly to a growing awareness of the destructive nature of factionalism, schools and universities showed greater sensitivity to multiculturalism by studying the experiences of groups whose viewpoints traditionally had been underrepresented in the curriculum, especially in accounts of American history and surveys of American literature. However, even the practice of multiculturalism sometimes fueled divisiveness, as the inclusion of minority figures inevitably required the exclusion of respected Anglo-American personalities from high school and college courses that did not have time to cover everyone. Consequently, the process of deciding whom to include and whom to omit from the curriculum became an inherently political act centering around race, gender, sexual preference, and ethnicity. At its best, multiculturalism broadened points of view, inspired a spirit of sympathy and compassion among divergent groups, and bred deeper, more fully nuanced cross-cultural and cross-gender understandings. But at its worst, it spawned intellectually stifling practices of "political correctness," or "PC," which pitted women and minorities against white men and tolerated only viewpoints that regarded women and minorities as victims of white-male-dominated social and economic forces. Although political correctness sometimes drew much-needed attention to long-neglected inequities and injustices, when practiced carelessly or abusively it tended to stereotype white men and Anglos as exploiters and women and ethnic minorities as their victims, thereby, in the words of Leonard Quart and Albert Auster, contributing to "the sacralization of victimhood in the nineties."[3] In this respect, political correctness further contributed to the spirit of divisiveness permeating the nation, even as it also ameliorated it.

Although the reasons for the collapse of the Soviet Union are still debated, its implosion meant that, after more than 50 years of cold war struggle, consumer capitalism had prevailed over state-run communism, and Western democracy had triumphed over totalitarian rule. The demise of the Soviet Union allowed the rapid spread of capitalism to Eastern European countries that had previously been subject to Communist domination. Even the cold war bastions of communism—China, Russia, and other countries that had made up the Soviet Union before its dissolution on December 31, 1991—quickly adopted their own version of a market economy, and the paradigm of a truly global economy began to emerge for the first time.

Of course, as in any economic shift, there were winners and losers in the global economy, and throughout the world and within the United States increasingly strong protests arose against the prospect of economic domination by multinational corporations that were viewed as unfriendly to labor, local industries, and the environment. Nonetheless, the trend toward a global economy remained strong, and regional trade, in particular, was encouraged by such treaties as the 1992 Maastricht Agreement, which formed the European Union; the agreement in 1991 among Brazil, Argentina, Uruguay, and Paraguay to form the Southern Cone Common Market (Mercosur) in South America; and the 1992 North American Free Trade Agreement (NAFTA) among Canada, Mexico, and the United States, which eliminated most trade restrictions within North America.

The progression toward a global economy has been linked to the triumph of corporate capitalism. Coinciding with the rise of consumerism and mass media during the second half of the 20th century, corporate capitalism flourished in the 1980s during the presidency of Ronald Reagan, who promoted corporation-friendly policies of deregulation and reduced taxes. It continued to flourish during the 1990s, despite a troubled economy in the first part of the decade that cost President George Herbert Walker Bush reelection in 1992. Bill Clinton, Bush's successor, also promoted corporate capitalism by winning congressional approval of the NAFTA agreement, balancing the federal budget, permitting mergers among large corporations, and pursuing fast-track approval for other international trade treaties. Although a Democrat with moderately liberal sensibilities, Clinton withstood opposition from some of his natural constituency, such as labor unions fearful of competition from low-paid workers in other nations and environmentalists who believed that international trade agreements would weaken U.S. regulations that protected air quality and natural resources.

Nonetheless, Clinton enjoyed a robust economy during his presidency, and he easily won reelection in 1996 by adhering to his 1992 campaign theme, "It's the economy, Stupid." In 1993, when he took office, the Dow-Jones average industrial index peaked at 3,799; by the time he departed office in 2001, it had topped 11,000. Nonprofit organizations, which played a significant role in shaping politics and addressing social needs, also flourished, as 42 percent of foundations that had accumulated $1 million or more in assets by 2003 were formed during the 1990s.[4] The growth in company-sponsored tax-deferred individual retirement accounts (IRAs) and other tax-deferred annuities and investment plans meant that a much larger portion of the public had savings invested in the stock market than ever before, and consequently, the success on Wall Street of the large corporations was shared by many working Americans.

The substantial increase in their investments led most Americans to discount another trend, alarming to some, that showed a rapidly growing division between the very wealthy and the rest of America. Between 1989 and 1999, the number of billionaires in the United States rose from 66 to 268, while the number of Americans living below the poverty line increased from 31.5 million to 34.5 million.[5] By 2000, 1.1 percent of the total personal income in the United States had been earned by just the wealthiest 400 taxpayers, more than double what the top 400 had accounted for in 1992 (0.5 percent). According to the Internal Revenue Service (IRS), the wealthiest 400 income earners garnered an average of $174 million in 2000, almost a fourfold increase from $46.8 million in 1992. Moreover, their relative share of taxes declined from a peak of 29.9 percent of their income in 1995, and 26.4 percent in 1992, to 22.3 percent in 2000. The reduction in their tax burden has been attributed to reduced tax rates on capital gains and increased donations to charity. Despite the decline in the percentage of income paid in taxes, the wealthiest 400, having earned substantially greater incomes, nonetheless paid more in taxes and assumed a larger proportion of the nation's tax burden by the end of the decade, paying 1.6 percent of all taxes in 2000, compared to 1.1 percent in 1992, with an average tax bill of $38.6 million. The IRS also reported that the number of Americans who had an annual income above $200,000 who paid no taxes at all rose from 37 in 1977 to 2,022 in 2000.[6]

In addition to salutary fiscal policies in the United States and Canada, the North American economy benefited from new technologies that were useful and appealing to businesses and consumers alike. Computer and telecommunications technologies, in particular, experienced enormous growth, in part due to such legislation as the Telecommunications Act of 1996, whose stated purpose was to promote competition, reduce regulation, and promote rapid development of new technology. In 1990, 25.4 percent of American households had at least one personal computer; by 1999, that figure was closer to 60 percent.[7] Moreover, a growing number of those without a home computer took advantage of free access in public facilities such as schools, universities, and libraries. Steady decreases in cost that were matched by steady increases in quality, capacity, and graphic and multimedia capabilities fueled the growth of personally owned computers. Moreover, the development in 1992 of the World Wide Web (also called the Internet, or simply the Web) undoubtedly attracted vast numbers of North Americans otherwise indifferent to or intimidated by computer technology. Although Internet connections to specific databases and to interactive computer bulletin boards had been available prior to 1992, the World Wide Web for the first time made individual documents universally available throughout the world, and it enabled users to move directly from one document to another document residing in an entirely different database, in an entirely different location. Moreover, high-speed search engines made each document, or Web page, readily accessible for reference.

Since its introduction to the public, the Web has played an increasingly important role in the cultures not only of the United States and Canada, but of all the technologically advanced nations of the world. In 1993, there were only 50 Web sites worldwide; by 2000, there were more than 50 million,[8] and throughout the 1990s, the Web transformed the ways people accessed information, conducted business, shared personal information, and otherwise interacted as members of society. Dubbed the information superhighway, the Internet was touted by politicians and investors as the technology of the future, and a general belief grew throughout society that it would soon revolutionize business, education, and home life. This expectation was energized by the pronouncements of politicians and business leaders, widespread media coverage, and the growing practice of "surfing the Web" to sample who and what were suddenly accessible in cyberspace. Electronic mail (e-mail) enabled friends to stay in touch easily, and instant messaging allowed people to send text messages back and forth in real time. Schools, corporations, and private citizens rushed to become "wired" into the Web, and many investors tried to get in on the ground floor by purchasing stock in start-up companies that proposed to sell goods and offer services via the Internet. Although many failed to live up to their expectations, these dotcoms—so called because of the *.com* suffix on their Internet addresses—became hot commodities in the mid-nineties, and many young, Internet-savvy entrepreneurs became millionaires overnight after their stock's initial public offering (IPO). Regions that could draw upon the graduates of some of the nation's best research universities flourished throughout much of the decade, especially California's so-called Silicon Valley between San Jose and Palo Alto, North Carolina's Research Triangle in the Raleigh-Durham area, and Greater Boston. Subsequently, the economies of these Internet-dependent areas were hit especially hard when the dotcom bubble burst at the end of the decade, following the failure of the Internet to meet the great expectations for profits.

But if the Internet did not generate the level of income anticipated by Wall Street, it quickly began to fulfill expectations that it would change society. Along with the advent of pocket-sized cellular telephones (cell phones), high-speed modems, enormous computer memory capacities made possible by ever-more-powerful microchips, Internet-equipped laptop computers, recordable compact computer disks (CDs), digital still cameras, video cameras, Web cameras, and other media devices, the Internet, for the first time in history, enabled businesses and average citizens throughout the world to communicate among themselves conveniently and inexpensively, with minimal government oversight. And in an era that was becoming increasingly dependent on computer technology, the Internet offered almost immediate transfer of digital information.

The most truly democratic international forum humanity has ever known, the Internet created an open, easily accessible, largely uncensored worldwide marketplace of ideas, as well as a marketplace for goods and services. As such, it was a double-edged sword that could both facilitate and undermine cooperation, goodwill, and the cultivation of common goals among individuals and communities. The Internet promoted greater regional, national, and global awareness among average citizens by encouraging personal communication among people of disparate nationalities, ethnicities, and socioeconomic groups. Anybody who believed he or she had a special insight into any topic of concern could now immediately publish that insight to the world, and the Internet accommodated information, analyses, and calls to action from a broad range of conflicting political viewpoints that were not commonly represented in the mainstream media. Moreover, cybermarkets such as e-Bay made it possible for private citizens throughout the world to barter and conduct individual transactions, as well as for small local businesses to advertise their services to an international clientele. Internet dating services and interest groups united people from diverse locations and backgrounds who shared common interests—not the least of which was sex, as attested by the proliferation of pornographic sites throughout the Web.

But the Internet provided no quality control on the accuracy of the information contained in Web sites or in the chains of e-mail that could assert any unsupported allegation or outright lie as undeniable fact and quickly spread it among millions of people throughout the world. The Internet gave an international platform to neo-Nazis, white supremacists, black supremacists, Islamic fundamentalists bent on *jihad,* or holy war, and other hate groups or hateful individuals who sometimes urged violent action against whole groups of people. It published instructions for making homemade bombs and other destructive devices, and it became an outlet for child pornography. Users could easily obtain anonymous e-mail accounts, a service that was useful to criminals, terrorists, and promulgators of unwanted e-mail advertisements ("spam," the cyber equivalent of junk mail), as well as to millions of legitimate users. The Internet offered new opportunities for grassroots democracy by giving forums to marginal candidates ignored by the mainstream media, and it enabled special interest groups across the political spectrum to organize mass campaigns to lobby politicians and regulators. But it did not hold anyone accountable for the truthfulness or completeness of the viewpoints expressed or the facts cited. E-mail made it easy for friends and relatives to stay in touch, but an e-mail etiquette quickly evolved. It favored short notes and missives that often truncated sentences and discouraged thorough discussions or deeply developed sentiments and ideas. Moreover, the emergence of destructive computer viruses that spread via e-mail attachments interjected an element of danger and suspicion into cyberspace.

Perhaps because the decade was so marked by extreme social, political, and even religious divisiveness, the U.S. presidents were typically regarded as moderates within their own party, and had to endure condemnation from both their own party's political extremes and the opposition. George Bush, a Republican who held office from January 1989 to January 1993, was often criticized by social conservatives for failure to advocate their agenda more strongly. Although he was more in step with fiscal conservatives and corporate interests, he alienated many of those when a failing economy in 1990 compelled him to renege on his 1988 campaign pledge that he would not raise taxes. Nonetheless, Bush's diplomatic skills as a coalition builder during the Persian Gulf War enabled him to achieve a nearly unanimous consensus among the bitterly fractious international community that Iraq's annexation of Kuwait could not be permitted to stand. And his success as a wartime president united the partisan American citizenry behind him, briefly making him the most popular American president since World War II, before the stagnant economy undermined his support.

When Bill Clinton, a Democrat, took office in January 1993, Democrats also controlled the Congress, and Clinton promoted an agenda designed to appeal to the more liberal wing of his party. In addition to appointing an unprecedented number of women, African Americans, and Hispanic Americans to top-level positions in order to make the government leadership "look more like America," Clinton submitted national health care legislation and tried to take executive action to permit homosexuals to serve in the armed forces. However, after both of these efforts failed and Republicans took control of Congress in 1994, Clinton moved closer to America's political center. In fact, when he reformed the welfare system and eliminated the federal deficit, some Republicans accused him of succeeding by appropriating their agenda.

Although Clinton failed to achieve his goal of providing humanitarian relief by intervening militarily to allow supplies to be delivered to civilians during Somalia's civil war in 1993, he won early success as an international power broker when he oversaw the negotiations that eventually resulted in a peace accord between Israel and the Palestine Liberation Organization (PLO). His threat in 1994 of military intervention in Haiti, coupled with last-minute diplomacy by former president Jimmy Carter, peacefully deposed a military junta and restored the democratically elected president Jean-Bertrand Aristide to power. Perhaps chastened by his experience in Somalia, Clinton declined to intervene in the genocide in Rwanda, a decision he later regretted. But he oversaw the diplomacy that ended the civil war in Bosnia, later obtained a commitment by the North Atlantic Treaty Organization (NATO) to halt Serbian atrocities in Kosovo, and authorized a brief but successful air war in 1999, which culminated in the ouster of Serbia's president, Slobodan Milošević, who was subsequently arrested for war crimes. Clinton also signed a 1994 pact in which North Korea agreed not to develop nuclear weapons in return for U.S. economic assistance, an agreement that North Korea renounced in 2002.

During Clinton's two terms as president the economy prospered and the country went from a budget deficit to a budget surplus. The nation remained largely at peace; home ownership was at its highest rate in U.S. history; unemployment dropped to its lowest rate in modern times; inflation fell to a 30-year low; the national crime rate dropped; and welfare rolls diminished. Nonetheless, the charismatic Clinton and his assertive liberal wife, Hillary Rodham Clinton, were viciously vilified by many conservatives who disliked him not only for his liberal agenda but also for what they believed were acts of moral misconduct, and who detested her for her aggressive, outspoken style, which represented much of what they found offensive about feminism. Thus, the last six years of Clinton's eight-year presidency were marked by passionately partisan confrontations with a Republican-led Congress, including a 1995 budget showdown in which Clinton prevailed after Republicans shut down the nonessential functions of the government.

Although Hillary Rodham Clinton maintained, perhaps with some legitimacy, that her husband was the target of a "vast right-wing conspiracy" to tarnish him and render him ineffective, ethical lapses in his personal conduct made it easy for his enemies to paint him as an immoral opportunist. Although Clinton was ultimately cleared of wrongdoing in the Whitewater affair, in which he was accused of illegal profiteering in an investment scheme while he was governor of Arkansas, and of other, unrelated charges that the independent counsel, Kenneth Starr, a conservative Republican loosely affiliated with some of Clinton's political enemies,[9] pursued, the repeated allegations undermined his appeal to the public and appeared to give some basis to Republican assertions that Republicans were more moral than Democrats. Among the charges that Starr investigated during his four-year inquiry were the suicide under questionable circumstances of Vincent Foster, a longtime friend of the Clintons; the so-called Travelgate allegations involving the firing of established White House workers; and the so-called Filegate, in which the Federal Bureau of Investigation (FBI) files of some Republicans were found in the White House.

In January 1998, Starr received allegations that Clinton had lied under oath when he claimed in his deposition for Paula Jones's civil lawsuit that he had not had sex with Monica Lewinsky, a former White House intern. After conducting an extensive investigation in which Clinton and Lewinsky were compelled to reveal intimate details about their relationship before a grand jury—testimony later released to the public—Starr accused the president of perjury and obstruction of justice. In December 1998, the Republican-controlled House of Representatives voted to impeach him for committing "high crimes and misdemeanors," as prescribed by the Constitution.

After a widely viewed televised Senate trial, Clinton was acquitted in February 1999. His approval ratings remained high throughout the process leading to the impeachment, and, ironically, his bitterest opponent, Newt Gingrich, resigned from his post as Speaker of the House shortly before the impeachment, after Democratic gains in the 1998 congressional elections suggested that the public objected more to the Republican leader's aggressive partisanship than to Clinton's sexual improprieties. Although he had pilloried Clinton for Whitewater, the Lewinsky affair, and other alleged misdeeds, Gingrich had been involved in questionable financial dealings that also eventually fell under scrutiny, as did his extramarital affair and those of other Republicans who led the attack on Clinton. Thus the impeachment process took a heavy toll on those who prosecuted it.

Nonetheless, the Lewinsky affair diminished Clinton's credibility with the American people, who widely believed that he had, in fact, lied about the liaison, regardless of whether that constituted sufficient grounds for removing him from office. Moreover, the impeachment, only the second in U.S. history, diverted Clinton's attention and resources and diminished his ability to focus the media on his political agenda. The affair thereby undermined his presidency, and the extensive media coverage of his testimony describing intimate sexual acts tarnished the dignity of the office of the president, as it blurred the line between legitimate, mainstream news reporting and lurid sensationalism. Arguably, the perception that Clinton was untrustworthy also provoked Vice President Al Gore to distance himself from the actual achievements of the Clinton presidency, a decision that weakened Gore's ultimately unsuccessful campaign for president in 2000.

Broadly speaking, science and culture were also greatly affected by both major innovations in computer technology and social fragmentation. The field of genetics made an enormous stride with the birth of the sheep Dolly, the first mammal to be born via cloning, rather than by a birth process involving the insemination of an ovum by a sperm. The federally sponsored Genome Project also achieved dramatic results during the decade. Charged in 1990 with identifying the approximately 30,000 genes in human deoxyribonucleic acid (DNA) and determining the sequences of the 3 billion chemical-base pairs that compose human DNA, the Genome Project issued a working draft of the entire human genome sequence in June 2000, well ahead of its initial 15-year schedule. Impressive as these feats were, the notion that humans might soon be able to control and manipulate the very creation and essential nature of life troubled many people, and genetics emerged as a new hotbed of controversy within the society. Proponents of scientific advancement contended with religious leaders and others concerned about the ethical implications of cloning, especially the cloning of human beings, which, after the birth of Dolly, seemed almost inevitable.

Moreover, antiabortion activists opposed using brain stem cells from aborted fetuses for genetic research, because they believed the practice would create an incentive for institutions to promote abortion. On the other hand, proponents of stem-cell research pointed to the potentially great advances in the treatment of many serious, even deadly, diseases that the research could make possible.

Technological and theoretical gains in astronomy and physics were equally impressive, if less controversial. Launched in 1990 into an orbit 375 miles above the Earth, the powerful *Hubble Space Telescope* afforded scientists views of the universe that extend back almost to the beginning of time and that provoked important new theories of cosmology, as well as providing spectacular photographs showing the immense diversity of colors, shapes, and sizes of galaxies and other cosmic phenomena. These images excited astronomers, who regarded the *Hubble* as the greatest boon to astronomy since the invention of the telescope, and they reignited a public interest in outer space that had waned after the manned Moon missions of the late 1960s and early 1970s. In 1991, an American astronomer discovered two planets orbiting a pulsar, or dying star, in the Earth's own Milky Way galaxy—the first sighting in history of planets orbiting a star other than the Sun. A meteorite believed to contain bacterialike life that originated on Mars was discovered on Earth in 1996, and photos from the *Galileo* space probe suggested that liquid water, whose presence is a precondition for carbon-based life, might exist beneath the surface of Europa, one of the moons of Mars. The rapid accumulation of evidence that extraterrestrial life might indeed be more than science fiction excited the public imagination. However, as with cloning, abortion, and other issues related to core beliefs about the nature of life and the appropriateness of interfering with it, even the possibility of life beyond the Earth created divisions among the populace, as some questioned whether the findings inherently contradicted the Bible—and, if they did, what the implications were.

At the other end of the cosmological scale, major gains occurred in subatomic physics, including the discoveries of the top quark, one of the basic particles of matter, and of the megaparticle, a form of matter consisting of a few thousand atoms, which Albert Einstein had predicted decades earlier, and of the fact that neutrinos have mass and may compose the so-called dark matter that, according to theoretical models, accounts for some 90 percent of the universe. Anthropology, chemistry, biology, medicine, meteorology, oceanography, and the other branches of science also enjoyed major discoveries, while comparatively new disciplines such as environmental science came more fully into their own in response to social and political controversies.

Literature, the fine arts, and popular culture also influenced and were influenced by social and political divisions within the society. The National Endowment for the Arts (NEA) fell under attack by conservatives who objected to government funding for artists such as Robert Mapplethorpe, whose sadomasochist and homoerotic photographs they found morally objectionable, pornographic, and even blasphemous. Black male rappers and gangsta artists were condemned for glorifying crime, including the killing of police officers, and for singing lyrics that degraded women and allegedly promulgated violence against them. In 1992, Vice President Dan Quayle condemned Murphy Brown, a popular television character played by Candice Bergen, because Brown chose to conceive a child out of wedlock and to raise it without a father. Viewers also clashed over Ridley Scott's sympathetic cinematic depiction of two women who become criminals after one of them is sexually assaulted in *Thelma & Louise* (1991).

In 1992, the film writer, actor, and director Woody Allen fell from favor among many cosmopolitan liberals—his core audience—after his affair with Soon-Yi Previn, the 19-year-old adopted daughter of the actress Mia Farrow, became public knowledge. Farrow, with whom Allen had long been professionally and romantically involved, subsequently accused him of sexually abusing their seven-year-old adopted daughter, Dylan. Although Allen was cleared of the charge, the scandal upset many of his fans who believed that his betrayal of Farrow contradicted the values of basic decency and sympathy for women projected in his films. Others were disillusioned because the scandal demolished their view of Allen and Farrow as an ideal progressive professional couple who had seemingly proved that it was possible to share love, family, and interesting work but maintain separate lives and separate residences, outside marriage.

O. J. Simpson, another greatly admired icon in the popular culture, fell even further from grace after DNA evidence identified him as the murderer of his wife, Nicole Simpson, and her friend Ronald Goldman in 1994. A handsome, wealthy, charismatic Hall of Fame football star who was also known for his work as a sports commentator, a star of television commercials, and an actor in the popular *Naked Gun* comedy films, Simpson had seemingly demonstrated that an African-American man could reach the pinnacle of 1990s white-dominated American society. Despite the DNA evidence, Simpson was acquitted in 1995 of killing his wife and Goldman, who were white, and the widely covered "trial of the century" fueled arguments over whether the very wealthy have access to a level of justice different from the one available to ordinary citizens. It also revealed strong differences in perceptions about the judicial system, as most nonblack Americans believed the DNA evidence was conclusive, and many black Americans found credible defense claims that Simpson was the victim of racism within the Los Angeles Police Department, which, the defense argued, had corrupted and manipulated evidence during its investigation. The controversy became further muddled after another jury, in a 1997 civil lawsuit, held Simpson responsible for battering Nicole and killing Goldman.

Issues of gender and race commanded the attention of national audiences in best-selling books such as John Gray's *Men Are from Mars, Women Are from Venus* (1992) and Clarissa Pinkola Estés's *Women Who Run with the Wolves* (1992). Another best seller, Richard J. Hernstein and Charles Murray's *The Bell*

Aggressive radio personalities such as Howard Stern (above) and Rush Limbaugh added a hard edge to American politics and culture. *(Photofest)*

Curve: Intelligence and Class Structure in American Life (1994), stirred controversy with research suggesting the existence of innate differences in natural intelligence among the races.

Whereas the popular daytime television talk-show hosts Oprah Winfrey and Rosie O'Donnell sought to foster a spirit of harmony and common humanity, they were largely exceptions, as competitors such as Jerry Springer and Ricki Lake hosted daytime shows in which participants revealed intimate, potentially humiliating secrets and bitterly accused one another before jeering and cheering audiences. The emerging cable television stations sought to tap into the growing market of younger, less traditional viewers by being sexier and more violent than network television and by otherwise presenting material that mainstream audiences often found offensive. Aggressive, highly partisan radio talk show hosts such as Rush Limbaugh and Howard Stern attracted huge nationwide audiences for their radio programs and best-selling books.

Gossip publications, daytime television talk shows, and new programs such as MTV's *The Real World,* which pioneered reality television by monitoring the daily life of young housemates, catered to an element of voyeurism that became increasingly pronounced throughout the decade. The voyeuristic spirit thrived not only in television, film, and fiction but also on the Internet, where Web cameras were used to spy on people in bathrooms, department store changing rooms, and other places considered private.

Related to this strain of voyeurism was a national obsession with celebrity, as average citizens competed to achieve fame by becoming the objects of voyeurism. In addition to people who revealed their body and/or their deepest secrets on national television when given the chance, some Internet users documented intimate details of their life in online journals called blogs and permitted Web surfers to look in on them and their companions via Web cameras, at any time of day, in any room of their dwelling. Certainly the Clinton-Lewinsky scandal appealed to the national preoccupation with both celebrity and voyeurism, and the aspects of the constitutional crisis related to them dominated the popular culture.

The 1990s chronicles North American life during this divisive period in American history. Although it centers on the United States, America did not exist in a vacuum, and significant international events are also treated. After an introductory chapter discussing some key developments from the 1980s, 10 chapters describe each year of the 1990s. Each chapter contains a narrative discussion, an annotated chronology, and a series of eyewitness accounts drawn from political documents, literary works, memoirs of private and public figures, and other sources. Each chapter describes the major political activity, as well as developments in science and technology, business and society, sports, entertainment, and the arts.

1

Prelude to the 1990s
The 1980s

The 1990s, which was dominated by a Democratic president and Republican Congresses, followed a decade dominated by Republican presidents and Democratic Congresses. Republican-formulated fiscal, social, and foreign policies shaped the 1980s, although these were tempered by the Democrats in the House and Senate.

Cold war politics greatly influenced the period. The cold war, which had been largely dormant during the so-called detente of the 1970s, reintensified after the Soviet Union (USSR) invaded Afghanistan in December 1979, an act that threatened U.S. interests and access to oil in the Persian Gulf. In response President Jimmy Carter, a Democrat, withdrew the Strategic Arms Limitation Treaty II (SALT II) from Senate consideration, canceled a major grain sale by the United States to the Soviet Union, and instituted a U.S. boycott of the 1980 Summer Olympics, which were held in Moscow.

With the election of Ronald Reagan in November 1980, the cold war entered its most confrontational stage since the conclusion of the 1962 Cuban missile crisis. Reagan, a conservative Republican, rejected the underlying assumption of detente, that the United States could peacefully coexist with the Soviet Union, which Reagan labeled an "evil empire." Consequently, during his first administration Reagan greatly increased defense spending; called for the creation of an expensive high-tech missile shield to protect North America from a Soviet attack, and adopted an uncompromisingly hard-line stand against the Soviets. However, after Mikhail Gorbachev assumed power in the Soviet Union in 1985, Reagan's position softened, and he negotiated arms limitation treaties with Gorbachev, as Gorbachev introduced internal reforms and new foreign policies that eventually led to the end of the cold war in 1990, and the dissolution of the Soviet Union in 1991. Reagan's supporters credit his hard-line policies with compelling the Soviets to divert enormous resources to their military defense, thereby undermining their domestic economy and eventually causing the 74-year communist experiment to fail. Others argue that the Soviet Union would have collapsed from its own inefficiency and rampant official corruption, regardless of Reagan's actions, and credit Gorbachev more than Reagan for

President Jimmy Carter's last year in office was dominated by the Iran hostage crisis. *(Photofest)*

the peaceful resolution of the cold war and the regime change in the USSR.

There is no dispute that Reagan's hard-line, anticommunist foreign policy and the military buildup that resulted from it shaped the mood of the United States, as well as the economy and domestic policies of the era. Reagan was a very popular president, and his high approval ratings derived in part from his seemingly unshakable belief that in the struggle against worldwide communism there existed clear choices between good and evil, and that the United States was therefore committed to opposing the totalitarian communist regimes for moral reasons, as well as for national security. In this respect, Reagan revived the original 1950s rhetoric that had also framed the cold war as a struggle between good and evil, a viewpoint that, since the failure of the Vietnam War, had been largely replaced by a pragmatic rhetoric of power politics and the widely held belief that peaceful coexistence with the Soviet empire was the best outcome the West could achieve within the context of a nuclear stalemate. The debacles of the 1960s and 1970s—the Vietnam War, the Watergate scandal, egregious abuses by U.S. intelligence agencies, and the seizure of American hostages in Iran—had dampened the national mood and created a pervading sense of pessimism that Reagan sought to reverse by reasserting America's might and its moral high ground. Reagan's campaign theme in 1984 was "It's morning in America," and, for many people, Reagan's assertive confidence and self-righteousness, along with his innate charisma and a growing economy, created a new era of optimism and good feeling.

For a significant minority of Americans, however, Reagan's policies produced despair. To them, his nuclear brinkmanship seemed delusional and suicidal; his hard-line anticommunism appeared overly simplistic and chauvinistic; his willingness to sacrifice social programs for military spending and tax reduction grossly distorted national priorities; and, in this group's view, Reagan's willingness to back repressive right-wing dictatorships abroad and to accept homelessness and a high unemployment rate at home as the price for healthy corporate profits undermined the nation's claim to moral superiority.

Similarly, for some, Reagan's alignment with the Moral Majority and other right-wing Christian groups conferred greater moral stature on the president by making him appear pious and committed to Christian values. But for others, this affiliation diminished his moral authority by linking him to groups they considered self-serving, narrow-minded, and intolerant. Citizens also passionately divided over the morality of Reagan's opposition to legalized abortion, which was perhaps the most divisive social issue of the decade. Reagan's position endeared him to those who regarded abortion as an unconscionable act of murder, but it alienated him from those who maintained that human life begins at birth, not at conception, and that the decision to abort should rest solely with the woman who carries the fetus and assumes the actual risks and consequences of childbirth, and not with the government.

Americans also divided over matters of race, gender, and the environment. American society in the 1980s expressed a strong, conservative backlash to the liberal policies of the 1960s and 1970s that promoted affirmative action, women's rights, homosexuals' rights, and environmental protection. Reagan successfully tapped into the sentiments that fueled this backlash, especially the resentment of white, middle-class, and working-class Americans, particularly men, who believed their rights were being trampled and their interests were being sacrificed in order to promote those of women and minorities. Representing a considerable portion of Reagan's political constituency, these voters, many of them working-class Democrats, believed that far from creating a more idealized society based on meritorious achievement, liberal programs that compensated for past inequities merely promoted mediocre women and minorities to key positions, while creating new inequities against the white male majority.

Reagan's vice president and successor, George Herbert Walker Bush, shared Reagan's basic viewpoint on both foreign affairs and domestic priorities, and he implemented policies consistent with Reagan's after he took office in January 1989. However, Bush lacked Reagan's charisma, and, before the 1991 Persian Gulf War, he failed to inspire the populace or gain its trust to the same degree as Reagan, especially among the Republicans' core base of social conservatives primarily concerned with making abortion illegal once more and promoting their notion of Christian values.

The combination of new wealth and new technologies enabled many North Americans to enjoy glitzy, on-the-go lifestyles that were widely celebrated in the media and by popular culture. By contrast to the Carters, who downplayed the privilege of the presidency, especially during the Iran crisis, when they did not want to appear to be insensitive to the plight of the hostages, the Reagans celebrated themselves and the nation with lavish inaugurations, White House receptions, and other forms of conspicuous consumption, such as the expensive designer dresses that the imperious first lady, Nancy Reagan, was fond of wearing. Through its disco music; flashy nightclubs; sexy fashion models; upscale advertising; international television hits such as *Dallas, Dynasty, Miami Vice,* and *Lifestyles of the Rich and Famous;* and youth-oriented cable stations such as MTV, the United States projected itself to the world as affluent, confident, dynamic, youth-oriented, sexually obsessed, and self-indulgent. Illegal drug trafficking and the violence associated with it became a growing problem throughout the decade, especially after the introduction of crack cocaine, an inexpensive and more highly addictive form of cocaine that became especially popular in poor communities. Although more expensive than crack, powdered cocaine became the drug of choice for many young urban professionals (sometimes known as yuppies) who could afford the illicit narcotic that afforded a rush of energy commensurate with fast-paced life.

Of course, not everyone approved of these values or lifestyles. Leftists denounced the materialistic indulgence of the wealthy at a time when unemployment and homelessness were increasing; feminists condemned the widespread use of sex for marketing purposes as exploitative; and some religious groups feared that the nation's proclivity for instant gratification and its tendency to understand success primarily in material terms undermined core Judeo-Christian values of hard work, humility, piety, and personal integrity.

Some people turned to Bible study, meditation, Eastern philosophies, and other forms of spiritual exploration and self-improvement, and the market for books on these subjects grew substantially, indicating a broadening interest among the general public, whose baby boomers, now "30-something," were entering a more mature phase of their life. The Christian Right, in particular, used television and other media both to promote a return to fundamentalist Christian practices and to denounce the society's sexual permissiveness, its growing tolerance for homosexuality, and its increasing acceptance of changing roles for women that, in contrast to biblical scripture, promoted women's equality with men at the workplace and at home.

Overall, the 1980s in the United States was a decade of great changes in society, business, and government. Pessimism and self-criticism spawned by the Vietnam War and other setbacks of the 1970s yielded to a greater spirit of optimism and self-celebration, as the nation reasserted itself as a military and economic superpower and opportunities abounded for personal growth, self-expression, and development. At the same time, however, conflicts with Islamic militants in the Middle East spawned a worldwide outbreak of terrorism directed against U.S. interests, and renewed cold war tensions between the superpowers rekindled the threat of a devastating nuclear war capable of eradicating all humanity and most other advanced life-forms on the planet.

THE COLD WAR AND OTHER INTERNATIONAL DEVELOPMENTS

The period between the mid-1970s and 1990 is remarkable for the worldwide ascendency of democracies over authoritarian regimes. The military rulers in Western Europe ceded power to elected governments in Greece (1974), Portugal (1976), and Spain (1977), and Turkey's military regime, which had seized power during a national emergency in 1980, restored civilian rule in 1983. Democracy also extended to other parts of the world where its traditions were less deeply rooted. In 1986, the military dictatorship of Ferdinand Marcos fell in the Philippines, and South Korea's military regime stepped down after permitting free elections in 1987. South Africa began moving toward majority rule in 1990, and in Latin America military regimes ceded power to democratically elected governments in Peru (1980), Argentina (1983), Uruguay (1984), Brazil (1985), El Salvador (1984), and Paraguay (1989). Haiti ended nearly 30 years of dictatorship in 1986, when President-for-Life Jean-Claude Duvalier fled to France after political unrest. In 1988, Chile's general Augusto Pinochet, who had assumed power in 1974 in a U.S.-backed coup, lost a constitutionally mandated referendum. He subsequently stepped down in favor of a democratically elected government in 1990, the same year that Nicaragua's Marxist Sandinista government fell from power in a national election. And in December 1989, a U.S. invasion ousted Panama's general Manuel Noriega and installed the winner of the presidential election, whose result Noriega had nullified. Thus, by the early 1990s, Cuba and Guyana were the only nations in the Western Hemisphere that did not have some viable form of democratic government. Moreover, after Soviet premier Mikhail Gorbachev announced in late 1988 that the Soviet Union planned to withdraw its troops from Eastern Europe and would not use its military to sustain the regimes there, the communist dictatorships in the so-called Iron Curtain countries quickly collapsed and were replaced by popularly elected governments. Along with their downfall occurred the conclusion of the cold war and, in 1991, the demise of the Soviet Union itself.

Cold war politics dominated U.S. foreign policy throughout the 1980s, and cold war allegiances, more than the democratic or authoritarian politics of a government, typically determined whether a country was treated as a friend or foe. Early in his presidency, Reagan initiated a number of policies, collectively known as the Reagan Doctrine, that opposed communist regimes and movements worldwide. U.S. support of rebels in Angola, Afghanistan, and Nicaragua, and of the military regime in El Salvador; U.S. intervention in the Lebanese civil war; and U.S. invasion of the Caribbean island of Grenada were applications of the Reagan Doctrine.

In 1981, Reagan approved a secret national security decision document that outlined a plan for prevailing in a protracted nuclear war, and during his first term defense spending increased by 40 percent, as the administration replenished ammunition stocks, funded the mobile MX missile, and reinstated production plans for the controversial B-1 bomber, which Carter had canceled. Reagan also achieved the European deployment of intermediate-range, nuclear-armed Pershing and cruise missiles, despite intense opposition by antinuclear activists in Great Britain, West Germany, and elsewhere in Western Europe.

Reagan's policies for winnable nuclear war replaced the doctrine of mutually assured destruction (MAD) that had dominated cold war strategic thinking since the 1960s. Reagan regarded MAD as dangerous, especially as he believed the Soviets had secretly repudiated the principles of detente and were themselves preparing to prevail in a nuclear war. His administration maintained, astonishingly to some, that enhanced civil defense efforts would enable most civilians to survive nuclear attacks and that the United States would be able to return to prewar economic levels in as little as two to four years, if it adopted Soviet civil defense practices.[1] In March 1983, Reagan proposed his controversial Strategic Defense Initiative (SDI), popularly known as Star Wars after a science fiction movie of the time. Intended to provide a shield of laser-armed satellites in outer space capable of shooting down missiles targeted at American cities and defense installations, SDI faced strong opposition from those who believed it was an expensive boondoggle that would never be able to achieve its mission but that would divert to corporate interests resources greatly needed for implementing social programs. Others maintained that it might even provoke a first strike by the Soviets, who feared they would become vulnerable if they allowed SDI to be completed. When Reagan was later persuaded that protecting every U.S. city was unrealistic, he revised SDI's mission to protect American missile sites against a first strike—in effect, returning to the policies of MAD.

In September 1983, after Soviet jets shot down a South Korean commercial jet that had strayed into Soviet airspace, superpower relations deteriorated to their lowest point since the Cuban missile crisis. Reagan cited the action as proof of Soviet barbarism, and Soviet foreign minister Gromyko warned that avoiding a nuclear war was the greatest problem then facing the world.[2] That fear was further exacerbated on October 23, after a car bomb killed some 240 U.S. Marines and 60 French soldiers serving on a peacekeeping mission in Beirut, Lebanon, and then again on October 25, when the United States invaded Grenada to overthrow the Marxist regime there, while also preparing NATO war games in Europe scheduled for early November. Soviet military intelligence incorrectly concluded that the war games, known as Able Archer 83, were intended as a prelude to an actual attack, and the Soviet Union went on high alert. Fortunately, the Soviet leadership did not order a preemptive strike and tensions eventually subsided.[3]

Even before taking office Reagan had denounced the Marxist Sandinistas in Nicaragua, who had deposed the dictator Anastasio Somoza in 1979, and, in 1981, Reagan directed the Central Intelligence Agency (CIA) to arm and organize rebels who were trying to depose the Sandinistas. However, Congress opposed the president's efforts, and in 1982 it passed the first Boland Amendment, forbidding the CIA to overthrow the Nicaraguan government. Nonetheless, the covert activities continued, largely directed by the National Security Council, and in 1984 the CIA secretly mined Nicaraguan harbors, an act of war. When these and other illegal covert activities became publicly known, Congress passed additional Boland Amendments denying government agencies funds to support military or paramilitary operations in Nicaragua directly or indirectly.

To bypass the Boland prohibitions, the Reagan administration sought ways to employ private sources to channel weapons and funds to the Nicaraguan rebels, known as contras. Its privatization of the country's handling of foreign affairs led directly to the Iran-contra affair of 1985 and 1986. Despite Reagan's pledge never to trade weapons for hostages, the Iran-contra affair involved the sale of U.S. weapons to Iran in return for the release of seven American hostages held by pro-Iranian terrorist groups in Lebanon. However, only three hostages were released, despite several transactions. The $48 million generated between September 1985 and October 1986 was diverted for various purposes, including arming the contras, running other covert operations, and establishing reserves for future operations. A 1987 congressional investigation concluded that many top administration officials were involved, including Reagan's National Security Advisors Robert McFarlane and John Poindexter and the CIA director William Casey. According to the U.S. Marine lieutenant colonel Oliver North, who distributed the money, the scheme was part of a more grandiose plan to create a "stand-alone," "off-the-shelf" covert capability that would extend throughout the world while evading congressional review.

Reagan gave a series of conflicting accounts of his own role but claimed to be unaware of any illegal activities or any arms for hostages trades. However, his self-proclaimed ignorance of this important operation conducted by top members of his own administration, in violation of his own publicly avowed principles, made him appear either dishonest or incompetent or both, and the incident seriously undermined his credibility and future effectiveness. During the 1988 presidential campaign Vice President Bush, the Republican candidate, claimed that he was "out of the loop" when decisions were being made about the Iran-contra deal. He thereby escaped serious political damage and easily won the election. However, new revelations by a special prosecutor a week prior to the 1992 elections hurt Bush's reelection bid, as documents showed him to be much more deeply inside the loop than he had represented.

During Reagan's second administration the United States took actions against hostile developing nations but adopted a more conciliatory tone toward the Soviets. Reagan continued to oppose the Sandinistas, and he supported the right-wing regime in El Salvador in its fight against Communist-supported insurgents. In 1986, he ordered attacks against Libya after alleged Libyan missile attacks on U.S. aircraft in the Gulf of Sirte. These policies provoked Soviet warnings and sparked acts of terrorism throughout Europe, to which Reagan responded by ordering more air strikes against Libya. In 1987, Reagan took steps to assist Iraq in its war against Iran, providing military escorts for Kuwaiti tankers carrying Iraqi oil through the Persian Gulf and authorizing some limited military actions against Iran in the gulf. The war concluded in summer 1988, shortly after a U.S. warship in the gulf shot down an Iranian passenger plane, killing 290 noncombatants. The United States maintained that the USS *Vincennes* mistook Iran Air Flight 655 for a hostile enemy plane, and the Reagan administration rejected comparisons to the Soviet downing of the South Korean passenger plane in 1983. Nonetheless, Iran's leaders may have interpreted the incident as an indication that the United States intended to intervene more forcefully, and the tragedy may have influenced their decision to accept a cease-fire less than two weeks later.

Other long-lasting regional conflicts concluded in the late 1980s, as the Soviets completed their military withdrawal from Afghanistan in February 1989. In early 1988, the United States participated in Angolan-Cuban talks that brought about a Cuban withdrawal from Angola and paved the way for Namibian independence.

Gorbachev became the Soviet premier in 1985 and quickly introduced economic reforms and new principles of freedom that, within a few years, led to the end of the cold war and the demise of international communism. After British prime minister Margaret Thatcher told Reagan that Gorbachev was more flexible and trustworthy than his predecessors, his stance toward the Soviet Union became increasingly conciliatory. In November 1985 Gorbachev and Reagan issued a joint statement declaring that nuclear war could never be won and during an October 1986 "minisummit" in Reykjavik, Iceland, they surprised the world and their own staffs by agreeing in principle to eliminate all intermediate-range missiles from Europe, eliminate all ballistic missiles over a 10-year period, and reduce other nuclear delivery systems. These agreements became the basis for the Strategic Arms Reduction Talks (START), which superceded the SALT talks and eventually produced the 1991 START Treaty. In December 1987, the two leaders signed the Intermediate Nuclear Forces (INF) Treaty to eliminate all intermediate-range nuclear weapons in Europe— the first cold war treaty that actually reduced the size of superpower nuclear arsenals, instead of merely limiting their rate of growth. In December 1988 Gorbachev further announced his intention unilaterally to downsize the Soviet army by a half-million soldiers and, even more importantly, to withdraw Soviet troops and tanks from Eastern Europe.

The removal of the Soviet military presence from the Iron Curtain countries was one of the long-standing U.S. cold war objectives, dating to the 1950s, and it signaled to reformers in those countries that they could act without fear of brutal Soviet retaliation, such as Hungary experienced in 1956 and Czechoslovakia in 1968. Consequently, in 1989, popular movements overthrew Communist dictatorships in Eastern Europe and replaced them by more democratic forms of government in Poland, Hungary, Yugoslavia, Bulgaria, Czechoslovakia, Romania, and East Germany, which, on November 10, dismantled the Berlin Wall and with it the most powerful and enduring symbol of the cold war. What remains truly remarkable is that these regionwide regime changes were generally peaceful and orderly, except in Romania, where the longtime Communist ruler and his wife were publicly executed.

Gorbachev's visit to Beijing in spring 1989 encouraged thousands of Chinese students to protest for freedom in Tiananmen Square. However, after protesters had some initial success, the military intervened and crushed the protest, which had been televised internationally, killing many of its leaders in public executions. Communism also persisted in Cuba, where, in April 1980, Cuba's premier, Fidel Castro, dealt with growing internal dissent by abruptly permitting anyone to emigrate. Soon thousands of Cuban exiles living in South Florida piloted fishing boats and other vessels, large and small, to Cuba's Mariel harbor to take friends and relatives back to the United States, and within about a month the Mariel boat lift carried some 125,000 Cuban refugees to America. Among them were hundreds of criminals and mentally ill patients who Castro insisted must be taken to the United States as a condition for allowing others to leave.

The decade also saw several important international conflicts in which direct U.S. participation was limited or nonexistent. Hoping to take advantage of disarray in the Iranian military caused by purges that followed the Islamic revolution of 1979, Iraq initiated the Iran-Iraq Gulf War in summer 1980. The war, which concluded in a stalemate in summer 1988 and produced casualties of 500,000 to 1 million—more than in World War I—featured Iraqi, and possibly Iranian, use of chemical weapons; assaults by both sides on oil tankers passing through the Persian Gulf; and long-range Scud missile attacks by both sides against civilian population centers. Iraq enjoyed support from other Persian Gulf states, the Soviet Union, and the United States, all interested in containing Iran's fundamentalist Islamic revolution. But although the war did succeed in curbing the spread of Iran's virulently anti-Western ideology, Iraq failed to achieve any of its own objectives—notably, it was unable to gain direct shipping access to the Persian Gulf, which it lost in 1969, when it lost access to the Shatt al-Arab, a deep-channel estuary at the Iranian border. However, the ongoing state of emergency did enable Iraq's dictator, Saddam Hussein, to consolidate his power at home and build up the large elite Republican Guard, personally loyal to him. It also left the nation with a standing army of some 1 million troops and large outstanding debts to Kuwait and other Persian Gulf states, thereby establishing conditions that gave rise to the Iraqi invasion and occupation of Kuwait in summer 1990 and the Persian Gulf War in winter 1991.

In spring 1982, Britain prevailed in its short Falklands War with Argentina, after Argentine troops invaded the British-owned Falkland Islands (also known as the Islas Malvinas). The defeat precipitated the resignation of Argentina's president, General Leopoldo Galtieri, and the restoration of democracy in 1983. In June 1982, Israeli forces invaded southern Lebanon in an effort to end attacks on their territory by the Palestine Liberation Organization (PLO) and to establish a friendly government in Lebanon. The invasion succeeded in driving the PLO from Beirut to Tripoli in northern Lebanon, but it also began a three-year-long Israeli occupation of southern Lebanon that was costly in lives, provoked international condemnation, and proved increasingly unpopular within Israel. More than 650 Israeli soldiers were killed and more than 4,000 were wounded during the occupation, which lasted through summer 1985. In December 1983 as Syria began to dominate Lebanon during its civil war, it forced the PLO from Tripoli to Tunisia.

Terrorism was rampant during the 1980s, especially during the middle of the decade, and much of it was related to conflicts in the Middle East. After the PLO's expulsion from Lebanon in 1982, pro-Palestinian and pro-Iranian militants committed several terrorist attacks on Israeli and U.S. interests, notably the kidnapping in 1985 of American citizens in Beirut, who became the hostages at the center of the Iran-contra affair; the hijacking of a TWA flight in June 1985, in which one American serviceman was killed and others were held as hostages; the abduction of the Mediterranean cruise ship *Achille Lauro* in October 1985, during which the hijackers ceremoniously murdered Leon Klinghoffer, an elderly, crippled Jewish-American man; a coordinated attack on civilians in December 1985, when terrorists opened fire with automatic weapons at crowded El Al counters at the Rome and Vienna airports, killing 14 and wounding at least 110; and an attack on a Jewish temple in Istanbul that killed 21 of the 29 worshippers there in 1986. U.S. clashes with Libyan naval forces off the Libyan coast in spring 1986 provoked the bombing of a TWA jet en route from Rome to Athens, in which four passengers were sucked out of the hole in the plane's side, and the bombing of a West Berlin discotheque popular with U.S. service personnel. Two people died and more than 150 were wounded. In response, Reagan ordered air strikes against sites inside Libya in an apparent effort to target the Libyan leader Colonel Muammar Qaddafi. Qaddafi survived, but his adopted daughter was killed along with other civilians in the raids, which provoked international protest and more terrorist reprisals, including the executions of British and American hostages in Lebanon. In December 1988, a bomb exploded aboard a Pan Am jet flying over Lockerbie, Scotland, killing all 259 aboard, as well as 11 people on the ground. Although Iranian terrorists were initially suspected of seeking revenge for the U.S. downing of an Air Iran plane over the Persian Gulf in July, Libya was later held responsible for the bombing, for which Abdel Basset Ali Megrahi, a Libyan intelligence officer, was convicted in 2001. In August 2003 Libya formally acknowledged that it was behind the terrorist act and agreed to pay $2.7 billion in compensation to the victims' families in return for the lifting of a United Nations (UN) trade embargo initiated in April 1992.

Several assassinations and assassination attempts undermined stability throughout the world. In March 1981, just two months after Reagan took office, John W. Hinckley, Jr., shot him in the chest but did not incapacitate him for very long. Hinckley was later found not guilty by reason of insanity and confined to a mental hospital. Less than two months later, Mehmet Ali Agça, a 23-year-old Turkish man who had escaped from prison, shot and severely wounded Pope John Paul II. Initially believed to be a lone fanatic with Islamic sympathies, Agça was later shown to have close connections to the Bulgarian secret service, which was working on behalf of the Soviet Union. In October 1981, Egypt's president Anwar Sadat was murdered by Egyptian soldiers who stepped out from a military parade and fired upon the president and others on the reviewing stand. The assassination was believed to be a response to Sadat's peace treaty with Israel and his crackdown on religious extremists. In September 1982, three months after the Israeli invasion of southern Lebanon, the president-elect of a new Lebanese government, Bashir Gemayel, was killed when a bomb exploded in the headquarters of his Christian Phalangist Party, which Lebanese Muslims accused of being affiliated with Israel. In August 1983, Benigno S. Aquino, Jr., the main political rival of the Philippine president Ferdinand Marcos, was assassinated while under the protection of a military escort as he deplaned to meet a group of supporters in Manila. Although Marcos denied complicity and denounced the act, he was widely believed to be responsible for the killing. Aquino's wife, Corazon, assumed her husband's political role and succeeded Marcos in 1986, after defeating him in a national election.

In October 1984, almost five months after authorizing a government assault that killed more than 400 protesting Sikhs who had occupied the sacred Golden Temple in Amritsar, in India's Punjab region, Prime Minister Indira Gandhi was shot down by two Sikh members of her personal bodyguard. Her son, Rajiv Gandhi, succeeded her. Swedish prime minister Olof Palme was assassinated in Stockholm while walking home from a movie with his wife in February 1986, and Pakistan's military ruler, Mohammad Zia ul-Haq, died along with the U.S. ambassador and most of Pakistan's military elite in a suspicious plane crash in August 1988. A joint U.S.-Pakistani committee concluded that the crash was caused by a criminal act of sabotage inside the aircraft, but no perpetrator has been identified. Lebanon's president René Moawad was killed by a car bomb in November 1989, after only 17 days in office. His death undermined hope for an agreement that would allow power sharing by Muslims and Christians in the nation.

GOVERNMENT AND SOCIETY

Reagan and his vice president, George Herbert Walker Bush, both believed that a strong economy was a primary national concern and they sought to create a business climate that would stimulate the economy and enable corporations to thrive. To this end, they cut some taxes, opposed increases of others, reduced government oversight and regulation of business, and scaled back environmental protections that interfered with corporate growth. Although they shared many values with social conservatives, such as opposition to abortion, they invested most of their political capital in their economic agendas, an emphasis that alienated some of their core conservative constituency from Bush, in particular. Efforts to appeal to that constituency included Reagan's appointment of the conservative Supreme Court justices Sandra Day O'Connor and Antonin Scalia and his elevation of William H. Rehnquist to chief justice. In 1987, however, Democrats in the Senate succeeded in blocking the appointment of Robert Bork, who had played a role in Nixon's Watergate cover-up and held views hostile to abortion rights, affirmative action, and broader interpretations of the First Amendment provisions for free speech. Reagan subsequently filled the vacancy with Anthony M. Kennedy.

The decade experienced a significant growth in homelessness, which resulted from both high levels of unemployment and reductions in spending on social programs. These included reductions in funding for inpatient care for indigents who were mentally ill. Consequently, many of the homeless were individuals who had mental and emotional illnesses. Other social ills included widespread illegal drug use and violent crime associated with it, growing numbers of gangs of out-of-control urban youth, and high levels of illiteracy among the adult population, the reversal of which became a favorite cause of First Lady Barbara Bush.

Acquired immunodeficiency syndrome (AIDS) was first isolated in 1983 as a new, deadly disease that attacks the body's immune system. At that time, homosexual men, Haitians, and intravenous drug users who shared needles were identified as the groups most affected. Reagan's refusal to increase funding for AIDS research sparked criticism from those fearing an AIDS epidemic, but the policy won approval from others, who pointed out that the number of people then affected by AIDS was much smaller than that of those affected by other diseases. Activists from the Christian Right proclaimed on religious television shows and from the pulpit that AIDS was divine punishment for homosexual permissiveness and sexual debauchery.

During the decade U.S. women crossed a number of important thresholds as Sandra Day O'Connor became the first female Supreme Court justice in 1981; the physicist Sally K. Ride became the first American woman to enter outer space in 1983; and in 1984 U.S. representative Geraldine Ferraro, a Democrat from Queens, New York, became the first woman to be nominated for vice president by a major political party. The movement to give women fully equal status found support within the National Council of Churches, which in 1983 released a gender-neutral translation of the Bible that omitted or altered traditional descriptions of God as a male.

Other religious groups, however, especially those on the Christian Right, vigorously opposed efforts to expand rights for women and homosexuals. Ironically, women sometimes assumed leadership positions in these efforts, notably Phyllis Schlafly and Anita Bryant, a popular evangelical singer and former beauty queen who, in the late 1970s, had led an unsuccessful effort to repeal a Miami-Dade County ordinance banning discrimination on the basis of sexual preference. Other leading voices from the Christian Right who opposed liberalization of traditional male-female roles and legitimization of homosexuality included Pat Robertson, founder of the Christian Broadcasting Network and leader of the Christian Coalition; the Reverend Jerry Falwell of the Moral Majority; and Pat Buchanan, a former presidential speechwriter. At the very extreme of the political Right were small groups of antigovernment survivalists, neo-Nazis, antitax activists, white supremacists, and others, who began to gather in mostly rural areas, especially in the far West. Some formed legally sanctioned militias, whose right to exist is explicitly stated in the Constitution. Others sometimes challenged the authority of the federal government in other, illegal ways.

BUSINESS

Shaped by large-scale governmental defense expenditures, reductions in spending for social programs, major tax cuts, and corporate-friendly policies for business regulation and environmental protection, the economy of the 1980s was generally strong in terms of growth in what was then called the gross national product (GNP; now called the gross domestic product, or GDP). The so-called Reaganomics that dominated the decade was based on a "trickle-down theory" that assumed tax cuts would stimulate business and thereby produce jobs and consequently reduce the need for welfare, and between 1983 and 1990, the United States experienced one of its longest periods of sustained economic growth. However, the combination of heavy defense spending and diminished tax revenues spawned large budget deficits, which fed inflation, led to high interest rates, and contributed to comparatively high levels of unemployment during the period. By the time Reagan left office the national debt had more than doubled, exceeding $3 trillion in 1988.

The early 1980s saw extreme fluctuations in the economy, as the GNP rose from 9 percent growth in 1980—the final year of Jimmy Carter's presidency—to 11.7 percent in 1981—Ronald Reagan's first year—and then dropped to 3.7 percent in 1982. By 1983, however, it stabilized at 7.6 percent and generally remained in the neighborhood of 7 percent growth per year for the rest of the decade. Overall, the stock market performed well, too. By 1989, the Dow-Jones industrial average, which had peaked in 1980 at 1,000, nearly tripled to 2,791, despite a stock market crash on "Black Monday," October 19, 1987, that saw a drop of 508 points, the largest single-day loss in history to that date. Overall, inflation fluctuated during the 1980s, dropping from 13.5 percent in 1980 and 10.2 percent in 1981 to 3.2 percent in 1983 and 1.9 percent in 1986 and back up to exceed 4.5 percent in 1988 and 1989. Unemployment fluctuated from 7.1 percent in 1980 and 7.6 percent in 1981 to 9.7 percent in 1982 and 9.6 percent in 1983 to around 7 percent in the middle of the decade to 5.3 percent in 1989.[4]

The period saw the accumulation of great personal and corporate wealth, especially among sophisticated investors and money managers who benefited from the corporate-friendly policies inspired by Reaganomics. Tax-deferred individual retirement accounts (IRAs) and other tax shelters available through payroll deductions encouraged middle-class workers to participate in the stock market at much higher levels than in the past. Overall, these investments both yielded good returns to investors and provided a vast new revenue stream of capital that fueled economic growth. Many individuals made fortunes managing these and other funds, sometimes trading so-called high risk junk bonds that were inexpensively priced or acting as "corporate raiders" who made "hostile takeovers" of undervalued publicly traded companies. Others became exceedingly wealthy by climbing to the top levels of their corporate ladder, after "superstars," such as Lee Iacocca, Chrysler Corporation's chief executive officer (CEO), convinced corporate boards that multibillion-dollar companies could maximize profits by hiring the most talented upper-management teams possible. These managers commanded huge salaries for their ability to create new markets and improve production efficiency, often by reducing the size of the labor force. As a result, the gap in compensation between labor and management grew significantly during the 1980s, as a hierarchical top-down corporate management structure increasingly became the model for institutional organization and compensation.

The loosened government regulation and lucrative investment opportunities not only created many legitimate fortunes, they also produced an environment that gave rise to major business scandals that required expensive taxpayer subsidies. Revelations of insider trading on Wall Street by such prominent figures as Ivan Boesky and executives from the investment firm of Drexel, Burnham, and Lambert provoked feelings of outrage and to some extent undermined public confidence in the integrity of Wall Street itself and of other previously respected institutions. Public cynicism was further exacerbated by the savings and loan (S&L) scandal of the late 1980s. Lax oversight, joined with a 150 percent increase in federal insurance coverage for S&L accounts and legal changes that permitted more aggressive lending practices, opened the door to negligent and fraudulent practices that, in 1989, required Congress to appropriate an additional $157 billion to pay off insurance claims for failed S&Ls. It also established the Resolution Trust Corporation, which sold off the assets of insolvent institutions at greatly reduced prices. One of the costliest and most publicized S&L failures to receive a government bailout was Silverado Savings, which was owned partly by Neil Bush, President Bush's son.

If Reagan, a former union president, won the backing of investors on Wall Street, his policies alienated him from organized labor, which dubbed the president a union buster when he fired 12,000 federal air traffic controllers in August 1981, after a three-day strike that crippled air transportation throughout the country. Small farmers also suffered during the Reagan years, as the number of small family-owned farms fell significantly as a result of falling prices and inflated credit costs. In the 1980s, therefore, a relatively small number of large, corporate-run farms accounted for an increasing portion of U.S. agricultural output.

Despite a regulatory environment that was generally favorable to corporate mergers and growth, in early 1982, the American Telephone and Telegraph Company (AT&T) agreed to settle an antitrust suit by divesting 22 local Bell System companies, the so-called Baby Bells. The settlement, which left the Baby Bells responsible for local phone service, while AT&T retained long-distance business, was the largest and most significant antitrust action since the dismantling of the Standard Oil trust in 1911, as it opened up the quickly evolving telecommunications industry for new competition—a development that had a profound impact on the business and technology environment of the 1990s.

NATURE AND THE ENVIRONMENT

The 1980s at once saw the loosening of environmental protections by Reagan and Secretary of the Interior James Watt and a growing recognition in other sectors of the society of the dangers of industrial and automotive pollution. As early as 1983, scientists warned of the harmful potential of global warming caused by a greenhouse effect that results from burning such fossil fuels as oil and gasoline. These warnings became more pronounced as the decade progressed. Also in 1983, researchers investigating possible environmental impacts of a nuclear war predicted that the widespread fires produced by a full-scale nuclear conflict would pour millions of tons of smoke and ash into the air, blocking out the Sun and producing a so-called nuclear winter that could potentially choke off plant production and exterminate all advanced forms of life.

The dramatic depletion of the ozone layer in the stratosphere, which filters out deadly ultraviolet radiation from the Sun, alarmed many researchers when readings taken in 1985 revealed a hole in the layer over Antarctica. Subsequent measurements showed that the hole was growing, and in 1987 nations throughout the world signed the Montreal Protocol to phase out the use of chlorofluorocarbons (CFCs), which were responsible for much of the ozone depletion. Subsequently, worldwide use of CFCs in refrigerants, aerosols, and solvents has significantly diminished, and the size of the hole in the ozone layer has stabilized.

Natural and human-caused disasters had profound impact on people and the environment during the 1980s. Among the most significant natural disasters was the volcanic eruption of Mount Saint Helens in Washington State in May 1980, which killed 57 people directly and produced devastating landslides, floods, and a massive cloud of ash that rained down upon everything within 300 miles. A cyclone in Bangladesh in May 1985 killed some 10,000 people; a powerful earthquake in Mexico City took the lives of thousands and destroyed large portions of the city in September 1985; a volcano erupted in northern Colombia in November 1985, burying two mountain towns in mud slides that killed up to 20,000; a volcanic eruption in the bottom of Lake Nios in Cameroon issued a toxic cloud of carbon dioxide gas that killed at least 1,200 people; and an earthquake struck Los Angeles in October 1987, killing six. With winds in excess of 180 miles per hour (mph) and the lowest barometric pressure ever recorded in the Western Hemisphere (888 millibars), Hurricane Gilbert inflicted ruinous damage on Jamaica in September 1988 before striking Mexico's Yucatán Peninsula and causing severe flooding in the Monterrey region. Altogether, 318 people died as a result of the storm. On December 7, 1988, a powerful earthquake struck Armenia, leaving some 500,000 homeless and killing perhaps as many as 40,000. In September 1989, Hurricane Hugo, a massive category 4 storm, devastated Puerto Rico and the Virgin Islands before striking the South Carolina and North Carolina coasts, where its 20-foot storm surge was the highest ever recorded on the East Coast. Altogether, Hugo killed 82 people and became, after Hurricane Andrew in 1992, the second costliest hurricane in U.S. history. A month later, on October 17, 1989, a strong earthquake struck the San Francisco Bay area, causing an estimated 270 deaths, severely damaging the Oakland Bay Bridge, and inflicting $1 billion to $3 billion worth of damage. Seats rocked and light towers swayed at Candlestick Park, where some 58,000 baseball fans had gathered for the third game of the World Series.

The most severe human-caused disasters included a toxic gas leak from a Union Carbide insecticide plant, which killed some 2,100 people in Bhopal, India, in December 1984. Eight months later toxic chemicals released from another Union Carbide plant resulted in severe eye, throat, and lung irritation for at least 135 residents near Charleston, West Virginia. A fire at a chemical warehouse in Basel, Switzerland, resulted in the discharge of more than 1,000 tons of toxic chemicals into the Rhine River, crippling the fisheries on the waterway and forcing the closure of drinking water plants. In March 1989 the oil tanker *Exxon Valdez* ran aground off Alaska's Prince William Sound while carrying more than 1 million barrels of oil, which spilled from the vessel and caused extensive environmental damage to what had been one of the most pristine areas in North America. The meltdown in April 1986 of a nuclear reactor in Chernobyl, in the Ukraine, was the worst nuclear disaster to date. Initially covered up by Soviet authorities, it subjected at least 400,000 people to unsafe levels of radioactivity, caused radiation sickness that killed at least 32 people in the region, and eventually resulted in birth defects and other radiation-induced ailments in thousands of humans and animals. The melt-down, which released more radioactivity than the atomic bombs dropped on Japan in World War II had, contaminated millions of acres of forest and farm-lands, as winds carried radioactive particles as far west as France and Italy.

SCIENCE AND TECHNOLOGY

The 1980s saw the first widespread use of personal computers, whose capaci-ties and capabilities grew geometrically throughout the decade, even while prices fell and computers became widely affordable. From its word-processing capabilities to its capacity to store and retrieve information, its calculating abili-ties, its facility for managing and effectively presenting data, and its ability to communicate and share information with other computers at remote sites, the personal computer was one of the most far-reaching technological innovations in human history.

The personal computer also contributed to and benefited from the emer-gence of the Internet, which was developed primarily in the 1980s. The Inter-net's roots trace back to the Advanced Research Projects Agency Network, a communications network among large so-called supercomputers developed by the U.S. Department of Defense in 1969. New technologies in the 1980s, however, enabled private computer users to interact with databases housed on mainframe computers and to communicate with one another through com-puter bulletin boards and early electronic mail (e-mail) systems. Research in the 1980s conducted by the British-born computer scientist Tim Berners-Lee also gave rise to the more versatile World Wide Web, which became available to the public in 1992. A downside of the increasing reliance on personal comput-ers was the emergence of computer viruses that could destroy the contents of individual personal computers linked to the Internet. One of the first large-scale worldwide viruses hit in November 1988 and damaged thousands of computers in North America.

The success of much of the new telecommunications technology depend-ed on improved satellite technology, and the decade saw important develop-ments in that field and in space exploration in general. Among these developments were the successful deployment in April 1981 of the first reusable space vehicle, the space shuttle *Columbia*. In January 1986, however, a second shuttle, the *Challenger*, exploded moments after takeoff, killing the entire crew of seven astronauts, including Christa McAuliffe, a teacher who had been chosen as the first private citizen to fly into outer space. In 1980, space probes to Mars and Venus discovered no signs of life on either planet. Launched in 1977, the space probe *Voyager 1* reached Jupiter in 1979, and in 1980, it showed that Saturn has at least 15 rings, not 12, as previously believed. *Voyager 2*, launched the same year, passed Jupiter in 1979, Saturn in 1981, Uranus in 1986, and Neptune in 1989. Both probes sent back informative data and impressive photographs that literally changed the way humans look at the planets. They then continued past the solar system into deep space, where, along with *Pioneer 10,* they presumably will endure even after the heat death of the Sun and the extinction of the solar system. In 1989 the *Galileo* probe began its long journey to Jupiter, which it reached in 1995.

LITERATURE, THE ARTS, SPORTS, AND POPULAR CULTURE

The arts and popular culture continued both to influence society and to be influenced by it. Sometimes these influences were dramatic, such as in 1980, when the rock musician and political activist John Lennon was assassinated outside his New York apartment by one of his fans, or in 1989, when Iran's Ayatollah Khomeini called for the assassination of the author Salman Rushdie, who, Khomeini maintained, had in his novel *Satanic Verses* slandered Islam's prophet, Muhammad. In 1985, a televised benefit concert focused international attention on the plight of America's small farmers, when such popular singers as Willie Nelson, John Mellencamp, and Neil Young joined other performers in Farm Aid. Other concerts protesting such matters as militarism, use of nuclear power, and environmental destruction also featured prominent performers.

Reagan's revival of a patriotic spirit found expression in a number of movies from the middle of the decade. Reagan, himself, invoked *Rambo* (1985), which starred Sylvester Stallone as a veteran who returns to Vietnam to rescue American prisoners of war (POWs) and vanquish their North Vietnamese captors. Stallone also directed and starred in the successful *Rocky* series about an underdog boxer from the streets of Philadelphia whose perseverance in the face of overwhelming odds makes him a hero. *Rocky 4* (1985) tapped into the patriotic fervor of the time, as the gritty and determined fighter prevails against a larger opponent from the Soviet Union. *Top Gun* (1986), directed by Tony Scott and starring Tom Cruise and Val Kilmer, also appealed to the militaristic sensibility of the times in its celebration of navy fighter pilots, and the story of the first American astronauts in Philip Kaufman's *The Right Stuff* (1983; based on Tom Wolfe's 1979 book of the same title) both struck a patriotic chord and appealed to the resurrected interest in space exploration. Taylor Hackford's *White Nights* (1985) contrasted American freedom with Soviet repression as Mikhail Baryshnikov and Gregory Hines starred as talented dancers exploited by the Soviets for cynical political purposes. *WarGames* (1983), directed by John Badham, issues a cautionary note about the dangers of accidental nuclear war; John Milius's widely publicized *Red Dawn* (1984) envisions American freedom fighters struggling against Soviet armies after American liberals surrender the United States to invading communist forces from Latin America. The movie appeared at a time when Reagan was warning that Soviet-supported troops in Nicaragua were only a day's drive from Texas.

Other movies that commented on the times included Sydney Pollack's *Tootsie* (1982), a comedy that explores sexual harassment experienced by successful women. Dustin Hoffman starred as an actor who pretends to be a woman in order to obtain an acting role and discovers that he is a better person in his female persona than his male self. Mike Nichols's *Silkwood* (1982) starred Meryl Streep and Cher in the real-life story of Karen Silkwood, who died in a suspicious car crash while threatening to expose shoddy practices at

In *White Nights* Mikhail Baryshnikov (right) and Gregory Hines (left) celebrated freedom of artistic expression amid cold war tensions. *(Photofest)*

the nuclear power plant where she worked. James L. Brooks's *Broadcast News* (1987) considers changing notions of journalistic integrity; Alan Parker's *Mississippi Burning* (1988) centers on racial strife during the 1960s Civil Rights movement; Spike Lee's *Do the Right Thing* (1989) depicts contemporary inner-city racial tensions; and Oliver Stone's *Wall Street* (1987) starred Michael Douglas in its exposé of corporate greed and manipulation. In *Ordinary People* (1980) Mary Tyler Moore and Donald Sutherland play parents in an American family made dysfunctional by the mother's emotional coldness. The film was the directorial debut of the actor Robert Redford, who, in 1984, founded the successful Sundance Film Festival as a venue for calling the work of independent filmmakers to public attention.

Steven Spielberg's *Raiders of the Lost Ark* (1981) starred Harrison Ford in his first of three movies about the adventures of swashbuckling archaeologist, Indiana Jones. One of the most successful and influential directors of the decade, Spielberg also directed the sequels, *Indiana Jones and the Temple of Doom* (1984) and *Indiana Jones and the Last Crusade* (1989), as well as *E. T. The Extra-Terrestrial* (1982), *Twilight Zone—The Movie* (1983), *The Color Purple* (1985), *Empire of the Sun* (1987), and *Always* (1989).

In *Sophie's Choice* (1982), which featured strong performances by Meryl Streep and Kevin Kline, Alan Pakula adapted William Styron's 1979 novel about the tortured relationship of a traumatized Holocaust survivor and her manic-depressive lover. Ben Kingsley starred in the title role of Sir Richard Attenborough's *Gandhi* (1982). Ridley Scott's *Blade Runner* (1982), based on Philip K. Dick's novel *Do Androids Dream of Electric Sheep?* (1968), addresses ethical problems that arise from advanced robotic technology. James Cameron also imagines the possibilities of futuristic technology in his action–adventure story *The Terminator* (1984), starring Arnold Schwarzenegger, and in *Aliens* (1986), the sequel to Scott's *Alien* (1979). Milos Forman's *Amadeus* (1984) highlights the lively and emotive music of Wolfgang Amadeus Mozart and offers a colorful characterization of the composer, as it enacts his suspected poisoning by a musical rival. Best known for his comic roles in such movies as

Do the Right Thing's depiction of inner-city racial conflict established Spike Lee (left) as an important film director and social commentator. *(Photofest)*

Ghostbusters (1984), Bill Murray starred in John Byrum's adaptation of Somerset Maugham's *The Razor's Edge* (1944), a story of the spiritual transformation of a shell-shocked World War I veteran who journeys to Tibet and then returns to the West. James Ivory won acclaim for his stylish adaptation of E. M. Forster novel, *A Room with a View* (novel 1908, film 1986).

Olivier Stone's *Platoon* (1986) drew attention to racial, cultural, and personal conflicts within an American military unit in Vietnam, and his *Born on the Fourth of July* starred Tom Cruise in the real-life story of Ron Kovic, a paralyzed Vietnam veteran who became an antiwar activist. *The Dead* (1987), John Huston's acclaimed adaptation of the story of an emotionally repressed marriage from James Joyce's *Dubliners* (1914), was the director's last film, and it starred his daughter, Anjelica Huston. In *Henry V,* Kenneth Branagh began the first in his highly praised series of cinematic interpretations of William Shakespeare's plays. Rob Reiner's comedy *When Harry Met Sally* (1989), starring Meg Ryan and Billy Crystal, explores the evolving relationship of two college acquaintances whose personalities and level of maturity develop over the years.

Mixing humor and pathos, Woody Allen's *Hannah and Her Sisters* (1986) shows the dynamics at play in the relationships among three sisters in a dysfunctional family. Allen also explores how personal growth through greater self-knowledge enables people to cope with and sometimes even transcend debilitating emotional traumas in *Zelig* (1983), *September* (1987), and *Another Woman* (1988). In *Crimes and Misdemeanors* (1989), Allen costarred with Martin Landau, Anjelica Huston, Alan Alda, and Mia Farrow in perhaps his most deeply philosophical movie, which raises fundamental questions about morality in a seemingly godless universe in which there are no guarantees that virtue will be rewarded or evil punished. One of the most prolific directors of the decade, who was more widely appreciated in Europe than in the United States, Allen also directed *Stardust Memories* (1980), a stream-of-consciousness story influenced by Federico Fellini's *8 1/2* (1963); *A Midsummer Night's Sex Comedy* (1982); *Broadway Danny Rose* (1984); *The Purple Rose of Cairo* (1985); *Radio Days* (1987); and *Oedipus Wrecks* (1989), which spoofs *Oedipus Rex,* Sophocles' classic Greek tragedy, which stands as Western culture's quintessential, if not archetypal, study of self-knowledge. Steven Soderbergh's low-budget *Sex, Lies, and Videotape* (1989) demonstrated to film distributors that independently made films were capable of attracting large audiences and reaping substantial profits. Consequently, the critically acclaimed film helped give a new generation of independent filmmakers access to broad national and worldwide audiences in the 1990s.

In the early 1980s, television programming capitalized on the public's attraction to the fast life of wealthy jet-setters of dubious morals, but later in the decade viewers opted for more wholesome, family-oriented shows. Immensely popular throughout the world, *Dallas,* a sexy soap opera about greedy, ambitious oilmen and their conniving families, received the highest, or second highest ratings of prime-time television show between 1980 and 1985. *Dynasty,* patterned after *Dallas,* premiered in 1981 and was among the five most widely viewed shows between 1982 and 1985, and *Dallas* spinoff *Knots Landing* and the *Dallas* imitator *Falcon Crest* also attracted large prime-time audiences between 1981 and 1985. Although not as popular, *Miami Vice,* which ran from 1984 to 1989, also earned a worldwide following through its use of rock music and fast-paced camera work and music video effects, as well as its steamy Miami setting with a Latin flavor. The show centers on a racially integrated team of police detectives who drive expensive sports cars and frequent lively nightclubs in their efforts to thwart rich but heartless drug dealers and their beautiful girlfriends.

Perhaps because the downsides of life in the fast lane became more apparent in the second half of the decade, by 1985 viewers demonstrated their preference for reassuring family-oriented situation comedies over dramas about morally deficient, profligate connivers. Between September 1985 and April 1990, *The Cosby Show* was the top-rated network program, and its spinoff, *A Different World,* was among the top four shows between 1987 and 1991. Starring the comedian Bill Cosby as a somewhat beleaguered, professional-class father and husband, *The Cosby Show* exudes much of the same appeal offered by such 1950s sitcoms as *Father Knows Best,* although, unlike any 1950s sitcom, it is about an African-American family. *Family Ties,* another family-oriented, professional-class sitcom, which was at one time President Reagan's favorite show,[5] starred Michael J. Fox as a brash, pro-Reagan teenager living in a family of liberals. *Roseanne,* which garnered top ratings soon after its debut in fall

1988 and ran through 1997, was a coarser, more hard-edged family sitcom about a working-class family who struggle to make ends meet and fulfill their obligations. Starring Roseanne Barr and John Goodman, it presents a darker, less idealized view of family dynamics than previously seen on American sitcoms.

Perhaps in response to consciousness-raising efforts by feminists and advocate groups for senior Americans such as the Gray Panthers, the networks altered their typical practice of omitting men and, especially, women older than age 40 from their programming and reaped the benefits of their decision, as several top shows in the late 1980s centered on women in their forties or older. *The Golden Girls* features four mature women living together in Miami, seeking to make the most of their so-called golden years; *Murder, She Wrote* starred Angela Lansbury as a middle-aged mystery writer with a knack for solving real murders; *Murphy Brown,* which debuted in 1988, starred Candice Bergen as a 40-something award-winning television journalist who is also a recovering alcoholic and an outspoken, opinionated liberal. Andy Griffith, who had starred as a clever but unpretentious North Carolina sheriff in *Andy of Mayberry* more than 25 years earlier, was 60 years old when his second hit show, *Matlock,* debuted in 1986.

Other popular shows in the latter part of the decade include *Cheers,* about a group of friends who meet regularly at a Boston bar; *L.A. Law,* featuring the dramas within a high-powered Los Angeles law firm; and *Kate & Allie,* about two divorcées and their children who share a New York apartment to make ends meet. *60 Minutes,* the CBS newsmagazine that began in 1968 and features well-documented investigative reporting, remained a top-rated show throughout the decade. Likewise, ABC's long-running *Monday Night Football* continued to attract large audiences.

As in the 1950s, which the 1980s in some ways mirrored, literature and theater of the Reagan era express cold war angst that was typically absent from television, with the exceptions of ABC's television movie *The Day After* (1983), which purports to offer a depressingly realistic scenario of life after a nuclear war, and the ABC miniseries *Amerika* (1987), which similarly treats the topic of life after the United States has capitulated to the Soviet Union rather than fight a nuclear war. Influential nonfiction that documents nuclear strategies and consequences included Robert Sheer's *With Enough Shovels: Reagan, Bush & Nuclear War* (1982) and Jonathan Schell's *The Fate of the Earth* (1982), which carefully considers several scenarios for nuclear war and concludes that a devastating nuclear winter would result from any large-scale nuclear exchange. Arthur's Kopit's play *End of the World* (1982) uses the film noir detective genre to suggest that nuclear war is inevitable, both because of the long-term logic of mutually assured destruction and because of an innate human impulse toward self-destruction.

Inspired by a real-life survivalist movement among individuals, most of them men, who did not trust the government to protect them in a post–nuclear war environment, survivalist fiction imagines postapocalyptic scenarios in which tough, independent people who have prepared for the disaster by arming and training themselves prevail in a lawless, hostile post–nuclear war environment. Among the more popular examples of that genre is Dean Ing's *Pulling Through* (1983). The Canadian author Margaret Atwood fashions a feminist nightmare in *The Handmaid's Tale* (1985), an imagined account of a postwar America stripped of its Constitution and ruled by extreme, misogynistic elements of the Christian Right. Carolyn See's *Golden Days* (1987) posits a more upbeat postapocalyptic future in its depiction of Californians whose pop psychology and Eastern mysticism enable them to face the postnuclear world with a positive attitude.

The political activism of the 1970s yielded a literary environment in the 1980s that was more open to and nurturing of the writings of women and minorities than at any previous time in American history, and several African-American women were among those to achieve special recognition. Alice Walker's *The Color Purple* won the 1982 National Book Award and the Pulitzer Prize in fiction; in 1985, Stephen Spielberg adapted it into a Academy Award–nominated film that starred Whoopi Goldberg, Danny Glover, and Oprah Winfrey. Toni Morrison published the novels *Tar Baby* (1981) and *Beloved* (1987), a Pulitzer Prize–winning story of a runaway slave who kills her child rather than allow her to be returned to bondage. Winfrey, a top-rated television talk-show host, produced and starred in the 1998 cinematic adaptation directed by Jonathan Demme and costarring Glover and Thandie Newton. Gloria Naylor won acclaim for *The Women of Brewster Place* (1982), which narrates the stories of several black women residing in the same housing project; and the poet Maya Angelou published several collections, including *The Heart of a Woman* (1981) and *All God's Children Need Traveling Shoes* (1986).

Other minority writers also found success during the decade. Maxine Hong Kingston and Amy Tan published widely read novels that explore the ethnic identities of Chinese Americans: Kingston's *China Men* (1980) and *Tripmaster Monkey: His Fake Book* (1989) and Tan's *The Joy Luck Club* (1989). Successful writers of Hispanic origin include Mexican-American Rolando Hinojosa (*Rites and Witnesses,* 1982), Mexican-American Sandra Cisneros (*The House on Mango Street,* 1983), and Cuban-American Oscar Hijuelos, who won the 1989 Pulitzer Prize for *The Mambo Kings Play Songs of Love*. Native American authors, notably Leslie Marmon Silko and N. Scott Momaday, also found new audiences among mainstream readers.

Before the 1980s, an openly homosexual point of view was largely absent from mainstream American literature; more commonly, homosexuality was represented as a form of moral perversion and/or a manifestation of weak character, especially in men. During the red scare of the 1950s it was often associated with vulnerability to communism. But in the 1980s a body of literature that presents homosexuality in a more sympathetic and humane light emerged. For instance, in addition to addressing matters of racial discrimination and identity, *The Color Purple* celebrates spiritual and physical love between women. Several gay authors published autobiographies presenting their experiences in an unwelcoming, if not outright hostile America; others wrote novels that describe the "coming out" experience in which gays openly acknowledge their homosexuality. Novels describing young men who come out to their parents include Edmund White's *A Boy's Own Story* (1980), Robert Ferro's *The Family of Max Desir* (1983), and David Leavitt's *The Lost Language of Cranes* (1986), in which the father also admits that he is gay. Paul Monette's *Borrowed Time: An AIDS Memoir* (1988) addresses the acquired immunodeficiency syndrome (AIDS) epidemic which was ravaging the homosexual community by the end of the decade and hit the literary and artistic communities especially hard.

Crime writers such as Elmore Leonard, James W. Hall, Edna Buchanan, and Carl Hiaasen explored ways to interject serious treatments of contemporary social and political matters into genre formulae. Judith Krantz and Danielle Steel continued to attract large, predominantly female audiences in such traditional genres as the romance novel, while a larger number of women than in the past were able to publish so-called literary fiction that had traditionally been dominated by men. Some, such as Atwood in *The Handmaid's Tale,* express strong feminist political sensibilities; others, such as Bobbie Ann Mason and Anne Tyler, address issues of female identity within the contexts of other issues. In Mason's *In Country* a young working-class woman achieves clarity about her personal identity and fundamental values by trying to comprehend the wartime experiences that traumatized Vietnam veterans and killed her father before she was born. Tyler garnered praise for *Dinner at the Homesick Restaurant* (1982), *The Accidental Tourist* (1985), and *Breathing Lessons,* which won the 1988 Pulitzer Prize. Other authors who received critical acclaim include Tama Janowitz, Joyce Carol Oates, Cynthia Ozick, Eudora Welty, and Alison Lurie, whose *Foreign Affairs* won the 1984 Pulitzer Prize.

A so-called minimalist style gained favor among the literati during the 1980s. Popularized by Raymond Carver, author of *What We Talk About When We Talk About Love* (1981) and *Cathedral* (1983); the short-story writer Donald Barthelme; and other *New Yorker* writers, it was notable for its subtle but provocative prose. William Kennedy won the 1983 Pulitzer Prize for *Ironweed,* a story of an elderly homeless couple that helped draw attention to the plight of the American homeless in the early 1980s. As does *In Country,* Don DeLillo's *White Noise,* winner of the 1985 National Book Award, shows how American culture is thoroughly embedded in consumer capitalism, as characters relate to one another primarily through consumer goods and advertisements, which they use as their essential points of reference in life. However, despite its postmodern sensibilities, *White Noise* ultimately concludes that a shared fear of death connects contemporary American consumers to humans throughout history. In *Libra* (1988), DeLillo creates a scenario for the Kennedy assassination in which two Central Intelligence Agency (CIA) operatives decide that an unsuccessful attempt to murder the president would unite the nation against the communist threat. Garrison Keillor, whose radio show *A Prairie Home Companion* enjoyed a national audience devoted to its wisdom and incisive but gentle humor, published several novels in that vein, notably *Lake Wobegon Days* (1985). Tom Wolfe's *The Bonfire of the Vanities* (1987) explores divisions and animosities based on class and race in a story of a wealthy young Wall Street investor who accidentally kills a black child while driving through the slums of the Bronx. In *The Dean's December* (1982) Nobel Prize winner Saul Bellow compares Communist and capitalist cultures in Bucharest and Chicago.

Theater flourished in the 1980s, and it covered a wide range of contemporary and historical subjects. Among the most influential and acclaimed dramatists were Woody Allen (*The Floating Light Bulb,* 1981), Wilson August (*Fences,* 1986, and the Pulitzer Prize–winning *The Piano Lesson,* 1989), David Edgar (*The Life and Adventures of Nicholas Nickleby,* 1981), Herb Gardner (*I'm Not Rappaport,* 1985), Tina Howe (*Coastal Disturbances,* 1986), David Henry Hwang

(*M. Butterfly,* 1988), David Mamet (*Edmond,* 1982; *Glengarry Glen Ross,* 1984; *Speed-the-Plow,* 1987; *Things Change,* 1988), Arthur Miller (*American Clock,* 1980), John Pielmeier (*Agnes of God,* 1982), Harold Pinter (*Betrayal,* 1980), David Rabe (*Hurlyburly,* 1984), Peter Shaffer (*Amadeus,* 1980), Sam Shepard (*True West,* 1980; *Fool for Love,* 1983), Neil Simon (*Brighton Beach Memoirs,* 1983; *Biloxi Blues,* 1985), Tom Stoppard (*The Real Thing,* 1984; *Artist Descending Staircase,* 1989), Jane Wagner (*The Search for Signs of Intelligent Life in the Universe,* 1985), Wendy Wasserstein (*The Heidi Chronicles,* 1989), Tennessee Williams (*Something Cloudy, Something Clear,* 1981), and Lanford Wilson (*Angels Fall,* 1982; *Burn This,* 1987). Andrew Lloyd Webber's *Cats* (1982), an adaptation of T. S. Eliot's whimsical book of poems *Old Possum's Book of Practical Cats* (1939), was among the most popular musicals of the decade. Webber also achieved success in *Joseph and the Amazing Technicolor Dreamcoat* (1982), on which he collaborated with Tim Rice, and in *The Phantom of the Opera* (1988), on which he collaborated with Richard Stilgoe and Charles Hart. Other top-rated musicals included Jerry Herman's *La Cage aux Folles* (1983), Stephen Sondheim's *Sunday in the Park with George* (1984), and Herbert Kretzmer and Claude-Michel Schönberg's adaptation of the Victor Hugo novel *Les Misérables* (1987).

Music evolved dramatically during the 1980s. The fusion of image and sound became more dominant as fast-paced music videos came into their own on newly available cable television channels such as MTV and on videotapes that entered the market with the introduction of affordable home video recorders in the early 1980s. Compact disc players, another new product, also greatly enhanced the quality of sound reproduction. Singers such as Bruce Springsteen, known as the Boss, and Billy Joel appealed to both patriotic and working-class sentiments in such albums as Springsteen's *Born in the U.S.A.* (1985) and Joel's hit single "Uptown Girl" (1984). On the other hand, some groups working more in the rock tradition challenged the establishment in their music or otherwise addressed political matters. These included the Police, Guns N' Roses, Fine Young Cannibals, and Pink Floyd, whose provocative cinematic rock opera *Pink Floyd—The Wall,* released as a film in 1982, explored the potential connection between nihilistic rock culture and neofascists in search of emotionally charged mass audiences. Sting, who left the Police in the mid-1980s, also articulated social concerns as a solo artist. Fleetwood Mac was another group known for its unique sound and engaging lyrics, which were more personally directed than political. Seemingly androgynous rock singers such as Michael Jackson, Boy George, Annie Lennox of the Eurythmics, Nick Rhodes of Duran Duran, and Grace Jones demonstrated international appeal through both their music and their unconventional and sometimes outrageous personality. They and bisexuals such as David Bowie and Elton John helped promote growing tolerance in Western societies for nontraditional sexual orientations, although acceptance remained far from complete in the 1980s. Top female vocalists included Madonna, a savvy self-promoter and businesswoman, as well as a talented performer, who climbed to fame in 1985 with her album *Like a Virgin.* Tina Turner projected an image of female strength and determination while resurrecting her career after a downturn in the 1970s, and Whitney Houston and the sensual-sounding Sade impressed listeners with their vocal abilities. Among the top male singers were Jackson, Sting, Springsteen, Prince, George Michael, and John Bon Jovi.

Music evolved in many other diverse areas, including the introduction of rap, black urban music with heavy rhymes, and punk, which was part of an antiestablishment social movement that emanated from Britain and sought to shock middle-class sensibilities with wild multicolored hairstyles, outrageous costumes, and slogans and lyrics calculated to offend conventional listeners. Jazz incorporated more Latin influences and otherwise fused with other kinds of music, while classical musicians experimented with new technologies and the very nature of sound and silence. Important jazz performers of the 1980s included Count Basie, Miles Davis, Branford Marsalis, Wynton Marsalis, Pat Metheny, Sarah Vaughan, Grover Washington, Jr., and the group Manhattan Transfer. Tito Puente and Celia Cruz continued to popularize traditional Latin salsa, as they had since the 1950s, and Gloria Estefan fused Latin sounds and rhythms with North American influences.

CHRONICLE OF EVENTS

1980

January 29: Six Americans who had been hiding in Tehran since the seizure of the American embassy in November 1979 escape from Iran by posing as Canadian diplomats. The escape is arranged by the Canadian government, which supplies diplomatic passports, and by the CIA, which forges Iranian visas in the passports.

February 2: The Federal Bureau of Investigation (FBI) announces it has conducted a two-year sting operation targeted at congressmen suspected of accepting bribes. One senator and four congressmen are indicted and later convicted as a result of Operation Abscam, short for Arab Scam, because FBI agents posed as wealthy Arab sheiks seeking political favors.

February 12–24: The Winter Olympics are held in Lake Placid, New York. The U.S. speed skater Eric Heiden wins a record five gold medals, and in a competition fraught with patriotic sentiment the United States defeats the Soviet Union in hockey and then goes on to win the gold medal by defeating Finland.

March 24: The Catholic archbishop Oscar Romero is assassinated in El Salvador while holding a mass in honor of a journalist who had opposed the government. Government-backed right-wing paramilitary groups are suspected of murdering Romero, an outspoken human rights advocate and promoter of economic and political reform.

April 4: A bus smashes into the Peruvian embassy in Havana, and the 25 Cubans inside seek political asylum. In response, Premier Fidel Castro permits all Cubans to leave the island, initiating the Mariel boat lift.

April 7: President Jimmy Carter severs diplomatic relations with Iran in response to the taking of hostages from the U.S. embassy in Tehran in November 1979.

April 18: Rhodesia becomes the independent state of Zimbabwe, and Robert Mugabe, the leader of Rhodesia's largest guerrilla army, becomes prime minister of the black-majority nation.

April 25: An attempt by U.S. commandos to free the Iranian hostages fails when American helicopters break down in a desert sandstorm, and eight soldiers die. Secretary of State Cyrus Vance subsequently resigns in protest over the action, which was taken over his objections.

May: Officials from New York State and the federal government agree on a plan to evacuate the 710 families remaining in the contaminated Love Canal area of Niagara Falls. Residents of homes near an abandoned chemical dump in the area have been found to have a disproportionately large number of chemically related illnesses, which they attribute to the leakage of toxic waste from the dump.

May 4: Yugoslavia's Marshal Tito dies and is succeeded by a collective rotating presidency.

May 18: Triggered by an earthquake centered beneath it, Mount Saint Helens, a volcano in southwest Washington State that had been dormant for 123 years, erupts, spewing tons of ash into the air, killing scores of people, and causing severe environmental damage.

May 20: Voters in Quebec, Canada, reject by a 3-2 ratio a proposal calling for the French-speaking province to become a sovereign state.

July 19: The Summer Olympics open in Moscow, but the United States boycotts the games to protest the Soviet invasion of Afghanistan.

August 11: China orders the removal of most public portraits, slogans, and poems of Mao Zedong.

August 24: The Polish government negotiates a settlement with the Solidarity Trade Union, providing the right of workers to unionize, reducing working hours, and permitting greater freedom for news media.

September 22: Iraq invades Iran, initiating the eight-year Gulf War, which produces casualties exceeding those in World War I.

November 4: The Republican candidate Ronald Reagan defeats the incumbent Jimmy Carter in the U.S. presidential election.

November 20: In China the radical Gang of Four, who had influenced Chairman Mao Zedong during his final year, stands trial for treason. Among the convicted is Jiang Qing, Mao's widow.

December 8: The songwriter, political activist, and former singer in the Beatles rock band John Lennon is assassinated outside his New York apartment building by a fan, Mark David Chapman.

1981

January 10: The Alabama Supreme Court nullifies a law prohibiting the use of obscene language in the presence of women.

January 20: Ronald Reagan is inaugurated as the 40th U.S. president, and George Herbert Walker Bush is sworn in as vice president.

January 20: Concurrent with Reagan's inauguration, 52 American hostages taken in 1979 from the U.S. embassy in Tehran, Iran, are released.

January 29: Reagan orders a 60-day freeze on implementing new government regulations.

January 31: The nuclear power plant in Indian Point, New York, is shut down after leaks are discovered.

February 9: After five months of serious labor unrest and massive demonstrations, Jozef Pinkowski is removed as prime minister of Poland and replaced by the more hard-line General Wojciech Jaruzelski.

March 30: Reagan is shot in the chest and severely wounded while returning to his limousine after addressing a labor meeting at the Washington Hilton Hotel, but he manages to joke with emergency room staff on his way to surgery. Press Secretary James S. Brady and two guards are also wounded. John W. Hinckley, Jr., is arrested on the scene.

April 11: Declining the use of a wheelchair, Reagan leaves the hospital and returns to the White House, where he continues his recovery from the assassination attempt.

April 12: The United States renews manned exploration of outer space with the inaugural flight of the space shuttle *Columbia.* The first reusable spacecraft, piloted by astronauts John W. Young and Captain Robert L. Crippen of the U.S. Navy, returns to Earth on April 14.

April 30: The Democratic senator Harrison A. Williams of New Jersey is convicted of bribery and conspiracy charges related to the FBI's Abscam sting operation. Williams is the first U.S. senator since 1905 to be convicted while in office and only the third in U.S. history.

May 10: François Mitterrand is elected the first Socialist president of France since the establishment of the Fifth Republic in 1958.

May 11: The Jamaican reggae performer Bob Marley dies of cancer in Miami at age 36.

May 13: Pope John Paul II is shot twice in the abdomen during an assassination attempt while riding in an open car in Saint Peter's Square in Vatican City. Police arrest the gunman, whom they identify as Mehmet Ali Agça. Agça is convicted on July 22 and sentenced to life in prison.

August 6: Reagan fires 12,000 striking federal air traffic controllers.

September 25: Sandra Day O'Connor is sworn in as the first female Supreme Court justice.

October 6: Egypt's president Anwar Sadat is assassinated by Egyptian soldiers participating in a military parade in Cairo. He is succeeded by Hosni Mubarak.

December: The United States grants economic and military assistance to El Salvador in order to combat leftist guerrillas.

December: Reagan directs the CIA to arm and organize Nicaraguan exiles who are attempting to overthrow the Communist Sandinista regime. These exiles become known as contras.

December 13: General Jaruzelski imposes martial law in Poland, bans Solidarity, and arrests its leader Lech Walesa.

1982

January 8: The Justice Department announces that the American Telephone and Telegraph Company (AT&T) has agreed to settle an antitrust suit by divesting 22 local Bell System companies.

April 2: The Falklands War between Argentina and Britain begins when thousands of Argentine soldiers invade the Falkland Islands (Islas Malvinas) off Argentina's southern coast.

May 30: Spain joins the North Atlantic Treaty Organization (NATO).

June 6: Some 60,000 Israeli troops invade Lebanon with the intention of ending guerrilla attacks against Israeli territory and driving the Palestine Liberation Organization (PLO) from the country.

June 12: More than 800,000 New Yorkers protest nuclear proliferation.

June 14: The Falklands War ends as Argentine forces surrender to Britain after their defeat at Goose Green in late May. Some 256 British and approximately 750 Argentine soldiers die in the fighting.

June 17: General Leopoldo Galtieri, Argentina's president and member of the ruling military junta, resigns.

June 21: A jury finds John W. Hinckley, Jr., not guilty by reason of insanity of attempting to assassinate Reagan. Hinckley is incarcerated in a mental institution.

June 25: Secretary of State Alexander Haig resigns as a result of disagreement with Reagan over foreign policy. He is replaced by George Shultz, who had been President Richard Nixon's secretary of the treasury.

August: Israeli troops force the PLO from Beirut. Many relocate in Tripoli, Lebanon, and in Cyprus.

September 1–12: The 12th Congress of the Chinese Communist Party restructures its constitution and elects Deng Xiaoping chairman of the new Central Advisory Commission.

September 14: Princess Grace of Monaco dies at age 52 in an automobile accident in Monte Carlo. Before marrying Prince Rainier III, the former Grace Kelly had been a widely admired movie star.

September 14: Bashir Gemayel, head of the Christian Phalangist Party and the president-elect of Lebanon, is assassinated in Beirut.

October 5: The manufacturers of Tylenol recall all bottles of the capsule form of the pain-relief drug after eight people are poisoned by pills that have been deliberately contaminated with strychnine. The incident leads to new safety controls on the packaging of medicines.

November 10: The Soviet premier Leonid Brezhnev dies.

November 12: Yuri Andropov, another elderly member of the Soviet Union's conservative, hard-line old guard and the former head of the KGB, the Soviet security organization, replaces Brezhnev as general secretary of the Communist Party.

November 12–14: The space shuttle *Columbia* makes its first fully operational flight.

November 22: Reagan announces his decision to deploy the controversial MX intercontinental ballistic missile (ICBM).

December 12: More than 20,000 British women surround the Greenham Common air base to protest peacefully the decision to install intermediate-range U.S. cruise missiles in England.

December 21: Reagan reluctantly signs into law the Intelligence Authorization Act, containing the first Boland amendment, which forbids the covert use of funds to overthrow the government of Nicaragua.

1983

January 25: Klaus Barbie, a World War II–era Nazi war criminal nicknamed the Butcher of Lyons, is arrested in La Paz, Bolivia.

March 8: Speaking before a convention of the National Association of Evangelicals in Orlando, Florida, Reagan denounces the Soviet Union as "the focus of evil in the modern world." Delegates respond enthusiastically, and a band plays "Onward Christian Soldiers."

March 23: Reagan proposes the Strategic Defense Initiative (SDI).

April 18: A car bomb explodes outside the U.S. embassy in Beirut, killing more than 40 people, including several Americans. Islamic terrorist groups are held responsible.

June 18: The 32-year-old physicist Sally K. Ride becomes the first American woman to enter outer space when she begins a six-day mission on the space shuttle *Challenger.* Some 250,000 spectators witness her return to Earth at Edwards Air Force Base in California on June 24.

August 4: Italy's first Socialist prime minister, Bettino Craxi, is sworn in as head of a coalition government.

August 22: Benigno S. Aquino, Jr., the main political rival of Philippine president Ferdinand Marcos, is assassinated in Manila.

September 1: Soviet jets shoot down a civilian South Korean passenger plane that has entered Soviet airspace, killing all 269 aboard, including an anti-Soviet U.S. congressman and 60 other American citizens. The downing of KAL Flight 007 provokes international outrage and elevates cold war tensions to their highest levels since the 1962 Cuban missile crisis.

October 17: The Environmental Protection Agency (EPA) and National Academy of Sciences publish reports predicting severe problems associated with global warming.

October 23: A terrorist car bomb in Beirut kills 241 U.S. Marines serving as peacekeepers in Lebanon, in accordance with the Reagan doctrine.

October 25: More than 1,900 U.S. Marines invade the Caribbean island of Grenada. They encounter minimal resistance, most of it from armed construction workers, and quickly depose Grenada's Marxist government.

October 31: Meeting in Washington for the World after Nuclear War Conference, scientists from the United States, the Soviet Union, and other nations warn that a devastating "nuclear winter" could follow a large-scale nuclear war.

November 14: The first U.S. cruise missiles arrive in England for deployment at the Greenham Common air base.

November 15: Peace activists at Greenham Common, most of them women, protest the deployment of the cruise missiles.

November 23: After U.S.-Soviet arms limitation negotiations break down, the Soviet Union announces that it will increase its nuclear forces.

December 20: Syria forces the PLO from Tripoli, Lebanon. The PLO leader Yasser Arafat relocates the organization in Tunisia.

1984

January: The CIA secretly mines harbors in Nicaragua.

January 18: Islamic terrorists assassinate Malcolm H. Kerr, the president of the American University in Beirut.

February 9: Soviet premier Yuri Andropov dies.

February 13: Konstantin Chernenko, another elderly hard-liner, is named general secretary of the Soviet Union's Communist Party.

February 29: Canada's prime minister Pierre Trudeau announces his resignation after serving as head of state and leader of the Liberal Party for 15 years.

April 30: At the conclusion of a six-day visit to China, Reagan signs cultural and scientific agreements and approves a tax accord that enables U.S. businesses to conduct business in China more easily.

June 5–7: Government troops sent to suppress violence in India's Punjab region assault the holiest of Sikh shrines, the Golden Temple in Amritsar, which is occupied by protesters who are calling for greater autonomy for the region. More than 400 Sikhs are killed, and protests break out throughout India, leaving at least 27 people dead.

July 12: The Democratic Party presidential candidate Walter Mondale names Geraldine Ferraro, a congresswoman from Queens, New York, as his running mate. Ferraro becomes the first woman to be nominated vice president by a major American political party. Mondale and Ferraro officially secure the party's nomination on July 19.

July 18: The nation experiences its largest death toll to date by a single gunman in a single day when an unemployed security guard carrying a semiautomatic rifle, a shotgun, and a pistol opens fire at a McDonald's restaurant in San Ysidro, California, killing 20 and wounding 16 before a police sharpshooter kills him.

July 28: The Olympic Summer Games open in Los Angeles. The Soviet Union and all its Eastern bloc allies, except Romania, boycott the games in retaliation for the U.S. boycott of the 1980 games in Moscow.

September 3: A bomb kills three people and wounds 40 others when it explodes in Montreal's principal railroad station. The bombing is believed to be connected to the visit of Pope John Paul II scheduled for the following week.

September 17: The Conservative Brian Mulroney becomes prime minister of Canada. His inauguration places conservative heads of state in all three North Atlantic, Anglo-American nations: Canada, Britain, and the United States. Reelected in 1988, Mulroney holds office through June 13, 1993.

September 20: Dozens are killed when the second car bomb in 17 months explodes outside the U.S. embassy in Beirut. Islamic terrorists claim responsibility.

October 31: India's prime minister Indira Gandhi is assassinated by two Sikh members of her personal security guard.

November 6: Reagan overwhelmingly wins reelection by defeating Carter's vice president, Walter Mondale.

December 3: A toxic gas leak from an insecticide plant owned by Union Carbide kills some 2,100 people in Bhopal, India.

December 19: Great Britain and China sign an accord in which Britain agrees to return control of Hong Kong to China in 1997, when Britain's 99-year lease on Hong Kong Island, Kowloon, and the New Territories expires.

1985

January 20: Reagan is officially inaugurated for his second term in a private ceremony.

January 20: The Washington Redskins defeat the Miami Dolphins 38-16 in Super Bowl XIX.

January 21: To preclude conflict with the Super Bowl, Reagan's public inauguration, followed by a parade and gala balls, takes place today.

March 10: Chernenko dies.

March 11: Mikhail Gorbachev succeeds Chernenko as general secretary of the Soviet Communist Party.

March 12–April 23: The United States and Soviet Union initiate a new round of Strategic Arms Reduction Talks (START) in Geneva.

May 1: The United States imposes a total trade and financial embargo on Nicaragua.

May 13: Philadelphia police end a 24-hour siege during which they fought with armed radicals by dropping a bomb on the inner-city apartment serving as headquarters for MOVE, a militant group who reject modern technology and consumerism. At least

11 people are killed and a residential city block is destroyed. Police blame MOVE for setting the fire by igniting gasoline, but in November, Police Commissioner George J. Sambor resigns as a result of protests of his handling of the incident.

June 10: Three years after invading Lebanon, Israel begins withdrawing its troops.

June 10: Thomas Sutherland becomes the eighth American to be kidnapped by Palestinians in Lebanon. He is freed on November 19, 1991, along with a British hostage, Terry Waite.

June 14: Demanding that Israel release 700 Shiite and Palestinian prisoners, Islamic terrorists associated with the Iranian-backed Hezbollah hijack TWA Flight 847. They kill a U.S. Navy diver, Robert Stethem, and take other Americans hostage. The hostages are released on June 30.

July 8: In a speech before the American Bar Association, Reagan accuses Iran, Libya, North Korea, Cuba, and Nicaragua of being a "confederation of terrorist states" that are carrying out "outright war" against the United States.

September 11: The Cincinnati Reds third baseman Pete Rose gets his 4,192th career hit to break Ty Cobb's 57-year-old record.

September 19: A powerful earthquake measuring 7.8 on the Richter scale kills some 20,000 people in Mexico City. An aftershock the next day measures 7.3.

October 1: In retaliation for the killings of three Israelis on Cyprus, Israeli jets attack PLO offices in Tunisia, killing 60.

October 7: Members of the Palestine Liberation Front hijack the Mediterranean cruise ship *Achille Lauro* and kill Leon Klinghoffer, a 69-year-old wheelchair-bound Jewish American from New York.

October 9: Hijackers of the *Achille Lauro* surrender in exchange for a pledge of safe passage. But when an Egyptian jet tries to fly them to freedom, U.S. Navy fighters intercept it and force it to land in Sicily, where the terrorists are taken into custody by Italian authorities. Italy's prime minister Bettino Craxi, however, rejects Reagan's request that U.S. forces assume custody of terrorist leader, Abu Abbas, insisting that Italy has sovereignty over the NATO base in Sicily. Abbas subsequently escapes and is convicted in absentia. He will be arrested in Baghdad in April 2003, after the U.S. invasion of Iraq that ousts Saddam Hussein.

November 14: The Nevada del Ruiz volcano erupts in northern Colombia, spawning mud slides that bury two mountain towns and kill some 20,000 people.

November 19–21: In Geneva, Reagan and Gorbachev hold their first of five summit meetings, after which they announce their agreement that nuclear war cannot be won and should never be fought and that neither side will seek military superiority.

December 5: The Dow-Jones industrial average sets a new record when it exceeds 1,500.

December 23: In response to a farming crisis, Reagan signs a $52 billion farm bill, the costliest in U.S. history, which is expected to favor large producers and accelerate the trend toward fewer, but larger, farms producing a greater share of the nation's food.

December 27: Pro-Palestinian terrorists open fire and hurl grenades at the crowded counters of El Al Israel Airlines in coordinated attacks at airports in Rome and Vienna, killing 14 and wounding at least 110.

December 30: After eight years martial law is lifted in Pakistan.

1986

January 28: The space shuttle *Challenger* explodes on takeoff, killing all seven astronauts aboard. Televised live and witnessed by millions, the disaster marks the beginning of a series of serious setbacks that will plague the National Aeronautics and Space Administration (NASA) through the end of the decade.

February 15: Despite allegations of election fraud, President Ferdinand Marcos is declared winner of the presidential elections in the Philippines; the United States refuses to accept the results.

February 25: After massive popular protests, defections within the army, and opposition from the United States, Marcos flees to Guam. Corazon Aquino, the widow of his major political opponent, receives U.S. recognition as winner of the popular election and, on February 27, she is sworn in as president.

February 24–March 6: The Congress of the Soviet Communist Party approves major changes to the membership of the Central Committee and Politburo and rejects outmoded thinking from the past.

March 12: A public referendum leaves Spain in NATO but removes it from the NATO military command structure and retains a ban on nuclear weapons on Spanish soil.

The televised explosion of the space shuttle *Challenger* horrified onlookers and set back the national space program. *(AP/ Wide World Photos)*

March 24: After alleged Libyan attacks on U.S. aircraft, U.S. warplanes bomb targets in Libya. The Soviet Union denounces the action as a threat to world security.

April 2: A bomb explodes during a Trans World Airlines (TWA) commercial flight from Rome to Athens, killing four passengers, who are sucked out of the hole in the plane's side. The Arab Revolutionary Cells takes responsibility, claiming the bombing is retaliation for U.S. action against Libya.

April 4: In West Berlin, Libyan agents explode a bomb in a crowded discotheque frequented by U.S. servicemen. Two people are killed and more than 150 wounded. One of those killed and more than 50 of those wounded are Americans.

April 15: In response to the recent bombings, the United States attacks terrorist bases in Libya, and Libya retaliates by aiming missiles at radar installations on the Italian island of Lampedusa. However, they fail to strike their targets.

April 17: Three British hostages are killed in retaliation for the U.S. attack on Libya.

April 18: U.S. hostage Peter Kilburn is executed in Beirut.

April 25–26: A core meltdown of the number 4 reactor at Chernobyl in the Ukraine results in the worst accident to date at a nuclear power plant. The Soviet government suppresses news of the accident for four days, as prevailing winds spread radioactive contamination to Western Europe.

May 19: China and Taiwan hold their first face-to-face talks since the founding of the People's Republic of China in 1949.

May 25: Millions of Americans, including Reagan, join hands to form a human chain in the Hands across America campaign to raise money for the homeless.

October 11–12: Reagan and Gorbachev meet in Reykjavik, Iceland, where the Soviets surprise U.S. negotiators by offering wide-ranging proposals to reduce strategic weapons by 50 percent and eliminate intermediate-range nuclear forces (INFs).

November 3: A Lebanese newspaper reports that in 1985 the United States secretly sold arms to Iran in return for Iran's promise to release American hostages held by terrorist groups in Lebanon. Investigation of these claims leads to the Iran-contra scandal.

November 13: Reagan acknowledges that his administration conducted a secret arms deal with Iran.

November 18: Ivan Boesky, one of the wealthiest and most prominent investors on Wall Street, pleads guilty to insider trading. He agrees to pay a $100 million fine and to assist the federal investigation of illegal activities. Other major Wall Street figures are subpoenaed, including employees of Drexel Burnham Lambert, a powerful agency known for using high-yield, high-risk junk bonds to facilitate corporate takeovers.

November 25: National Security Advisor John Poindexter and Lieutenant Colonel Oliver North are dismissed from their jobs for their roles in the Iran-contra affair.

December 15: Shortly before he is to testify before a Senate panel about his role in the Iran-contra affair, CIA director William J. Casey suffers a stroke. He will undergo brain surgery three days later and die of nervous-system lymphoma on May 6, 1987, without ever commenting publicly about his role.

December 21: The Census Bureau announces that by the year 2000, the world's population will exceed 6 billion.

December 30: For the first time in his presidency Reagan experiences a sharp drop in public approval, from 67 to 46 percent, after his admission in a weekly radio broadcast that "mistakes were made" in the handling of the Iran-contra affair.

1987

February 28: Gorbachev drops his demand that the United States repudiate the Strategic Defense Initiative (SDI) as part of an agreement to eliminate intermediate nuclear weapons in Europe. This act resolves the only remaining outstanding difference over the INF treaty to eliminate all intermediate-range nuclear missiles in Europe.

March 19: Claiming that he was tricked into a sexual encounter with a woman, the evangelist Jim Bakker resigns from his popular television ministry. The Reverend Jerry Falwell, the founder of the Moral Majority, replaces Bakker as head of the Praise the Lord (PTL) ministry, which has been receiving some $100 million a year in contributions from viewers.

May 8: Senator Gary Hart, a top contender, drops out of the race for the Democratic presidential nomination after the discovery of his sexual tryst with a 27-year-old model, Donna Rice, during a trip to Bimini on a friend's yacht, *Monkey Business.*

May 15: After testimony on May 6 by General Richard Secord that claims that the president knew of the diversion of funds to the contras, Reagan takes responsibility for initiating the plan to use private money to aid the rebels.

May 17: An Iraqi jet fires on the USS *Stark,* which is in the Persian Gulf to escort Kuwaiti oil tankers transporting Iraqi oil, killing 37 crew members. Iraq apologizes for what it maintains was a mistake, and the United States accepts the explanation and declines to retaliate for the attack.

June 11: The Conservative Margaret Thatcher wins reelection, the first British prime minister in 160 years to be elected to a third term.

June 21: For the first time in Soviet history, reforms allow voters to choose from more than one candidate in some local elections.

August 17: Rudolf Hess commits suicide at the Spandau Prison in West Berlin, where he had been in solitary confinement since the end of World War II. The 93-year-old Hess, who had been part of Nazi leader Adolf Hitler's inner circle, was serving a life sentence for war crimes.

October 1: An earthquake measuring 6.1 on the Richter scale strikes close to Los Angeles, killing six and causing limited damage.

October 19: On so-called Black Monday the Dow-Jones industrial average loses 508 points in the largest single-day loss in the history of the market.

The crash sparks fears of an impending economic depression, which does not occur.

November 18: Democratic Party–dominated Senate and House panels release a joint report holding Reagan responsible for the Iran-contra fiasco and accusing the administration of permitting pervasive dishonesty and tolerating lack of adherence to proper procedures and legal requirements at the highest levels of government. But the report falls short of accusing Reagan of illegal action. Republicans on the panel issue a minority report refuting these conclusions and accusing the majority of conducting partisan politics.

December 8: Gorbachev and Reagan sign the INF treaty.

December 15: Maintaining that his new ideas require a voice, Gary Hart reenters the race for the Democratic presidential nomination.

1988

January 1: Gorbachev policies of *perestroika*—the liberalization of the Soviet economy in which private enterprises play a considerably larger role—take effect.

January 29: Angolan-Cuban talks begin with U.S. participation.

February 5: The U.S. Justice Department indicts Panama's leader, General Manuel Noriega, on two counts of drug smuggling dating from 1981. The indictment accuses Noriega of accepting bribes and kickbacks and assisting a multimillion-dollar drug cartel based in Colombia.

February 8: Gorbachev announces that Soviet troops will begin withdrawing from Afghanistan on May 15 and will complete the troop removal by February 15, 1989.

February 21: The popular television evangelist Jimmy Swaggart resigns his ministry after admitting that he had sex with a prostitute, Debra Murphee. Swaggart, who owns three luxury homes and who labeled his fellow television evangelist Jim Bakker a "cancer on the body of Christ" after Bakker confessed to adultery in 1987, faces the collapse of an organization that takes in some $140 million per year in contributions from viewers in 140 nations.

March 23: Nicaragua's ruling Sandinista government signs a 60-day cease-fire agreement with contra leaders.

April 4: Arizona's state senate votes overwhelmingly to remove Governor Evan Meecham from office for financial impropriety and obstruction of justice. This is the first time since 1929 that a governor is removed.

May 15: The Soviet Union begins withdrawing its troops from Afghanistan.

May 29: Reagan begins a four-day visit to Moscow and endorses Gorbachev's reforms.

June 9: The cease-fire between the Sandinistas and contras ends without a permanent peace agreement.

June 23: Testifying before a congressional committee, James E. Hansen, head of the Institute for Space Studies, attributes the year's exceptionally high summer temperatures to global warming that is caused by an increase in the level of carbon dioxide in the Earth's atmosphere—the so-called greenhouse effect. Noting that the Great Plains, South, and Midwest are experiencing their worst drought in 50 years, Hansen points out that the four hottest years of the century have occurred during the 1980s and warns that temperatures in the higher latitudes could rise by 20 degrees by the year 2500.

June 28–July 1: The Soviet Communist Party approves six resolutions for Gorbachev's *perestroika*.

July 1: Iraq admits that it used chemical weapons during an attack in March on the Iranian-occupied Iraqi town of Halabja, in which almost 5,000 Kurds were killed by mustard gas and cyanide. Iraq accuses Iran of using chemical weapons first.

July 3: The U.S. warship *Vincennes,* on patrol in the Persian Gulf, shoots down an Iranian passenger plane, killing all 290 people aboard.

July 18: Iran formally accepts United Nations (UN) Resolution 598 calling for a cease-fire in the Iran-Iraq Gulf War.

July 21: Massachusetts governor Michael Dukakis accepts the Democratic Party's nomination for president. Texas senator Lloyd Bentsen is his running mate.

July 31: King Hussein relinquishes Jordan's claim to the Israeli-occupied West Bank, which Hussein envisions as a future independent Palestinian state.

August 17: Pakistan's military ruler, Mohammad Zia ul-Haq, dies in a plane crash, along with the American ambassador, Arnold Raphael, and most of Pakistan's military elite. A U.S.-Pakistani commission later concludes that the crash resulted from sabotage inside the plane.

August 18: Vice President George H. W. Bush receives the Republican nomination for president. The Indiana senator J. Danforth Quayle is his running mate.

September 17–October 2: The Soviet Union wins the most medals in the Summer Olympics held in Seoul, Korea.

November 8: Bush defeats Dukakis in the U.S. presidential election.

December 2: After her People's Party wins parliamentary elections in Pakistan, 35-year-old Benazir Bhutto becomes the world's youngest prime minister and the first woman in centuries to rule an Islamic state.

December 7: Gorbachev announces plans unilaterally to reduce Soviet armed forces by 500,000 troops and cut conventional arms.

December 22: Angola, South Africa, and Cuba agree to grant Namibia independence from South Africa as of January 1, 1989. The agreement also calls for the withdrawal of Cuban troops.

December 28: All 259 people aboard Pan Am Flight 103 are killed, along with 11 people on the ground, when a bomb explodes inside the plane as it flies over Lockerbie, Scotland. Libyan agents are held responsible.

1989

January 4: U.S. Navy fighter planes shoot down two Libyan military jets over international waters off the coast of Libya. The United States claims that its warplanes acted in self-defense; Libya claims that its planes were unarmed and on routine maneuvers.

January 11: Cuba begins withdrawing troops from Angola.

January 17: An unemployed welder opens fire with an automatic assault rifle at an elementary school in Stockton, California, killing five children and wounding 30 others before killing himself.

January 20: George H. W. Bush is inaugurated as the 41st U.S. president.

January 24: The serial killer Theodore "Ted" Bundy is executed in Florida. Some 200 people standing outside the Florida State Prison in Starke cheer the announcement of the murderer's death.

February 3: The Soviet Union acknowledges that between 1927 and 1953 its leader, Joseph Stalin, was responsible for the death by execution, hard labor, famine, and farm collectivization of some 20 million Soviet citizens and for the arrest and displacement of 20 million more. This is the first comprehensive acknowledgment of Stalin's crimes made public in the Soviet Union.

February 14: Iran's leader, Ayatollah Ruhollah Khomeini, issues a fatwa, condemning the Indian-born novelist Salman Rushdie to death for his depiction of Islam's Prophet, Muhammad, in his novel *Satanic Verses.* Khomeini also offers a $1 million reward to anyone who kills the author; $3 million if the assassin is Iranian. Rushdie subsequently goes into hiding.

February 28: Two bookstores in Berkeley, California, are firebombed for selling *Satanic Verses.*

March 24: The oil tanker *Exxon Valdez* runs aground off the coast of Alaska, leaving an oil spill that covers 500 square miles and causes extensive environmental damage.

March 26: The Soviet Union holds its first democratic elections as citizens elect representatives to the Congress of People's Deputies, which, one month later, elects Gorbachev president of the Soviet Union.

April 5: The Polish government and Solidarity labor union agree to hold free parliamentary elections in June.

April 15–June 4: Chinese students protest in prodemocracy marches in Tiananmen Square until they are suppressed by military force on June 4.

May 4: The space probe *Magellan* is launched from the space shuttle *Atlantis,* en route to Venus, where it will send radar images of the planet's surface back to Earth, some 800 million miles away. Traveling 6,000 miles per hour, *Magellan* is expected to arrive at Venus in August 1990.

May 31: Jim Wright, the Democratic Speaker of the House of Representatives, steps down from his post and offers to resign from the House after revelations that he has committed financial improprieties.

June 3: Ayatollah Khomeini dies in Iran of an illness believed to be cancer.

June 4: Solidarity wins the first partially democratic elections in Poland, and on August 24 its nominee, Tadeusz Mazowiecki, becomes the first non–Communist Party prime minister in the Eastern bloc.

June 21: The Supreme Court rules that flag burning is protected by the Constitution as a form of political speech.

July 31: Shiite Muslims who belong to a pro-Iranian militia group hang Lieutenant Colonel William R. Higgins, who was captured on February 17, 1988, while serving as a member of a UN observer group in Lebanon. The captors, who release a videotape of Higgins hanging by a noose, claim that the execution is retaliation for Israel's kidnapping of Sheik Abdul Karim Obeid, a leader of another pro-Iranian party.

August 7: The leaders of Costa Rica, El Salvador, Guatemala, Honduras, and Nicaragua sign the Latin Accord, which declares that by December 8, Nicaraguan contra armies based in Honduras must be disbanded. The United States denounces this decision.

August 24: Commissioner A. Bartlett Giamatti bans Pete Rose from major league baseball for allegedly gambling on baseball games. Rose holds baseball's all-time record for most hits in a career.

September 10: Hungary opens its borders with Austria, thereby enabling 60,000 East Germans to cross into Western Europe. Most are destined for West Germany.

October 17: A powerful earthquake measuring 6.9 on the Richter scale strikes the San Francisco Bay region, causing hundreds of deaths and extensive damage to buildings and infrastructure.

October 18: East Germany's Communist Party removes Erich Honecker, its hard-line leader for 18 years, and appoints Egon Krenz to replace him.

October 19: The Hungarian parliament concludes more than 40 years of single-party Communist rule when it legalizes opposition political parties and calls for multiparty elections in 1990.

October 23: On the 33rd anniversary of the 1956 Hungarian Revolution, a new Hungarian Republic is declared. The Hungarian Communist Party dissolves after renouncing Marxism-Leninism in favor of social democracy.

October 23: The Soviet foreign minister, Eduard Shevardnadze, acknowledges that the Soviet Union's ill-fated invasion of Afghanistan in 1979 violated Soviet law and "civilian norms" and that the Krasnoyarsk radar station in Siberia violates the Anti-Ballistic Missile Treaty, as the United States has maintained since 1983.

October 25: Yugoslavia's Communist Party endorses free elections, political pluralism, labor unions, and greater individual freedoms.

October 28: The Flag Protection Act of 1989, passed in response to the Supreme Court decision of June 21, 1989, permitting flag burning, takes effect.

November 4: A powerful computer virus attacks thousands of computers throughout North America.

November 7: Willi Stoph resigns as prime minister of East Germany; most of the Politburo resigns the next day.

November 9: East Germany removes virtually all travel restrictions to West Germany.

November 10: East Germany dismantles the Berlin Wall and opens access to West Germany, permitting free travel between East and West Berlin for the first time since 1961.

November 10: Todor Zhivkov, Bulgaria's long-reigning head of the Communist Party, resigns and is subsequently expelled from the party.

November 15: Solidarity leader Lech Walesa asks the United States for economic assistance similar to that provided by the Marshall Plan in the late 1940s to stabilize European governments vulnerable to Communist takeover.

December 7: Prime Minister Ladislav Adamec of Czechoslovakia steps down after a coalition of non-Communist parties demands his resignation. Marian Calfa replaces him and announces his intention to form a multiparty system.

December 17: *The Simpsons* debuts on the Fox Network.

December 20: A force of 24,000 U.S. troops invades Panama after Noriega refuses to honor the results of a presidential election won by his opponent, Guillermo Endara. Endara is sworn in at a U.S. military base, and Noriega takes refuge inside the Vatican embassy in Panama City until early January 1990, when he surrenders and is taken to Miami to stand trial on charges of drug trafficking.

The destruction of the Berlin Wall emerged as the most powerful symbol of Eastern Europe's repudiation of communism. *(AP/Wide World Photos)*

December 22: Nicolae Ceauçescu, president of Romania's Communist Party, and his wife are overthrown by the army and executed on Christmas Day, after being hastily convicted of genocide and gross misuse of power.

December 28: Alexander Dubček, who had been deposed as leader of Czechoslovakia's Communist Party after the 1968 Prague Spring, is elected chairman of the Czech parliament.

December 29: Václav Havel, a prominent playwright, philosopher, and government protester, is inaugurated president of Czechoslovakia.

EYEWITNESS TESTIMONY

1980

Mood is, in fact, the fulcrum upon which U.S.-Soviet relations now teeter. *Detente,* if not dead, is mortally wounded. So is SALT II, the keystone of *detente.*

Most of all, [President] Jimmy Carter's mood has changed. Events in Iran [the seizure of the U.S. embassy and taking of U.S. hostages] heated his seeming indecision cherry-red. Afghanistan may have annealed him into what the Soviets obviously thought he was not: a steely leader prepared to defend his people's vital interests, at whatever sacrifice that defense demands.

A Miami Herald *editorial of January 6, 1980, commenting on President Jimmy Carter's responses to the Soviet invasion of Afghanistan in December 1979, in* Editorials On File, *January 1–15, 1980, p. 6.*

President Carter should follow through on his proposal for boycotting the 1980 Olympics or moving them—an idea endorsed by British Prime Minister Thatcher—to demonstrate disapproval of the Soviet invasion of Afghanistan. There might not be time to move the games or organize alternative games. There is time for a boycott.

Mr. Carter can put aside any worry that a boycott would politicize the Olympics. Politics have been part and parcel of the Olympics for years now. What of Hitler's propaganda efforts at the 1936 games in Berlin? What of the assassinations of Israelis by Arab terrorists in Munich in 1972?

To Soviet leaders, every encounter with the outside world is a political event, an opportunity to assert the superiority of Marxist-Leninism as it is practiced in the USSR. . . .

A boycott led by the U.S. and Britain would have the support of millions whose admiration of the spirit of Olympic competition is secondary to abhorrence of naked aggression.

A News and Courier *(Charleston, South Carolina) editorial of January 22, 1980, endorsing President Jimmy Carter's proposal to boycott the Summer Olympic Games in Moscow, in* Editorials On File, *January 16–31, 1980, p. 108.*

In the beginning [Secretary of State Cyrus] Vance seemed exactly right for a Carter administration. His instincts were sound, his morals impeccable, his behavior understated and thoroughly decent. Here indeed was a man who believed with the president . . . that morality was the "fundamental precept" on which to build a realistic and enduring foreign policy.

How long ago all that seems now. In the past year everything that Vance has stood for throughout his years as a liberal-to-moderate career diplomat—strategic arms control, detente with the Soviet Union—began to fall apart. What was a man like Vance to do after the Soviet invasion of Afghanistan? How could he argue any longer . . . that peaceful coexistence is what the Russians want above all else? . . .

The failure of a decent and competent man like Cyrus Vance to find a home in an administration that made decency its guiding principle is another devastating comment on the steady deterioration of the foreign policy goals of the past 20 years. And who, now, can even imagine a time when it will be possible for another Cyrus Vance to serve as this nation's secretary of state?

An Atlanta Constitution *editorial of April 29, 1980, commenting on the resignation of Secretary of State Cyrus Vance after the failed U.S. military effort to rescue the American hostages in Iran, in* Editorials On File, *April 16–30, 1980, p. 463.*

There you go again [to President Carter]. . . .

Are you better off than you were four years ago? . . .

Is America as respected throughout the world as it was?

The Republican presidential nominee Ronald Reagan asking rhetorical questions of President Jimmy Carter during their televised debate of October 28, 1980. Available online. URL: http://www.pbs.org/ newshour/debatingourdestiny/80debates/cart1.html.

I am a 60-year-old man but I know what a teenage girl must feel like when she swoons over her favorite rock star. Every time I hear or think that phrase "There you go again," I hear Mr. Reagan's deep, mellow voice speaking with just the right touch of irony. I hear it and I swoon.

When I first heard Mr. Reagan saying that phrase in the 1980 debate with Mr. Carter, I was in my "in between" phase. I was in between being a liberal and conservative. The moment I heard Mr. Reagan say, "there you go again," I knew this man was something very special. I knew that what he stood for was something very special. My conservative side had won over and defeated my liberal side at that moment and forever.

Citizen Jeff Gordon recalling on June 7, 2004, the impact of Ronald Reagan's performance in his second debate with President Jimmy Carter on October 28, 1980. Available online. URL: http://www.freerepublic.com/focus/f-news/1148991/posts.

1981

Enough of this back up and retreating. Enough of this lip service and no action. It's time to begin to train. It is time to begin to reclaim this country for white people. Now I want you to understand that they're not going to give it back to us. If you want it, you're gonna have to get it the way the founding fathers got it—Blood! Blood! Blood! . . .

Never let any race but the white race rule this country.

White supremacist and militia founder Louis Beam addressing members of his Texas Emergence Reserve militia in 1981, in Morris Dees, Gathering Storm: America's Militia Threat *(1996), p. 3.*

The business of our nation goes forward. These United States are confronted with an economic affliction of great proportions. We suffer from the longest and one of the worst sustained inflations in our national history. It distorts our economic decisions, penalizes thrift, and crushes the struggling young and the fixed-income elderly alike. It threatens to shatter the lives of millions of our people.

Idle industries have cast workers into unemployment, causing human misery and personal indignity. Those who do work are denied a fair return for their labor by a tax system which penalizes successful achievement and keeps us from maintaining full productivity.

But great as our tax burden is, it has not kept pace with public spending. For decades, we have piled deficit upon deficit, mortgaging our future and our children's future for the temporary convenience of the present. To continue this long trend is to guarantee tremendous social, cultural, political, and economic upheavals. . . .

It is my intention to curb the size and influence of the Federal establishment and to demand recognition of the distinction between the powers granted to the Federal Government and those reserved to the States or to the people. All of us need to be reminded that the Federal Government did not create the States; the States created the Federal Government.

Now, so there will be no misunderstanding, it is not my intention to do away with government. It is, rather, to make it work—work with us, not over us; to stand by our side, not ride on our back. Government can and must provide opportunity, not smother it; foster productivity, not stifle it. . . .

The crisis we are facing today does not require of us the kind of sacrifice that [the World War I casualty] Martin Treptow and so many thousands of others were called upon to make. It does require, however, our best effort, and our willingness to believe in ourselves and to believe in our capacity to perform great

President Ronald Reagan promised to renew optimism in America. *(Photofest)*

deeds; to believe that together, with God's help, we can and will resolve the problems which now confront us.

And, after all, why shouldn't we believe that? We are Americans. God bless you, and thank you.

From President Ronald Reagan's first inaugural speech on January 20, 1981. Available online. URL: http://www.geocities.com/sentryusa2000/ HOREV_FirstInaugural.htm.

[Weinberger] seemed to go out of his way to oppose Israel on any issue and to blame the Israelis for every problem in the Middle East. In our planning for counterterrorist operations, he apparently feared that if we went after Palestinian terrorists, we would offend and alienate Arab governments—particularly if we acted in cooperation with the Israelis.

Weinberger's anti-Israel tilt was an underlying current in almost every Mideast issue. Some people explained it by pointing to his years with the Bechtel Corporation. . . . Others believed it was more complicated, and had to do with his sensitivity about his own Jewish ancestry.

Lieutenant Colonel Oliver North (retired) describing in 1991 an anti-Israeli bias in the Mideast policies of Defense Secretary Caspar Weinberger, who served from January 21, 1981, to November 23, 1987, in North, Under Fire *(1992), pp. 154–155.*

In the past, it was possible to destroy a village, a town, a region, even a country. Now it is the whole planet that has come under threat. This fact should fully compel everyone to face a basic moral consideration: from now on, it is only through a conscious choice and then deliberate policy that humanity can survive.

Pope John Paul II addressing the threat of nuclear war in February 1981, in Jonathan Schell, The Abolition *(2000), p. 3.*

What a way to come to California! . . . I think we're back in the space business to stay.

Captain Robert L. Crippen, pilot of the first flight of the space shuttle Columbia *on April 14, 1981, celebrating the mission's accomplishment, in John Noble Wilford, "Crippen Says That Nation Is 'Back in the Space Business to Stay,'"* New York Times, *April 15, 1981, p. 1.*

I am killing the pope as a protest against the imperialism of the Soviet Union and the United States and against the genocide . . . in El Salvador and Afghanistan.

Text of a note found in the possession of Mehmet Ali Agça after he was arrested for shooting Pope John Paul II on May 13, 1981, in Clifton Daniel, ed., 20th Century Day by Day *(2000), p. 1189.*

If there are enough shovels to go around, everybody's going to make it. . . . You've got to be in a hole. . . . The dirt is really the thing that protects you from the blast as well as the radiation, if there's radiation. It protects you from the heat. You know, dirt is just great stuff. . . .

If we don't protect our society [against nuclear attack], we've not been able to calculate recovery time because we've lost so many people, it's beyond calculation. It would take a couple of generations, probably more. You'd lose half the people in the country. With protection of people only, your recovery time to prewar [gross national product] GNP levels would probably be six or eight years. If we used the Russian methods for protecting both the people and the industrial means of production, recovery times could be two to four years.

Deputy Undersecretary of Defense for Strategic and Theater Nuclear Forces Thomas K. Jones arguing in autumn 1981 for enhanced civil defense protections against nuclear attack in Robert Scheer, With Enough Shovels: Reagan, Bush and Nuclear War *(1982), pp. 18–25.*

1982

One way to begin to grasp the destructive power of present-day nuclear weapons is to describe the consequences of . . . a one-megaton bomb, which possesses eight times the explosive power of the Hiroshima bomb. . . . Burst some eighty-five hundred feet above the Empire State Building [in New York City], a one-megaton bomb would gut or flatten almost every building between Battery Park and 125th Street. . . .

A dazzling white light from the fireball would illumine the scene, continuing for perhaps thirty seconds. Simultaneously, searing heat would ignite everything flammable and start to melt windows, cars, buses, lampposts, and everything else made of metal or glass. People in the street would immediately catch fire. . . . About five seconds after the light appeared, the blast wave would strike, laden with the debris of a now nonexistent midtown. Some buildings might be crushed, as though a giant fist had squeezed them on all sides. . . . The four-hundred-mile-an-hour wind would blow from south to north . . . and then blow in the reverse direction with diminished intensity. While these things were happening, the fireball would be burning in the sky for the ten seconds of the thermal pulse. . . . A mass fire . . . renders shelters useless by burning up all the oxygen in the air and creating toxic gasses, so that anyone inside the shelters is asphyxiated, and also by heating the ground to such high temperatures that the shelters turn, in effect, into ovens, cremating the people inside them. . . .

A description of the effects of a one-megaton bomb . . . gives some notion of . . . a megaton of nuclear explosive power, but a weapon that is more likely to be used against New York is the twenty-megaton bomb. . . . The Soviet Union is estimated to have at least a hundred and thirteen twenty-megaton bombs in its nuclear arsenal.

Author Jonathan Schell describing in 1982 the likely effects of a nuclear attack on New York City, in Schell, The Fate of the Earth *(2000), pp. 47–52.*

President Reagan's plan for revitalizing distressed cities and producing jobs for unemployed urban dwellers equals his sand-bagging efforts in flood-stricken Fort Wayne: All show, no impact.

The enterprise zone concept centers around lowering corporate taxes and cutting government red tape to bring companies into blighted areas. . . .

It's a beautiful dream until reality casts a shadow.

First of all, up to 75 areas could be designated enterprise zones over a three-year period. That's only 1 1/2 zones per state. Cities, both large and small, will be fighting each other for precious designation thus polarizing areas instead of promoting needed interregional cooperation.

And the proposal offers no help on the basic services and amenities that are necessary to attract successful businesses to any area: schools, low crime rates, police and fire protection, adequate public transportation, roads, water and sewer lines, fine arts projects. In

fact, Reagan-proposed cuts already have curtailed many of those.

A Dayton Daily News *(Dayton, Ohio) editorial of April 3, 1982, deriding President Ronald Reagan's proposal to create free enterprise zones to revive blighted inner cities, in* Editorials On File, *April 1–15, 1982, p. 363.*

Mistakes have to be corrected. Congress should pass President Reagan's proposed $98.3 billion tax increase. It will begin to correct the excesses of the president's 25 percent across-the-board income tax cuts passed last year. . . .

The president's tax-cut measure is spread across three years. It includes not only individual income-tax cuts, but various tax incentives for businesses. The idea was the cuts and incentives would be used for investment, boosting the economy out of the recession and increasing employment. The result would be sufficient increases in tax revenues to offset the tax cut.

It hasn't worked out that way. Lenders and investors saw huge deficits building because of the tax cuts—deficits that would have to be financed. This has kept interest rates high and has discouraged consumers and businesses from borrowing for purchases or expansion. So recession and unemployment continue, and the deficits rise higher and higher. . . . [The] $98.3 billion tax increase should help keep future rates lower than they would be otherwise.

An Atlanta Constitutional *editorial of August 18, 1982, supporting President Ronald Reagan's proposed tax increase, in* Editorials On File, *August 16–31, 1982, p. 936.*

Sometimes statistics point to what is in many people's minds. Such a statistic is this: 400,000 of the 9 million Americans required by a 1980 law to register for the draft have not done so. Consider how improbable that would have seemed 20 years ago, before Vietnam, in an America as close to D-Day as we are today to the Gulf of Tonkin resolution [which gave congressional authorization for the U.S. military intervention in Vietnam]. Then, it was taken for granted that society had a legitimate right to conscript young men and that the armed forces had a legitimate use for their services. Today, apparently, these things are no longer taken for granted. . . .

One reason has been that our highest officials themselves have been hesitant in defining and enforcing society's interest. The draft registration law was passed at the urging of President Carter, as one response (the now defunct grain embargo was another) to the Soviet invasion of Afghanistan. Candidate Ronald Reagan in 1980 attacked the law as immoral, and President Reagan in 1981 said he would not enforce it. Only this year did the administration change its mind. . . .

If society is to assert a claim to young men's services—even as unintrusive a means as a requirement to register—it needs to make plain to them why that claim is legitimate.

A Washington Post *editorial of November 17, 1982, commenting on enforcement of a 1980 law requiring draft registration for young American men, in* Editorials On File, *November 16–30, 1982, p. 1509.*

1983

If history teaches anything, it teaches that simple-minded appeasement or wishful thinking about our adversaries is folly. It means the betrayal of our past, the squandering of our freedom.

So, I urge you to speak out against those who would place the United States in a position of military and moral inferiority. . . . So, in your discussions of the nuclear freeze proposals, I urge you to beware the temptation of pride—the temptation of blithely declaring yourselves above it all and label[ing] both sides equally at fault, to ignore the facts of history and the aggressive impulses of an evil empire, to simply call the arms race a giant misunderstanding and thereby remove yourself from the struggle between right and wrong and good and evil. . . .

While America's military strength is important, let me add here that I've always maintained that the struggle now going on for the world will never be decided by bombs or rockets, by armies or military might. The real crisis we face today is a spiritual one; at root, it is a test of moral will and faith.

From President Ronald Reagan's so-called evil empire speech on March 8, 1983. Available online. URL:http://www.awesome80s. com/Awesome80s/News/1983/March/ 8-Reagan_Evil_Empire_Speech.a sp.

Dr. Sally Ride became America's first female astronaut when she rode the space shuttle *Challenger* into outer space in June 1983. *(AP/Wide World Photos)*

Have you ever been to Disneyland? This was definitely an E ticket.

Dr. Sally Ride, the first American female astronaut to enter outer space, describing her flight on the space shuttle Challenger, *which lasted June 18–June 24, 1983, in "Challenger: Ride, Sally Ride,"* Newsweek, *June 27, 1983, p. 34.*

I speak for all Americans and for the people everywhere who cherish civilized values in protesting the Soviet attack on an unarmed civilian passenger plane. Words can scarcely express our revulsion at this horrifying act of violence.

The United States joins with other members of the international community in demanding a full explanation for this appalling and wanton misdeed. The Soviet statements to this moment have totally failed to explain how or why this tragedy has occurred. Indeed, the whole incident appears to be inexplicable to civilized people everywhere.

President Ronald Reagan decrying the downing of South Korean Airline Flight 007 on September 1, 1983, in Steven Weisman, "President Demands Explanation for 'Horrifying Act of Violence'," New York Times, September 2, 1983, p. 1.

Problem number one for the world is to avoid nuclear war.

Soviet foreign minister Andrei Gromyko warning on September 8, 1983, of the danger of superpower confrontation after the Soviet downing of Korean Airlines Flight 007 on September 1, 1983, in Martin Walker, The Cold War: A History (1993), p. 276.

I haven't seen carnage like that since Vietnam.

The U.S. Marine spokesman Major Robert Jordan describing the October 23, 1983, bombing of the U.S. Marine barracks in Beirut, Lebanon, which killed 241 marines, in Thomas L. Friedman, "Truck Loaded with TNT Wrecks Headquarters of a Marine Unit," New York Times, October 24, 1983, p. 1.

After the bombing [of the U.S. Marine barracks] things started to heat up so we began the arduous task of properly fortifying our positions. . . . Then, on December 7, 1983, my platoon became engaged in a furious duel with Druse militiamen who began firing at us from strong points three hundred yards out in the town of Burj al Burajinah, a place we dubbed "Hooterville.". . . The deadly chatter of automatic weapons fire cut through the air. Sand bags burst open. . . . By early evening the fighting had simmered down; however, artillery and heavy mortars echoed across the airstrip throughout the night. When morning came we stood on full alert. . . . One of the company's forward observation posts had sustained a direct hit from a 122 mm rocket. That attack killed eight Golf Company Marines. I had gone to boot camp with two of the men and a third had received news about his newborn son just two days before.

Our sense of loss had little time to fester. . . . On January 31, 1984, second platoon became engaged in the hottest battle yet with Amal fighters who had entrenched themselves behind the 12-foot wall of a construction company, a place we called "The Café

Daniel." The battle became so intense that we had to be re-supplied with additional ammunition. By late evening the fighting began to taper off. Lance Corporal Dramis was observing the enemy position through a pair of binoculars when a single shot cracked through the afternoon calm. I looked over my right shoulder and saw Dramis stumble out of the observation post. He fell on his back convulsing, kicking the red clay with his heels, his flailing hands grasping at his chest. People from the command post began screaming, "Corpsman Up!" Dramis was medevaced on the back of a Jeep, blood-covered battle dressings snapping in the breeze, our navy corpsman, "Doc" Lou, feverishly working to save his life, frantically begging Dramis not to die—"Don't die on me Dramis, don't die!"

Former U.S. Marine Thaddeus "Ted" Randall describing his experience as a peacekeeper in Beirut, Lebanon, in the months after the October 23, 1983, bombing of the U.S. Marine barracks that killed 241 marines, in Randall, Long Range Patrol: Exploring the Warrior Mystique (2002), pp. 4–5.

1984

Looking within themselves at the nuclear peril prepared people for action, and also was in itself a kind of action . . . within the privacy of each person's soul. Because this preparatory action . . . was not yet a political action, and prescribed no political course, it seemed to some as if it were nothing. That may be one reason the public awakening caught so many politicians and so much of the press by surprise; it had come about in domains of existence—the moral and spiritual—in which they ordinarily take little professional interest. . . . The new disturbances were, in fact, seismic. Suddenly people were awash in fathomless questions of human existence. How did it happen . . . that we have become the underwriters of the slaughter of billions of innocent people? Can such slaughter be justified? How? What is the meaning of human life on earth? What would its extermination mean? What does it mean about us that we have built the equipment with which to carry out that extermination and are apparently prepared to perform the act? What does it mean that we—one link in the chain of the generations—are prepared to cut the chain, and set adrift in darkness all the future generations of human beings?

What is our responsibility to these unborn people, and how can we fulfill it?

Author Jonathan Schell reviewing in 1984 some of the moral questions raised by growing popular awareness of the nuclear peril, in Schell, The Abolition *(2000), pp. 11–12.*

There's a glitter to nuclear weapons. I had sensed it in others and [while observing a nuclear test] *felt it in myself.* If you come to these things as a scientist, it is irresistible, to feel it's there in your hands, so to speak, the ability to release this energy that fuels the stars! . . . to make it do your bidding! To make it perform these miracles! To lift a million tons of rock into the sky. And all from a thimbleful of stuff. *Irresistible!*

Fictional character Philip Stone describing the seductive thrill inherent in nuclear weaponry in Arthur Kopit's play End of the World *(1984), p. 94.*

We lived on a high floor, overlooking the river, the Hudson. . . . And I looked down at this tiny creature [his infant son] . . . and I realized I had never had anyone completely in my power before! . . . And I'd never know what that *meant*! . . . And I saw I was standing near a window. . . . And I thought: I could . . . *drop him out*! And I went *toward* the window, because I couldn't believe this thought had come into my head—*where had it come from?* Not one part of me felt anything for this boy but love, not one part! . . . and I was thinking, I can throw him out of here! . . . and then he will be falling . . . and as he's falling, I will be *unable to get him back*! . . . And I felt a *thrill*! I FELT A THRILL! IT WAS THERE!

Fictional character Michael Trent describing the seductive, self-destructive allure of doom in Arthur Kopit's play End of the World *(1984), p. 94.*

As the story of the B1 [bomber] illustrates, this close alliance [among top military leaders, defense contractors, and congressmen]—christened the "military-industrial complex" by President Eisenhower—has developed a weapons' buying system that produces profits and promotions in peacetime, even if it provides questionable tools for war.

It is an alliance well beyond checks. Indeed, the defense establishment has become so powerful that, in the case of the new B1 bomber, even Defense Secretary Caspar Weinberger got only the answers the

plane's proponents wanted him to have when he questioned the wisdom of buying another bomber.

Correspondent Frank Greve analyzing the Reagan administration's support of the controversial B1 bomber in Greve, "The B1 Bomber," Miami Herald, *February 12, 1984, p. 1E.*

You don't need to know the full details of National Security Decision Directive 138 to start worrying about it. The directive authorizes preemptive strikes and reprisal raids against terrorists; allows for intensification of FBI and CIA anti-terrorist intelligence gathering; creates anti-terrorist strike forces in the FBI, the CIA and the Pentagon; and places the counter-terrorist units of the armed forces under a central command. And, oh yes, it approves of domestic as well as foreign anti-terrorist activity and it fails to make a clear distinction between preemptive strikes and assassination. . . .

There is broad frustration over the administration's failure to prevent terrorist activity, and so this directive is somewhat soothing. But there is also legitimate suspicion that the directive resulted from the bombing of the Marine headquarters in Beirut last fall, which was the result of military bungling, not impotence. Thus, although President Reagan is correct to formulate anti-terrorist procedures, this directive goes too far. The authority to launch preemptive strikes dilutes appropriate diplomatic efforts and threatens civil liberties.

A Plain Dealer *(Cleveland, Ohio) editorial of April 17, 1984, criticizing President Ronald Reagan's National Security Directive permitting preemptive strikes against terrorist organizations, in* Editorials On File, *April 16–30, 1984, p. 440.*

The Reagan administration's announced plans to take the offensive against worldwide terrorism couldn't have come at a better time. To fanatics fighting "war on the cheap," the upcoming Democratic and Republican national conventions and Olympic games will surely be inviting targets. Recommendations like preventive raids on terrorists and large rewards for providing information about suspects deserve congressional approval. . . .

To this point; however, America's intelligence has been pretty poor. If the Ford administration started the emasculation of the FBI and CIA in the post-Watergate era, then Carter officials finished the job.

Obsessed with protecting individuals' civil rights, they ignored their responsibility when it came to protecting people from the attacks of armed subversives. . . .

Congress should approve such preventive measures with reasonable speed because of upcoming events. Taking the offense against terrorism will generate the best defense against it.

> *A* Richmond Times Dispatch *(Richmond, Virginia)*
> *editorial of April 21, 1984, endorsing President Ronald*
> *Reagan's National Security Directive permitting*
> *preemptive strikes against terrorist organizations, in*
> Editorials On File, *April 16–30, 1984, p. 440.*

In June of 1984, I was contacted by a Mr. Casey who then was head of the CIA in the United States of America. . . . He requested me to assist in the sale of [arms] to Iran in exchange for hostages held.

These hostages were being held in Lebanon, so in June of 1984, I started [attending] a series of meetings in London. . . . During these series of meetings, it was discussed as to how one could get the hostages released, ways of doing it, some of them improper, some of them proper.

> *British intelligence agent Leslie Aspin describing the*
> *beginnings of the Iran-contra arms-for-hostage exchange*
> *in June 1984, from the unedited transcript of his sworn*
> *statement to his British attorney on May 1, 1987, in*
> *John Loftus and Mark Aarons,* The Secret War against
> the Jews *(1994), p. 438.*

Denied funding by Congress, the President turned to third countries and private sources [to raise money for the antigovernment Contras in Nicaragua]. Between June 1984 and the beginning of 1986, the President, his National Security Adviser, and the [National Security Council] NSC staff secretly raised $34 million for the Contras from other countries. An additional $2.7 million was provided for the Contras during 1985 and 1986 from private contributors, who were addressed by [Lieutenant Colonel Oliver] North and occasionally granted photo opportunities with the President. In the middle of this period, Assistant Secretary of State A. Langhorne Motley—from whom these contributions were concealed—gave his assurance to Congress that the Administration was not "soliciting and/or encouraging third countries" to give funds to the Contras because, as he conceded, the Boland Amendment prohibited such solicitation. . . .

The diversion [of profits from arm sales to Iran] . . . was not an isolated act by the NSC staff. [National Security Advisor John] Poindexter saw it as "implementing" the President's secret policy that had been in effect since 1984. . . .

According to North, CIA Director [William] Casey saw the "diversion" as part of a more grandiose plan to use the Enterprise as a "stand-alone," "off-the-shelf," covert capacity that would act throughout the world while evading Congressional review. . . .

All told, the Enterprise received nearly $48 million from the sale of arms to the Contras and Iran, and in contributions directed to it by North. A total of $16.5 million was used to purchase the arms sold to (and paid for by) the Contras; $15.2 million was spent on Iran . . . [intermediaries] took $6.6 million in commissions and other profit distributions; almost $1 million went for other covert operations sponsored by North; $4.2 million was held in reserve for use in future operations. . . .

The United States simultaneously pursued two contradictory foreign policies—a public one and a secret one:

The public policy was not to make any concessions for the release of hostages lest such concessions encourage more hostage-taking. At the same time, the United States was secretly trading weapons to get the hostages [in Lebanon] back.

The public policy was to ban arms shipments to Iran and to exhort other Governments to observe this embargo. At the same time, the United States was secretly selling sophisticated missiles to Iran and promising more.

The public policy was to improve relations with Iraq. At the same time, the United States secretly shared military intelligence on Iraq with Iran and North told the Iranians in contradiction to United States policy that the United States would help promote the overthrow of the Iraqi head of government.

> *A description of the U.S.-Iran arms-for-hostages*
> *arrangement that took place between June 1984 and late*
> *1986, in* Report of the Congressional Committees
> Investigating the Iran-contra Affair
> *(November 1987), pp. 3–12.*

1985

When I took this oath four years ago, I did so in a time of economic stress. Voices were raised saying we had to look to our past for the greatness and glory. But we, the present-day Americans, are not given to looking backward. In this blessed land, there is always a better tomorrow. . . .

That system has never failed us, but, for a time, we failed the system. We asked things of government that government was not equipped to give. We yielded authority to the National Government that properly belonged to States or to local governments or to the people themselves. We allowed taxes and inflation to rob us of our earnings and savings and watched the great industrial machine that had made us the most productive people on Earth slow down and the number of unemployed increase.

By 1980, we knew it was time to renew our faith, to strive with all our strength toward the ultimate in individual freedom consistent with an orderly society.

We believed then and now there are no limits to growth and human progress when men and women are free to follow their dreams.

And we were right to believe that. Tax rates have been reduced, inflation cut dramatically, and more people are employed than ever before in our history.

We are creating a nation once again vibrant, robust, and alive. But there are many mountains yet to climb. We will not rest until every American enjoys the fullness of freedom, dignity, and opportunity as our birthright. It is our birthright as citizens of this great Republic, and we'll meet this challenge.

These will be years when Americans have restored their confidence and tradition of progress; when our values of faith, family, work, and neighborhood were restated for a modern age; when our economy was finally freed from government's grip; when we made sincere efforts at meaningful arms reduction, rebuilding our defenses, our economy, and developing new technologies, and helped preserve peace in a troubled world; when Americans courageously supported the struggle for liberty, self-government, and free enterprise throughout the world, and turned the tide of history away from totalitarian darkness and into the warm sunlight of human freedom.

My fellow citizens, our Nation is poised for greatness. We must do what we know is right and do it with all our might. Let history say of us, "These were golden years—when the American Revolution was

President Ronald Reagan invoked the determined, patriotic spirit of *Rambo* to describe America's cold war resolve. *(Photofest)*

reborn, when freedom gained new life, when America reached for her best."

From President Ronald Reagan's second inaugural speech on January 21, 1985. Available online. URL: http://www.bartleby.com/124/pres61.html.

After seeing the movie *Rambo*, I'll know what to do the next time something like this happens.

President Ronald Reagan commenting on the June 14, 1985, hijacking of a TWA flight carrying 104 Americans, in Lois Gordon and Alan Gordon, American Chronicle *(1999), p. 804.*

Good morning children of the '80s. This is your Woodstock, and it's long overdue.

Singer Joan Baez addressing the Live Aid concert for African famine relief on July 13, 1985, in Clifton Daniel, 20th Century Day by Day *(2000), p. 1262.*

Because he was an American, because he was a Jew and because he was a free man.

New York senator Daniel Moynihan accounting on October 20, 1985, for why pro-Palestinian hijackers of the cruise ship Achille Lauro *killed a wheelchair-bound passenger, Leon Klinghoffer, on October 7, 1985, in Clifton Daniel,* 20th Century Day by Day *(2000), p. 1,268.*

1986

Ladies and gentlemen, I'd planned to speak to you tonight to report on the state of the Union, but the events of earlier today have led me to change these plans. Today is a day for mourning and remembering. Nancy and I are pained to the core by the tragedy of the shuttle *Challenger*. . . . This is truly a national loss.

Nineteen years ago, almost to the day, we lost three astronauts in a terrible accident on the ground. But we've never lost an astronaut in flight. We've never had a tragedy like this. And perhaps we've forgotten the courage it took for the crew of the shuttle. But they, the *Challenger* Seven, were aware of the dangers, overcame them, and did their jobs brilliantly. We mourn seven heroes: Michael Smith, Dick Scobee, Judith Resnik, Ronald McNair, Ellison Omizuka, Gregory Jarvis, and Christa McAuliffe. We mourn their loss as a nation together. . . .

I want to say something to the schoolchildren of America who were watching the live coverage of the shuttle's takeoff. I know it is hard to understand, but sometimes painful things like this happen. It's all part of the process of exploration and discovery. It's all part of taking a chance and expanding man's horizons. The future doesn't belong to the fainthearted; it belongs to the brave. The *Challenger* crew was pulling us into the future and we'll continue to follow them.

I've always had great faith in and respect for our space program, and what happened today does nothing to diminish it. We don't hide our space program. We don't keep secrets and cover things up. We do it all up front and in public. That's the way freedom is, and we wouldn't change it for a minute. We'll continue our quest in space. . . .

The crew of the space shuttle *Challenger* honored us by the manner in which they lived their lives. We will never forget them, nor the last time we saw them, this morning, as they prepared for their journey and waved goodbye and "slipped the surly bonds of earth" to "touch the face of God."

President Ronald Reagan commemorating on January 28, 1986, the astronauts who died aboard the space shuttle Challenger *earlier that day, in Robert Torricelli and Andrew Carroll, eds.,* In Our Own Words *(1999), pp. 367–368.*

When I learned what NASA did with the numbers [estimating a failure rate of one in 100,000 for shuttle booster rockets], I was really outraged. Their number was absolutely arbitrary—they made it up—and I think that's criminally fast and loose.

Robert K. Weatherwax, author of a 1983 air force study that predicted a failure rate of one in 70 for shuttle booster rockets, responding to revelations that in 1983 NASA had officially estimated the failure rate to be more than 10,000 times greater, in Mark Thompson, "NASA Rejected Three U.S. Studies Warning of Booster Rocket Blast," Miami Herald, *June 1, 1986, p. 1A.*

It was a warm summer night in 1986 at [Pastor Richard] Butler's Survivalist compound north of Coeur d'Alene, Idaho, and the Christian Identity movement had just staged the major event of its liturgical year—the annual cross burning and anointing of new members as "Aryan warriors." . . .

On the Sunday morning following the Saturday-night cross burning, Butler . . . anointed two hundred new "warriors." . . . One wore the dress blues of the United States Marine Corps. Another wore the badge of the Pennsylvania highway patrol. Others wore the blue shirts with red swastika arm patches of Butler's Aryan Nations compound. . . .

[T]he neo-Nazi movement is utterly sexist as well as racist. . . . [Women's] role is to serve as planting ground for the "white seed" so their warrior husbands can propagate the race before they raise their swords against ZOG [Zionist Occupational Government—the movement's term for the U.S. government]. . . .

After a few hours of hearing Identity sermons outlining how the international Jewish conspiracy manufactured the lie about six million people dying in Hitler's Holocaust, how Anne Frank's diary was a "Jew forgery" and how "Negroes have their particularly bad smell because of the way the beasts' body oils accumulate in their unnaturally thick skins," it is tempting simply to hate these "Christians" right back. It's easy to fall into the spirit of hatred in a church with romanticized portraits of Adolf Hitler and Rudolf Hess on the wall in place of saints, with pamphlet racks in the back offering *The Holy Book of Adolf Hitler; The Negro: Serpent, Beast and Devil;* and *The International Jew. . . .*

The bizarre religion unites numerous segments of the Survival Right that in the past had been so inclined toward internecine squabbling that the prospect of joint action was remote. Further, the doctrine of hatred preached from Identity pulpits transforms the sort of violence advocated by the fringes of the Survival Right from furtive sin to virtue praised by one's congregation.

James Coates describing a meeting of the extreme Right
Identity Christians in summer 1986, in Coates,
Armed and Dangerous: The Rise of the
Survivalist Right *(1987), pp. 77–80.*

1987

What will the late 1980s and 1990s hold [for the criminal justice system]? It appears that the current system [based on punishment and retribution] will crumble by the late 1980s and that alternative values and methods will emerge. While vindictiveness runs deep as a value, it is usually a symptom of hard times. Americans are a pragmatic lot who will not spend huge resources on locking up fellow citizens. Neither will they agree to wholesale slaughter under the revived death penalty statutes.

Already, retribution is being replaced by the more pragmatic deterrence as the prevailing value in the justice system. Sentence-reform commissions in states across the nation are recommending more use of mandatory prison terms, but shorter terms—relying on certainty of punishment rather than severity of punishment for deterrence. . . .

The best sign that this [practice of longer prison sentences] will change by the late 1980s or early 1990s is the generally falling crime rate. All indicators . . . show that street crime is falling—by as much as 10% in one year. While some argue that deterrence is working, a better explanation might be that the population is getting older and there are fewer individuals in the crime-prone teens and early 20s. . . . And, yes, through selective prosecution of "career criminals," some of the 10% of the offenders who commit up to 90% of the street crimes are in prison. Two problem areas that could slow or reverse

this trend toward less street crime involve the breakdown of the family and the emptying of the mental hospitals. . . .

The values of the 1990s may involve a search for a middle ground between unrealistic optimism of changing all lawbreakers into law abiders and the pessimism and uncertainty that has resulted in the "lock 'em up and throw away the key" attitude.

Professor Gene Stephens considering in January 1987
the likely course of U.S. criminal justice in the 1990s,
in Edward Cornish, ed., The 1990s and Beyond
(1990), pp. 96–104.

If I had to choose just one thing to remember from the Iran-contra mess . . . what I would choose to remember is how easily, how comfortably, how casually, a group of wealthy people in America purchased a private foreign policy.

The millionaires who testified last week [before a congressional investigative committee] . . . Ellen Garwood, William O'Boyle, Joseph Coors—regarded the chance to build a nice little army in Nicaragua like the chance to build a hospital wing in their hometown or a college library at their alma mater.

The fund-raisers presented them with a catalogue of goodies to pick and choose from, everything from planes to boats, complete with a price tag. A truly generous contributor might get a plaque on the plane bearing his name, the way hospital elevators proclaim their donor. . . . They [the donors] are . . . the logical extension of the Reagan era's rule by the rich. . . .

One of the precious things that the rich can buy in America is "out.". . . They can buy out of consensus-building, buy out of community, buy out of compromising, buy out of, around, or over the common will. . . .

The Reagan Administration, rife with attitudes and emblems of these rich, regarded the congressional "no" to supplying *contras* as a traffic jam they could fly over. The adventure capitalists, for their part, sprang for the planes. They bought out of the system.

And for a while in America, the rich had not only their own private estates. They had their own private foreign policy.

Columnist Ellen Goodman decrying the privatizing of
U.S. foreign policy during the Iran-contra affair in
Goodman, "Foreign Policy for Fun and Profit,"
Miami Herald, *May 30, 1987, p. 19A.*

Modern theories of guerrilla warfare . . . developed from the late 1940s to the early 1960s. World War II represented the culmination of state-organized violence. Since then, there has been a long-range trend toward the "privatization" of violence.

Terrorism has become a routine way of focusing attention on a dispute, of bringing pressure on a government. New causes and new groups have emerged—Armenian terrorists, Sikh terrorists, issue oriented groups opposed to nuclear power, abortion, technology, pollution, animal vivisection, etc. There certainly will be no lack of causes.

There are economic incentives to the use of terrorist tactics. Kidnaping and extortion based upon threats of violence have become routine means of financing revolutionary movements.

A semipermanent infrastructure of support has emerged. Behind the terrorist groups, and supporting them often without regard to ideology or cause, is an ephemeral but resilient network of connections, alliances, safe houses, arms suppliers, and provisioners of counterfeit documents and other services. This network resembles the infrastructure that supports organized crime.

States have recognized in terrorism a useful weapon and are exploiting it for their own purposes. To a certain extent, international terrorism has become institutionalized. . . .

All these reasons suggest that terrorism as we know it now is likely to persist as a mode of political expression for various groups and as a means of warfare among states. . . . It is a ragged increase, with peaks and valleys, but the overall trajectory [of the incidence of terrorism] is clearly upward.

Political scientist Brian Michael Jenkins, a former Green Beret captain and a specialist on terrorism for the RAND Corporation, anticipating in July 1987 that international terrorism will increase during the 1990s, in Edward Cornish, ed., The 1990s and Beyond *(1990), pp. 90–95.*

The left at its core understands in a way Grant understood after Shiloh that this is a civil war, that only one side will prevail, and that the other side will be relegated to history. This war has to be fought with the scale and duration and savagery that is only true of civil wars. While we are lucky in this country that our civil wars are fought at the ballot box, not on the battlefields, nonetheless it is a civil war.

Congressman Newt Gingrich of Georgia declaring in 1988 that the Senate's rejection on October 23, 1987, of the Supreme Court nomination of Robert Bork signaled a civil war between U.S. liberals and conservatives, in David Brock, Blinded by the Right *(2002), p. 47.*

AIDS has been compared to the Black Death, which swept through Europe along the trade routes from Italy to Sweden in 1347–1350, killing some 30 million people out of a population of 75 million in four years. AIDS probably has the same high mortality rate, but it has such a slow development and low infectivity that it could be called the Black Death in Slow Motion. . . .

With a projection of about 100 million people infected worldwide by 1991, or 2% of the world's population, the total death from AIDS in the 1990s could be 50 million—more than the Black Death. . . .

If the AIDS epidemic in the United States does go on growing after 1991 . . . much greater effects on society can be imagined. Fears will multiply . . . and our social behavior and arrangements will become increasingly reminiscent of life during earlier plagues.

Hospitals will be desperately overcrowded, and many AIDS patients will die at home or be abandoned. Burials will be replaced by cremation. . . . Attitudes of hopelessness and sadness will alternate with an "eat, drink, and be merry philosophy.". . .

The U.S. economy—built on consumer growth—will stagnate, with buildings and property abandoned. . . . The move away from urban life to rural areas will accelerate. We could see on the one hand [rural] survivalist camps and on the other hand large sections of great cities becoming derelict, abandoned to the poor, the sick, and the gangs.

Yet all is not negative. . . . The environment will improve. . . . The loss of top workers will accelerate automation. . . . With a wider variety of jobs paying higher wages to attract a shrinking work force . . . work may be less constraining and leisure even more varied than today. . . .

The greatest political danger after 1991 might be the power of new Hate Parties, with leaders promising to purge scapegoats and straighten things out.

Biophysicist John Platt predicting in November 1987 the impact of the AIDS epidemic in the 1990s, in Edward Cornish, ed., The 1990s and Beyond *(1990), pp. 53–59.*

Even for this city, which long ago mislaid its sense of wonder, this was a thrilling day, bathed in a glow of satisfaction at what has been achieved and of optimism about what may be just ahead.

Often Washington looks on the dark side, especially where the Soviet Union is concerned, but there were few in the capital who failed to feel a frisson of excitement as Mikhail S. Gorbachev stepped from his limousine and grasped Ronald Reagan's hand, few in the country who were immune to the drama of television pictures of the two leaders in profile with the red Soviet flag whipping in the wind behind them.

> *Political analyst R. W. Apple describing the popular response to Ronald Reagan's and Mikhail Gorbachev's signing of the INF treaty on December 8, 1987, in Apple, "A Tempered Optimism," New York Times, December 9, 1987, p. 1.*

1988

The entire record of this [Reagan-Bush] administration will be an issue in the [forthcoming presidential election] when I am the [Republican] nominee. That means the people will evaluate how we dealt with the economy, with the creation of jobs and with our educational system. It means our record of dealing with the Soviets, with our allies and the developing nations will be evaluated. . . . When the entire record is examined, the scales tip strongly in our favor. I believe my experience gives me the best opportunity to build on what we have done well and gives me the insight to avoid mistakes.

> *Vice President George H. W. Bush explaining on January 14, 1988, why he should be elected president in November, in Alan F. Pater and Jason R. Pater, eds., What They Said in 1988 (1989), pp. 211–212.*

We're inheritors of great wealth in this country. We've forgotten all the sacrifices that the people who've gone before us made to give us this wonderful life we have. We accept it, we take it for granted, we think it's our birthright. The facts are, it's precious, it's fragile, it can disappear on us in a moment. It's like quicksilver. If this is going to be a country that's owned by its people, then the owners have got to be active in the management of the country. It's that simple. The wimps are us.

> *Industrialist Ross Perot in the June 1988 issue of Esquire magazine calling for greater public participation in the political process, in Alan F. Pater and Jason R. Pater, eds., What They Said in 1988 (1989), p. 16.*

"American Abstract art is a lie, a sham, a cover-up for a poverty of spirit," he [the artist Philip Guston] wrote. "A mask to mask the fear of revealing oneself." He began to draw and paint a repentant catalogue of all the mundane objects that had been excluded from his art for the past quarter century: old shoes, rusted nails, mended rags, brick walls, cigarette butts. . . . His fluent style became halting, and, as time passed, the figures in his once high-minded paintings and drawings came to recall the characters in the comic strips of the thirties and forties: the guys at "Our Boarding House" or the bums in "Powerhouse Pepper." People who admired Guston tried to discern some saving political content in the new work, but most people found it painful, or even embarrassing, to look at what seemed so relentless an act of remorse and self-repudiation.

And yet less than a decade after his death Guston's apostasy has become a new faith. . . . Guston is now seen as more prophet than penitent. His late paintings are regarded as the precursors of the expressionist figurative painting of the eighties, and the blunt candor of his late drawings is thought to have recalled art to its responsibility to tell the truth about the world around it.

> *Writer Adam Gopnik describing the new popularity of the work of the late artist Philip Guston in Gopnik, "Cyclops," New Yorker, October 3, 1988, p. 95.*

But I'm also someone who balances budgets, something he [the Republican nominee, Vice President George H. W. Bush] has never done. I mean, I'm fiscally a lot more conservative than George Bush. . . . Like most Americans, I'm liberal in some ways and conservative in others. I was always taught that the first thing a conservative did was pay his bills.

> *Democratic presidential nominee Michael Dukakis describing himself as a fiscal conservative on November 1, 1988, in Alan F. Pater and Jason R. Pater, eds., What They Said in 1988 (1989), p. 224.*

1989

In 1989 . . . 60 percent of the teenagers in a nationwide sample named drug abuse as the most serious problem facing them. This figure was up from 35 percent in 1983 and 27 percent in 1977. Peer pressure was the next most frequently mentioned problem, with 13 percent of the teens listing it as the most serious issue. There was a slight decrease in the percentage of teenagers who ranked alcohol abuse and teenage pregnancy as the most serious problem of youth.

A new concern which emerged in the 1989 survey did not appear in earlier samplings. For the first time, 3 percent of teenagers contacted listed teenage gangs as the most serious problems facing their age group. Only 1 percent of the teens surveyed cited suicide as the biggest issue facing them.

An unexpected finding was the drop in the number of teenagers who listed the generation gap as the most serious problem they faced. In 1977, 20 percent of teens surveyed put parent-child conflicts at the top of their list, while only 1 percent of the teenagers placed such problems first in the 1989 survey.

Although it did not appear in the Gallup survey, an abiding concern of many teenagers I talk with is the divorce—real or imagined—of their parents. Even for teenagers whose parents are happily married, divorce is still a concern because so many of their friends' parents are divorced.

Perhaps the most important thing we can do to help teenagers is to take their anxieties and concerns seriously. . . . If we say it and mean it (if we are ready to be there whenever our teenager is ready to talk, and not just when we are ready to listen), the teenager will eventually talk about his or her worries when the time is right. . . . Discussing problems is one of the healthiest ways for teenagers to handle their anxieties.

David Elkind, a professor of child study, commenting in 1993 on the results of a 1989 Gallup survey showing American teenagers' ranking of their greatest concerns as the 1990s approached, in Elkind, Parenting Your Teenager in the '90s *(1993), pp. 12–13.*

I come before you and assume the Presidency at a moment rich with promise. We live in a peaceful, prosperous time, but we can make it better. For a new breeze is blowing, and a world refreshed by freedom seems reborn; for in man's heart, if not in fact, the day of the dictator is over. The totalitarian era is passing, its old ideas blown away like leaves from an ancient, lifeless tree. . . .

Great nations of the world are moving toward democracy through the door to freedom. Men and women of the world move toward free markets through the door to prosperity. The people of the world agitate for free expression and free thought through the door to the moral and intellectual satisfactions that only liberty allows. . . .

America is never wholly herself unless she is engaged in high moral principle. We as a people have such a purpose today. It is to make kinder the face of the Nation and gentler the face of the world. My friends, we have work to do. There are the homeless, lost and roaming. There are the children who have nothing, no love, no normalcy. There are those who cannot free themselves of enslavement to whatever addiction—drugs, welfare, the demoralization that rules the slums. There is crime to be conquered, the rough crime of the streets. There are young women to be helped who are about to become mothers of children they can't care for and might not love. They need our care, our guidance, and our education, though we bless them for choosing life.

The old solution, the old way, was to think that public money alone could end these problems. But we have learned that is not so. And in any case, our funds are low. We have a deficit to bring down. We have more will than wallet; but will is what we need. . . .

I am speaking of a new engagement in the lives of others, a new activism, hands-on and involved, that gets the job done. . . .

I have spoken of a thousand points of light, of all the community organizations that are spread like stars throughout the Nation, doing good. We will work hand in hand, encouraging, sometimes leading, sometimes being led, rewarding. We will work on this in the White House, in the Cabinet agencies. I will go to the people and the programs that are the brighter points of light, and I will ask every member of my government to become involved. . . .

Great nations like great men must keep their word. When America says something, America means it, whether a treaty or an agreement or a vow made on marble steps. We will always try to speak clearly, for candor is a compliment, but subtlety, too, is good and has its place. While keeping our alliances and friendships around the world strong, ever strong, we will continue the new closeness with the Soviet Union, consistent both with our security and with progress. One might say that our new relationship in part reflects the triumph of hope and strength over experience. But hope is good, and so are strength and vigilance.

From the inaugural speech of President George H. W. Bush given on January 20, 1989. Available online. URL: http://www.bartleby.com/124.

As a Marine, I was taught to fight, and fight hard, for as long as it takes to prevail.

Lieutenant Colonel Oliver North reacting to his conviction on charges related to the Iran-contra scandal on May 4, 1989, in Clifton Daniel, ed., 20th Century Day by Day (2000), p. 1331.

It's become a grant agency rather than a credit program.

Agriculture secretary Clayton Yeutter describing the Farmers Home Administration's lending policies, which were expected to result in losses of approximately $22.2 billion between 1990 and 1992, in Rich Thomas, "Harvest of Red Ink," Newsweek, September 18, 1989, p. 38.

We are on your side; we are and remain one nation. We belong together.

West Germany's chancellor, Helmut Kohl, addressing the people of East Germany after the destruction of the Berlin Wall on November 10, 1989, in Clifton Daniel, ed., 20th Century Day by Day (2000), p. 1343.

A hands-across-Prague protest designed as a human chain became instead a merry dance, a living tableau from a Brueghel painting, as laughing, skipping people in warm mufflers and long scarves formed an endless twisting snake around the trees, through the snowy park, up to the floodlit spires . . . then helter-skelter slithered giggling down steep, slippery, narrow cobble streets, and holding hands with exaggerated formality with a pastiche mazurka, passed across the fifteenth century Charles Bridge, watched by stern statues of all the saints. . . .

Rumours abounded of tanks on the city outskirts. But everyone, including the party, knew the simple truth: without Soviet military and political armour behind it, the threat of armed intervention was hollow.

British journalist Peter Millar describing on November 26, 1989, the popular response in Prague to the collapse of Czechoslovakia's Communist regime, in Martin Gilbert, A History of the Twentieth Century, vol. 3 (2000), p. 681.

2

The Cold War Ends; The New World Order Begins
1990

The 20th century did not go gently to its conclusion. From its opening year, the final decade of the millennium witnessed radical changes to established social, cultural, and political systems throughout the world. Even before President George H. W. Bush declared in November, "We have closed a chapter of history. The cold war is over," the old world order had begun to crumble and the stirrings of a new one had begun. Premier Mikhail Gorbachev's declaration in late 1989 that the Soviet Union would no longer militarily sustain the Communist governments in Eastern Europe unleashed a powerful force for change that repudiated the communist economic system and the totalitarian regimes that had dominated the region since the late 1940s. The drive in those nations toward representative government and free-market economies acquired an unstoppable momentum, and the rapid changes throughout Eastern Europe caught virtually every political observer by surprise, including the intelligence agencies of the United States and its allies. In addition to the regime changes that occurred in late 1989 in East Germany, Hungary, Bulgaria, Czechoslovakia, and Romania, by the end of 1990, the opposition leader Lech Walesa had been elected president of Poland; Germany was reunified after 45 years of division into Communist and democratic republics; and even the Soviet Union expanded civil liberties, held its first multiparty elections since the Communist Party took power in 1917, and entertained declarations of sovereignty by several of the Soviet republics, including Russia itself.

The forces for change extended to Central America as well, as a democratic election in Nicaragua deposed the Marxist Sandinista regime that had so vexed Ronald Reagan during the 1980s, and Panama's dictator, Manuel Noriega, surrendered to U.S. forces after taking refuge in the Vatican embassy during the U.S. invasion of December 1989. Noriega was then taken to Miami, where he was later tried for and convicted of drug trafficking. In Africa, the white supremacist government in South Africa freed the longtime political prisoner Nelson Mandela, setting the stage for the termination of apartheid in 1991 and establishment of black majority rule in 1993; and in the Middle East, North and South Yemen ended decades of conflict and merged to form the Republic of Yemen.

But Iraq's invasion of Kuwait in early August was the greatest force for world change in 1990, as the United States assembled a military coalition of former cold war allies and adversaries, along with several Islam-dominated Arab nations, to block a possible Iraqi incursion into oil-rich Saudi Arabia. This action, known as Operation Desert Shield, set the stage for the 1991 Persian Gulf War.

But the dazzling international events only partially distracted attention from a faltering economy that finally provoked Bush to contradict his 1988 campaign promise that he would not raise taxes. Dissatisfaction over this reversal, rising unemployment, the weak economy, and revelations that the president's son had been involved in a costly savings-and-loan failure contributed to voter dissatisfaction in the November midterm elections that enabled Democrats to gain additional seats in Congress, where they already enjoyed a majority in both houses.

The ever-changing face of America continued to evolve as the 1990 U.S. census estimated that one-quarter of the population were members of minority groups and that Asians and Pacific Islanders were now the fastest growing minority. These and other demographic changes that slightly diminished the predominance of the Anglo white majority had long-term social and political consequences that reverberated throughout the decade.

Advances in science and technology accelerated changes in human understanding and human capacity to do things never before accomplished. These included the first use of human gene therapy, the launching of the *Hubble Space Telescope,* and new evidence supporting the big bang theory of the origin of the universe. Closer to home, the growing popularity of gangsta rap gave expression to a different explosion of violent energy, and the culture wars intensified as controversies erupted over federal funding of the arts. Using satellite technology, Cable Network News (CNN) asserted itself as a worldwide media force by offering round-the-clock live reportage from Baghdad and the Persian Gulf.

INTERNATIONAL DEVELOPMENTS

The End of the Cold War

In 1990, the fall of the old world order that had dominated international relations since the end of World War II intersected with the rise of a new world order that saw the United States as the sole superpower and the most potent military power in history. The Soviet Union's decision to withdraw its troops from Eastern Europe and allow those nations to be ruled by non-Communist, democratically based governments, and its acquiescence to the reunification of a democratic Germany fulfilled the key U.S. cold war objectives dating back to the late 1940s.

At the beginning of the year, the Soviets agreed to remove their troops from Hungary and Czechoslovakia, and by the end of September, they had consented to withdraw entirely from Eastern Europe. The dissident playwright Václav Havel, who had been elected interim president of Czechoslovakia in December 1989, was reelected on a permanent basis in July, becoming the first non-Communist leader of that country since 1948. Another anticommunist activist who had also been imprisoned by his nation's Communist regime in the 1980s rose to the height of power, as the Solidarity labor union leader Lech Walesa was overwhelmingly elected president of Poland. The Soviets also conceded the accuracy of a long-standing accusation they had consistently denied throughout the cold war: that at the end of World War II their troops had massacred some 15,000 Polish officers—their ostensible allies—in order to facilitate Soviet domination in the postwar era.

Free, multiparty elections took place for the first time in more than 50 years throughout Eastern Europe and within the Soviet Union itself for the first time since its founding in 1917. Those elections produced declarations of sovereignty by several of the republics within the Soviet federation, including Lithuania, Estonia, and Russia. Free elections also facilitated the ascension to national prominence of Moscow's former mayor, Boris Yeltsin, an advocate of rapid reform whom the parliament elected president of the republic of Russia, despite Gorbachev's support for a rival candidate. In July, Yeltsin quit the Communist Party and demanded greater movement toward a free market economy. However, Gorbachev, who received the 1990 Nobel Peace Prize for his role in transforming Eastern Europe, otherwise consolidated his power throughout the year, as he oversaw the transfer of authority from the Communist Party, which he still led, to elected government institutions, which he also headed in his new capacity as the Soviet Union's first executive president. Concerned over the vast powers that were accruing to the office of executive president, his critics warned that Gorbachev was creating a dictatorship.

The reunification of Germany as a single democratic nation with ties to the West—a major cold war objective of the United States—was achieved incrementally throughout the year. Although it gratified many Germans who had been separated from family members and friends since the erection of the Berlin Wall in 1961, the reunification also raised concerns that prosperous West Germany would have to absorb the financial difficulties of Communist East Germany, whose economy had been suffering for years. The first step occurred in May, when East Germany accepted West Germany's much stronger deutschmark as the currency for both republics. Soon afterward, free passage between East and West Berlin was permitted, and East Germany adopted West Germany's monetary, economic, and social laws. In September, East and West Germany signed a peace treaty with Great Britain, France, the United States, and the Soviet Union officially concluding World War II and arranging the complete withdrawal of Soviet troops from Europe. Finally, on October 3, Germany was officially reunited into a single nation for the first time since the end of World War II. In December, West Germany's leader, Helmut Kohl, was elected chancellor of the new Federal Republic of Germany in the first nationwide elections since Adolf Hitler attained power in 1933.

The cold war concluded in mid-November, when leaders of all the European states, the United States, Canada, and the Soviet Union signed a new charter regulating relations among themselves and approved a nonaggression pact between cold war adversaries, the North Atlantic Treaty Organization (NATO), and the Warsaw Pact, which voted in February 1991 to dissolve as a military alliance. They also signed the Treaty on Conventional Forces in Europe (CFE), which dramatically reduced nonnuclear arsenals in Europe. The signing of the Charter of Paris on November 21 put an official end to the cold war and the nuclear stalemate that had dominated world politics throughout the second half of the 20th century.

Iraq's Invasion of Kuwait and Operation Desert Shield

Even as the cold war raced to a conclusion, producing talk of an anticipated "peace dividend" that would result from reduced military spending in a less threatening world, Iraq's president Saddam Hussein made bold moves that ultimately provoked the United States to assert itself as the world's sole remaining superpower. Iraq's Gulf War with Iran throughout most of the 1980s had concluded in 1988 in a stalemate that failed to secure any of Saddam Hussein's objectives. But the ongoing conflict did enable him to consolidate his power at home by creating the large elite Republican Guard, which was personally loyal to him, and by leaving him in charge of a standing army of some 1 million troops who were well equipped with modern Soviet arms. After Israel, Iraq boasted the most powerful military force in the Middle East.

Iraq had accumulated large debts to Kuwait and other Persian Gulf states, which had lent vast sums to help finance the war that suppressed Iran's fundamentalist Islamic revolution, a revolution that threatened to topple their wealthy secular rulers. Unlike the other Gulf states, Kuwait angered Saddam Hussein by refusing to forgive its loans to Iraq, despite Saddam Hussein's claim that Iraq had waged the war on its behalf. Saddam Hussein also accused Kuwait of stealing billions of dollars worth of oil by drilling into Iraq's part of the Rumalia oil field, which spans their border. And he denounced Kuwait for undermining the Iraqi economy by driving down the price of oil by selling more than the quota agreed upon by the Organization of Petroleum Exporting

Iraqi president Saddam Hussein threatened the world's oil supply when he invaded and annexed Kuwait in August 1990. *(AP/Wide World Photos)*

Countries (OPEC). In addition, Saddam Hussein had aspirations of personal aggrandizement, as he desired to create a new Babylon that would again unite the entire Arab world, as it had in biblical times, with Iraq at its center and with him the new Nebuchadnezzar, the conqueror of Israel.

Saddam Hussein made his first public accusations against Kuwait in late May, at an emergency meeting of the Arab League. He reiterated the charges throughout the summer, and in late July, Iraq began massing troops at the border. On July 25, Saddam Hussein conferred with the U.S. ambassador, April Glaspie, to learn how the United States would respond to an Iraqi military action. According to a secretly made transcript of the meeting, which Iraq later leaked to the press and which the State Department did not deny, Glaspie replied that the United States took no official position on Arab-Arab conflicts, such as Iraq's border disagreement with Kuwait.[1] Moreover, throughout the week members of the State Department and the administration made statements suggesting tolerance of Iraq's aggressive behavior. These statements, and Glaspie's, were later cited by critics who maintained that Bush, who also regarded Iraq as a bulwark against Iran, gave Saddam Hussein tacit approval to invade Kuwait, probably with the expectation that the outcome would be an adjustment of the border boundaries and possibly some concessions on Iraq's outstanding debt and its claims that Kuwait was selling more oil than permitted. More cynical critics speculated that Bush might have been "setting up" Saddam Hussein by encouraging him to take aggressive action, so the United States could intervene and possibly depose him or diminish his power.

Whether or not the administration intended to encourage Saddam Hussein, on August 1, Iraqi diplomats walked out on an emergency meeting in Jeddah mediated by Saudi Arabia's king Fahd, and Iraqi troops crossed into Kuwait during the early morning of August 2, local time. By the end of the day, Iraqi troops had captured Kuwait City; deposed the royal family, some of whom were killed in the fighting; and established defensive positions close to the Saudi border. That evening, Bush met in Aspen, Colorado, with Britain's prime minister, Margaret Thatcher, who urged him to oppose the invasion strenuously, and the United Nations (UN) Security Council passed Resolution 660 condemning the invasion and calling for Iraq's immediate withdrawal from Kuwait. Ignoring the storm of protest from the international community, Iraq annexed Kuwait on August 8, wiping out its $13 billion debt and resolving its oil disputes in a single stroke.

An Iraqi conquest of thinly defended Saudi Arabia was now possible, as Iraq continued to reinforce its troops at the Saudi border. Such a conquest, coupled with Iraq's control over Kuwait, would have taken the world's most abundant oil reserves from conservative, pro-West Arab regimes and placed them instead under Saddam Hussein's personal control. This contingency was clearly in the best interests of neither the United States, the Western industrialized nations, nor Saudi Arabia itself. Therefore, on August 6, after meeting with Defense Secretary Richard Cheney and being briefed by General Norman Schwarzkopf, commander in chief of the U.S. Central Command, King Fahd agreed to allow the United States to send troops to protect his country. The agreement stipulated that the U.S. military presence would be temporary, and U.S. personnel would respect the Saudis' traditions and religious customs. In return, Saudi Arabia agreed to increase its oil production to compensate for the

Soldiers patrolled the Saudi desert in Black Hawk helicopters during Operation Desert Shield. *(U.S. Department of Defense)*

oil lost when Iraq stopped exporting its own oil and Kuwait's. Saudi Arabia later also agreed to pay for most of the expenses incurred by the United States for its defense.

Operation Desert Shield was immediately initiated to implement this agreement. Invoking the 1979 Carter Doctrine, which, after the Soviet invasion of Afghanistan, asserted that any attempt to gain control of the Persian Gulf would be treated as an assault on U.S. vital interests, Bush announced the U.S. military response in a televised address to the nation on August 8, and the first troops departed immediately thereafter. Overall, Bush enjoyed wide public support for his efforts to protect Saudi Arabia, although the later decision to fight an offensive war was more controversial.

Saddam Hussein gave credence to the threat by moving more troops into Kuwait and further strengthening Iraqi defenses along the Saudi border. He also tried to gain additional leverage by taking hostage thousands of Westerners who had been caught in Kuwait during the invasion and by seizing the foreign embassies there and forcing diplomats to relocate in Iraq. Some of the hostages were positioned close to military sites, making them "human shields" who would die if the sites were attacked by coalition air strikes. These actions also provoked UN condemnation, and Saddam Hussein released all the hostages by the end of the year.

Meanwhile, Bush worked to assemble a coalition of nations to block further Iraqi advances and enforce a UN-mandated embargo against Iraq. Eventually, the coalition numbered 36 nations, most of them NATO countries but also such Arab nations as Egypt, Syria, and the Persian Gulf states, and even some members of the Warsaw Pact. The nascent coalition defenses remained vulnerable to an Iraqi assault throughout August and September, when it was believed that an invasion could occur at any time. The heavily outnumbered coalition forces were too small and underequipped to stop an attack, and their mission would have been to fight a delaying action until reinforcements could be assembled and deployed. But by the beginning of October, enough troops and equipment had been moved to the region that the defense of Saudi Arabia was considered secure. Subsequently, both as a means of pressuring Saddam Hussein to leave Kuwait and as a prelude to waging war if he did not, the United States continued to increase its troop strength in the region. On November 8, two days after the midterm congressional elections, Bush ordered an additional 150,000 air, sea, and ground troops to the Persian Gulf, and on November 14, Cheney authorized the call-up of 80,000 more army reserves and 15,000 Marine Corps reserves. By the end of the year, some 325,000 American troops and 540,000 total coalition troops from 31 countries were stationed in the region. Iraq, which had begun conscripting 17-year-old boys, was estimated to have deployed 43 divisions, consisting of 540,000 troops supported by 4,200 tanks, 2,800 armored personnel carriers, and 3,100 pieces of artillery.[2]

Bush spent the Thanksgiving holiday in Saudi Arabia with the troops. A week later, on November 29, the UN Security Council authorized war against Iraq if it did not withdraw from Kuwait. The following day, Bush offered for the first time to negotiate directly with Iraq and suggested that Secretary of State James Baker and Iraqi foreign minister Tariq Aziz meet. On December 18, however, a tentative meeting in Washington, D.C., was canceled when the two sides could not agree on terms for a reciprocal visit in Iraq. The meeting, eventually held on January 9, produced no results. Operation Desert Shield ended and Operation Desert Storm began on January 16, 1991, when the United States–led coalition began its air war.

Although most Americans supported the defensive operation, Desert Shield met some opposition, both in the United States and in Saudi Arabia. In particular, the matter of respecting the Saudis' Islamic customs posed a sensitive and somewhat complicated problem. Throughout Desert Shield and Desert Storm, the U.S. Central Command tried to isolate American troops from the Saudi population to prevent cultural clashes. The deference to Saudi custom, at the expense of the personal freedoms of U.S. personnel, especially female soldiers, highlighted the fact that American troops were being sent to protect a nondemocratic monarchy that deprived its citizens of many of the personal and political freedoms Americans have traditionally cherished. The disenfranchisement of Saudi women and the imposition of stringent limitations on their behavior, in accordance with Islamic tradition, struck an especially raw nerve among many Americans still celebrating the expanded rights and opportunities U.S. women had acquired during the cold war era. Paradoxically, American women played a much larger role and were given far greater responsibilities in the Persian Gulf War than in any previous war, but they were constrained by the coalition's need to respect Islamic culture.

The Saudis, in turn, were concerned that the American presence might provoke Saudi citizens to emulate the behavior of American soldiers, in violation of Islamic tradition. A highly publicized demonstration by Saudi women who drove cars around Riyadh demanding driving privileges was the most visible example of the effect of the American influence on Saudi citizens during Operation Desert Shield.

GOVERNMENT AND SOCIETY

The 1990 census listed the total U.S. residential population as 248.7 million, an increase from 1980 of 22.2 million, or 9.8 percent. Blacks, Hispanics, Asians, and Native Americans accounted for more than half of the overall increase, and Hispanics for the largest share. However, Asians and Pacific Islanders were the fastest-growing minority. Although the total number of white Americans grew by 11 million to 209 million, the percentage of whites within the population declined to 80.3 percent, compared to 83.1 percent in 1980, and the percentage of non-Hispanic whites dropped from 80 percent in 1980 to 76 percent in 1990. The census also showed that for the first time more than half of all Americans lived in urban areas of 1 million or more people; the New York City area (18 million) and Los Angeles (14.5 million) showed the largest populations. The fastest-growing metropolitan areas were in the so-called Sun Belt states of the South and West, led by Orlando, Phoenix, Sacramento, San Diego, Dallas, and Atlanta. The census also noted the continued decline in numbers of the traditional family, defined as a married couple with one or more children below the age of 18. Such traditional families accounted for only 26 percent of the nation's 93.3 million households, down from 31 percent in 1980. Conversely, the number of single parents grew by 41 percent—approximately 80 percent of single parents were women—and almost one-quarter of the children born in 1990 were born to unmarried parents (23.3 percent). The census also found that American children's chances of growing up in poverty rose to 36 percent after their parents separated or divorced, compared to 19 percent for children whose parents remained together.[3]

The census itself became the center of controversy, as several cities, states, and organizations sought to employ commonly used statistical adjustments to account for a possible undercount, especially among minority residents. As the census is the basis for determining the number of seats that states hold in the U.S. House of Representatives, the argument had significant political implications. Proponents of the adjustments argued that undercounting resulted in underrepresentation of the actual centers of population; opponents argued that the constitutional mandate for the census had no provision for adjustments.

Americans in 1990 were living longer than in previous years. A study conducted by the Department of Health and Human Services revealed that the average life expectancy was 75 years, up from 74.8 in 1986 and 70.9 in 1970. African Americans had an expectancy of 69.4 years, compared to 75.6 for whites, although black women could, on average, expect to live to 73.6 years, compared to 72.2 for white men. The rates of infant mortality and of death of heart disease and stroke were also in decline.[4]

Despite the increase in longevity, public health issues ranging from air pollution to cigarette smoking to legalized abortion to the widespread use of illegal drugs remained in the forefront of the public consciousness. The pervasiveness of illegal cocaine use throughout all strata of society became especially apparent when Marion Barry, mayor of Washington, D.C., was caught on videotape smoking crack cocaine. Moreover, some 375,000 "crack babies" faced a life marred by birth defects after being born to crack-addicted mothers.[5] The National College Athletic Association (NCAA) deemed it necessary to mandate year-round drug testing for some 18,500 football players, who were to be tested for both illegal street drugs and prohibited performance-enhancing supplements. Connections between illegal drug trafficking and respected financial institutions became public when two subsidiaries of the Luxembourg-based Bank of Credit & Commerce International Holdings (BCCI) pled guilty to charges that they helped the Colombian Medellín drug cartel launder more than $32 million in illegal profits through secret accounts around the world.

Race relations, always a sensitive issue in the United States, were exacerbated by a string of bombings in the South in late 1989 and 1990. Moreover, Charles Stuart, a white upper-middle-class Bostonian who identified a black suspect in the 1989 murder of his pregnant wife, committed suicide in January, after his brothers and sister revealed that Stuart himself had shot his wife and their unborn child, who died weeks after surviving an emergency caesarean birth. The supposed shooting of the Stuarts, whom the media had labeled a "Camelot couple" who had risen from the working class to wealth, attracted widespread newspaper and television coverage, which stirred antiblack sentiments within the city. The subsequent revelation that Stuart carried out the murder with the intention of blaming an innocent black man provoked anger and resentment among African Americans, many of whom believed that racial prejudice had led the media to embrace Stuart's lurid story eagerly and the police to search numerous young black men throughout the city.

Similar charges of racism emerged in New York City after the acquittal of the alleged ringleader of a white mob who had murdered Yusuf Hawkins, a black teenager who was killed in 1989, after he entered the predominantly white Bensonhurst neighborhood in Brooklyn. Even though another member of the mob was convicted, the acquittal of 19-year-old Keith Mondello provoked outrage, especially because Mondello had earlier confessed to leading the bat-wielding group who chased Hawkins before he was shot to death. The controversy that followed the trial pitted New York City's first black mayor, David Dinkins, against the black activist the Reverend Al Sharpton, who called for a rally that would paralyze the city. At the national level, in October Bush vetoed the Civil Rights Act of 1990, although it contained provisions he endorsed, because he maintained it would introduce racial quotas into the workplace.

Another high-profile mob attack of 1989 was resolved in 1990, when three black teenagers were convicted of beating and raping Trisha Meili, a young white woman who had been jogging through New York City's Central Park. (The convictions were overturned in December 2002 after deoxyribonucleic acid [DNA] evidence corroborated a jailhouse confession by a convicted rapist who maintained that he alone had committed the crime.) Although the attack on Meili, then identified in the media only as the "Central Park jogger," was originally attributed to racial and class tensions and to a so-called teenage practice of wilding, it soon was recast by the media and various organizations, such as the National Organization for Women, as a gender crime. As such, it was used to draw attention to increasing incidents of violence against women throughout the nation. According to figures released by the Senate Judiciary Committee in 1990, one woman was raped every six minutes in the United States and 16 women confronted a rapist every hour, making the U.S. rate of rape 13 times greater than Britain's and more than 20 times greater than Japan's. Moreover, 3 to 4 million American women, more than 1 million of whom required medical assistance, were battered each year. Seventy-five percent of all women could expect to be victims of violent crime during their lifetime.[6]

In general, violence in the United States approached record levels, and firearms continued to play an increasing role in the commission of crimes. The alarming rate of violent crime led to vocal demands for stricter gun control, especially among liberals, and equally passionate opposition by the National Rifle Association (NRA) and other conservative groups who maintained that corrupted moral values, not weapons, were the core problem. Drug use and drug trafficking, television violence, and the breakdown of the nuclear family were also cited as explanations for the surge in violence. Bush signed legislation requiring the federal government to track hate crimes motivated by racial, ethnic, or sexual prejudice.

Legalized abortion remained a contentious issue as well, even within the First Family, as President Bush and his sons voiced their opposition at a family gathering, while First Lady Barbara Bush and the other women in attendance expressed pro-choice sentiments.[7] Equally divided was the American Bar Association, which voted to endorse a constitutional amendment that would guarantee women's right to have abortions and then later rescinded the vote and adopted a neutral position. Connecticut, meanwhile, enacted similar legislation to guarantee the right to abortion, even if the Supreme Court were to reverse the *Roe v. Wade* decision, which legalized the practice in 1973. Although the Supreme Court did not strike down that landmark decision, it did narrow the right to abortion by allowing states to require pregnant girls to notify both of their parents of their intention to abort a fetus, provided the states also allowed them to obtain a judge's permission instead of notifying their parents.

A federally funded study conducted by the Johns Hopkins University School of Hygiene and Public Health concluded that after two years black inner-city teenagers who had abortions fared better economically, educationally, and emotionally than those who gave birth. And a panel of the American Psychological Association reported that abortions performed in the first trimester of pregnancy caused little long-term psychological distress. Nonetheless, antiabortion sentiment remained strong throughout the country, and antiabortion activists continued to represent a potent political force. In April, Vice President Dan Quayle appeared before a massive antiabortion rally in Washington, D.C., and Bush addressed the group by telephone.

The Supreme Court also reflected the social, political, and ideological divisions within the nation. Thirty-seven decisions, almost a quarter of the 129 rulings the Court rendered during its term, were decided by 5-4 votes. Of these, the conservative bloc, led by Chief Justice William H. Rehnquist, prevailed in 25 cases, and the liberal bloc, headed by Justice William J. Brennan, Jr., prevailed in 11 decisions. Justice Byron R. White emerged as the swing vote in most of these cases. Brennan resigned shortly after the session ended, concluding nearly 34 years on the Court, and Bush replaced him with David Souter, a relatively unknown justice who had moderately conservative sensibilities.

Significant Supreme Court decisions during the year included rulings that juries did not have to represent a cross section of the community in order to be considered impartial; that prosecutors could introduce improperly obtained evidence to contradict a defendant's false or inconsistent testimony; that the government could limit political spending by corporations; that individuals had a "right to die" when faced with a terminal illness, but that states could withhold that right from people who were in a coma who had not previously expressed their desire to die if they were reduced to living in a permanently "vegetative" condition; that states could tax religious organizations on the sale of religious material; that a company could bring suit against competitors who bribe foreign officials; and that alcohol checkpoints on public roads did not violate Fourth Amendment provisions against unreasonable search and seizure. The Court also struck down a controversial law forbidding the burning or defacing of the American flag, saying that such legislation violated the First Amendment's guarantee of free speech. The Flag Protection Act of 1989 had been passed in response to a previous Supreme Court decision in 1989 that permitted flag-burning as a constitutionally guaranteed form of free speech.

In verdicts that would later be struck down because the prosecutors violated the immunity provisions of the defendants' 1987 congressional testimonies, Lieutenant Colonel Oliver North and former National Security Advisor Admiral John Poindexter were convicted in federal court for their roles in the Iran-contra affair. Poindexter's trial was notable for the videotaped testimony of former president Ronald Reagan, who maintained that he, Reagan, had never ordered any of the illegal actions committed in conjunction with the arms-for-hostages scandal.

BUSINESS

The year saw a weakening of the economy, as the gross national product (GNP) fell after a record eight years of growth. The Dow-Jones industrial average fluctuated between 2,365 and 2,999.75; the GNP was an anemic 0.9 percent; inflation rose from 4.6 percent in 1989 to 5.4 percent; and unemployment rose from 5.3 percent in 1989 to 6.1 percent.[8] Most analysts concurred that the economy entered into a recession in the year's fourth quarter, an assessment that was seemingly shared by the Federal Reserve Board, which cut its discount rate for the first time since 1986.

Major business scandals also undermined public confidence in the business climate. The Office of Thrift Supervision reported that savings & loan (S&Ls) institutions lost $19.17 billion in 1989, and estimates of the total cost of the S&L debacle were around $300 billion over 10 years, much of it due to fraud.[9] The renowned junk bond specialist Michael Milken pled guilty to securities fraud. His company, Drexel Lambert Burnham, outraged investors by distributing $200 million in bonuses for top executives shortly before declaring bankruptcy. Neil Bush, the president's son, was implicated in a costly scandal centering around the collapse of the Denver-based Silverado S&L. Five U.S. senators, Alan Cranston, Dennis DeConcini, John Glenn, Donald W. Riegle, Jr., and John McCain, were implicated in another high-profile S&L scandal involving Charles Keating's failed Lincoln S&L. In 1991, a Senate ethics panel cleared the others of illegal behavior but found that there was "substantial credible evidence" that Cranston, a long-serving California Democrat, had acted improperly and possibly illegally. The recently formed Resolution Trust Company (RTC) was charged with disposing of the assets accumulated from the bankrupt S&Ls—mostly real estate and art—and critics accused the administration of arranging "fire sales" in which well-connected investors were able to acquire valuable properties at prices well below market value. A government directive for the RTC to sell off its real estate holdings as quickly as possible also upset bankers, who feared the properties held by the trust would be dumped onto an already weak real estate market.

The marketing and manufacture of cigarettes also became a public health issue in 1990. The Environmental Protection Agency (EPA) tentatively concluded that secondhand smoke was causing more than 3,000 cases of lung cancer yearly, and the health and human services secretary, Louis W. Sullivan, called for states to protect children by banning cigarette-vending machines. The R. J. Reynolds Company was heavily criticized for its plans to market two new cigarette brands, Uptown and Dakota, to African Americans and to young poorly educated white women, respectively. Reynolds canceled Uptown after charges by Sullivan that targeting black Americans as potential consumers of the cancer-causing product was an act of cynical racism. Harvard University became the most prominent academic institution to divest its investments in tobacco stocks.

Marketing to young people also stirred controversy with the introduction of Channel One, a commercially sponsored television news program made especially for broadcast in public schools, where sponsors then gained access to a captive audience of teenagers.

NATURE AND THE ENVIRONMENT

The harmful environmental impact of certain corporate and industrial practices provoked controversy that was manifested in a variety of venues throughout the decade, as legislation, legal action, and populist protest sought to compel businesses to modify their behavior. Although businesses often thwarted or reduced the scope of proposed legislation that might require costly modifications, as they did with the Clean Air Act of 1990, the 1990s saw significant growth in corporate responsiveness to environmental concerns. Most of this growth took place during the Clinton years, but it was apparent as early as 1990, when 93 nations, including the United States, signed an agreement to banish by the end of the century chlorofluorocarbons (CFCs), which deplete the Earth's ozone layer, and to establish a fund to help developing nations phase out the use of such chemicals. In addition, a national grassroots campaign formed to limit the use of polystyrene, or Styrofoam®, which poses an environmental hazard because it is not biodegradable. Environmental activists targeted the McDonald's hamburger chain, picketing local restaurants with slogans such as "Get Your Styrofoam off Our Planet!" and with drawings of coffee cups marked with a skull and crossbones, the international icon for poison. In November, McDonald's agreed to phase out its use of Styrofoam® and to substitute biodegradable materials. Subsequently, other corporations also adopted more environmentally friendly practices, as they tried both to prevent the negative effect of public protest and to cash in on a growing public demand for so-called green products believed to reduce harm to nature.

As the market for recycled paper products, plastics, and other materials subsequently grew, the waste management industry created a more central role for recycling. The recycling industry was greatly bolstered by local legislation across the country that mandated residential recycling of paper, plastic, and aluminum. In 1990, for instance, California enacted the especially ambitious Integrated Solid Waste Management Act, which requires cities to reduce waste by 25 percent in 1995 and 50 percent in 2000. By 1997, waste was recycled nationwide at the rate of approximately 47 millions tons per year, up from 8 million tons per year in 1970.[10]

Other environmentally related business developments included a major oil spill from an Exxon refinery into New York Harbor and the release of a study by the American Lung Association showing that health-care costs resulting from air pollution by automobiles ranged from $40 to $50 billion annually. The announcement was timed to coincide with debate over the Clean Air Act of 1990, which Congress passed to reduce levels of automobile emissions, industrial toxic air pollutants, CFCs, and smokestack emissions from electric utilities. The final legislation was a compromise intended to balance business and environmental interests.

The fact that global surface temperatures in 1990 were higher than in any year since records were first kept in the 19th century gave new credence to claims that global warming was already in progress, although critics of the hypothesis maintained that the high temperatures could be simply an anomaly or the result of natural, rather than human-made, causes. More than 700 scientists, including 49 Nobel Prize winners, signed a petition stating that the problem of global warming was urgent and required immediate action, but Bush declined to take additional, potentially costly steps that would have required businesses to reduce the emissions that were the suspected causes. Nonetheless, publicity surrounding global warming and other environmental concerns prompted greater public awareness of the problem and stimulated renewed interest in Earth Day, whose 20th anniversary was widely celebrated throughout the nation. In New York City alone some 750,000 people gathered in Central Park for Earth Day activities.

Science and Technology

The launch of the *Hubble Space Telescope* put into orbit one of the most powerful and effective tools for space exploration ever constructed. The *Hubble,* unlike telescopes on Earth, does not suffer from distortion caused by the Earth's atmosphere, and it has produced photographs from near and deep space that have radically altered astronomers' literal and conceptual views of the cosmos and have inspired artists and ordinary citizens with their beauty. The large reflecting telescope with mirrors ground to near perfection was initially a profound disappointment, however, because its pictures were out of focus as a result of a misalignment of the two mirrors. This problem was corrected in 1993. Also in 1990, the *Magellan* space probe, named after the Spanish explorer who first circumnavigated the Earth, took off to explore Venus, and the *Ulysses,* named after the Greek mythological hero of the *Odyssey,* was deployed from the space shuttle *Discovery* to survey the polar regions of the Sun. The *Cosmic Background Explorer* satellite, which was launched in late 1989, produced new measurements that supported the big bang theory of the origin of the universe.

The introduction of the third version of Microsoft's Windows© contributed substantially to the rapid growth in the worldwide use of personal computers by offering a computer operating system that was both comprehensible and affordable to middle-class and working-class users. As did the system used by Microsoft's less successful competitor, Apple, Windows version 3.0 employed a comparatively easy-to-use point-and-click system that was visually oriented, instead of word-oriented, and hence more user friendly.

In medical science, a new study challenged the widely held, scientifically endorsed belief that oat bran fiber reduces cholesterol level; a four-year-old girl who had the immune system disorder adenosine deaminase deficiency (ADA) became the first person to receive human gene therapy; and calcium was shown to slow osteoporosis in postmenopausal women. The National Academy of Science and the National Research Council found that the United States was a decade behind other countries in developing new birth control methods, a lag that, among other things, led to increased rates of abortion. According to the report, about half of the nation's approximately 1.5 million abortions resulted from contraceptive failure.[11]

LITERATURE, THE ARTS, SPORTS, AND POPULAR CULTURE

Black gangsta rappers expressing their experiences of and feelings about inner-city violence attracted large new national audiences in 1990. The music's hard, sometimes harsh, insistent beat; its rage at social hypocrisy and injustice; and its expressed need to lash out violently at something, perhaps anything, found ready listeners among teenagers and young adults not only in impoverished inner-city neighborhoods but also in white, middle-class and upper-class suburbs. The lyrics often expressed a machismo that denigrated women, regularly referring to them as "bitches" and reducing them in the rawest terms to their sexual organs. In this regard, gangsta rap repudiated the nation's growing feminist movement, which was generally supported in other art forms. Made either deliberately or as an unintended side effect of young male performers using their music to claim their territory and declare that they have come of age as men, this repudiation of female equality represented a new assault on feminism from a largely unexpected quarter, especially as many feminists regarded the inner-city poor as fellow victims of a white male patriarchy. Very different in both its messages and its messengers from the critiques of feminism issued by conservative and religious groups, gangsta rap nonetheless shared with those groups a worldview that made men paramount and regarded women primarily in terms of their sexual or childbearing capacity. Among its top performers were Ice Cube, Geto Boys, and N.W.A. MC Hammer, a more traditional rapper in the hip-hop tradition, sold more than 4 million copies of his album *Please Hammer, Don't Hurt 'Em,* the best-selling rap album to that date.[12] The group Milli Vanilli, winners of the 1990 Best New Artist award issued by the recording industry, had their prize revoked when it was revealed that the group's ostensible performers, Rob Pilatus and Fab Morvan, had not performed any of the vocals on their album, *Girl You Know It's True.* Pilatus attempted suicide, and, although they'd sold 10 million albums and had three top-rated singles, Milli Vanilli has since essentially been written out of the living history of popular music, as most radio stations across the nation stopped playing their music.

Rapper MC Hammer's album *Please Hammer, Don't Hurt 'Em* sold 4 million copies. *(Photofest)*

On the other end of the cultural spectrum, New York's Metropolitan Opera performed a widely viewed, critically acclaimed, and nationally televised production of Richard Wagner's *Ring* cycle. Popular songs of the year included Mariah Carey's "Vision of Love," Janet Jackson's "Escapade," Michael Bolton's "How Am I Supposed to Live without You?" and Garth Brooks's "Unanswered Prayers." Jackson, Bolton, Kathy Mattea, Johnny Gill, and Billy Joel released best-selling albums. Phil Collins won the Grammy Award for his single "Another Day in Paradise," and Quincy Jones won for his album *Back on the Block*. The pianist Harry Connick, Jr., revived 1940s swing style, and Wynton Marsalis and his brother, Branford Marsalis, won large followings with their revival of classical jazz and jazz-rock fusion. The singer Bobby Darin and the groups the Four Seasons, the Four Tops, the Kinks, the Platters, and Simon and Garfunkle were inducted into the Rock and Roll Hall of Fame, along with the songwriting team of Gerry Goffin and Carole King, and the team of Eddie Holland, Brian Holland, and Lamont Dozier, who wrote many of the hit songs recorded by Motown artists. Louis Armstrong, Charlie Christian, and Ma Rainey were also inducted as major early influences on rock.

The nation's cultural divisions were also played out in the visual arts, both in the artworks that were created—many of which expressed extremely liberal points of view that championed the rights of women and homosexuals—and in the politics surrounding the federal and state funding of such works. The Cincinnati Contemporary Arts Center and its director, Dennis Barrie, were indicted on obscenity charges for displaying in an exhibit of 175 photographs by Robert Mapplethorpe, seven pictures depicting naked children or homosexual acts. In a separate action, the National Council on the Arts rescinded two $40,000 grants it had awarded to the University of Pennsylvania's Institute of Contemporary Art, whose retrospective of Mapplethorpe's work sparked objections to using federal monies to fund work that many Americans regarded as obscene and/or morally offensive. Under pressure from conservative politicians, the National Endowment for the Arts (NEA) rejected grant applications from four performance artists who had been recommended by one of its review panels of artists and art managers. The rejected works involved nudity associated with feminist issues, homosexuality and AIDS, and a performance piece by John Fleck, who appeared nude and urinated on stage. In response to efforts by conservative legislators to slash funding for the NEA, several well-known actors, including Kevin Kline, Kathleen Turner, and Morgan Freeman, and the theater producer Joseph Papp met with legislators to defend the endowment.

Elsewhere in the world of art, Vincent van Gogh's *Portrait of Dr. Gachet* became the most expensive painting ever auctioned when it was sold for $82.5 million. Pierre Auguste Renoir's *Au Moulin de la Galette* was the second most expensive at $78.1 million.

With the publication of *Rabbit at Rest,* which won the Pulitzer Prize in fiction, the acclaimed novelist John Updike concluded a series he had begun in 1960 centering around the life of his middle-American antihero, Rabbit Angstrom. The series chronicled not only the adult life of the onetime high school basketball star but also the evolution of American society between 1960 and 1990. The poets Dave Smith and Maya Angelou published *Cuba Night* and *I Shall Not Be Moved,* respectively, and the reclusive author Thomas Pynchon released *Vineland,* his first novel since his surreal masterpiece of 1973, *Gravity's Rainbow.* Other works of fiction by major figures included *Natural Selection* by Frederick Barthelme, who, as did Updike, wrote about dissatisfied middle-class men struggling to find meaning and value in their life and relationships, and Joyce Carol Oates's *Because It Is Bitter, and Because It Is My Heart,* which mixes love, racial discord, and violence in a story about a murder in an industrial town in 1956. John Edgar Wideman won the PEN/Faulkner Award for Fiction for his novel *Philadelphia Fire,* based on the 1985 police firebombing of a housing complex, part of which was occupied by members of the radical group MOVE.

In their statistically informed *Megatrends 2000: Ten New Directions for the 1990's* John Naisbitt and Patricia Aburdene identified dominant socioeconomic developments they anticipated for the decade, including a growing global economy, replacement of government welfare services with private enterprise programs, and the emergence of a strong Pacific Rim market centered in Tokyo, Seoul, Shanghai, Taipei, Hong Kong, and Singapore. They also argued that throughout the world women would achieve parity with men within their professions; that the approaching millennium would stimulate a strong resurgence in the arts, ethnic cultures, and religion; and that major breakthroughs in genetics and biochemistry would yield both exciting new possibilities and frightening dangers. Financial scandal was the topic of much of the year's nonfiction, including Brian Burrough and John Helyar's *Barbarians at the Gate: The Fall of R.J.R. Nabisco.* Edward O. Wilson and Bert Hölldobler won the Pulitzer Prize in nonfiction for their study of insect behavior, *The Ants.*

August Wilson won the 1990 Pulitzer Prize in drama for *The Piano Lesson,* about a 20th-century black family who inherit the piano owned by the white plantation family who had once also owned their forebears. Frank Galati won the Tony Award for his dramatic adaptation of *The Grapes of Wrath* (1939), John Steinbeck's best-selling novel about migrant farm workers during the Great

Depression, and Cy Coleman, David Zippel, and Larry Gelbart won the Tony Award for their musical *City of Angels.* John Guare's *Six Degrees of Separation* tells about a high-society gathering that is transformed when a young black man, who claims to be the son of the actor Sidney Poitier, appears. Audiences were also receptive to William Nicholson's affirmation of religious faith in the face of personal difficulties in *Shadowlands,* which describes the meeting of the Irish writer and scholar C. S. Lewis and American poet Joy Gresham and their efforts to reconcile religious faith with the challenges of life and relationships. The Canadian playwright Craig Lucas's *Prelude to a Kiss* is a gentle comedy about a young, frightened bride who inadvertently swaps souls with an elderly man who wants to reclaim his youth as he gives her a good luck kiss at her wedding. Norman René directed the 1992 film adaptation, which starred Meg Ryan and Alec Baldwin.

Kevin Costner's Academy Award–winning *Dances with Wolves* appealed to liberal sentiments in its celebrations of Sioux Indians on the American frontier in the 19th century. The film contrasts the Native Americans' spirituality and their practice of living in harmony with nature with the warlike aspirations of the U.S. Army, which is driving them from their home. Penny Marshall's *Awakenings* also pits the underdog against a more powerful force in its factually based depiction of a doctor who fights the medical establishment in order to use an experimental drug for a group of catatonic patients. Marshall's brother, Garry Marshall, directed Richard Gere and Julia Roberts in *Pretty Woman,* the successful story of a would-be prostitute who falls in love with a prosperous businessman.

Crime and intrigue feature prominently in the popular and critically acclaimed films of 1990, in treatments that range from serious to absurd. Warren Beatty directed himself, Al Pacino, and Madonna in *Dick Tracy,* a campy, entertaining musical comedy, which showcases Madonna's singing as well as her acting in the role of a gangster's moll. The first major feature film to employ a digital soundtrack, *Dick Tracy* is based on a 1940s comic strip about an ultrastraight, dedicated crime fighter. The criminal underworld is treated more seriously and depicted more violently in Martin Scorsese's *Goodfellas* and Francis Ford Coppola's *The Godfather Part III,* which concludes the saga of the Corleone family, which began with *The Godfather* in 1972. Jeremy Irons won the Academy Award as best actor for his role as Claus von Bulow in *Reversal of Fortune.* Based on a highly publicized real-life court case in which von Bulow successfully appealed his conviction for the attempted murder of his wife, *Reversal of Fortune* deals with the moral and legal considerations inherent in the case of a wealthy couple whose marriage has gone awry. Kathy Bates won the Academy Award for best actress for her role as a deranged fan of pulp fiction in Rob Reiner's *Misery,*

Madonna, who starred as a gangster's moll in *Dick Tracy,* proved to be a forceful and savvy businesswoman, as well as a versatile and controversial performer. *(Photofest)*

an adaptation of a Stephen King horror story. Arnold Schwarzenegger starred in Paul Verhoeven's futuristic action/adventure film *Total Recall,* which was adapted from "We Can Remember It for You Wholesale" (1966), a short story by the celebrated science fiction writer Philip K. Dick. Chris Columbus's *Home Alone* starred Macauley Culkin as a young boy who uses his wits to fight off home invaders when his family travels to Europe on vacation and accidentally leaves him behind. Steve Barron's *Teenage Mutant Ninja Turtles* also appealed to young audiences in its depiction of unlikely animated superheroes who rescue a damsel in distress.

Notable foreign films included Giuseppe Tornatore's *Cinema Paradiso,* a heartwarming story about a boy who befriends a movie projectionist in a small town in Italy; the Spanish director Pedro Almodóvar's *Tie Me Up, Tie Me Down,* about the romance of a soft-core porn star and a recently released psychiatric patient; and the Italian director Franco Zeffirelli's excellent adaptation of William Shakespeare's *Hamlet,* starring Mel Gibson, Glenn Close, and Helena Bonham Carter. Gibson's performance as the emotionally unstable prince of Denmark draws effectively on the actor's previous roles as a similar type of bipolar personality in his popular *Lethal Weapon* movies.

Responding to complaints about the sex and violence younger viewers routinely witness in movies, the Hollywood motion picture industry introduced a new NC-17 rating banning viewers younger than 17 from attending. Because some chains promised not to screen films with the NC-17 rating, Hollywood studios sought to tailor their movies' content to avoid the designation. Consequently, no major studio produced a big-budget NC-17-rated film until 1995, when Metro Goldwyn Mayer/United Artists released *Showgirls,* about Las Vegas strippers.

Many of the top television shows broke away from stereotypes by featuring intelligent and accomplished women and minorities and/or working-class parents. The most watched television show of the 1990–91 season was *Cheers,* a sitcom set in a working-class Boston bar "where everyone knows your name." *Cheers* also won the 1991 Emmy Award for the season. It was followed in the ratings by *60 Minutes,* a long-running newsmagazine; *Roseanne,* a hard-edged sitcom about a working-class family struggling to make ends meet; *The Cosby Show,* a sitcom about a professional-class black family starring Bill Cosby and Phylicia Rashad; and *A Different World,* a spinoff of *The Cosby Show* centered on the family's teenage daughter who goes away to college. Also popular was *Murphy Brown,* a sitcom that starred Candice Bergen as an extremely successful hard-edged, opinionated liberal television news reporter and recovering alcoholic. *Murphy Brown* won the 1990 Emmy Award as outstanding comedy of the 1989–90 season. *L.A. Law,* a drama about a high-power Los Angeles law firm, which began in 1986, won the award as outstanding dramatic series for both 1989–90 and 1990–91. Angela Lansbury starred as a crafty and insightful mystery writer who solves real crimes in the popular series *Murder, She Wrote.* The independent film director David Lynch introduced a surreal and absurdist sensibility, never before seen on prime time television, in his offbeat murder mystery series *Twin Peaks,* while Matt Groening took television animation to a new level with rich writing and cleverly developed characters in *The Simpsons,* an insightful satire of American families, schools, and institutions that debuted in mid-December 1989. The Cable Satellite Public Affairs Network (C-SPAN)

The Simpsons used a cartoon format for presenting sophisticated social satire on network television. *(Photofest)*

enjoyed unusually large audiences when it broadcast complete coverage of congressional deliberations and military briefings about the situation in Kuwait.

Not initially a success, *Seinfeld* debuted on May 31 and went on to become a long-running, top-rated sitcom that dominated 1990s television comedy. Starring Jerry Seinfeld, Julia Louis-Dreyfus, Jason Alexander, and Michael Richards as unmarried, self-absorbed 30-something New Yorkers caught up in the minutiae of dating, working, and dealing with their outspoken Jewish, White Anglo-Saxon Protestant (WASP), and ethnic parents, the show "about nothing" became what many still consider the best television comedy ever aired.

In addition to its imaginative writing and talented cast, *Seinfeld* regularly features a broad range of economic, ethnic, religious, and racial groups. By showing the main characters interacting on an equal or even a less than equal footing with, for instance, high-powered African-American and Chinese-American attorneys, menacing homosexuals, ingratiating Pakistanis, intimidating Middle Eastern chefs, and gossiping Jewish rabbis, the immensely popular show repudiates cultural stereotypes, and broadcasts a truly multicultural view of urban America rarely shown on network television comedies. In addition, *Seinfeld* reinforced the movement toward greater gender equality in American society in the 1990s. By routinely presenting women who are intelligent, articulate, decisive, ambitious, assertive, empowered, and sexually active, the show communicates that such women are desirable and worthy of emulation. On *Seinfeld* women and minorities do not restrict their personal aspirations to traditional roles, and they are accepted for their lifestyle choices, even when those choices are eccentric or absurd and become the object of the humor. Indeed, their idiosyncrasies compel viewers to relate to them as distinct individuals instead of members of an ethnic group or gender. These characters typically have strong opinions about what they want, and many occupy positions of authority. At the same time, although the show thus shatters demeaning stereotypes, it also shuns the clichés promulgated by those proponents of political correctness who present women and minorities as always virtuous and often victimized.

Sports remained one of the nation's favorite pastimes. Led by quarterback Joe Montana and receiver Jerry Rice, the San Francisco 49ers concluded the 1989 season by defeating the Denver Broncos 55-10 in the National Football League (NFL) Super Bowl XXIV. The record-setting rout made the 49ers, along with the Pittsburgh Steelers, the only teams to win four Super Bowl championships. Philadelphia's quarterback, Randall Cunningham, was the most valuable player (MVP) of the 1990 season. The University of Colorado and Georgia Tech split the national college championship, and Brigham Young's Ty Detmer won the Heisman Trophy. The NFL changed policies to allow college juniors to enter its annual draft and added two teams to its playoff format, to include three division winners and three wild card teams in each conference.

The Cincinnati Reds defeated the Oakland As in four games to win Major League Baseball's World Series. Barry Bonds of the Pittsburgh Pirates was the National League's MVP; Oakland's Rickey Henderson was the American League's. Pittsburgh's Doug Drabek and Oakland's Bob Welch won their leagues' Cy Young Awards for best pitcher, and Nolan Ryan of the Texas Rangers pitched a record sixth no-hitter. The Detroit Tiger Cecil Fielder led the Major Leagues with 51 home runs. Cincinnati's retired second baseman Joe Morgan and Baltimore Oriole retired pitcher Jim Palmer became the 20th and 21st players to be elected to the Hall of Fame in their first year of eligibility. Less gloriously, Pete Rose, a Hall of Fame–caliber player who had starred with Morgan on the Reds during the 1970s but who was banished from major league baseball in 1989 for gambling, received a five-month prison sentence for income tax evasion.

The Detroit Pistons defeated the Portland Trail Blazers to win the National Basketball Association (NBA) championship. However, victory celebrations in Detroit degenerated into deadly riots that killed eight people. Magic Johnson of the Los Angeles Lakers was the league's MVP. The University of Nevada at Las Vegas won the college championship, and La Salle's Lionel Simmons was voted College Player of the Year. Canada's Edmonton Oilers won hockey's Stanley Cup, and Hale Irwin won golf's U.S. Open. Nineteen-year-old Pete Sampras became the youngest man to win the U.S. Tennis Open when he defeated his rival Andre Agassi, while Gabriela Sabatini won the women's competition. Ridden by Craig Perret, Unbridled won the Kentucky Derby. James "Buster" Douglas knocked out champion Mike Tyson in 10 rounds to claim the world heavyweight boxing title.

CHRONICLE OF EVENTS

January 1: For the first time in 30 years, Cuba joins the UN Security Council.

January 1: The Panama Canal passes to Panamanian control, fulfilling the terms of the 1977 Panama Canal Treaty.

January 2: Damage to an underwater pipeline emanating from Exxon's Bayway Refinery in New Jersey releases between 200,000 and 500,000 gallons of oil into New York Harbor.

January 2: The rock musician Paul McCartney, a former member of the popular 1960s band the Beatles, makes his first stage appearance in 13 years.

January 3: The newly formed federal Resolution Trust Company is directed to sell off real estate holdings it has acquired from insolvent savings and loan institutions as quickly as possible.

January 3: The former Panamanian president Manuel Noriega, who was ousted by U.S. forces on December 20, 1989, surrenders to U.S. authorities after taking refuge in the Vatican embassy in Panama City.

January 4: Noriega is imprisoned in Miami after being formally charged for drug trafficking in a U.S. federal court.

January 5: Susan Eisenhower, granddaughter of the cold war–era president Dwight Eisenhower, announces her engagement to Roald Z. Sagdeyev, the former head of the Soviet space program. The couple receives congratulations from both Bush and Gorbachev.

January 6: The Iraqi army displays its enhanced surface-to-surface missiles, which can strike targets within a 600-mile range.

January 9: A federally funded assessment of progress in U.S. education reports that students' reading and writing skills made no significant gain during the 1980s, despite some advances by minority students.

January 10: China lifts martial law, which had prevailed in Beijing since the Tiananmen Square protests of May 1989.

January 12: Bush calls for a reduction in the capital gains tax rate, as well as tougher antidrug and anticrime legislation.

January 12: The space shuttle *Columbia* demonstrates its versatility by capturing a malfunctioning satellite for repair.

January 18: After the successful invasion of Panama, polls show that Bush has a 79 percent approval rating, the highest of any president since World War II.

January 18: Gorbachev orders 11,000 troops to the Soviet republic of Azerbaijan to suppress ethnic fighting between Azeris and Armenians and to halt separatist insurrection.

January 19: Marion Barry, mayor of Washington, D.C., is arrested for drug use after being videotaped smoking crack cocaine.

January 19: After public charges of cynical racism by Health and Human Services secretary Louis W. Sullivan, the R. J. Reynolds Tobacco Company cancels plans to test market Uptown, a new cigarette brand that was to be directed at black smokers.

January 23: The Soviet Union agrees to remove its troops from Hungary.

January 25: The actress Ava Gardner dies at age 68.

January 25: Pakistan's premier Benazir Bhutto becomes the first world leader in modern times to give birth while in office.

January 28: The San Francisco 49ers defeat the Denver Broncos 55-10 to win football's Super Bowl XXIV.

January 31: In his State of the Union address, Bush calls for U.S. and Soviet troop reductions in Europe.

February 2: South Africa lifts the ban on the African National Congress (ANC).

February 7: Congress approves a $42 million request for emergency aid to Panama.

February 7: The Communist Party in the Soviet Union agrees to relinquish the monopoly on power that it has held since 1917.

February 11: South Africa frees political prisoner Nelson Mandela, the leader of the ANC who has been imprisoned for some 27 years.

February 11: James "Buster" Douglas claims the world heavyweight boxing title after knocking out Mike Tyson, the reigning champion, in 10 rounds.

February 14: The Perrier company withdraws its entire stock of 160 million bottles of carbonated water from the world market after discovering traces of benzene in the product.

February 24: The first multiparty elections since 1917 take place within the Soviet Union when Lithuanians vote for a new parliament.

February 26: The Soviet Union agrees to remove its troops from Czechoslovakia.

February 26: The Nicaraguan opposition leader Violeta Chamorro defeats President Daniel Ortega in the first free elections in that country since 1979. Ortega agrees to accept the outcome of the election.

March 6: The Soviet parliament permits ownership of private property.

March 10: Haiti's president Prosper Avril is removed from office 18 months after seizing power in a coup.

March 11: Patricio Aylwin is sworn in as president of Chile, becoming that country's first democratically elected president since the overthrow of Salvador Allende in 1973.

March 11: Lithuania declares its independence from the Soviet Union.

March 15: Iraq hangs the British journalist Farzad Bazoft for alleged spying.

March 15: Gorbachev is elected first executive president of the Soviet Union.

March 20: Imelda Marcos, wife of the former Philippine president Ferdinand Marcos, goes on trial in the United States on charges of racketeering, embezzlement, and bribery.

March 21: Namibia, the last European colony in Africa, becomes an independent nation after 105 years of colonial rule.

March 22: Dr. Gerald Bull is assassinated. Bull had been designing a "supergun"—a long-range artillery weapon with nuclear capacities—for Iraq. Israeli agents are suspected to be responsible for Bull's murder.

March 25: Estonia votes for independence from the Soviet Union.

March 25: A fire in an overcrowded unlicensed discotheque in the Bronx, New York, kills 87 people, many of them illegal immigrants from Honduras and the Dominican Republic.

March 28: Britain announces that its customs officials have foiled a plan to smuggle to Iraq American-made capacitors capable of triggering a nuclear device.

March 30–April 2: A poll conducted by the *New York Times* and CBS News shows that Bush enjoys a 56 percent approval rating among black Americans, the highest of any Republican president since Dwight Eisenhower.

April 3: The jazz vocalist Sarah Vaughan dies at age 66.

April 4: Belgium's king Baudouin steps down for 24 hours to allow passage of a bill legalizing abortion.

April 5: The entrepreneur Donald Trump opens the Trump Taj Mahal, a lavish gambling casino in Atlantic City, New Jersey.

April 7: The former national security advisor Admiral John Poindexter is convicted for his role in the Iran-contra affair. The conviction is later overturned on a technicality, and Poindexter later serves in the administration of President George W. Bush.

April 10: As part of $211 million program to fight tobacco use, California initiates a $28.6 million anti-smoking campaign.

April 11: British police seize parts for a British-made supergun about to be shipped to Iraq.

April 13: The Soviet Union admits that its troops massacred some 15,000 Polish officers at the end of World War II.

April 15: The Swedish-born actress Greta Garbo dies at the age of 84.

April 22: Robert Polhill, who had been held hostage in Lebanon since the mid-1980s, is released by the pro-Iranian group, the Islamic Jihad.

April 22: Americans throughout the country celebrate the 20th anniversary of Earth Day.

April 25: The space shuttle *Discovery* launches the *Hubble Space Telescope* into orbit around the Earth, where it can view outer space without distortion from the Earth's atmosphere.

April 28: A massive antiabortion rally endorsed by Bush and Quayle attracts some 200,000 protesters in Washington, D.C.

April 30: The Islamic Jihad frees Frank Reed, a U.S. college administrator who has been held hostage in Lebanon since the mid-1980s.

May 1: Gorbachev is jeered by crowds in Moscow during the traditional May Day celebration.

May 3: The Iraqi foreign minister Tariq Aziz criticizes unnamed OPEC members who have exceeded their oil production quotas.

May 14: Some 250,000 people march through Paris in protest against recent outbreaks of anti-Semitism in France.

May 16: Thirty-four nations, including the United States, sign an agreement pledging to reduce chemical emissions harmful to the ozone layer.

May 16: The entertainer Sammy Davis, Jr., dies at age 64.

May 18: Germany takes a critical step toward reunification when East and West Germany agree to adopt a single currency, the West German deutschmark.

May 22: After decades of conflict, Marxist South Yemen merges with pro-Western North Yemen to form a new state, the Republic of Yemen.

May 24: Japan officially apologizes to Korea for abuses Japanese occupiers committed between 1910 and 1945.

May 28: Saddam Hussein hosts an emergency summit meeting of the Arab League in which he justifies his military buildup, denounces Israel and the United States, asserts himself as leader and protector of the Arab community, and threatens Kuwait for driving down the price of oil and stealing oil from Iraq's Rumalia field at the Kuwaiti border. This is Saddam Hussein's first public denunciation of Kuwait.

Seinfeld, starring Jerry Seinfeld (center), Julia Louis-Dreyfus (left), Michael Richards (above), and Jason Alexander (right), was widely regarded as one of the best situation comedies of all time. *(Photofest)*

May 29: The parliament of the republic of Russia elects Boris Yeltsin as president, selecting him over a rival candidate backed by Gorbachev.

May 29: Rickey Henderson, an outfielder for the Oakland As, sets a new record when he steals his 893rd base against the Toronto Blue Jays.

May 31: Seinfeld debuts on NBC.

June 1–3: Bush and Gorbachev hold a summit meeting in Washington, D.C., in which the United States and the Soviet Union agree to cut their nuclear stockpiles but fail to reach an accord on the Soviets' desire to modernize their SS-18 missiles, which are the central weapons in their nuclear arsenal.

June 1: U.S. Navy ships arrive off Monrovia to help evacuate U.S. citizens in Liberia as rebel troops advance toward the capital.

June 10: The dissident writer Václav Havel's Civic Forum Party wins the first free elections held in Czechoslovakia in 40 years.

June 10: Alberto Fujimori is elected president of Peru.

June 12: The Russian Federation, the largest republic in the Soviet Union, declares its state sovereignty.

June 14: Riots break out in Detroit after the Detroit Pistons win the NBA basketball championship. Eight people are killed and dozens of others are wounded as crowds overturn cars, smash windows, and loot stores in celebration.

June 20: The recently freed South African political prisoner Nelson Mandela receives a ticker tape welcome on his first visit to New York City.

June 22: Canadian voters reject the 1987 Meech Lake Accord, which would have granted French-speaking Quebec province special status within the Canadian union.

June 22: East Germany dismantles Checkpoint Charlie, which had been erected in 1961 as a cold war crossing point through the Berlin Wall.

June 23: A scientific study shows that the world's ozone layer is being destroyed faster than previously estimated.

June 26: Contradicting his 1988 campaign pledge not to raise taxes, Bush responds to pressures from a sluggish economy by increasing taxes to trim the budget deficit.

June 27: The National Aeronautics and Space Administration (NASA) announces that the $1.5 billion *Hubble Space Telescope* has serious defects.

June 29: Representatives from 93 nations agree to banish ozone-depleting CFCs by the end of the century.

July 1: East Germany adopts West Germany's monetary, economic, and social laws.

July 2: Some 1,400 Muslim pilgrims are crushed to death and suffocated when an air-conditioning failure in a tunnel connecting the Great Mosque to the holy site of Mount Arafat near Mecca, Saudi Arabia, produces panic inside the tunnel, which is filled to more than five times its capacity.

July 7: Martina Navratilova sets a new record when she wins her ninth tennis championship at Wimbledon, England.

July 10: Neil Bush, son of President George H. W. Bush, is implicated in the collapse of the Denver-based Silverado Banking, Savings and Loan Association.

July 13: Yeltsin resigns from the Communist Party.

July 16: In an open letter to the Arab League, Saddam Hussein accuses Kuwait of stealing $2.4 billion of oil by drilling into the Rumalia oil field. He further accuses Kuwait of military aggression because the Kuwaitis have advanced their border and customs posts northward. Kuwait accuses Iraq of trying to intimidate it and other countries to cancel Iraq's war debts.

July 16: Nine hundred people die in the Philippines when an earthquake measuring 7.7 on the Richter scale, the strongest in 14 years, strikes near Baguio, a popular mountain resort.

July 19: The $21 million Richard Nixon Library opens in Yorba Linda, California. President Bush and the former presidents Gerald Ford and Ronald Reagan join Nixon at the ceremonies.

July 19: The baseball star Pete Rose is sentenced to five months in jail for federal tax evasion. Rose is also fined $50,000 and ordered to perform 1,000 hours of community service, stay in a halfway house or community treatment facility for three months after fulfilling his prison term, and receive psychiatric treatment for his gambling addiction.

July 20: Justice William Brennan resigns after nearly 34 years on the Supreme Court.

July 20: The Iran-contra conviction of Oliver North is overturned because the prosecution failed to demonstrate that witnesses' testimony was not influenced by North's congressional testimony, which was protected by immunity from prosecution.

July 21: The U.S. Central Command learns that about 3,000 military vehicles are moving from Baghdad toward Kuwait and that an Iraqi armored division has deployed to an area just across the border. By the next day Iraq has massed some 30,000 troops at the Kuwaiti border, and Kuwait reinstates its state of military alert.

July 25: The U.S. ambassador, April Glaspie, meets to discuss the situation in Kuwait with Saddam Hussein and, according to a secretly made transcript released by Iraq, indicates that the United States will not intervene in a war between the two countries.

July 26: Approximately 120,000 Iraqi troops are now positioned to attack Kuwait.

July 27: The World Health Organization reports that AIDS is "a major cause of death" of women between the ages of 20 and 40 in the Americas, Western Europe, and sub-Saharan Africa.

July 31: U.S. Central Command informs the Joint Chiefs of Staff that Iraq appears ready to invade Kuwait.

July 31–August 1: Saudi Arabia's king Fahd hosts a meeting in Jeddah of high-level Iraqi and Kuwaiti officials. After making intractable demands that the Kuwaitis do not accept, the Iraqis walk out of the meeting in protest.

August 1 (August 2, local time): Armored divisions of Iraq's Republican Guard overrun a Kuwaiti brigade stationed at the border around 2:00 A.M. local time. The armored divisions then proceed to the capital, Kuwait City, about 50 miles to the south. At the same time Republican Guard special forces attack Kuwait City by helicopter, and sea commandos seize the southern coastal road leading to the capital. By 5:30 A.M. the armored divisions arrive and the battle for the city begins. By 2:20 P.M. the battle concludes and Iraq controls the capital. Iraqi troops then continue on to the Saudi border, where they establish defensive positions.

August 2: Bush meets in Aspen, Colorado, with Prime Minister Thatcher of Britain, who encourages him to take a hard line against Saddam Hussein.

August 2: The Security Council passes Resolution 660 condemning the invasion and demanding Iraq's withdrawal from Kuwait by a vote of 14-0-1, with Yemen abstaining.

August 3: Oil prices jump to $26 per barrel on the world oil market.

August 3: Despite promising to withdraw, Iraq sends reinforcements into Kuwait and masses troops close to the Saudi Arabia border, prompting fears that it plans to invade Saudi Arabia.

August 3: Meeting in Cairo, Egypt, the Arab League condemns the invasion.

August 4: The European Community freezes Iraqi and Kuwaiti assets.

August 5: Bush publicly denounces Iraq and declares his determination not to allow the Iraqi conquest of Kuwait to stand.

August 5: U.S. warships begin to deploy in the Persian Gulf and Red Sea to defend Saudi Arabia.

August 6: With Cuba and Yemen abstaining, the Security Council passes Resolution 661 imposing a worldwide embargo on Iraq.

August 6: Operation Desert Shield begins after Cheney and Schwarzkopf meet with King Fahd in Saudi Arabia, where they agree that the United States will send troops and other military assistance to help defend against a possible Iraqi attack.

August 6: Saudi Arabia agrees to increase its oil production by 2 million barrels a day to help compensate for the 4.1 million barrels lost to the world market when Iraq stopped exporting its own oil and Kuwait's.

August 6: British, American, and German nationals are taken from Kuwait to Baghdad. These become the first of Iraq's hostages.

August 7: The new government in Kuwait installed by Iraq declares the Republic of Kuwait; however, no outside country recognizes it.

August 8: Pakistan's president Gulam Ishaq Khan fires Prime Minister Benazir Bhutto and dissolves her government.

August 8: In a televised address Bush announces that he is ordering U.S. troops to Saudi Arabia. Elements of the 82nd and 101st Airborne Divisions depart for Saudi Arabia within hours and arrive the next day.

August 8: Britain pledges to contribute to a multinational force to defend Saudi Arabia and immediately to reinforce its naval fleet in the Persian Gulf.

August 8: Iraq announces that it has annexed Kuwait.

August 9: The Security Council unanimously passes Resolution 662 rejecting Iraq's annexation of Kuwait.

August 9: Turkey consents to allow U.S. planes to use its air bases and expand its military presence in Turkey.

August 9: Saddam Hussein sends a message to Bush declaring that Iraq has no plans to invade Saudi Arabia.

August 9: Mexico and Venezuela announce they will increase their oil production to help compensate for oil controlled by Iraq.

August 9: Iraq closes its borders and bars foreign nationals from leaving either Iraq or Kuwait. It further demands that all foreign embassies in Kuwait close by August 24 and their diplomatic staff be transferred to Baghdad.

August 10: The *Magellan* space probe is launched to explore Venus.

August 10: As the Royal Saudi Air Force, U.S. Air Force, and U.S. Navy begin Exercise Arabian Gulf to coordinate air operations over the Persian Gulf, Saddam Hussein calls for a jihad, or holy war, to liberate Mecca and Medina, Islam's holiest cities, which are located in Saudi Arabia.

August 12: Saddam Hussein tries to link the Iraqi occupation of Kuwait to Israel's occupation of Palestinian-inhabited territories conquered in 1967 and Syria's occupation of Lebanon by offering to begin negotiations to resolve "all issues of occupation" in the Middle East. The United States emphatically refuses to accept this linkage as a precondition for Iraqi withdrawal from Kuwait.

August 12: The first American fatality of Operation Desert Shield occurs when an air force sergeant is struck by a military truck in Saudi Arabia.

August 12: Anti-Western demonstrations in Jordan, Yemen, southern Lebanon, and Somalia support Saddam Hussein.

August 12: President Rafsanjani of Iran condemns the presence of U.S. and other foreign troops in the Persian Gulf.

August 13: Jordan's King Hussein condemns the presence of Western troops in Arab lands and claims that the West is more interested in preserving its access to oil than in helping the region.

August 13: France declares that British and U.S. naval policy amounts to a blockade that exceeds the measures authorized by the Security Council and refuses to participate.

August 15: To secure Iraq's eastern border and transfer some 300,000 additional troops from there to the Kuwaiti and Saudi borders safely, Saddam Hussein offers major concessions to Iran for a treaty to end the Iran-Iraq Gulf War, which has been in a state of cease-fire since 1988.

August 15: Iraq requires all Westerners in Kuwait, including 4,000 British and 2,500 U.S. citizens, to report to three hotels.

August 15: Syria announces the deployment of troops to Saudi Arabia.

August 15: Palestinians hold a general strike in the Israeli-occupied territories to protest the U.S. military presence in Saudi Arabia.

August 18: The Security Council passes Resolution 664 demanding the release of foreign nationals being held as human shields in Iraq and calling for the return of thousands of Kuwaiti citizens who have been forcibly removed to Iraq.

August 20: George Steinbrenner, principal owner of the New York Yankees, relinquishes management control over the team as a penalty for his association with the gambler Howard Spira.

August 21: Saddam Hussein warns the Western allies that if they attack Iraq, the "mother of all battles" will ensue.

August 23: The Republic of Armenia declares its independence from the Soviet Union.

August 25: The Security Council passes Resolution 665 calling on member nations to enforce sanctions against Iraq and authorizing the use of force to maintain the embargo.

August 25: After talks with Saddam Hussein, Austria's president Kurt Waldheim secures the release of 96 Austrian hostages. Austria subsequently declines to join the coalition against Iraq.

August 26–28: Five students—four women and one man—are found murdered in their respective apartments in Gainesville, Florida. Three of the women are found nude and one is decapitated, with her head placed on a shelf.

August 29: Iraq announces that all female and child hostages will be released.

August 30: Iraq announces that it will launch attacks against Israel and Saudi Arabia if war breaks out.

August 30: The U.S. politician Jesse Jackson meets in Baghdad with Aziz.

August 30: Police arrest 18-year-old Edward Lewis Humphrey for the murder earlier in the week of the five students in Gainesville, Florida.

August 31: The United States agrees to advance Israel $1 billion in military equipment.

September 4: For the first time since 1950, North Korea's prime minister travels to South Korea to participate in talks there.

September 5: The USS *Acadia* departs San Diego for the Persian Gulf with 360 women among its crew of 1,260. This is the first time a combined crew of American men and women have served together in wartime conditions.

September 9: The former immigration processing center at Ellis Island, New York, which served as a gateway to the United States for millions of immigrants, is dedicated as a museum after a $156 million renovation.

September 9: Nineteen-year-old Pete Sampras defeats his rival Andre Agassi to become the youngest winner of the U.S. Tennis Open.

September 9: Bush and Gorbachev issue a joint declaration condemning Iraq and threatening repercussions if it does not withdraw from Kuwait.

September 10: Iran officially restores diplomatic relations with Iraq, and Saddam Hussein offers free oil to any nation that ships goods to Iraq, in violation of the UN embargo.

At age 19, Pete Sampras defeated Andre Agassi (left) to become the youngest man ever to win the U.S. Tennis Open. *(AP/Wide World Photos)*

September 12: World War II officially concludes as East and West Germany, Great Britain, France, the United States, and the Soviet Union sign the Treaty on the Final Settlement with Respect to Germany. The treaty also arranges for the complete withdrawal of Soviet troops from Eastern Europe.

September 13: The Security Council passes Resolution 666 reaffirming that Iraq is responsible for the well-being of foreign hostages and establishing guidelines for mercy shipments of medical supplies to Iraq. Cuba and Yemen oppose the resolution.

September 13: The U.S. House of Representatives passes legislation requiring the allies to assume more of the costs of Operation Desert Shield.

September 13: The Muslim League passes the so-called Mecca Declaration, which approves Saudi Arabia's request for U.S. assistance and condemns Iraq's violation of the Tenets of the Faith of Islam by invading Kuwait.

September 14: Iraqi soldiers break into the remaining Western embassies in Kuwait and take several diplomats hostage.

September 15: After the raid on its embassy in Kuwait, France announces that it will send 4,000 troops to Saudi Arabia in addition to the French light armor and helicopters already deployed. Eventually France commits some 14,000 troops, 40 fighter planes, and 14 ships.

September 15: West Germany agrees to contribute $2 billion in military and financial aid.

September 16: The Security Council unanimously passes Resolution 667 condemning Iraqi actions against diplomats and demanding the immediate release of hostages.

September 17: President Corazon Aquino states that she wants the United States to remove its bases in the Philippines.

September 18: Argentina becomes the first Latin American country to join the coalition against Iraq when it commits naval and air force units.

September 24: The Soviet parliament gives Gorbachev near-dictatorial powers to handle every aspect of reform.

September 24: For the first time since 1980, world oil prices reach $40 per barrel.

September 24: The Security Council unanimously passes Resolution 669 to examine requests for humanitarian shipments to Iraq and Kuwait.

September 24: President Mitterrand of France presents a four-stage plan to the United Nations calling for free elections in Kuwait, the restoration of Kuwait's sovereignty, and an international conference on all major issues in the Middle East.

September 25: The Security Council passes Resolution 670, which establishes an air blockade of Iraq and calls for Iraqi ships to be detained.

September 26: The Soviet parliament votes to give its citizens full religious freedom, reversing 70 years of religious suppression.

September 28: The first British ground troops embark for Saudi Arabia. Eventually 9,000 soldiers and 120 tanks will join the coalition force.

September 30: The Soviet Union announces that it will resume diplomatic relations with Israel, which have been severed since 1967.

September 30: The Soviet Union announces that it will support the coalition against Iraq, but that its troops will serve only under UN auspices and not under the United States or NATO command.

September 30: Two Air Force crewmen are killed when their jet crashes on a training mission in Oman, becoming the first Americans to die on military maneuvers during Desert Shield.

September 30: As of this date the U.S. Transportation Command has airlifted 115,826 tons of cargo and 127,739 military and other support personnel in 3,541 flights to the Persian Gulf region. Iraq has stationed 22 army divisions in the Kuwait theater.

October 1: The U.S. House of Representatives votes 380–29 to support Bush's actions in the Middle East but underscores its desire for a diplomatic resolution.

October 1: Addressing the UN General Assembly, Bush maintains that the United States is still seeking a diplomatic solution.

October 1: Operation Camel Sand, the first amphibious rehearsal in Desert Shield, is held in Oman.

October 2: The U.S. Senate votes 96–3 to endorse Bush's efforts.

October 2: Saudi Arabia dismisses a French peace initiative linking the Palestinian issue to the occupation of Kuwait.

October 2: A report by Amnesty International accuses Iraqis of widespread killings and human rights violations in Kuwait.

October 2: The U.S. Senate votes overwhelmingly to confirm David Souter as Supreme Court justice.

October 3: Germany is officially reunited into a single nation.

October 3: The U.S. Senate overwhelmingly supports the deployment of troops to the Gulf region.

October 7: Israeli authorities begin distributing gas masks to civilians.

October 9: David Souter is sworn in as Supreme Court justice.

October 9: Iraq announces that it will attack Saudi Arabia and Israel with long-range missiles if a war begins.

October 11: Schwarzkopf briefs Bush on initial plans for Operation Desert Storm, the offensive to drive Iraq from Kuwait.

October 14: The composer/conductor Leonard Bernstein dies at age 72.

October 15: Gorbachev wins the Nobel Prize in peace.

October 15: Bush signs legislation to compensate victims of radiation exposure caused by open-air nuclear tests conducted during the 1950s.

October 16: The jazz performer Art Blakey dies at age 71.

October 20: The Cincinnati Reds conclude a four-game sweep over the favored Oakland As to win baseball's World Series.

October 20: The first large protests against the American military involvement in the Middle East take place within the United States, notably in New York, Boston, San Francisco, and Los Angeles. Other protests occur in Paris.

October 21: Powell flies to Saudi Arabia to discuss plans for a ground offensive with Schwarzkopf. To reduce the likelihood of heavy casualties, they agree to more than double the U.S. military force in the region.

October 24: Labor Secretary Elizabeth Dole, the highest-ranking woman in the Bush administration, resigns after 22 months in office to assume the presidency of the American Red Cross.

October 26: A senior engineer for the Kuwait Oil Company claims that Iraq has placed explosives on 300 Kuwaiti oil wells so it can destroy them if necessary.

October 27: Congress passes the Clean Air Act of 1990.

October 29: The Security Council passes Resolution 674 demanding that Iraq cease its mistreatment of Kuwaiti citizens and foreign nationals and reminding Iraq that it is liable for damages.

November 1: The Italian businessman Giancarlo Parretti purchases the Hollywood film production company Metro Goldwyn Mayer for $1.3 billion.

November 5: In Manhattan, a gunman of Egyptian descent assassinates Rabbi Meir Kahane, founder of the Jewish Defense League and an anti-Arab militant.

November 6: Democrats gain eight seats in the House of Representatives and one in the Senate in the midterm congressional elections, giving them strong majorities in both legislative chambers.

November 7: After the former West German chancellor Willy Brandt meets in Baghdad with Saddam Hussein, Aziz, and the Palestine Liberation Organization (PLO) chairman, Yasser Arafat, Iraq releases 120 hostages, most of them Germans.

November 8: Bush orders an additional 150,000 air, sea, and ground troops to the Persian Gulf, enabling Schwarzkopf and his staff to prepare for Desert Storm, the United States–led coalition's air and ground offensive war.

November 9: Mary Robinson is elected the first female president of Ireland.

November 13: Saudi Arabia bans women from driving automobiles.

November 14: Cheney authorizes the call-up of 80,000 army reserves and 15,000 Marine Corps reserves.

November 17–19: Leaders of all the European states, the United States, Canada, and the Soviet Union meet in Paris to sign a new charter regulating relations among all the participants, a nonaggression agreement between NATO and the Warsaw Pact, and the Treaty on Conventional Forces in Europe (CFE), which reduces arsenals in Europe.

November 19: The National Academy of Recording Arts and Sciences rescinds the Grammy Award to Milli Vanilli as Best New Artist. It is the first time in the 33-year history of the Grammys that an award has been revoked.

November 20: Fifty-three representatives and one senator file suit in U.S. Federal District Court seeking an injunction to prevent Bush from going to war without first gaining congressional approval. The judge rejects the request but indicates he will reconsider if the full Congress requests it.

November 21: International leaders sign the Charter of Paris, and Bush declares the official end of the cold war.

November 21: Bush meets with King Fahd and the emir of Kuwait. The leaders reiterate their call for an unconditional Iraqi withdrawal.

November 21: The so-called junk-bond king, Michael Milken, formerly of the Drexel Burnham Lambert investment company, receives a 10-year prison sentence and $600 million fine for securities violations.

November 22: Bush and congressional leaders spend the Thanksgiving holiday with U.S. troops in Saudi Arabia.

November 22: British prime minister Margaret Thatcher resigns after 11 years in office.

November 27: John Major, a member of Thatcher's Conservative Party, becomes Britain's prime minister.

November 27: The Senate Armed Services Committee opens the first congressional hearing on the Persian Gulf crisis.

November 28: Federal Reserve chairman Alan Greenspan declares that the U.S. economy has entered a "meaningful downturn" but refrains from concluding that it will be a recession.

November 28: The Security Council passes Resolution 677 condemning Iraq's destruction of Kuwait's civil records and its attempt to absorb Kuwait demographically.

November 29: Over opposition from Cuba and Yemen, the Security Council passes Resolution 678 authorizing war against Iraq. China abstains.

November 30: For the first time, Bush offers to negotiate directly with Iraq and suggests a meeting of Secretary of State James Baker and Iraqi foreign minister Tariq Aziz.

December 1: The 30.7-mile Channel Tunnel joining England and France is completed.

December 1: Led by Andre Agassi and Michael Chang, the U.S. Davis Cup tennis team wins its first championship since 1982.

President George H. W. Bush visited U.S. troops in Saudi Arabia on Thanksgiving Day. *(George Bush Presidential Library and Museum)*

December 1: Cheney increases to 115,000 the number of U.S. army reservists called to active duty. Two days later he increases the U.S. Marine call-up to 23,000, along with an additional 63,000 U.S. national guard and reserves.

December 2: The U.S. composer Aaron Copland dies at age 90.

December 6: Iraq announces that it will free the remaining Western hostages. The first American hostages are released on December 10, and the last group leaves Baghdad on December 14.

December 9: Lech Walesa is elected president of Poland.

December 10: The Communist Party, led by Slobodan Milošević, wins the popular election in Yugoslavia's Republic of Serbia.

December 11: Czechoslovakia deploys a chemical decontamination battalion, the first detachment of Warsaw Pact troops to join the coalition forces in the Gulf.

December 12: The United States agrees to provide a food aid package to the Soviet Union, which has been suffering from famine.

December 16: The four phases of Operation Desert Storm are articulated: a strategic air campaign against targets inside Iraq, a campaign to achieve air dominance over the Kuwaiti theater, battlefield preparation involving bomb attacks against the Iraqi army, and a ground attack.

December 17: Jean-Bertrand Aristide is elected president of Haiti.

December 18: Fabio Ochoa, one of the leaders of the notorious Medellín drug cartel, surrenders to Colombian authorities.

December 20: By this date 280,000 U.S. troops are in the Middle East.

December 20: In an interview on German television Saddam Hussein asserts that once 5,000 U.S. troops have been killed, Bush will be forced to call off the war if he starts one.

December 21: Twenty-one sailors of the U.S.S. *Saratoga* die while returning from liberty when their ferry capsizes off Haifa, Israel.

December 24: In an interview on Spanish television Saddam Hussein declares that Israel will be Iraq's first target in a war, whether or not it participates in action against Iraq.

December 26: The chess master Garry Kasparov retains his world title by defeating his Soviet rival, Anatoly Karpov.

December 28: The Defense Department announces that for the first time in history U.S. troops will be vaccinated against chemical and biological weapons.

December 30: An Iraqi spokesman declares that any attempt to force Iraqi troops from Kuwait will result in an Islamic holy war and that American targets throughout the world will be subject to terrorist attacks.

EYEWITNESS TESTIMONY

No one has ever led your life before; no one has ever negotiated his or her way to the twenty-first century before—especially not with your particular set of personal, family, ethical, social, and professional circumstances. No one has ever yet faced the challenges and opportunities that will appear before you in the near and distant future—especially not from your unique perspective. In short, every approaching moment of each of our lives represents unknown territory for us all: uncharted ground. Alas that we were not born with a written instruction manual—or better yet, a map, a treasure map, to show us the way through the maze of desires, expectations, and obligations that fill our days and define our various relationships to people, society, and ourselves. . . .

I typically work with clients who feel lost in the bewildering environment of their lives. They say they don't know what they feel or what they want from life. They are unclear about where they are going, and they don't know for sure where they have been. These clients complain of feeling helpless, out of control, confused, disoriented, and generally unhappy. They are not fulfilled souls. They need a treasure map to lead them back to a more productive and satisfying path.

Health and education specialist Nicholas Mason, Ph.D., describing the emotional state of many of his clients during the 1990s, in Mason, Following Your Treasure Map *(2001), p. 10.*

Theoretically, managers know they need an educated work-force who can think for themselves—but for years they've discouraged that and even organized jobs so they didn't need it. Most managers are a long way from abandoning traditional, hierarchical organizations.

Professor Thomas Bailey commenting in 1990 on hierarchical corporate structures in Alan F. Pater and Jason R. Pater, eds., What They Said in 1990 *(1991), p. 32.*

Do you want nuns washing your underwear for the rest of your life?

The Vatican emissary to Panama, Monseigneur José Laboa, describing the arguments he used to convince Panama's deposed president Manuel Noriega, who had taken refuge in the Vatican's embassy, to surrender to U.S. forces on January 3, 1990, in "Overheard," Newsweek, *January 15, 1990, p. 13.*

Our full liberation from the dictatorship of Noriega is now complete. All Panamanians feel great jubilation because we know now that a new day has begun, a new day of democracy and being brothers again, so as to reconstruct our country.

Panama's vice president, Ricardo Arias Calderón, on January 3, 1990, celebrating the surrender of President Manuel Noriega to U.S. forces earlier the same day, in Larry Rohter, "As Word Spreads in Panama, Thousands Turn Out to Cheer," New York Times, *January 4, 1990, p. 1.*

Minutes after she heard that Charles Stuart had jumped off the Tobin Bridge, New York literary agent Jane Dystel phoned Joe Sharkey, a former *Wall Street Journal* reporter. That afternoon, Sharkey was in Boston interviewing figures in the Stuart case, and a few days later . . . "we had a 26-page [book] proposal on the editor's desk."

What took them so long? Assistant editor Colleen Mohyde of Little, Brown in Boston saw the first of many proposals the day after Stuart's suicide. "The fastest response I've ever seen," she says. . . .

When the subject is a juicy crime, many book publishers demand speed, not style, depth, or perspective. . . . "It's a family story. That makes it appealing," says William Grose, editorial director of Pocket Books. "And it's about upwardly mobile Yuppies—a perfect fable from the '80s for the '90s."

James N. Baker reporting on the book industry's response to Charles Stuart's suicide on January 4, 1990, shortly after it was revealed that Stuart, not a black assailant, had murdered his wife and unborn child, in Baker, "Writers and Agents: The Rush to Cash In," Newsweek, *January 22, 1990, p. 20.*

Just as President Bush is willing to issue a bounty for Noriega, it must be done for this.

Civil rights activist Jesse Jackson calling for a reward for the capture of those responsible for a series of racially directed bombings in the South during 1989 and 1990, in "Overheard," Newsweek, *January 15, 1990, p. 13.*

In every decade a new political player steps up to the table and reshuffles the cards. In the 1970s it was the oil-exporting countries. In the '80s President Reagan dealt out tax cuts, rousing the country into a festival of spending and debt. The 1990s might have been 10 years at hard labor, paying the bills, except for another turn of events: the fall of the Berlin wall. . . .

Without peace, without slower growth in the military budget, the economy has a tough row to hoe. . . . Peace offers the country an unexpected chance to climb down from the elephant debt of the Reagan years. If the savings are used to reduce the general deficit, interest rates should come down. . . . That would boost housing, construction and business investment and induce faster growth.

You will instantly object that any money drawn from the Pentagon would simply be spent on something else. Too true. But if the government reallocates arms dollars to investments that raise productivity—like better transport systems or worker-training programs—the country would still come out ahead.

Columnist Jane Bryant Quinn discussing an anticipated peace dividend from the cessation of the cold war in Quinn, "Laying Bets on the 90s," Newsweek, *January 15, 1990, p. 53.*

We have waited too long for our freedom. We can wait no longer. Now is the time to intensify the struggle on all fronts. To relax our efforts now would be a mistake which generations to come will not [be] able to forgive.

Political activist Nelson Mandela stating his intention, after his release from prison on February 11, 1990, to continue the quest for equality of nonwhites in South Africa, in Christopher S. Wren, "Mandela Freed, Urges Step-Up in Pressure to End White Rule," New York Times, *February 12, 1990, p. 1.*

Like everyone else, Hollywood was ill-prepared for the end of the Cold War and the post–Cold War era. Even a year after the fall of the Berlin Wall, the film industry was still producing films that reeked of the Cold War, albeit with faint hints of the coming collapse of communism. The most popular of these was action-film director John McTiernan's . . . *The Hunt for Red October* (1990). The film is based on a [1984] Tom Clancy techno-thriller that . . . sold as many as five million copies. . . .

What is interesting about a mechanical film like *The Hunt for Red October,* especially in light of the Cold War's end, are its political assumptions, not its aesthetics. The most striking was that Soviet naval officers, certainly among the most privileged group in their society, had become so disillusioned with their country and its ideology . . . that they felt compelled to defect. . . .

Of course, these assumptions . . . point to the widely held belief, even before the fall of the Berlin Wall . . . that faith in the Soviet system had almost disappeared. They also implicitly acknowledge the fact that despite this the Cold War left such a dangerous residue of mistrust that one mistake might still lead to catastrophe. And that there was still a need for reasonable men . . . to overcome the last vestiges of Cold War paranoia.

Film scholars Leonard Quart and Albert Auster discussing the political assumptions inherent in the movie The Hunt for Red October, *which opened in late February 1990, in Quart and Auster,* American Film and Society since 1945 *(2002), pp. 170–171.*

[I am] more talented than any Bob Dylan or Paul McCartney. Mick Jagger can't produce a sound. I'm the new Elvis.

Millie Vanilli "singer" Rob Pilatus, who was later found not to be performing any of the songs on his award-winning albums, boasting in Jay Cocks, "Two Scoops of Vanilli," Time, *March 5, 1990, p. 69.*

The Hubble is the single most important instrument ever made in astronomy. . . . Hubble is unique. Nothing else can do what it can do. Once it's gone, we're going to be paralyzed. We've gotten hooked. We're addicted.

Astronomer Sandra Faber, remarking in 2003 on the eventual demise of the Hubble Space Telescope, *which was launched into orbit around the Earth on April 25, 1990, in Dennis Overbye, "As Clock Ticks for Hubble, Some Plead for a Reprieve,"* New York Times, *July 27, 2003.*

Americans did not fight the wars of the 20th Century to make the world safe for green vegetables.

Richard Darman, director of the Office of Management and Budget, deriding the environmental movement during a commencement address at Harvard University in May 1990, in Michael Zimmerman, professor of biology, in "But Some Administration Appointees Reveal Their Flat-Earth View of Nature," Miami Herald, *October 6, 1991, p. 8C.*

The excessive hoarding of riches by some denies them to the majority, and thus the very wealth that is accumulated generates poverty. . . .

Launched in 1990, the *Hubble Space Telescope* began sending back high-quality photos from near and deep space after astronauts repaired it in December 1993. *(AP/Wide World Photos)*

We must not forget that often it is the poor who are forced to make sacrifices while the possessors of great riches do not show themselves ready to renounce their privileges for the good of others.

Pope John Paul II addressing business executives in Durango, Mexico, on May 9, 1990, in "John Paul II Criticizes Capitalism," Miami Herald, May 10, 1990, p. 12A.

The two contractors aren't meeting their deadlines, costs are running 24 percent higher than the statutory cap, and in test after test, [the Advanced Medium Range Air-to-Air Missile] AMRAAM gets an "F" for reliability. This is a good opportunity to stop another Pentagon boondoggle before it gets too far down the tracks.

Representative Denny Smith of Oregon on May 9, 1990, urging cancellation of AMRAAM after it failed a series of performance tests, in Mark Thompson, "Congress Asked to Deny Funds for Failed Missile," Miami Herald, May 10, 1990, p. 11A.

[The Advanced Medium Range Air-to-Air Missile] AMRAAM is the most successful air-to-air missile that

we've ever had at this point in time. I think the operational performance of AMRAAM is unparalleled.

Major General John E. Jaquish, director of U.S. Air Force tactical programs, defending the AMRAAM, in Mark Thompson, "Congress Asked to Deny Funds for Failed Missile," Miami Herald, May 10, 1990, p. 11A.

The shift from fighting "for civil rights" to fighting "against racism" was a shift from seeking and finding common ground to a position that has been disastrously divisive. To fight against racism divides humanity into "us against them." It leads to a self-definition as "victim," and anyone who defines himself as a victim has found a way to keep himself in a perpetual state of self-righteous self-pity and anger. And that, in a nutshell, is the state of black America today.

Professor Julius Lester discussing on May 11, 1990, the state of the Civil Rights movement in the 1990s, in Alan F. Pater and Jason R. Pater, eds., What They Said in 1990 (1991), p. 24.

I ask those of you who grieve Yusuf not to be swayed by those who would use this occasion to spread their venom and cause our city more pain. The answer to racism cannot be further assault on our people, our institutions and our civic pride.

New York City's mayor David Dinkins responding to calls from the Reverend Al Sharpton, an activist, for rallies that would shut down the city after the acquittal of one of Yusuf Hawkins's accused murderers, in George Hackett, "No Justice, No Peace," Newsweek, May 28, 1990, p. 19.

We are in a transitional period right now . . . fascinating and exhilarating times . . . learning to adjust to the changes and the choices we . . . men and women . . . are facing.

Maybe we should adjust faster, maybe we should adjust slower. But whatever the era, whatever the times, one thing will never change: Fathers and mothers, if you have children—they must come first. You must read to your children, hug your children, and you must love your children. Your success as a family . . . our success as a society depends not on what happens in the White House, but on what happens inside your house.

For over 50 years, it was said that the winner of Wellesley's annual hoop race would be the first to get married. Now they say the winner will be the first to become a C.E.O. Both of those stereotypes show too little tolerance for those who want to know where the mermaids stand. So I want to offer you today a new legend: The winner of the hoop race will be the first to realize her dream . . . not society's dreams . . . her own personal dream. And who knows? Somewhere out in this audience may even be someone who will one day follow in my footsteps, and preside over the White House as the President's spouse.

I wish him well!

First Lady Barbara Bush addressing the graduates of Wellesley College on June 1, 1990. Available online. URL: http://www.americanrhetoric.com/ speeches/barbarabush.html.

We as a nation are doomed to a severe chastening from the hand of God. Abortion is the symbol of our decline, the slaughter of the most innocent. What kind of justice is it, when 10 of us are fined $450,000 for trying to stop the murder of innocent babies [by blocking the entrances to abortion clinics], while the homosexuals who entered [New York City's] St. Patrick's Cathedral and disrupted Mass are fined $100 each. I tell you, if we were homosexual, we'd be treated a lot better in the courts. . . . In 30 years, we're going to have forced abortion. I can already write the decision about how in a society with limited resources we can only accommodate the needs of the most by limiting each family to two babies. You say that's far-fetched, but what would you have said 30 years ago if I'd told you we would be killing 1.5 million babies a year, and having Gay Pride week and AIDS and no prayer [allowed] in public schools? The feminists got what they wanted, but are women better off with pornography and no-fault divorce and irresponsible fathers who don't pay child support? I don't think so.

The antiabortion activist and founder of Operation Rescue Randall Terry, condemning legalized abortion on June 11, 1990, in Alan F. Pater and Jason R. Pater, eds., What They Said in 1990 (1991), pp. 28–29.

Now we have minorities and feminists and the left allied with fundamentalists who believe some communitarian values take precedence. To them, group rights are more important than individual rights. The First Amendment is being embattled from all sides. Some say racist speech on campus should be an exception [to freedom of speech]. All of these people believe they have a special pleading.

Law professor Nadine Strossen discussing on June 29, 1990, then-current assaults on the right to free speech in Alan F. Pater and Jason R. Pater, eds., What They Said in 1990 (1991), p. 28.

I have great confidence in the integrity and honor of my son. And for those who want to challenge it, whether they're in Congress or elsewhere, let the system work and then we can all make a conclusion as to his honor and his integrity.

President George H.W. Bush on July 11, 1990, defending his son, Neil Bush, who was implicated in the failure of the Silverado Savings & Loan, in Thomas E. Hitchings, ed., Facts On File Yearbook 1990 *(1991), p. 532.*

There's a kind of hysteria going on that's making it hard for artists to work. It's like a throwback to the dark ages where artists are suddenly suspicious characters because one or two have done something controversial.

Actor Kevin Kline on July 12, 1990, protesting congressional efforts to cut funding for the NEA because some of the projects it supported were considered obscene, in Thomas E. Hitchings, ed., Facts On File Yearbook 1990 *(1991), p. 537.*

A central problem in this case is that many grand jury and trial witnesses were thoroughly soaked in [Oliver] North's immunized testimony, but no effort was made to determine what effect, if any, this extensive exposure had on their testimony. . . .

[For the case to proceed, the prosecution] must proceed witness-by-witness; if necessary . . . line-by-line and item-by-item.

U.S. District Judge Gerhard A. Gesell overturning on July 20, 1990, the conviction of Lieutenant Colonel Oliver North for crimes associated with the 1987 Iran-contra affair, in Thomas E. Hitchings, ed., Facts On File Yearbook 1990 *(1991), pp. 552–553.*

We have no opinion on Arab-Arab conflicts, like your border disagreement with Kuwait. . . . President Bush is an intelligent man. He is not going to declare an economic war against Iraq.

U.S. Ambassador April Glaspie responding on July 25, 1990, to Iraq's president Saddam Hussein, who indicated he was contemplating war with Kuwait, as recorded in a secretly made transcript leaked by Iraq but partially repudiated by Glaspie in 1991, in Con Coughlin, Saddam: King of Terror *(2002), p. 250.*

I was a cardiologist in China, where I practiced both Western medicine and traditional Chinese medicine. I had been an emergency room physician as well. In August 1990, I was accepted into a university program to study psychology in New York City, but, having lived my life under the communist economic system, I did not realize that I would also be expected to pay for food and housing. I just naturally assumed these would be taken care of, and so I arrived with less than $200, where I was expected to survive in one of the world's most expensive cities. As a result, I had to drop out of the program and earn my living doing essentially sweatshop work for a dollar an hour.

I rented a room in Queens, and one day, just before she was to go away on a trip, my landlady developed a very painful foot condition. I did acupuncture on her, and the pain went away, and she was able to travel without a problem. When she returned, she told some of her friends, and I soon began to develop a small clientele. But this was a difficult time for me, as I knew few people and had very little money, and thus had very limited opportunities to pursue my interests. I was beginning to get down about this when, one night, I had a dream in which Chairman Mao Zedong, who died years before, assured me that everything would turn out fine. (I had mixed feelings about Mao. My family and I had suffered during the Cultural Revolution of the 1960s, but Mao had resisted Western-influenced efforts to eradicate Chinese medicine, which he called China's gift to the world, and I have always appreciated that.)

Soon after my dream, my landlady's son David, a Buddhist, came to visit. David was so impressed by my acupuncture that he offered to help me establish a practice in South Florida, where he lived. And so I moved to Miami, where I soon developed a thriving practice. (Miami's tropical setting reminded me of another dream—one that I had as a little girl in which I saw myself living in a land of palm trees.) David, who was born in Taiwan, also taught me about Buddhism, about which I knew very little,

because in communist China religious practices were forbidden. My Buddhist practices, which I learned in the United States, have greatly enriched my life. More than ten years later David, who had always remained a good friend, unexpectedly proposed to me, and we are now a happily married, Chinese couple—something that never would have happened if he had stayed in Taiwan or I had stayed in China.

Xiaolin Mary Tan, doctor of Chinese medicine, describing her experience of immigrating to the United States in August 1990, in private correspondence with the author.

On August 2, 1990, it could be said that George Bush's media prospects were dire. The budget, prisons, drugs, inner cities, AIDS, crack, crime, and the homeless were exhibiting an obdurate, malicious, even perverse inclination to resist all solution.

There was also the $500 billion S&L scandal. While one could not yet speak of it as a cancer upon the presidency—no, not so bad as Watergate—still, it was a damn chancre at least, and the president's son, whether innocent, guilty, or somewhat smudged, was going to be treated by the media for the next six months as a blot on the Bush escutcheon. The media would not be the media if they did not have the instincts of a lynch mob.

Author Norman Mailer describing President George H. W. Bush's political situation on August 1 (August 2, local time) 1990, the day of the Iraqi invasion of Kuwait, in Mailer, "How the Wimp Won the War," Vanity Fair, *May 1991, p. 138.*

I view very seriously our determination to reverse this aggression. There are an awful lot of countries that are in total accord with what I've just said, and we will be working with them all for collective action. This will not stand, this aggression against Kuwait.

President George H. W. Bush announcing his opposition to Iraq's annexation of Kuwait on August 5, 1990, in U.S. Department of Defense, Conduct of the Persian Gulf War: Final Report to Congress *(1992), p. 31.*

Our overwhelming approval is not a sign that the Senate intends to be lax about exercising its advise-and-consent power, or intends to use that power only to screen out extremist nominees. Rather it is a sign that we take this power seriously, and that we intend to exercise it responsibly. And in doing so, Judge Souter falls within the sphere of candidates acceptable to the Senate.

Democratic senator Joseph Biden of Delaware, chairman of the Senate Judiciary Committee, commenting on the Senate's approval on October 2, 1990, of Judge David Souter's nomination to the Supreme Court, in Richard L. Berke, "Senate Confirms Souter, 90 to 9, As Supreme Court's 105th Justice," New York Times, October 3, 1990, p. 1.

Forty-five years after it was carved up in defeat and disgrace, Germany was reunited today in a midnight celebration of pealing bells, national hymns and the jubilant blare of good old German oom-pah-pah.

At the stroke of midnight Tuesday, a copy of the American Liberty Bell, a gift from the United States at the height of the cold war, tolled from the Town Hall, and the black, red and gold banner of the Federal Republic of Germany rose slowly before the Reichstag, the scarred seat of past German Parliaments.

Then the President, Richard von Weizsäcker . . . proclaimed from the steps of the Reichstag: "In free self-determination, we want to achieve the unity in freedom of Germany. We are aware of our responsibility for these tasks before God and the people. We want to serve peace in the world in a united Europe."

Journalist Serge Schmemann describing ceremonies celebrating the unification of Germany on October 3, 1990, in Schmemann, "Two Germanys United after 45 Years with Jubilation and a Vow of Peace," New York Times, October 3, 1990, p. 1.

If the women's movement did any harm at all, it gave the woman who stayed at home an inferiority complex. I think it dissolved a lot of marriages. Women would say, "There has to be more out there," and there wasn't necessarily anything more or better. . . .

The signing of the Charter of Paris on November 21, 1990, officially ended the cold war. *(AP/Wide World Photos)*

Fortunately, today, if you stay home to raise a family, no one condemns you.

Television journalist Barbara Walters, in November 1990, discussing the status of women, in Alan F. Pater and Jason R. Pater, eds., What They Said in 1990 *(1991), p. 30.*

In signing the Charter of Paris this morning, we have closed a chapter of history. I'm about to sign this, and we are closing a chapter in history. The cold war is over, and now we move on to working . . . for a peaceful and stable Europe.

President George H. W. Bush declaring the end of the cold war on November 21, 1990. Available online. URL: http://bushlibrary.tamu.edu/research/ papers/1990/90112101.html.

It was a rare and great moment in history. The end of an era of enormous and unrelenting hostility had come in an instant. And, most incredible of all, without a single shot being fired.

The final collapse of Soviet power and the dissolution of its empire brought to a close the greatest transformation of the international system since World War I and concluded nearly eight decades of upheaval and conflict. The world we had encountered in January 1989 had been defined by superpower rivalry. The Cold War struggle had shaped our assumptions about international and domestic politics, our institutions and processes, our armed forces and military strategy. In a blink of an eye, they were gone. We were suddenly in a unique position, without experience, without precedent, and standing alone at the height of power. It was, it is, an unparalleled situation in history, one which presents us with the rarest opportunity to shape the world and the deepest responsibility to do so wisely for the benefit of not just the United States but all nations.

Former national security advisor Brent Scowcroft reflecting, in 1998, about the end of the cold war, which officially concluded on November 21, 1990, in Stephen Ambrose and Douglas Brinkley, eds., Witness to America *(1999), p. 579.*

The importance of presidential leadership is probably greater now than ever. From a domestic perspective the president must take seriously his constitutional role as the chief foreign policy-maker, developing objectives and setting priorities, doing what is right for all even if it is unpopular, and then rallying the country. The challenge of presidential leadership in foreign affairs is not to listen to consensus, but to forge it at home and abroad. Nowhere is this leadership more critical than in creating a new domestic consensus for the American role in the world. There should be no question that we must face future challenges head on, without reverting to the isolationism and protectionism of the earlier part of the century. Our nation can no longer afford to retire selfishly behind its borders as soon as international conditions seem to recede from crisis, to be brought out again only by the onrush of the next great upheaval. This was a pattern I was determined to break as we moved beyond the Cold War, and it is one we must continue to put behind us.

Former president George H. W. Bush reflecting, in 1998, about presidential leadership after the cold war, which officially concluded on November 21, 1990, in Stephen Ambrose and Douglas Brinkley, eds., Witness to America *(1999), p. 580.*

3

Desert Storm and the New World Order

1991

From war in Kuwait to mass murders in a Texas diner and in a modest Milwaukee apartment to inner-city gang wars to high-profile police brutality to racial conflict to growing awareness of the so-called date-rape phenomenon, 1991 was a year dominated by violence at home and abroad. The Persian Gulf War took place in January and February, and viewers throughout the world watched on television as America's professional military forces, armed with never-before-used high-tech weaponry, quickly overwhelmed the much-heralded Iraqi army and liberated Kuwait. The conflict, which greatly enhanced Bush's popularity, introduced satellite technology to the battlefield and to media coverage of hostilities. Overall, the Persian Gulf War changed both the way war was fought and the way war news was reported

Other significant international developments included the final breakup of the Soviet Union and ascension of Boris Yeltsin to power in Russia; the withdrawal of Slovenia, Macedonia, and Croatia from Yugoslavia, followed by the outbreak of a prolonged civil war in the Balkan region; the removal of Soviet troops from Cuba; the repeal of apartheid in South Africa; the downfall of Somalia's long-reigning socialist dictator, General Mohammed Siad Barre; and a short-lived peace agreement that temporarily ended Angola's 15-year civil war.

Violence dominated the American domestic landscape in a number of ways. On October 16, George Hennard, a lone gunman, committed the worst mass shooting in U.S. history when he randomly murdered 23 people, including himself, outside Dallas, Texas, and wounded 23 more. Another mass murderer, Jeffrey L. Dahmer, was linked to the killings of at least 15 boys and young men after police discovered dismembered heads and other body parts in his Milwaukee apartment. The gruesome case, which involved cannibalism and homosexual necrophilia, became a source of morbid fascination for many Americans, as did the year's winner of the Academy Award for best film, *The Silence of the Lambs,* which also featured particularly gruesome, sadistic, and perverse acts of murder. Overall, a record 23,300 homicides were reported throughout the nation for the year.[1] Moreover, almost one-fourth of high school students surveyed by the Centers for Disease Control claimed they had "seriously thought" about committing suicide within the year.[2] As the nation remained divided over whether to treat homosexuality as acceptable or aberrant behavior, in terms of both social norms and legally permitted practices, acquired immunodeficiency syndrome (AIDS) continued to claim the lives of a growing number of Americans. And it killed many more throughout the world, especially in Africa.

INTERNATIONAL DEVELOPMENTS

The Persian Gulf War and Operation Desert Storm

Throughout the fall of 1990, the United States–led coalition increased its military strength in the Persian Gulf region, and the United Nations issued increasingly stronger edicts against Iraq, including one that authorized war if Iraq did not withdraw from Kuwait by January 15, 1991. However, for both the public and the Bush administration, the specter of the Vietnam War loomed large over the prospect of a new large-scale foreign intervention—the first conflict, apart from the brief small-scale invasions of Grenada and Panama, since American troops left Vietnam in 1973. Consequently, unlike the nearly unanimous support expressed for the defense of Saudi Arabia against an Iraqi invasion, the American public response was divided over the prospect of waging an offensive war against Iraq, especially because of the large number of anticipated casualties expected from a head-on assault against well-armed, firmly entrenched Iraqi forces. The military, led by Chairman of the Joint Chiefs of Staff general Colin Powell and U.S. Army general Norman Schwarzkopf, was determined to wage a swift, decisive offensive characterized by overwhelming American force, rather than fight a prolonged war in which U.S. military power would increase by increments in response to enemy provocations, as occurred during the Vietnam War.

As chairman of the Joint Chiefs of Staff, General Colin Powell oversaw the fighting during Operation Desert Storm. *(U.S. Army)*

Between late November 1990 and early January 1991, antiwar protests reminiscent of the Vietnam War era broke out across the country. Even such ranking government officials and former officials as Senator Sam Nunn, the respected conservative head of the Senate Armed Services Committee; Admiral William Crowe, a former chairman of the Joint Chiefs of Staff; and Robert McNamara, the former secretary of defense, who was the architect of the Vietnam War, spoke of their fears of massive U.S. casualties and their belief that it would be safer and better policy to allow the economic depravation caused by the trade embargo to compel Iraq to withdraw from Kuwait—probably after a year or two of occupation. Although he did not express it publicly, within the administration Colin Powell also argued initially for a similar course of restraint.[3]

Others opposed an offensive war because they viewed it primarily as an act of U.S. imperialism aimed mostly at benefiting the oil industry, with which Bush had close personal and political connections. Some Americans objected to sending U.S. troops to restore a nondemocratic Kuwaiti monarchy who deprived their citizens of many basic human rights. Still other citizens believed American soldiers were being used essentially as hired guns to fight for Saudis and Kuwaitis, who had done little to protect themselves. Some Jewish Americans, and other Americans as well, feared that Saddam would carry out his threat to attack Israel with chemical weapons if the allies started a war, and they did not consider Kuwait worth that risk. Moreover, the largely pro-Iraqi U.S. foreign policy up to the moment of the Kuwait invasion made the administration's anti–Saddam Hussein rhetoric appear hypocritical. If, as Bush maintained, Saddam Hussein was another Hitler, then why had Bush and Reagan supported him for the past several years?

Bush's attempt to garner public support for the war during this period was further complicated by satellite-based television news coverage that included live reporting from Baghdad. Through his access to Cable Network News (CNN) and other international media outlets, Saddam Hussein was able to present his case directly to the American public. This was the first time that an enemy leader had the capability to appeal directly to the U.S. people before the outbreak of war. Cognizant of the large shadow that Vietnam still cast upon the American psyche, Saddam Hussein made explicit references to it, warning that the United States faced a war even more terrible.

Nonetheless, Bush remained convinced that the coalition would not remain together indefinitely, and he was aware that if he did not initiate an offensive by the end of February or early March, sandstorms, intense heat, and other adverse desert conditions would make military action difficult and unreliable until the following autumn. He therefore continued to take a hard line against Saddam Hussein—at times the animosity between the leaders appeared to be personal. And the administration continued to press its case before Congress and the American people. On January 12, after the failure of a last-ditch diplomatic effort to convince Iraq to withdraw by the January 15 deadline, the majority of Congress voted to authorize war.

The initial phase of Operation Desert Storm, an air campaign, began on January 17 (local time, eastern, standard time January 16 [EST]). Its objectives were to achieve complete air supremacy; disrupt Iraqi command and control; destroy Iraqi chemical, biological, and nuclear weapons stockpiles and/or production facilities; and weaken Iraqi ground forces and defensive fortifications through repeated bombings. Iraq's offensive response occurred on January 18, when it launched the first of 40 Scud missiles that it fired upon Israel during the war. Saddam Hussein hoped to provoke Israel to retaliate and thereby create a rift within the coalition, as the Arab countries presumably would refuse to fight alongside Israel. To forestall this scenario, the United States sent batteries of Patriot antimissile missiles and missile crews to Israel and, over Schwarzkopf's objections, made destroying Iraqi Scud launchers a major military priority in the air campaign, even though these were not of great importance to Schwarzkopf's campaign against the Iraqi defenses.

Although Saddam Hussein had threatened to attack Israel and the coalition troops with chemical weapons, he did not do so, presumably because he feared nuclear retaliation. He did, however, launch a vindictive scorched earth policy

Tomahawk cruise missiles launched at sea struck targets in Iraq. *(U.S. Department of Defense)*

against Kuwait during the air campaign, setting more than 450 of its oil wells aflame and pumping approximately 8 million barrels of oil into the Persian Gulf, possibly with the intention of polluting the desalination plants that supplied Saudi Arabia and the coalition forces with fresh water. Although these tactics caused enormous environmental damage to Kuwait and the Persian Gulf, they failed to help Iraq's cause. The desalination plants were not affected by the oil slick, which covered some 350 square miles. And, ironically, the burning oil wells placed Iraqi troops at an even greater disadvantage because during the ground war Iraqi tank crews were blinded by the burning oil. But American crews, equipped with thermal gunsights, could locate and target Iraqi tanks and armored vehicles not visible through the dense smoke.

Although some officials estimated that capping all the fires would take two to three years, the last was extinguished in about 10 months, in early November 1991.

As the air war proceeded, Schwarzkopf secretly redeployed most of his armored divisions several hundred miles to the west along the Saudi Arabia–Iraq border so he could launch a surprise attack against the Iraqi flank. This westward shift, known as Operation Hail Mary, was a major logistical achievement. More than 270,000 U.S., British, and French troops, along with their tanks and equipment and enough food, water, and ammunition to sustain them in the desert for 60 days, secretly moved across the desert to positions as far as 260 miles inland.[4] At the same time, the First Marine Expeditionary Force and the Joint Forces Command, which included Arab units from Egypt, Syria, and the Persian Gulf states, also redeployed from their positions by the Saudi coast to new attack positions farther inland and closer to the Kuwait border.

The air campaign concluded on February 24, after achieving its objectives. Schwarzkopf initiated a two-pronged ground attack on that date. The first was an assault by U.S. Marines and pan-Arab forces against the Iraqi fortifications in Kuwait. After breaching the Iraqi defenses they proceeded directly north to Kuwait City, which they liberated on February 27. The second prong constituted the main coalition assault, as U.S. and British armored divisions west of the Iraqi lines crossed into Iraq and then swung around to attack the exposed flank of the elite Republican Guard armored divisions, which were unprepared for the surprise strike from the west. Farther to the west, a French armored division and U.S. airborne troops protected the allied flank against a counterattack. During 100 hours of fighting, the allies trapped most of the Republican Guard in a pocket in northern Kuwait, inflicted heavy casualties, and destroyed most of Iraq's tanks and armored vehicles.

Altogether, in four days of ground fighting, the allies destroyed about 3,800 tanks, 1,450 armored personnel carriers, and 2,900 pieces of artillery. They took some 86,000 prisoners and rendered at least 36 of Iraq's 43 combat divisions ineffective.[5] Approximately 2,300 Iraqi civilians died in the bombings and another 6,000 were wounded. Additional civilian casualties followed from the poor sanitary conditions and breakdown in support services caused by the air attacks. By contrast, fewer than 300 coalition troops died in combat, and 42 coalition troops were captured. After the war, however, tens of thousands of veterans—as many as one-third of those who served in the Middle East—began experiencing such symptoms as fatigue, nausea, depression, severe headaches, memory loss, disturbed sleep, dizziness, sexual impotence, muscle pain and fatigue, rashes, confusion, and inability to concentrate. As of 2005, efforts to treat and fully account for the so-called Gulf War syndrome remained unsuccessful.

Bush concluded offensive actions at 8:00 A.M. on February 28 (local time, midnight February 27 EST). At that point all of the coalition's stated objectives had been achieved: Iraqi troops had been forced from Kuwait and Iraq's ability to wage offensive war within the region had been eliminated. But several hundred Iraqi tanks were able to escape back into Iraq, and these were soon used to suppress rebellions within Iraq by disaffected Kurds and Shiite Muslims and to enable Saddam Hussein to retain power. Bush's decision to end the war

M-1A1 Abrams tanks from the 1st Armored Cavalry Division raced through the desert at record-setting speeds during Operation Desert Storm. *(U.S. Department of Defense)*

before the Republican Guard was completely destroyed remains one of the most controversial aspects of the war. Bush justified the decision by pointing out that the UN mandate did not authorize the overthrow of Saddam Hussein and that an attempt to do so might have caused the allied coalition to disintegrate. He also pointed to the likelihood of high casualties to coalition troops that would result from intense street fighting within Iraq.

The Persian Gulf War was the first American war waged by all-volunteer military forces. Moreover, women military personnel were more fully involved in all phases of the war, including combat operations, than in any previous U.S. military action. The war introduced many highly sophisticated computerized weapons and advanced satellite technology. Satellite communications systems and cable television also permitted instantaneous and nearly continuous media coverage. At the same time, the U.S. military subjected battlefront journalists to more stringent restrictions than ever before.

OTHER INTERNATIONAL DEVELOPMENTS

During the spring and summer, the Soviet Union moved rapidly toward its dissolution as Gorbachev's near-dictatorial powers and problematic economic policies were attacked by a range of adversaries. In June, Boris Yeltsin, running as an independent party candidate, defeated the Gorbachev-backed Communist Party nominee in Russia's first popular presidential election. In July, Gorbachev failed to garner significant financial support from the leaders of the seven leading industrialized nations at the so-called G-7 meeting, because his economic reforms were not considered extensive enough to create a viable free-market economy. But at the end of the month he and Bush signed the Strategic Arms Reduction Treaty (START), which reduced each side's nuclear arsenal by one-third. Less than three weeks later, Gorbachev was temporarily deposed when a group of Communist hard-liners arrested him at his summer residence in the Crimea and attempted to seize power. But Yeltsin suppressed what he denounced as a cynical right-wing coup by rallying popular support against it and winning the backing of most of the military. Gorbachev returned to power two days later, but his influence was greatly weakened, as was the standing of the Communist Party, which Yeltsin suspended in Russia. About two weeks later, on September 5, the Soviet Supreme Legislature voted the Union of Soviet Socialist Republics out of existence, ending almost 74 years of Communist rule. Most of the power was transferred to the individual republics, and work was begun to formulate a new treaty among them. This was concluded in December, with 11 of the 15 republics joining the Commonwealth of Independent States. On December 25 Gorbachev resigned, and the Soviet Union officially ceased to exist. Control of the Soviet nuclear arsenal passed to Yeltsin in his capacity as president of Russia.

Meanwhile, Yugoslavia, which had been unified under Communist Party rule during the cold war, moved rapidly toward civil war, as the Serb-dominated Yugoslavian military, directed by Premier Slobodan Milošević, attacked strategic points in the breakaway republic of Croatia, including its capital, Zagreb; historic Dubrovnik, which had long been internationally celebrated for its Venetian architecture and baroque churches; and Vukovar, which surrendered after a three-month siege.

The struggle between democratic and military rule continued elsewhere in the world. After replacing the Duvalier dictatorship in February, Haiti's first democratically elected president, Jean-Bertrand Aristide, a Roman Catholic priest, promptly retired six of the eight generals in the army's high command. Nonetheless, Aristide's presidency remained tasked with dealing with opposition from Duvalier loyalists, as well as the nation's persistent widespread poverty, and he was deposed by a military coup in late September. In Thailand, a military coup seized power over U.S. objections.

GOVERNMENT AND SOCIETY

Bush made his second Supreme Court appointment when he replaced the liberal Justice Thurgood Marshall, America's first African-American justice, who retired after serving for 24 years, with Clarence Thomas, an ultraconservative African American. Thomas won Senate confirmation by a narrow 52-48 vote after Anita Hill, a liberal African-American law professor at the University of Oklahoma, charged that Thomas had sexually harassed her when she served as his aide years earlier. The widely publicized confirmation hearings, which revealed predictable divisions between liberals and conservatives, also exposed political differences within the traditionally liberal African-American community. Also, women were more likely than men to believe Hill, whose veracity was impossible either to prove or to disprove. The fact that Hill waited until Thomas was nominated to speak out against him further clouded the issue, as it suggested that she was driven more by liberal politics than by a sincere desire for justice, although Hill maintained in her congressional testimony that she was not responsible for the timing of her charges or even for her decision to make them public (see Appendix 1).

Before Thomas's appointment, the Supreme Court had made several far-reaching decisions. It ruled that no constitutional basis exists for restricting the size of punitive damage awards in civil lawsuits; that the telephone book white pages are not subject to copyright protection; that coercion of confessions does not automatically void a criminal conviction if a guilty verdict can be sustained by other, independently obtained evidence; that federal law barring employment discrimination does not apply to the operation of U.S. companies outside the country; that employers cannot unilaterally bar women from jobs in which they might face exposure to materials harmful to a developing fetus. The Court also upheld a New York State "lemon law" protecting consumers who purchase chronically defective automobiles, and it tightened the standards that state prisoners, including those awaiting execution, must meet in order to file a second challenge to the constitutionality of their conviction. After Thomas assumed his seat on the bench, the Court unanimously struck down New York State's so-called Son of Sam law, which prohibited criminals from profiting by selling the stories of their crimes for books or movies.

New studies showed that the gap between the country's wealthiest citizens and the rest of the nation was widening, and divisions among social and economic classes were exacerbated by a perception that wealthy investors were taking advantage of the S&L and other business scandals to make huge profits at the expense of ordinary citizens. The Census Bureau issued a report indicating that according to data collected in 1988, the top 20 percent of the nation's most wealthy households were the only group who had experienced a significance increase in net worth since a comparable 1984 study and controlled 44 percent of the total national wealth. The same study showed that the average white household had an eight times higher net worth than Hispanic households and 10 times higher than black households.[6] Another report based on data from a 1989 study conducted by the University of Chicago's National Opinion Research Center showed that white Americans continued to have negative stereotypes about blacks and Hispanics concerning matters of wealth, willingness to work, intelligence, proclivity for violence, patriotism, and willingness to rely on welfare; a separate report by the Sentencing Project used data from 1990 to show that the United States had the highest rate of prison incarceration in the world.[7]

The tradition of Gay and Lesbian Day began at Disney World in Orlando, Florida, on the first Saturday of June. The gathering of homosexuals inside the theme park, after they had paid for full admission, not only afforded a day of entertainment for the participants but also publicly asserted the homosexual community's belief that gays are normal citizens entitled to engage openly in mainstream American life. Presumably the location was chosen in part because of Disney World's reputation as a wholesome place for family entertainment, and the event drew sharp criticism from conservative and religious groups who regarded the practice of homosexual acts as not only aberrant, but even immoral and/or blasphemous. Although located in the midst of Florida's so-called Bible Belt, Disney, which was one of the first major U.S. corporations to extend health benefits to same-sex partners of its employees, refused to prohibit the profitable gathering, which generated some 2,500 paid admissions. Disney did not, however, organize or promote Gay and Lesbian Day, which was initiated instead by users of a local gay-oriented computer bulletin board. Thus, the event was one of the first large-scale instances in which the Internet was used to galvanize social and political action.

Congress passed and Bush signed the Civil Rights Act of 1991, which reversed several recent Supreme Court rulings that limited the redress of victims of discrimination in the workplace. The act permitted victims to receive awards for punitive damages when discrimination is intentional; it established a Glass Ceiling commission to recommend ways to remove barriers to women and minorities seeking advancement to upper-echelon positions; and it forbade race norming, the practice of adjusting test scores according to race. The Supreme Court let stand a New Jersey Supreme Court decision that an all-male eating club at Princeton University practiced illegal gender discrimination when it refused to allow women to join. And it ruled that court-mandated requirements for busing of students to achieve racial integration in public schools could be terminated if the school districts demonstrated that they had done everything practical to eliminate vestiges of past discrimination.

Vestiges of implicitly condoned racism remained evident in some government agencies and local police departments. Most notoriously, four white policemen were indicted in Los Angeles after they were videotaped brutally beating Rodney King, a black motorist whom they arrested after a high-speed chase. Although some defended the officers, who were dealing with an unruly lawbreaker, the severity of the beating, which was broadcast nationwide, outraged many Americans of all backgrounds, and the subsequent acquittal of the officers in 1992 sparked devastating riots in the city. Elsewhere, violence erupted between Hasidic Jews and African Americans in the Crown Heights section of Brooklyn after a car driven by a Hasidic Jew struck two black children, killing one. Three days of rioting followed as gangs of blacks shouting anti-Semitic slogans smashed Jewish-owned stores and killed a Jewish scholar visiting from Australia. Racial politics were interjected into professional football when the National Football League voted to move Super Bowl XXVII from Phoenix to Pasadena, California, to protest Arizona's failure to implement a paid state holiday commemorating the civil rights leader Martin Luther King, Jr. In Canada, the government agreed to permit indigenous Canadians to govern themselves.

Domestic violence and other violence against women remained a national concern. The prevalence of sexual assaults on women by friends and acquaintances drew public attention, as the term *date rape* entered the common parlance, and surveys indicated that 21 percent of all women questioned reported being harassed at work.[8] In Maryland, Governor William D. Schaefer commuted prison sentences of eight women who had been convicted of killing or assaulting men who had abused them.

The devastating impact of the AIDS epidemic, which began in 1983, continued to become more pronounced, especially within the high-profile arts and entertainment industries. Freddie Mercury, the flamboyant lead singer of the British rock group Queen and an avowed bisexual, died at age 45 of the disease; the British film director Tony Richardson died at age 63; and Magic Johnson, one of the most popular and most talented basketball players in National Basketball Association (NBA) history, announced that he was quitting the sport after testing positive for the AIDS virus, which he contracted through unprotected heterosexual sex. Additional dangers from AIDS became apparent when Kimberley Bergalis, a 23-year-old health worker, died after contracting the disease while having dental work performed by an infected dentist.

Though a study by the New York–based Alan Guttmacher Institute found that the overall abortion rate in the United States declined by 6 percent between 1980 and 1987,[9] abortion remained a contentious issue throughout the nation. Congress passed legislation allowing doctors at federally funded clinics to counsel women about abortion, but Bush vetoed the bill. The South Dakota legislature narrowly defeated one of the toughest antiabortion bills in the nation, through which all abortions would have been prohibited, except in cases of rape, incest, threat to the health of the mother, or severe handicap of the fetus. Governor George A. Sinner vetoed similar legislation in North Dakota, and Maryland enacted a law designed to protect women's right to abortion in the event that a new Supreme Court decision were to permit the individual states to make the procedure illegal. On the other hand, the Mississippi state legislature overrode a veto by Governor Ray Mabus in order to enact legislation that required doctors to provide information about the medical risks of and alternatives to abortion and mandated that women wait 24 hours after receiving the information before having the procedure. In an 8-1 decision, the Supreme Court of Canada ruled that a fetus is not a person and is therefore not entitled to legal protection until it has completely left its mother's body.

Throughout the 20th century American family units became increasingly smaller and more autonomous, as the extended family, which included parents, grandparents, and children living together or close by and regularly interacting as a social unit, fragmented. After World War II millions of so-called nuclear families, which consisted solely of parents and children who lived and functioned apart from grandparents, populated the American suburbs. Increasing divorce rates within nuclear families in the second half of the century, along with greater acceptance of single parenthood and nontraditional sexual and living arrangements, led, by 1991, to further fragmentation of the family, as evidenced by the 41 percent increase since 1980 in the number of single parents and 80 percent increase in that of unmarried couples living together. More than one-quarter of all babies in 1991 were born to single women.[10] More liberal sexual mores were also evident among teenagers, as a survey of more than 11,000 high school students conducted by the Centers for Disease Control showed that 54 percent had experienced sexual intercourse, including 40 percent of ninth graders and 72 percent of 12th graders. Sixty-one percent of boys and 48 percent of girls reported having had intercourse; 78 percent of those who were sexually active used some form of birth control. Four percent had contracted a sexually transmitted disease.[11]

BUSINESS

As part of a worldwide economic decline that was exacerbated by higher oil costs caused by the crisis in the Middle East, the U.S. economy began the year in a downturn that was marked by high inflation and significant job losses. In January, every sector except retailing and health services experienced job losses, and by December, the unemployment rate was at a five-and-a-half-year high, at 7.1 percent.[12] In addition, farm prices rose and additional S&Ls failed. By the end of the year, the United States was experiencing the recession that would go on to dominate presidential politics in the 1992 election. General Motors lost a world-record $4.5 billion in 1991. Although it earned $4 billion in overseas profits, these were offset by a loss of $8.5 billion in North America, where the automaker closed 21 plants and laid off 70,000 workers. Ford reported losing $2.3 billion, its largest decline ever, and IBM lost $564 million, its first annual loss.[13] The airlines, in particular, felt the impact of both increased costs and reduced public travel during wartime, and by the end of the year, two long-established Miami-based airlines went out of business. Eastern failed in January, and Pan Am, which had pioneered the aviation industry 64 years earlier, ceased operations in December. At the same time, inflation created additional strains to the economy. Even the cost of first-class postage rose almost 20 percent, from 25 cents to 29 cents. Nonetheless, although the unemployment rate rose from 6.1 percent to 6.7 percent, in other respects the economy improved from 1990, as inflation dropped from 5.4 percent to 4.2 percent, and the GNP rose from a stagnant 0.9 percent to 2.8 percent. The Dow Jones industrial average peaked at 3,169, 169 points higher than in 1990; it had a low of 2,470, 105 points higher than the low in 1990.[14]

The S&L scandal continued to deplete the public reserves as Congress approved a $78 billion funding package for the Resolution Trust Corporation, the agency charged with bailing out insolvent S&Ls. Moreover, the Bush administration diverted monies from the Federal Reserve to recapitalize the Federal Deposit Insurance Corporation's Bank Insurance Fund, which had been depleted by claims stemming from failed S&Ls.

Forbes magazine reported that although the family of the Wal-Mart founder Sam Moore Walton claimed total assets of $18.5 billion, the single wealthiest individual in the world was Taikichiro Mori, a Japanese real estate investor who had assets of $15 billion. He was followed by another Japanese investor, who had $14 billion in assets, and the United States–based Du Pont family, who had $10 billion. At the other end of the economic scale, workers receiving the minimum wage saw their income increase by 45 cents an hour, to $4.25. The so-called training wage, a minimum wage for teenagers, increased to $3.62 an hour.

Important international business developments included an agreement by Brazil, Argentina, Uruguay, and Paraguay to form the Southern Cone Common Market (Mercosur) in South America. Financial scandal intertwined with international intrigue, as the demise of the British-based Bank of Commerce and Credit International (BCCI) revealed instances of massive fraud, as well as revelations that the bank had been used by Arab terrorist groups. The controversial British publisher Robert Maxwell was found dead under suspicious circumstances aboard his yacht. After his death, the tycoon's international business empire collapsed amid accusations of massive fraud.

NATURE AND THE ENVIRONMENT

An 11-year study conducted by researchers at the University of California at Los Angeles concluded that prolonged exposure to air pollution can seriously harm lung tissue and cause deterioration of people's capacity to breathe. Other matters affecting the environment included a multinational treaty banning mining and oil exploration in the Antarctic for at least 50 years. Alaska and the U.S. federal government agreed to a plea bargain by the Exxon Corporation concerning the devastating 1989 oil spill from the *Exxon Valdez* tanker in Alaska's Prince William Sound. Exxon and a subsidiary agreed to pay a fine of $100 million, the largest ever assessed for pollution.

Among the year's natural disasters was a so-called perfect storm in the North Atlantic, the product of a rare confluence of three tumultuous weather systems that generated waves 10 stories high and winds 120 miles an hour. The October nor'easter sank the *Andrea Gail,* a commercial fishing boat with a six-man crew, which mistakenly headed toward its center while trying to outrun the tempest. Hurricane Bob, a category 2 hurricane, struck Rhode Island and damaged Cape Cod and southeast Massachusetts, destroying more than 50 homes and causing extensive erosion. A tropical storm in the Philippines unleashed floods that killed 4,000 people. Fires destroyed buildings and killed 19 people when they raged through the hills just beyond Berkeley and Oakland, California. Altogether, the Federal Emergency Management Agency (FEMA) estimated that it would spend $323.2 million from the President's Disaster Relief Fund for regions in the United States declared disaster areas.

SCIENCE

For the first time, scientists produced a significant amount of energy from the process of nuclear fusion. The joint effort by researchers of the European Community, Sweden, and Switzerland held out promise for a clean and inexpensive source of abundant energy that would be safer than existing processes for nuclear fission.

The possibility that life might exist elsewhere in the universe appeared more likely when a team of British astronomers published an article claiming to have discovered the first planet known to exist outside the solar system, a planet orbiting a pulsar, or dying star, some 30,000 light-years from Earth. The authors later retracted their finding, citing an error in their calculations, but later in the year, the American astronomer Alexander Wolszczan discovered two extrasolar planets orbiting a different pulsar—this one in the Earth's own galaxy, the Milky Way. Wolszczan published the results in January 1992. Although it was deemed very unlikely that life would be sustainable on a planet orbiting a dying star, the discoveries gave credence to the hypothesis that other stars also have planetary systems and that planets may, in fact, be common objects in the universe.

Apple and IBM agreed to make their computers compatible, with interchangeable programs and components, thereby rectifying a significant impediment to computer users who exchanged software and other computer files. The companies also agreed to develop a powerful new generation of microprocessors.

Medical studies showed that regular use of aspirin reduced the risk of death from colon cancer; the use of estrogen by women after menopause reduced their risk of heart disease by almost 50 percent; prostate-specific antigen (PSA) tests, combined with a rectal examination, were highly effective in the early detection of prostate cancer in men; and taxol, a derivative from the yew tree, was effective in treating lung, breast, and ovarian cancers. Medical researchers reported at the First International Symposium on the Psychological and Pharmacological Effects of Camellia Sinensis [tea] that green tea contains a strong agent that retards cancer. A successful transplant of a small intestine was performed at the University of Pittsburgh, and a successful heart surgery was performed on a fetus within the womb. On the other hand, concerns arose that Halcion, a tranquilizer widely prescribed for treating chronic insomnia, might be connected to a syndrome that produced depression, amnesia, hallucinations, and anxiety. The drug was subsequently removed from the market in the United Kingdom, Brazil, Argentina, Norway, Denmark, and the Netherlands. The United States, Canada, and other nations reduced the recommended dosage and duration of treatment and changed the labeling to increase users' awareness of possible adverse side effects.

The well-preserved 4,000-year-old remains of a Bronze Age hunter were discovered in the Austrian Alps.

LITERATURE, THE ARTS, SPORTS, AND POPULAR CULTURE

Violence, a persistent feature of many aspects of American society in 1991, features prominently in the mass culture as well, in such movies as *The Silence of the Lambs,* which won Academy Awards for best picture, best director (Jonathan Demme), best actress (Jodie Foster), and best actor (Anthony Hopkins); Barry Levinson's *Bugsy;* James Cameron's *Terminator 2: Judgment Day;* and Ridley Scott's *Thelma & Louise,* which starred Susan Sarandon and Geena Davis as working-class buddies who become fugitives from justice when one kills a man after he sexually assaults the other. Many feminist viewers applauded the growth in strength, confidence, and independence experienced by the protagonists as they assert themselves, sometimes violently, against men who harass or threaten them. Other viewers deplored the film's celebration of what they perceived as male bashing and lawlessness. Spike Lee's *Jungle Fever,* which features stunning, almost mythic visuals of an inner-city crack house, examines the pressures faced by interracial couples, and John Singleton's *Boyz N the Hood,* a film about violent life in inner-city Los Angeles, prompted gang-related violence throughout the country, including a shooting death outside Chicago, despite the director's intention to "increase the peace" and repudiate gang culture. David Mamet's *Homicide* presents the social, as well as forensic, problems of solving the murder of an elderly Jewish woman in a predominantly African-American neighborhood. Oliver Stone's *JFK,* a controversial revisionist account of the assassination of President John F. Kennedy, centers on one of the most far-reaching acts of violence in America's recent political history.

Other notable films of the year included Terry Gilliam's *The Fisher King,* which starred Robin Williams and Jeff Bridges in a bizarre but life-affirming treatment of the medieval quest for the Holy Grail. Gus Van Sant, Jr.'s, *My Own Private Idaho,* which invokes William Shakespeare's *Henry IV* plays, starred River Phoenix as a lonesome young hustler suffering from nacrolepsy, who is befriended by the son of the mayor of Portland, Oregon, played by Keanu Reeves. Billy Crystal and Jack Palance starred in *City Slickers,* a comedy that appealed to the mystique of the Old West as urban yuppies address their midlife crises by joining an old-fashioned cattle drive. In Joel Coen's *Barton*

Fink, an independently made film that won the grand prize at the 1991 Cannes Film Festival, Jon Turturro plays a gifted playwright who, while struggling to succeed as a Hollywood screenwriter, provokes the wrath of his neighbor, a mass murderer played by John Goodman, whose pride is stung by the writer's elitism and narcissism. Also set during the 1930s Great Depression, John Avnet's *Fried Green Tomatoes,* which starred Jessica Tandy and Kathy Bates, depicts a storyteller whose tales heal and encourage the women she befriends. As did *Thelma & Louise,* the movie struck an unexpectedly strong chord among many female viewers, and it received Academy Award nominations for best supporting actress (Tandy) and best adapted screenplay (Fannie Flagg and Carol Sobieski). The actress Demi Moore appeared nude on the cover of the August issue of *Vanity Fair* magazine while eight months pregnant, in an apparent effort to demonstrate the beauty of pregnancy. Soon afterward, her husband, actor Bruce Willis, appeared on the cover of *Spy* magazine, made up also to appear several months pregnant.

Expressions of violence also extended to music, particularly in gangsta rap, which continued to gain popularity as it both revealed and reveled in the violent, antiauthoritarian gang culture of the inner cities. The antiestablishment message of grunge rock gained national prominence when Kurt Cobain's Seattle-based band Nirvana sold 10 million copies of its album *Nevermind,* featuring the hit single "Smells Like Teen Spirit," and the Smashing Pumpkins issued their hit album *Gish,* named after the silent film star Lillian Gish. A synthesis of punk, heavy metal, and contemporary alternative music modes, grunge's anticorporate, antimaterialistic message, and its expressions of despair, self-loathing, and absence of personal control over life, attracted large followings among disaffected Generation Xers—the generation, born in the 1960s, that followed the post–World War II baby boom generation.[15]

Michael Jackson, a far more mainstream figure who was then one of the most popular musicians in the world, was pressured to cut a section from his single "Black or White" that featured his smashing a car window with a crowbar and grabbing his crotch, because some viewers found the scene excessively lewd and violent. Both Jackson and his sister, Janet Jackson, signed record-setting contracts with recording studios that called for each artist to receive in excess of $40 million for making multiple albums. Michael Jackson's contract also called on him to form his own label for promoting the work of new artists.

Among the most popular albums of the year were Madonna's *The Immaculate Collection,* Bonnie Raitt's *Luck of the Draw,* Guns N' Roses's *Use Your Illusion I* and *II,* and *Mariah Carey,* by Mariah Carey. Natalie Cole won a Grammy Award for best album for *Unforgettable, with You,* which featured her Grammy-winning single "Unforgettable," for which she used editing technology to produce a duet with her late father, Nat "King" Cole, who originally made the song famous. The album sold some 14 million copies. Women made many of the other top hit singles of the year, including Whitney Houston's "All the Man I Need," Paula Abdul's "Rush Rush," and Bette Middler's "From a Distance."

Violence directly invaded the realm of literature when two of the translators of Salman Rushdie's *Satanic Verses* were attacked, presumably by Iranian agents. Hitoshi Igarashi, the novel's Japanese translator, was murdered in Tokyo less than two weeks after the book's Italian translator was stabbed by an Iranian

who demanded Rushdie's address. Iran's late religious leader Ayatollah Ruhollah Khomeini had condemned Rushdie to death in 1989 for writing the novel,
which Khomeini maintained insulted Islam. Rushdie, who was living in hiding, later made his first trip outside Britain since 1989, when he appeared, with
no prior announcement, at a forum on the First Amendment at Columbia
University's Graduate School of Journalism in New York. The South African
novelist Nadine Gordimer, who became the seventh woman to win the Nobel
Prize in literature, was honored for her body of work revealing the abuses of
apartheid. The crime writers Carl Hiaasen (*Native Tongue*), James W. Hall (*Bones
of Coral*), and Les Standiford (*Spill*) wove gruesome tales of violence and retribution around biological warfare, ecoterrorism, corporate greed, and other top-
ical misdeeds. Less focused on brutality, Douglas Coupland's *Generation X: Tales
for an Accelerated Culture* brought attention to the special trials and tribulations
faced by the generation newly emerging in the 1990s. The Persian Gulf War
made the interplay between the modern West and medieval Baghdad in John
Barth's *The Last Voyage of Somebody the Sailor* resonate in new, unanticipated
ways.

Violence against women is the subject of Susan Faludi's critically acclaimed
nonfiction book *Backlash: The Undeclared War against American Women*. Author
Kitty Kelley published *Nancy Reagan: The Unauthorized Biography,* a controversial, unflattering, unauthorized representation of the former first lady, which
became one of the fastest-selling books in American publishing history.
Because Ronald Reagan remained a popular figure among many Americans,
Kelley's allegations that he and his wife smoked marijuana when he was governor of California and that Nancy Reagan controlled his agenda when he was
president were vehemently denied by many of his supporters, as well as by the
Reagans themselves. Jane Smiley won the Pulitzer Prize in fiction for *A Thou-
sand Acres,* a retelling of Shakespeare's *King Lear* set in an Iowa farm, and Daniel
Yergin won the prize in nonfiction for his timely book, *The Prize: The Epic
Quest for Oil, Money, and Power.*

Neil Simon's *Lost in Yonkers* won the Pulitzer Prize in drama and the Tony
Award for its story about two young boys compelled to live with their tyranni-
cal grandmother while their father takes a job in another state. *The Will Rogers
Follies,* based on the popular wry social commentator of the Great Depression
era, won the Tony Award as best musical. *Miss Saigon,* adapted by Claude-
Michel Schönberg, Richard Maltby, Jr., and Alain Boubil from Giacomo Puccini's 1904 opera *Madama Butterfly* and set during and after the Vietnam War, was
another successful musical which opened on Broadway in 1991. *Riverdance,* an
Irish dance revue, fused ancient Celtic musical traditions with contemporary
sensibilities.

Museum exhibitions continued to fuel political dissension. "The West as
America: Reinterpreting Images of the Frontier," an exhibition curated by
William Truettner at the National Museum of American Art in Washington,
D.C., challenged more traditional, heroic representations of the white settlers in
America by highlighting the violence and racism exhibited by a significant
number of them. Hostile audience response compelled Truettner to modify or
replace certain exhibition labels. Shown in Chicago and Los Angeles, "Degenerate Art: The Fate of the Avant-Garde in Nazi Germany" brought a different
awareness of the problem of censoring and politicizing art. The philanthropist

Walter H. Annenberg announced his intention to bequeath his $1 billion art collection to the Metropolitan Museum of Art in New York City, and a painting by Vincent van Gogh that had been discovered on the wall of a private home in Milwaukee sold for $1.4 million at auction.

Coverage of the Persian Gulf War was the year's major development on television. *Time* magazine named as its man of the year Ted Turner, the founder of CNN. Employing new satellite technology, CNN provided virtually continuous coverage of the ongoing crisis, and during the early part of the war CNN journalists were permitted to file reports from Iraq. The network's reporting from Baghdad was so timely that even some of the government decision-makers relied on it for up-to-date intelligence. Such live coverage from the enemy capital during wartime was unprecedented, as viewers throughout the world were able to watch a war commence when reporters in Baghdad broadcast live video coverage of the initial air raids on the morning of January 17.

On the other hand, strict military censorship limited U.S. reporters' access to information and to the battlefield to a far greater extent than in previous wars, and Iraqi censorship skewed reporting from Baghdad. Indeed, both the Iraqis and the allies were aware of the impact of television on public support for the war; both tried to take advantage of it; and actions of both were influenced by it. For instance, after an American attack on an Iraqi bomb shelter on February 13 killed more than 200 civilians, Iraq accused the allies of targeting noncombatants. CNN broadcast images of the ruined Al Firdos bunker and the casualties, and its on-the-spot reporter, Peter Arnett, reported the Iraqi government's insistence that the facility had been used solely as a civilian bomb shelter. Arnett added that he personally could perceive no evidence of any military function. Despite the fact that CNN later presented military experts who pointed out considerable evidence suggesting that the bunker had, in fact, also been a military command and control facility, Iraq scored a public relations victory, and allied targeting practices were subsequently altered. The adverse television coverage of this event also increased the pressure to end the air campaign and begin the ground war. Similarly, anticipation of the public response to televised carnage on the so-called Highway to Hell, in which hundreds of Iraqis were killed while fleeing Kuwait on February 26 and 27, influenced Bush's decision to terminate the fighting soon afterward, before the Iraqi forces were entirely destroyed.

Throughout the war administration officials and military officers briefed the public, and several generals emerged as admired media figures who held their own against a sometimes combative press corps. Among these were Schwarzkopf; Lieutenant General Thomas Kelly, the Joint Chiefs of Staff operations officer; and the U.S. Marine brigadier general Richard Neal. In addition to providing basic information, these briefings were designed to build public confidence and sustain support, and the impressive, computerized weaponry received considerable attention. In his most memorable briefing Schwarzkopf showed video footage of a video-guided "smart bomb" entering the headquarters of his Iraqi counterpart. The television display of the high-tech U.S. arsenal led many Americans at home to liken their experience of the war to a sophisticated video game, a perception that lent an aspect of unreality to the death and devastation on the battlegrounds. Moreover, administration officials further sanitized the war by not showing dead bodies or providing the body counts that had been a daily feature of Vietnam War reporting.

One of the most controversial aspects of the media coverage was the restriction of reporters' movement and access to information. These policies resulted from a report by the Sidle Commission about the 1983 Grenada invasion, in which press access to military operations was also restricted. Many observers believe that these policies were meant to prevent the kind of negative reporting that many in the government and military believed influenced the public against the Vietnam War in the 1960s and 1970s. Instead of having open access to the battlefield, as they had in Vietnam, journalists reporting on Grenada and the Persian Gulf War were restricted to limited-sized press pools supervised by military personnel.

Other events that garnered large audiences for live television coverage of history in the making included the Soviet coup against Gorbachev, Clarence Thomas and Anita Hill's testimonies before Congress, and the rape trial of William Kennedy Smith, nephew of Senator Edward Kennedy and the late president John F. Kennedy.

Perhaps because the public sought relief from the war news, comedies were the most popular television shows of the year. Although the top-rated show of the fall season was CBS's long-running newsmagazine *60 Minutes,* the next five were comedies: *Roseanne; Murphy Brown; Cheers,* which won the 1991 Emmy Award for outstanding comedy series; *Home Improvement;* and *Designing Women. Northern Exposure* a quirky new dramatic series about eccentric characters in small-town Alaska, won the Emmy Award in 1992 for the 1991–92 season. *L.A. Law* repeated as the Emmy winner in 1991, for the 1990–91 season. Disappointing the longtime guest host David Letterman, NBC selected comedian Jay Leno to replace Johnny Carson as host of *The Tonight Show,* after Carson announced his plans to retire in 1992. Letterman subsequently hosted a competing show on CBS.

In sports, the New York Giants concluded the 1990 football season in January 1991, when they defeated the Buffalo Bills 20-19 in Super Bowl XXV, the most closely matched Super Bowl ever played. Buffalo missed a potential game-winning field goal with four seconds left to play. Led by the most valuable player (MVP) running back Thurman Thomas, Buffalo again won the 1991 American Football Conference title but lost in Super Bowl XXVI to the Washington Redskins in January 1992. By refusing to hear the Players Association's challenge to the league's free agency system, the Supreme Court let stand a lower court ruling that the National Football League (NFL) was immune to antitrust action. The World League of American Football, a European and North American affiliate of the NFL, began playing during the NFL's off-season in the spring and summer. The Associated Press named the University of Miami the best college team for the 1991 season, and the United Press International poll chose the University of Washington. Both teams had a perfect 11-0 record. The University of Michigan's Desmond Howard won the Heisman Trophy.

Interest in Major League Baseball remained strong in the United States and Canada, as total attendance rose by 3 percent from 1990 to 56,880,512 admissions,[16] and the Toronto Blue Jays became the first team to attract more than 4 million fans. The Blue Jays, however, lost the American League championship to the Minnesota Twins, who went on to win the World Series by defeating the Atlanta Braves in the 10th inning of the seventh game. The Twins and the

Braves were the first teams to go from last place to first in a single year. Atlanta's Terry Pendleton and Baltimore's Cal Ripken, Jr., won the National and American League MVP awards, respectively, and Atlanta's Tom Glavine and Boston's Roger Clemens won the Cy Young Award for best pitcher in each league. Jose Conseco of the Oakland Athletics and the Detroit Tiger Cecil Fielder, who led the Major Leagues in 1990, shared the 1991 home run championship with 44 apiece. Rickey Henderson of the Oakland Athletics broke Lou Brock's record when he stole his 939th base in a game against the New York Yankees, and the Texas Ranger Nolan Ryan recorded his seventh career no-hitter when he shut out the hot-hitting Blue Jays. No other pitcher in the modern era had previously thrown more than four career no-hitters (Sandy Koufax). Retired batting champion Rod Carew and retired pitchers Ferguson Jenkins and Gaylord Perry were enshrined in Major League Baseball's Hall of Fame, while Pete Rose, baseball's all-time leader in hits and games played, was barred from eligibility for the Hall as a result of prior disciplinary action taken for his gambling on baseball.

The perennial star Magic Johnson quit playing professional basketball after revealing that he had contracted AIDS through heterosexual sex. Johnson's longtime rival, Larry Bird of the Boston Celtics, became the fifth player in NBA history to score 20,000 points in his career, and 5,000 rebounds and 5,000 assists. But the Chicago Bulls, led by MVP Michael Jordan, defeated Johnson's Los Angeles Lakers to win their first league championship. Jordan and the Bulls went on to dominate the NBA throughout most of the 1990s. Duke University won the closely watched college championship, and Larry Johnson of the University of Nevada at Las Vegas was the college player of the year.

The Pittsburgh Penguins won their first Stanley Cup when they defeated the Minnesota North Stars in the National Hockey League finals. Stephan Edberg and Monica Seles won the singles championships in the U.S. Tennis Open, and Payne Stewart won the United States Golf Association (USGA) Open. The U.S. women's team won its first World Cup in soccer in a tournament played in China. Strike the Gold, ridden by Chris Antley, prevailed in the Kentucky Derby, and the former world heavyweight boxing champion Mike Tyson was indicted on charges of raping an 18-year-old contestant in the Miss Black America beauty pageant. Tyson's successor, Evander Holyfield, retained the title after scoring a technical knockout of Bert Cooper.

CHRONICLE OF EVENTS

January 1: By this date 325,000 U.S. troops are stationed in the Middle East.

January 4: The United States and Iraq agree to a U.S. proposal that Iraqi foreign minister Tariq Aziz and U.S. secretary of state James Baker hold talks January 9 in Geneva, Switzerland.

January 7: Israeli foreign minister David Levy states that Israel is willing to enter a comprehensive Middle East peace process after the Gulf crisis has been resolved.

January 7: U.S. intelligence estimates that Iraq has deployed 35 divisions, consisting of 542,000 troops, 4,300 tanks, and 3,100 pieces of artillery in the Kuwaiti theater of operations.

January 9: The Geneva meeting of Baker and Aziz takes place but yields no results.

January 10: The French defense minister, Jean-Pierre Chevènement, calls for the United States to agree to an international peace conference on the Middle East as a face-saving mechanism that will allow Saddam Hussein to withdraw from Kuwait before the January 15 deadline.

January 11: Saddam Hussein once more calls for an Islamic holy war and urges that Islamic leaders prepare their followers for the Great Mother of All Battles.

January 11: Saudi Arabia agrees to pay up to half the cost of deploying U.S. forces in the Gulf.

January 12: Congress votes to permit the use of military force to remove Iraq from Kuwait 52-47 in the Senate and 250-183 in the House.

The United States rejects France's proposal for an international peace conference on the Middle East.

January 13: First Lady Barbara Bush breaks her leg in a sledding accident.

January 15: France proposes that the Security Council hold an international conference on the Palestinian situation if Iraq agrees to withdraw from Kuwait. The United States, Great Britain, and the Soviet Union reject the plan.

January 16: An hour before Desert Storm commences, Baker notifies Soviet premier Gorbachev, who, in turn, warns Saddam Hussein to withdraw from Kuwait immediately.

January 16: Operation Desert Storm begins at 5:00 P.M. EST (1:00 A.M. January 17, local time), when allied missiles strike at early warning radar sites in Iraq.

January 17: The air assault on Baghdad is broadcast live by CNN camera crews and CNN correspondents Bernard Shaw, John Holliman, and Peter Arnett.

After destroying Iraqi surface-to-air missiles in Kuwait, the United States launches its first long-range precision tactical missile strike in history. As of this date, 425,000 U.S. troops are in the region, along with ground forces of 18 other countries and ships of 13 others.

January 18: Iraq launches its first Scud missile attack against Israel, injuring 12 civilians. In response American jets attack the missile launching sites. During the war a total of 40 Scuds are launched against Israel, killing four civilians and wounding 289.

January 18: The Miami-based Eastern Airlines ceases operations.

Virtually undetectable Stealth F-117A bombers dropped laser-guided "smart bombs" on Iraqi targets. *(U.S. Department of Defense)*

January 18: An asteroid has a near miss with Earth.

January 20: Schwarzkopf reports that coalition bombers have "thoroughly damaged" Iraq's nuclear research reactors.

Saddam Hussein asks other Arabs to join in a *jihad,* a holy war, against the allies.

A mysterious explosion above Khafji, Saudi Arabia, produces a mist that burns the skin of personnel on the ground and triggers chemical alarms. The Pentagon later claims the mist was rocket propellant from an Iraqi Scud missile that detonated in the air, but some veterans who were present believe the mist was an Iraqi gas attack.

President François Mitterrand announces that France will attack Iraq if necessary.

January 20: Some 100,000 demonstrators in Moscow protest the Soviet army's military intervention in Lithuania, where violence earlier erupted over Lithuania's desire for sovereignty.

January 21: Iraq announces that prisoners of war (POWs) will be used as human shields around strategic targets inside Iraq.

January 22: Iraq ignites oil storage tanks in Kuwait at Mina Abdullah, Ash Shuaiba, and Wafra. By the end of the war more than 450 oil wells will be ignited.

January 22: Pope John Paul II issues an encyclical urging Roman Catholics to spread Christian doctrine throughout the world, even in Islamic countries where it is forbidden. The pope also criticizes religious relativism among Christians who maintain that one religion is as good as another.

January 23: Japan agrees to increase its support for the war by $9 billion.

January 24: Navy sea, air, and land (SEAL) teams reclaim the first piece of Kuwaiti territory when they capture Qaruh Island, take 67 prisoners, and raise the Kuwaiti flag.

In the only attempted Iraqi offensive air strike of the war, two Iraqi Mirage jets attack allied ships in the Persian Gulf, but a Saudi fighter shoots them down. The Canadian Air Force participates in its first combat mission since World War II.

January 25: Iraq begins releasing millions of barrels of oil from Kuwait's Sea Island oil tanker terminal into the Persian Gulf. Within two days the oil slick is 35 miles long and 10 miles wide.

January 26: The coalition air campaign attacks military storage facilities and Republican Guard troop fortifications to prepare the battlefield for the ground attack.

More than 20 Iraqi warplanes flee to Iran. Eventually, more than 80 planes—10 percent of the Iraqi air force—manage to escape destruction by flying to Iran, where they are all impounded.

January 26: Somalia's dictator, 80-year-old General Mohammed Siad Barre, flees Mogadishu, leaving the city in a state of chaos.

January 27: Schwarzkopf announces that the coalition has achieved air supremacy. This is accomplished against some of the most heavily defended airspace in the history of warfare.

U.S. Air Force jets use laser-guided bombs to sever the manifold pipelines feeding the oil spill from Kuwait's Sea Island oil tanker terminal.

January 27: The New York Giants defeat the Buffalo Bills 20-19 to win football's Super Bowl XXV.

January 29: Iraqi launches its only ground offensive of the war, as armored divisions invade border regions in Saudi Arabia near the coast. U.S. Marines stop the attack, but 13 marines are killed, 11 by friendly fire from their own troops. Another Iraqi force occupies the abandoned Saudi town of Khafji, trapping two marine reconnaissance teams inside. The marines hide in houses and cellars for almost two days, while ordering "danger close" fire support and close air support to fight off the Iraqis.

Iraqi soldiers capture Army Specialists Melissa Rathbun-Nealy and David Lockett when they inadvertently drive their truck into Iraqi-occupied Khafji. Rathbun-Nealy, the driver, becomes the first female POW.

January 29: Chevènement resigns in opposition to Mitterrand's support of the war.

January 30: Oil from the Sea Island terminal stops flowing into the Persian Gulf.

January 31: After suffering heavy casualties, Iraq withdraws its troops from the Saudi border areas they occupied on January 29.

Using intelligence obtained from the Kuwaiti resistance, a U.S. Marine jet drops a laser-guided smart bomb on a building near Ash Shuaiba where high-ranking Iraqi generals are meeting. The commander of Iraq's III Corps is killed.

In Kuwait, 14 Americans are killed when their helicopter crashes into the Persian Gulf. This is the greatest number of U.S. casualties in a single incident during the air campaign and the second-highest number of U.S. combat deaths due to a single cause in Operation Desert Storm.

January 31: The U.S. State Department announces that 70 terrorist attacks have been conducted against coalition countries.

February 1: Albania and the United States restore diplomatic relations after 52 years.

February 2: By this date all 13 of Iraq's ships capable of firing antiship missiles and all of its patrol boats have been damaged or destroyed, except one that escaped to Iran. The Iraqi navy is judged to be no longer combat-effective.

February 3: The U.S. Army VIIth Corps completes its shift 150 miles to the west, and the XVIII Airborne Corps completes its western redeployment 250 miles inland. They then prepare for the ground offensive.

For the first time, a remotely piloted vehicle (RPV) is used in combat to spot gunfire.

February 4: Winnie Mandela, wife of Nelson Mandela, stands trial in South Africa for complicity in the kidnapping and beating of four black youths.

February 5: Two thousand retired marines below the age of 60 are called to active duty.

February 5: General Motors lays off 15,000 workers after a large decline in car sales.

February 7: Jean-Bertrand Aristide, a Roman Catholic priest and Haiti's first democratically elected president, takes office.

February 9: Bush approves Schwarzkopf's recommendation that the ground attack begin between February 21 and 24.

February 11: 300 Afghani Mujahidin soldiers join the coalition against Iraq. By this date 510,000 U.S. troops are committed to the war.

February 12: The Soviet diplomat Yevgeni Primakov meets with Saddam Hussein and tries, but fails, to convince him to withdraw from Kuwait before the ground offensive begins.

February 13: U.S. precision bombs kill 204 noncombatants when they strike the Al Firdos bunker in Baghdad. The United States maintains the bunker was a camouflaged fortified command and control facility, but Iraq insists it was solely a civilian bomb shelter.

February 15: Cuban president Fidel Castro asserts his support of Iraq.

February 19: Iraq announces that it will accept a Soviet peace proposal calling for it to withdraw immediately from Kuwait and for the coalition to halt its attacks and void all UN resolutions against Iraq. Bush rejects the proposal.

February 19: Boris Yeltsin criticizes Gorbachev's vast powers and policies and calls for his resignation.

February 21: Aziz returns to Moscow and negotiates a new eight-point plan with Gorbachev.

February 22: Bush delivers an ultimatum that Iraq must begin a large-scale withdrawal from Kuwait by noon (EST) the following day and complete the evacuation within one week or face a ground war.

February 23: After Iraq fails to withdraw by noon, Bush authorizes Schwarzkopf to commence a ground campaign.

February 24: At 4:00 A.M. local time forces from the United States, Great Britain, France, Kuwait, Saudi Arabia, United Arab Emirates, Bahrain, Qatar, Oman, Syria, and Egypt initiate a ground offensive against Iraq.

February 25: After determining that the Iraqis are not counterattacking, Schwarzkopf decides to cut off and destroy the retreating Republican Guard. In the most decisive military maneuver in Desert Storm, he orders the VII Corps to begin to turn clockwise to the east to attack Republican Guard tanks and armored vehicles.

Farther to the west, the 24th Mechanized Infantry Division concludes its drive northward into the Euphrates River valley near Nasiriya. Between the afternoons of February 24 and 25, the division covers almost 150 miles in 24 hours, faster than any mechanized ground force had ever traveled during warfare. Meanwhile, the 1st Infantry Division completes breaching the Iraqi defenses, and the British 1st Armoured Division moves through newly opened lanes and turns east, securing the allies' southern flank.

In Kuwait, the first Marine Expeditionary Force wins decisive tank battles against stiff Iraqi resistance near the burning Burqan oil field. It then proceeds toward its final objective, Kuwait International Airport and the suburb of Al-Jahra. Late that night marine aircraft detect Iraqi convoys fleeing Kuwait City, and throughout the next two days they attack trucks, private cars, and other vehicles carrying fleeing Iraqi soldiers, damaging and destroying 3,000–4,000 vehicles along the so-called Highway to Hell.

In Dhahran, Saudi Arabia, debris from an exploding Scud missile kills 28 U.S. Army Reserve personnel from the 14th Quartermaster Detachment and wounds

The greatest number of U.S. casualties from a single incident occurred on February 25, 1991, when an Iraqi Scud missile struck a warehouse in Dhahran, Saudi Arabia. *(U.S. Department of Defense)*

100—the highest death toll for coalition forces in any single incident.

February 25: The Warsaw Pact, a cold-war alliance of Eastern European Communist regimes, votes to dissolve its military structures by March 31.

February 26: Saddam Hussein announces that Iraq is withdrawing its troops from Kuwait. Insisting that the Iraqi pullback is a military retreat, not a withdrawal, Bush vows to continue prosecuting the war. By the end of the day, the allies have destroyed more than 21 Iraqi divisions.

The U.S. 24th Mechanized Infantry Division seals off the Euphrates River valley by cutting off the strategic Highway 8. The XVIIth Corps and the British 1st Armoured Division begin their assaults against the Republican Guard's armored divisions in the largest tank battle since World War II.

In the desert to the west, the French 6th Light Armored Division captures the strategic As Salman airfield and then joins the U.S. 101st Airborne Division in the Euphrates River valley. Less than two Iraqi brigades now stand between the allied forces and Baghdad.

In Kuwait, throngs of Iraqi soldiers surrender to the 1st Marine Division as it proceeds toward Kuwait City. The 2nd Marine Division captures the suburb of Al-Jahra after heavy resistance. After an afternoon tank battle, 12 marines of the Second Force Reconnaissance unit become the first Americans to enter Kuwait City, where they recapture the U.S. embassy.

February 27: The 1st Marine Division captures Kuwait International Airport.

After overwhelming allied victories on the battlefield, Bush declares that Kuwait has been liberated, Iraq has been defeated, and all coalition offensive combat operations will cease at midnight EST (8:00 A.M. February 28, local time). In reply, Iraq declares its intention to comply with the terms of a UN cease-fire.

February 28: At 8:00 A.M. local time (midnight February 27 EST) the cease-fire takes effect.

February 28: Christian Brando, son of the actor Marlon Brando, is jailed for 10 years for the 1990 murder of his half sister's lover.

March 1: Iraq officially agrees to abide by Security Council Resolution 660 calling for it to withdraw from Kuwait. The U.S., British, French, and Canadian embassies reopen in Kuwait, and the international airport becomes operational.

An Iraqi brigade attacks the 3rd Armored Cavalry Regiment, which destroys the unit in an hour-long battle near the Rumalia oil field.

March 2: The Security Council passes Resolution 686 setting down the conditions for a cease-fire.

March 3: Iraqi generals meet with Schwarzkopf and other coalition military leaders. They accept the UN's terms for a cease-fire and agree to release some POWs immediately.

Inspired by Bush's call for Iraqi citizens to overthrow Saddam Hussein, Shiite Muslims in southern Iraq rebel and take control of several areas, including Nasiriyah.

March 3: Four white Los Angeles policemen are caught on videotape brutally beating Rodney King, a 25-year-old black motorist. The officers are indicted on March 15.

March 5: Kurds in northern Iraq revolt.

March 7: Saddam Hussein orders the Republican Guard to suppress both the Shiite and Kurdish insurrections.

March 8: Operation Desert Farewell begins as the first 5,000 American troops leave for home. The harbor of Kuwait City reopens after two weeks of minesweeping.

March 10: The United States announces that it will not actively support the rebellions against Saddam Hussein because these are "Iraqi internal affairs."

March 12: The United States and the PLO conduct high-level talks for the first time since summer 1990.

March 13: The Exxon Corporation pleads guilty to four misdemeanor environmental charges and agrees to pay $100 million in fines for pollution caused by the 1989 *Exxon Valdez* oil tanker spill in Prince William Sound, Alaska.

March 13: President Bush and Canadian prime minister Brian Mulroney meet in Ottawa, where they discuss Bush's opposition to Mulroney's proposal for international talks on controlling weapons of mass destruction. Although they fail to find common ground on that topic, they sign an accord on acid rain.

March 14: The emir of Kuwait, Sheik Jaber Al-Sabah, returns to Kuwait City from his exile in Saudi Arabia.

March 20: The popular singer Michael Jackson signs a $1 billion multiyear contract with Sony.

March 20: The Cuban air force pilot Major Orestes Froilán Lorenzo Pérez flies his fighter plane beneath U.S. radar and lands at the U.S. naval station in Key West, Florida, where he defects.

March 20–21: April Glaspie, the outgoing U.S. ambassador to Iraq, testifies before the Senate Foreign Relations Committee, breaking an almost eight-month silence over the administration's response to Iraqi provocations against Kuwait immediately before Iraq's invasion of Kuwait.

March 22: The Security Council ends its embargo on food shipments to Iraq and eases sanctions on other forms of humanitarian aid.

March 26: The Bush administration formally refuses to aid Iraqi rebels seeking to overthrow Saddam Hussein.

March 27: The United States announces that in compliance with the 1987 U.S.-Soviet INF treaty, it has withdrawn the last of its medium-range nuclear missiles from Europe.

March 28: Florida's former governor, Bob Martinez, replaces William J. Bennett as so-called drug czar—director of national drug control policy.

March 28: Iraqi troops loyal to Saddam Hussein suppress the Shiite rebellion when they recapture the city of Kerbala.

April 1: The minimum wage increases from $3.80 to $4.25 per hour.

April 3: Security Council Resolution 687 establishes the terms for the formal cessation of hostilities.

April 3: Yugoslavia sends troops to suppress an independence movement in Croatia.

April 7: The United States inaugurates Operation Provide Comfort to send humanitarian aid and security assistance to Kurds in northern Iraq.

April 9: The Security Council passes Resolution 689 establishing an observer mission to monitor the permanent cease-fire.

April 9: The Republic of Georgia, birthplace of Joseph Stalin, votes for independence from the Soviet Union.

April 11: The Security Council announces that Operation Desert Storm has officially concluded.

April 12: Turkey votes to rescind a 1983 law forbidding Kurds to speak the Kurdish language.

April 13: The Kurdish rebellion in northern Iraq ends after defeats that create some 2 million Kurdish refugees.

April 18: Iraq reports that it still has 10,000 nerve-gas warheads, 1,000 tons of mustard and nerve gas, 1,500 chemical weapons, and 30 Scud missiles.

April 20: British, French, and U.S. troops begin erecting refugee camps for 500,000 displaced Kurds.

April 26: More than 70 tornadoes sweep through Kansas, killing 26.

May 3: Bush denies allegations that he played an active role in the 1980s Iran-contra scandal.

May 4: Bush is hospitalized for an erratic heartbeat after experiencing fatigue and shortness of breath while jogging. He is released on May 6.

May 7: The United States completes its withdrawal of forces from southern Iraq.

May 8: William H. Webster resigns as director of the Central Intelligence Agency (CIA), a post he has held since 1987.

May 10: To address the city's financial crisis, New York's mayor, David Dinkins, presents a so-called doomsday budget that will cut $1.5 billion and lay off 29,000 workers, including 2,800 teachers.

May 18: The restored Kuwaiti government begins trials of 200 alleged collaborators, most of whom are convicted and sentenced to death.

May 23–24: Both houses of Congress vote to give Bush so-called fast track authority to negotiate international trade agreements.

May 25: Cuba completes its troop withdrawal from Angola.

May 25: The Pittsburgh Penguins defeat the Minnesota North Stars to claim their first National Hockey League (NHL) championship.

May 30: A study conducted by the Environmental Protection Agency concludes that secondhand cigarette smoke kills 53,000 nonsmoking Americans annually, including 37,000 who die of heart disease.

May 31: India's premier, Rajiv Gandhi, is assassinated by a suicide bomber.

May 31: Rival factions end Angola's 16-year civil war when they sign a cease-fire and agree to establish a democracy.

June 6: The jazz pioneer Stan Getz dies at age 64.

June 8: Louisiana State University defeats Wichita State 6-3 to win the College World Series.

June 10: Crowds cheer troops returning from the war against Iraq as they parade down Broadway in New York City.

June 12: The Chicago Bulls defeat the Los Angeles Lakers to claim their first NBA championship.

June 13: Running as an independent party candidate, Boris Yeltsin defeats the Communist Party candidate in Russia's first popular presidential election.

June 17: South Africa's parliament repeals the 1950 Population Registration Act, which made apartheid official policy.

June 19: Pablo Escobar, the head of a powerful drug cartel in Medellín, surrenders to Colombian police.

June 21: In Germany, citizens vote to restore Berlin as the newly reunited nation's capital.

June 25: Croatia and Slovenia declare their independence from the Federal Republic of Yugoslavia. In response, Premier Slobodan Milošević orders Yugoslav forces, composed primarily of Serbs, to advance on the capital cities, Zagreb and Ljubljana.

June 26: In response to objections by human rights organizations and world governments, Kuwaiti authorities commute the death sentences given to collaborators to life in prison.

June 27: Justice Thurgood Marshall announces his retirement from the Supreme Court after 24 years on the bench.

July 1–5: Lebanese troops seize territory controlled by the PLO in the port city of Sidon, in southern Lebanon, thereby depriving the PLO of a base of operations against Israel.

July 4: The National Civil Rights Museum opens in Memphis, Tennessee, at the site where the civil rights leader Martin Luther King, Jr., was assassinated in 1968.

July 11: A total eclipse of the Sun is visible across parts of Central and South America and Hawaii.

July 12: The opening of the movie *Boyz N the Hood* sparks gang fights in cities throughout the United States.

July 22: Police arrest 31-year-old Jeffrey L. Dahmer after discovering human heads and other body parts in his Milwaukee apartment.

July 31: Bush and Gorbachev sign the START treaty, which cuts the nuclear arsenals of the United States and Soviet Union by one-third. As a symbolic gesture, they write their signatures with pens made of metal taken from scrapped missiles.

August 2: Health officials confirm a policy that forbids entry into the United States of foreigners carrying the AIDS virus.

August 17: More than 1,000 young Germans wearing Nazi armbands and shouting "Heil Hitler" march through Bayreuth, Germany, on the anniversary of the death of Hitler's deputy Rudolph Hess. This is only one of several neo-Nazi demonstrations taking place throughout Europe, especially in Germany, Poland, France, and Belgium.

August 19: Violence breaks out between Hasidic Jews and African Americans in Brooklyn, New York, after a car driven by a Hasidic Jew strikes two black children, killing one. Three days of rioting follow as gangs of blacks shouting anti-Semitic slogans smash Jewish-owned stores and kill a Jewish scholar from Australia.

August 19: Striking with sustained winds of 75 to 100 mph and gusts up to 125 mph, Hurricane Bob passes over Block Island and makes landfall at Newport, Rhode Island. Buzzards Bay, off Cape Cod, is hardest hit as it endures a storm surge of 12–15 feet.

August 19: A small group of Communist Party hard-liners seize power in the Soviet Union and place Gorbachev under house arrest in his vacation home in the Crimea. Yeltsin denounces the action as a cynical right-wing coup and rallies public sentiment and the resources of Russia against it.

August 21: The coup in the Soviet Union fails after the military supports Yeltsin, and Gorbachev returns to power as premier.

August 23: Gorbachev appears before the Russian parliament to thank Yeltsin and the people of Russia for foiling the coup. At Yeltsin's insistence, he also reads a list of coup supporters, many of whom hold top positions in the government and party, and he declares that the entire Soviet government will have to resign. Yeltsin suspends the Russian Communist Party and shuts down *Pravda,* the party's newspaper, while many senior party leaders throughout the Soviet Union resign from the Politburo.

August 28: One of the worst subway crashes in the history of New York City kills five and injures more than 200 commuters.

September 5: The Soviet Supreme Legislature votes to dissolve the Soviet Union.

September 11: Gorbachev announces that the Soviet Union will withdraw 11,000 troops from Cuba, leaving only a token training force on the island, which has had a Soviet military presence since 1961.

September 12: The Soviet Union announces that 400,000 people were contaminated by radioactivity in the 1986 nuclear meltdown at Chernobyl.

September 13: The retired chief of the secret service, Pierre Marion, reveals that for the past decade French agents have been spying on U.S. firms based in France, seeking computer plans and secrets about fiber optics.

September 16: The Philippine senate votes not to renew the lease on the U.S. naval base at Subic Bay.

September 24: The grunge band Nirvana releases its album *Nevermind,* which debuts at 144 on the Billboard 200.

September 25: The drug trial of Manuel Noriega, the former president of Panama, begins in Miami after months of secret hearings concerning the release to the defense of classified government documents.

September 27: Bush announces that the United States will unilaterally remove all its tactical nuclear weapons from Europe and Asia and cancels the 24-hour alert status of Strategic Air Command bombers.

September 28: The jazz pioneer Miles Davis dies at age 65.

September 29: Led by David Stockton, the U.S. golf team wins the Ryder Cup.

September 30: A military coup drives into exile Haiti's first democratically elected president, Jean-Bertrand Aristide.

October 1: The city of Leningrad officially reverts to its pre-Soviet name, Petrograd, or Saint Petersburg, and the Soviet Union restores full diplomatic relations with Israel, which it had severed in 1967, after Israel's six-day war with Soviet-allied Arab countries.

October 3: Speaker of the House Thomas S. Foley announces that the House Bank will close by the end of the year after the General Accounting Office reveals that representatives have bounced thousands of dollars worth of checks.

October 6: The actress Elizabeth Taylor marries her eighth husband, Larry Fortensky, a builder.

October 7: Yugoslav aircraft bomb the Croatian capital, Zagreb.

October 11: Anita Hill testifies at the Senate confirmation hearing for Clarence Thomas that Thomas sexually harassed her when she worked for him between 1981 and 1983. Thomas testifies in his own defense, calling Hill's accusations part of a "high-tech lynching."

October 16: In the worst single incident of mass murder in U.S. history, George Hennard, a 35-year-old trucker, drives his pickup truck through a restaurant window in Killeen, Texas, outside Dallas, and opens fire with two semiautomatic pistols. He kills 22 before shooting himself to death after being wounded by police officers.

October 16: By a vote of 52–48, the U.S. Senate confirms Bush's appointment of Clarence Thomas to the Supreme Court.

October 26: Yugoslav forces tighten their siege around the ancient Croatian city of Dubrovnik, amid fears for its historic buildings and treasures.

November 5: The body of Robert Maxwell, a British publishing magnate and the recent owner of the *New York Daily News,* is found floating naked off the Canary Islands, sparking speculation that he has been murdered. Two days later, Maxwell's publishing empire collapses amid charges of massive fraud.

November 8: The Los Angeles Lakers star Magic Johnson announces that he is ending his basketball career because he has contracted AIDS. The three-time MVP states that he will now devote his time to elevating awareness of the danger of contracting AIDS through unprotected heterosexual sex.

November 14: The United States and Britain charge two Libyan intelligence officers with planting the bomb that blew up Pan American's Flight 103 over Lockerbie, Scotland, in December 1988.

November 16: Democrat Edwin Edwards is elected governor of Louisiana when he defeats the Republican nominee, the former Ku Klux Klan grand wizard David Duke.

November 23: The Croatian city Vukovar surrenders to Yugoslav forces after a three-month siege kills some 1,000 people.

November 24: Freddie Mercury, the lead singer of the rock group Queen and an avowed bisexual, dies of AIDS at age 45.

December 3: White House chief of staff John Sununu resigns.

December 4: Pan American Airlines ceases operations.

December 5: Terry Anderson, the last of the Reagan-era hostages held in Lebanon, is freed after more than six and a half years of captivity.

December 11: The high-profile date rape trial of William Kennedy Smith ends after a jury acquits the

Basketball star Earvin "Magic" Johnson retired after learning he had contracted acquired immunodeficiency syndrome (AIDS). *(Photofest)*

wealthy nephew of Massachusetts senator Edward Kennedy.

December 13: North Korea and South Korea sign a nonaggression pact.

December 16: The United Nations repeals a 1975 resolution condemning Zionism as fundamentally racist.

December 21: Eleven of the 15 former Soviet republics join to form the Commonwealth of Independent States.

December 25: Gorbachev resigns and the Soviet Union officially ceases to exist.

December 31: A peace agreement ending the civil war in El Salvador is reached at the United Nations.

EYEWITNESS TESTIMONY

The term *Generation X* has become a derisive media catchphrase, a snide put-down for those, like me, who were born between 1961 and 1981—children of Baby Boomers. The group is, we're told, "numb and dumb," lazy underachievers, apathetic "boomerangers" who slink home to the parental nest after graduating from college, as if being born into an era of reduced economic expectations is a character defect. . . .

Young people find themselves compelled to improvise in order to survive. . . . This streetwise instinct is grounded in disillusionment with many aspects of American life, an understandable reaction which, in kinder times, would have been praised as pragmatism. . . . If they appear aloof, it is because they are wary of cliches and propaganda, and because theirs is a legacy of smashed idols. If they seem inclined to take short cuts to reach a desired result, their rationale is that old-fashioned integrity is for those who can afford it.

The young have few heroes, and are nonpolitical in the traditional two-party-sense. Weaned on Watergate, on debunked and deposed political candidates, hyena scholars and yellow journalism, the students in my class tend to admire those who live by what they preach: consumer advocate Ralph Nader, whose austere lifestyle matches his public convictions; former President Jimmy Carter, who takes up hammer and nails to build homes for the poor. . . . In other words, respect is granted to those elders who "walk the talk," in Twelve Step parlance. . . .

If we want to talk about generational accomplishment, consider this. Young people have effectively disposed of two of America's most enduring and time-honored myths: the rags-to-riches ethic of Horatio Alger and the soul-shrinking Puritan work ethic. Perhaps, some will argue, they had no choice, as American society copes with a rapidly changing world economy.

History professor Douglas Brinkley writing on April 3, 1994, about the so-called Generation X, a term that became popular in the United States around 1991, in Stephen Ambrose and David Brinkley, eds., Witness to America *(1999), pp. 574–577.*

Mr. William Brady was the Battalion Logistics (noncommissioned officer) NCO with the 217th Maintenance Battalion. Around midnight on January 18, or possibly very early on the 19th, Mr. Brady was awakened by what he believed to be a SCUD intercepted by a Patriot directly over his unit's position. He said there was a deafening sound, a flash of light, and everything shook. Chemical alarms were going off everywhere, and there was sheer panic. He remembered the chemical litmus paper turning red, and a positive reading from an M-256 kit. Mr. Brady said that his nose began to run, and he smelled and tasted sulfur. He began coughing up blood a couple of days after the attack, and continued to do so "the whole time we were there after the attack.". . .

Eventually they were told to come to Group Headquartrers (Hq.) for a message that Hq. didn't want to radio over. The message said that what they heard was a sonic boom, and instructed them to perform another test. The second test [for chemicals], performed several hours after the initial test, was negative. Members of the unit were told that the M9 paper had turned red as a result of exposure to diesel fumes. The message also gave the "all clear". . . but, Mr. Brady recalled, everyone was afraid to unmask. . . . They were told that while they were out riding around (without a radio), there had been another attack.

Beginning on January 22, Mr. Brady began getting too sick to work. He had been taking the nerve agent pre-treatment pills since about January 17, and had been getting severe headaches from them. Approximately three days after the attack, his eyes began to burn, he developed a high fever, and "taking a breath of air made his lungs feel like they were burning up." He also had diarrhea, sores, nausea, and a runny nose. On January 24, he went to the 13th Evacuation Hospital, which had no beds available for him. He described the hospital as completely filled with people that seemed to have the same illness that he had. His January 26 diary entry said: "I'd rather die than feel like this."

Mr. Brady stated during the interview that he "is convinced that there was a chemical attack." He reported that "everyone started getting pneumonia or flu-like symptoms after the attack,". . . that the nerve agent pre-treatment pills "were useless,". . . and that he is convinced that the PB tabs gave people headaches, but that they also "got hit with a nerve agent."

An account of an alleged chemical attack on American troops at Log Base Alpha in Saudi Arabia during the Persian Gulf War on January 18, 1991, reported in Senator Donald W. Riegle, Jr., "U.S. Chemical and Biological Warfare–Related Dual Use Exports to Iraq and Their Possible Impact on the Health Consequences of the Gulf War," May 25, 1994. Available online. URL: http://www.gulfweb.org/bigdoc/report/r_2_3.html.

George Bush and the Pentagon, with the generous assistance of Saddam Hussein, have apparently invented a new kind of war. It's a war that you can watch and enjoy on television, but one in which hardly anybody gets killed. . . .

The obvious question: . . . are both sides seeking to downplay the horrors of war out of fear that public support may rapidly erode if there is too much evidence of bloodshed? . . .

We know that both sides are engaged in a massive propaganda war. And both are capable of considerable manipulation of information.

Saddam has total, dictatorial control over information from Iraq. And the Pentagon, with White House approval, has established the most elaborate system of control and censorship over information since World War II. . . .

The model for Pentagon control of information about casualties and the horrors of war was developed, honed, and polished in the U.S. invasions of Grenada in 1983 and Panama in 1989.

The Reagan administration simply kept the press out of Grenada. It then inflated the size of Cuban resistance, understated the number of Grenada dead, and concealed military mistakes. . . . By the time the bad news was released, the public was in apparent ecstasy over an apparent success.

In Panama, the Bush Administration . . . controlled information to the point that TV presented an impression of a virtually bloodless conflict. . . .

What you are going to get from the Pentagon in the Persian Gulf is the good news, the successes. . . . You're not going to see bodies being brought back home in caskets. . . .

It's OK to die for your country. The Pentagon just doesn't want too many people to know about it.

Columnist James McCartney writing about the Defense Department's control of information during the Persian Gulf War in McCartney, "Americans Protected from Bad News," Miami Herald, January 28, 1991, p. 17A.

It certainly didn't look like a token fight on Friday morning. The battle unfolded against a surrealistic backdrop: more than two dozen burning Kuwaiti oil wells, each shooting orange jets of flame 50 or 60 feet into the air and throwing off vast clouds of black smoke. The smoke blew across the battlefield from northwest to southeast, forming a thick curtain above the Iraqi positions, against which the fireballs from Iraqi targets hit on the ground and the white puffs of American airburst shells were starkly outlined. The sky above the American positions was clear blue, so that the white trailers of the Tiger Brigade multiple rocket-launched projectiles stood out like fat yarns of white wool. . . .

Two Marines were wounded; two others had what will surely be one of this war's most miraculous escapes. As Colonel [John] Sylvester described it, "There were two Marines driving in a Humvee, both of them in the front seat. An Iraqi mortar round landed in the back seat, exploding the ordinance in the Hummer and blowing the whole thing to shreds. The blast blew both men out of the vehicle and neither has a scratch on him—although you would hardly recognize the thing they were driving in."

Journalist Tony Clifton reporting on the battle for Kuwait's oil fields on February 25, 1991, in Clifton, "Going into Battle with the Tiger Brigade," Newsweek, March 4, 1991, p. 24.

It should be clearly understood that the option of going all the way to Baghdad was never considered. . . . There was not a single head of state, diplomat, Middle East expert, or military leader who, as far as I am aware, advocated continuing the war and seizing Baghdad. The United Nations resolutions that provided the legal basis for our military operations in the gulf were clear in their intent: kick the Iraqi military force out of Kuwait. We had authority to take whatever actions were necessary to accomplish that mission, including attacks into Iraq; but we had no authority to invade Iraq for the purpose of capturing the entire country or its capital.

If we look back to the Vietnam War we should recognize that one of the reasons we lost world support for our actions was that we had no internationally recognized legitimacy for our intervention in Vietnam. In the gulf the case was exactly the opposite; we had no less than nine United Nations resolutions authorizing our actions, and we had the support of virtually the entire world. But that support was for us to kick Iraq out of Kuwait, not to capture Baghdad. . . .

Had the United States and the United Kingdom gone on alone to capture Baghdad, under the provisions of the Geneva and Hague conventions we would have been considered occupying powers and therefore would have been responsible for *all* the costs of maintaining or restoring government, education, and other services for the people of Iraq. From the brief time we did spend occupying Iraqi territory after the war, I am certain that had we taken all of Iraq, we would have been like the dinosaur in the tar pit—we would still be there and we, not the United Nations, would be bearing the costs of that occupation.

General Norman Schwarzkopf discussing in his book It Doesn't Take a Hero *(1992) President George H.W. Bush's decision on February 27, 1991, to end combat operations in the Persian Gulf War, quoted in Stephen Ambrose and Douglas Brinkley,* Witness to America *(1999), pp. 559–560.*

General Norman Schwarzkopf was the supreme commander of the allied forces during Operation Desert Storm. *(U.S. Department of Defense)*

There's enough dissent and disorder that it appears that Iraq citizens are trying to do something about it. We'll wait and see how it plays out.

President George H.W. Bush explaining his decision on March 26, 1991, not to afford U.S. assistance to Iraqi rebels trying to overthrow Saddam Hussein, in Hitchings, ed., Facts On File Yearbook 1991 *(1992), p. 213.*

"Graduate of the Thelma and Louise Finishing School"

"Thelma and Louise were right."

Buttons worn by pro-abortion-rights protestors at a Washington, D.C., rally in April 1992, referring to the independence and assertiveness shown by the violent title characters of the film Thelma & Louise, *which was released in May 1991, in Michael Bernard-Donals and Richard R. Glejzer, eds.,* Rhetoric in an Antifoundational World *(1998), pp. 152–153.*

You always see women as adversaries. It's as if the interesting relationship between women is adversarial; they're in competition for a man . . . or their characters are just so weak that they naturally are aggressive towards other females. I have never found that to be true in my own life—ever. . . .

I wanted to write a movie that I could go to as a woman and not be really upset and offended by. . . . I really wanted to write a movie where women were going to go in there and feel good about being women. I myself have experienced going into movies where so often I'm *embarrassed* . . . by the behavior of the women on the screen . . . by the audience's response to the women on the screen. And I just don't think that most of the things that I see represented in women on the screen are in any way indicative of the reality of most women's lives or most women's psychologies or personalities or emotions or motivations.

Screenwriter Callie Khouri discussing her motivation for writing Thelma & Louise, *which was released in May 1991, in Kari J. Winter, "On Being an Outlaw: A Conversation with Callie Khouri,"* Hurricane Alice, *Spring 1992, pp. 6–8.*

Thelma & Louise is a thumpingly adventurous road pic about two regular gals who shoot down a would-be rapist and wind up on the lam in their '66 T-bird. Even those who don't rally to pic's fed-up feminist outcry will take to its comedy, momentum, and dazzling visuals. This could be the pic that drags sidelined MGM/Pathé back out onto the road. . . .

Despite some delectably funny scenes between the sexes, Scott's latest pic isn't about women vs. men. It's about freedom, like any good road picture.

From "Thelma & Louise," a review in Variety, *May 13, 1991, reprinted in Paul M. Sammon,* Ridley Scott *(1999), pp. 143–144.*

The old days when the American worker earning $12 an hour could beat a guy on the other side of the world earning a dollar an hour, because he was 20 times as productive, are gone.

Representative Don J. Pease speaking on May 23, 1991, in opposition to granting fast-track authority to President Bush for negotiating international trade agreements, in Hitchings, ed., Facts On File Yearbook 1991 *(1992), p. 393.*

[U.S. military intelligence reports were] caveated, footnoted and watered down. . . . There were so many disclaimers that by the time you got done reading many of the intelligence estimates . . . no matter what happened, they would have been right.

General Norman Schwarzkopf complaining on June 12, 1991, about the quality of intelligence reports he received during Operation Desert Storm, in Hitchings, ed., Facts On File Yearbook 1991 *(1992), p. 535.*

We are deeply disturbed by the events of the last hours in the Soviet Union and condemn the unconstitutional resort to force. While the situation continues to evolve and information remains incomplete, the apparent unconstitutional removal of President Gorbachev, the declaration of a state of emergency, and the deployment of Soviet military forces in Moscow and other cities raise the most serious questions about the future course of the Soviet Union. This misguided and illegitimate effort bypasses both Soviet law and the will of the Soviet peoples.

Accordingly, we support President Yeltsin's call for "restoration of legally elected organs of power and

Thelma & Louise afforded many women a visceral sense of "payback" against abusive men. *(Photofest)*

the reaffirmation of the post of USSR President M. S. Gorbachev.". . .

We believe the policies of reform in the Soviet Union must continue. . . .

We support all constitutionally elected leaders and oppose the use of force or intimidation [to] suppress them or restrict their right to free speech.

We oppose . . . the use of force or intimidation [to] suppress or replace democratically elected governments. . . .

We will avoid . . . actions that would lend legitimacy or support this *coup* effort.

We have no interest in a new cold war or in the exacerbation of East-West tensions.

At the same time, we will not support economic aid programs if adherence to extra-constitutional means continues.

President George H. W. Bush's statement on August 19, 1991, condemning the ongoing coup in the Soviet Union, in Edward H. Judge and John W. Langdon, eds., The Cold War: A History through Documents *(1999), p. 259.*

This is not disaster, it is merely a change. The area won't have disappeared, it will just be under water. Where you now have cows, you will have fish.

J. R. Spradley, a member of the U.S. delegation to an international conference on the greenhouse effect, describing the benefits of elevated sea levels to a representative from Bangladesh, which might lose up to 10 percent of its land area to rising oceans, in Michael Zimmerman, "But Some Administration Appointees Reveal Their Flat-Earth View of Nature," Miami Herald, *October 6, 1991, p. 3C.*

After enduring three and a half months tied to the liberal Democrats' whipping post, and surviving a last minute "high-tech lynching" attempt, Clarence Thomas is finally an associate justice of the Supreme Court. . . .

The nomination of Clarence Thomas to fill the seat vacated by Thurgood Marshall was a stroke of political genius. If Thomas was confirmed, the seat would continue to be occupied by a black, albeit a black conservative Republican. If Thomas was not confirmed, the liberal Democrats and the civil-rights establishment risked losing black representation on the Supreme Court altogether.

The liberal Democrats were forced into a quandary over how to oppose a black man brought up in poverty and discrimination. . . . They couldn't get him in the regular committee hearings, so they resorted to a traditional method of dealing with an offending black—lynching. Only this time, it wasn't ignorant rednecks trying to string up an unfortunate Negro accused of raping a white woman, it was liberal Democrats going after a man with the effrontery to call into question the sacred cows of the liberal civil-rights establishment. . . .

The white liberal master and his "civil-rights" overseers want blacks to think themselves incapable of taking care of themselves. The white liberal master wants blacks to believe that they are dependent on him for all that they receive. The white liberal master wants blacks to always be welfare slaves and entitlement addicts on his liberal plantation.

Clarence Thomas and others like him are runaway slaves from the liberal plantation. They no longer believe the lies of the white liberal master and his "civil-rights" overseers.

They long for the freedom to make the most of their lives and to enjoy the blessings of America for which their ancestors sweated and cried, bled and died. Anyone for a second Emancipation Proclamation?

Columnist James M. Wallace commenting on October 24, 1991, on liberal opposition to the nomination of Clarence Thomas to the U.S. Supreme Court during hearings conducted in early October 1991, in Wallace, "Thomas Escapes the Fury of Liberal Persecution" (1991). Available online. URL: www.compleatheretic. com/pubs/columns/thomas.html.

Anita Hill is no feminist heroine. A week ago, in the tense climax of the Senate Judiciary Committee's hearings into the nomination of Clarence Thomas to the Supreme Court, the important issue of sexual harassment, one of the solid innovations of contemporary feminism, was used and abused for political purposes.

In an atrocious public spectacle worthy of the show trials of a totalitarian regime, uncorroborated allegations about verbal exchanges ten years old were paraded on the nation's television screens. The Judiciary Committee should have thoroughly investigated the charges but conducted the proceedings privately. It was an appalling injustice to both Anita Hill and Clarence Thomas to pit them and their supporters against each other. The Senate turned itself into the Roman Colosseum, with decadent, jaded patricians waving thumbs down over a blood-drenched arena.

Professor Camille Paglia discussing the October 11, 1991, testimony in the Clarence Thomas confirmation hearings, in Paglia, Sex, Art, and American Culture (1992). Available online. URL: www.uiowa.edu/ ~030116/153/articles/paglia.htm.

It is remarkable that the person most responsible for this fiasco has managed thus far to avoid blame. I refer, of course, to the president and his administration. George Bush nominated Clarence Thomas despite the fact that Thomas has never tried a case in his life; despite the fact that Thomas has had only a brief and undistinguished judicial career; despite the fact that the sum total of Thomas' legal experience is less than 7 years....

It was the Bush Administration's decision to stress Clarence Thomas' character as his most important qualification for the position. Given that the nominee's integrity was to be featured so prominently, it seems that at a minimum the administration should have assured itself that the nominee was as pure as Caesar's wife. There is an office in the Department of Justice that exists for the purpose of identifying and recommending candidates for federal judgeships. Before any person is nominated, the FBI investigates his or her background. Given the controversy the Thomas nomination was sure to engender, the FBI should have interviewed all of Thomas' present and former top aides, including Anita Hill. Had they done so, they would have learned of her allegations before the nomination was announced publicly or would have had a statement from her indicating the conduct later complained of did not occur. In the former case, Bush would not have nominated Thomas. In the latter, Anita Hill would be subject to the devastating charge of recent fabrication....

Political commentator Gregory Berry writing about the hearings for Clarence Thomas's nomination to the U.S. Supreme Court on October 11, 1991, in Berry, "Speaking Truth to Power: Anita Hill v. Clarence Thomas" (June 9, 2004). Available online. URL:http://users.erols.com/gberry/politics/ anitahil.htm.

There's an indifference to the contributions one can make [as a female senator addressing foreign policy issues]. What I can resent is indifference. I was never once asked by anyone at the White House or by any of my colleagues about how I reacted to Anita Hill's public allegations of sexual harassment or how I thought the allegations should be handled.

Senator Nancy Kassebaum of Kansas describing her experience as a female Republican senator during the Clarence Thomas confirmation hearings on October 11, 1991, in Wendy Kaminer, "Crashing the Locker Room," Atlantic, July 1992, pp. 59–60.

Much, indeed most, of our [the airline industry's] problems can be attributed to managements who seem to believe their mission in life is to put every living human being on an airplane at any price. This get-'em-on-the plane mentality is exacerbated by the fact that more than 25 percent of our industry's capacity is being operated by bankrupt and near-bankrupt carriers.

Robert L. Crandall, chairman of AMR Corporation (American Airlines), discussing on October 15, 1991, the financial difficulties faced by the airline industry, in Alan F. Pater and Jason R. Pater, eds., What They Said in 1991 (1992), p. 162.

We have to deal with our own self interests. At some point you have to decide what you stand for. [The United States] is out of the electronics business, the [video cassette recorder] VCR business, and soon we could be out of the car business.

Lee Iacocca, chairman of the Chrysler Corporation, discussing on October 15, 1991, the desirability of legislation to restrict imports of Japanese automobiles in Alan F. Pater and Jason R. Pater, eds., What They Said in 1991 (1992), p. 163.

I'm presenting what I call a countermyth to the myth of the Warren Commission.

Film director Oliver Stone describing his artistic goal for his movie JFK, in Lance Morrow and Martha Smilgis, "Plunging into the Labyrinth," Time, December 23, 1991, pp. 74–76.

Dear fellow countrymen, compatriots. Due to the situation which has evolved as a result of the formation of the Commonwealth of Independent States, I hereby discontinue my activities at the post of President of the Union of Soviet Socialist Republics. I am making this decision on considerations of principle. . . . I support the preservation of the union state and the integrity of this country. The developments took a different course. The policy prevailed of dismembering this country and disuniting the state, which is something I cannot subscribe to. . . .

Destiny so ruled that when I found myself at the helm of this state it already was clear that something was wrong in this country. We had a lot of everything—land, oil, gas, other natural resources—and there was intellect and talent in abundance. However, we were living much worse than people in the industrialized countries were living and we were increasingly lagging behind them. The reason was obvious even then. This country was suffocating in the shackles of the bureaucratic command system. Doomed to cater to ideology, and suffer and carry the onerous burden of an arms-race, it found itself at the breaking point. . . .

This society has acquired freedom. It has been freed politically and spiritually, and this is the most important achievement that we have [not] yet fully come to grips with. And we haven't, because we haven't learned to use freedom yet. . . .

Free elections have become a reality. Free press, freedom of worship, representative legislatures and a multi-party system have become reality. . . .

We're living in a new world. An end has been put to the cold war and to the arms race, as well as to the mad militarization of the country, which has crippled our economy, public attitudes and morals. The threat of nuclear war has been removed. . . .

Of course, there were mistakes that could have been avoided, and many of the things we did could have been done better. But I am positive that sooner or later, some day our common efforts will bear fruit

The Soviet premier Mikhail Gorbachev's reforms helped end Communist domination of Eastern Europe and bring about the dissolution of the Soviet Union. *(Photofest)*

and our nations will live in a prosperous, democratic society.

Mikhail Gorbachev announcing his resignation as president of the Soviet Union on December 25, 1991, in Edward H. Judge and John W. Langdon, eds., The Cold War: A History through Documents *(1999), pp. 262–263.*

4

"It's the Economy, Stupid"
1992

Throughout the decade, social unrest over ethnic affiliation, religion, race, and national identity fragmented, and, in some cases, destroyed, several established societies across the world. At the same time, economic forces prompted the creation of larger, more centralized financial institutions and political entities. The resulting push and pull between impulses toward division and those toward unity was particularly evident in 1992, the year that marked the 500th anniversary of Christopher Columbus's discovery of the Americas and saw the election of Bill Clinton as president.

Czechoslovakia, a former Iron Curtain nation that had been ruled for more than 40 years by a Communist regime and for seven years before that by Nazi occupation, agreed to terms of a so-called velvet divorce calling for the country to split amicably at midnight on December 31 into two new nations, Slovakia and the Czech Republic, each dominated by a different ethnic group. The breakup of Yugoslavia was far more brutal, as civil war continued in Croatia and a vicious, genocidal campaign to remove Muslims from Bosnia-Herzegovina began after that republic seceded from the Serb-dominated Yugoslav federation.

Violence erupted elsewhere too. In Africa, the Tutsi-ruled government of Burundi suppressed an insurrection and then executed some 1,000 Hutu; civil war rekindled in Angola after a 1991 peace agreement collapsed; violence between political factions killed thousands in South Africa; and feuding warlords prevented international famine relief from reaching thousands of starving people in Somalia. Religious riots spread throughout northern India after Hindus destroyed the ancient Muslim Babri Masjid mosque in the Hindu holy city of Ayodhya, and Tamil revolutionaries in Sri Lanka continued their 10-year insurgency. The Communist regime in Afghanistan ceded power to a coalition of Islamic rebels, who then battled one another to gain control. Closer to home, the Irish Republican Army (IRA) bombed government and commercial centers in Northern Ireland and Britain, and race riots in Los Angeles killed more than 50 people and caused an estimated $1 billion of damage after four white police officers were acquitted of using excessive force while arresting a black motorist, despite a widely viewed videotape showing them beating the man.

At the same time, important steps were taken toward forging greater international cooperation over key political and economic issues. Bush and Yeltsin declared a new era of "friendship and partnership"; the United States sent food relief and economic aid to its former cold war foes in the former Soviet Union and Eastern Europe; and the United States and Russia agreed on language in the second Strategic Arms Reduction Treaty (START II) calling for further reductions in their nuclear arsenals.

Continuing a process that began with the formation of the Common Market in 1957, Europe became more fully integrated as a political and economic community with the ratification of the so-called Maastricht Treaty, which created the European Union (EU), effective November 1, 1993. The EU would provide common citizenship among its 12 member nations, establish common economic and defense policies, and call for a single European currency by 2000. Six months later, the United States, Canada, and Mexico created the world's wealthiest trading bloc when they signed the North American Free Trade Agreement (NAFTA), which called for the eventual elimination of trade barriers. The election of moderate Labor Party leader Yitzhak Rabin as Israel's prime minister inspired hope that some new accommodation between Israelis and Palestinians might be reached. And gestures of conciliation were made by King Juan Carlos of Spain, who went to a synagogue in Madrid to apologize to Chaim Herzog, the Israeli president, for the actions of the Inquisition, which brutally drove the Jewish population from Spain 500 years earlier. In a similar demonstration of goodwill, Emperor Akihito became the first Japanese monarch ever to visit China, which suffered widespread atrocities at the hands of Japanese soldiers during the occupation of the 1930s and 1940s.

Although politically influential elements in both the Republican and the Democratic Parties pushed candidates to support social positions that were considered extreme by so-called middle Americans, both parties nominated presidential candidates closer to the political center than most of their rivals. President Bush's probusiness policies endeared him to fiscal conservatives, although his reluctant decision to raise taxes in 1990 and the persistence of the weak economy eroded that support, and the third-party candidacy of the Texas billionaire Ross Perot, who campaigned on his economic plan, attracted voters who might otherwise have chosen Bush for fiscal reasons. Many social conservatives who doubted the depth of Bush's commitment to their beliefs were attracted to the hard-liner Pat Buchanan. Yet whereas fiscal conservatives could vote for Perot, social conservatives had no one but Bush to turn to in the general election after Democrats nominated Arkansas governor Bill Clinton, a fiscally moderate Democrat whose advocacy of women's rights, homosexuals' rights, and abortion rights were anathema to social conservatives but dear to many liberals. Clinton's focus throughout the campaign remained on the economy, and by promising both to create more jobs and to stimulate the economy with innovative initiatives that broke from traditional Democratic practices, Clinton was able to garner enough votes from political moderates and even from some fiscal conservatives to supplement his liberal base and win the presidency.

INTERNATIONAL DEVELOPMENTS

Civil War in the Balkans

Although the formation of the European Union created cooperation among some nations, internal strife tore others apart. In Yugoslavia, the civil war that began in June 1991 when Croatia and Slovenia seceded from the Yugoslav federation spread to Bosnia in March 1992, after the republic of Bosnia-Herzegovina also voted for independence. Yugoslav forces renewed their attack on Croatia in September 1991 and continued it throughout that year. After reports of atrocities committed by Yugoslav troops and local ethnic Serbian guerrillas and the downing in early January 1992 of a helicopter carrying European monitors, the European Community (EC) officially recognized the republics of Croatia and Slovenia, an act that signaled the dissolution of Yugoslavia. (The United States recognized the independence of these republics and Bosnia in April.) Nonetheless, the fighting continued throughout Croatia, and, fearing the violence could have even more far-reaching consequences for Europe (World War I began in the region), the United Nations sent a peacekeeping force of 14,000 troops in February.

The Orthodox Christian Serbian minority in Bosnia-Herzegovina, which wanted to remain affiliated with Yugoslavia, largely boycotted the election calling for independence. Immediately afterward, Bosnia was attacked by both Yugoslavia and Croatia, who were determined to protect and advance the interests of their minority Serb and Croat populations against Bosnia's Muslim majority. (The composition of Bosnia's 3 million inhabitants was roughly 44 percent Muslim, 31 percent Serb, and 17 percent Croat.[1]) The Bosnian army was not as well equipped as its foes, and it suffered far more acutely than its enemies from an international arms embargo that had been imposed on the entire region in 1991. Consequently, much of the country was quickly overrun by the combined forces of the Yugoslav military and local Bosnian Serb militias, who began a practice, in their words, of "ethnic cleansing" that entailed the massacre and forced removal of the Muslim population. In April, the Bosnian capital, Sarajevo, which hitherto had been a model of ethnic coexistence and had been showcased to the world as the host city for the 1984 Winter Olympics, fell under fire from Serbian artillery. After a brief cease-fire collapsed, the siege continued in May, although in July, UN peacekeepers from Canada took control of the airport and began airlifting humanitarian aid. In northern Bosnia, Muslims were forced from their homes, and hundreds were slaughtered or sent to concentration camps. In August, the Security Council denounced the war crimes and authorized further military action to provide humanitarian relief.

By the end of August, Yugoslav and Serb forces commanded 70 percent of the country. They declared the region under their control the Republika Srpska (the Serbian Republic), with its capital at Rule. Serbia and Montenegro, the remaining Yugoslav republics, dissolved the old federation and declared a new Yugoslav state, now known as Serbia. Serbia's premier Slobodan Milošević then transferred Yugoslav soldiers who were Bosnian Serbs to the army of the Serbian Republic, along with all of the armaments and supplies already there. This allowed the Serbs to maintain that their offensive was part of a civil war, and not an invasion of one sovereign nation by another.

The Bosnian Serbs, now in control of the occupied territories, continued their genocidal ethnic cleansing. And the Serbian air force continued to conduct air strikes against Bosnian targets, leading the United Nations to establish an exclusionary "no-fly" zone over Bosnia and to embargo Serbian shipping. Sarajevo remained under siege from Bosnian Serbs, who pressed on in their fight to remove Muslims from other regions of the country as well.

Other International Developments

Recollections of genocide earlier in the century also surfaced in Germany, where extreme right-wing anti-immigration political parties made substantial gains in state elections. One such party, headed by a former Nazi SS officer, won 11 percent of the vote in Baden-Württemberg, Germany's most affluent state. In another state, a neofascist party took almost 7 percent. Shortly after the elections, Josef Schwammberger, an 80-year-old former SS officer and concentration camp commandant, was sentenced to life in prison for atrocities committed during World War II.

The Soviet Union had officially dissolved in December 1991, and in 1992 the newly independent republics had to address their political differences and common interests, as well as the problems and opportunities inherent in international trade and diplomacy, especially with Western Europe and the United States, their former cold war enemies. As the former Soviet Union continued to suffer from serious economic woes, the international community airlifted food and medical supplies to Russia and other newly independent republics.

China introduced reforms that repudiated communist principles in favor of an economic philosophy more similar to Western-style capitalism. The new policies included an end to jobs-for-life employment guarantees and a greater role for stock markets. The economic liberalization was not accompanied by political reforms or enhanced civil liberties for Chinese citizens, however, and China further asserted itself as a military power by testing a one-megaton nuclear device. Elsewhere in Asia, military rule ended in Thailand, where a coup had seized control in 1991.

El Salvador's 12-year civil war concluded after the rightist government signed a peace agreement with leftist insurgents calling for a cease-fire, the dismantling of rebel forces, a 50 percent reduction of the government's military forces by 1994, the dissolution of the Salvadoran military intelligence units, creation of a new civilian police force that would include former rebel combatants, freeing of political prisoners, establishment of a so-called Truth Commission to investigate claims of human-rights abuses, and establishment of the Farabundo Marti National Liberation Front (FMLN) as a legitimate political party. Backed by the military, Peru's president, Alberto Fujimori, established himself as a virtual dictator after he first declared a state of emergency and then suspended the constitution and disbanded the Congress. Fujimori also intensified efforts to suppress a 12-year rebellion in the nation's remote regions. These succeeded when government troops captured the leader of the vicious, rural Maoist revolutionary group Shining Path. Manuel Noriega, the former dictator of Panama who was ousted by a U.S. invasion in December 1990, was convicted of drug trafficking and sentenced to 40 years in prison after a seven-month trial in Miami. Growing poverty and political unrest in Haiti led hundreds of refugees to risk a dangerous ocean crossing in unreliable vessels in hopes of entering the United States, but President Bush ordered the Coast Guard to intercept their boats and return them to Haiti.

In an effort to compel Libya to surrender two agents suspected of engineering the 1988 bombing of a Pan Am jet over Lockerbie, Scotland, the United Nations imposed an embargo on air traffic and arms sales to the African nation. Elections were canceled in Algeria, and the military took control of the government after preliminary results showed that Islamic fundamentalists would easily prevail. A subsequent crackdown on the fundamentalists provoked resistance that intensified throughout the decade and that, in 1992, led to the assassination of President Mohammed Boudiaf. Tunisia's president also called for a crackdown on Islamic militants who were using religion to acquire political power. In December Bush deployed 28,000 troops to Somalia after the United Nations authorized military intervention to distribute humanitarian supplies to famine-starved Somalis, whose aid shipments were being stolen by warring factions.

GOVERNMENT AND SOCIETY

The Presidential Election

The presidential election was the dominant political event in the United States. Although Clinton eventually won by focusing on the nation's ailing financial health—he had placed a sign in his campaign strategy room reminding him that "It's the economy, Stupid"—other issues affecting the election included expanded civil rights for women, homosexuals, and racial and ethnic minorities; illegal immigration; abortion rights; national health insurance; and the problem of balancing environmental and public health needs with pressures to reduce environmental regulation in order to spark economic revival and promote job creation and the interests of industry. Ultimately, in the November elections, Democrats retained control of both congressional chambers, and women and members of minority groups gained seats in Congress.

Bush, the incumbent, was the clear choice for his party's renomination, despite criticism of his economic policies by many Republicans. His campaign focused on his foreign policy achievements, particularly the overwhelming success of the Persian Gulf War. He also stressed his commitment to family values, which he maintained was evident in his opposition to abortion, advocacy of private school vouchers, and a proposed $500 per child tax credit. Opponents, however, pointed to his veto of a family leave bill a month before the election as evidence that he cared more about corporate profits than the well-being of families. Bush's supporters countered that a vibrant economy that produced jobs and other social benefits was crucial for the preservation of strong families. Bush also advocated reducing the capital gains tax and providing other tax breaks and changes in regulatory policies to stimulate business; changing banking laws to permit banking across state lines and allowing banks to offer additional financial services; expanding the federal death penalty to apply to more crimes; and easing restrictions on oil and gas exploration in the Arctic National Wildlife Refuge.

Bush faced a stiff challenge for the Republican nomination from the popular syndicated columnist and television personality Pat Buchanan, whose isolationist, protectionist, anti-immigration, antiabortion, antifeminist, and antihomosexual positions appealed to the right wing of the party and won him nearly a quarter of the votes in the primaries. The effect of Buchanan's candidacy was to push Bush farther to the Right on social issues than he might otherwise have gone, and Buchanan, who called for a freeze on federal spending, reduced federal regulation, and restrictions on immigration to preserve the nation's "Euro-American" nature, was allowed to voice his views at the Republican convention, even though his positions, considered extreme by many, may have alienated undecided voters.

In the general election Bush was further undermined by Ross Perot's third-party candidacy, which attacked Bush's economic policies and tapped into voter dissatisfaction with the two dominant political parties. Perot garnered 19 percent of the popular vote, enough to tip the balance in favor of Clinton, who received 43 percent to Bush's 38 percent. Senator Al Gore of Tennessee was elected vice president.

Clinton defeated a pool of contenders for the Democratic nomination that included the former California governor Jerry Brown, Senator Tom Harkin (Iowa), Senator Bob Kerrey (Nebraska), and Senator Paul Tsongas (Massachusetts). Known for liberal positions, Brown campaigned for term limits for elected officials, campaign reform, elimination of capital punishment, cuts in defense spending, and a so-called flat income tax of 13 or 14 percent to replace the existing graduated income tax. He opposed nuclear power and vouchers for private school education. Harkin, who positioned himself as a populist, shared Brown's positions on defense spending, the death penalty, and nuclear power. He proposed providing a free college education to students in return for commitments of national service, a moratorium on arms sales to the Middle East, and protectionist trade policies. Kerrey—not to be confused with the 2004 Democratic presidential nominee Senator John Kerry of Massachusetts—was a decorated Vietnam War veteran who, in 2001, was accused of participating in war atrocities against civilians. In 1992, however, he promoted his service record and appealed more to conservative and middle-of-the road voters by supporting the death penalty, endorsing requirements that minors obtain parental or judicial consent before having an abortion, and advocating fiscal policies that would promote trade and corporate research. He promoted universal health insurance, a middle-income tax cut, and reduction of government bureaucracy, including eliminating the Departments of Commerce, Labor, and Agriculture. Tsongas also ran as an "aggressively pro-business Democrat," who would create tax credits for business investments in plants, equipment, and research. He favored loosening antitrust laws to promote cooperative research among companies, but he advocated tax increases on gasoline to finance public works and promote conservation.

Pat Buchanan, who opposed illegal immigration, legalized abortion, homosexuals' rights, women's liberation, and the global economy, made a strong showing in the Republican primaries. (Photofest)

The billionaire third-party candidate Ross Perot gained many supporters by calling for a simplified tax code and economic reforms. *(Photofest)*

Clinton, too, appealed to moderate, middle-class voters and corporate interests by advocating a middle-class tax cut combined with an upper-class tax increase, tax credits for the working poor, welfare reform that included job training and health care for welfare recipients, reduced capital gains taxes for investments in new businesses, and creation of an agency to support corporate research and development. He did not oppose nuclear power per se but did not favor building more plants. Although he endorsed the Persian Gulf War, Clinton, as did Bush, favored a large cut in defense spending. He advocated parental choice for public schools but opposed vouchers for private schools. He supported the death penalty and requirements that minors obtain parental or judicial consent before having an abortion, as well as "boot camps" for children convicted of nonviolent crimes.

The campaign was not without its sensational moments. Clinton was accused of dodging the draft during the Vietnam War (unlike Bush, who had been a combat pilot during World War II); having a long-standing affair with Gennifer Flowers, which he denied; and smoking marijuana when he was younger—to which he famously replied, perhaps with tongue in check, that he had smoked it once, but "didn't inhale." Clinton and his wife, Hillary Rodham Clinton, a prominent attorney, presented themselves as having a modern professional marriage that included dedication to their careers, as well as to their daughter, Chelsea, and each other. Hillary Rodham Clinton drew both strong praise and vicious condemnation as an independent, outspoken, high-powered professional woman, and she angered many men and women when she seemingly demeaned homemakers who "stayed home and baked cookies and had teas," instead of pursuing a career, as she had, and when she asserted her autonomy within her marriage, maintaining, "I'm not some little woman . . . standing by my man like Tammy Wynette" (who had recorded the popular song "Stand By Your Man").

Bush's vow to do "whatever it takes to be reelected" was regarded as ominous by many. Even more ominous was the revelation, reminiscent of the Watergate-era abuses by President Nixon, that members of Bush's administration had improperly searched the passport records of Clinton and his mother. Although better known for his manipulation of charts and statistics than the English language, Ross Perot cleverly turned Bush's past pronouncements against him by declaring, "The total national debt was only $1 trillion in 1980. . . . It is now $4 trillion. Maybe it *was* voodoo economics [Bush's term for Reagan's financial plans when Bush ran against Reagan for the Republican nomination in 1980] . . . Whatever it was, we are in deep voodoo."[2]

Other Developments

Once more the nation was made painfully aware of how much race remained an explosive issue in America when riots broke out in Los Angeles on April 29, after the acquittal of four white policemen charged with beating Rodney King, a black motorist, in 1991. The trial had been moved to Simi Valley, a largely white community north of Los Angeles, because a judge ruled that the officers could not receive a fair hearing in Los Angeles. The jury found them not guilty of illegally beating King, despite an amateur videotape that recorded their striking him savagely. The video had been broadcast nationwide, and to many viewers it appeared to offer compelling evidence that the police had used excessive force. The apparent injustice enraged many blacks and other inner-city minorities who interpreted the acquittal as an endorsement of institutionalized brutal racist violence against them. Los Angeles suffered from a four-day rampage during which 6,000 national guardsmen and 4,000 marines and army troops were ordered in to restore peace, and more than 5,000 people were arrested. Even firefighters were assaulted as they sought to extinguish flames in the inner city where the rioters resided.

The riots revealed antagonisms not just between blacks and whites but also between blacks and Asian shop owners, many of whom lost successful establishments they had operated for years. The violence left more than 50 people dead, 2,500 injured, and approximately 1,100 stores and business destroyed.[3] Property damage was estimated at approximately $1 billion.[4] To alleviate circumstances believed to have contributed to the uprising, Bush allocated $19 million to fund an antidrug and antigang campaign.

The riots revealed the breadth, as well as the depth, of latent anger in inner-city Los Angeles. Although the destruction was typically represented in the media and in public and political discourse as perpetrated mostly by blacks, in fact, of the first 5,438 people arrested, only 37 percent were black. Fifty-one percent were Hispanic, and the rest were either white or members of other ethnic groups.[5]

An incident in Idaho four months later fueled another form of antigovernment rage. Although not generally sympathetic to the Los Angeles rioters, white supremacists, members of right-wing separatist groups, some libertarians, and other citizens more broadly concerned about governmental abuse of power denounced the killing by federal agents of the wife and 14-year-old son of fugitive Randy Weaver. A federal marshal also died in the two gun battles outside Weaver's remote cabin in Ruby Ridge, Idaho, close to the Canadian border. The shootings occurred as federal agents tried to arrest Weaver for selling illegal sawed-off shotguns to a federal undercover agent with whom Weaver had discussed forming an organization to fight the *Zionist Organized Government*—a term for the U.S. government used by some white supremacist groups. Affiliated with the white separatist organization Aryan Nations, Weaver had, in 1985, been accused by his neighbors of threatening to kill President Reagan and Idaho governor John Evans, but no charges were filed against him.

Because of these allegations and other uncontested statements, the Bureau of Alcohol, Tobacco, and Firearms (ATF) decided to try to arrest Weaver on August 21, through a nonconfrontational undercover plan in which they hoped to catch him unsuspecting. Weaver surprised the agents, however, and he, his dog, and his son, Sammy, chased them into the woods beyond the cabin, where a gunfight broke out in which Sammy and Deputy Marshal William Degan were killed. The next day Weaver and his friend Kevin Harris were wounded, and Weaver's wife, Vicki, was killed by federal snipers who fired two shots when Harris and Weaver ran outside with the apparent intention, the agents maintained, of shooting at a government helicopter. Vicki, standing inside behind the door and carrying her 10-month-old daughter, was killed by the same shot that wounded Harris.

After an eight-day standoff, Weaver and Harris surrendered. They were acquitted in 1993 of murdering Degan, although Weaver was convicted, and briefly jailed, for failing to appear for his initial court appearance and for committing an offense while on release. A Justice Department investigation released in 1995 was unable to determine whether Weaver or the marshals initiated the first gun battle. But it concluded that the ATF agents had acted properly when they formulated their undercover plan; that their participation in the gunfight was justified under the circumstances; and that they did not intentionally shoot Sammy, of whose death they were unaware until the following day. Nor did they cover up their roles or distort the facts to provoke a more severe federal response, as their critics had charged.

The task force, however, criticized the FBI agents in charge for the way they conducted negotiations, communicated with FBI headquarters, documented decisions, and secured the site. Its most severe condemnation was of the rules of engagement that instructed the special Hostage Rescue Team sent in on August 22 to "shoot all armed adult males appearing outside the cabin." The task force argued that these conditions "may have created an atmosphere that encouraged the use of deadly force thereby having the effect of contributing to an unintentional death." The report further found that the rules of engagement "not only departed from the FBI's standard deadly force policy but also contravened the Constitution of the United States."[6] Throughout the 1990s the Ruby Ridge incident, along with the 1993 raid against the Branch Davidians in Waco, Texas, fueled charges, made most vocally by those on the far Right, that the United States had become a police state that routinely and brutally squelched the rights of individual Americans.

Violent crime, punishment, and federal informants also figured in the murder conviction of John Gotti, the 51-year-old head of New York's leading organized crime family. The guilty verdict returned against the Teflon Don of organized crime—so labeled because of the inability of prosecutors to make charges stick in three earlier trials—was based mainly on testimony by one of his chief assistants, Salvatore Gravano, who violated the so-called Mafia code by cooperating with the government and testifying against a fellow member of his crime family. In another closely watched trial, 17-year-old Amy Fisher pleaded guilty to shooting the wife of her alleged lover, 42-year-old Joey Buttafuoco. The lurid crime mixing sexual passion and violence inspired two television movies during the year. Jeffrey Dahmer, a serial killer who had murdered 15 homosexual young men and boys in 1991 and had eaten some of them, received 15 consecutive life sentences for his sensational crime. Overall, the rate of prison incarcerations had doubled in the United States since 1980, as 455 per 100,000 citizens were jailed—the highest percentage per capita in the world.[7]

Institutional violence against women was at the center of the Tailhook scandal, in which revelations of widespread sexual harassment at the 1991 Tailhook Association convention for naval aviators prompted the resignation of Secretary of the Navy H. Lawrence Garrett III. During the convention at least

26 women, half of them naval officers, were harassed by drunken navy airmen, apparently with the tacit approval of senior military personnel.

Despite oppressive conditions in some inner cities and the persistence of a tradition of machismo in military and other institutions, women and minorities made some substantial gains in 1992. More women than ever before ran for congressional office during the so-called Year of the Woman, and Carol Moseley Braun, an Illinois Democrat, became the first black woman elected to the U.S. Senate. Four other women were also elected to that chamber, and the total number of women in Congress rose from 28 to 42. Thirty-six-year-old Leah Sears-Collins became the first black woman to serve on the Supreme Court of Georgia when she was appointed to complete the term of a retiring justice. Mae C. Jemison became the first black woman to fly into space, and Mona Van Duyn was appointed the nation's first female poet laureate. The introduction of the vaginal pouch, also known as the female condom, gave women greater control over their body by better enabling them to prevent pregnancy and avoid contracting AIDS and other sexually transmitted diseases. Anglican churches in England and Australia changed their rules to allow women to become priests.

Abortion continued to divide the nation bitterly. A 5-4 Supreme Court ruling giving states the power to restrict but not outlaw abortions troubled both supporters and foes of abortion rights. Supporters, such as Clinton, viewed the ruling as encroaching upon women's rights, and he warned that the right to abortions, which he maintained should be safe, legal, and rare, were "hanging by a thread." President Bush, on the other hand, praised the Court's "reasonable restrictions," while antiabortion activists decried the ruling's failure to overturn the 1973 *Roe v. Wade* decision that legalized the practice. The Court further upheld a federal ban on the importation of RU-486, a so-called morning-after birth control pill legal in France and England but banned in the United States. The French company that manufactured the pill had declined to seek U.S. approval as a result of threats of boycotts and violence from so-called prolife activists who maintained that life begins at conception and that anything done to terminate pregnancy even hours afterward constitutes a form of abortion. In other decisions, the Supreme Court enforced restrictions on prayer in public schools and overturned a local ordinance outlawing cross burning. The Twenty-seventh Amendment to the Constitution forbidding U.S. senators and representatives from giving themselves pay raises during their present term in office, was ratified. But Bush failed to win congressional passage of a constitutional amendment calling for a balanced federal budget.

BUSINESS

Although the economy improved significantly during the year, the upturn was too late to help Bush in the presidential election, in which his loss was attributed mainly to the recession and high levels of unemployment. The year's GNP rose to 4.0 percent, up from 2.8 percent in 1991. Inflation dropped to 3.0 percent, but unemployment increased by more than 0.5 percent, to 7.4 percent, its highest rate in five years. The Dow-Jones industrial average rose about 250 points to a high of 3,413. The poverty rate rose to 14.2 percent, its highest level since 1983.[8] TWA airlines and Macy's department store, long-established and well respected institutions, filed for bankruptcy, and General Motors recorded a $23.5 billion loss, its largest ever.[9] The rest of the world also suffered from economic hard times; in Canada, Olympia & York, the world's largest real estate company, filed for bankruptcy after its debt exceeded $12 billion.

The business development with the most far-reaching consequences occurred in August with the signing of NAFTA, in which the United States, Canada, and Mexico agreed to create the world's largest and wealthiest trading partnership. The agreement called for the elimination over the next 15 years of tariffs and other trade barriers among the participating countries. The treaty, for which President Clinton won congressional ratification in 1993, was hailed by corporations, which looked forward to expanded markets and opportunities to avail themselves of inexpensive Mexican labor. Supporters maintained that industrial jobs lost to foreign labor would be offset by new jobs in other business sectors created to fill the increased demand for U.S. products and services. They further argued that the pact would stimulate the Mexican economy, which in turn would improve wages and working conditions there, thereby reducing the incentive for illegal immigration to the United States, an ongoing problem that remained a social and economic concern throughout the decade. Labor groups, however, opposed NAFTA because they feared that well-paying American jobs would be replaced by low-paying ones, or by jobs for which displaced workers had little training or aptitude. Many in the agriculture industry also feared competition from Mexico, where growers did not have to comply with the same standards and health and labor regulations as their American counterparts, and they argued that NAFTA would permit importation of foods treated with harmful pesticides banned in the United States. Environmentalists feared the agreement would degrade existing U.S. standards for pollution control and reduction.

President Bush had earlier also won trade concessions while on a 10-day tour of Asia in January. Yet, despite agreements by Japan nearly to double the value of United States–made auto parts it would import between 1991 and 1995; to increase sales in Japan of United States–made cars, computer, and supplies; and to stimulate its economic growth, Bush was criticized by U.S. automakers, and even by leaders of his own party, for failure to gain sufficient concessions. Others maintained that it was unseemly for the leader of the free world to be acting as if he were selling cars. Democratic leaders complained that Bush's election-year effort would fail to produce more jobs or higher wages for Americans, a position that, polls showed, was shared by the majority of the public.

Moreover, the administration was less successful at finding common ground with some of its European trading partners. On the day after Bush lost the presidential election, the administration imposed a 200 percent tariff on $300 million worth of EC imports, and a trade war threatened. Two weeks later, in a compromise agreement, the EC agreed to curb farm subsidies, and the United States agreed to drop demands for firm limits on the production of oilseeds.

The Dow-Corning Corporation was accused of allowing silicone-gel breast implants to be inserted in women before the company received results from safety tests run on animals, and the Food and Drug Administration (FDA), acting on evidence that the implants were linked to immune-system and connective-tissue disorders, called for a voluntary moratorium on their sale and implantation. Internal memoranda showed that the company had also instructed its sales representatives to understate the possibility that silicone might leak into the body.

The exportation of American culture to the rest of the world continued with the opening of Euro Disneyland outside Paris. Patterned after Disney's American-based theme parks, Euro Disneyland was the product of a 1987 agreement among the French government, the Walt Disney Company, the Ile-de-France Regional Counsel, the Seine-et-Marne Departmental Counsel, the Parisian public transport authority, and the Public Planning Board for the new town of Marne-la-Vallée. Initial interest was smaller than anticipated, however, and Euro Disneyland fell almost 1 million visitors short of its originally anticipated attendance for the year.

NATURE AND THE ENVIRONMENT

Global warming garnered increasingly serious attention as a growing body of scientific evidence continued to support the likelihood that the threat was real. The depth of international concern became apparent when representatives of 153 countries met in June at the Earth Summit in Rio de Janeiro, Brazil, and signed treaties designed to curb global warming and protect the diversity of the world's plant and animal species. Political differences erupted, however, between wealthy, industrialized countries—which generated most of the climate-altering pollution and which had destroyed much of their own forests and wildlife habitats—and poorer, largely nonindustrialized nations—which produced far fewer pollutants and faced the greatest restrictions on developing their rain forests and natural resources, while also trying to overcome the burdens of poverty. Efforts by the poorer nations to have the United States, Britain, Japan, and Germany double levels of aid by 2000 failed, and the results of the summit were widely greeted with skepticism.

In addition to global warming, the deterioration of the ozone layer, which filters out dangerous ultraviolet radiation from the Sun, remained a concern, as record levels of ozone-depleting chlorofluorocarbons (CFCs) and bromines were detected above New England and eastern Canada. Pollution was also a growing concern for the nation's food supply. At a time when many people were choosing to eat more fish as part of a healthier diet, *Consumer Reports* magazine revealed that a high percentage of fish sold in the Chicago and New York markets had been contaminated by bacteria and pollutants, including cancer-causing polychlorinated biphenyls (PCBs) and mercury, which has been linked to birth defects.

Hurricane Andrew struck Miami on August 24, as a category 5 hurricane on the five-point Saffir-Simpson scale, with measured wind gusts exceeding 175 mph. It was the costliest hurricane on record in terms of dollars, causing 23 deaths in the United States, plus three in the Bahamas, and creating $26.5 billion in damage in the United States, of which $1 billion occurred in Louisiana and the rest in south Florida, in Greater Miami. The Bahamas suffered an additional $250 million in destruction.[10] Other natural disasters of the year included an earthquake in eastern Turkey that killed more than 1,000 people, floods in India and Pakistan that killed some 2,500, and an earthquake in Indonesia that took 1,500 lives. Foremost among the human-caused environmental disasters was the grounding of a Greek oil tanker whose oil spill despoiled the Spanish coastline, dumping some 21.5 million gallons of crude oil off the coast of La Coruña, about twice the amount spilled in 1989 by the *Exxon Valdez* in Prince William Sound, Alaska.

SCIENCE AND TECHNOLOGY

The World Wide Web was born in April, when the European Particle Physics Laboratory (CERN) in Geneva, Switzerland, gave full public access to an international network of computer sites accessible to computers anywhere throughout the globe. The Web was made possible by software technology developed by the British-born computer scientist Tim Berners-Lee, along with his colleague Robert Cailliau. Although Internet connections to specific databases and to interactive computer bulletin boards had been available previously, the Web for the first time made individual documents universally available throughout the world by giving each document a Web address, called a universal resource locator (URL). It further enabled users to link directly from one document to another in an entirely different database housed on a different computer, perhaps in another part of the world. Moreover, high-speed search engines made each document, or Web page, readily referable.

The World Wide Web, sometimes called the Internet (although there is a technical difference), was one of the most important developments of the 20th century. It changed the way ordinary people throughout the industrialized world conducted business, accessed information, developed private relationships, and promoted their wares, their accomplishments, their interests, and even their bodies. It enabled small businesses to advertise inexpensively to a worldwide market, facilitated grassroots political action, made e-mail a popular form of interpersonal communication for both private and business uses, and changed the dating habits of millions. It also energized a worldwide pornography industry that was among the first to flourish in the new medium.

Human understanding of the workings of the universe continued to expand as the *Mars Observer* was launched to study Mars. In a setback, however, the *Magellan* probe orbiting Venus inexplicably lost the use of one of the antennae constructed to transmit data back to Earth. Ground-based telescopes confirmed the existence of a 10th planet some 3,700,000,000 miles from the Sun. In January, the astronomer Alexander Wolszczan published his discovery, made in 1991, of two planets outside the solar system—the first sighting of planets beyond the solar system. Other astronomers sighted two black holes in binary star systems, confirming the existence of the theoretically predicted indentations in the fabric of spacetime that have at their core matter so dense that their gravitational field precludes light from escaping. Data culled in 1991 from the *Cosmic Background Explorer* raised additional questions about the fabric of outer space when it revealed unexpected ripples in the background microwave radiation that fills the cosmos. These discoveries are directly related to modern applications of relativity theory that scientists have been using to predict and confirm the origin of the universe, its direction of motion, and its characteristics, including the existence of black holes. Scientists on the space shuttle *Discovery* conducted experiments on the effects of weightlessness on crystals and biological subjects.

Delving into the past, archaeologists in Saudi Arabia discovered the 4,000-year-old site of Ubar, an ancient trade center referred to in the Koran. New findings suggested that primates originated in Africa, and in Kenya the anthropologist Maeve Leakey discovered the oldest humanoid fossil known to that date, tracing back some 25 million years to the period when human evolution diverged from that of apes.

Medical science also saw many new advances. One of the most far-reaching was the publication of the first two maps of human chromosomes, the product of the Human Genome Project, which began in 1990 to determine the sequence of all human genes. Chronic fatigue syndrome, sometimes known as the yuppie flu for its tendency to afflict professionals in high-stress, fast-paced jobs, was linked to inflammation of the brain. The genes for muscular dystrophy and Marfan's syndrome were identified; the medication Caprotil was shown significantly to reduce the death rate of patients who had heart failure; high-density lipoprotein (HDL), the so-called good cholesterol, was shown to play a greater role in reducing heart disease than previously recognized; and high levels of blood fats, or triglycerides, were shown to be a substantial risk for heart attack. Angioplasty, a procedure that employs a balloon to open obstructed heart arteries, was demonstrated to be more effective than prescription of standard medications, and use of a fiber-optic monitor inserted through the rectum into the colon was shown to provide early detection and removal of colon cancer. Contrary to conventional belief, dyslexia among children was shown to be reversible. A 35-year-old man who received a liver transplant from a baboon lived for 71 days before dying of stroke.

Even as great strides were being made in medical research and treatment, interest in chiropractic, acupuncture, hypnotherapy, herbal treatments, massage therapy, Chinese medicine, Reiki, and other forms of so-called alternative medicine continued to grow among the public and to gain limited degrees of begrudging, often qualified respect from the medical community. The extent to which alternative approaches to good health had moved into the mainstream became apparent with the establishment of the Office of Alternative Medicine within the National Institutes of Health.

LITERATURE, THE ARTS, SPORTS, AND POPULAR CULTURE

When the singer Paul Simon toured South Africa in January, he became the first international pop star to perform there since the end of apartheid. Singer Sineád O'Connor also entered the political arena when she tore up a photograph of Pope John Paul II on the television comedy show *Saturday Night Live,* and the alternative band Rage against the Machine, whose musicians were self-proclaimed Marxists, issued its debut album, *Rage against the Machine,* which condemned racism, cynical politics, and social injustice. The lyrics of Ice-T's rap number "Cop Killer" provoked outrage among many middle Americans who believed the song celebrated acts of violence against law enforcement officials. Hip hop came into its own with the nationwide success of *The Chronic* by Dr. Dre (Andre Young), who had helped pioneer gansta rap in 1989 as a member of Niggaz With Attitude (N.W.A.).

Among the year's top singles were R.E.M.'s "Losing My Religion," Bonnie Raitt's "Something to Talk About," Prince and the N.P.G.s' "Diamonds and Pearls," and "I Will Always Love You," a Dolly Parton song that Whitney Houston revived for her acting debut with Kevin Costner in Mick Jackson's film *The Bodyguard.* Best-selling albums included Michael Jackson's *Dangerous,* Vanessa Williams's *Comfort Zone,* Garth Brooks's *Ropin' the Wind,* U2's *Achtung Baby,* and Eric Clapton's Grammy Award–winning *Unplugged,* whose standout number "Tears in Heaven" also won for best song. Several top recording artists signed multimillion-dollar contracts with major studios, including Prince ($100 million), Madonna ($50 million), and Michael Jackson, who sold HBO television the rights to broadcast his *Dangerous* concert for $20 million.

Jazz received recognition and support when the Lila Wallace–*Reader's Digest* Foundation donated $1 million in grants for jazz concerts and jazz education programs; the saxophonist/composer Steve Lacy won a MacArthur "genius" award for creativity; and the pianist Billy Taylor received the National Medal of Arts, an honor also bestowed upon the Grand Ole Opry performer Minnie Pearl, banjo player Earl Scruggs, and opera singer Marilyn Horne, as well as actor James Earl Jones, sculptor Allan Houser, architects Robert Venturi and Denise Scott Brown, and film director Robert Wise. Composer Philip Glass commemorated the 500th anniversary of Columbus's expedition to the New World with a $2 million production of his new opera *The Voyage,* which celebrated Columbus's spirit of discovery.

Jazz pianist Billy Taylor was honored for his achievements. *(Photofest)*

The arrival of Europeans in the New World in 1492 was also the subject of social controversy, as Columbus's world-altering achievements and his brutal crimes against humanity were often framed in a context of political correctness that emphasized the harsh enslavement suffered by the indigenous American Indian population during Columbus's reign as governor of Hispaniola. Such arguments called attention to a long-neglected dark side of the discovery of the Americas, but they often downplayed the magnitude of the bright side: how, as much as anything else, Columbus's discovery of the New World sparked the end of the intellectually stifling, authoritarian medieval sensibility that predominated throughout Europe and energized the movement toward a freer, more diverse, diffuse, and intellectually open modern world, with all of its subsequent unimaginable horrors and awe-inspiring achievements.

In *Columbus: The New World Order* Peter Schumann's Bread and Puppet Theater used giant puppet masks to highlight the cruelty that the Spanish explorers inflicted on the indigenous inhabitants and to point out the hypocrisy inherent in Columbus's invocation of Christianity to justify the horrors his men committed. The title further punned on the phrase *new world,* which in Columbus's time referred to the Americas, but in the aftermath of the cold war evoked Bush's declaration of an American-led "new world order." The satirical puppet play thereby linked the past with the present, suggesting that a strain of hypocrisy, violence, and brutally has persisted throughout American history from the time of Columbus to the present.

In his cinematic treatment of the explorer's life, the director Ridley Scott tries to retain sympathy for Columbus by showing him as the victim of ruthless Spanish nobility, who undermine Columbus's efforts to treat the Indians fairly and ultimately force him from office. The exquisite photography of the lush tropical rain forest communicates how the New World must have appeared to be the Garden of Eden to the Spaniards from parched Iberia. And although he is fully dedicated to rational thought, Scott's Columbus, played by Gérard Depardieu, is nonetheless driven by a passionate quest to discover a new world where humanity can reinvent itself and start anew to create paradise on Earth.

Clint Eastwood's *Unforgiven* garnered Academy Awards for best picture, director, and actor (Eastwood). Set in Wyoming in the 1880s, the modern-day western tells the story of William Munny, a retired killer played by Eastwood who is driven by economic necessity to return to his former trade. Like many viewers in 1992 suffering from high unemployment, Munny is unable to sustain himself and his two children by hard work alone. And so, he rides off to earn the reward offered for killing two men who have mutilated a prostitute because she had inadvertently trivialized the manhood of one of them. The

Gérard Depardieu celebrated Christopher Columbus's belief in reason and imagination in Ridley Scott's *1492*. *(Photofest)*

movie thus makes a timely appeal to Americans suffering from the recession, while it embraced "politically correct" liberal values by showing disempowered women victimized by greedy, insensitive men and by highlighting the close friendship of the white protagonist, Munny, and his closest friend, a black man married to a Native American woman.

Emma Thompson won the Academy Award as best actress for her role in James Ivory's adaptation of E. M. Forster's novel *Howard's End* (1910). The film, much praised for its exquisite photography, period costumes, and set designs, costarred Anthony Hopkins, Vanessa Redgrave, and Helena Bonham Carter. In *Turn of the Screw* Rusty Lemorande adapts another novel by a major turn-of-the-century novelist, Henry James. Also remarkable for its cinematography is Michael Mann's remake of *The Last of the Mohicans,* adapted from the 18th-century novel by James Fenimore Cooper, in which Daniel Day Lewis plays Hawkeye, an American frontiersman during the French and Indian War. Jack Nicholson, Tom Cruise, and Demi Moore starred in Rob Reiner's *A Few Good Men,* which explores conflicts between the necessary exercise of power and the constraints of the law. Michael Douglas and Sharon Stone starred in Paul Verhoeven's *Basic Instinct,* a sexy and clever detective story; in *Scent of a Woman* Al Pacino plays a blind suicidal retired military officer who regains his will to live after sharing what he intended to be his final weekend with a college student hired to look after him (Chris O'Donnell). Penny Marshall's *A League of Their Own,* starring Geena Davis, Tom Hanks, Madonna, and Rosie O'Donnell, appealed to the public's growing appreciation of women's sports and athleticism. About a women's baseball league founded during World War II while many male players were overseas fighting, the movie suggests feminist sentiments by exposing the sexism and male condescension endured by female athletes. However, it also endorsed family values, as the star player was dedicated to her soldier/husband, who remained her first priority. Notable comedies included *Wayne's World,* a spinoff of a *Saturday Night Live* television skit in which Mike Myers and Dana Carvey play music-crazed teenagers who have a local cable-access television show, and *The Player,* Robert Altman's independently made satire of the Hollywood film industry.

Other independently made films included Spike Lee's *Malcolm X,* in which Denzel Washington plays the black activist and Nation of Islam leader who was assassinated in 1965; John Sayles's *Passion Fish,* the story of a woman struggling to readjust to life after a debilitating traffic accident; *Reservoir Dogs,* Quentin Tarantino's directorial debut about a jewelry heist gone wrong; and *A River Runs Through It,* Robert Redford's adaptation of Professor Norman Maclean's novel about the relationship between two Montana brothers (Brad Pitt and Craig Sheffer) raised by their father, a stern minister who has a passion for fly-fishing. Tim Robbins starred in and directed *Bob Roberts,* a scathing political satire directed against the religious right wing. Notable foreign-made films included Régis Wargnier's *Indochine,* starring Catherine Deneuve in a story about Vietnam before World War II, when it is still a French colony; and Neil Jordan's *The Crying Game,* a drama about the conflict in Northern Ireland in which little is as it appears.

Woody Allen released two of his most provocative movies in 1992, both starring him and his longtime acting partner and romantic companion, Mia Farrow. In *Shadows and Fog,* costarring Kathy Bates, John Cusak, Jodie Foster,

Julie Kavner, Madonna, and John Malkovich, Allen evokes the tragically surreal sensibility of Franz Kafka and the dark cinematographic style of Fritz Lang and other German Expressionists in a story of a man wrongly accused. In *Husbands and Wives,* about two couples whose marriages dissolve, Allen plays a professor of writing attracted to one of his star students. Farrow plays Allen's passively manipulative, chronically dissatisfied wife.

But it was the dissolution of Allen's real-life partnership with Farrow that became a notorious public scandal after the revelation that the 56-year-old Allen had been having an affair with Farrow's adopted daughter, Soon-Yi Previn, then a college coed (now Allen's wife and mother of their adopted children). The scandal intensified after Farrow accused Allen of sexually abusing their young jointly adopted daughter, Dylan. An investigation subsequently found insufficient grounds for filing criminal charges of abuse against Allen, but Allen's stature among his admirers was greatly diminished. Farrow and Allen had been widely admired as the ideal professional couple who successfully shared love, family, and interesting work but maintained separate lives. Consequently, the exposure of the duplicity and instability in their relationship left many feeling angry and betrayed and fueled arguments by social conservatives critical of the nontraditional, quasi-independent union Allen and Farrow had forged outside wedlock.

Social conservatives were also disturbed by Madonna's book *Sex,* a celebration of sexual passion that featured graphic pictures of activities ranging from heterosexual to bisexual to bestial couplings. Costing almost $50 a copy, it nonetheless sold some half-million copies in the first week, grossing $25 million. Another popular hit was *Millie's Book,* the purported autobiography of the Bush-family's dog, ghostwritten by First Lady Barbara Bush. Perot's *United We Stand* and Gore's *The Earth in the Balance: Healing the Global Environment* were also best-sellers.

Violence figures prominently in much of the literary writing of the year. In *Jazz,* Toni Morrison, who went on to win the 1993 Nobel Prize in literature, employs a narrative structure influenced by the improvisational nature of jazz music to tell the multifaceted story of a murder set amid the Harlem jazz scene of the 1920s; Richard Price's *Clockers* provided a more contemporary story of drugs and inner-city crime. On the other hand, Donna Tart's *The Secret History* imagines the crime and punishments of privileged white students—brilliant but morally deficient classics majors at an elite New England college. Terry McMillan's *Waiting to Exhale* addresses the problems of affluent black Americans in its story of four professional women who face reentering the dating scene in their late thirties. Susan Sontag's *The Volcano Lover: A Romance* depicts self-absorbed aristocrats whose life of art, love, and professional pursuits is overwhelmed by the French Revolution. The popular authors Stephen King, John Grisham, Danielle Steel, Sidney Sheldon, Anne Rice, and James A. Michener also published new fiction. The long-lost first half of Mark Twain's manuscript of *Adventures of Huckleberry Finn* was discovered in an attic and reunited with the second half in the Buffalo Public Library.

The Canadian author Michael Ondaatje's best-selling novel *The English Patient,* a World War II love story, won the 1992 Governor General's Award for fiction and shared the 1992 Booker Prize in Great Britain—the first time a

Canadian won that award. The Mexican author Laura Esquivel's love story *Like Water for Chocolate* also won critical acclaim for its magical realism and provoked considerable discussion among readers, especially women who responded strongly to the repressive family dynamics it portrayed. Robert Olen Butler received the Pulitzer Prize in fiction for *A Good Scent from a Strange Mountain,* a collection of stories about the Vietnam War told in the voices of the Vietnamese people.

Among the year's notable nonfiction was Norman Maclean's *Young Men and Fire,* a National Book Award winner about the deaths in 1949 of 13 Forest Service firefighters killed in a fire in Montana; Dan Wakefield's *New York in the Fifties,* a memoir of the Greenwich Village Beat and literary scenes; James Gleick's *Genius: The Life and Science of Richard Feynman,* about the Nobel Prize–winning theoretical physicist; Harvard professor Edward O' Wilson's *The Diversity of Life,* an environmentally sensitive survey of the way new life is created on Earth and recent human activity that has been destroying it; *Debating P.C.: The Controversy over Political Correctness on College Campuses,* edited by Paul Berman; *It Doesn't Take a Hero,* the autobiography of the Persian Gulf war hero General Norman Schwarzkopf; *Summer Meditations* by Václav Havel, Czechoslovakia's president; Clarissa Pinkola Estés's *Women Who Run with the Wolves,* a Jungian-influenced study that applies the lessons of folk tales to contemporary women's issues; John Gray's best-selling *Men Are from Mars, Women Are from Venus,* intended to help men and women better understand one another; and Francis Fukuyama's *The End of History and the Last Man,* which argues that after the collapse of worldwide communism, the historical evolution of human society reached its pinnacle with the success of liberal capitalist democracy. Drawing on the early 19th-century philosopher Georg Hegel, who also influenced the founder of communism, Karl Marx, Fukuyama argues that with the demise of communism and triumph of capitalist democracy, human society has arrived at a point where it no longer needs to continue to evolve in order to ensure citizens personal freedoms and provide for their security and material comforts and needs. Toni Morrison published *Playing in the Dark: Whiteness and the Literary Imagination,* a work of criticism, and edited and wrote the introduction to *Race-ing Justice, En-gendering Power: Essays on Anita Hill, Clarence Thomas, and the Construction of Social Reality.* Garry Wills won the Pulitzer Prize in nonfiction for *Lincoln at Gettysburg: The Words That Remade America.*

A copy of the first *Superman* comic book from 1938 sold for $82,500, and, after proclaiming, "Silence equals death," Northstar, a hero of Marvel comics, reveals that he is homosexual.

Two of television's most memorable moments of the year occurred in May. On May 22, Johnny Carson taped his final program as host of NBC's *The Tonight Show,* a late-night talk show he had hosted since taking over from Jack Paar on October 1, 1962. Television's highest-paid personality, Carson was attracting some 15 million viewers a night at the time of his retirement and earning $2,380 per minute of air time.[11] On May 18, the television character Murphy Brown, a highly accomplished 42-year-old, single professional woman, gave birth on her sitcom to a son. Played by Candice Bergen, who originated the character in 1988, Brown is an outspoken advocate of women's rights and liberal causes. Her decision not to marry the willing father, or another suitor, but to raise the child alone, won approval from some feminists, who applauded the show's advocacy of women's right to make lifestyle choices for themselves. But it was widely condemned by conservatives and others who believed Murphy's choice undermined family values. Vice President Dan Quayle, in particular, was ridiculed for attacking a television character; nonetheless, he expressed the views of many Americans when he condemned Murphy for dismissing the importance to a child's upbringing of a father or father figure. The convicted murderer Roger Coleman captured public sympathy when he proclaimed his innocence on *Donahue* and other television shows, but he failed to pass a lie detector test and went on to be executed for the 1981 rape and murder of a Virginia woman.

CBS's long-running newsmagazine *60 Minutes* remained the top-rated show throughout the year, followed in the fall season by the sitcoms *Roseanne, Murphy Brown, Home Improvement,* and Angela Lansbury's detective show *Murder, She Wrote. Murphy Brown* won the Emmy as best comedy of 1992; *Northern Exposure* was chosen as best dramatic series. The debut of MTV's *The Real World* pioneered the kind of reality programming that went on to dominate the ratings in the early 21st century. With cameras recording their conversations and actions throughout the house at all hours of the day, several young housemates pursue their personal and professional ambitions.

The arts and theater communities were especially hard hit by the ongoing AIDS epidemic, and the difficulties faced by homosexuals in the late 20th century were among the top issues explored on Broadway during the 1990s. *Millennium Approaches,* the first part of Tony Kushner's two-part *Angels in America* drama about gay men dealing with AIDS during the Reagan presidency, opened in 1992 and won the 1993 Pulitzer Prize and 1993 Tony Award as best play. Robert Schenkkan's *The Kentucky Cycle,* about conflicts among Indians, Irish immigrants, black slaves, and early American white pioneers, won the 1992 Pulitzer Prize in drama. Brian Friel's *Dancing at Lughnasa,* about five unmarried Irish sisters, won the 1992 Tony Award as best play, and the revival of George and Ira Gershwin's *Crazy for You* as best musical. Among the other top-rated Broadway openings were Herb Gardner's *Conversations with My Father,* starring Judd Hirsch and David Margulies; Ariel Dorfman's *Death and the Maiden,* starring Glenn Close, Richard Dreyfus, and Gene Hackman; August Wilson's *Two Trains Running,* with the Tony Award–winner Lawrence Fishburne and Cynthia Martell; and Neil Simon's *Jake's Women,* starring Alan Alda, Helen Shaver, and Kate Burton.

In sports, a study reported in the British science magazine *Nature* noted that female runners were becoming more competitive with men and that, although the fastest women still would not qualify for the men's 1992 Olympic events, statistical projections suggested they might equal, or even exceed, men's performance during the 21st century, especially in long-distance events that depend on endurance, such as the marathon.

The Washington Redskins became the champions of the 1991 professional football season in January, when they defeated the Buffalo Bills in Super Bowl XXVI. The Bills again won their conference title in the 1992 season but lost 52-17 to the Dallas Cowboys in Super Bowl XXVII, played in January 1993. The San Francisco 49er quarterback Steve Young was the league's most valuable player (MVP). The University of Alabama was named the top college team, and the University of Miami quarterback, Gino Torretta, won the Heisman trophy.

The pitchers Rollie Fingers and Tom Seaver, who received the strongest vote of any player in history (98.8 percent), were elected to Major League Baseball's Hall of Fame. Commissioner Fay Vincent resigned under pressure after trying to realign the leagues, and Bud Selig, the Milwaukee Brewers's owner, was appointed temporary commissioner. The Seattle Mariners became the first Major League team to have foreign owners when a Japanese-based group led by Hiroshi Yamauchi of the Nintendo Corporation purchased the team.

In league play, the Toronto Blue Jays defeated the Atlanta Braves in seven games to claim the World Series title. The Pittsburgh Pirate slugger Barry Bonds was the National League's MVP. The naming of Oakland Athletics relief pitcher Dennis Eckersley instead of an "everyday player" as the American League MVP was controversial, as pitchers, who generally play only every fourth day, have their own Cy Young Award. Eckersley and Greg Maddux of the Chicago Cubs were their league's Cy Young winners. Juan Gonzalez of the Texas Rangers led the Major Leagues with 43 home runs. Milwaukee's Robin Yount and Kansas City's George Brett became the 17th and 18th players in Major League history to produce 3,000 hits.

The Boston Celtics basketball star Larry Bird retired after 13 seasons, and the era that had been dominated by Bird and Los Angeles Laker standouts Kareem Abdul-Jabbar and Magic Johnson yielded to a new era dominated by Michael Jordan and the Chicago Bulls. The Bulls won the 1992 NBA championship, defeating the Portland Trailblazers, and Jordan was MVP. Led by Player of the Year Christian Laettner, Duke University was the year's top college basketball team.

Hockey's Pittsburgh Penguins won their second consecutive Stanley Cup, and Manon Rheaume became the first woman to play for any of the major professional sports leagues when she played goaltender for the NHL's Tampa Bay Lightning in a preseason hockey game against the Saint Louis Blues. The golfer Tom Kite won the USGA open, and Stephen Edberg and Monica Seles prevailed in the singles events at the U.S. Tennis Open in New York. Tennis player Martina Navratilova set a new record when she defeated Jana Novona, also from Czechoslovakia, to win her 158th championship. The retired tennis champion Arthur Ashe revealed that he had contracted AIDS through blood transfusions administered after a heart attack. Ashe, who in 1968 became the first black man to win a Grand Slam tennis event, the U.S. Open, died in February 1993. Riddick Bowe took boxing's heavyweight title from Evander Holyfield, and the former heavyweight champion Mike Tyson was sentenced to 10 years in prison after being convicted of raping a contestant in the Miss Black America beauty contest. Ridden by Pat Day, the 17-1 longshot Lil E. Tee won the Kentucky Derby.

The 1992 Olympic Games were notable as the last time that the summer and winter competitions were held during the same year. To facilitate the new staggered schedule, the next winter Olympics were planned for 1994, and the summer games for 1996. Held in February in Albertville, France, the 1992 winter competition moved the Olympics into the post–cold war era, as a single German team featured athletes from both the former East and former West

Germany; and the Baltic states Lithuania, Latvia, and Estonia competed as independent nations for the first time since World War II. Competing as the Unified Team, athletes from the former Soviet Union participated as a single squad. Kristi Yamaguchi became the first American to win a gold medal in figure skating since Dorothy Hamill had in 1976. Although Germany won the most medals (26), U.S. women also garnered gold medals for speed skating and downhill skiing. The summer games took place in Barcelona, Spain. Playing together for the final time as a single squad, the Unified Team won the most medals, followed by the United States. A U.S. "Dream Team" basketball squad, including NBA stars Bird, Johnson, Jordan, Karl Malone, Scottie Pippen, Patrick Ewing, John Stockton, and Charles Barkley, dominated all opposition. Americans also won gold medals in several track events, as Mike Barroman and Kevin Young set world records in the 200- and 400-meter races, respectively.

Chronicle of Events

January 1: Egypt's Boutros Boutros-Ghali becomes UN secretary-general.

January 1: Serbia and Croatia allow deployment of UN peacekeeping troops.

January 5: UN efforts fail to secure a cease-fire in Somalia.

January 5–6: The IRA detonates two large bombs in Belfast's commercial center. Another IRA bomb explodes in the government center of London on January 10.

January 6: As a result of newly raised safety concerns, the FDA places a moratorium on the sale and implantation of silicone-gel breast implants.

January 6: The *New York Times* runs an op-ed piece maintaining that a 15-year-old Kuwaiti woman whose 1990 congressional testimony about Iraqi atrocities helped secure popular support for the Persian Gulf War was actually the daughter of Kuwait's ambassador to the United States.

January 6: A Quebec Superior Court grants a 25-year-old woman "the right to die," when it approves her petition to compel doctors to disconnect her from the respirator that has been sustaining her life for more than two years.

January 7: A Yugoslavian air force jet shoots down an unarmed helicopter that is part of the EC's observer mission in Croatia. Five observers are killed.

January 8: Suffering from the flu, President Bush collapses at a state dinner in Japan, where he is visiting for three days as part of a 10-day tour of Asia.

January 11: The singer Paul Simon and his band begin their tour of South Africa in celebration of the end of apartheid. Simon is the first major artist to

Singer Paul Simon celebrated the end of apartheid by performing on tour in South Africa. *(Photofest)*

perform in South Africa since the end of a worldwide cultural boycott.

January 11: To forestall a political victory by Algeria's Islamic fundamentalists, President Chadli Benjedid resigns and cedes power to the military, which, on January 12, cancels a runoff election scheduled for January 16, in which the fundamentalists were expected to gain a majority in parliament. On January 22, the government arrests the leader of the fundamentalists and bans all nonreligious activities in Algeria's mosques.

January 13: The mass murderer Jeffrey L. Dahmer pleads guilty (though insane) to killing 15 young men and boys, most of them black homosexuals, in his Milwaukee apartment.

January 15: The European Community recognizes the independence of Yugoslavia's breakaway republics, Croatia and Slovenia.

January 16: The government of El Salvador concludes 12 years of civil war when it signs a peace agreement with leftist rebels.

January 17: The astronomer Alexander Wolszczan of Pennsylvania State University publishes an article in the journal *Science* citing his discovery in late 1991 of two extrasolar planets orbiting a pulsar within the Milky Way.

January 17–30: Arkansas governor Bill Clinton, a candidate for the Democratic nomination for president, becomes the subject of media reports that he has had a 12-year extramarital affair.

January 20: A riot breaks out in Denver, Colorado, between Ku Klux Klansmen and civil rights supporters celebrating the national holiday honoring the Reverend Martin Luther King, Jr., who had been assassinated. In Phoenix, some 5,000 demonstrators march in support of recognizing the holiday in Arizona, the only state in the country that does not officially observe it, although New Hampshire designates it as a tribute to civil rights in general, and not solely to King.

January 20: In Cuba, Eduardo Díaz Betancourt, the leader of three exiles arrested on charges of terrorism in December 1991, is executed by a firing squad, sparking international protest.

January 22: Roberta Bondar becomes the second Canadian, and the first Canadian woman, to travel into outer space, when she joins the crew of the U.S. space shuttle *Discovery.*

January 30: In his State of the Union address Bush proposes to stimulate the economy by ordering a 90-day moratorium on new government regulations, decreased federal withholding from employee paychecks, and accelerated government spending and by proposing reductions in the capital gains tax and other tax breaks, and the extension of unemployment benefits. Bush also announces cuts in defense spending.

February 1: Bush and Yeltsin meet at Camp David, Maryland, and declare a new era of "friendship and partnership" between the United States and Russia.

February 3: Record levels of CFCs and bromine are measured in the atmosphere above New England and eastern Canada.

February 7: Meeting in the Dutch town of Maastricht, foreigner ministers of the 12 nations in the European Community sign the Treaty on the European Union and the Final Act.

February 8–23: The Winter Olympic Games are played in Albertville, France.

February 17: Jeffrey Dahmer receives 15 consecutive life terms in prison for murdering 15 boys and young men in 1991. He later receives a 16th life sentence for a murder he committed in 1978.

February 20: The United Nations votes to send 16,000 peacekeeping troops to enforce a cease-fire in Cambodia.

February 21: The Security Council votes to send a 14,000-troop peacekeeping force to Croatia.

February 24: The grunge musicians Kurt Cobain of Nirvana and Hole's Courtney Love marry.

February 24: The U.S. Postal Service unveils two potential designs for its proposed Elvis Presley stamp for consumers to vote on. The portrait of Presley as he looked during the 1950s, the so-called young Elvis, prevails over that of a much older-looking Presley from the 1970s and is issued the following January.

March 1: Muslim and Croatian communities in Bosnia vote for independence from Yugoslavia, prompting military action by Bosnian Serbs who want to remain affiliated with the Serb-dominated federation and by invading Yugoslav and Croatian forces.

March 6: The final episode of the popular *Cosby Show* airs on NBC.

March 6: The Michelangelo computer virus is launched on the 517th anniversary of the artist's birthday. The virus goes on to infect approximately 1 million IBM and IBM-compatible computers.

March 10: Clinton asserts himself as front-runner for the Democratic presidential nomination after

The Cosby Show, which ran from 1984 to 1992, was the top-rated network program between 1985 and 1990. *(Photofest)*

winning eight primary victories on so-called Super Tuesday.

March 10: The former Soviet foreign minister Eduard Shevardnadze is elected interim president of the Republic of Georgia.

March 11: The former president Richard Nixon, who presided over the thawing of U.S.–Soviet relations in the 1970s, criticizes Bush, a fellow Republican, for not offering sufficient economic aid to Russia.

March 17: White South Africans vote to endorse President Frederik de Klerk's plan to extend equal legal status to black citizens, prompting de Klerk to declare, "Today, we have closed the book on apartheid."

March 17: A bomb explodes outside the Israeli embassy in Buenos Aires, Argentina, killing 10 people.

March 20: Prime Minister Li Peng calls for economic reforms to make China's economy more similar to Western capitalism.

March 27: Police in Philadelphia arrest a man who has AIDS for infecting several hundred teenage boys with human immunodeficiency virus (HIV) through sexual relations.

March 31: As a gesture of reconciliation, King Juan Carlos of Spain meets in a Jewish synagogue in Madrid with Israeli president Chaim Herzog exactly 500 years after the Inquisition drove the Jews from Spain in 1492. The king receives blessings from a rabbi.

April 2: The organized crime leader John Gotti is convicted on five counts of murder. He is sentenced to life in prison on June 23.

April 6: The United States recognizes the newly independent states of Slovenia, Croatia, and Bosnia-Herzegovina, which have separated from Yugoslavia.

April 9: Prime Minister John Major leads his Conservative Party to its fourth consecutive victory in Britain's general elections.

April 9: A Miami jury finds Manuel Noriega, Panama's former president, guilty of drug trafficking.

April 12: Euro Disneyland opens in France.

April 13: Chicago's downtown district is flooded and its infrastructure damaged when some 250 million gallons of water leak from the Chicago River, overflowing into basements and tunnels and causing power outages.

April 21: Serbian forces allied with Bosnian Serbs fire on Sarajevo, the capital of Bosnia, held by a combined Muslim and Croat force.

April 23: European monitors negotiate a cease-fire in Bosnia.

April 23: The Cosmic Background Explorer (COBE) discovers ripples in the background microwave radiation that fills outer space.

April 29: A jury acquits four white Los Angeles policemen accused of illegally beating black motorist Rodney King during a widely viewed videotaped arrest. Four days of rioting ensue.

May 9: An explosion in the Westray coal mine in Plymouth, Nova Scotia, kills 26 miners and closes the state-of-the-art facility just eight months after its opening.

May 12: Serbs break the cease-fire and renew their shelling of Sarajevo.

May 18: The UN high commissioner for refugees announces that 1 million people have been made homeless as a consequence of the fighting in Bosnia and that tens of thousands are seeking sanctuary in other countries.

May 18: The television character Murphy Brown, a 42-year-old single professional woman, gives birth on her sitcom to a son, after choosing to bear and raise the child alone.

May 19: Quayle condemns the writers of *Murphy Brown* for denigrating the importance of fathers in child rearing.

June 1: The government of Taiwan apologizes for the death of 28,000 civilians who were killed during political protests in 1947.

June 3–14: Leaders of countries throughout the world attend an Earth Summit on economic development and the environment in Rio de Janeiro, Brazil.

June 16: Caspar Weinberger, who had served as secretary of defense under Reagan, is indicted for lying to Congress about the Iran-contra affair.

June 16: The last two Western hostages held in the Middle East, the Germans Heinrich Strubig and Thomas Kemptner, are released.

June 16: Fidel Ramos is elected president of the Philippines.

June 23: Labor candidate Yitzhak Rabin is elected prime minister of Israel.

June 29: President Mohammed Boudiaf of Algeria is assassinated. Islamic fundamentalists are believed to be responsible.

July 1: Two months after the riots, Willie Williams replaces Daryl Gates as chief of the Los Angeles Police Department.

July 2: Canadian troops push through a Serb roadblock and take positions around the Sarajevo airport, which they open to flights carrying food and medicine for inhabitants of the besieged city.

July 5: The American Andre Agassi and Steffi Graf of Germany win the singles championships at the Wimbledon tennis tournament.

July 6: The Russian Kirov Opera performs for the first time in the United States.

July 8: Thomas Klestil becomes president of Austria, replacing Kurt Waldheim, a former officer in the Nazi army, who, as president, had been snubbed by Western leaders after revelations of his complicity in the Holocaust during World War II.

July 9: Astronauts on the space shuttle *Columbia* conclude NASA's longest shuttle mission to this date, a 14-day stay in space during which they circle the Earth 221 times and travel 5.76 million miles.

July 9: Clinton selects Gore as his running mate.

July 10: Noriega is sentenced to 40 years in prison.

July 10: Poland installs its first female prime minister.

July 16: Clinton wins the Democratic nomination for president, and the billionaire Ross Perot withdraws as a third-party candidate.

July 17: After a declaration of sovereignty by Slovakia and the pending breakup of Czechoslovakia it implies, Czech president Václav Havel resigns.

July 22: Pablo Escobar, head of the Medellín cocaine cartel, escapes from his luxurious ranchlike prison in Colombia, where he has been confined since his capture in June 1991.

July 24: Thousands of Bosnian Muslims flee the northern town of Bosanski to escape ethnic cleansing.

July 25–August 9: The Summer Olympics are played in Barcelona, Spain.

July 28: The ruling Islamic regime in Afghanistan bans women from appearing on television.

August 3: Russia and the Ukraine place the former Soviet Black Sea Fleet under their joint command.

August 3: France ratifies the nuclear nonproliferation treaty.

August 4: The Security Council condemns concentration camps that Serbs have erected in Bosnia to facilitate ethnic cleansing.

August 11: The largest shopping mall in the United States opens in Bloomington, Minnesota. Housing more than 300 stores and covering 4.2 million square feet, it has cost $625 million.[12]

August 11: The United States agrees to furnish $10 billion in loan guarantees to Israel after Rabin agrees to limit expansion of Jewish settlement on the West Bank and Gaza Strip.

August 12: Leaders of the United States, Canada, and Mexico sign NAFTA.

August 14: The Security Council authorizes military action in support of humanitarian relief operations in Bosnia.

August 18: Larry Bird of the Boston Celtics retires from professional basketball after completing a 13-year career in which he was named MVP three times (1984–86).

August 20: Republicans renominate Bush and Quayle as their choices for president and vice president in the upcoming election.

August 21–22: Vicki and Sammy Weaver, the wife and 14-year-old son of the fugitive Randy Weaver, and Deputy Marshal William Degan are killed in gunfights at Weaver's cabin in Ruby Ridge, Idaho, as federal agents attempt to arrest Weaver, a fugitive wanted for selling illegal weapons. The standoff will end on August 31, with the surrender of Weaver and his 25-year-old friend Kevin Harris, who will subsequently be tried for and acquitted of killing Degan.

August 24: Hurricane Andrew becomes the most expensive natural disaster in U.S. history after it strikes south Florida, just south of Miami, with winds up to 175 mph.

September 4: Todor Zhivkov is sentenced to seven years in prison for crimes committed during his 35 years as head of the Communist regime in Bulgaria.

September 12: Forces in Peru capture Abimael Guzman, the leader of the Maoist guerrilla insurgency known as Shining Path, which had been terrorizing the nation since 1980.

September 12: Mark Lee and Jan Davis become the first married couple to enter outer space when they begin a mission together on the space shuttle *Endeavor,* along with the first black woman to fly into space, Mae Jemison, and Mamoru Mohri, the first Japanese astronaut to go into space aboard an American spacecraft.

September 14: Floods kill some 2,500 people in India and Pakistan.

September 21: Ending a 130-year break, the Vatican restores diplomatic relations with Mexico.

September 23: The 20-year-old goalie Manon Rheaume becomes the first woman to play in any of the four major professional sports leagues when, as a member of the NHL's Tampa Bay Lightning, she enters a preseason hockey game against the Saint Louis Blues.

September 25: NASA launches the *Mars Observer* to study Mars and the Martian environment. It also carries high-energy astrophysics instruments, including a gamma ray spectrometer.

September 25: A 12-year-old Florida boy wins his lawsuit petitioning to be "divorced" from his biological parents, who, he claims, have neglected him.

September 28: Observation by astronomers confirms the existence of a 10th planet at the edge of the solar system.

October 1: By this date some 300,000 Somalis are estimated to have died of famine and thousands more of factional warfare that has both killed people outright and prevented humanitarian aid from reaching others in dire need.

October 1: Perot reenters the presidential race as a third-party candidate.

October 2: The UN Security Council votes to use frozen Iraqi assets to compensate victims of the Kuwaiti invasion and to defray the cost of the Persian Gulf War.

October 3: Tens of thousands of Germans commemorate the second anniversary of German reunification by marching in protest against the recent wave of neo-Nazi attacks on immigrants.

October 9: The UN imposes an air exclusion zone over Bosnia.

October 13: Police in Germany seize more than four pounds of uranium that originated in the former Soviet Union, fueling concerns that the corrupt and chaotic conditions there might enable rogue nations or terrorist organizations to acquire material necessary for making nuclear bombs.

October 19: Bosnian Serbs massacre the Muslim population of the village of Vlasenica.

October 23: The former head of France's National Blood Transfusion Center receives a four-year prison sentence for his role in the distribution of HIV-contaminated blood.

October 24: The Toronto Blue Jays defeat the Atlanta Braves in the seventh game of baseball's World Series.

October 24: In an effort to encourage freedom and market economies, Bush signs the Freedom Support Act providing financial and technical assistance to most of the states of the former Soviet Union.

October 25: German and British veterans of the World War II battle of El Alamein in the Egyptian desert reunite.

October 26: Canadian voters reject a constitutional proposal that would have given French-speaking Quebec greater autonomy and special status within the Canadian confederation.

October 31: Guerrilla attacks in Angola shatter a 1991 cease-fire and renew civil war.

October 31: A Vatican commission of historical, scientific, and theological inquiry absolves Galileo Galilei of heresy charges for which he was condemned in 1633.

November 2: Iran increases its bounty for the killing of British citizen Salman Rushdie, author of *Satanic Verses.*

November 4: Clinton defeats Bush to win the U.S. presidential election. Al Gore is elected vice president.

November 5: Playing in Belgrade, in defiance of an embargo on Serbia, the American chess master Bobbie Fischer defeats Russian Boris Spassky in a replay of their famous cold war contest of 1972, which Fischer also won.

November 11: Anglican churches in England vote to allow women to become priests. Anglican churches in Australia will do likewise on November 21.

November 16: The Roman Catholic Church adopts a new universal catechism for the first time in four centuries.

December 3: The Security Council approves direct humanitarian intervention in Somalia to distribute food and medical supplies to starving Somalis.

December 4: Bush authorizes Operation Restore Hope, sending 28,000 troops to Somalia to assist famine-stricken Somalis.

December 7: Religious riots across northern India kill hundreds of people after Hindus destroy an ancient Muslim mosque in the Hindu holy city of Ayodhya.

December 9: The first contingent of U.S. Marines in Somalia is met by hordes of photographers and camera crews as they storm ashore before dawn.

December 20: Bush and Britain's prime minister John Major agree to establish a no-fly zone over Bosnia from which Serbian aircraft are banned.

December 24: Outgoing president George H. W. Bush pardons six officials charged or convicted in the Iran-contra affair, including Weinberger.

December 29: The United States and Russia agree on language calling for further reductions of their nuclear stockpiles in START II, which Bush and Yeltsin will sign on January 3, 1993.

December 31: Bush flies to Mogadishu, the capital of Somalia, to review relief efforts.

Eyewitness Testimony

The English Patient began with a vision: a burning man in the desert.

> *Canadian author Michael Ondaatje describing the genesis of his best-selling 1992 novel* The English Patient, *in Lauri Seidlitz,* The 1990s *(2000), p. 25.*

I was inspired by the conviction behind the music and the sincerity behind the lyrics. It's not like they were the first band [to fuse hard rock and rap], but they were the first to do it right.

> *Singer Chino Moreno of the Deftones commenting on the music of the politically inspired band Rage against the Machine, who in 1992 released their first album, "The Greatest Albums of the '90s," Spin, September 1999, p. 132.*

The twentieth century, it is safe to say, has made all of us into deep historical pessimists. . . .

The pessimism of the twentieth century stands in sharp contrast to the optimism of the previous one [which was] . . . by and large a century of peace and unprecedented increases in material well-being. There were two broad grounds for optimism . . . the belief that modern science would improve human life by conquering disease and poverty . . . [and] free democratic governments would continue to spread to more and more countries around the world. . . .

The extreme pessimism of our own century is due at least in part to the cruelty with which these earlier expectations were shattered. The First World War was a critical event in the undermining of Europe's self-confidence. The war of course brought down the old political order . . . but its deeper impact was psychological. . . . The virtues of loyalty, hard work, perseverance, and patriotism were brought to bear in the systematic and pointless slaughter of other men. . . .

If modern science made possible weapons of unprecedented destructiveness . . . modern politics create a state of unprecedented power. . . . In our own time, one of the clearest manifestations of our pessimism was the almost universal belief in the permanence of a vigorous, communist-totalitarian alternative to Western liberal democracy. . . .

[Nonetheless] as we reach the 1990s, the world as a whole . . . has gotten *better* in certain distinct ways. . . . Authoritarian dictatorships of all kinds, both on the Right and on the Left, have been collapsing. . . . If the early twentieth century's major political innovation was the invention of the strong states of totalitarian Germany or Russia . . . then the past few decades have revealed a tremendous weakness at their core. And this weakness, so massive and unexpected, suggests that the pessimistic lessons about history that our century supposedly taught us need to be rethought from the beginning.

> *Historian Francis Fukuyama arguing in 1992 that the fact that liberal democracy prevailed over fascist and communist totalitarianism is the basis for historical optimism, in Fukuyama,* The End of History and the Last Man *(1993), pp. 3–12.*

Healthy wolves and healthy women share certain psychic characteristics: keen sensing, playful spirit, and a heightened capacity for devotion. Wolves and women are relational by nature, inquiring, possessed of great endurance and strength. They are deeply intuitive, intensely concerned with their young, their mates, and their pack. They are experienced in adapting to constantly changing circumstances; they are fiercely stalwart and very brave.

Yet both have been hounded, harassed, and falsely imputed to be devouring and devious, overly aggressive, of less value than those who are their detractors. They are the targets of those who would clean up the wilds as well as the wildish environs of the psyche, extincting the instinctual, and leaving no trace of it behind. The predation of wolves and women by those who misunderstand them is strikingly similar. . . .

What are some of the feeling-toned symptoms of a disrupted relationship with the wildish force in the psyche? To chronically feel, think, or act in any of the following ways is to have partially severed or lost entirely the relationship with the deep instinctual psyche: . . . feeling extraordinarily dry, fatigued, frail, depressed, confused, gagged, muzzled, unaroused. Feeling frightened . . . or weak, without inspiration, without animation, without soulfulness, without meaning, shame-bearing, chronically fuming, volatile, stuck, uncreative, compressed, crazed. . . .

The wild nature carries the bundles for healing; she carries everything a woman needs to be and know. . . . To adjoin the instinctual nature does not mean to come undone, change everything from left to right . . . to act crazy or out of control. . . .

It means to establish territory, to find one's pack, to be in one's body with certainty and pride regardless of the body's gifts and limitations, to speak and act in one's behalf, to be aware, alert, to draw on the innate feminine powers of intuition and sensing. . . .

Jungian psychoanalyst Clarissa Pinkola Estés, Ph.D., discussing women's need to remain attuned to their natural wolflike instincts in Estés, Women Who Run with the Wolves *(1992), pp. 2–11.*

Why did I stay with Woody Allen when so much was wrong? How can I explain it to my children, when even to me it is incomprehensible and unforgivable? Was he only an illusion I loved all along? What was missing in me that compelled me to hold it all in place? When did the illusion become a lie? Why did I expose my children to his disregard for so long, and place them at risk? Why did I allow therapists to override my maternal instincts and doubt my own eyes?

I could protest that I didn't know—how could I have known—what he was capable of. How could I believe it? I could argue that the world I had occupied with him for a quarter of my life was so utterly removed from any other that it was impossible for me to envision a life for myself beyond it. Every aspect of my existence was interwoven with his.

I could tell my children all this, but no explanation seems adequate. In the end all I can do is accept my share of responsibility, and hope they can find it in their hearts to forgive me.

Actress Mia Farrow trying to comprehend her love relationship with the actor/director Woody Allen, which ended on January 13, 1992, when she discovered Allen was having an affair with her adopted daughter, Soon-Yi Previn, in Farrow, What Falls Away *(1997), pp. 237–238.*

As human beings on the surface we have a very short-term [idea] of survival—we need to think more about the survival of the planet as a whole. We're so small we think the horizon goes on forever. When you're in space, you realize it doesn't.

Astronaut Roberta Bondar, the first Canadian woman to travel to outer space, commenting on the perspective she gained from her voyage on the U.S. space shuttle Discovery, *which began on January 22, 1992, in Lauri Seidlitz,* The 1990s *(2000), p. 26.*

Crime is out of control. Criminals have no fear of punishment. Prisons are overcrowded so they know they will not be imprisoned long. . . .

Taxes are a joke. Regardless of what a political candidate "promises," they will increase taxes. More taxes are always the answer to government mismanagement. . . .

The "American Dream" of the middle class has all but disappeared, substituted with people struggling just to buy next week's groceries. Heaven forbid the car breaks down! . . .

What is it going to take to open up the eyes of our elected officials. AMERICA IS IN SERIOUS DECLINE.

We have no proverbial tea to dump; should we instead sink a ship full of Japanese imports? Is a Civil War imminent? Do we have to shed blood to reform the current system? I hope it doesn't come to that! But it might.

A letter to the editor published by the future Oklahoma City bomber Timothy McVeigh in the Lockport, New York, Union-Sun & Journal *in February 1992, in Morris Dees,* Gathering Storm: America's Militias *(1996), pp. 154–155.*

Down with Jews and Germans. Poland for the Poles.

Anti-Semitic and antiforeign slogans chanted by protesting members of the Polish National Community Party—many of them skinheads—on February 15, 1992, in Martin Gilbert, A History of the Twentieth Century, *vol. 3 (2000), pp. 739–740.*

You don't build economic strength by taxing economic strength. If you tax wealth, you diminish wealth. If you diminish wealth, you diminish investment. The fewer the investments, the fewer jobs.

Vice President Dan Quayle justifying administration-supported tax cuts for business on February 27, 1992, in Alan F. Pater and Jason R. Pater, eds., What They Said in 1992 *(1993), p. 107.*

Some contemporary defenders of fee-for-[medical] service . . . reject the distinctions . . . between business and medical practice, claiming that medicine is just another market—admittedly with more imperfections than most, but a market nonetheless. They profess they do not see much difference between medical care and any other important economic commodity, such as food, clothing, or housing. Such critics dismiss the notion of a *de facto* social contract in medical care. They assert that physicians and private hospitals owe nothing to society and should be free to sell or otherwise dispose of their services in any lawful manner they choose.

Until recently such views had little influence. Most people considered medical care to be a social good, not a commodity, and physicians acted as if they agreed. . . . The situation is now rapidly changing. In the past two decades or so health care has become commercialized as never before, and professionalism in medicine seems to be giving way to entrepreneurialism. The health-care system is now widely regarded as an industry, and medical practice as a competitive business.

Arnold S. Relman, M.D., discussing the growing influence of economic forces on medical decisions in "What Market Values Are Doing to Medicine," Atlantic, March 1992, p. 101.

If anybody will listen, I have said there is one priority that faces this country. That is to stop the decline of the job base. Because if we continue to lay off tens of thousands of people, we lose taxpayers and get welfare users. A welfare user gets more money from the government than a blue-collar worker pays in taxes every month. So it's more than a double kill. We take in a trillion dollars a year. We spend a trillion four. . . . The way out of debt is the expanded job base. If you don't have that, you can't make this country work.

The third-party presidential candidate Ross Perot explaining his position on the economy on April 27, 1992, in Alan F. Pater and Jason R. Pater, eds., What They Said in 1992 (1993), p. 105.

The riots were pretty, even on that old TV. The flames, the excitement, the helicopter shots. It was *The Year of Living Dangerously* in real life. I figured that was the reason the rioters had done it in the first place. They were as desperate as the rest of us for something to happen, something big, something significant. The [Rodney] King verdict was chickenshit, of course, but it was just a key to the door. When they got started out here in the street, they said, Hey, we can do this. We can ravage this fucking city, this fucking shithole. We can tear it apart and burn it down. . . . They can't do anything worse to us than they've already done. You could see their minds working there on the TV, see them getting more and more excited, getting the thrill of smacking people with boards, yanking people out of cars, standing in the middle of the road where you don't belong and pissing like there was no tomorrow. It was day and night drama, something to tell the kids. I wasn't being cynical, either. The riot guys felt bad about their lives. You got a sense of how bad looking at them work. . . .

On screen the guys were beating up Reginald Denny, the truckdriver. The one guy drop-kicked him and another guy hit him with a rock. Denny wasn't looking too good. He was kind of splattered on the road there, didn't know where he was, his big truck was right there with its door open, but it didn't offer any protection at all. They showed the attack on him four or five times, and it was hard to watch over and over. I understood it and it still made me angry, like I wanted some avenger to swoop in and kick these kids' asses.

The fictional character Del describing the experience of watching the televised Los Angeles riots, which began on April 29, 1992, in Frederick Barthelme, Painted Desert (1995), pp. 22–23.

Yesterday afternoon, National Guard troops drove down Figueroa Street and occupied this country's second-largest city. . . .

Inside the [Mount Zion Missionary Baptist Church], President Bush was rubbing elbows at an ecumenical service with a select group of the city's elite. . . . The president's staff and Secret Service, fearing protests by angry residents, had turned the trucks loaded with food donated for victims of last week's riot into temporary shields, blocking sight lines for the ordinary people who had come to get a glimpse of their president. Call it food for defense.

Like everything else about Bush's short trip . . . the scene in front of the church showed just how isolated this Yale preppie is from the people he governs. "We've seen the tip of his hair," said Luis Limon. "He didn't even as much as wave.". . .

Inside, Bush tried his best to be relevant. "We've seen the hatred. We've got to heal and see the love," said the man who captured the White House . . . by milking racist images like that of Willie Horton. But even this appeal for healing was hollow and rife with political partisanship. The neighborhood's top black official, Democratic Senator Diane Watson, for instance, wasn't even invited to the service or to Bush's meeting with black leaders afterward. . . . [The actor and relief organizer] Edward James Olmos . . . emerged from the church furious that [a top Hispanic official, Gloria] Molina and other key Latino leaders had been neglected and that the riots continue to be characterized as a "black problem."

Olmos has good reason to be angry. . . . Of the first 5,438 people arrested, only 37 percent were black, while 51 percent were Hispanic and the rest were either white or of other races. . . .

The evidence is in. There is so much anger and frustration among the forgotten have-nots of this country and it has been building for so long that when it erupts . . . it becomes a sight more ghastly than any we have yet imagined. This was, after all, the riot America has always feared—the one that spilled out of the ghetto and into every corner of town.

Newspaper reporter Juan Gonzalez describing in May 1992 President Bush's visit to Los Angeles soon after the riots in Los Angeles that lasted from April 29 to May 3, 1992, in James Haley, ed., Post–Cold War America: 1992–Present *(2003), pp. 30–39.*

We believe that many of the root problems that have resulted in inner-city difficulties were started in the '60s and '70s and that they have failed.

Marlin Fitzwater, Bush's press secretary, commenting on May 4, 1992, on the Los Angeles riots that lasted from April 29 to May 3, in Hitchings, ed., Facts On File Yearbook 1992 *(1993), p. 213.*

When hip-hop began its development some 15 years ago in New York, it was dismissed as a passing fad . . . until the release of Public Enemy's ground-breaking 1988 album, "It Takes a Nation of Millions to Hold Us Back." Suddenly, rap was [perceived as] . . . a method of conveying political statements and promoting a world view that wasn't reflected in the mainstream media. It was also a perfect medium for teaching a young, impressionable audience about their culture and for motivating them to question the society they lived in.

While the music media fell over themselves discussing the new political rap and its influences, from the Nation of Islam to the Afrocentricity movement, another genre of socially infused hip-hop was evolving. Gangsta rap had its first major success [in 1989] with L.A. group N.W.A., whose second album, *Straight Outta Compton,* went platinum in the United States. . . . The music emphasized the rough street sensibilities from which it sprang, and the listeners loved it.

What began as a cousin to its more serious Afrocentric and political rap relatives has since become the new patriarch in the hip-hop musical family. . . .

Critics of gansta rap argue that it's not constructive criticism or commentary on the social problems being described. . . . People were shocked by the amount of violence described in the track ["F—Tha Police" from N.W.A.'s *Straight Outta Compton* album]. . . . Three years later, though, the group's detractors were forced to swallow those words when an 81-second home video of Rodney King being brutally beaten by L.A. police surfaced. After the [subsequent] L.A. riots . . . N.W.A.'s defense of "F—Tha Police" as a "revenge fantasy" seems less like a copout and more like a prescient view of how people felt in neighborhoods like Compton. *Straight Outta Compton,* despite its profanity, violence, and misogyny, contains undeniable truths.

Music industry executive Ian Steaman discussing on September 19, 1992, the status of hip-hop and gansta rap after the Los Angeles riots of April 29–May 3, 1992, in James Haley, ed., Post–Cold War America: 1992–Present *(2003), pp. 40–43.*

Russia is still [a threat in Asia and the Pacific]. You don't see the same changes in the Russian military structure when you sit in Japan and look west as you do when you sit in Berlin and look east. China is a major power center, and that alone is ample justification for continued U.S. presence in this part of the world.

Lieutenant General Richard Hawley, commander of U.S. forces in Japan, commenting on May 5, 1992, on military threats posed by China and Russia, in Alan F. Pater and Jason R. Pater, eds., What They Said in 1992 *(1993), p. 280.*

It doesn't help matters when prime-time TV has Murphy Brown, a character who supposedly epitomizes today's intelligent, highly paid professional woman, mocking the importance of fathers by bearing a child alone and calling it just another lifestyle choice.

Vice President Dan Quayle, on May 19, 1992, criticizing the television character Murphy Brown for choosing to have a child out of wedlock and raise it alone, in Tim Brooks and Earle Marsh, The Complete Directory to Prime Time Network and Cable TV Shows: 1946–Present *(1999), p. 694.*

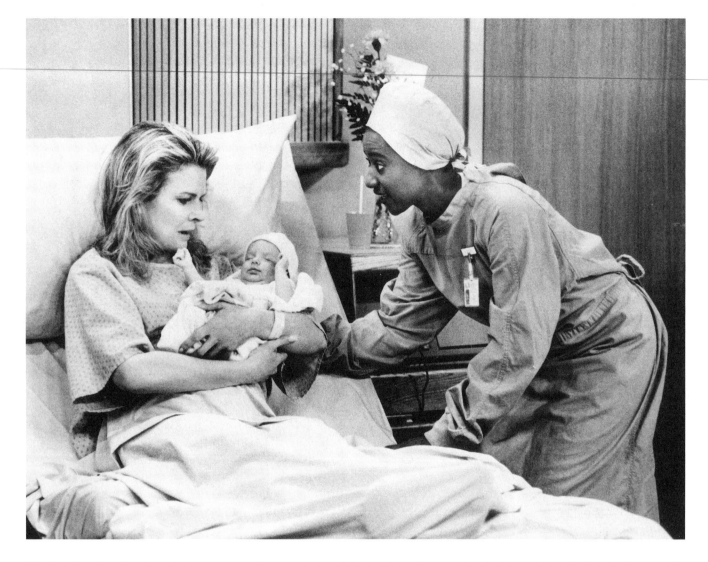

Vice President Dan Quayle sparked controversy when he condemned the television character Murphy Brown (played by Candice Bergen, left) for choosing to raise her child without a father. *(Photofest)*

I doubt there has been a time in the recent history of our country when there has been a greater disparity between what the American people want and expect from their government and what both political parties provide for them.

> *Hamilton Jordan, adviser to the independent presidential candidate Ross Perot, discussing on June 3, 1992, the popular discontent with the Democratic and Republican Parties, in Alan F. Pater and Jason R. Pater, eds.,* What They Said in 1992 *(1993), p. 153.*

The same women have been talking optimism for a long time, but here we are, in 1992, and we have only twenty-eight women in the House. . . . Something like the Gulf War rolls around, and the mood changes overnight. You could change the polls in two days if you suddenly got everyone in their flight suits bombing [Libya's president] Qaddafi. The testosterone is flowing, and everyone's cheering—guys in the reserves put on their suits and they run the military hardware in the mall and crawl all over it. Great images.

> *Congresswoman Pat Schroeder of Colorado commenting on the comparatively small number of female representatives in Congress, in Wendy Kaminer, "Crashing the Locker Room,"* Atlantic, *July 1992, p. 65.*

Too much compassion makes people clutch at their wallets.

Polling expert Celinda Lake explaining why she believes the combination of liberal and traditionally feminine values is a political liability, in Wendy Kaminer, "Crashing the Locker Room," Atlantic, July 1992, p. 65.

I have found that good taste, oddly enough, plays an important role in politics. . . . Good taste is a visible manifestation of human sensibility toward the world, environment, people. I came to this castle and to other governmental residences inherited from Communism, and I was confronted with tasteless furniture and many tasteless pictures. Only then did I realize how closely the bad taste of former rulers was connected with their bad way of ruling.

I also realized how important good taste was for politics. During political talks, the feeling of how and when to convey something, of how long to speak, whether to interrupt or not, the degree of attention, how to address the public, forms to be used not to offend someone's dignity, and, on the other hand, to say what has to be said, all these play a major role. All such political behavior relates to good taste in a broader sense. What I really have in mind is something more than just knowing which tie to match a particular shirt.

Václav Havel, former president of Czechoslovakia, discussing the political importance of tasteful behavior, in an interview published on August 3, 1992, in Alan F. Pater and Jason R. Pater, eds., What They Said in 1992 (1993), p. 152.

Woody Allen having non-incest with a non-daughter to whom he was a non-father because they were a non-family fits the Democratic platform perfectly.

Representative Newt Gingrich of Georgia smearing the Democratic Party in late August 1992, in George F. Will, "No One Is Safe from GOP Attack Dogs," Miami Herald, September 1, 1992, p. 39A.

Just after dusk the winds started to increase, but it was impossible to see what was going on outside, shuttered as we were. When the power failed around 10:00, my wife, three young daughters, and I gathered in the master bedroom, and we replaced the television with the Weather Channel's radio news. The sounds of the wind became louder, and the east wall of the

house was being pounded by something. Fearful that the shutters might give, we moved to a more interior bedroom but soon experienced water dripping from the ceiling fan. So we retreated into the hallway. I took the three twin mattresses from the beds and propped them against closed bedroom doors, and we endured the strongest part of the hurricane huddled in the dark, my wife and daughters backed into a linen closet and I leaning against the opposite wall, a wall that would later expand and contract, pulsating with the different pressure in the room on the other side.

Except for a flashlight we were in total darkness; so what I remember most of that early morning, as the worst of the storm moved through, are the sounds. The wind was howling madly, and the eerie noises penetrating it sounded at some times like a locomotive or a huge truck, and at others like the screeching of a Jimi Hendrix guitar riff. Mixed in with these were the quieter but distinct sounds of glass shattering in the master bedroom and the family room.

When, sometime after 6 A.M., we had enough natural light to see the damage, my wife screamed that the house was on fire! She had looked up to see the early morning Sun beaming through a narrow hole in the roof. Everything was a total mess. Strewn throughout the devastated master bedroom were broken window and mirror glass and pieces of tan, rust, and brick colored barrel tiles from my neighbor's roof. The drapes were wrapped around the remaining blades of the ceiling fan. Something had punched a

Hurricane Andrew, a powerful category 5 storm, devastated much of south Florida. *(AP/Wide World Photos)*

huge gash in the door of the walk-in closet, and clothes were scattered throughout the room. The shutters had blown away from the 16 feet of sliding glass doors in the family room, leaving books and furniture and glass everywhere. Outside, my huge mango tree was on its side, the roots pulled up as the winds lifted the 40-foot canopy. Several queen palms were down, and only a few scraps remained from a gazebo I had built for the kids. The chain link fence was now irregularly serpentine and a few posts had been pulled out of the ground, along with 18 inches of the concrete into which they had been sunk. The pool was full of leaves, branches, a bicycle tire (not mine), and some other oddities. Less than a mile to the east, neighbors had dead fish in their yards and pools.

A few days later when I got back to the house, I could only salvage a few things. Although some in my area were living in trailers parked in the yards of their damaged homes, my neighbor, a Florida Highway Patrol trooper, advised against it: there was much looting and some gunfire after dark, as well as packs of stray dogs. There was no way to secure these broken homes. One day I saw four very young, armed National Guardsmen marching in step down my street.

Professor Donald G. Watson describing his experience of Hurricane Andrew, which struck south Florida in the early morning of August 2, 1992, in private correspondence with the author on September 13, 2004.

Peter Schumann's Bread and Puppet Theater has never shrunk from taking on issues whose scope more than matches the dimensions of the giant puppet masks and figures that the company commonly uses. . . . And in "Columbus: The New World Order,". . . the topic is nothing less than Christopher Columbus's voyage to the New World in 1492 and its consequences. With Mr. Schumann being devoutly pacifist and left-wing, the fable that unfolds is a brutal tale of conquest, destruction and oppression that ends with an ambiguous warning. . . .

Among the play's more insistent themes is the invocation of Christianity to justify all the conquest and bloodshed. . . .

Another recurrent motif is the image of everyday people turned into grotesque automatons. In the first part they are sailors dressed in identical prison-stripe uniforms who hold up placards that give the percentages from bogus public-opinion polls. Later they reappear as literally faceless bureaucrats in baggy suits and eyeless, lipless shoe-shaped masks, spouting clichés like "have a nice day" while marching around in formation.

In the most gripping scene the cutout figures of babies in their mothers' arms are wrenched from their grasp by the conquerors wearing hooks and cables as the eggheaded figure of Columbus, looking a bit like George Washington, watches impassively. . . . The section ends with the establishment of "the New World order" and the waving of that [American] flag.

Theater critic Stephen Holden reviewing Peter Schumann's antiwar play Columbus: The New World Order, *in Holden, "Pastiche of Columbus, Politics and Puppets, Tinged with Pathos,"* New York Times, *September 9, 1992, p. C15.*

There's a new paradigm of international competition and that paradigm is based on dynamism, on the capacity of firms to innovate and upgrade the sophistication of how they compete. Now success depends on relentless investment by companies . . . not just in physical assets, but also in less tangible assets such as research and development, training, supplier relationships, and the losses required to gain access to foreign markets.

What's the problem? We [in the United States] invested a significantly lower rate in plant and equipment than our major international rivals. We simply don't have a large enough pool of investment capital. We're not saving enough, either in households or in government. In addition to this inadequate pool of capital, our policies are too erratic. We keep changing the tax code. We keep changing the rules. And this instability causes companies to waiver, to hold back from investment.

Economist Michael Porter discussing the need for greater investment capital at an economic conference convened by President-elect Bill Clinton on December 14, 1992, in Alan F. Pater and Jason R. Pater, eds., What They Said in 1992 *(1993), p. 107.*

5

Don't Ask; Don't Tell
1993

After taking office on January 20, Bill Clinton suffered several setbacks in the first year of his presidency. His efforts to integrate homosexuals into the military met stiff resistance, and in the end he had to accept an indecisive "Don't ask; don't tell" policy on homosexuality that retained the ban on gays' serving in the armed services but protected servicemen and servicewomen from being questioned about their sexual preferences. Likewise, Clinton's ambitious plan for a national health care system, formulated in 1993 under the leadership of his controversial wife, Hillary Rodham Clinton, also eventually failed, and Clinton's continued support of Bush's peacekeeping effort in Somalia led to a humiliating withdrawal at year's end.

Barely a month after Clinton took office, Islamic terrorists exploded a car bomb in the parking garage of New York's World Trade Center. Six people were killed and hundreds more suffered injuries in what was then the worst terrorist attack in U.S. history. In June, FBI agents foiled a related plan to blow up the UN headquarters and the Lincoln and Holland Tunnels in New York City. In between, federal agents outside Waco, Texas, conducted a bloody assault on the heavily armed compound of the religious leader David Koresh and his followers, the Branch Davidians. The raid, which concluded a 51-day siege, killed Koresh and some 75 others, including at least 17 children who were inside the compound. Four FBI agents had been killed and 12 were injured in an earlier raid in February that precipitated the siege. The newly appointed attorney general, Janet Reno, the first woman to hold that cabinet post, won praise from some for her forthright assumption of responsibility for the deadly attack, but the large number of casualties also provoked others to condemn Reno, Clinton, and the federal government.

Clinton's greatest successes during the year were in the realm of foreign diplomacy. He asserted himself as a major world leader by brokering a peace agreement between the longtime enemies Israel and the Palestine Liberation Organization (PLO). And, enlisting the aid of top Republicans, he won congressional approval for the controversial North American Free Trade Agreement (NAFTA), which Bush had negotiated in 1992. Clinton further demonstrated his commitment to a global economy by convening in Seattle the first Asia-Pacific Economic Cooperation summit among 15 nations of the so-called Pacific Rim. Although at the beginning of the year the economy was sluggish, by December modest improvement was apparent.

Serbia's genocidal ethnic cleansing in Bosnia continued to shock the world and provoke calls for international intervention, while full-scale fighting also broke out between Bosnia and Croatia. But other long-standing foes reconciled. In addition to the agreement between Israel and the PLO, the Communist People's Republic of China began talks with Taiwan-based Nationalist China, the first negotiation since the Communists drove the Nationalists from the mainland in 1948. White rule ended in South Africa, as the parliament voted itself out of existence, and Great Britain and Ireland signed an agreement outlining a plan to end the violence in Northern Ireland. Japan formally apologized for forcing thousands of women into sexual slavery during World War II.

Elsewhere, women were elected to top leadership positions in Canada and Turkey, and Boris Yeltsin consolidated his control in Russia, after he suppressed a coup attempt by former hard-line Communists. The World Bank reported that the life expectancy in developing countries had risen from 46 to 63 years since 1960.

INTERNATIONAL DEVELOPMENTS

At the beginning of the year, Bush and Yeltsin signed the second Strategic Arms Reduction Treaty (START II) calling for their nuclear stockpiles to be reduced by two-thirds by 2003. Anxious to complete the accord as part of his presidential legacy, Bush negotiated START II in the final six months of 1992 and signed it before Clinton took office in 1993. By comparison, some cold war-era arms limitation treaties that simply slowed the growth of nuclear arsenals but did not reduce them necessitated up to 10 years of negotiation. The broadest disarmament agreement in history, START II nonetheless allowed the United States to retain 3,500 nuclear weapons and Russia 3,000. It called for elimination of controversial multiple warheads (multiple independently targetable reentry vehicles, or MIRVs) on all land-based intercontinental missiles, a provision that would phase out the Soviet SS-18 missile and the U.S. MX missile (Peacekeeper), which Reagan had introduced in 1982 over considerable opposition. Analysts generally believed that the United States gained more from START II, as it cut deeply into the Russian's strength—land-based missiles—but did not limit submarine-based MIRVs, a field the United States dominated.

Less than two weeks after signing START II, Bush initiated the first allied offensive against Iraq since the conclusion of the 1991 Persian Gulf War, when he authorized U.S., British, and French warplanes to destroy illegal Iraqi missile sites in the so-called no-fly zone, which Iraqi aircraft were forbidden to enter. Four days later, he ordered cruise missile strikes against a suspected nuclear-weapons production plant near Baghdad after Iraq refused to comply with UN resolutions calling for international weapons inspections. One off-course missile struck a Baghdad hotel, killing two Iraqi civilians and prompting critics to condemn the decision to route the attack over the heavily populated city. Two days later, Iraq agreed to permit weapons inspections, as called for by the 1991 peace agreement, and to stop attacking allied planes patrolling the no-fly zones that protected enclaves of Kurds and Shiite Muslims from Iraqi air strikes. Although Iraq's president Saddam Hussein may have been hoping to take advantage of the transition between the Bush and Clinton administrations by defying the UN resolutions, Clinton affirmed his support of Bush's decisions.

President Clinton also maintained Bush's policies of providing aid to Russia, pursuing the NAFTA initiative, and contributing militarily to the humanitarian UN intervention in Somalia, which began in December 1992. Clinton succeeded in winning congressional ratification of NAFTA, despite intense opposition within his own party. But the peacekeeping mission failed to stabilize conditions in the famine-struck nation victimized by civil war. Violence there escalated throughout the year, especially after June, when the United Nations ordered the arrest of one of the Somali war lords, General Mohammed Farah Aidid, after his troops attacked U.S. peacekeepers. Attempts to capture Aidid led to deadly fighting between Aidid's supporters and UN peacekeepers, in which numerous civilians were killed, along with combatants. After 12 American soldiers died in an unsuccessful attack on Aidid in October, Clinton ordered heavy armor and an additional 15,000 troops to Somalia. At the same time, he placated critics of the increasingly murky mission by announcing U.S. troops would begin to withdraw in December and, except for a small contingent, leave the country completely by the end of March 1994.

The much-heralded peace agreement between Israel and the PLO created hope for genuine peace and gave Clinton his first major achievement in international diplomacy. The Oslo Accords, so called because they began as secret negotiations in Norway, resulted days after the PLO reversed its long-held position and affirmed Israel's right to exist as a nation, and Israel acknowledged the PLO as the legitimate representative of the Palestinian people. Highlighted by a handshake between Israel's prime minister Yitzhak Rabin and the PLO leader Yasser Arafat, the agreement established a process by which Palestinians would gain local autonomy, while Israelis retained strategic and military control over the region. The PLO agreed to repudiate terrorist attacks against Israel, cooperate with Israel in preventing them, and use its police force to suppress them. In return, Israel consented to a phased-in process in which it would remove its troops from the occupied territories and permit the creation of a semiautonomous Palestinian authority. The treaty called for interim Palestinian self-rule in parts of the Israeli-occupied Gaza Strip and West Bank, Israeli troop withdrawal from Gaza and Jericho by the end of the year, a five-year phased-in process that would provide internationally supervised elections to create a governing Palestinian Authority in the occupied territories, redeployment of Israeli forces outside populated areas, and direct ongoing negotiations between Israel and the PLO to resolve remaining issues, notably the status of Jerusalem, a city sacred to both Jews and Muslims that both Israel and the PLO claim as their capital; the status of Israeli settlements in the West Bank; the establishment of final borders; and the right of return for Palestinians who left Israel after it gained independence in 1948. On September 14, the day after the agreement was signed, Israel and Jordan also agreed to establish an "agenda for peace," and they signed a peace treaty in 1994.

A December agreement between Britain's prime minister John Major and Ireland's prime minister Albert Reynolds also sparked hope for an end to the long and bloody conflict in Northern Ireland between majority Protestants, who wished to remain affiliated with Great Britain, and minority Catholics, led by the outlawed Irish Republican Army (IRA), who sought removal of British troops and ultimate reunification with the Catholic-dominated Republic of Ireland, from which Northern Ireland had separated after Ireland's independence in 1949. Labeled a "framework for lasting peace," the agreement conditionally called for participation in subsequent negotiations by Sinn Féin, the political wing of the IRA, if the IRA agreed to cease its long-standing terrorist campaign in both Northern Ireland and England permanently. The accord also declared that the ultimate fate of Northern Ireland should be determined by a majority of its residents, the Republic of Ireland would remove from its constitution claim to six Northern Irish counties, and Britain would not oppose ultimate reunification of Northern Ireland and Ireland, if a majority of voters in Northern Ireland agreed.

Elsewhere in Europe, the European Union officially came into being on November 1. Less than a week later, Belgium, France, and Germany formed the Eurocorps, a joint military force intended as a prototype for a future European army. Meanwhile the situation in Bosnia continued to deteriorate, as Croatia invaded the fledgling nation and Bosnian Serbs continued their practice of ethnic cleansing. Croatian forces fomented international outrage after they destroyed the widely admired 16th-century Stari Most bridge, which spanned the Neretva River in Mostar, Bosnia, while Bosnian Serbs continued shelling civilians inside Sarajevo. Reluctant to be drawn into a morass of centuries-old ethnic animosities, the foreign ministers of Britain, France, Spain, Russia, and the United States agreed in May not to threaten air strikes against the Bosnian Serbs, but to create UN-protected safe havens where Bosnian Muslims could seek refuge. Under the rules of engagement, however, UN soldiers could fire if they were fired on, but could not if only Muslim civilians were targeted. Clinton, concerned about the potential outbreak of regional warfare involving Albania, Greece, Turkey, and Bulgaria, warned Milošević that the United States would respond militarily if Serbia allowed the Yugoslav civil war to spread to the predominantly Muslim province of Kosovo, within Serbia.

A bloody daylong battle broke out in the Russian parliament building after former Soviet hard-liner troops tried to seize control of the government in early October. Forces loyal to Yeltsin suppressed the coup, which was led by Russia's vice president and other ranking government officials, but the incident left Yeltsin dependent on the military. Popular dissatisfaction with Yeltsin became evident in the success in the December parliamentary elections of the ultranationalist Vladimir Zhirinovsky, a development that threatened to slow Yeltsin's program of social and economic reforms and provoked concerns about growing anti-Semitism and neofascism in the former Communist country.

Clinton threatened North Korea in November that the United States would take military action if it attacked South Korea or developed nuclear weapons. China's Communist Party leader, Jiang Zemin, consolidated his power when he also assumed the nation's presidency. Japan formally apologized for forcing tens of thousands of women, most of them Koreans but also other Asians and some Europeans, into sexual slavery during its occupation of Korea and China between 1932 and 1945. However, it offered no compensation to victims.

Despite threats of violence by white supremacists, South Africa's parliament set the stage for ending white-minority rule when it ratified a new constitution and voted itself out of existence on December 22. The move followed U.S. legislation revoking the last of the sanctions against South Africa, most of which had been terminated in 1991, after President Frederik de Klerk began to dismantle the harsh segregationist policies of apartheid. Clinton also announced an investment initiative intended to support South Africa's black communities.

Paraguay held its first fully democratic election since its founding 182 years earlier in May, and in December Colombian police killed Pablo Escobar, the escaped head of the Medellín drug cartel. Haiti's democratically elected president Jean-Bertrand Aristide signed a UN-brokered agreement with the military rulers who deposed him in 1991, calling for his reinstatement by October 30 and amnesty for those responsible for the coup. However, although the military junta, led by General Raoul Cédras, permitted human-rights observers to enter Haiti, they reneged on the agreement, and Aristide's return was delayed until October 1994.

GOVERNMENT AND SOCIETY

Declaring that the administration should "look more like America," Clinton appointed a historic number of women and minorities to the cabinet and other influential positions. Notably, the Dade County state attorney Janet Reno became the highest-ranking woman in the history of the executive branch when Clinton made her the nation's first female attorney general. His initial two choices for the post, also women, withdrew from consideration after revelations that they had hired illegal aliens as domestic workers. Two other women also received cabinet appointments, as did African Americans and Hispanics. Warren M. Christopher, considered a skilled negotiator committed to promoting U.S. commercial interests and reform in Eastern Europe, was secretary of state, and Les Aspin, chairman of the House Armed Services Committee, became secretary of defense. In August, Clinton appointed Ruth Bader Ginsburg to fill the Supreme Court vacancy created by the retiring justice Byron R. White, a Kennedy appointee. Ginsburg became the second female Supreme Court justice in American history after the Reagan appointee Sandra Day O'Connor.

The first legislation Clinton signed was a family leave bill, which guaranteed workers up to 12 weeks of unpaid leave a year to cope with family emergencies. Bush had twice vetoed similar legislation, citing concerns that it would be too costly for businesses. But neither of Clinton's two major initiatives of 1993 fared well. His plan to end prohibitions against homosexuals' serving in the military was opposed by conservatives and top military leaders. In the end, he settled for a compromise, "Don't ask; don't tell" policy in which homosexuals remained banned from service and homosexual activity remained forbidden, but military personnel were strictly limited in their ability to question or investigate suspected homosexuals. The compromise, generally regarded as a political defeat for Clinton, was opposed by members of both the military and the homosexual communities. Some liberalization of military policy did occur when, as a result of the expanded role of women in the Persian Gulf War, the secretary of defense lifted rules that prevented women in the navy and air force from flying in combat.

In his first year, Clinton developed a plan for universal health insurance for all Americans, a proposal first made by President Harry S. Truman in the 1940s. Clinton's plan, which envisioned a system of managed competition to provide health insurance for all U.S. citizens and legal aliens, would have cost $350 billion and been funded from anticipated savings in Medicare, Medicaid, and other health systems and from so-called sin taxes on tobacco. It would also require employers to contribute 80 percent of their workers' health-care premiums. According to Clinton, his plan would reduce the federal deficit by $91 billion, cut overall health-care expenditures by more than $120 billion annually, and provide coverage to an estimated 37 million uninsured Americans. It would require every American to enroll in one of three types of insurance options ranging from comparatively low-priced health maintenance organizations (HMOs) to more costly fee-for-service options that would require higher copayments but give patients greater flexibility in their choice of health-care providers. Each option would include hospital care, doctor care, emergency services, pregnancy-related services, hospice and home care, prescription drug benefits, limited mental health and substance abuse treatment, and preventative dental and eye care for all children less than 18 years old.

The health-care reform was formulated by a task force, chaired by First Lady Hillary Rodham Clinton, which studied data collected from physicians, pharmaceutical and insurance companies, and some 700,000 Americans who submitted letters describing their experiences with the current system. Hillary Clinton was criticized by some because of her lack of governmental experience and by others who felt the Clintons were improperly politicizing the role of the First Lady, who is not an elected official. Opponents further believed the proposal would place a great financial burden on employers, result in excessive government regulation, impair the overall quality of health care, ultimately require increased taxes, and inflate the federal deficit. Concerted opposition by Republicans, conservative Democrats, and several advocacy groups, including small businesses, insurers, pharmaceutical companies, and health-care providers, ultimately defeated the plan in 1994.

Abortion remained a polarizing issue. In a move condemned by the Vatican and antiabortion activists, Clinton overturned several restrictions imposed during the Reagan and Bush administrations, including a so-called gag rule at federally funded family clinics that had banned anyone but doctors from discussing abortions with patients and restrictions on using fetuses from elective abortions in federally funded medical research. On the other hand, opponents of abortion rights cheered a Supreme Court ruling that civil rights law did not prohibit them from blockading abortion clinics. The decision permitted

President Bill Clinton and First Lady Hillary Rodham Clinton worked closely together throughout his presidency. *(AP/Wide World Photos)*

antiabortion protesters to continue to picket abortion clinics throughout the country, often preventing patients from entering or berating them as they did. Growing violence against the clinics and practitioners intensified during the year, culminating in bombings, acts of arson, and the assassination of David Gunn, a physician, outside the abortion clinic where he worked in Pensacola, Florida. Another doctor known for performing abortions was wounded in a similar incident in Wichita, Kansas, and a third was killed in Alabama, although whether the murder was related to his job was unclear. Late in the year, Congress passed legislation aimed at protecting abortion clinics, staff, and patients from attacks, blockades, and acts of intimidation.

Many of those against abortion opposed any practice that caused an unnatural end to human life, except, in some cases, the death penalty for commission of capital crimes. Consequently, doctor-assisted suicides for terminally ill patients were another point of contention between so-called prolife and pro-choice activists. Oregon passed a controversial law permitting the practice, but Dr. Jack Kevorkian, a retired pathologist popularly known as the suicide doctor or Doctor Death, was arrested in Michigan for violating a law prohibiting assisted suicides. A circuit court dismissed the charge after ruling that the law was unconstitutional. The Supreme Court of Canada ruled that a terminally ill woman was not entitled to a doctor-assisted suicide.

Large-scale violence rocked the United States twice in the winter and spring. The first occurred in February, when Islamic extremists, followers of the Egyptian mullah Sheikh Omar Abdul Rahman detonated an automobile filled with 1,500 pounds of explosives in the underground parking garage of New York City's World Trade Center. Six people died, a thousand more were injured, and $500 million worth of damage resulted. Nonetheless, the attack failed to achieve its objective of razing the world's second-tallest office building, a symbol of the secular consumer capitalism that the militants believed undermined Islamic practice. Rahman and several of his disciples subsequently received life sentences when they were convicted.

Two days later, on February 28, the saga of the Branch Davidians began, when four federal agents from the Bureau of Alcohol, Tobacco, and Firearms (ATF) were killed and 16 more wounded while attempting to arrest David Koresh, the leader of the approximately 95 heavily armed members of the apocalyptic Branch Davidian cult, a spinoff segment of the Seventh-Day Adventists, who resided in a compound near Waco, Texas. Two cult members were also killed in the exchange of gunfire that began when the Davidians opened fire on the agents as they unsuccessfully attempted to seize Koresh and confiscate the Davidians' arsenal, which included guns, ammunition, hand grenades, explosives, and .50-caliber rifles that had a range of close to two miles and were capable of shooting down airplanes. Koresh considered himself a messianic figure chosen by God to facilitate the end of the world, a precondition for the second coming of Jesus, as predicted in Revelations in the New Testament. Koresh had also been accused of having sex with teenage girls within the community whom he had taken as his "spiritual wives," ostensibly as part of his plan to produce a line of children destined to rule the world.

A six-month siege followed the shootings. Finally, believing Koresh and his followers could hold out for another year and fearing that the danger to the children within the compound was intensifying, Reno authorized a federal assault. On April 19, FBI agents in armored vehicles attacked the compound and pumped tear gas into the holes in the wall, hoping to force the Davidians to surrender. A fire soon broke out, however, and quickly engulfed the fortress, as agents and television crews watched helplessly. Some 100 Davidians died among the flames, among them Koresh and at least 17 children.

Long-lasting controversy arose immediately, as many believed the federal agents were responsible for igniting the inferno, especially after the government admitted in 1999 that it had pumped flammable material into the compound before the fire erupted. But an independent investigation in 2000, led by the former Republican senator John Danforth, determined that the pyrotechnic devices had been fired in a different direction from the building, four hours before the fire began. The commission concluded that the Davidians, not the government, were responsible for the conflagration. Nonetheless, immediately after the incident many Americans, particularly those on the extreme Right and some members of the local militias that were then becoming popular throughout the country, regarded the Davidians as martyrs to a repressive federal government intent on suppressing their rights, especially their constitutional right to bear arms. One such person was Timothy McVeigh, who, in 1995, blew up the federal building in Oklahoma City, Oklahoma, partly in retaliation for the Waco incident. Other citizens less sympathetic to Koresh and his followers nonetheless decried the handling of the raid that left so many dead, and several agents were later disciplined for acting improperly.

Colin Ferguson, a 35-year-old mentally disturbed gunman, further shocked the nation when he opened fire on a crowded Long Island commuter train, killing six riders and wounding 18 others. Carolyn McCarthy, the wife of one of the victims, who advocated tighter gun control, was subsequently elected to Congress.

Domestic violence against men dramatically caught the public's attention after Lorena Bobbitt severed the penis of her sleeping husband, whom she claimed had sexually abused her. Britain opened its first shelter for men battered by their partner.

In late December the so-called Whitewater affair began when federal investigators, responding to accusations that Clinton had abused his power as governor of Arkansas, subpoenaed and received from the Clintons financial records relating to the Whitewater Development Corporation, a defunct Arkansas real-estate firm they owned with Arkansas financier James McDougal and his wife, Susan McDougal. Also in December, Arkansas state troopers accused Clinton of abusing the powers of his office by coercing women to have affairs with him when he was governor. They also portrayed Hillary Clinton as a power-hungry shrew. Their allegations were never substantiated, however, and several were disproved. David Brock, the journalist who broke the story for the conservative magazine *American Spectator,* later repudiated it. Brock admitted he had published the accusation as part of a right-wing effort to discredit Clinton and said that anti-Clinton activists had paid $6,700 to each of the two troopers who had accused Clinton in the article.[1] At the time, however, although the mainstream press condemned Brock's story as tasteless and inappropriate, it initially reported it as potentially credible, and large segments of the population accepted it as fundamentally accurate.

Overall, the Supreme Court practiced judicial restraint by avoiding opportunities to impose its own interpretations of the law. Significant decisions included rulings that states could issue the death penalty to teenagers convicted of murder, workers did not need to prove they suffered serious psychological damage to win sexual harassment suits against an employer, public agencies could require contractors to employ only union labor for public construction projects, states were authorized to impose specific sentencing guidelines for hate crimes, and the government could not ban the killing of animals for religious rituals. It affirmed the constitutionality of the government policy of intercepting boat loads of Haitian refugees on the high seas and returning them to Haiti, and it disallowed a woman's claim that she should control seven frozen embryos that she and her former husband had conceived through in vitro fertilization but that, since the dissolution of their marriage, he no longer wanted to allow to progress to term.

Asia remained the fastest-growing source of immigration to North America, and Canada reported that Chinese had become its third most commonly used language, after English and French. Canada elected its first female prime minister, Kim Campbell, but the Conservative politician was ousted in November by a Liberal Party election landslide that installed Jean Chretien as the nation's top official.

BUSINESS

Although the economy improved in late 1993, the unemployment rate remained high, at 7.5 percent, up from 7.4 percent in 1992. The gross national product, now known as the gross domestic product (GDP), fell by 1.1 percent to 2.9 percent.[2] Some 26.6 million Americans received government food stamps.[3] Inflation, however, decreased from 3.0 percent in 1992 to 2.7 percent in 1993, and the Dow-Jones industrial average rose by more than 11 percent, from a 1992 high of 3,413 to a 1993 high of 3,799. Home interest rates dropped to their lowest levels in 30 years,[4] and after-tax profits for U.S. corporations rose by 6.7 percent, from $232.5 billion reported in 1992 to $249.1 billion.[5]

Clinton's economic policies centered around reduction of the federal budget deficit, which had grown to about $332 billion under the Reagan and Bush administrations. To achieve this, Clinton cut crop subsidies, defense expenditures, pay raises for federal workers, and Medicare payments to doctors, hospitals, and laboratories. He raised taxes for corporations and wealthy private citizens and expanded taxes on Social Security benefits. Middle-income families also paid somewhat higher income taxes and were subject to an across-the board 2.9 percent Medicare tax and a 4.3-cent-per-gallon tax on gasoline and other transportation fuels, which was calculated to help the environment by encouraging greater energy efficiency. Spending increases went to fund tax credits for the working poor, food stamps, child foster care, and free immunizations of uninsured children. Clinton also proposed short- and long-term spending initiatives to stimulate the construction industry and promote private-sector investment and improvements to the nation's infrastructure, but a Republican filibuster killed his stimulus plan.

North American firms moved to take advantage of an enormous new market that was opening to them, as reforms in China moved the Communist country toward a Western-style economy and fuller integration with the world economy. American Telephone & Telegraph Company (AT&T) signed a potentially lucrative contract to develop telephone and data-transmission services and an extensive corporate communications network in the world's most populous nation. The agreement would allow communications equipment and other electronic devices to be manufactured by joint ventures of AT&T and Chinese companies appointed by their government. AT&T also contracted with Nationalist China to upgrade its telecommunications network. The Coca-Cola Company, already the world's largest soft-drink producer, agreed to supplement existing plants along the Chinese coast by investing $150 million to construct 10 new bottling plants in China's interior regions.

NATURE AND THE ENVIRONMENT

Pointing to the adverse health, economic, and quality-of-life effects of air and water pollution, Clinton and Gore had campaigned promising greater environmental protections. Soon after taking office, the administration began implementing policies toward that end. It negotiated with the state of Florida and several sugar-cane producers a multimillion-dollar plan to restore the Everglades, which was suffering from the effects of agriculture in the region. The negotiations culminated with Florida's passage in 1994 of the Everglades Forever Act, which allocated more than $685 million over several years for Everglades restoration, and of the federal government's Water Resources Development Act of 1996, which included $75 million for the world's largest fresh-water marsh. The administration also introduced legislation to protect other wetland areas and imposed stringent environmental regulations on public lands used for grazing of livestock.

Nonetheless, pollution and global warming remained ongoing concerns, as UN scientists recorded record-low ozone levels over the Western Hemisphere. Despite opposition by car makers, the Environmental Protection Agency (EPA) ruled that it would allow California and other states to require antipollution standards more rigorous than federal requirements. But, resisting pressure from medical and environmental groups, the EPA refused to impose stricter standards for allowable smog.

In January, just five weeks after an oil tanker broke up off the coast of Spain, the U.S.-owned *Braer* was driven aground in a heavy North Sea storm, spilling some 26 million gallons of crude oil onto the Shetland Islands off the coast of Scotland. Government scientists disputed a study made by Exxon claiming that between 73 and 91 percent of the oil spilled by the *Exxon Valdez* in 1989 off Alaska's Prince William Sound had been cleaned up and that the waterway had almost fully recovered. Russia acknowledged that during the cold war the Soviet Union systematically dumped nuclear waste into the arctic seas.

Record-setting weather wrecked havoc throughout the nation. A late-winter blizzard packing winds above 100 mph covered much of the South with ice and snow, spawning dozens of tornadoes and trapping 117 schoolchildren camping in the Great Smoky Mountains, before moving on to the Northeast, where it also caused major damage. Dubbed the Storm of the Century, the blizzard, which originated in the Gulf of Mexico, was responsible for 213 deaths, most of them along the East Coast but also as far north as Canada and as far south as Cuba. In June and July, record flooding in the Midwest killed at least 50 people, destroyed approximately 38,000 homes, left some 20 million acres of farmland across eight states under water, rendered the upper Mississippi River unnavigable, and caused approximately $12 billion in damage. In the fall, fires destroyed some 200,000 acres in Southern California, destroyed more than 1,000 homes, and killed at least three people. In central India an earthquake killed some 30,000 people.

SCIENCE AND TECHNOLOGY

Scientists suffered setbacks after Congress voted not to fund a costly superconducting supercollider that would have permitted more complete study of high-energy physics, and the *Mars Observer,* whose mission was to explore the Martian environment, permanently lost contact with Earth as it began to maneuver into orbit around the planet. On the other hand, the United States and Russia agreed to build jointly an international space station, and astronauts aboard the space shuttle succeeded in repairing and upgrading the *Hubble Space Telescope,* which immediately began sending back to Earth high-quality photographs of deep space, some of which later prompted important advances in several branches of astronomy. Scientists at the Princeton Plasma Physics Laboratory made a breakthrough in nuclear fusion, a process considered safer and potentially more efficient and less costly than fission methods used in nuclear power plants.

Oceanographers discovered a vast range of volcanoes beneath the depths of the Pacific Ocean, and geologists in Greenland drilled a record 10,021 feet through the polar ice cap to extract an ice core deposited a quarter-million years ago. The fossil of the most primitive dinosaur known to date, a carnivorous eoraptor, was uncovered in Argentina. Archaeologists found an Aramaic stone monument referring to King David, the first known reference to the king of ancient Israel outside the Bible.

A federal study found traces of a nicotine by-product in the blood of smokers and nonsmokers alike, indicating that secondhand smoke is potentially harmful to nonsmokers. Subsequently, the EPA designated secondhand smoke as a carcinogen. On the other hand, a small study of pregnant women suggested that moderate amounts of coffee and other caffeinated beverages do not harm the fetus in the womb.

A panel of scientists asserted that to date no evidence supported a commonly held belief that cellular telephones cause brain cancer, although they acknowledged that limited data concerning the effects on humans of the low-level radiation released by household appliances had been collected. An article published in the *Journal of the American Medical Association* concluded that vasectomy increases men's likelihood of development of prostate cancer, and baldness at the top of a man's head was correlated to increased likelihood of heart attack. Researchers located the gene whose mutation is responsible for the onset of Lou Gehrig's disease (amyotrophic lateral sclerosis, or ALS), and the Centers for Disease Control and Prevention found that the number of new AIDS cases among heterosexuals had increased by 111 percent, from 49,016 in 1992 to 103,500 in 1993. This increase was significantly greater than the 75 percent rate of growth the centers had projected for 1993.[6] Alcoholism among young people remained a national concern as well, as a study published in the *Journal of the American Medical Association* in 1994 reported that 44 percent of college students polled in 1993 had practiced "binge drinking," defined as five consecutive alcoholic drinks for men, four for women, within two weeks of being surveyed.

The Department of Energy announced that approximately 800 people had been exposed to radiation in experiments performed by the government between the 1940s and 1960s, including prisoners at the Oregon State Prison whose testicles were subjected to radioactivity to determine its effects on sperm production and 19 mentally retarded boys at the Fernald State School in Waltham, Massachusetts, who, between 1946 and 1956, were used in a study of the digestive system.

LITERATURE, THE ARTS, SPORTS, AND POPULAR CULTURE

Illiteracy remained a national problem, as an Education Department study showed that nearly half of U.S. adults possessed inadequate reading or math skills. Some 40 to 44 million adults functioned at the lowest levels of literacy, and an additional 50 million ranked at the second-lowest level. One-fourth of 12th graders could not read properly.[7] Nonetheless, large numbers of Americans could and did read, and several new novels by established genre writers were best-sellers, among them John Grisham's legal thriller *The Client*, Stephen King and Anne Rice's horror stories *Nightmares and Dreamscapes* and *Lasher*; Danielle Steel's romance *Vanished*; and Tom Clancy and Robert Ludlum's stories of action and intrigue, *Without Remorse* and *The Scorpio Illusion*.

Throughout the 1980s and 1990s literature and the arts became battlegrounds for the so-called culture wars, which pitted social conservatives, who called for the nation to return to so-called traditional American values rooted in Christian teachings and the Protestant work ethic, against social progressives, who pointed out that those values, which emanated primarily from comparatively static, homogenous, male-dominated, agrarian societies, had often been discriminatory, unnecessarily restrictive, and selectively applied. Liberals were typically more supportive of efforts to promote living and working arrangements, sexual practices, and social behavior more closely attuned to a continuously evolving, culturally diverse, highly mobile, high-tech urban society. On the other hand, many conservatives were convinced that the progressives' lifestyles were simply decadent, self-indulgent, licentious, morally reprehensible, and sinful.

The year's nonfiction was the battlefield for several skirmishes in the culture wars, as the former secretary of education William J. Bennett, a social conservative, garnered headlines with his best-selling *Book of Virtues,* a compilation of stories chosen by Bennett to illustrate specific moral virtues in action. As Bennett and others call for a return to what they regarded a Victorian sensibility that promoted more circumspect sexual behavior and greater emphasis on good manners and respectful codes of behavior, the historian Peter Gay's *The Cultivation of Hatred* argues that the Victorian virtues were never broadly or consistently practiced in 19th-century Britain. Instead, Gay argues, Victorian culture was shaped by an underlying conviction that human nature is inherently sinful and evil, and this belief fostered violent, abusive behavior within families and by the dominant social and political institutions, which employed sanctimonious Victorian religions, political expediency, and scientific beliefs to justify brutal acts of aggression practiced by colonialists, racists, and extreme nationalists.

In *Moral Sense* the sociologist James Q. Wilson attacks moral relativism, arguing that a moral sensibility is the product of a child's earliest familial experiences. Wilson maintains that self-restraints on impulses and desire are built into the "primitive" limbic brain. He further proposes that men and women differ innately in their moral orientation, as men are more inclined to emphasize justice and emotional control and women to stress sympathy, caring, and cooperation. The law professor Steven L. Carter claims in *The Culture of Disbelief* that American legal and political practices harm the nation by trivializing religion and by requiring the religiously faithful to subordinate their moral sensibilities to a deliberately secular social order. Although he affirms the need to maintain the constitutional separation of church and state, Carter insists that the society has to find ways in which religious faith can shape public life. And in *Culture of Complaint* Robert Hughes lashes out at the divisiveness, suspicion, and ill will spawned by the angry rhetoric of extremists on both sides of the culture wars. David Remnick's *Lenin's Tomb: The Last Days of the Soviet Empire* received the Pulitzer Prize in nonfiction.

Toni Morrison was awarded the Nobel Prize in literature, the first African-American woman to receive the world's highest literary honor. Works of literary fiction included Philip Roth's *Operation Shylock: A Confession,* an award-winning self-reflexive, darkly comic novel in which the author appears both as a character and as an imposter of himself; Bobbie Ann Mason's *Feather Crowns,* about the birth in the Kentucky backwoods of the world's first surviving quintuplets; Alan Lightman's *Einstein's Dream,* 30 scientifically informed fictional dreams about places where time behaves quite differently; and Annie Proulx's *The Shipping News,* which won the Pulitzer Prize for its story of the personal growth of a Newfoundland fisherman.

60 Minutes, CBS's perennially highly rated newsmagazine, was the top-rated show for the 1993–94 season. Otherwise, comedy remained popular on television. The final episode of *Cheers,* which starred Ted Danson and Kirstie Alley, attracted some 98 million viewers, and the next six top shows were situation comedies: *Home Improvement, Seinfeld, Roseanne, Grace under Fire, Coach,* and *Frasier,* a new spinoff from *Cheers* that centers on the neurotic psychiatrist Frasier Crane, played by Kelsey Grammar. The show, which won the Emmy Award as outstanding comedy series every year from 1994 to 1998, costarred David Hyde Pierce, John Mahoney, and Jane Leeves. *Seinfeld* won the award in 1993; *Picket Fences* was the Emmy winner for outstanding drama series. The debut of *NYPD Blue,* a gritty police drama, introduced new levels of nudity and profane language to prime-time television, and the Fox Network's *The X-Files,* in which government agents investigate supernatural phenomena, attracted a large cult following.

Other new sitcoms included *Ellen* and *Grace under Fire.* As had *Seinfeld,* these featured actors who became prominent as stand-up comedians, Ellen DeGeneres and Brett Butler. An immediate success that was often compared to

Roseanne for its focus on working-class mothers, *Grace under Fire* appeals to the growing national concern for women's equality in the workplace. Butler plays a feisty single mother who has divorced her abusive "knuckle-dragging, cousin-loving, beer-sucking, redneck husband" and taken a job at an oil refinery. Known as a "quota babe" because she has obtained employment through an affirmative action program, she trades barbs with the men at work.

Upset that NBC hired Jay Leno to replace Johnny Carson on *The Tonight Show,* David Letterman left the network and started his own late-night talk show on CBS. Somewhat more sophisticated and acerbic than Leno, Letterman attracted a dedicated following, but his ratings failed to match those of Leno, who appealed to a broader spectrum of America. Martha Stewart gave a tone of class and elegance to daytime television with her syndicated show *Martha Stewart Living,* which was also the title of her magazine. By 1995, the Emmy Award–winning program, which gave information about gardening, entertaining, decorating, cooking, and housekeeping, had attracted some 5 million viewers and established Stewart as an arbiter and prime example of good taste.

The growing success of genetic research sparked interest in stories of deoxyribonucleic acid (DNA) gone awry. The most successful of these was Steven Spielberg's film *Jurassic Park,* based on Michael Crichton's best-selling 1990 action novel about genetic experimentation that revives long-extinct dinosaurs. Spielberg won the Academy Award as best director and for best picture for his other major hit of the year, *Schindler's List,* about a Christian German who risks his own life and comfortable status in Third Reich Germany to save Jews during the Holocaust. The movie was one of several efforts by Spielberg to prevent the Holocaust from fading from memory: He also sponsored a project to collect oral histories from Holocaust survivors and timed the opening of *Schindler's List* to coincide with that of the U.S. Holocaust Memorial Museum in Washington, D.C.

Concern about AIDS and the rights of homosexuals found expression in Jonathan Demme's *Philadelphia,* for which Tom Hanks won the Oscar as best

Stephen Spielberg's *Jurassic Park* tapped into anxieties about genetic engineering gone awry. *(Photofest)*

Meg Ryan (left), Ross Malinger (middle), and Tom Hanks (right) starred in the sentimental comedy *Sleepless in Seattle.* *(Photofest)*

actor. Holly Hunter won as best actress for her role as a 19th-century mute Scotswoman who travels to New Zealand in Jane Campion's *The Piano.* Harvey Keitel costarred. *The Piano* was one of several artfully made films to gain public support. Others included Martin Scorsese's *The Age of Innocence,* starring Michelle Pfeiffer, Winona Ryder, and Daniel Day-Lewis and based on the 1920 novel by Edith Wharton; James Ivory's *Remains of the Day,* starring Anthony Hopkins and Emma Thompson and based on the 1989 novel by Kazuo Ishiguro; and Kenneth Branagh's adaptation of William Shakespeare's comedy *Much Ado about Nothing.*

Notable box-office hits included Adrian Lyne's *Indecent Proposal,* with Robert Redford and Demi Moore; Sidney Pollack's adaptation of Grisham's *The Firm,* a story of young lawyers that featured Tom Cruise and Gene Hackman; Andrew Davis's *The Fugitive,* starring Harrison Ford and Tommy Lee Jones and based on the 1960s television drama about a wrongly accused man; and the comedies *Sleepless in Seattle;* Nora Ephron's remake of Leo McCarey's *An Affair to Remember* (1957), starring Tom Hanks and Meg Ryan; and Chris Columbus's *Mrs. Doubtfire,* starring Robin Williams as a man who disguises himself as an English nanny so he can be near his children after his separation from his wife. In Joel Schumacher's *Falling Down* Michael Douglas plays a bigoted middle-class white man in Los Angeles who, after being laid off from his job, vents his frustrations in a shooting spree that targets ethnic minorities. All of the top five box-office stars and eight of the top 10 were men: Cruise, Williams, Ford, and Hanks, Clint Eastwood, Kevin Costner, Mel Gibson, and Sylvester Stallone. Julia Roberts and Whoopi Goldberg were the only women in the category. The up-and-coming star River Phoenix died of a drug overdose at age 23.

Angels in America: Millennium Approaches won the 1993 Pulitzer Prize in drama and the Tony Award as best play. The first part of Tony Kushner's two-part play about homosexuals living through the AIDS epidemic in the 1980s, it follows the life of two AIDS-infected homosexual men who have very different personal outlooks and political points of view. One of them is the attorney Roy Cohn, who worked in the 1950s for Senator Joseph McCarthy and, although he never acknowledged his homosexuality, later died of AIDS and was widely believed to be secretly gay. In the play, Cohn loathes his own homosexuality, which he rejects as a source of weakness. The other man is fundamentally optimistic, is open to miracles, and regards his homosexuality as a source of strength. The second part, *Angels in America: Perestroika,* which opened in late 1993, won the 1994 Tony Award. John Kander and Fred Ebb's adaptation of Manuel Puig's *Kiss of the Spider Woman* (1979), about the growing love between a political prisoner in Latin America and his cellmate, an apolitical homosexual obsessed with popular culture, won the Tony Award as best musical. Nathan Lane starred in Neil Simon's comedy *Laughter on the 23rd Floor,* and Lynn Redgrave appeared in her one-woman performance *Shakespeare for My Father. The Who's Tommy,* by Peter Townshend, which pioneered the rock-opera genre in the 1970s, enjoyed a Broadway revival.

Among the best-selling music albums were Aerosmith's *Get a Grip,* Mariah Carey's *Music Box, janet* by Janet Jackson, *Ten* by Pearl Jam, *Plush* by the Stone Temple Pilots, and Lenny Kravitz's *Gonna Go My Way.* There was a revival of 1940s big-band swing music, and rap and jazz fused to create new hybrid styles. Notably, Digable Planets mixed rap and cool jazz, and Greg Osby fused street jazz and rap. Many classical orchestras, already facing economic difficulties, struggled to gain younger audiences, and some, including the Buffalo and Houston Symphonies, had to cancel their seasons. Country music regained its popularity, as Billy Ray Cyrus's *Some Gave All* was the fastest-selling debut album in history. The U.S. Postal Service issued a stamp of Elvis Presley featuring a picture of the so-called King of Rock 'n' Roll as he appeared in the 1950s, when he first became famous among teenage baby boomers. That portrait prevailed in a 1991 national referendum over a picture depicting Presley as he appeared in his Las Vegas period, during the 1970s.

In sports, the Toronto Blue Jays defeated the Philadelphia Phillies in six games to win baseball's World Series. San Francisco's Barry Bonds was named National League MVP for the third time in four years, and Frank Thomas of the Chicago White Sox won the title in the American League. The Atlanta Brave Greg Maddux and Jack McDowell of the White Sox won the National and American League Cy Young Award as best pitcher. For the second year in a row, Juan Gonzales of the Texas Rangers led the Major Leagues in home runs, this time with 46. Carlton Fisk set records for the most games played as a catcher and most home runs as a catcher, before being released by the Chicago White Sox at age 45. Paul Molitor and Dave Winfield had their 3,000th hits, and the pitcher Nolan Ryan and the third baseman George Brett, both future Hall of Fame players, retired.

Enjoying record-setting attendance, Major League Baseball introduced two new expansion teams, the Florida Marlins and Colorado Rockies. It also voted to expand the number of divisions to a total of six, three in each league, and to introduce an additional round of playoffs. Marge Schott, owner of the Cincinnati franchise and baseball's only female owner, was fined $25,000 and suspended for a year for racial slurs and anti-Semitic statements she had made in 1992.

The basketball star Michael Jordan retired after leading the Chicago Bulls to their third consecutive National Basketball Association (NBA) title. *(AP/Wide World Photos)*

For the second consecutive year, the Dallas Cowboys defeated the Buffalo Bills in the Super Bowl, played in January 1994, and the Dallas running back Emmitt Smith was named the NFL's MVP. Florida State University was the national champion in college football, and its quarterback, Charlie Ward, won the Heisman Trophy before joining the New York Knicks professional basketball team. Don Shula of the Miami Dolphins broke George Halas's record for most wins as a head coach with his 325th game, and the league instituted new free agency rules that provided greater opportunities for players and yielded larger contracts.

Led by Michael Jordan, the Chicago Bulls won their third consecutive NBA title; Phoenix's Charles Barkley was league MVP. Claiming that he had nothing left to prove, Jordan, one of the best players in NBA history, retired shortly after the apparently random murder of his father. The University of North Carolina was the top college basketball team, and Indiana's Clabert Cheaney was player of the year. The Montreal Canadiens won hockey's Stanley Cup; the golfer Lee Janzen won the USGA Open; and Pete Sampras and Steffi Graf prevailed in the singles events in the U.S. Tennis Open. The former tennis star Arthur Ashe died of AIDS contracted through a blood transfusion, and the career of the top-rated tennis star Monica Seles had an abrupt, although temporary, halt when a fan enamored of Graf, Seles's chief rival, stabbed Seles with a knife during a match in Hamburg, Germany. Julie Korone became the first female jockey to win a Triple Crown race when her horse, Colonial Affair, placed first in the Belmont Stakes, and Sea Hero, ridden by Jerry Bailey, won the Kentucky Derby. The underdog, Evander Holyfield, defeated Riddick Bowe to claim boxing's heavyweight title.

CHRONICLE OF EVENTS

January 1: At the stroke of midnight, Czechoslovakia splits into two sovereign nations, Slovakia and the Czech Republic.

January 3: In Moscow, Bush and Yeltsin sign START II, calling for a two-thirds reduction in their nuclear arsenals.

January 6: The jazz pioneer Dizzy Gillespie dies at age 75.

January 14: Five Somali women are stoned to death for committing adultery.

January 15: Italian police capture Salvatore "Toto" Riina, the head of the Sicilian Mafia, who had been wanted in connection with more than 100 murders and political assassinations, including the 1992 killing of a judge who was prosecuting Mafia crimes.

January 17: Bush orders a missile attack on a suspected nuclear-weapons plant outside Baghdad.

January 20: Bill Clinton is inaugurated 42nd president of the United States, and Al Gore is sworn in as vice president.

January 25: Clinton appoints his wife, Hillary Rodham Clinton, to head a task force charged with formulating a plan to provide universal health care insurance for all Americans.

January 29: Clinton announces his interim policy ending the ban on homosexuals in the armed forces, pending a decision on whether to make the ban permanent.

January 31: Arguing that Ayatollah Ruhollah Khomeini is dead and therefore unable to rescind his edict, Iran's president Ali Akbar Rafsanjani reaffirms Khomeini's 1989 fatwa, or death sentence, on the British novelist Salman Rushdie for allegedly blaspheming Islam in *Satanic Verses.*

January 31: The Dallas Cowboys rout the Buffalo Bills 52-17 to win Super Bowl XXVII.

February 4: The National Research Council issues a study concluding that the AIDS epidemic has had minimal impact on the lives of most Americans because most of its victims are members of "marginalized" portions of the population.

February 5: Clinton signs his first bill, the Family and Medical Leave Act.

February 8: The independent prosecutor Lawrence E. Walsh makes public 49 pages of excerpts related to the Iran-contra scandal from the former defense secretary Caspar Weinberger's diary. Walsh also criticizes Bush for pardoning Weinberger before he could be tried, stating that a trial would have revealed new evidence that the Reagan administration tried to cover up the illegal arms deal.

February 17: Clinton submits his economic program to Congress. Intended to reduce the annual budget by 38 percent by 1997, it calls for increased taxes for corporations and very wealthy private citizens, as well as significant spending cuts.

February 19: The Security Council extends its peacekeeping mission in Croatia.

February 22: The Security Council unanimously votes to create an international court to try war crimes committed in the former Yugoslavia.

February 26: Islamic militants explode a large car bomb in the parking garage of the World Trade Center in New York City. Six people are killed and a 100-foot crater is formed beneath the building, which remains standing and intact.

February 28: Four ATF agents are killed and 16 are injured while trying unsuccessfully to arrest the Branch Davidian leader David Koresh in his heavily armed compound outside Waco, Texas. Two Davidians are also killed.

March 1: Clinton threatens U.S. military intervention if Serbia allows the Yugoslav civil war to spread to Kosovo.

March 5: The American sprinter Ben Johnson is suspended for life and stripped of his gold medal from the 1988 Olympics after he tests positive for performance-enhancing drugs.

March 7: Warring Afghan leaders sign a peace agreement concluding fighting that began after the fall of the Communist government in spring 1992.

March 10: David Gunn, M.D., is shot to death by an antiabortion activist, Michael F. Griffin, during a protest rally outside Gunn's abortion clinic in Pensacola, Florida. Gunn had previously been threatened and harassed by abortion opponents and had been featured on a "Wanted" poster issued by the antiabortion group Operation Rescue, which Griffin had recently joined.

March 12: Janet Reno takes office, becoming the nation's first female U.S. attorney general. She announces that she will determine whether the Justice Department should investigate Gunn's death.

March 12: A wave of car bombings kills some 300 people in Bombay, India.

Islamic extremists tried unsuccessfully to blow up New York's World Trade Center. *(AP/Wide World Photos)*

March 13–14: A late winter blizzard kills 213 people, most of them along the East Coast, others in Canada and Cuba.

March 25: President Frederik de Klerk acknowledges that South Africa built six nuclear bombs but maintains they are no longer intact.

March 29: Édouard Balladur is installed as prime minister of France after an overwhelming victory in the general election by a right-wing political coalition.

April 17: A federal jury convicts two officers charged with violating the civil rights of black motorist Rodney King, whom they brutally beat during a traffic arrest. Two other officers are acquitted. Clinton and Reno applaud the conviction of the officers, whose acquittal on state charges stem-

ming from the same incident sparked the 1992 Los Angeles riot.

April 19: The Branch Davidian leader David Koresh and some 100 of his followers, including at least 17 children, are killed in a fire that consumes their compound outside Waco, Texas, after FBI agents assault the structure with tear gas. The fire is believed to have been set by the Davidians themselves.

April 22: Timed to commemorate the 50th anniversary of the Jewish rebellion in Warsaw, Poland, against the Nazi occupiers during World War II, the Holocaust Museum, built with private donations, opens in Washington, D.C.

April 28: Between 200,000 and 1 million girls and young women between the ages of nine and 15 witness their parents' performing their jobs in the first national Take Our Daughters to Work Day, which was initiated by Ms. Foundation to raise self-esteem and provide a concrete sense of career opportunities available to women.

April 30: A fan of her rival Steffi Graf stabs the tennis star Monica Seles during a match in Hamburg, Germany.

May 13: Reagan's cold war Strategic Defense Initiative (popularly known as Star Wars) is officially terminated.

May 19: The so-called Travelgate scandal begins when seven members of the White House travel office are fired, allegedly for financial mismanagement and possible corruption.

May 20: The final episode of *Cheers* attracts 98 million viewers and obtains the second-highest Nielsen ratings ever for an episodic program.

May 22: Meeting in Washington, D.C., foreign ministers of Britain, France, Spain, Russia, and the United States decide to create safe areas for Bosnian Muslims where they will be protected by UN forces.

May 25: Five of the fired workers in the White House travel office are reinstated after new information suggests they may have been let go to allow Clinton's friends and relatives to obtain a share of the White House travel business.

May 27: A powerful car bomb damages Florence's famed Uffizi Gallery, killing the caretaker and his family and destroying a number of paintings and sculptures.

June 5: In Somalia, troops loyal to General Mohammed Farah Aidid kill 24 Pakistani peacekeepers, the largest single-day casualty toll for UN soldiers since 1961.

Cheers, starring Ted Danson (left), Woody Harrelson (right), and Kirstie Alley (across), ended after a successful nine-year run. *(Photofest)*

June 6: The Security Council orders the arrest of Somalia's General Aidid.

June 11: Ruling on an appeal by Ernesto Pichardo, a priest of the Afro-Cuban Santeria religion, practiced by an estimated 50,000 people in South Florida, the Supreme Court unanimously overturns a ban by the city of Hialeah, Florida, on animal sacrifice in religious rituals. The sacrificed barnyard animals are typically eaten in a sacred meal.

June 12: Some 20 Somalis are killed when UN forces raid General Aidid's stronghold.

June 13: Kim Campbell becomes Canada's first female prime minister when she is chosen head of the Progressive Conservative Party and replaces the outgoing prime minister Brian Mulroney.

June 13: The Yale-educated economist Tansu Ciller is elected head of Turkey's ruling True Path Party and becomes that country's first female prime minister.

June 17: General Aidid goes into hiding after UN troops fail to capture him during an attack on his home and command center. The United Nations issues a formal warrant for his arrest.

June 21: Basque separatists detonate a car bomb that kills five senior military officers in Madrid, Spain. Two others are also killed and 24 are wounded.

June 24: FBI agents arrest eight followers of the Egyptian mullah Sheikh Omar Abdul Rahman for planning a series of terrorist attacks on New York City landmarks, including the UN headquarters and the Lincoln and Holland Tunnels.

June 26: U.S. missiles aimed at Iraq's intelligence headquarters kill six people in Baghdad.

July 4: Sheila Widnall is named secretary of the U.S. Air Force, the first woman to head one of the military services.

July 8: Seven Islamic militants are executed in Egypt for attacks on Western tourists.

July 12: Three hundred U.S. troops arrive in Macedonia as UN peacekeepers.

July 12: A U.S. helicopter attack on General Aidid's stronghold kills more than 50 Somalis. In retaliation, a large crowd of Aidid's supporters seize and kill four Western journalists.

July 18: The Mississippi River crests at a record 47 feet, as flooding in the Midwest reaches its worst levels in history.

July 19: The Clinton administration announces its compromise "Don't ask; don't tell" policy on homosexuals in the military.

July 20: The deputy White House counsel Vince Foster, a childhood friend of Clinton's, is found dead of a bullet wound to the head. Although the death is ruled a suicide—a conclusion later also reached by the independent council Kenneth Starr—some of Clinton's critics on the political Right promulgate rumors claiming Foster was murdered to cover up Clinton's alleged financial improprieties concerning the Whitewater Development Corporation.

August 10: Ruth Bader Ginsburg is sworn in as Supreme Court justice.

August 11: Canada ends its 15-year embargo on humanitarian aid to Cuba.

August 12: An elite force of 400 U.S. Army Rangers charged with capturing General Aidid and subduing his forces arrives in Somalia.

August 21: NASA loses contact with the *Mars Observer* as it begins its maneuvering sequence for orbiting Mars. Scientists later conclude an explosion of the fuel and oxidizer elements probably destroyed the space probe.

August 21: Islamic militants in Algeria assassinate the former prime minister Kasdi Merbah and members of his family.

August 26: Yeltsin apologizes to leaders of the Czech Republic for the Soviet invasion that crushed the Prague Spring, which had temporarily conferred greater personal and artistic liberties on Czechoslovakia in 1968.

August 28: Sheikh Omar Abdel Rahman and 14 other Islamic militants are indicted for the World Trade Center bombing of February 28.

September 9: The Senate passes a nonbinding resolution calling on Clinton to clarify U.S. objectives in Somalia by October 15 and obtain congressional approval for further military involvement. The House passes a similar resolution on September 28.

September 10: The Palestinian Liberation Organization (PLO) unequivocally affirms Israel's right to exist, and Israel recognizes the PLO as the sole representative of the Palestinians—concessions neither side had previously made. U.S.–PLO talks, which had been suspended since a 1990 PLO terrorist assault on an Israeli beach, are resumed.

September 13: At the White House, Rabin and Arafat sign the so-called Oslo Accords, a Clinton-brokered accord that establishes a plan for peace in the Middle East.

September 23: Clinton presents his health-care reform proposal before a joint session of Congress.

September 25: Three U.S. soldiers die when their Blackhawk helicopter is shot down by a rocket-propelled grenade launcher fired by General Aidid's forces in Somalia. The incident later becomes the subject of Mark Bowden's 1999 book and Ridley Scott's film *Black Hawk Down* (2002).

October: New software is introduced to make "surfing" the World Wide Web easier. It soon attracts millions of new users to the Internet.

October 3–4: Twelve U.S. soldiers are killed, more than 70 are wounded, one is captured, and several are declared missing during a 15-hour gunfight with rebels loyal to General Aidid in Mogadishu, Somalia.

October 4: Despite pressure from some members of Congress, Clinton deploys an additional 220 troops, as well as tanks and armor, to bolster the U.S. presence in Somalia.

October 4: Soldiers loyal to Yeltsin subdue a coup attempt by hard-liners of the former Soviet Union.

October 7: Clinton orders an additional 15,000 troops to Somalia but establishes a deadline of March 31, 1994, for a full U.S. troop removal.

October 7: The author Toni Morrison receives the Nobel Prize in literature.

October 20: Benazir Bhutto gains power as prime minister of Pakistan.

October 27: Clinton presents an amended version of his health-care reform package to Congress.

November 1: The European Union begins existence with the implementation of the 1992 Maastricht Treaty.

November 2: The United States and China resume high-level military contacts, which had been suspended since 1989.

November 4: Jean Chrétien replaces the Conservative Party leader Kim Campbell as prime minister of Canada after a landslide Liberal Party victory.

November 9: Invading Croatian forces destroy the 16th-century Stari Most bridge, which spanned the Neretva River in Mostar, Bosnia.

December 2: The escaped drug lord Pablo Escobar is killed in Colombia.

December 2–12: Space-shuttle astronauts repair the defective mirror system on the *Hubble Space Telescope* and upgrade equipment and computers.

December 7: Gunman Colin Ferguson opens fire on passengers aboard a crowded Long Island Railroad commuter train, killing six.

December 17: The first U.S. combat troops begin their withdrawal from Somalia. Except for a small contingent left behind, the withdrawal is completed on March 25, 1994.

December 18: Two state troopers claim that Clinton had frequent extramarital affairs while governor of Arkansas. Clinton denies the allegations, and David Brock, the journalist who broke the story, later repudiates it.

December 21: Alina Castro, daughter of Cuba's dictator, Fidel Castro, seeks political asylum in the United States.

December 23: Bill Clinton and Hillary Rodham Clinton release to federal investigators financial records relating to the Whitewater Development Corporation.

EYEWITNESS TESTIMONY

In Britain we tend to view America in overly idealised or cynical ways—either way, we often mistake our simplistic perception(s) for the thing itself. The very thing we admire in American culture—its images, its icons, its *modernity*—is the thing we distrust the most. We tend to call facile this reliance on image, this redemption through heroes. But our disaffection reeks of the addict's disavowal of their drug: it is precisely because so many of our modern images/heroes *are* American that we resent this particular "special relationship."...

[Hollywood's epic movie biographies about dominating historical personalities] are mega-budget excursions into the safer past of American history; slices of history which were bridging moments, rites of passage, written in blood and riven with contradiction. But they still convey some basic, bitter truth about contemporary America, and perhaps a wider contemporary truth: although they are about magnetic galvanising personae, prophet figures, power beasts led to slaughter, the reading they invite is one of milder, degraded wish-fulfillment: look, they seem to be saying, look at these figures we once produced.... Where are they now we need them? The age of the power patriarch is over....

In the UK, we are stuck at the George Bush stage; stuck with a figurehead who is no more than a minor career man who happened to find himself in the right place at the wrong time: a little clerk of a man who literally embodies nothing. *Nothing.*...

At least Clinton seems to have realised that—beyond the washes and wipes of imagistic self-congratulation—it all has to start with a brutal *economic* reappraisal.

British journalist and cultural commentator Ian Penman
analyzing Hollywood film biographies and
American leadership in 1993, in Penman,
Vital Signs *(1998), pp. 323–24.*

In many disciplines, technical obsolescence has become an occupational problem to which vocational education training and retraining is seen as a possible solution. Many years ago the knowledge and skills gained through vocational training programs could remain useful for several years. However, today the usefulness of knowledge and skills has become short lived because of the exponential growth of new knowledge and emerging work environments....

Contemporary vocational education philosophies must be concerned not only with the development of entry-level occupational skills in graduates, but also with the need to upgrade and maintain graduates' knowledge base and occupational skills in keeping with the dynamics of society. To this end, the knowledge and skills students learn must be generically focused. The vocational educator must take into consideration all of these entities.

A true vocational education philosophy should be developed based on societal needs, human values, furthering national development, and intrinsic and extrinsic satisfaction derived from the acquisition and use of marketable skills.

Professor Henry James Findlay, Ed.D., writing in 1993
about the need for a new philosophy of vocational
education in the 1990s, in Craig Anderson and
Lary C. Rampp, eds., Vocational Education in the
1990s, vol. 2, A Sourcebook for Strategies,
Methods, and Materials *(1993), p. 25.*

Today, a generation raised in the shadows of the Cold War assumes new responsibilities in a world warmed by the sunshine of freedom but threatened still by ancient hatreds and new plagues.

Raised in unrivaled prosperity, we inherit an economy that is still the world's strongest, but is weakened by business failures, stagnant wages, increasing inequality, and deep divisions among our people....

This new world has already enriched the lives of millions of Americans who are able to compete and win in it. But when most people are working harder for less; when others cannot work at all; when the cost of health care devastates families and threatens to bankrupt many of our enterprises, great and small; when fear of crime robs law-abiding citizens of their freedom; and when millions of poor children cannot even imagine the lives we are calling them to lead—we have not made change....

We know we have to face hard truths and take strong steps. But we have not done so. Instead, we have drifted, and that drifting has eroded our resources, fractured our economy, and shaken our confidence....

It is time to break the bad habit of expecting something for nothing, from our government or from each other. Let us all take more responsibility, not only for ourselves and our families but for our communities and our country. To renew America, we must revitalize our democracy. . . .

To renew America, we must meet challenges abroad as well as at home. There is no longer division between what is foreign and what is domestic—the world economy, the world environment, the world AIDS crisis, the world arms race—they affect us all.

Today, as an old order passes, the new world is more free but less stable. Communism's collapse has called forth old animosities and new dangers. Clearly America must continue to lead the world we did so much to make.

While America rebuilds at home, we will not shrink from the challenges, nor fail to seize the opportunities, of this new world. Together with our friends and allies, we will work to shape change, lest it engulf us.

> *From President Bill Clinton's first inauguration speech on January 20, 1993. Available online. URL: http://www.bartleby.com/124/.*

The culture of poverty in this country has become institutionalized to an extent that is surprising to me and many others. Poverty has been with us since the beginning of time, and in many cultures there is a permanent underclass with all the problems that that suggests. It is contrary to the American ethos and history of progress that we would see that developing and becoming institutionalized in our country. There is nothing new about having poor people in our midst. What is very new is that we now have the institutionalization of that culture of poverty in ways that are difficult to reconcile with the whole concept of upward mobility, change, the American dream. And so those observers . . . who point that out as one of our major problems are absolutely right.

> *First Lady Hillary Rodham Clinton on February 15, 1993, decrying the institutionalization of a culture of poverty, in Alan F. Pater and Jason R. Pater, eds.,* What They Said in 1993 *(1994), pp. 202–203.*

It depended on where you were in the towers when it came. For some the warning was a trembling underfoot or just a blank computer screen and flickering lights. For others, it was a shocking noise. One woman was blown out of her high heels. Another, desk chair and all, sank into the floor. And then,

instantly it seemed, came the billowing smoke and the chilling realization that you had to get out of there.

There were those who panicked, those who cooly absorbed it, those who got sick to their stomach and those who saw the face of death. No one was sure what had happened. . . . But thousands of people in the World Trade Center yesterday afternoon knew they were in the grip of one of the most dreaded urban nightmares: they were in the city's tallest building and something was very wrong.

> *Journalist N. R. Kleinfeld describing the bombing of New York's World Trade Center on February 26, 1993, in Kleinfeld, "First, Darkness, Then Came the Smoke,"* New York Times, *February 27, 1993, p. 1.*

New York is the city of crime, the Mafia, and organized gangsters who are stronger than armies. It is the jungle where one cannot move without fearing for one's life. New York is the capital of the Jews with all their perversions, including politics, sex, media, forgery, cinema, drugs, and money laundering. It is the greatest arena for crime, most terrible fortress of discrimination, and ugliest example of class and race oppression.

> *Excerpt from a 1993 column in the comparatively progressive daily Arabic newspaper in Beirut, Lebanon, al-Safir, discounting the likelihood that Arabs were responsible for the World Trade Center bombing of February 26, 1993, in James Haley, ed.,* Post–Cold War America: 1992–Present *(2003), p. 49.*

What kind of man can rape a young girl, repeatedly cheat on his wife, beat his year-old son, then look you in the eye and call himself Jesus Christ? More important, what kind of people can look at such a man and believe him?

These people have been holed up in a compound in Waco, Texas, with their "spiritual leader." Vernon Howell, who has convinced his followers that he is the son of God, reportedly is responsible for a 45-minute shootout on Sunday that caused the deaths of four federal agents and two of the group's followers.

About 100 federal agents of the Bureau of Alcohol, Tobacco and Firearms had tried to serve arrest and search warrants on Vernon Howell for firearms charges. The battle erupted when three people tried to shoot their way out of the compound. At least 10 children were allowed to leave, but it remains surrounded by 400 federal officers and local police. . . .

There is a huge difference, which is also a fine line, between legitimate religion and madness. Vernon Howell, who is also known as David Koresh but who should never be known as Jesus Christ, is on the wrong side of that line. So are his followers.

From a March 3, 1993, editorial in the Detroit Free Press *commenting on the lethal gun battle on February 28, 1993, between law enforcement officers and Branch Davidian followers of David Koresh, in* Editorials On File, *March 1–15, 1993, p. 275.*

While Gunn's death is unfortunate, it's also true that quite a number of babies' lives will be saved.

Don Teshman, national director of the antiabortion organization Rescue America, commenting on March 10, 1993, about the assassination that day of David Gunn, M.D., during a protest rally outside the Pensacola, Florida, abortion clinic where Gunn worked, in Thomas E. Hitchings, ed., Facts On File Yearbook 1993 *(1994), p. 186.*

Just as there should be a federal remedy for racial discrimination and for gender discrimination, I think in this instance . . . there has got to be a federal response to interference through physical conduct which restrains access to a woman's right to choose.

Attorney General Janet Reno responding on March 12, 1993, to the practice of antiabortion protesters of blocking access to abortion clinics, in Thomas E. Hitchings, ed., Facts On File Yearbook 1993 *(1994), p. 186.*

It was based on what we knew then. Based on what we know now, it was obviously wrong.

Attorney General Janet Reno commenting on the Larry King radio show on April 19, 1993, about her decision to authorize a federal raid earlier that day on the Branch Davidian compound outside Waco, Texas, in Stephen Labaton, "Reno Sees Error in Move on Cult," New York Times, *April 20, 1993, p. 1.*

We need to be honest about one central fact: We have no way to predict the size, length and casualties of a peacemaking effort. If we find ourselves involved in a conflict in which American casualties mount, in which there is no end in sight, in which we take sides in a foreign civil war, in which American fighting men and women have great difficulty distinguishing between friend and foe, then I suggest that

The deadly federal raid on the Branch Davidian compound in Waco, Texas, outraged many Americans. *(AP/Wide World Photos)*

American support for military involvement would rapidly evaporate.

Senator John McCain of Arizona testifying before the Senate on April 21, 1993, about the dangers inherent in assuming a peacekeeping role in the former Yugoslavia, in Alan F. Pater and Jason R. Pater, eds., What They Said in 1993 *(1994), p. 322.*

During the week of April 5, the FBI advised me that they were developing a plan for the possible use of tear gas in an effort to increase the pressure on those in the compound to surrender. . . . The threshold question I asked was whether the gas would cause permanent injury to the children. I did not even want to consider the matter further if we could not be certain about this factor. The FBI assured me that the gas would not cause permanent injury. . . .

Then the primary question I asked again and again . . . was: "Why now? Why not wait?" I asked about their food and water supply and was told that it could last at least a year or more. . . . I became convinced that short of allowing David Koresh to go free, he was not coming out voluntarily.

Given that unacceptable result, in light of the fact that he was such a dangerous criminal, allowing the status quo to remain was not going to lead to an ultimate peaceful resolution and eliminate any risk to the safety of the innocent children in the compound, the public at large or the government agents at the scene. On the contrary, the passage of time only increased the likelihood of incidents and possible injuries and attendant injuries and harm.

Attorney General Janet Reno testifying before the House Judiciary Committee on April 28, 1993, about her decision to authorize a federal raid on the Branch Davidian compound outside Waco, Texas, on April 19, 1993, in James Haley, ed., Post–Cold War America, 1992–Present *(2003), p. 61.*

But even as Mr. Kushner portrays an America of lies and cowardice to match [Roy] Cohn's cynical view, he envisions another America of truth and beauty, the paradise imagined by both his Jewish and Mormon characters' ancestors as they made their crossing to the new land. *Angels in America* not only charts the split of its two central couples but it also implicitly sets its two gay men with AIDS against each other in a battle over their visions of the future. While the fatalistic, self-loathing Cohn ridicules gay men as political weaklings with "zero clout" doomed to defeat, the younger, equally ill Prior sees the reverse. "I am a gay man, and I am used to pressure. . . . I am tough and strong." Possessed by scriptural visions he describes as "very Steven Spielberg," even when in abject pain, Prior is Mr. Kushner's prophet of hope in the midst of apocalypse.

Theater critic Frank Rich reviewing Tony Kushner's play Angels in America: Millennium Approaches *on May 5, 1993, in* New York Times Theater Reviews: 1993–1994 *(1996), p. 75.*

The latest holiday on the national calendar is "Take a Daughter to Work Day," an invention of the Ms. Foundation, which pretty much tells you what it's all about.

For anyone who misses the point, working mothers and fathers are supposed to take their daughters along for a day's look at what they do for a living. The purpose is to show girls career opportunities they might not otherwise have imagined.

Boys, presumably, already know all about those opportunities.

These excused absences occurred on a school day, suggesting that sponsors believe that whatever girls might have learned in a classroom that day did not compare in value to watching a parent earn a living. . . . It's a trendy idea. And a good one too. . . .

Some jobs are plain dirty, sweaty, uncomfortable and with poor reward. . . . Our daughters need to see

and know this work too—so that they will understand why they should study hard, apply themselves, and aspire to something more. . . .

In many [professional] families, Take-Your-Daughter Day was undoubtedly an interesting educational experience. But the daughters of professionals are not the ones who need the lesson in the reality of working in America.

From a May 13, 1993, editorial in The Saginaw News *(Michigan) discussing Take Our Daughters to Work Day, which took place on April 28, in* Editorials On File, *May 1–15, 1993, p. 539.*

If the international community is not ready to defend the principles which it itself has proclaimed as its foundation, let it say so openly, both to the people of Bosnia and to the people of the world. Let it proclaim a new code of behavior in which force will be the first and the last argument.

Bosnia's president Alija Izetbegović denouncing a decision by Western leaders on May 22, 1993, not to launch air strikes against Bosnian Serbs practicing genocidal ethnic cleansing, but instead to create safe havens for Muslims within Bosnia, in Noel Malcolm, Bosnia: A Short History *(1996), p. 251.*

I learned one thing. When you bring something forward that is outside the Judeo-Christian tradition, the dominant culture is going to cause you problems.

Santeria priest Ernesto Pichardo commenting on the Supreme Court decision, delivered on June 11, 1993, upholding his religious right to sacrifice barnyard animals in religious rituals, in Richard Willing, "Courts Asked to Consider Culture," USA Today. *Available online. URL: http://www.usatoday.com/news/washington/judicial/2004-05-24-courts-culture_x.htm.*

Of the more than half a million U.S. troops deployed to the Persian Gulf during Operations Desert Shield and Desert Storm, approximately 7 percent (about 41,000) were women. The deployment of so many women renewed debate about whether restrictions that prohibit the assignment of women to combat positions and units should be removed. The Persian Gulf War provided the first opportunity to evaluate some of the salient issues in that debate on the basis of a large-scale, lengthy military deployment involving a hostile situation. . . .

Four of the most frequently raised issues in the debate . . . focus on whether combat and noncombat role distinctions made in women's assignments have any meaning in modern warfare; women cannot endure the hardships of a lengthy hostile deployment and perform assigned tasks without mission impairment; the presence of women negatively affects unit cohesion and, therefore, unit performance; and women impede the ability of units to deploy due to lost time for reasons such as pregnancy. . . .

Overall, the unit commanders and focus group participants gave primarily positive assessments of women's performance in the Persian Gulf War. Women . . . worked on a broad spectrum of assignments and tasks during the deployment. Focus group discussions indicated that women and men endured similar harsh encampment facilities and conditions. Health and hygiene problems during the deployment were considered inconsequential for both men and women. Cohesion in mixed gender units was generally considered to be effective during deployment, and the unit commanders and focus group participants often described cohesion as being best while the units were deployed. The groups . . . cited pregnancy as a cause for women returning early from deployment or not deploying at all, but generally identified few actual cases.

Findings from the General Accounting Office's Report to the Secretary of Defense, "Women in the Military: Deployment in the Persian Gulf War," July 1993, pp. 2–3.

Our society is failing to protect its children, and it fails them even more once they are in crisis. . . . We can no longer confine our focus to narrow legal issues, but must look for ways in which legal changes may redress broad social problems.

From an August 1993 report by the American Bar Association calling for changes in the legal system to place greater emphasis on the best interests of children and less emphasis on the rights of parents and interested adults, in Editorials On File, *August 1–15, p. 977.*

The sad journey of 2-year-old Jessica from Michigan to her birth parents in Iowa sends a chilling message to any couple thinking of adopting a child. If there is any flaw in the adoption procedure and a custody case gets to court, the rights of the birth parents will be paramount. . . .

Justice John Paul Stevens of the US Supreme Court summed up the current state of legal thinking when he refused the DeBoers' [adoptive parents'] plea for a hearing with this argument: "Neither Iowa law, Michigan law nor federal law authorizes unrelated persons to retain custody of a child whose natural parents have not been found to be unfit simply because they may be better able to provide for her future and her education.". . .

If a country consciously set out to discourage adoption, it would establish policies just like those that have grown up willy-nilly in the United States. Children suffer grievously if they do not have parents who are able and willing to give them intense, consistent love and care. Qualified couples should be encouraged to adopt children without worry that they might face a struggle like the one endured by Roberta and Jan DeBoer.

From an August 13, 1993, editorial in the Boston Globe *reacting to the decision issued by Supreme Court justice John Paul Stevens on July 26, 1993, allowing two-year-old Jessica DeBoer to be returned to her natural parents, despite objections by her adoptive parents, in* Editorials On File, *August 1–15, p. 975.*

We the soldiers who have returned from battle stained with blood, we who have fought against you, the Palestinians, we say to you in a loud clear voice: "Enough of blood and tears! Enough!"

Israeli prime minister Yitzhak Rabin calling for peace upon signing the Oslo Accords in Washington, D.C., on September 13, 1993, in Thomas L. Friedman, "Rabin and Arafat Seal Their Accord as Clinton Applauds 'Brave Gamble,' " New York Times, September 14, 1993, p. 1.

Our two peoples are awaiting today this historic hope and they want to give peace a real chance.

PLO chairman Yasser Arafat anticipating peace upon signing the Oslo Accords in Washington, D.C., on September 13, 1993, in Thomas L. Friedman, "Rabin and Arafat Seal Their Accord as Clinton Applauds 'Brave Gamble,' " New York Times, September 14, 1993, p. 1.

On television, single parenting is suddenly chic. More middle-class whites are having children out of wedlock, and many children are being brought up by hired hands and a bewildering rotation of boyfriends and girlfriends. Sixty years ago people understood that children need the loving care of their parents. Will it take another 60 years to understand that again?

Sociologist Amitai Etzioni criticizing the trendiness of single parenting among middle-class Americans, on October 25, 1993, in Alan F. Pater and Jason R. Pater, eds., What They Said in 1993 *(1994), p. 203.*

The other day the mayor of Baltimore . . . told me a story . . . of a young man who had been killed—eighteen years old—on Halloween. He always went out with the little bitty kids so they could trick-or-treat safely. And across the street from where they were walking on Halloween, a fourteen-year-old boy gave a thirteen-year-old boy a gun and dared him to shoot the eighteen-year-old boy, and he shot him dead. . . .

More than 37,000 people die from gunshot wounds in this country every year. Gunfire is the leading cause of death in young men. And now that we've all gotten so cool that everybody can get a semiautomatic weapon, a person shot now is three times more likely to die than fifteen years ago, because they're likely to have three bullets in them. One hundred and sixty thousand children stay home from school every day because they are scared they will be hurt in their school.

The famous African American sociologist William Julius Wilson has written a stunning book called *The Truly Disadvantaged,* in which he chronicles in breathtaking terms how the inner cities of our country have crumbled as work has disappeared. And we must find a way, through public and private sources, to enhance the attractiveness of the American people who live there to get investment there. We cannot, I submit to you, repair the American community and restore the American family until we provide the structure, the value, the discipline, and the reward that work gives. . . .

So I say to you, we have to make a partnership—all the government agencies, all the business folks. But where there are no families, where there is no order, where there is no hope . . . who will be there to give structure, discipline, and love to these children? You must do that. And we must help you.

President Bill Clinton addressing a predominantly African-American church in Memphis, Tennessee, on November 13, 1993, in Robert Torricelli and Andrew Carroll, eds., In Our Own Words *(1999), pp. 405–406.*

If you end the first half of an epic play with an angel crashing through a Manhattan ceiling to visit a young man ravaged by AIDS, what do you do for an encore?

If you are Tony Kushner . . . you follow the angel up into the stratosphere, then come back home with a healing vision of heaven on Earth. . . .

The opening questions are asked by a blind character who never reappears: a blind Russian man who is the world's oldest living Bolshevik. *Perestroika* is aptly titled not because it has much to do with the former Soviet Union but because it burrows into that historical moment of change when all the old orders, from Communism to Reaganism, are splintering, and

Tony Kushner's *Angels in America* received critical acclaim for its study of how acquired immunodeficiency syndrome (AIDS)–stricken patients faced their impending fates. *(Photofest)*

no one knows what apocalypse or paradise the next millennium might bring. "How are we to proceed without theory?" asks the cross, aged Bolshevik. Not the least of Mr. Kushner's many achievements is his refusal to adhere to any theatrical or political theory. *Angels in America* expands in complexity as it moves forward, unwilling to replace gods that failed with new ones any more than it follows any textbook rules of drama.

> *Theater critic Frank Rich reviewing Tony Kushner's play* Angels in America: Perestroika, *on November 23, 1993, in* New York Times Theater Reviews: 1993–1994 *(1996), p. 192.*

But at the end of the day, the allegations [made by Arkansas state troopers of then-governor Bill Clinton's sexual misconduct] couldn't be verified, the troopers hadn't been able to affix specific dates or times to any of the events described, and I had to make a leap of faith in accepting their word.

I bought it all because I wanted to. War for war's sake was really the only way I knew since coming to Washington seven years before. I also had career considerations. The Anita Hill experience was still fresh in my mind. . . . I had slain a liberal Goliath, and I was casting around for the next big prey. That Clinton was the first Democratic president in my adult lifetime—personally reviled by the [right-wing] movement, my audience, even if not by me—made him an especially inviting target. . . .

Indeed, Troopergate can perhaps best be understood as having nothing to do with the Clintons, but rather as an extension of a form of warfare I had learned to perfect in writing *The Real Anita Hill*—a cruel smear disguised as a thorough "investigation." As I had heedlessly appropriated the Republican attacks on women witnesses in the [Clarence] Thomas hearing, so did I appropriate the troopers' misogynistic rendering of Hillary Clinton. Having invented a "kinky" sex life for Anita Hill, I had little trouble making what may have been a few extramarital dalliances by Clinton appear deviant and strange. "Bill Clinton is a bizarre guy," I said with a smirk, appearing on CNN's *Crossfire* to debate the trooper piece. But it was me, a sexually repressed closeted gay man, detailing Clinton's alleged infidelities to forward the right-wing political agenda, who was the bizarre guy. . . .

[The article published in the January 1994 issue of *American Spectator*] left such an indelible image in the minds of the media and the public . . . that it would be possible in the future to say and write and broadcast any crazy thing about the first couple and get away with it.

> *Author David Brock describing his personal and political motivations on December 18, 1993, when he broke the so-called Troopergate story alleging that Bill Clinton had abused his power as governor of Arkansas by having adulterous affairs, in Brock,* Blinded by the Right *(2002), pp. 149–151.*

6

The Contract with America and the Crime of the Century
1994

Overall, in 1994 the nation moved toward the political center, as the economy improved and several international conflicts eased, but bitter bipartisan politics scuttled much of the Democrats' domestic agenda, most notably Clinton's effort to provide universal health care for all Americans. Clinton achieved international victories by winning an agreement from North Korea not to develop its nuclear capabilities, reaching an accord with Cuba to halt the mass exodus of refugees to the United States, and, with assistance from last-minute negotiations by former president Jimmy Carter, effecting the resignation of the junta that had ousted Haiti's democratically elected president Jean-Bertrand Aristide in 1991. Carter also helped negotiate a late-year cease-fire in Bosnia.

Clinton took steps to encourage international trade, including ending a trade embargo on Vietnam and dropping the linkage between China's human rights abuses and its ability to conduct business with the United States. The nation enjoyed an increase in the GDP of more than 50 percent and a decrease in unemployment.

Nonetheless, in November the Democrats lost both bodies of Congress in the midterm elections, giving Republicans total control of the legislative branch for the first time in 40 years. Clinton interpreted the Republican victory as the public's repudiation of some of his more liberal policies, and he subsequently moved more to the political center. The Georgia congressman Newt Gingrich, an outspoken foe of Clinton's, was elected Speaker of the House after engineering the Republican victory with his Contract with America—a promise to introduce specific acts of legislative reform within the first 100 days of the new Congress. Gingrich also attacked Clinton's moral character, accusing him of complicity in the Whitewater affair, whose investigation was later led by Kenneth Starr, who succeeded Robert Fiske as independent counsel.

Matters of race and genetics captured public attention in such books as *The Bell Curve,* a controversial scientific study that suggests that intelligence is largely predetermined by genetics. Sharp divisions over homosexuals' rights, women's rights, and abortion rights also divided the country, and the AIDS pandemic persisted throughout the United States and the rest of the world, especially in sub-Saharan Africa. In the United States, as AIDS continued to decimate homosexual and artistic communities, it also spread to a greater number of heterosexuals. Crime and punishment remained a prominent concern, as Congress passed a compromise crime bill, and the U.S. prison population exceeded 1 million inmates for the first time.

But the most sensational of the year's crimes involved the arrest of the former football star O. J. Simpson, a handsome, charismatic African American who had been widely popular among both blacks and whites, and who had risen to the top of white-dominated American society before being charged with what soon became known as the Crime of the Century: the murders of his white wife, Nicole Brown Simpson, and her white friend Ronald Goldman. Simpson's arrest followed a sensational nationally televised low-speed car chase along a Los Angeles freeway, and it once again put in focus how deeply race still divided the nation, especially in terms of beliefs about the fundamental honesty and good intentions of police and the justice system and about the credibility of DNA evidence, as Simpson's DNA was linked to the stabbings. Throughout the remainder of 1994, the so-called O. J. Trial, which culminated in October 1995 with Simpson's acquittal, received intense media scrutiny and provoked public commentary, as it evoked wide-ranging responses among different demographic groups regarding matters of celebrity, wealth, race, jurisprudence, domestic violence, police prejudice, and the privileged status of athletes in American society.

INTERNATIONAL DEVELOPMENTS

Although the world continued to experience violent upheaval, especially in the Balkans and Africa, several significant steps toward peace and unification also occurred. After the Irish Republican Army (IRA) agreed to a cease-fire in Northern Ireland and mainland Britain, peace talks began between Britain and the IRA. The political activist Nelson Mandela, who spent 27 years as a political prisoner in South Africa for his opposition to apartheid, was elected president of South Africa under the country's new majority-rule constitution. Upon taking office Mandela stressed the importance of reconciliation and financial responsibility, and South Africa rejoined the British Commonwealth after a 33-year estrangement. The opening in May of the Channel Tunnel, which introduced direct train travel between London and Paris, created a more literal sort of unity, as the British Isles were for the first time connected directly to mainland Europe.

The cold-war era continued to slip into the past, as Clinton visited Russia in January to support Yeltsin's economic and political reforms; the International Monetary Fund (IMF) agreed to release the remaining $1.5 billion of a $3 billion fast track loan to Russia; and Russia and the Western allies withdrew the last of their cold-war forces stationed in Germany. Clinton extended the U.S. moratorium on nuclear testing to September 1995 and cancelled the $8 billion Doomsday Project, designed to keep the government functioning in the aftermath of a nuclear war. After weeks of bargaining to ensure its continued status as a major power, Russia joined the North Atlantic Treaty Organization's (NATO's) Partnership for Peace program, which allied it with its former cold-war enemies. Russia also signed a pact of friendship and military cooperation with Georgia and an agreement with China not to target each other with nuclear missiles. After German authorities arrested several smugglers trying to take plutonium out of the former Soviet Union, Russia also agreed to work with German authorities to prevent the theft of that key ingredient for nuclear bombs. Aleksandr Solzhenitsyn, the Nobel Prize–winning Soviet dissident, returned to Russia after 20 years of exile. The world-famous author was appalled by the post-Soviet political situation, however, which he called a "sham democracy," and he criticized Yeltsin's movement toward Western capitalism as a form of "privateering." In December, Yeltsin ordered Russian troops to attack Muslim secessionists in the breakaway republic of Chechnya, initiating an armed struggle that persisted throughout the rest of the decade.

Jewish and Islamic extremists tried to scuttle the peace process by killing civilians in the Middle East and throughout the world. Notably, a Jewish West Bank settler slaughtered 29 Palestinian worshipers at prayer in Hebron, and Iranian-backed Muslim terrorists exploded a powerful car bomb outside a Jewish community center in Buenos Aires, Chile, which killed more than 100 people. Nonetheless, the Israeli prime minister Yitzhak Rabin and the Palestine Liberation Organization (PLO) leader Yasser Arafat signed the Cairo Agreement, and Israel established peaceful relations with Jordan for the first time in its history. The Cairo Agreement established the Palestinian Authority and installed Arafat as its chairman, in return for assurances that the Palestinian Authority would cooperate with Israeli security forces and take real steps to stop terrorist attacks against Israel by Islamic militants based in the West Bank and Gaza. However, Arafat jeopardized the pact a few days later when, while speaking in a mosque in Johannesburg, South Africa, he vowed that Palestinians would continue their *jihad,* commonly translated as "holy war," until they had liberated Jerusalem. After Rabin warned that further violence and terror would negate the agreement that recognized Palestinian authority and prompted an Israeli troop withdrawal, Arafat explained that by *jihad* he had really meant a sacred campaign. But his speech, although playing well to Islamic audiences, undermined Israeli confidence in the Palestinians' actual intentions as partners in peace.

The spirit of goodwill between Israel and Jordan seemed more genuine, as leaders of the neighboring countries, signed in a Washington, D.C., ceremony arranged by Clinton, a July declaration ending the official state of warfare that had lasted since Israel's founding in 1948. After concluding a formal treaty in October, the countries further established cooperative economic ventures and agreed to share water and electrical resources. Rabin, Arafat, and Israel's foreign minister, Shimon Peres, received the Nobel Prize in peace for their efforts to end the violence in the region. Israel also established full diplomatic ties with the Vatican.

Another moment of peace and reconciliation occurred when last-minute diplomatic efforts led by the former president Jimmy Carter, the former chairman of the Joint Chiefs of Staff Colin Powell, and Senator Sam Nunn forestalled a UN-authorized invasion of Haiti, as the ruling military leaders agreed to step down and allow Jean-Bertrand Aristide, who had been elected in 1990 and deposed in 1991, to reassume the presidency. While announcing the agreement to the nation, Clinton revealed that, at the time the agreement was reached, 61 U.S. warplanes were already en route to Haiti to spearhead a military action to overthrow the junta. Some 20,000 U.S. troops then landed unopposed and briefly served as peacekeepers as Aristide dismantled the military and began to establish a new police force, which was subsequently accused of corruption and excessive violence.

Carter's diplomacy also helped convince North Korea to renounce its nuclear-weapons development program in return for U.S. assistance and guarantees. The agreement was reached after North Korea's founding leader, Kim Il Sung, died after 46 years of rule and was succeeded by his son, Kim Jong Il, and it forestalled Clinton's plans to launch a preemptive attack on the country's nuclear facilities after North Korea threatened to withdraw from the Nuclear Non-Proliferation Treaty, which had been in effect since 1985. In return for North Korea's agreement to freeze its graphite reactors, to stop construction of two additional reactors, and to permit UN inspectors on the sites to assure compliance, the United States, Japan, and South Korea pledged to help the North Koreans build two 1,000-megawatt light-water reactors for generating electricity without producing by-products that could be used to make weapons-grade plutonium.

After threatening to overwhelm the United States with boat loads of refugees, who during July were fleeing to America at the rate of almost 1,000 per day, Cuba concluded a pact in which it agreed to restrain its citizens from leaving the island, using "mainly persuasive measures," in return for U.S. acceptance of 20,000 legal immigrants per year, up from the existing yearly quota of 3,000. Clinton hoped the agreement would protect the safety of the refugees, many of whom died trying to cross the shark-infested Florida Straits on makeshift rafts and boats, and forestall a repeat of the 1980 Mariel boat lift, in which some 125,000 refugees arrived in south Florida in a single month. However, the arrangement angered many Cuban exiles and others who deplored the idea of compelling freedom-

Anxious to flee the repressive Castro regime, Cuban refugees fled to the United States on improvised rafts. (*AP/Wide World Photos*)

seeking people to remain confined without basic civil liberties on an island ruled by a Communist dictator. The government of Mexico reached a peace agreement with Zapatista rebels, descendants of indigenous Mayans in the southern province of Chiapas, who were demanding ownership of their ancestral homelands. Luis Donaldo Colosio, the candidate of Mexico's long-ruling party who had been virtually assured of winning the upcoming presidential election, died in Tijuana, the victim of an unrelated assassination. Ernesto Zedillo, the party's new nominee, was subsequently elected. North Yemen declared a cease-fire with South Yemen, which was trying to secede.

But while these movements toward peace and reconciliation occurred elsewhere, the conflict in Bosnia intensified throughout the year, and NATO, acting as the military arm of the United Nations, was drawn further into the fighting. A NATO threat to bomb Serbian artillery positions around Sarajevo, combined with political pressure from Russia, Serbia's traditional ally, succeeded in securing the withdrawal of those weapons, but only after a Serbian mortar shell killed 68 people in a downtown marketplace in early February. Weeks later, NATO conducted its first offensive military action since the formation of the alliance in 1949, as U.S. warplanes shot down Serbian aircraft that violated a no-fly zone established to protect Bosnian Muslims. Conditions within Sarajevo soon improved, and Bosnian Muslims and Bosnian Croats agreed to end their infighting by establishing a Muslim-Croat federation. By the end of March, some 20,000 people felt safe enough to attend a soccer match in the city's stadium, which two months earlier had been a regular target of Serbian artillery fire. But conditions quickly deteriorated as Bosnian Serbs reintensified their attacks, and by late summer they had repositioned their heavy weaponry around Muslim enclaves. In September, Pope John Paul II canceled a mass he planned to celebrate in Sarajevo because conditions there were too dangerous, and by the end of the year, NATO planes were conducting their heaviest attacks of the war against Serbian air bases. However, in late December, Carter unexpectedly convinced Milošević to agree to a cease-fire, and a four-month truce took effect on January 1, 1995.

Fears that the fighting in Bosnia might trigger a broader regional conflict became more real as Greece, concerned that the Republic of Macedonia would make claims on the northern Greek region also called Macedonia, demanded that the Republic of Macedonia change its name. Although hostilities did not break out, Greece closed its border and took other measures to pressure the former Yugoslav republic, which had gained sovereignty in 1991.

The other large-scale genocidal campaign of the decade began in Rwanda in April, after that country's president and the president of neighboring Burundi were killed when their plane was shot down as they returned from peace talks in Tanzania. The Rwandan president—and the prime minister, who was assassinated the following day along with 10 UN soldiers assigned to protect him—were members of the ruling Watutsi people, also known as Batutsi, or simply Tutsi. The vast majority of Rwandans, however, were Hutu, members of Bantu tribal groups throughout sub-Saharan Africa. The Hutu opposed to the Tutsi-dominated Rwandan Patriotic Front (RTF) were believed to be responsible for the assassinations. Despite the presence of 2,500 UN peacekeeping forces, civil war began after the assassinations, and within three weeks some 200,000 people died. Within months the number of deaths reached or exceeded a half-million. Although both sides committed atrocities, the minority Tutsi and their supporters were the overwhelming victims. Furthermore, hundreds of thousands of Tutsi refugees fled to Tanzania. Nonetheless, the RTF succeeded in gaining military control over the capital city, Kigali, and three-quarters of the countryside. This development led some 1.2 million Hutu to take shelter in UN-protected enclaves within Rwanda and another 2 million to seek refuge in neighboring Zaire, causing instability there and eventually forcing Zaire to turn away additional refugees and close its border with Rwanda.[1] By the end of the year, the worst of the killing was over, and the United Nations established an international criminal tribunal to prosecute those responsible for genocide. The Tutsi-dominated government, under pressure from the United Nations, initiated policies of reconciliation. Hutu moderates were appointed president and premier, and the military established centers of reeducation where defeated Hutu soldiers could be integrated into a new Rwandan army composed of elements of both peoples. Although the situation ultimately stabilized, the international community was criticized for failing to acknowledge the genocide sooner and assume its UN-mandated responsibilities for intervening in such situations more quickly, when their intervention could possibly have saved tens of thousands of lives. In fact, many countries, including the United States, refrained from using the term *genocide* in order to avoid incurring a legal responsibility to intervene to stop the killings. Clinton later admitted that his failure to take quicker action in Rwanda was one of his main regrets as president.

U.S. forces completed their withdrawal from Somalia in late March, after achieving mixed results. The famine that had plagued the nation ended; about three-quarters of a million children received vaccinations; thousands of new wells were constructed; and tens of thousands of children were enrolled in schools. But looting and banditry remained rampant, and armed factions continued to hijack relief convoys and otherwise impede the distribution of humanitarian aid supplies. The U.S. public generally regarded the intervention in Somalia as a failure in foreign policy.

India, a nuclear-armed nation, tested a missile capable of reaching targets in China, and Turkey launched a major land and air assault against Kurdish strongholds in the eastern province of Tunceli. Iraq provoked fears of another invasion after it deployed two divisions of the Republican Guard to the Kuwaiti border, but they pulled back and the situation quickly defused after Clinton ordered a large and rapid deployment of U.S. forces in the region. Silvio Berlusconi, a right-wing media mogul, was elected prime minister of Italy, despite concerns about his alliance with a neofascist party and fears about the confluence of the powers of the media and the state that his election effected. Accusations of corruption, for which he was later convicted, led Berlusconi to resign before the year's end. Officials at the 10th International Conference on AIDS announced that more than 17 million people had been infected by the AIDS-producing HIV, some 10 million of them in sub-Saharan Africa.

GOVERNMENT AND SOCIETY

Clinton narrowly won passage of a $30.2 billion crime bill, the result of a bipartisan compromise. The bill funded construction of new prisons and the hiring of an additional 100,000 police officers to patrol the streets. It also banned certain kinds of assault weapons—to the chagrin of the National Rifle Association (NRA) and other opponents of gun control—and it expanded the federal death penalty to apply to more than 50 crimes; mandated life imprisonment for anyone convicted of a federal crime who had two prior convictions for serious state or federal crimes; required that communities be notified when a convicted sex offender moved there; and permitted accusations of past sexual offenses to be used as evidence in federal criminal trials, even if the defendant had not been charged in those cases. The compromise reduced from $1.2 billion to $380 million the funding Clinton sought for community prevention programs, which many Republicans regarded as frivolous. In a separate action also opposed by the NRA, the Bureau of Alcohol, Tobacco, and Firearms (AFT) banned certain armor-piercing bullets, popularly known as cop killers for their ability to penetrate the protective body gear worn by police officers.

Although Clinton lauded the passage of the anticrime legislation as a great example of the way bipartisan cooperation could yield positive results for the country, he was unable to gain a similar consensus for his much-heralded plan for health-care reform, which failed to win congressional approval. Overall, political gridlock characterized the 103rd Congress, as other legislation also fell victim to partisan disagreements among Democrats and to Republican filibusters. Among the failed legislative initiatives were a $16.2 billion economic-stimulus bill, campaign-finance reform, revisions intended to strengthen federal mining and clean-water laws, and a proposed revamping of the Superfund toxic-waste cleanup program.

Many observers believed that Republican intransigence stemmed in part from a desire to avoid handing Clinton victories before the midterm congressional elections, in which they expected to pick up seats and perhaps take control of one or both houses of Congress. If that was their goal, they succeeded, as Republicans gained nine Senate seats and 52 seats in the House of Representatives to win control of both houses of Congress for the first time since 1954, when Dwight Eisenhower was president. They concluded the year with 53 Senate seats and 230 in the House. Democrats had 47 Senate seats and 204 in the House. There was also one independent seat in the House.

Much of the Republicans' success, especially in the House, resulted from efforts by the Georgia representative Newt Gingrich, a passionate Clinton critic. Through his Contract with America Gingrich aspired to "restore the bonds of trust between the people and their elected representatives" by reducing congressional waste and fraud, cutting the costs of running Congress, requiring zero-based budgeting, imposing term limits on congressional committee chairs, and requiring that all tax increases pass by a 60 percent margin or better. The contract further called for quick passage of 10 bills intended to strengthen families, produce a balanced budget amendment, fight crime by imposing tougher sentences, cut welfare programs, provide middle-class tax relief, increase military spending, repeal tax hikes on Social Security earnings, give incentives to small businesses, place reasonable limits on punitive damages awarded by juries, and impose term limits on career politicians. After the election, Republicans nominated Gingrich by unanimous acclaim to be the next Speaker of the House. Dick Armey, a Texas Republican, was elected House majority leader; Robert Dole of Kansas became the Senate majority leader, while Richard

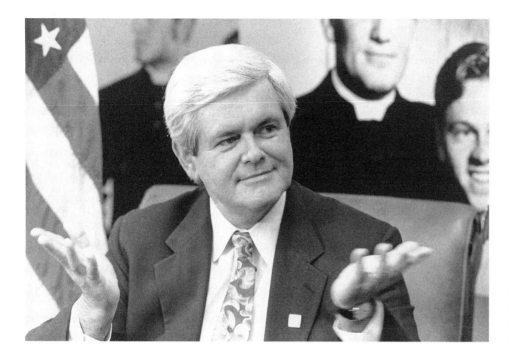

Newt Gingrich was elected Speaker of the House after Republicans took control of Congress in the midterm elections. *(Photofest)*

Gephardt, a Missouri Democrat, became minority leader in the House and Tom Daschle of South Dakota was elected minority leader in the Senate.

The so-called Whitewater investigation began in December 1993, when the Justice Department subpoenaed documents belonging to Bill and Hillary Rodham Clinton to determine whether Clinton had improperly used his political influence in his real-estate and financial dealings with his business partner, James B. McDougal, in the late 1970s. The investigation was made public in January 1994, and throughout his presidency Clinton was dogged by charges, especially by his critics on the political Right, that he had illegally used his position as governor for personal gain. McDougal, owner of the Madison Guaranty Savings and Loan, which failed in 1989, was then under federal investigation concerning allegations that he had illegally diverted funds to various political campaigns, including Clinton's campaign for governor. Investigators further probed the dealings of the Whitewater Development Corporation, a defunct real-estate venture owned jointly by the Clintons and McDougal and his wife, Susan.

Although the Clintons maintained they were simply "passive investors" in the venture, in which they claimed they lost money, the specter of foul play surfaced after it was learned that Clinton's friend and former personal lawyer, the former deputy White House counsel Vincent W. Foster, Jr., had been handling affairs related to Whitewater before his apparent suicide in July 1993. Although authorities ruled the death a suicide, rumors circulated, especially among Clinton's critics on the political Right, that Foster was murdered to stop him from revealing potentially harmful information about Clinton's business transactions and political dealings. At Clinton's request, Attorney General Janet Reno appointed Robert B. Fiske, a former federal prosecutor, as special counsel with broad authority to review all of the charges associated with Whitewater. After the Senate reenacted the independent-counsel legislation that had expired in 1992, when Republicans blocked its renewal to protest the prolonged Iran-contra investigation of the Reagan administration, Reno asked a panel of federal judges to appoint Fiske to that position, which provided greater autonomy because an independent counsel, unlike a special counsel, does not report to the attorney general, who is a political appointee. But in August, the panel instead replaced Fiske with Kenneth Starr, a conservative Republican who had served in a top legal position in the Bush administration, prompting Democrats to question whether Starr could conduct an impartial investigation. Both Fiske and Starr ultimately concurred that Foster's death was a suicide, and ultimately neither found grounds for indicting Clinton for his dealings with McDougal. Committee hearings conducted in 1995 by the Republican-controlled House and Senate also concluded without finding significant evidence of wrongdoing. Nonetheless, rumors of financial improprieties associated with Whitewater and complicity in Foster's death continued to circulate throughout the remainder of Clinton's time in office.

In addition to fending off accusations of wrongdoing in his Whitewater dealings, Clinton had to defend himself against new charges of sexual harassment when Paula Corbin Jones, a former employee of the Arkansas state government, filed a civil lawsuit claiming that Clinton had made "persistent and continuous" unwanted advances toward her during a business conference in May 1991, when Clinton was governor. After a 1997 Supreme Court decision allowed the lawsuit to proceed while Clinton was in office, the case went to trial in 1998, when a judge dismissed the suit as being without merit. However, to avoid a lengthy appeal, Clinton settled the case in 1998 by agreeing to pay Jones $850,000, without acknowledging any wrongdoing. But the accusation tarnished Clinton's reputation and placed many feminists in an awkward position, as they deplored acts of sexual harassment, on the one hand, but generally applauded Clinton's domestic agenda, which sought to broaden rights and opportunities for women. Moreover, a deposition Clinton gave in January 1998 for the Paula Jones lawsuit, in which he denied having a sexual relationship with former White House intern Monica Lewinsky, led to a broader investigation that resulted in Starr's 1998 recommendation to Congress that Clinton be impeached for committing perjury and obstructing justice.

In response to antiabortion protests that often harassed or intimidated doctors, staff, and patients attempting to enter abortion clinics, Clinton, who maintained that abortions should be "safe, legal, and rare," signed the Federal Access to Clinic Entrances Act, making it a crime to harm individuals entering or leaving abortion clinics. Moreover, the Supreme Court ruled that abortion clinics could, to protect patients and others from physical and verbal intimidation, keep the protestors 36 feet away from their buildings without violating the demonstrators' First Amendment right to free speech. Opponents of abortion were further distressed when the French firm that manufactured the RU-486, a pill that could induce abortions, donated its U.S. patent rights to a nonprofit contraceptive research group, thereby raising prospects that the drug, already legal in China, France, Great Britain, and Sweden, would soon become available in the United States. Abortion opponents feared the pill would increase the number of abortions performed each year because it promised to make the termination of newly created embryos easier and more private. Two antiabortion militants, Michael Griffin and Rachelle Shannon, were convicted of shooting doctors in 1993 who performed abortions. Griffin's victim, Dr. David Gunn, died of his wounds; Shannon's was superficially injured. Another antiabortion militant, Paul J. Hill, was arrested for the fatal shooting of Dr. John Bayard Britton and a companion outside a clinic in Pensacola, Florida. Hill, who had previously defended killing doctors who perform abortions on such national television shows as *Donahue* and *Nightline,* was convicted in October of violating the Freedom of Access to Clinics Act, after the judge denied his attempt to present a so-called necessity defense in which he maintained the shooting was justified because it prevented a greater harm—an abortion. Hill was the first person to be charged under the act. A month later he was also convicted of murder under state law and condemned to death. Britton was the third doctor to be assassinated since March 1993, and his death prompted an FBI investigation into a possible conspiracy of militant antiabortion activists pursuing a program of planned murders. Although the Republican Party did not support the violent acts of extremists, it had long endorsed the antiabortion movement and was officially committed to reversing the 1973 Supreme Court ruling that legalized the practice. Nonetheless, a *New York Times* poll

To counter growing violence against doctors performing abortions, Congress passed the Federal Access to Clinic Entrances Act. *(AP/Wide World Photos)*

concluded that the Republican rank and file were largely split on the abortion question, and that nearly 40 percent favored broad abortion rights.

One of the greatest security failures in the nation's history came to light in February when a Central Intelligence Agency (CIA) counterintelligence officer, Aldrich Ames, and his Colombian-born wife were arrested for selling secret information to the Soviet Union and Russia over the previous nine years, a period that included the final five years of the cold war. According to the *Wall Street Journal,* Aimes was the highest-ranking U.S. government official ever accused of spying, and the secrets he and Maria del Rosario Casas Ames passed on, in exchange for more than $2.5 million, seriously undermined U.S. intelligence networks. A draft report issued by the CIA revealed that Ames exposed 55 clandestine U.S. and allied operations and exposed the identity of 34 secret agents. Revelations of the prolonged spying by the Russians and Soviets further called into question both the ability of the CIA to police itself and U.S. support of Russia in the post–cold war era, and they prompted the CIA director, R. James Woolsey, Jr., to resign at the end of the year amid criticism of his handling of internal security and his failure to restructure the organization in a manner properly suited to the needs of post–cold war intelligence.

Changes in educational philosophy surfaced when the most commonly used college entrance exam, the Scholastic Aptitude Test (SAT), was overhauled for the first time in 20 years. The new version placed greater emphasis on critical thinking skills and reading comprehension, and, in recognition of the growing role of computers and technology in daily life, for the first time students were allowed to use calculators for the math sections. In addition to fueling a demand for commercial preparatory courses to help students raise their scores, the changes in the test reflected a growing consensus among educators, businessmen and businesswomen, and other professionals that current and future business environments call for enhanced problem-solving capabilities and deeper comprehension of fundamental issues. The vast majority of students in 1994 took the older version, and though the changes were made partly in response to accusations that the older exam was biased against females and minorities, as well as that it did not reliably predict future college achievement, the 1994 test results showed a slight narrowing of the gender gap. Young men still tested better than young women, but their scores decreased overall, while women's improved. The average verbal score for women was 421, up one point from 1993, and 425 for men, down three points from 1993. Overall, men scored 501 on math, down one point, while women scored 460, up three points.[2]

In its major rulings for the year the Supreme Court decided that jurors cannot be excluded on the basis of gender; governments are limited in their ability to require property owners to reserve portions of their land for public use; written, visual, and musical parodies are, in some cases, exempt from copyright law; a school board cannot carve out a specially designed school district to accommodate the special needs of a religious group; and passengers bumped from airplane flights as a result of overbooking may sue airlines in state courts. The Court declined to hear a case brought by Vietnam War veterans exposed to Agent Orange who did not begin experiencing adverse effects until after a 1984 class-action lawsuit was initiated against the companies who manufactured the defoliant. Justice Harry A. Blackmun argued in a 22-page dissent to an 8-1 ruling that the death penalty is unconstitutional because the legal system has proved incapable of administering capital punishment fairly. Blackmun, a Nixon appointee best known for writing the landmark *Roe v. Wade* decision that legalized abortion, resigned from the bench at age 85 in June. After the Senate majority leader, George Mitchell, declined Clinton's offer to nominate him as Blackmun's replacement so he could work instead to pass Clinton's health-care reform bill, Clinton appointed Stephen G. Breyer, who was generally regarded as a nonideological pragmatist and consensus builder.

In November former president Ronald Reagan published a letter to the nation acknowledging that he had a deteriorating condition, Alzheimer's disease, and Richard Nixon, the only U.S. president to resign from office, died in April at age 81 after complications of a severe stroke. Despite the disgrace of his ostensible crimes associated with the Watergate scandal (a grand jury had named him an unindicted coconspirator), in his later years Nixon was treated as an elder statesman and he was consulted on matters of foreign policy, and Clinton, who was among those to eulogize him, declared a national day of mourning. Also attending the funeral were the former presidents who followed Nixon: Gerald Ford, Jimmy Carter, Ronald Reagan, and George H. Bush, as well as Nixon's vice president, Spiro T. Agnew, who also resigned in disgrace, and the former Watergate figures G. Gordon Liddy, who planned the infamous 1972 break-in into the headquarters of the Democratic National Committee, and Charles Colson, architect of the cover-up that brought down Nixon.

Although the O. J. Simpson case demonstrated the depth of the racial divide remaining in America, a modicum of racial healing occurred in February after Byron De La Beckwith was convicted of and sentenced to life in prison for the 1963 assassination of the civil-rights activist Medgar Evers. In 1964, two trials with all-white juries had failed to reach a verdict, despite compelling evidence against Beckwith, then a member of the white supremacist organization the Ku Klux Klan. In another move toward racial healing, the Atlanta-Fulton County Recreation Authority voted unanimously to remove the Georgia state flag from Atlanta-Fulton County Stadium, in deference to the sentiments of those offended by the Confederate "stars and bars" battle insignia that had been added to the flag in 1956, in protest of federal efforts at desegregation. The practice of flying all or part of the Confederate flag in government buildings and public facilities continued to be a contentious issue in Georgia and national politics throughout much of the decade.

BUSINESS

The economic turnaround that began to surge in late 1993 continued throughout 1994, as the GDP grew to 4.5 percent, up from 2.9 percent in 1993; the unemployment rate dropped from 7.5 percent to 6.1 percent; the Dow-Jones industrial average rose nearly 200 points to a high of 3,978, up from 3,799; and the inflation rate remained constant at a relatively low 2.7 percent.[3]

Clinton's decision to end the economic embargo against Vietnam, which had begun in 1975, angered many veterans and others who remained opposed to the nondemocratic Communist regime there. Given Clinton's own record of avoiding service in Vietnam, this was an especially sensitive issue for him.

Manufacturers, however, were cheered by the opening of a large new market that had been off-limits to them since the end of the Vietnam War. Clinton also canceled the policy of linking trade policies with China to China's human rights performance when he extended its most-favored-nation trade status for another year, a gesture that angered many liberals. In a further move toward a global economy, the 18 members of the Asia Pacific Economic Cooperation forum agreed to create the world's largest free-trade zone by 2020.

Clinton's support of big business and the global economy distanced him from many traditional Democrats, especially organized labor, who feared that good-paying jobs would be lost to workers overseas eager to accept lower wages. But Clinton won support from Wall Street and moderate Democrats. Having gained passage of the NAFTA treaty in 1993, Clinton in 1994 won bipartisan approval in the Senate to implement the Uruguay round provisions of the General Agreement on Tariffs and Trade (GATT). These provisions, designed to promote international trade, made broad cuts in tariffs throughout the world.

The Clinton administration also generally looked favorably on corporate mergers, and the year saw several mergers of conglomerates. Despite keen competition from QVC, another leading telecommunications firm, Viacom succeeded in convincing Paramount to accept a $9.8 billion merger offer. Rupert Murdoch's Fox Broadcasting Company acquired New World Communications Group and lured 12 affiliates of the major networks to affiliate with Fox. The defense contractors Lockheed and Martin Marietta likewise merged. Microsoft, the computer software giant, and McCaw Cellular Communications agreed to spend $9 billion to send 840 satellites into orbit to relay information around the world. Home shopping via television continued to emerge as a significant industry, as some $1 billion worth of merchandise was sold on television shopping shows in 1994.[4]

As corporate profits rose, so did the salary of top executives, whose total compensation continued to outpace at geometric levels that of workers. According to *Business Week,* the nation's highest compensated executive in 1994 was Charles Locke, chairman and executive officer of Morton International, whose pay totaled $25,928,000. The 10th-most-highly compensated executive earned $14,572,000. Altogether, the average compensation for the two highest-paid executives at each of 371 companies surveyed had increased by 10 percent since 1993, and a record 537 of these earned more than $1 million. However, including stock options and other long-term pay, the average total pay of the 742 executives fell by 25 percent, to $2,880,975.[5]

A seven-year government investigation of bribery, bid rigging, and secret funding in pursuit of government defense contracts ended when Litton Industries pleaded guilty to conspiracy charges. Overall, the investigation led to convictions of 54 individuals, including former senior government officials, and 10 corporations; fines in excess of $250 million were assessed against perpetrators. Dow Corning, Bristol-Myers-Squibb, Baxter International, and 3M—the four largest U.S. producers of silicone breast implants—agreed to pay a $4.3 billion settlement with women who had been harmed by defective implants. However, the court rejected the offer as insufficient after more than 400,000 women signed up for compensation. Later in the year a study published in the *New England Journal of Medicine* found no evidence that the leaks caused diseases or disorders. Although Europe remained wary of genetically engineered produce, the United States took an important step toward official acceptance of such fruits and vegetables when the FDA approved the sale of the first genetically engineered tomato.

Data collected by Statistics Canada and published by the *Toronto Globe and Mail* showed that the income gap between English-speaking and French-speaking Canadians widened by almost 6 percent between 1977 and 1992. In 1977, French-speaking individuals earned 4.4 percent less than their English-speaking counterparts; in 1992, they earned 10.3 percent less. French-speaking households in 1992 earned 14.1 percent less, up from 9.9 percent less in 1977.[6]

NATURE AND THE ENVIRONMENT

A major earthquake struck in Northridge, California, 20 miles north of Los Angeles in the San Fernando valley on January 17, inflicting enormous damage to the metropolis. Fifty-seven people were killed and hundreds were left homeless as freeways crumbled, buildings collapsed, and broken gas and water lines caused fires and flooding that inflicted property damage estimated to exceed $7 billion. Five hundred people died in Egypt in November when a flash flood caused a fuel depot to explode. In January, fierce storms on the Sun released waves of electromagnetic radiation, 100 times stronger than any previously measured, into the solar system. These disrupted electronic communications and disabled two of Canada's telecommunications satellites.

Environmental disasters caused by human activity included the leakage of thousands of tons of crude oil from a Russian pipeline in the arctic, after a dam in Siberia collapsed on October 1. The spill was approximately eight times greater than the *Exxon Valdez* oil spill in 1989. A federal jury ordered Exxon to pay a record $5 billion in punitive damages to more than 10,000 Alaskan commercial fishermen and 4,000 Alaska Natives whose livelihood was ruined by the *Exxon Valdez* accident that spilled some 11 million gallons of heavy crude oil in Alaska's Prince William Sound. Joseph Hazelwood, the captain of the *Exxon Valdez,* who testified that he lied to the Coast Guard about his alcohol consumption before the ship's grounding, was ordered to pay a symbolic fee of $1. Hazelwood maintained that Exxon knew about his drinking problem but did nothing about it. The monetary judgment against Exxon, the largest ever imposed in an environmental pollution case and the largest ever ordered against a company, was later reduced to $4 billion but then raised again in 2004, with billions of dollars of new interest charges added. That judgment was appealed and a final resolution remains pending as of this writing. The EPA reported results of a controversial study that showed that the greatest threat of dioxin, a by-product of certain industrial processes, is not cancer, as commonly assumed, but damage to the immune system and to the development of the fetus.

SCIENCE AND TECHNOLOGY

Space exploration continued to reveal exciting new vistas, as astronomers at a Dutch observatory discovered a previously unknown galaxy, Dwingeloo 1, located relatively close, about 10 million light-years from Earth, behind the constellation Cassiopeia. NASA released images from the Orion nebula that confirmed the birth of planets around newborn stars; the space shuttle *Endeavor* carried out a mission to map remote regions of the Earth and measure seasonal and environmental changes on the Earth's surface; and the shuttle *Atlantis* studied depletion of ozone in the Earth's atmosphere. The *Galileo* space probe made a surprising discovery, a moon orbiting an asteroid, and the *Clementine 1* space probe initiated the first U.S. lunar exploration mission since 1972. Unfortunately, it went out of control, but not before mapping portions of the Moon's surface and discovering dense polar ice caps, which excited many because water is considered a necessary precondition for the evolution of life forms and because an existing water supply would make lunar exploration and eventual settlement more feasible. Astronomers used the Internet and other high-tech methods to distribute to the public photos of the spectacular collision of a disintegrating comet, Shoemaker-Levy 9, with the planet Jupiter.

At the other end of the cosmic spectrum, physicists using an atomic accelerator discovered the so-called Top quark, a subatomic particle whose existence had been predicted 20 years earlier but never confirmed. Along with leptons, quarks are considered the building blocks of matter, and the Top was the sixth quark to be identified, after the Charm, Strange, Up, Down, and Bottom quarks.

Anthropologists in Ethiopia discovered a complete skull of *Australopithecus afarensis,* the earliest known ancestor of humans, dating back some 4.5 million years, which could possibly be the long-sought missing link between humans and apes; meanwhile researchers in northern Pakistan found what they believed might be the missing link to modern whales when they uncovered fossil remains of a 50-million-year-old mammal, a land-based creature from which sea-born whales may have evolved.

A sedentary lifestyle, coupled with increasing reliance on fast foods rich in fat, carbohydrates, and sugar, was held largely accountable for a national trend of increasing obesity among adults and children, as one-third of the adult population was estimated to be at least 20 pounds overweight.[7] The World Health Organization announced that polio was now completely eradicated from the Western Hemisphere. Medical studies showed that people in their eighties and nineties benefit significantly from regular exercise; that elderly patients undergoing kidney dialysis face poor chances for long-term survival and the likelihood of prolonged periods of weakness and fatigue; that anger increases the risk of heart attack for up to two hours in people who have heart disease; that small doses of aspirin taken daily help heart attack and stroke survivors prevent recurring complications; that needle-swap programs for drug users are effective in reducing the risk of transmitting, HIV, the AIDS-causing virus; that women who smoke a pack of cigarettes daily throughout their adult life face increased risk of development of bone deterioration known as osteoporosis, but that women who drink a glass of milk daily can compensate for bone loss caused by coffee drinking.

The integrity of all medical studies was undermined when a U.S. inquiry revealed that a Canadian researcher, Dr. Roger Poisson, had knowingly and improperly enrolled approximately 100 patients in a 1985 landmark study of breast cancer, updated in 1989. Apparently motivated by a desire to have the largest database possible, Poisson's research group kept two sets of data for each patient labeled "true" and "false" in order to include patients who failed to qualify for the study. After the revelation of Poisson's duplicity, researchers at the University of Pittsburgh removed his data from the study and reevaluated its results, which had played a significant role in changing the way the disease was treated. They concluded that the study's findings remained the same, but the now-smaller population of patients made the results less statistically compelling, a fact that impeded general acceptance of the alternatives to mastectomy that the study recommended.

LITERATURE, THE ARTS, SPORTS, AND POPULAR CULTURE

One of the most controversial works of nonfiction was Richard J. Herrnstein and Charles Murray's *The Bell Curve: Intelligence and Class Structure in American Life*, a genetically based study that nurtures arguments by white supremacists and others who believe that certain races are inherently smarter than others, at least in the specific ways intelligence is defined in the book. Other race-related books that attracted interest were Professor Henry Louis Gates's *Colored People, A Memoir*, and Jane Mayer and Jill Abramson's *Strange Justice: The Selling of Clarence Thomas*. In *The Death of Common Sense: How Law Is Suffocating America*, Philip K. Howard appeals to the notion that contemporary life is becoming increasingly rooted in abstraction and losing a fundamental connection to ordinary experience. Howard illustrates ways that legal requirements and restrictions impede the application of simple and potentially successful solutions to matters of public concern. Jonathan Weiner's *The Beak of the Finch: A Story of Evolution in Our Time* won the Pulitzer Prize in nonfiction, and Lynn H. Nicholas's *The Rape of Europa: The Fate of Europe's Treasures in the Third Reich and the Second World War*, about the Nazi plundering of the art collections of the countries they conquered, won the National Book Award in nonfiction.

Carol Shields, an American-born author living in Canada, won the Pulitzer Prize and the National Book Award in fiction for her novel *The Stone Diaries*, which presents the broad range of experiences of a Canadian woman whose life spans the years from 1905 to 1985. Other notable fiction included John Updike's *Brazil*, a retelling of the Tristan and Isolde myth featuring a black beach boy who falls in love with the affluent daughter of a career diplomat on a beach in Rio de Janeiro; *The Crossing*, the bleak second novel in Cormac McCarthy's Border trilogy about a boy who runs away to Mexico in the 1930s; Joseph Heller's *Closing Time*, the sequel to his darkly humorous *Catch-22* (1961); John Barth's experimental *Once Upon a Time*, about a writer and his wife who sail into a time warp in Chesapeake Bay; David Guterson's popular *Snow Falling on Cedars*, about the difficult relations between white and Japanese Americans in a small town in the Northwest after World War II; John Dufresne's darkly humorous *Louisiana Power & Light*, about a group of eccentric southern characters; Rick Moody's *The Ice Storm*, an exposé of privileged suburban American life during the 1970s sexual revolution, which became the basis of the popular film by the same title (1997); Jayne Anne Phillips's *Shelter*, about the violent encounter of a group of Girl Guide campers with a former convict, his young abused son, and a demented loner who regards himself as God's instrument; and the National Book Award winner *A Frolic of His Own*,

William Gaddis's satiric telling of the legal woes of the grandson of a Confederate soldier who hires a substitute to escape a deadly battle and later becomes a Supreme Court judge.

Edward Albee's *Three Tall Women,* about three women at pivotal moments of their life, won the 1994 Pulitzer Prize in drama. Tony Kushner's *Angels in America: Perestroika,* which opened in late 1993, won the Tony Award as best play. Arthur Miller, another long-established playwright, debuted on Broadway *Broken Glass,* a play about sexual repression and sexual reawakening. Laurence Holder's *Red Channels* (the title taken from the 1950 publication that was used to create the blacklists), addressed the blacklisting of politically active writers, actors, and directors during the 1950s Red Scare. Stephen Sondheim and James Lapine won the Tony Award for best musical for *Passion,* which attempts to evoke and explore a wide range of emotions. However, many of the season's most popular musicals were either revivals of musicals of earlier eras, such as Oscar Hammerstein II and Jerome Kern's *Show Boat,* about a Mississippi riverboat, and Richard Adler and Jerry Ross's *Damn Yankees,* the 1950s story of an ardent baseball fan who sells his soul to the devil so his perennially losing team can unseat the perennially victorious New York Yankees. Others adapted movies from earlier times, such as Andrew Lloyd Webber's tale of a fading actress, *Sunset Boulevard,* which opened late in the year and won the 1995 Tony Award. *Jelly Roll!,* celebrating the music of the late jazz pianist "Jelly Roll" Morton, also opened. Mikhail Baryshnikov starred in the New York City Ballet's performance of *A Suite for Dances* choreographed by Jerome Robbins. The pianist Van Cliburn, who gained international celebrity when, at the height of the cold war in 1958, he won the coveted International Tchaikovsky Competition in Moscow, made a comeback tour of nine cities.

Perhaps in response to the growing accusations of scandal, the nation's desire for simple wisdom and uncomplicated morality was reflected in the success of Robert Zemeckis's Academy Award–winning film *Forrest Gump,* which starred Tom Hanks as a simple-minded but virtuous man who participates in the making of history by adhering to his core beliefs. Hanks won the award as best actor. In addition to the acting, award-winning direction, and story, the film's technical achievements were greatly admired. In particular, many viewers were impressed by the movie's ability to insert a fictional character into actual documentary footage of historical events convincingly, a technique first mastered in 1983 by the cinematographer Gordon Willis in Woody Allen's *Zelig.* On the other end of the moral spectrum, is Quentin Tarantino's *Pulp Fiction,* a popular and critically acclaimed story about gangster hit men that employs a complicated postmodern stream-of-consciousness narrative framework to tell a violent story of sadistic killings. Oliver Stone's *Natural Born Killers* also follows the careers of mass murderers in a brutal, but ironic and sometimes comically postmodern fashion, as it tells the story of a modern-day Bonnie and Clyde who "know the difference between right and wrong" but "just don't give a damn." Institutional corruption is highlighted in Robert Redford's *Quiz Show,* about dishonesty in the popular high-stakes television quiz shows of the 1950s. Woody Allen creates rich sets and costumes from the 1920s as he equates the morality of artists with that of Prohibition-era gangsters in his provocative comedy *Bullets over Broadway,* for which Dianne Wiest won an Academy Award as best supporting actress. *Mary Shelley's Frankenstein* starred the director Kenneth Branagh, Robert De Niro, and Helena Bonham Carter in a cinematic adaptation of the 19th-century novel about human aspirations for godlike power. Jessica Lange won the Academy Award as best actress in Tony Richardson's *Blue Sky*, which costars Tommy Lee Jones in a story about an army nuclear engineer in the early 1960s who opposes aboveground nuclear testing but whose ability to prevail in his work is undermined by his marriage to a mentally ill woman who cannot conform to the social and moral expectations of the army base. Steven James's acclaimed documentary *Hoop Dreams* follows the lives of inner-city high school students who dream of becoming professional basketball players.

On television, the historian Ken Burns released his popular series *Baseball*, a study of the national pastime, and the enduring shows *ER* and *Friends* made their debut, as did *Touched by an Angel*. The most widely viewed shows in the 1994–95 season were the sitcoms *Seinfeld, Home Improvement, Grace under Fire, Friends,* and *Roseanne* and the dramas *ER*, about the staff of a hospital emergency room; *NYPD Blue,* a gritty police show; and the enduring murder mystery *Murder, She Wrote.* The perennially popular *60 Minutes* and *Monday Night Football* also ranked among the top-10 offerings. *Frasier* won the Emmy Award as outstanding comedy, and *Picket Fences* repeated as the winner for outstanding drama.

Although symphonies throughout the country struggled to remain financially viable, more than 1 billion people worldwide watched a live broadcast of a Los Angeles concert by the so-called Three Tenors: the opera stars José Carreras, Plácido Domingo, and Luciano Pavarotti. Some 350,000 people attended a concert celebrating the 25th anniversary of the Woodstock rock festival of 1969, but the reenactment was marred by violence. Fans of gangsta rap were shocked when the rapper Tupac Shakur was shot and wounded at his recording studio the day before he was convicted by a New York jury of sexually abusing a woman in 1993. Shakur, who received a year-and-a-half prison sentence for the abuse, was acquitted of more serious weapons and sodomy charges. Kurt Cobain, the 27-year-old leader of the band Nirvana, committed suicide, distressing thousands of fans of the anticorporate grunge scene. (*Rolling Stone* magazine later named Cobain its Artist of the Decade.[8]) Some fans of the late Elvis Presley were upset, others perplexed, when his daughter, Lisa Marie Presley, married the eccentric performer Michael Jackson. Jackson's fans were also dismayed and/or defensive after Jackson settled a civil lawsuit out of court, reportedly for $5 million, with the family of a 14-year-old boy who claimed the singer had sexually molested him. A judge in Rome ordered an injunction banning the sale of Jackson's *Dangerous* album after ruling that Jackson's song on the album "Will You Be There?" plagiarized "I Cigni di Balaka" (The Swans of Balaka) by the Italian singer Al Bano. Top albums included Eric Clapton's *From the Cradle,* Pink Floyd's *The Division Bell,* R. Kelly's *12 Play,* and *Toni Braxton* by Toni Braxton. Sheryl Crow won the Grammy Award for best record for *All I Wanna Do,* Tony Bennett's *MTV Unplugged* won as best album, and Bruce Springsteen's "Streets of Philadelphia" was named best song. Frank Sinatra received the Lifetime Achievement award. The three surviving members of the Beatles secretly recorded additional music for some of John Lennon's old unfinished demonstration recordings.

Although Major League Baseball owners and players agreed to realign divisions for the 1994 season, breaking each league into three divisions, and owners agreed to some revenue sharing among richer and poor teams, for the first time since 1904, the World Series was cancelled after the owners ended the season prematurely in response to a player strike that began in August, after the players rejected the owners' insistence on a salary cap. It was estimated that the teams would lose $500 million to $600 million in revenues, while the players would collectively lose about $230 million in income. Before its premature conclusion, the season saw an unprecedented number of home runs, leading to widespread speculation that the baseballs were being "juiced" to be more lively and put more offense in the game. Sluggers Jeff Bagwell of the Houston Astros and Frank Thomas of the Chicago White Sox were named MVP of the National and American Leagues. Atlanta's Greg Maddux became the first pitcher to win the Cy Young Award three years in a row; Kansas City's David Cone won the award in the American League. San Francisco's Matt Williams hit 43 home runs to lead the Major Leagues. The Philadelphia Phillies left-handed pitcher Steve Carlton, baseball's only four-time winner of the Cy Young Award to that date, was elected to the Hall of Fame in his first year of eligibility.

Led by the MVP quarterback Steve Young, the San Francisco 49ers defeated the San Diego Chargers in Super Bowl XXIX, which was played in January 1995, making the 49ers the first team to win five Super Bowl championships. After a feud with the Dallas Cowboys owner, Jerry Jones, the Dallas head coach, Jimmy Johnson, resigned after leading the Cowboys to two successive Super Bowl victories in 1992 and 1993. The University of Nebraska was the top college football team, and the University of Colorado's Rashaan Salaam won the Heisman Trophy.

Center Hakeem Olajuwon, the league's MVP, led the Houston Rockets to their first NBA championship, when they defeated the New York Knicks in the seventh game of the title series. The former Los Angeles Laker standout Earvin "Magic" Johnson, who quit professional basketball in 1991 after being diagnosed with AIDS, replaced Randy Pfund as the Lakers' coach. The University of Arkansas won the National College Athletic Association (NCAA) basketball tournament, and Purdue's Glenn Robinson was the college player of the year.

American Andre Agassi, a favorite among young tennis enthusiasts, and Arantxa Sanchez Vicario of Spain won the singles events at the U.S. Open, and Martina Navratilova retired at age 38, after 20 years of professional competition and 167 singles championships. The tennis star Vitas Gerulaitis died of carbon monoxide poisoning while sleeping in a poolside cottage at a friend's house. Golfer Ernie Els won the U.S. PGA championship, and Tiger Woods, at age 18, became the youngest player ever to win the U.S. Amateur Golf Championship. He was also the first person to win both the Amateur and the Junior Amateur championships, and the first black competitor to win the Amateur, although he later pointed out that his heritage includes a mix of ethnic origins of which he is equally proud. Although an impasse in labor negotiations delayed the opening of the NHL season, play eventually began, and the New York Rangers went on to win hockey's Stanley Cup, while the Los Angeles Kings center, Wayne Gretzky, formerly of the Edmonton Oilers, broke Gordie Howe's NHL record for most career goals when he scored for the 802nd time. Michael

Moorer defeated defending champion Evander Holyfield to become the first left-handed boxer to win the world heavyweight championship. However, the former champion George Foreman, age 45, then defeated Moorer to regain the title he had lost to Muhammad Ali 20 years earlier. Go for Gin, ridden by Chris McCarron, won the Kentucky Derby.

The United States took 13 medals in the Winter Olympics, including six first-place finishes, the most medals ever won by Americans in the winter games. But the violence plaguing the rest of society spread to the normally genteel sport of figure skating, as the 1992 Olympic medalist Nancy Kerrigan was attacked and beaten on her knee as she practiced for the national figure-skating championships in Detroit. Rival skater Tonya Harding later pleaded guilty to conspiring with her former bodyguard and former husband to cover up the attack, although she denied foreknowledge of it. Although forced to withdraw from that competition, Kerrigan went on to win a silver medal in the Winter Olympics the following month. Harding placed eighth. After her plea agreement, Harding, who won the national championship in Detroit, was compelled to resign from the U.S. Figure Skating Association (USFSA) and withdraw from the U.S. team competing in upcoming world championships, thereby ending her amateur career. She was also fined, ordered to undergo a psychiatric evaluation and perform 500 hours of community service, but she was not imprisoned. Her ex-husband, former bodyguard, and two other men received prison sentences for their roles in the crime. The USFSA further stripped Harding of her championship title and banned her from competition for life. Just a few weeks after the attack on Kerrigan, women's winter sports suffered another tragic setback when the slalom ski champion Ulrike Maier died after a high-speed crash on the Kandahar course in Germany. The popular Brazilian racing-car driver Ayrton Senna and the Austrian driver Roland Ratzenberg died in crashes during the San Marino Grand Prix.

CHRONICLE OF EVENTS

January 1: The Zapatista National Liberation Army (ZNLA), a little-known group of rebels of Mayan descent named after Emiliano Zapata, a leader of the 1910 Mexican revolution, declare war against the federal government and seize four towns in Chiapas, Mexico.

January 4: The ZNLA rebels withdraw after a government counterattack.

January 5: The Justice Department discloses that in late 1993 it subpoenaed documents belonging to President Clinton and Hillary Rodham Clinton concerning their real-estate and business dealings with the Arkansas financier James B. McDougal. This is the beginning of the so-called Whitewater investigation.

The 1992 Olympic medalist Nancy Kerrigan went on to win the silver medal in the 1994 Winter Games, despite an assault that damaged her knee earlier in the year. *(Photofest)*

January 6: The figure skater Nancy Kerrigan is beaten on the right knee by a man wielding a crowbar as she practices for the national championships in Detroit.

January 6: Jeffrey David Powell, a former member of the Weather Underground, a 1960s radical group, surrenders to authorities in Chicago after almost 24 years as a fugitive. He is sentenced to 18 months' probation and fined $500 for striking a police officer on the head with a lead pipe during a Vietnam War protest rally in October 1969.

January 13: At a champagne dinner for the Russian leader at the U.S. embassy in Moscow, President Clinton urges Yeltsin to continue his economic and political reforms.

January 17: Measuring 6.6 on the Richter scale, the Northridge earthquake strikes 20 miles outside Los Angeles, killing 57 people and causing extensive property damage.

January 18: In the final report on his costly six-and-a-half-year investigation of the Iran-contra scandal, the independent counsel Lawrence E. Walsh clears former Presidents Reagan and Bush of criminal activity but charges that in 1986 and 1987 senior administration officials engaged in a "concerted effort" to deceive Congress and the American public. He further maintains that Reagan, at the least, acquiesced in the cover-up and that Bush deliberately impeded the investigation.

January 20: Reno appoints the New York attorney and former federal prosecutor Robert B. Fiske, Jr., to serve as special counsel to investigate allegations in the Whitewater affair. She gives Fiske broad jurisdiction to look into the Clintons' dealings with Madison Guaranty Savings & Loan, the Whitewater Development Corporation, Capital Management Services, and the apparent suicide of Clinton's friend and former personal attorney Vince Foster. Both Clinton and his Republican critics applaud the appointment.

January 21: Lorena Bobbitt is found not guilty by reason of temporary insanity for her 1993 attack on her sleeping husband, in which she severed his penis.

January 25: In his State of the Union address Clinton calls for legislation on universal health insurance, crime prevention, welfare reform, job training for the unemployed, gun control, drug treatment, and urban renewal.

January 25: A civil suit contending that the singer Michael Jackson sexually molested a 14-year-old boy is dropped amid rumors that Jackson paid $5 million to settle the case out of court.

January 30: The Dallas Cowboys hand the Buffalo Bills their fourth straight Super Bowl loss, winning Super Bowl XXVIII 30-13.

February 2: Disney's popular animated film *The Lion King* premiers.

February 3: Clinton ends the U.S. economic embargo on Vietnam that had been in effect since 1975.

February 3: Yeltsin and Eduard Shevardnadze, the president of Georgia, sign a treaty of friendship and military cooperation between Russia and Georgia.

February 3: Sergei Krikalev becomes the first Russian cosmonaut to fly into space aboard a U.S. spaceship when he joins the crew of the space shuttle *Discovery.*

February 5: A Serbian mortar shell kills 68 people in a marketplace in Sarajevo.

February 9: NATO issues an ultimatum to Serbia to withdraw its heavy weapons around Sarajevo or face air strikes against its positions. Bosnian Serbs agree to a British-brokered cease-fire.

February 11: Serbian forces begin to withdraw their heavily artillery from Sarajevo.

February 12–27: The Winter Olympics are played in Lillehammer, Norway.

February 12: Sue Rodriguez, a terminally ill patient who had unsuccessfully fought a long battle in the Canadian courts to win the right to have a doctor-assisted suicide, kills herself.

February 15: Danny Rollings, described as a drifter from Louisiana, pleads guilty to the 1990 killings of five college students in Gainesville, Florida. Four of the victims were women who had been raped, mutilated, and/or decapitated.

February 22: CIA counterintelligence officer Aldrich Ames and his wife are arrested for selling secret information to the Soviet Union and Russia over the preceding nine years.

February 23: The largely conservative Russian parliament overwhelmingly votes to grant amnesty to pro-Communist hard-liners who participated in the August 1991 coup attempt against Gorbachev and to those who tried to depose Yeltsin in October 1993.

February 25: Dr. Baruch Goldstein, a Jewish settler opposed to the ongoing peace process with the Palestine Liberation Organization (PLO), kills 29 worshipers when he opens fire with an automatic rifle on a roomful of Muslims praying in the Ibrahim Mosque in Hebron, on the West Bank. When Goldstein runs out of ammunition, the survivors beat him to death. Riots erupt throughout the Israeli-occupied territories.

February 28: NATO forces take their first offensive action in the 45 years of the organization's existence when NATO planes shoot down four Serbian planes that violate a no-fly zone established to protect Bosnian Muslims.

February 28: The Defense Department's controversial compromise "Don't ask; don't tell" policy for homosexuals who serve in the military takes effect.

March 4: A federal jury in New York City finds all four Arab defendants guilty of bombing the World Trade Center in February 1993.

March 5: Michael Griffin, a member of the antiabortion group Operation Rescue, is convicted of killing Dr. David Gunn in 1993, outside his clinic in Pensacola, Florida. Griffin is subsequently sentenced to 25 years to life in prison.

March 7: Under new Defense Department rules, 60 women join the crew of the aircraft carrier *Eisenhower.* These are the first American women ever assigned to navy sea combat duty.

March 9: The Supreme Court justice Anthony Kennedy criticizes Congress's practice of imposing mandatory minimum sentences for some federal crimes.

March 14: Associate Attorney General Webster Hubble, a close friend of the Clintons, abruptly resigns after controversy about his billing practices at the Rose Law Firm in Little Rock, Arkansas.

March 15: The United States extends its voluntary moratorium on nuclear testing to September 30, 1995, and the United States and Russia agree to permit each other's specialists to inspect sites where plutonium triggers from dismantled nuclear warheads are stored.

March 16: Reagan sends a letter to Oliver North, a former member of his national security staff, criticizing North for making "false statements" about Reagan's role in the Iran-contra arms-for-hostages scandal.

March 18: Bosnian Muslims and Croats agree to establish a Muslim-Croat federation. Britain's prime minister, John Major, visits Sarajevo.

March 22: The Arkansas businessman David Hale, the only person to date publicly to accuse the

Clintons of wrongdoing in the Whitewater affair, pleads guilty to two felony counts of conspiring to defraud the federal Small Business Administration.

March 24: Jim Leach, the ranking Republican on the House Banking Committee, accuses Clinton's partner, James McDougal, of using the Whitewater venture to skim federally insured deposits from a savings and loan (S&L) institution. He further accuses Clinton of knowing about this diversion of funds and charges that federal officials pressured investigators not to investigate Whitewater. That evening, in a prime-time news conference, Clinton presents an extensive defense of his role in the investment deal.

March 25: Except for a minimal contingent left behind, the last U.S. troops leave Somalia.

March 25: The Clintons make public their tax records from 1977 to 1979, detailing their Whitewater losses and revealing details about earnings from commodity trades reported by Hillary Clinton.

April 6: The presidents of neighboring Rwanda and Burundi die when their plane is shot down while returning from peace talks in Tanzania. On the following day, the Rwandan prime minister and 10 Belgian soldiers assigned by the UN to protect him are assassinated in Kigali, the Rwandan capital. The death of these Tutsi leaders leads to genocidal massacres along tribal lines.

April 8: Kurt Cobain, lead singer of the Seattle grunge band Nirvana, commits suicide at age 27. Subsequently, millions of fans tune in to an around-the-clock tribute to him aired on MTV.

April 8: A Defense Department policy banning tobacco smoking in the workplace, including all buildings, vehicles, and aircraft, takes effect.

April 17: Despite NATO air strikes against them, Bosnian Serb armored forces enter the UN-designated safe haven for Muslims in Goražde, Bosnia. The troops withdraw on April 24, as UN peacekeepers approach the city.

April 22: Former president Richard M. Nixon dies at age 81 after a stroke.

April 24: The University of Arkansas defeats Duke 76-72 to claim the NCAA basketball title.

April 28: Former CIA counterintelligence agent Aldrich Ames pleads guilty to spying for the former Soviet Union and Russia and is sentenced to life in prison. Ames's wife, Rosario Ames, also pleads guilty but, as part of a plea agreement, receives a reduced prison sentence.

The apparent suicide of the tormented rock star Kurt Cobain was a deep blow to fans of alternative music. *(Photofest)*

April 29: The first all-race elections are held in South Africa. Former political prisoner Nelson Mandela wins the presidency.

April 29: For the first time a U.S. president meets with Native American tribal leaders when Clinton hosts 322 representatives of the nation's 547 federally recognized American Indian and Alaska Native tribes.

May 3: Florida governor Lawton Chiles signs the Everglades Forever Act, a $685 million bill authorizing a cleanup of the Everglades to be funded jointly by Florida, the federal government, and local sugar producers.

May 4: The Israeli leader Yitzhak Rabin and the PLO leader Yasser Arafat sign the Cairo Agreement, also known as Oslo I, creating the Palestinian National Authority and giving further autonomy to Palestinians in Gaza and the West Bank.

May 6: Queen Elizabeth II of England and President François Mitterrand of France open the Channel Tunnel, thus for the first time linking Britain and France and permitting train travel between London and Paris.

May 6: Paula Jones files a civil lawsuit accusing Clinton of sexually harassing her in 1991, while he was governor of Arkansas.

May 9: Ernesto Balladares is elected president of Panama.

May 10: Nelson Mandela is inaugurated president of South Africa.

May 17: The 1988 campaign committee of former president George H. W. Bush agrees to pay a civil fine of $40,000 for violations of spending and donation rules.

May 19: Jacqueline Kennedy Onassis, widow of the assassinated president John F. Kennedy, dies of cancer at age 64. She is buried beside Kennedy in Arlington National Cemetery outside Washington, D.C.

May 25: The Senate votes to renew the statute providing for the appointment of independent counsels to investigate alleged wrongdoing by top officials in the executive branch. Clinton signs it into law on June 30. The vote facilitates investigation of Clinton's role in the Whitewater affair.

May 27: The dissident author Aleksandr Solzhenitsyn returns to Russia after 20 years of enforced exile.

May 31: Representative Dan Rostenkowski of Illinois, the powerful chairman of the House Ways and Means Committee and a strong political ally of Clinton's, is indicted for embezzlement, fraud, and obstruction of justice.

June 1: South Africa is readmitted to the British Commonwealth after a 33-year absence.

June 1: A U.S. District Court jury in Los Angeles refuses to award punitive damages to the black motorist Rodney King in a civil lawsuit against six police officers whose videotaped beating of him in May 1991 triggered the Los Angeles riots.

June 4: Virginia Republicans nominate Oliver North, who became prominent for his central role in the Iran-contra affair, as their nominee for the U.S. Senate in the upcoming November election.

June 4: Islamic fundamentalists issue a death warrant for the Bangladesh author Taslima Nasrin, who has denounced the Muslim religion as oppressive to women and called for major revisions to the Qu'ran (Koran). She flees Bangladesh on August 10.

June 6: Clinton visits Normandy Beach in France to commemorate the 50th anniversary of the World War II D-day invasion.

June 13: The bodies of Nicole Brown Simpson, the former wife of the retired football star and media celebrity O. J. Simpson, and her friend Ronald Goldman are found at her townhouse in the wealthy Los Angeles community of Brentwood, where they have been stabbed to death.

June 17: Viewers throughout the country watch a televised 90-minute low-speed car chase in which O. J. Simpson sits in the back of his white Ford Bronco, apparently contemplating suicide with a gun to his head, while police cars follow and crowds gather along the interstate to cheer him and chant his nickname, "Juice." When he returns home and is speaking to his mother, Simpson is arrested for the deaths of Goldman and Nicole Brown Simpson. O. J. Simpson's friend and former teammate Al Cowlings, the driver of the vehicle, is arrested for aiding and abetting a fugitive.

Former football star O. J. Simpson was charged with the murder of his ex-wife, Nicole Brown Simpson, and her friend Ronald Goldman after a televised low-speed car chase. *(Photofest)*

June 19: Ernesto Samper is elected president of Colombia.

June 20: O. J. Simpson pleads not guilty to murder charges.

June 21: Occidental Petroleum Corporation settles a 14-year-old lawsuit when it agrees to pay the state of New York $98 million to defray costs stemming from contamination caused by Occidental's burial of some 22,000 tons of toxic waste at the Love Canal housing subdivision in Niagara Falls between 1942 and 1953. Discovered in 1978, the waste was shown to cause health problems and birth defects, and the area was evacuated by federal mandate.

June 22: The Houston Rockets defeat the New York Knicks to win their first NBA basketball championship.

June 27: In part to address criticism that his administration has been indecisive in handling the health-care reform initiative and in pursuing a resolute foreign policy, particularly in regard to Bosnia and Haiti, Clinton announces that Leon E. Panetta will replace his childhood friend Thomas F. McLarty III as chief of staff, and he names David Gergen, a former Reagan strategist, as adviser on foreign policy, answering both to him and to Secretary of State Warren Christopher.

June 29: Japan elects Tomiichi Murayama, its first Socialist prime minister since 1948.

June 30: The Supreme Court votes 6-3 to uphold an injunction restricting harassment by antiabortion protesters outside abortion clinics.

June 30: The International Earth Rotation Service advances the world's atomic clocks by one second.

July 8: Premier Kim Il Sung, who had led North Korea since its founding in 1948, dies at age 82. He is succeeded by his son, Kim Jong Il.

July 12: Arafat establishes his residence and headquarters for the Palestinian National Authority in the Gaza Strip.

July 18: Approximately 100 people, mostly Jews, are killed when Iranian-backed Muslim terrorists explode a massive bomb at a Jewish community center in Buenos Aires, Argentina.

July 25: In a ceremony in Washington, D.C., Rabin and King Hussein sign a declaration that concludes a 46-year-old state of war between Israel and Jordan. They conclude a formal treaty on October 26.

July 26: A car bomb outside the Israeli embassy in London injures 14 people.

July 31: The Security Council votes to authorize a United States–led invasion of Haiti to depose the ruling military junta and restore the democratically elected president, Jean-Bertrand Aristide.

August 5: In an unexpected decision, a panel of three federal judges removes special counsel Fiske from the Whitewater investigation and names Kenneth Starr independent counsel to head the ongoing inquiry into Clinton's business dealings while governor of Arkansas.

August 8: The first border crossing is opened between Israel and Jordan.

August 12: North Korea and the United States reach a tentative agreement intended to guarantee North Korea's security against nuclear attack, establish full political and economic relations between the nations, and assure that North Korea will terminate its program to build nuclear weapons.

August 12: Major league baseball players go on strike.

August 14: Some 350,000 people attend a rock concert in Saugerties, New York, to celebrate the 25th anniversary of the Woodstock festival.

August 14: Ilich Ramirez Sanchez, the Venezuelan-born international terrorist widely known as Carlos, or the Jackal, is captured in Sudan. He is extradited to France on August 15 to stand trial for murders he allegedly committed in the 1970s and 1980s.

August 22: Ernesto Zedillo, candidate of the ruling Institutional Revolutionary Party, is elected president of Mexico.

August 28: The United States compensates the families of two British officers killed in northern Iraq when Americans fighters mistook their UN helicopters for Iraqi aircraft and shot them down.

August 30: The 81-year-old civil rights pioneer Rosa Parks is robbed of about $50 and beaten in her house in Detroit. The next day two of her neighbors apprehend the suspect, Joseph Skipper, a 28-year-old black man who was seeking money to buy crack cocaine.

August 31: The last Russian troops leave the former East Germany, some 50 years after Soviet forces crossed into Germany during World War II. The last British, French, and American troops stationed in Berlin depart the following week.

August 31: The IRA announces a cease-fire in both Northern Ireland and the British mainland.

September 8: All 132 passengers and crew members aboard USAir Flight 427 die when their plane crashes in Aliquippa, Pennsylvania, outside Pittsburgh. This is the fifth USAir flight to crash in five years.

September 9: Cuba agrees to restrain refugees fleeing to the United States by raft and boat, and the United States agrees to increase the number of legal immigrants it will permit to enter the country by 27,000.

September 10: Arantxa Sánchez-Vicario of Spain wins the women's singles championship in tennis's U.S. Open.

September 11: Andre Agassi of the United States wins the men's singles competition at the U.S. Open.

September 12: An unemployed truck driver is killed when his light plane crashes on the White House lawn.

September 13: Clinton signs the anticrime bill into law.

September 14: The acting baseball commissioner Allan H. (Bud) Selig announces the cancellation of the remainder of the season, including the World Series, as a result of the strike by the players' union.

September 18: Former president Jimmy Carter, retired general Colin Powell, and Senator Sam Nunn convince Haiti's ruling military junta to step down by October 15 in exchange for an amnesty from the Haitian parliament.

September 19: A contingent of 3,000 U.S. troops lands unopposed in Haiti, where they will enforce the restoration to power of President Jean-Bertrand Aristide.

September 26: Senate majority leader George Mitchell concedes that he will not be able to pass a bill calling for universal health care this year.

September 26: Jury selection for the murder trial of O. J. Simpson begins in Los Angeles.

September 27: Standing beneath patriotic banners of red, white, and blue bunting, 350 Republican candidates for Congress gather on the steps of the Capitol in Washington, D.C., to sign the Contract with America, a legislative plan drawn up by Congressman Newt Gingrich of Georgia. The contract promises action on 10 bills that promote specific conservative initiatives within the first 100 days after the election of a Republican House of Representatives.

September 28: More than 900 passengers die when the ferry *Estonia* sinks in the Baltic Sea.

September 29: The Smithsonian Institution's National Air and Space Museum in Washington, D.C., announces that it will significantly revise its planned exhibit featuring the fuselage of the *Enola Gay,* the airplane that dropped the atomic bomb on Hiroshima, Japan, in 1945. The original plan had been criticized as overly politically correct: ignoring the Japanese attack on Pearl Harbor and Japanese war atrocities, representing the plight of Japanese victims of the bombing in an overly sympathetic manner, and failing to acknowledge the casualties the bombing prevented among Japanese civilians who would have been subject to further conventional air attacks and a full-scale invasion, civilians suffering under Japanese occupation throughout Asia and the Pacific, and U.S. servicemen, up to 1 million of whom were expected to become casualties in the invasion of the Japanese home islands if the atomic bomb had not caused the quick surrender.

September 30: Named by Clinton to replace the retiring justice Harry Blackmun, Stephen G. Breyer is seated on the Supreme Court.

October 3: Secretary of Agriculture Mike Espy, the first African American to serve in that cabinet position, announces he will resign effective December 31 in response to a growing ethics scandal surrounding charges that he had improperly received gifts from Tyson Foods, an Arkansas-based agribusiness company affected by policies promulgated by the Department of Agriculture.

October 3: Brazil elects as president Finance Minister Fernando Enrique Cardoso, an economic reformer who campaigned by promising to cut the 50-percent-a-month inflation rate to single digits.

October 14: Rabin, Arafat, and the Israeli foreign minister Shimon Peres are awarded the Nobel Peace Prize as architects of the Israeli-Palestinian accords.

October 15: Aristide returns to power in Haiti after three years of exile.

October 19: A suicide bomb kills 22 Israelis near Tel Aviv. The Islamic militant group Hamas takes credit.

October 21: Britain lifts its ban prohibiting Sinn Féin members from entering mainland Britain and reopens the border crossings between Northern Ireland and the Republic of Ireland.

October 26: Israel and Jordan conclude a formal peace treaty in which Israel returns several parcels of land in the Arava valley and in a region south of the Sea of Galilee.

October 27: After witnessing the peace treaty between Israel and Jordan, Clinton travels to Syria, the first U.S. president to do so in 20 years. However, he fails to gain concessions on peace with Israel.

October 29: No one is harmed after a convicted felon armed with a semiautomatic assault rifle fires 27 rounds at the north face of the White House. Francisco Martin Duran, an army veteran and ex-con, is subdued by Secret Service agents and bystanders. After an investigation to verify that Clinton was, indeed, his target, Duran is charged on November 17 with attempting to assassinate the president and is convicted in April 1995.

October 31: An American Airlines flight crashes in Indiana, killing all 68 people aboard.

November 5: Former president Ronald Reagan announces to the nation that he has Alzheimer's disease.

November 8: Republicans pick up nine Senate seats and over 52 seats in the House of Representatives to gain control of both houses of Congress in the midterm elections. Several incumbent Democratic governors are also defeated, including New York's Mario Cuomo, who loses to the Republican George Pataki.

November 10: Jordan's king Hussein makes his first visit to Israel.

November 18: Fighting between Islamic fundamentalists and the police force of the newly created Palestinian National Authority kills 14 people in the Gaza Strip.

November 18: The renowned big band leader Cabell "Cab" Calloway dies at age 76.

November 21: NATO warplanes conduct their heaviest bombing raid to date against a Serb-held airfield in Croatia used to attack a Muslim safe haven in Bosnia.

November 28: Julio Sanguinetti is elected president of Uruguay.

November 30: The Italian cruise ship *Achille Lauro*, the target of a notorious terrorist hijacking in 1985, catches fire and sinks in the Indian Ocean.

November 30: The rapper Tupac Shakur is shot in his recording studio and wounded in the head, left arm, thigh, and groin. He is also robbed of approximately $45,000 worth of jewelry.

December 2: A Los Angeles jury convicts Heidi Fleiss, who was arrested in 1993 for running a high-class prostitution service in Hollywood, of pandering.

December 8: Jury selection in the O. J. Simpson murder trial ends with the seating of eight black jurors, two Hispanics, one white, and one person identified as half white and half American Indian.

December 9: Peace talks between Britain and the IRA begin in Belfast, Northern Ireland.

December 11: Russian troops invade the republic of Chechnya to prevent it from seceding.

December 15: The United Nations admits its 185th member, the Republic of Palau, the last remaining UN Trust Territory in the western Pacific.

December 17: A gunman fires at least four small-caliber bullets at the White House while the Clintons are asleep. No one is injured and no suspects are identified.

December 19: Carter negotiates a cease-fire in Bosnia and an agreement by Serbs to negotiate a long-term peace agreement.

December 20: A U.S. Parks officer shoots a homeless man, Macelino Corniel, in front of the White House after Corniel brandishes a large hunting knife at officers. Corniel dies the next day.

December 24: Former president Carter negotiates a temporary cease-fire between Bosnian Serbs and the Muslim-Croat government of Bosnia. The armistice will go into effect on January 1, 1995, and last four months.

December 24: The Rams play their last football game in Los Angeles, before moving to Saint Louis in 1995. They had been in Los Angeles since 1946.

December 26: French commandos kill four Algerian Islamic fundamentalists who hijacked an Air France Airbus in Algiers on Christmas Eve.

December 28: The target of criticism about the Aldrich Ames spy case, CIA director R. James Woolsey, Jr., announces his resignation effective at the end of the year.

December 31: The World Trade Organization replaces the General Agreement on Tariffs and Trade (GATT).

December 31: Russian troops storm Grozny, the capital of Chechnya.

EYEWITNESS TESTIMONY

At the beginning of the twentieth century, the average life expectancy was 47 years; today it is 75 years. Census data for the United States reveal that for the first time in the history of our young country there are more older Americans than younger ones. . . . The fastest growing segment of the aging population is those over 85 years of age, many of whom require physical, emotional, and financial support. . . .

It is predicted that today's nursing students will spend 75 percent of their working lives treating people over 65. Heart disease, cancer, stroke, unintentional injuries (such as falls, fires, and accidents, and respiratory problems) continue to lead the cause of death for many older Americans. . . .

Coupled with the graying of America is the "browning of America," or the rise in multiculturalism. Unfortunately, this trend is being regarded less attentively than is warranted. Our population will no longer be predominantly white, as nearly 1 in 4 Americans has African, Asian, Hispanic, or Native American ancestry. . . .

As multiculturalism takes hold, more of the population requiring health care services will be nonwhite. However, the registered nurse population does not show any increase in the number or proportion of nurses from minority racial/ethnic backgrounds. . . .

Although the nursing profession has always been characterized as a predominantly female profession, we are beginning to witness a more female work force in general. . . . Yet dominance in nursing does not translate into dominant influence in health care . . . Nurses, therefore, must bond with other women to create a new awareness and response to the long neglected issues of women in the mainstream of American society. . . . Our survival and economic growth in the twenty-first century depends on our responsiveness as a nation to the status and condition of women as full partners.

Vernice D. Ferguson, M.A., R.N., F.A.A.N.,
F.R.C.N., discussing in 1994 the challenges facing
nurses in the 1990s, in Ora L. Strickland and Dorothy
J. Fishman, eds., Nursing Issues in the 1990s *(1994),*
pp. 5–7.

I couldn't stop screaming as I ran out of the house. I looked up and all I could see was darkness coming toward us, and it got real windy. I thought the sun was exploding.

The 19-year-old survivor Eric Wyler describing the Los
Angeles earthquake of January 17, 1994, in Seth
Mydans, "Severe Earthquake Hits Los Angeles; At Least
30 Killed; Freeways Collapse," New York Times,
January 18, 1994, p. 1.

If you send me legislation that does not guarantee every American private health insurance that can never be taken away, you will force me to take this pen, veto the legislation, and we'll come right back here and start all over again.

President Bill Clinton calling for universal health care for
all Americans in his State of the Union address on
January 25, 1994, in Martin Gilbert, A History of
the Twentieth Century, *vol. 3 (2000), p. 767.*

It was a long hard struggle to bring this issue of physician-assisted suicide to the public at a critical time in my life. I hope that my efforts will not have been in vain and that . . . the minister of justice will introduce legislation into Parliament soon so that terminally ill people have another option available thereby permitting physician-assisted suicide.

Sue Rodriguez, a terminally ill Canadian advocate of
doctor-assisted suicide, in a message released after
she killed herself on February 12, 1994,
in Thomas E. Hitchings, ed., Facts On File
Yearbook 1994 *(1995),*
p. 130.

Some say that the Cold War is over and Russia lost. That is not true. The Communists, the Soviet Communists, lost the Cold War. But democratic Russia, under the courageous leadership of [President] Boris Yeltsin, gave the knockout blow to Soviet Communism.

Former president Richard Nixon at a reception in
Moscow on March 10, 1994, crediting Boris Yeltsin for
his role in terminating Communist rule in the former
Soviet Union, in Alan F. Pater and Jason R. Pater, eds.,
What They Said in 1994 *(1995), p. 307.*

Time is running out. [China's strategy] is to suppress [Tibetans] completely and in the meantime to increase the Chinese population [in Tibet] so that in a few years' time, the Tibetans become insignificant in their own land. Some of my friends call this the "Final Solution" of the Tibet issue.

The Dalai Lama speaking out against Chinese repression of Tibetans in a Los Angeles Times *interview published on May 15, 1994, in Alan F. Pater and Jason R. Pater, eds.,* What They Said in 1994 *(1995), p. 278.*

This accounting is not what it should have been. We've been trying to reconstruct the stuff from the early days and having a hard time.

Energy Department spokesman Michael Gauldin describing problems in accounting for the nation's plutonium supplies, in William J. Broad, "Experts Say U.S. Fails to Account for Its Plutonium," New York Times, *May 20, 1994, p. 1.*

Ah, the media war against Serbia. They have produced *mountains* of lies! And the average American *believes* media. They are not informed at all. [Yugoslavia] is a moral failure not only of journalism, it is as well, indirectly, a moral failure of democracy. . . . Yugoslavia was disintegrated with the pressure of different foreign factors which were following their interests. They supported disintegration, they supported secession! And in the same time, they have punished loyalty to your home country. Who is guilty [according to the media]? All who are fighting for integration, for preservation of integrity to their country, were punished.

Serbia's president Slobodan Milošević decrying the press accounts of the Balkans conflict in the June issue of Vanity Fair, *in Alan F. Pater and Jason R. Pater, eds.,* What They Said in 1994 *(1995), p. 307.*

What I recall most from those days [after O. J. Simpson's arrest for murder] is the anger, the free-floating racial hostility one encountered everywhere.

I'm thinking of a white colleague with whom I was having a minor and, I thought, friendly disagreement one day about some aspect of the trial. Suddenly he opened up on me, saying I was one of those blacks too blinded by blackness to see Simpson's obvious guilt.

He stalked away still ranting and I don't think he ever heard me say—though I said it several times—that I thought Simpson was guilty too.

At that moment, I was not somebody he knew. I was simply blackness, with all its perceived blights and inadequacies. It was a scene that was being enacted nationwide. And if you've never had your individuality denied by somebody you thought you knew, you can't begin to understand what a betrayal it is.

But then, the Simpson case was a racial Rorschach test, an ink blot upon which the nation projected its deepest irresolution about sex and race.

White people looked at it and saw the sad story of a man who fell to earth after seeming to have "transcended" his race. Blacks . . . saw fuel for the conspiracy theory which says that "they" will always bring a successful brother down.

Columnist Leonard Pitts, Jr., writing 10 years later about the arrest on June 17, 1994, of the retired football star O. J. Simpson for the murder of his former wife, Nicole Brown Simpson, and her friend Ronald Goldman, in Pitts, "Simpson Case Exposed Raw Feelings on Race," Miami Herald, *June 14, 2004, p. 1B.*

Child-care workers agree that children in residential treatment today are likely to be far more disturbed than the children who were in need of protective services twenty years ago and who, in turn, were probably more disturbed than the good-hearted orphans with chips on their shoulders who preceded them. These kids have had it with parents—biological, adoptive, or foster—and the feeling is usually mutual. These kids do not trust adults, especially parents. They cannot tolerate the intensity of family life, nor do they behave well enough to attend public school. During a first screening at a residential treatment center a psychiatrist often asks a child, "If you had three wishes, what would they be?" Twenty years ago a typical answer was, "I want a basketball," or "I wish my father didn't drink." Today, according to Nan Dale, the executive director of . . . a resident treatment center for boys . . . one is likely to hear "I wish I had a gun so I could blow my father's head off." Child care professionals call these young people "children of rage." . . .

An institution provides some children with a first chance to be taken care of by adults who do not hit or even yell.

Author Mary-Lou Weisman describing the challenges of dealing with angry institutionalized children in Weisman, "When Parents Are Not in the Best Interests of the Child," Atlantic, *July 1994, pp. 43–44, 57.*

Hit and run tactics will be our method of fighting. . . . We will destroy targets such as telephone relay centers, bridges, fuel storage tanks, communication towers, radio stations, airports. . . . Human targets will be engaged when it is beneficial to the cause to eliminate particular individuals who oppose us (troops, police, political figures, snitches . . .).

An excerpt from the draft of an antigovernment newsletter article written by James Roy Mullins, founder of the Blue Ridge Hunt Club militia, who was arrested for possessing hand grenades and other illegal weapons in late July 1994, in Morris Dees, Gathering Storm: America's Militias *(1996), p. 130.*

The whole authoritarian set of mind depends on suppression of individual thought, suppression of eccentric thought, suppression of inerrancy in the interpretation of the Bible, or of Marx, or *Mein Kampf,* or Mao's *Little Red Book* in favor of mass thought, mass buzz words, party lines. They all want to eliminate or get rid of the alien, or the stranger, or the Jews, or the gays, or the Gypsies, or the artists, or whoever are their infidels. And they're all willing to commit murder for it, whether Hitler or Stalin or Mao or the Ayatollah, and I have no doubt that if Rush Limbaugh or Pat Robertson or Ollie North ever got real power, there would be concentration camps and mass death. There already are in the police-state aspect of the "war on drugs."

Left-wing poet Allen Ginsberg denouncing authoritarianism, in Matthew Rothschild, "Allen Ginsberg," The Progressive, *August 1994. Available online. URL: http://www.progressive.org/ ginzroth9408.htm.*

The [Clinton] Administration has a problem with foreign intervention. It wants to do good around the world, mostly for humanitarian reasons. . . . But the American people, who were willing to shed blood in the Cold War when it was a form of self-defense, aren't convinced that they want to shed blood in a series of what appear to be humanitarian causes.

Professor Michael Mandelbaum discussing in the August 1, 1994, Los Angeles Times *the popular resistance in the United States to military intervention for international peacekeeping and nation-building efforts, in Alan F. Pater and Jason R. Pater, eds.,* What They Said in 1994 *(1995), p. 231.*

One of the great ironies of American drug policy is that anti-drug laws over the past century have tended to

become most punitive long after the use of a drug has peaked. David Musto, professor at Yale Medical School and the preeminent historian of American narcotics policy, explains that when drug use is at its height, so is tolerance; but as drugs recede from middle-class homes, their users are marginalized, scapegoated, and more readily punished. The price that society pays for harsh sanctions becomes invisible to most people. Musto thinks that our nation's drug laws reflect cultural changes after the fact; though extreme punishments may help to limit a drug epidemic, the principal causes of its rise and fall lie elsewhere. This theory is supported by recent history. Marijuana use among the young peaked in 1979; strict federal laws were passed seven years later, when use had already fallen by 43 percent; and the explanation most young people gave for quitting marijuana was a concern about the perceived health risks, not fear of imprisonment. A drug culture is once again emerging on college campuses, despite the existence of draconian mandatory minimums.

Author Eric Schlosser discussing strict sentencing requirements for marijuana-related crimes in Schlosser, "Marijuana and the Law," Atlantic, *September 1994, p. 94.*

In no case should abortion be promoted as a method of family planning. All governments and relevant intergovernmental and nongovernmental organizations are urged to strengthen their commitment to women's health, to deal with the health impact of unsafe abortion as a major health concern and to reduce the recourse to abortion through expanded improved family planning services. Prevention of unwanted pregnancies must always be given the highest priority, and all attempts should be made to eliminate the need for abortion. Women who have unwanted pregnancies should have ready access to reliable information and compassionate counseling. . . . In circumstances in which abortion is not against the law, such abortion should be safe. In all cases, women should have access to quality services for the management of complications arising from abortion. Post-abortion counseling, education and family-planning services should be offered promptly which [would] also help to avoid repeat abortions.

Text from a paragraph on abortion issues adopted on September 9, 1994, by delegates to the UN Conference on Population and Development held in Cairo, Egypt, in Thomas E. Hitchings, ed., Facts On File Yearbook 1994 *(1995), p. 677.*

We're in danger of losing the House in November, maybe even the Senate.

Yes, the economic plan is paying off: More than four million new jobs have been added, paying better on average than the old; the economy is growing nicely. But there's a huge amount of frustration and disillusionment in the land. Only a relatively few are sharing in the newfound prosperity. . . .

Only the richest five percent of Americans are gaining much ground. In fact, their share of the national income in 1993 (48.2 percent) is the highest on record, while the share going to the bottom three-fifths is the lowest on record. The gap is the widest since the Census began collecting the data almost thirty years ago.

Nor is the recovery improving the lives of a large group of American children: 22.7 percent of them were impoverished in 1993, a higher proportion than in 1992—in fact, the highest since 1964. In 1977, by contrast, only 16.2 percent of American children were in poverty.

In 1992, Americans voted for "change" because so many were losing ground. Your economic plan spurred the recovery, but didn't stop the slide. As a result, these Americans feel betrayed. They're likely to vote for "change" again in 1994. . . .

The most important thing you (and other Democrats) need to do between now and the midterm election is *acknowledge* the problem. Recognize the frustrations and fears of a large segment of the workforce. Talk about the challenge of widening inequality. Talk about the responsibilities of profitable corporations to share the good times with their employees.

Former secretary of labor Robert B. Reich communicating concerns about the upcoming midterm elections in a memorandum to President Bill Clinton dated September 30, 1994, in Reich, Locked in the Cabinet *(1997), pp. 194–195.*

Adolescence is a modern social invention, designed to deal with a modern social problem: the lengthening period between biological and social maturity. Earlier in the nation's history girls entered puberty and left school at about the same time—around age fifteen or sixteen. . . . By the beginning of this century, however, the age of menarche was declining and the period of formal schooling was lengthening. At the same time, parents, churches, and schools were relaxing their close supervision of young women. . . . Under these new social conditions youthful risk-taking became perilous, its penalties more severe.

As a social invention, therefore, adolescence represented a clear effort to define, order and regulate a life stage that was becoming socially chaotic. Among other things, adolescence provided institutional reinforcement for the moratorium on youthful sexual activity, giving young people the opportunity to acquire the competencies and credentials of adulthood before they took on the responsibilities of marriage and parenthood.

In the past decade or so, however, a new way of thinking about teenage sexuality has emerged. . . . The new approach contends that teenagers should be expected to express themselves sexually as part of their normal growing up, but should be able to do so protected from the risks of early sexual activity. . . .

These competing traditions assign radically different responsibilities to adults. In the classic model, adults are the custodians of the moratorium. . . . In the contemporary model . . . [the adult's] job is to train teenagers in the management of her own sexuality and to provide access to contraceptives. . . .

In the past decade the [contemporary] technocratic approach has gained ground while the classic approach has steadily lost it. This has brought a corresponding shift in adult responsibility. Increasingly, the litmus test of adult concern is one of access: will grown-ups give teenagers the skills and tools to manage their sex lives?

Author Barbara Doe Whitehead discussing evolving notions about adolescent sexuality in Whitehead, "The Failure of Sex Education," Atlantic, *October 1994, p. 80.*

We must prove that the Mediterranean can become a region of solidarity and equilibrium, a true Sea of Galilee, around which the three religions and the sons of Abraham, united by historical bonds, will be able to build a magnificent bridge for the century to come.

King Hussein of Jordan addressing an economic summit of U.S., European, Israeli, and Arab business representatives in Casablanca, Morocco, on October 29, 1994, three days after concluding a peace treaty with Israel, in Martin Gilbert, A History of the Twentieth Century, *vol. 3 (2000), p. 774.*

As President Bill Clinton looked on, Prime Minister Rabin of Israel (right) and King Hussein of Jordan (left) ended the official state of war that had lasted since 1948. *(AP/Wide World Photos)*

Rejecting the House's gentlemanly ways, he [Gingrich] waged such constant guerrilla war against the Democrats he was attacked for McCarthyism. . . . Gingrich himself, bombastic and ruthless, would be the most dramatic change imaginable, a change the administration can only dread.

> *Television reporter Eric Engberg anticipating the consequences for President Bill Clinton of a Republican victory in the upcoming congressional elections, on the* CBS Evening News, *November 2, 1994. Available online. URL: http://secure.mediaresearch.org/ news/nq/1995/nq19950508.html.*

My fellow Americans, I have recently been told that I am one of the millions of Americans who will be afflicted with Alzheimer's disease.

Upon learning this news, Nancy and I had to decide whether as private citizens we would keep this a private matter or whether we would make this news known in a public way. In the past, Nancy suffered from breast cancer and I had my cancer surgeries. We found through our open disclosures we were able to raise public awareness. . . .

So now we feel it is important to share it with you. In opening our hearts, we hope this might promote greater awareness of this condition. Perhaps it will encourage a clearer understanding of the individuals and families who are affected by it.

At the moment I feel just fine. I intend to live the remainder of the years God gives me on this Earth doing the things I have always done. I will continue to share life's journey with my beloved Nancy and my family. . . .

Unfortunately, as Alzheimer's disease progresses, the family often bears a heavy burden. I only wish there was some way I could spare Nancy from this painful experience. When the time comes, I am confident that with your help she will face it with faith and courage....

I now begin the journey that will lead me into the sunset of my life. I know that for America there will always be a bright dawn ahead.

Thank you, my friends. May God always bless you.

Ronald Reagan's letter to America, issued November 5, 1994, announcing that he suffered from Alzheimer's disease, in Reagan, "Announcement of Alzheimer's Disease—November 5, 1994." Available online, URL: http://www.reagan.com/ronald/speeches/rrspeech05.shtml.

[Oliver North is a] document-shredding, Constitution-trashing, Commander-in-Chief-bashing, Congress-thrashing, uniform-shaming, Ayatollah-loving, arms-dealing, criminal-protecting, resume-enhancing, Noriega-coddling, Social-Security–threatening, public-school-denigrating, Swiss-banking-law–breaking, letterfaking, self-serving, election-losing, snake-oil salesman who can't tell the difference between the truth and a lie.

Democratic senator Charles S. Robb of Virginia smearing his Republican challenger, the Iran-contra figure Oliver North, whom Robb defeated on November 8, 1994, in Lois Gordon and Alan Gordon, American Chronicle *(1999), p. 889.*

It was an immoderate campaign, coarse in its tone and unedifying in its substance, and the nation's politics are likely to stay that way for the next two years and beyond.

Dissatisfaction with President Clinton, with liberalism, with the Democratic Party and with Washington in general combined to create a surge by Republicans, especially conservative Republicans. If not quite a tidal wave, yesterday's results swept dozens of incumbents from office and set up two years of intense political confrontation between the White House and Congress....

This was a realigning election that put the final nails in the coffin of the Solid South, the regional bastion upon which Democratic power was once built....

Stated most simply, the message from the electorate was disgust with big government and impatience with

government activism, two of the things with which the Democrats are most closely identified.

Political commentator R. W. Apple, Jr., analyzing the results of the midterm elections held on November 8, 1994, in Apple, "A Vote against Clinton," New York Times, *November 9, 1994, p. 1.*

One day after the election, he [Newt Gingrich] called Hillary and me "counterculture McGovernicks," his ultimate condemnation.

The epithet . . . was correct in some respects. We had supported McGovern, and we weren't part of the culture that Gingrich wanted to dominate America: the self-righteous, condemning, Absolute Truth–claiming dark side of white southern conservatism. . . . I knew the dark side all too well. Since I was a boy, I had watched people assert their piety and moral superiority as justifications for claiming an entitlement to political power, and for demonizing those who begged to differ with them, usually over civil rights....

I had been raised not to look down on anyone and not to blame others for my own problems or shortcomings. That's exactly what the "New Right" message did . . . "they" were always right, "we" were always wrong; "we" were responsible for all the problems, even though "they" had controlled the presidency for all but six of the last twenty-six years....

Of course there were political and personal excesses in the 1960s, but the decade . . . also produced advances in civil rights, women's rights, a clean environment, workplace safety, and opportunities for the poor. The Democrats believed in and worked for those things. So did a lot of traditional Republicans....

The core of his [Gingrich's] argument was not just that his ideas were better than ours; he said his *values* were better than ours because Democrats were weak on family, work, welfare, crime, and defense, and because, being crippled by the self-indulgent sixties, we couldn't draw distinctions between right and wrong.

The political power of his theory was that it forcefully and clearly confirmed the negative stereotypes of Democrats that Republicans had been working to embed in the nation's consciousness since 1968. . . . The problem with his theory was that it didn't fit the facts.

Former president Bill Clinton responding to Congressman Newt Gingrich's negative characterizations of liberal Democrats on November 9, 1994, in Clinton, My Life *(2004), pp. 633–635.*

In these parts, we don't have much use for such ideas as taking children away from young unwed mothers and putting them in orphanages. Come to think of it, "Newt Gingrich" could be the name of a villain in a Dickens novel.

From "A Reading from The Newt Testament," San Francisco Examiner, November 20, 1994, an editorial condemning a Republican proposal to place children of unwed mothers in orphanages, quoted in Richard B. McKenzie, ed., Rethinking Orphanages for the 21st Century *(1999). Available online. URL: http://www.gsm.uci.edu/~mckenzie/ rethink/mck97-ch6.htm.*

[We would] see literally thousands and thousands of people on our streets, seeing the unbelievable and absurd idea of putting children into orphanages because their mothers couldn't find jobs.

First Lady Hillary Rodham Clinton condemning Republican proposals for welfare reform in a speech before the New York Women's Agenda on November 30, 1994, quoted in Richard B. McKenzie, ed., Rethinking Orphanages for the 21st Century *(1999). Available online. URL: http://www.gsm.uci.edu/~mckenzie/ rethink/mck97-ch6.htm.*

Woody Allen compared the morality of artists and writers to that of gangsters in *Bullets over Broadway,* which starred Dianne Wiest and John Cusack (above). *(Photofest)*

"Don't speak!"

Dianne Wiest's frequently quoted line in Woody Allen's Prohibition-era gangster comedy Bullets over Broadway, *which opened in December 1994.*

I don't understand liberals who live in enclaves of safety who say, "Oh, this would be a terrible thing. Look at the Norman Rockwell family that would break up." The fact is we are allowing a brutalization and a degradation of children in this country, a destructiveness. We say to a 13 year old drug addict who is pregnant, you know, "Put your baby in a Dumpster, that's OK, but we're not going to give you a boarding school, we're not going to give you a place for that child to grow up. . . .

[In response to First Lady Hillary Rodham Clinton's characterization of this proposal as "unbelievable"] I'd ask her to go to Blockbuster and rent the Mickey Rooney movie about Boy's Town.

Congressman Newt Gingrich responding on Meet the Press *on December 4, 1994, to criticism of his proposal to place children of unwed mothers in orphanages, quoted in Richard B. McKenzie, ed.,* Rethinking Orphanages for the 21st Century *(1999). Available online. URL:http://www.gsm.uci.edu/ ~mckenzie/rethink/mck97-ch6.htm.*

7
Terror in the Heartland
1995

Domestic terrorism shook a sense of national security that most Americans had experienced throughout their life. Exactly two years after an FBI raid killed David Koresh and scores of his heavily armed Branch Davidian followers in Waco, Texas, a homemade car bomb demolished the Alfred P. Murrah Federal Building in Oklahoma City, Oklahoma, killing 169 people, including children in a day-care center inside the building, and one unborn baby. Timothy McVeigh, a Persian Gulf War veteran linked to antigovernment, white supremacist, and militia groups, was later convicted and executed for the crime. A few months later a different sort of violent antiestablishment sensibility contributed to the climate of fear, when the Unabomber, an elusive sender of deadly letter bombs, published a long manifesto condemning "industrial–technological society" in the *Washington Post* and *New York Times*. Moreover, the release of a deadly nerve gas in the Tokyo subway system by domestic terrorists in Japan demonstrated the vulnerability of all modern cities to lethal attacks by small but well-armed fringe groups. Overall, the number of international terrorist attacks increased in 1995 to 440, up from 322 in 1994. Of those, 99 were attacks on U.S. interests, up from 66 in 1994. According to the State Department, the total number of deaths internationally decreased from 314 to 165, but the number of wounded rose from 66 to 6,291—many of them affected by the gas attacks on the Japanese transit system.[1]

The former football star O. J. Simpson's acquittal of charges that he murdered his wife and her friend fueled still another kind of insecurity when it sparked a nationwide debate about the efficacy and fairness of America's judicial system.

Anxieties over pending disaster were also fueled by scientific evidence showing that the overall temperature of the Earth is rising and that industrial pollution is a leading, and preventable, cause of global warming. Many people feared that ongoing government foot dragging and industry inaction ignored a catastrophe in the making; others maintained that the danger of global warming was overblown and that the greater threat were from hysterical demands for costly improvements that could potentially cripple businesses and damage the economy.

Citizens' faith in the competence and/or good intentions of the federal government was further tested when, 20 years after the fall of the U.S. embassy in Saigon, the former secretary of defense Robert S. McNamara published *In Retrospect: The Tragedy and Lessons of Vietnam*. McNamara, who presided over the Vietnam War from its beginnings in the early 1960s through 1968, admitted that the Kennedy and Johnson administrations had failed to formulate, even among themselves, a clear idea of what they were trying to accomplish by the fighting—as war protesters had maintained at the time, to little avail.

INTERNATIONAL DEVELOPMENTS

NATO and the United States became more deeply involved in the fighting in the former Yugoslavia after a shaky four-month cease-fire expired in May. Serb forces renewed their offensive in Croatia, and, in late May, Bosnian Serbs seized UN peacekeepers and unarmed military observers and used them as human shields to protect their military operations in Bosnia. After Bosnian Serbs threatened to execute some of the peacekeepers in July, the United Nations abandoned its thinly staffed defense of Srebrenica, which had been designated as a safe haven for Bosnian Muslims. Bosnian Serb troops then seized Srebrenica and Zepa, another safe haven, forcing tens of thousands of people to flee and executing thousands more, partly in revenge for earlier atrocities perpetrated by Muslims against Serbs and partly in pursuit of their goal of "ethnically cleansing" Muslims from that region of the country.

The fortunes of war, which had mainly favored Serb and Bosnian Serb forces from the beginning, began to change in late July, when Bosnian Croats and Bosnian Muslims allied with the army of Croatia, which crossed the border into Bosnia and won key victories over Serbian forces there. In early August, the Croatian army also drove Bosnian Serbs from Krajina, the predominantly Serb region of Croatia that had earlier fallen under Bosnian Serb control. When the town of Knin fell, some 150,000 Croat Serbs fled to sections of Bosnia then held by Bosnian Serbs. Others were raped, tortured, and massacred by Croat forces seeking, with success, to "cleanse" the region of ethnic Serbs. At roughly the same time, the United Nations deployed a Rapid Reaction Force of 1,200 British and French soldiers to assist in the defense of Sarajevo. After Bosnian Serb shelling killed 37 civilians in the marketplace, NATO planes began attacking Serb positions around the city.

Finally, in September, under threat of continuing NATO air strikes and pressure from Serbia's president, Slobodan Milošević, who feared NATO would attack Serbia itself, the Bosnian Serbs ended their siege of Sarajevo, which had begun in 1992. On September 8, foreign ministers of Serbia, Croatia, and Bosnia, meeting in Geneva under the auspices of the U.S. assistant secretary of state, Richard Holbrooke, agreed in principle that Bosnia would remain a separate sovereign state with a single president but would be partitioned into two self-governing democratic entities, one predominantly Serb, to be known as Republika Srpska (the Serbian Republic), and the other, called the Federation of Bosnia and Herzegovina, to be dominated by Muslims and Croats. Under Clinton's personal supervision, the final details were negotiated in Dayton, Ohio, and the so-called Dayton peace accord was signed in Paris on December 14. The agreement also called for introduction into the region of 60,000 NATO peacekeeping troops, including some 20,000 Americans. Meanwhile, two leaders of the Bosnian Serbs, Radovan Karadžić and Ratko Mladić, were formally charged with war crimes in the World Court in the Hague. Milošević was also later tried for war crimes, including that he was personally responsible for the massacre of 7,000 Muslim men and boys from Srebrenica. Overall, civilians suffered the greatest casualties from the conflict, which left 200,000 dead and 2 million homeless from the time the fighting began in 1992. The United Nations high commissioner for refugees announced that his office was caring for 27 million refugees worldwide, three times as many as in 1985.[2]

Deadly terrorist attacks took place in Israel, where Palestinian suicide bombers struck civilian targets and where, in November, Prime Minister Yitzhak Rabin was assassinated by a Jewish extremist opposed to Rabin's efforts toward conciliation with the Palestinians. Rabin died less than two months after signing the Oslo II accord, a Clinton-brokered agreement with Arafat granting Palestinians self-determination on the West Bank of the Jordan River in return for guarantees of Israel's security. Rabin was succeeded by Shimon Peres.

Egypt's president Hosni Mubarak survived an assassination attempt made while he was visiting Ethiopia. Elsewhere, massacres continued in Rwanda, as Tutsi soldiers slaughtered thousands in a Hutu refugee camp; fighting continued between government troops and Islamic separatists in India's Kashmir region; the Turkish army raided Kurdish bases in Iraq; fighting between the secular government of Algeria and Islamic rebels prompted the U.S. State Department to advise Americans to travel with "substantial armed protection"; and Clinton suspended all U.S. trade with Iran in response to its support of terrorism and its continuing efforts to acquire nuclear weapons.

Members of the Japanese religious sect Aum Shinrikyo (Supreme Truth) terrorized commuters in Tokyo in March by unleashing the deadly World War II–era nerve gas Sarin on five subway trains, killing eight and injuring more than 4,000. Subsequent gas attacks in Yokohama injured hundreds more. Along with several of his followers, Shoko Asahara, the leader of the cult, was quickly arrested for the Tokyo attack and later pleaded guilty. He was convicted in 2004 and sentenced to death along with 11 others.

Russia negotiated a broad trade agreement with the European Union but failed to prevent NATO from proceeding with its plan to admit former Soviet allies from the cold war into the military coalition that had been formed almost 50 years earlier to oppose Soviet expansion. Russia's president Boris Yeltsin initially refused to acknowledge the existence of an ongoing insurgency in Chechnya, much less consent to Clinton's call in May for a negotiated settlement. But he was soon compelled to confront the situation, while being twice hospitalized for health problems, after Chechen rebels seized 2,000 hostages in June. Hundreds were killed when Russian troops unsuccessfully attacked the hospital where the hostages were held. Finally, both sides agreed that the rebels would release the hostages in return for safe passage home and a Russian promise to open peace talks with the Chechen leader General Dzhokhar Dudayev. Early talks were unsuccessful, but an agreement was reached in December granting Chechnya greater autonomy than any other republic in the Russian Federation, allowing the Chechen government to open its own consulates and trade missions abroad, guaranteeing that Chechen draftees would not be required to serve beyond the borders of Chechnya, and granting amnesty to rebel fighters who surrendered their weapons.

France ended 14 years of Socialist Party rule with the election as president of the Conservative Party leader Jacques Chirac. France subsequently provoked widespread international outrage when it began testing a series of nuclear bombs in the South Pacific, about 750 miles from Tahiti. Chirac argued that the tests were necessary to ensure the effectiveness of the newest generation of nuclear warheads, and French officials maintained that after the conclusion of this round of tests in May 1996, France would end its nuclear testing program altogether and sign a comprehensive global test ban treaty. French officials tried to allay fears about potential pollution by claiming that the basalt rock deep beneath the coral-ringed test site would prevent radioactivity from leaking into the sea. But this assurance was indignantly disputed by thousands of protesters across the world, especially in such Pacific Ocean nations as Australia, New Zealand, and Japan, where boycotts of French products were organized. Environmental groups such as Greenpeace also denounced France's unilateral decision to test nuclear weapons at a time when other major nuclear powers such as Britain and the United States were both reducing stockpiles and renouncing nuclear testing. French military units forcibly prevented Greenpeace ships from disrupting the tests.

Although the United States generally cultivated improved relations with China throughout the decade, especially in matters of trade, close ties became more problematic after the Chinese government jailed an additional 17 dissidents shortly before the sixth anniversary of the Tiananmen Square protest, and after the CIA accused China of selling missile technology to Iran and Pakistan. Clinton also continued to pursue closer links to Vietnam as, after lifting the trade embargo in 1994, he granted full diplomatic relations in July 1995.

Closer to home, voters in Quebec narrowly voted to remain federated with Canada, and Jean-Bertrand Aristide, Haiti's first democratically elected president, who returned to power with U.S. assistance in 1994, forced 43 senior army officers, including all generals and lieutenant generals, to retire, thereby removing the last of those who held senior positions in the military government that had overthrown him in 1991. Aristide's supporters won an overwhelming majority in subsequent elections. Alberto Fujimori was overwhelmingly reelected president of Peru, Carlos Menem was reelected president of Argentina, and Colombia arrested the coleaders of the Cali drug cartel.

GOVERNMENT AND SOCIETY

The April 19 bombing of the Alfred P. Murrah federal building in Oklahoma City was the most deadly episode of domestic terrorism ever experienced in the United States to that date. Initially, much of the public suspected it was the work of anti-American Arabs and Islamic extremists, although both the government and the media took steps to discourage a rush to judgment. Ethnic and/or religious prejudice may have contributed to the public's immediate inclination to blame Muslim extremists, but its general suspicion of Islam-inspired terrorism was rooted in many compelling episodes from recent history: the convictions in 1994 of Muslim terrorists for the 1993 bombing of the World Trade Center; the virulent denunciations of America broadcast by Saddam Hussein and loudly embraced by hundreds of thousands of Arabs in Jordan, Egypt, and the West Bank during the Persian Gulf War; numerous deadly

The bombing of the federal building in Oklahoma City was the most deadly act of domestic terrorism in the nation's history, to that date. *(AP/Wide World Photos)*

attacks on American troops and civilians by Islamic militants throughout the 1980s; and, in the 1990s, the common practice of Islamic insurgents in Israel, Algeria, Chechnya, Chile, the Philippines, and elsewhere of bombing civilian centers.

Nonetheless, within two days the FBI arrested Timothy McVeigh, a 27-year-old white American from Michigan, and his associate, Terry Nichols. Both men were ultimately convicted in federal court, and McVeigh was executed in 2001 for the actual bombing. Nichols was sentenced to life in prison for assisting him. In 2004, he was convicted of murder in state court and sentenced to life in prison without the possibility of parole.

McVeigh had become disaffected with the U.S. government while serving in the Persian Gulf War and then turned against it more forcefully after federal agents raided the Branch Davidian compound in Waco. Part of McVeigh's motive for attacking the federal building was to retaliate for the Waco raid and for other federal assaults on armed resisters that McVeigh, Nichols, and their cohorts deplored as unlawful governmental trampling on the rights of individual citizens. The bombing was especially upsetting because it apparently targeted the children of federal workers in a day-care center inside the building, and because the attack took place in Oklahoma City, a small, conservative, comparatively homogeneous, relatively religious city populated mostly by whites and located in the center of the country, where it had seemed insulated from the social and political upheaval associated with the more culturally and ethnically diverse East and West Coasts.

The Oklahoma City bombing called national attention to the proliferation of far-Right citizen militias, several of whom were known for antigovernment, white supremacist, and/or anti-Semitic sympathies. McVeigh and Nichols had been affiliated with such a militia in Michigan. Many local militias were quick to dissociate themselves from these sentiments and portrayed themselves as concerned citizens dedicated to personal and national security, exercising their constitutionally guaranteed right to bear arms. Ever vigilant against any effort to curtail that right, the politically influential National Rifle Association (NRA) added its voice to those condemning efforts by the FBI, the ATF, and other federal law enforcement agencies to restrict those rights. In a fund-raising letter sent just a month after the Oklahoma City bombing, the NRA angered many Americans, even many of its own members, by describing federal agents as "jack-booted government thugs" wearing "Nazi bucket helmets." Among those to protest the comparison of federal law enforcement agents to Nazi storm troopers was the former president George H. W. Bush, a lifelong NRA member, who publicly resigned in protest.

Unlike in his first two years in office, when Democrats controlled both chambers of Congress, Clinton was faced in 1995 with a Republican-dominated House and Senate. Claiming to have received the message voters sent in the 1994 midterm elections that unseated many liberal Democrats, he moved closer to the political center and scaled down his ambitions for a liberal domestic agenda. In his State of the Union address Clinton promised to make the government smaller and more efficient. He also called for more college loans, a tax cut for the middle class, and increased funding for immunization against childhood diseases, school lunches, the Head Start program, and medical care and nutrition for pregnant women and infants. Acknowledging that his administration "bit off more than we could chew" with its efforts in 1993–94 to provide universal health insurance, Clinton now promoted more modest health care reform. He also announced his intention to increase military spending by $25 billion over the next six years, most of it earmarked for pay increases for personnel; to provide economic assistance to Mexico; and to reform the "failed welfare system," while providing opportunities for America's poor to lift themselves from poverty. Alluding to representatives who lost their seats in Congress for supporting the 1994 crime bill and the Brady bill, which together restricted the sale of handguns and banned certain assault weapons, Clinton vowed not to let those acts be repealed. He also called for efforts to combat both domestic and international terrorism and closed by urging Americans to participate more in the civic life of their community.

Pitted against Clinton's agenda was the Republicans' Contract with America, which House Speaker Newt Gingrich had crafted and used with great success in the 1994 elections. The contract called for passage of a constitutional amendment requiring a balanced federal budget by 2004, as well as other legislation intended to strengthen families, require tougher mandatory sentences for criminals, reduce welfare programs, provide middle-class tax relief, increase military spending, create incentives for small businesses, limit jury awards for punitive damages, forbid the passage of "unfunded mandates" that require state compliance but provide inadequate funding for implementation, and impose term limits on career politicians. Gingrich fulfilled his contractual obligation to submit legislation addressing each of these issues within the first 100 days of the new session, and the House passed everything but the bill calling for term limits. However, only five of the measures in the contract were enacted into law by the end of the year.

Some of the proposals of the contract overlapped with Clinton's agenda, especially in such areas as middle-class tax cuts and increased military spending, which were achieved in 1995. However, the balanced budget amendment failed by one vote to gain the necessary two-thirds majority in the Senate.

Congress passed and Clinton signed legislation to deter Congress from passing unfunded mandates, but the final, weakened version did not ban them outright, as required by the contract. As part of the contract's commitment to reduce government regulation, the House voted to scale back the 1972 Clean Water Act by reducing wetlands protection and easing regulations preventing industries and municipalities from discharging polluted runoff into lakes and rivers. Clinton threatened to veto the bill if the Senate passed it, and it ended the year in a standoff. Ultimately, the revisions failed to become law. In January 1996, Clinton vetoed a welfare reform bill because he believed it provided inadequate incentives for finding work and threatened to increase the suffering of poor children. However, he signed different welfare reform legislation in 1996.

Although Clinton and most Democrats opposed the balanced budget amendment, he shared the Republicans' goal of eliminating the deficit, which he believed undermined the economy. But they differed sharply over how to achieve this, and the year concluded with a dramatic budget showdown between the president and Congress that resulted in the longest shutdown of nonessential government operations in history. Clinton threatened to veto a defense-spending bill calling for $7 billion more than the significant increase he had already requested. But he allowed it to become law without his signature, as he feared he would otherwise lose necessary support for the peacekeeping mission in Bosnia. He did veto debt-limit legislation that would have kept the government functioning in the absence of a complete budget appropriation but would have compelled him by the end of the year either to reach a new budget agreement largely on Republican terms or to risk the government's going into default. Clinton later signed a second continuing resolution that temporarily ended the budget impasse but did not resolve the stalemate. However, his refusal to sign another stopgap budget bill because it would require increased Medicare premiums forced the temporary closings of museums, national parks, and other nonessential government operations. Finally, on January 6, 1996, Clinton signed a stopgap funding bill that ended the shutdown. Overall, 280,000 workers were furloughed throughout most of December and early January, and another 480,000 deemed essential to government operations worked without pay.

In the aftermath of his political victory over the budget, Clinton emerged as a considerably stronger leader, while Gingrich, who decided in December not to seek the Republican nomination for president in 1996, began his political decline. The public largely approved of Clinton's refusal to cave in to Gingrich's aggressive, partisan political style, and the majority of Americans blamed the Republicans in Congress for the government shutdown. In particular, many Americans were put off by what they perceived as Gingrich's arrogance, especially after Gingrich stated that he had placed several provisions offensive to Clinton in one of the funding bills Clinton vetoed, because he felt snubbed that he had to exit from the rear of the presidential airplane upon returning from Rabin's funeral in Israel. Clinton's approval ratings, on the other hand, passed 50 percent for the first time in his presidency.

At the same time, the public, angered by the government's inability to conduct its business, complained about the intensely partisan nature of American politics, in which political opponents were increasingly cast as dangerous enemies who threatened to corrupt society by undermining fundamental moral, religious, and American values. But outcries for a more bipartisan, cooperative spirit that would place the nation's overall best interests before those of ideologically driven power brokers had little impact.

Although the crime rate actually fell significantly in 1995, violent crime nonetheless preoccupied many Americans. The acquittal of O. J. Simpson of murdering his former wife and her friend once more revealed the intensity of the racial divisions still present in American society, as well as the differing perceptions among ethnic groups of the overall fairness of the judicial system. The entire trial, which lasted from September 26, 1994, to October 3, 1995, was televised live, and the judge, attorneys, and some of the witnesses became national celebrities and ongoing subjects for television talk shows and satires and for impassioned commentary among citizens in general.

Testimony during the trial provided clear evidence of racism within the Los Angeles Police Department, lending credence to the defense claim that Simpson was the victim of racially motivated police evidence tampering. Nonetheless, seemingly conclusive DNA evidence appeared to link Simpson, an African American, to the deaths.

The outcome was largely approved by black Americans throughout the country, many of whom, feeling that the systemic racism of the police and judicial systems had been exposed and repudiated, burst out in spontaneous celebration when the verdict was announced. Conversely, whites overwhelmingly condemned the acquittal, which many believed allowed yet another celebrity literally to get away with cold-blooded murder.[3] Some critics questioned the selection of the predominantly black jury, which included 10 women and two men, of whom one was Hispanic and two were white,[4] and they complained of a two-tiered justice system in America, one for the wealthy who could afford the very best legal representation and the other for the rest of the citizenry.

Blacks and whites also split over their assessment of the Million Man March on Washington organized by the Nation of Islam leader Louis Farrakhan, which was attended by approximately 400,000 African-American men in October. Two black political activists, the Reverend Jesse Jackson and the Reverend Al Sharpton, were among those who participated. Regarded with suspicion by many whites, who pointed to Farrakhan's public denunciations of the white establishment, Jews, Asians, and homosexuals, and by some feminists, who were disturbed by the exclusion of women from the rally, Farrakhan nonetheless won some praise among both blacks and whites for his message that black men need to acknowledge their own shortcomings and seek greater responsibility for their family and for his condemnation of violence, drug use, and abusive behavior toward women, all of which he maintained were destroying black families and communities.

Americans of all races widely approved the guilty verdict of the Muslim leader Sheik Omar Abdel Rahman on 48 charges of conspiring to wage a "war of urban terrorism" against the United States, although many Americans of Arab descent also feared an anti-Arab backlash. Abdel Rahman was found guilty of masterminding failed efforts in 1993 to bomb the United Nations building, bridges, and other public sites in and near New York City; for plotting to assassinate political leaders, including Egypt's president Hosni Mubarak, and for directing the terrorist group that murdered the radical Jewish leader Rabbi Meir Kahane in 1990. He was later also linked to the 1993 World Trade Center bombing, and his Islam-based revolutionary action inspired Osama bin Laden and the al-Qaeda terrorist network that destroyed the World Trade Center and attacked the Pentagon in 2001.

The Unabomber, later identified as the former math professor Theodore Kaczynski, promised to "desist from terrorism" if a major newspaper would publish his rambling 35,000-word manifesto condemning Western society's reliance on science and technology; if they did not, he would continue his bombing campaign. Since 1978, Kaczynski had sent letter bombs to scientists, university professors, business leaders, and others identified with the "industrial-technological society," which he believed was creating a social, psychological, and environmental "disaster for the human race" and constricting the individual's ability to "control the circumstances of one's own life." Because three people had been killed and more than two dozen wounded between 1978 and 1995, the FBI took Kaczynski's threat seriously and encouraged the *Washington Post* and *New York Times* to publish the piece, entitled "Industrial Society and Its Future," and they did on September 19. Ironically, the treatise's publication led to Kaczynski's capture in 1996, as his brother recognized the writing style and alerted the FBI that Kaczynski might be the Unabomber.

Many of Kaczynski's anti-industrial sentiments were shared by a growing number of Americans, who expressed them less violently, but often vociferously: Grunge, a form of musical and social expression popular among younger Americans, complained that lifestyles built around the corporate workplace were meaningless and spiritually unrewarding; environmental activists pointed to the rapid destruction and degradation of nature associated with a high-tech consumer culture; and laid-off workers who had lost well-paying jobs "outsourced" to laborers in other countries decried the growing global economy that threatened to shred the middle class and create a two-class American society of rich and poor. Nonetheless, the combined forces of technology and consumerism continued to drive worldwide economies and make the nation, and much of the world, increasingly dependent on multinational corporations. And the increasing numbers of cellular telephones, Internet services, e-mail, and other forms of telecommunications were rapidly becoming integral parts of people's life, shaping the ways they interacted with one another and greatly expanding the range of opportunities, resources, and experiences available to them. By 1995, more than 7 million people subscribed to America Online, Prodigy, Compuserve, or other online services.[5]

The nation remained divided over recent court rulings that opened previously all-male institutions to women. After fighting two years of legal battles that culminated in a Supreme Court victory, Shannon Faulkner enrolled as the first female cadet in the history of the Citadel, a state-supported military academy in Charleston, South Carolina. Her male classmates deeply resented what they regarded as the tarnishing of a long southern tradition, and Faulkner arrived at the school accompanied by federal marshals after receiving death threats. She withdrew a few days later after collapsing, along with four male cadets, of heat exhaustion during the first day of the so-called hell week of intensive workouts. To those opposed to greater roles for women in military and other traditionally male bastions, Faulkner's withdrawal demonstrated that women are not capable of competing equally with men. But many supporters of women's rights whose main point was that qualified women should have equal opportunity to succeed or fail to men's, nonetheless praised Faulkner for pressing forward with her court battle and enrolling in the academy, despite the intense vitriol directed against her by her classmates and others.

The Harvard professor Robert Putnam published data showing that contemporary Americans were less engaged civically and less connected socially than Americans of the previous generation. Fewer voted, were politically active, attended church, participated in Parent–Teacher Associations (PTAs) and other school organizations, or otherwise engaged in communal activities. Even informal interactions among small groups of friends had diminished. In his article "Bowling Alone" (updated and expanded as a book in 2000) Putnam attributed this breakdown of community to the prevalence of television, which people often watched alone and which, even when viewed in couples or groups, became the focal point of attention and discouraged personal interactions among those present. Putnam also pointed to increased demands from the workplace on individuals' time and energy and to the effects of urban sprawl, which made commuting and other forms of travel within communities more stressful and time consuming. The article apparently resonated for many Americans, as it became the subject of magazine articles and television talk shows. It also provoked objections from so-called soccer moms who spent much of their time facilitating their children's group activities. Putnam's discussion of the adverse implications of social disengagement for sustaining a vital democracy attracted the special attention of Bill Clinton, who had addressed the problem in his State of the Union speech and met with Putnam at Camp David.

The sexual revolution that began in the 1960s continued to spread to younger Americans, as a 1995 study showed that more than 80 percent had lost their virginity as teenagers. The average age for males' first sexual experience was 16; it was 17 for females.[6] Although much of this activity was consensual, peer pressure was identified as a significant influence among sexually active teenagers. Date rape by friends or acquaintances also emerged as a growing concern, especially as many young men and women did not regard it as actual rape.

The Supreme Court ruled that police holding search warrants need to announce themselves before entering a home to conduct a search; judges can overrule juries' sentencing recommendations in death-penalty cases; evidence obtained through good-faith use of an invalid arrest warrant is admissible; Amtrak is a federal agency and is therefore bound to respect First Amendment free-speech rights; anonymous political literature is protected under the First Amendment and cannot be banned by legislatures; investors are entitled to receive punitive damages from securities firms that mishandle their accounts; companies can change their employee-benefits plans, even if doing so cancels medical benefits of retired workers; companies can trademark distinctive colors used to identify their products; cities cannot use residential zoning laws to bar the establishment of group homes for handicapped people, including recovering substance abusers; organizers of a Saint Patrick's Day parade in Boston have the constitutional right to exclude gay rights advocates from marching in their parade; random drug testing for student athletes is constitutional; and race cannot be the predominant factor in determining electoral districts. By a 5-4 vote, the Court also declared unconstitutional the Gun-Free School Zones Act, which made possession of a firearm within 1,000 feet of a school a federal offense. The Supreme Court of Canada ruled 5-4 that protections from discrimination apply to homosexuals, though sexual orientation is not specifically mentioned in Canada's Charter of Rights and Freedoms.

BUSINESS

Although the Dow-Jones industrial average suffered a 100-point drop in December, the largest single-day drop in four years, overall the economy fared well in 1995. The Dow-Jones average rose from a high of 3,978 in 1994 to 5,216 in 1995, an extraordinary increase of more than 33 percent. Inflation dropped by 0.2 percent to 2.5 percent, and the GDP continued to grow at a healthy rate of 4.5 percent. The unemployment rate fell to 5.6 percent.[7] Moreover, according to the Census Bureau, poverty declined from 14.5 percent in 1994 to 13.8 percent, with 1.6 million fewer people living at or below the poverty level than in 1994. The poverty rate among black Americans declined to 29.3 percent, down 1.3 percent from 1994—the lowest rate since records were first kept in 1959. Elderly Americans replaced working-age people as the group who had the lowest percentage of poverty. The median household income rose by 2.7 percent to $34,074, the first increase in inflation-adjusted median household income since 1989. However, earnings for full-time workers declined by 0.7 percent for men and 1.5 percent for women, causing some analysts to speculate that the gain in household income derived from the larger number of household members who were working than in 1994.[8]

The year began with the appointment of a new secretary of the treasury, as Robert E. Rubin replaced Lloyd M. Bentsen, Jr., who announced his retirement in December 1994. During his confirmation hearings Rubin attributed the ongoing economic recovery and the ability to provide middle-class tax relief to the Clinton administration's deficit reduction policies, which he pledged to support.

Mexico, which sharply devalued the peso in December 1994, suffered from a monetary crisis that threatened to undermine its entire economy. Although critics warned that a bailout would harm the U.S. economy and questioned Mexico's ability ever to repay any loans it might receive, Clinton heeded economists who feared that severe ongoing devaluation of the peso would undermine the stability of the U.S. dollar and the currencies of other industrial countries. Others predicted that the deteriorating Mexican economy would further drain government resources and create further social problems by increasing illegal immigration into the United States. Therefore, despite congressional opposition, Clinton authorized a $20 billion line of credit to rescue Mexico's economy. The agreement, in addition to a $30 billion loan from the International Monetary Fund (IMF) and the central banks of several Western nations, required Mexico to adopt austere policies to curb inflation and enhance its economic self-sufficiency, measures intended to stimulate the country's stagnant economy.

Clinton's dealings with China and Japan were less friendly. At the beginning of February, he threatened to impose punitive tariffs on China in retaliation for its ongoing tolerance of copyright infringements. China responded by threatening to raise tariffs on U.S. products. Altogether, more than $1 billion worth of Chinese-made goods would have been affected, but the dispute was resolved on the day that the 100 percent tariffs were to go into effect, when China agreed to take a number of actions to enforce international copyright laws and curtail the manufacturing of pirated U.S. goods. In May, Clinton imposed a punitive 100 percent tariff on 13 models of luxury cars to retaliate for Japan's failure to open its domestic car market to U.S. automakers. The following month the two countries reached a broad agreement on automotive trade that concluded a two-year dispute. These conflicts notwithstanding, as Asian markets continued to open, U.S. industries prospered, especially those associated with agriculture, and the export of farm goods reached record levels. However, overall the United States recorded a $111.04 billion trade deficit, an increase in the deficit of 4.5 percent from 1994 and the greatest deficit since 1988.[9]

A new market without borders opened in cyberspace with the founding of eBay, an online auction house that facilitated high-volume and low-volume trading among private individuals, as well as companies.

NATURE AND THE ENVIRONMENT

Earthquakes were among the most destructive natural disasters, as a strong earthquake in Kobe, Japan, killed some 4,000 people in January, after buildings believed to be earthquake resistant collapsed and fires ran out of control throughout the city. Earthquakes also killed 2,000 on Russia's Sakhalin Island and more than 60 in west-central Mexico, near the coastal port of Manzanillo. Floods in the Netherlands provoked fears in February that dams might break and forced hundreds of thousands of people to evacuate. Severe winter flooding in California was responsible for the death of 15 and some $2 billion worth of damage, and during the summer the Mississippi and Missouri Rivers flooded in Missouri and Illinois.

Fears that in an era of biological terrorism an antibiotic-resistant virus might unleash a massive, unstoppable epidemic were fanned with the outbreak in Zaire of an epidemic caused by the Ebola virus, in May, which, according to the World Health Organization, had killed 244 of the 315 people known to have been infected.[10]

New evidence surfaced to support the theory of global warming, as 1995 proved to be the warmest year on record since scientists began keeping records in 1866. Environmentalists argued that the widening hole in the ozone layer above Antarctica and the breaking away of a massive iceberg from Antarctica demonstrated that the worldwide trend toward rising temperatures was a real and present danger. And they and others pointed to health hazards associated with pollution and dangers to business and society emanating from rising oceans and other potential long-term effects of global warming. (In fact, more than 500 people died in northern India as temperatures reached 113 degrees during the hottest summer of the century, and more than 570 died in Chicago, where temperatures peaked around 106 degrees.) However, many top business leaders, especially those in heavy industries, resisted these conclusions, insisting instead that global warming remains just a theoretical possibility; that the current temperature increases may be just a temporary fluctuation or anomaly and not necessarily part of a long-term trend; and that more scientific study and consensus are prerequisites for expensive factory upgrades. The World Bank released a report warning of an imminent worldwide water crisis resulting from rapid worldwide population growth and increased water pollution by industry, household waste, and agricultural chemicals.

Archaeologists studying slabs of sediment in the Yucatán Peninsula in Mexico unearthed conclusive evidence that a period of severe drought prevailed between A.D. 800 and 1000, coinciding with and possibly contributing to the decline of the Mayan civilization.

SCIENCE AND TECHNOLOGY

Big science once again captured the public imagination when the *Galileo* space probe sent back the first closeup photographs of Jupiter and its moons, and astronomers in Hawaii discovered the most distant galaxy yet observed, some 15 billion miles from Earth. Other astronomers in the United States and Japan announced that they had found the most direct and definitive evidence to date confirming the existence of theoretically predicated black holes, and scientists at Switzerland's Geneva Observatory sighted the first extrasolar planet orbiting a sunlike "live" star, 51 Pegasi—the 51st brightest star in the southern constellation Pegasus. (The first extrasolar planets were discovered in 1991.) Closer to Earth, the U.S. space shuttle *Discovery* overcame concerns about a fuel leak and docked with the Russian *Mir* space station, uniting U.S. and Russian crews for the first time since the cold-war detente of the 1970s. *Discovery* was piloted by Lieutenant Colonel Eileen Collins, the first American woman to command a space shuttle.

The Indian physicist Satyenda Bose created a "super atom," a new state of matter whose existence Albert Einstein had predicted 70 years earlier, and scientists at the Los Alamos National Laboratory in New Mexico generated preliminary evidence that the subatomic particles called neutrinos possess small amounts of mass, leading to speculation that they may account for much of the 90 percent of so-called missing matter in the universe—matter that was theoretically predicated to exist but was unaccounted for. Other scientists at Los Alamos developed a new superconducting tape composed of metal and ceramic materials capable of carrying significantly more electrical current than existing "high-temperature" superconductors.

Researchers at Yale University found that the brains of men and women function differently when processing language, and scientists at the University of Pennsylvania reported that men experience greater activity in certain parts of their brain and women experience greater activity in other parts of theirs. The study added further support to a hypothesis that by reason of their biological makeup, men are more inclined to express emotions through instrumental means, such as fighting, and women are more prone to express emotions symbolically through language.

Recent advances in medical treatment for AIDS, including expensive drug "cocktails" that mix several medications, began to show significant results, as 5 to 10 percent of those infected with HIV were surviving longer than 10 years. The FDA approved vaccinations for hepatitis A and chicken pox, and a study showed that people who took four to six aspirin weekly for 20 years were significantly less likely to have colon cancer.

The role of genetics in medical science continued to expand as the researcher Craig Venter decoded the entire genome of an influenza bacterium. Scientists at Johns Hopkins University isolated the gene linked to the onset of adult diabetes (type II) and to obesity, and investigators at the Washington University suggested that there could be a genetic predisposition to smoke tobacco. Physicians at the National Institutes of Health found the first effective treatment for sickle cell anemia, a disease that primarily affects African Americans. A previously approved treatment for blood pressure, however, calcium-channel-blocking drugs, was associated with a 60 percent higher risk of heart attack in those who used it, compared to patients taking other kinds of blood pressure medication.

The debate continued over whether exposure to high levels of electromagnetism from utility lines increases the risk for cancer, as a study in the *American Journal of Epidemiology* demonstrated that workers exposed to high levels of low-frequency electromagnetic radiation were roughly twice as likely as others to die of brain cancer. However, the researchers did not have sufficient data to conclude whether low-frequency magnetic radiation was responsible for the increased risk.

The impact of socioeconomic factors on individual health has been at the heart of many debates over public policy for decades. Researchers at the Centers for Disease Control and Prevention found that women who live in poverty and uneducated women of all races are more likely to bear mildly retarded children than other mothers. The scientists studying 10-year-old children in Atlanta found that 0.84 percent were mildly retarded and 0.36 percent were severely retarded. In the study mothers who did not finish high school were four times more likely to have mildly retarded children than more highly educated women. Black children were 2.6 times more likely to be mildly retarded than white children, but when preventable socioeconomic factors were taken into account, that figure was cut in half. Teenage mothers were slightly more likely to have retarded children. One of the researchers, Carolyn Drews, pointed to the results of the study to refute the claims made by the popular book *The Bell Curve* (1994), which argues that race exerts a greater influence on intelligence than social and economic background and environment.

The relationships of diet and exercise to disease continued to attract scientific attention, as the largest study to that date surprised researchers when it did not demonstrate that eating large amounts of fish or fish oil reduces the risk of heart disease, despite considerable prior speculation to that effect. However, a different study revealed that middle-aged men who ate large amounts of fruits and vegetables were less likely to suffer strokes in later life. A Harvard study of 17,300 middle-aged male Harvard graduates showed that regular vigorous exercise increases life expectancy significantly, but moderate exercise does not, although it may offer other kinds of benefits. A separate, smaller study, however, found that even moderate exercise offers benefits for longevity. Another study reported that women who are mildly to moderately overweight or who experience mild to moderate weight gain in middle age have a significantly increased chance of premature death. A separate study found similar results for men.

The body of a 500-year-old Inca girl believed to have been killed as a human sacrifice was discovered in good condition, dressed in ceremonial clothes, frozen in ice in the Peruvian Andes. More than 300 drawings of mammoths, wooly rhinoceroses, bears, and other Ice Age creatures that lived 17,000 to 20,000 years ago were found in France near Avignon. Archaeologists in Argentina discovered the fossil remains of a carnivorous dinosaur believed to be larger even than *Tyrannosaurus rex,* which had previously been believed to be the largest of the dinosaur species.

LITERATURE, THE ARTS, SPORTS, AND POPULAR CULTURE

As the preliminaries began for the 1996 campaign season, deep divisions over fundamental questions about the role of the arts and humanities became enmeshed in presidential politics. Candidates and critics on both sides of the culture wars argued—often stridently and with no real interest in true dialogue—about the appropriateness of artists', especially musicians', filmmakers', and performance artists', attacking the society's core values, deviating from the norms of acceptable sexual behavior, and celebrating violence, racism, sexist attitudes, and other behavior anathema to most citizens. Several artists, such as the singer Barbra Streisand, who delivered a public address at Harvard entitled "The Artist as Citizen," spoke about the importance of retaining broad artistic freedom to sustain a vital democracy capable of continuously examining and correcting itself as necessary. Others, not exclusively but especially on the political Right, condemned violent and sexually explicit songs and videos as morally degenerate, anarchistic, and especially harmful to children still developing their values, psyche, and views of reality.

In this spirit, the Republican-dominated Congress maintained its attack on the National Endowment for the Arts (NEA), which, among its many programs, sometimes funded projects that represented America in a negative fashion, degraded Christian icons, or otherwise offended public sensibilities about good taste, proper public behavior, and religious reverence. These outrages, intended to be outrageous, became frequent targets for candidates seeking office. For instance, Robert Dole of Kansas, the Senate majority leader and a contender for the Republican nomination for president, attacked the U.S. entertainment industry for promoting music and films whose emphases on violence and sex "debase our nation and threaten our children." He further criticized multilingual education programs and blamed a liberal "intellectual elite" in the nation's universities, museums, and cultural institutions for engaging in a campaign to tarnish American history and undermine "traditional American values."

The cold war and its implications featured significantly in the year's nonfiction. In addition to *In Retrospect,* Robert McNamara's insider's view of the management and mismanagement of the Vietnam War, Richard Rhodes's *Dark Sun: The Making of the Hydrogen Bomb* provides an intimate look at the interplay between science and politics at an earlier but perhaps even more critical moment of the cold war. Cold war politics is also the subject of *The Secret World of American Communism,* by Harvey Klehr, John Earl Haynes, and Fridrikh Firsov, who used recently declassified documents from the former Soviet Union to demonstrate the large extent to which the American Communist Party had been under the direct control of the Soviet Union, which funded the organization, controlled its policies, directed subversive activities, and used it to recruit and oversee spies. Colin Powell, the future secretary of state, who had served in Vietnam and presided over the Persian Gulf War as chairman of the Joint Chiefs of Staff, published his autobiography, *My American Journey*. And Tina Rosenberg won the National Book Award and the Pulitzer Prize in nonfiction with *The Haunted Land: Facing Europe's Ghosts after Communism*, which asks how the countries of Eastern Europe will come to terms with their Communist past and how they will deal with citizens who actively supported repressive Communist regimes.

Other nonfiction expressed a growing perception that legalities and technicalities inhibit people from assuming personal responsibility and preclude direct, straightforward solutions to social problems. As well as in Philip K. Howard's *The Death of Common Sense: How Law Is Suffocating America*, which appeared in December 1994, this sentiment found expression in the historian Gertrude Himmelfarb's *The De-Moralization of Society: From Victorian Virtues to Modern Values*, which advocates the Victorian values of hard work, thrift, deferral of gratification, and self-reliance. Gingrich's *To Renew America* also argues for earlier values in its call for commonsense government, greater local authority to make decisions and solve problems, increased assumption of personal responsibility, and shifting of power from the federal government to the people. However, Gingrich's $4.5 million advance from his publisher, which he returned after a storm of public criticism, attracted more attention than his arguments. In *Emotional Intelligence: Why It Can Matter More Than IQ*, Daniel Goleman argues that the capacity to be emotionally well balanced often plays a greater role in determining a person's success in life than raw intellectual capability. John F. Kennedy, Jr., the son of the late president John F. Kennedy, founded *George*, a political magazine.

Stories about journeys of self-discovery and personal growth resonated with contemporary readers, whose own life, or that of their friends, relatives, or associates, was likewise marked by experiences emanating from broken marriages, troubled children, intrusive technologies, and a strange new world of postmodern sensibilities, relationships, and living and working arrangements that, collectively, sometimes created a vague, bewildering sense that life is nothing like what they expected. In 1995, road trips were an especially effective means for exploring perceptions, beliefs, and emotions elicited by unsettling, sometimes painful events that placed the characters on the path to self-discovery. Richard Ford's *Independence Day*, his sequel to *The Sportswriter* (1986), won the Pulitzer Prize for its depiction of a middle-aged divorced man who retains feelings for his former wife, even as he participates in a relationship with a new lover and copes with the mood swings of his troubled teenage son, with whom he drives to the sports halls of fame. In *Painted Desert* Frederick Barthelme uses a postmodern road journey through the American West to explore the personal growth of a middle-aged, divorced man beginning life anew in a contemporary America obsessed by outpourings of violence that he and his Generation X girlfriend encounter electronically, through the media and the Internet, and as entertainment in tourist attractions and other forms of popular culture. James Redfield's *The Celestine Prophecy* uses an American's travels in Peru to present a New Age philosophy for personal growth. Redfield originally self-published the novel, whose success then attracted a mainstream publisher and made it a best seller. Russell Banks's *Rule of the Bone* is in many ways a 1990s version of

Mark Twain's *Adventures of Huckleberry Finn.* The protagonist, the Bone, is, as is Huck, a 14-year-old boy who runs away from an abusive home life and affiliates himself with people from the underclass of American society, biker gangs, a fast-talking producer of child pornography, and a black Jamaican who, as does Huck's Jim, befriends the Bone and, with the assistance of Rastafarian philosophy and ample marijuana, helps him find direction in his life. *The First Man,* the unfinished autobiographical novel by Albert Camus, another coming-of-age story, is set in Algeria. It was published posthumously 34 years after the manuscript was taken from the wreckage of the car accident that killed the acclaimed Algerian-born French existentialist novelist. Philip Roth won the National Book Award for his darkly humorous *Sabbath's Theater,* which explores the inner life of a 64-year-old man driven by profound emotions and a powerful libido. In *The Wedding* Dorothy West, the last surviving member of the Harlem Renaissance, explores the web of racial tensions and conflicted feelings that surface within a well-to-do black family whose daughter decides to marry a white jazz musician. Jane Smiley satirizes American university life in *Moo,* and in Salman Rushdie's *The Moor's Last Sigh,* a Spanish Moor speaks from the grave to tell the story of a complex family history connecting India and Spain. Best-selling fiction also included novels by such established genre writers as John Grisham (*The Rainmaker*), Michael Crichton (*The Lost World*), Stephen King (*Rose Madder*), Mary Higgins Clark (*Silent Night*), and Danielle Steel (*Five Days in Paris* and *Lightning*).

Terrence McNally won the 1995 Tony Award for his serious comedy *Love! Valour! Compassion!* starring Nathan Lane and Anthony Heald, which presents the ongoing lives of three gay men as they meet regularly throughout the summer, contending with AIDS and other challenges. Jason Robards and Blythe Danner appeared in Harold Pinter's *Moonlight,* a story about a family who come to terms with themselves as they accept the father's impending death; *Death Defying Acts,* a trilogy of one-act plays by Woody Allen, Elaine May, and David Mamet, won critical acclaim; Allen's *Central Park West* received particular praise. Emily Mann's *Having Our Say* featured Mary Alice and Gloria Forster as two African-American sisters more than 100 years old who reflect on their family's difficult history in America; and Blair Brown and Victor Garber starred in *Arcadia,* Tom Stoppard's comically philosophical drama in which characters from different moments in history contemplate such questions as the nature of truth, differences in romantic and classical temperaments, and the influence of sex, "the attraction which Newton left out," on the ways lives evolve. Shirley Knight starred in Horton Foote's Pulitzer Prize–winning *The Young Man from Atlanta,* about the ways the death of their child under mysterious circumstances transforms the lives of the affluent parents.

Andrew Lloyd Webber, Christopher Hampton, and Don Black won the Tony Award for their musical *Sunset Boulevard,* which opened in late 1994. Other musicals included revivals of Henri Mancini and Leslie Bricusse's *Victor/Victoria,* with Julie Andrews, Tony Roberts, and Michael Nouri, and Frank Loesser's *How to Succeed in Business Without Really Trying,* starring Matthew Broderick.

Except Sandra Bullock and Demi Moore, who ranked sixth and eighth, respectively, all of the top-10 box-office stars were men, led by Tom Hanks, Jim Carrey, Brad Pitt, Harrison Ford, and Robin Williams. Several of the year's most acclaimed films appealed to a sense of courage and adventure. Mel Gibson directed and starred in *Braveheart,* an epic about a medieval Scottish aristocrat who avenges himself on the king of England, for which Gibson won Academy Awards for best picture and best director. Ron Howard's *Apollo 13* featured Tom Hanks, Bill Paxton, Ed White, and Kevin Bacon in a well-made dramatic reenactment of the ill-fated *Apollo 13* mission to the Moon in the 1970s. Susan Sarandon won the Academy Award as best actress for her performance in Tim Robbins's *Dead Man Walking,* the story of a nun who befriends a murderer on death row (Sean Penn). Oliver Stone's *Nixon* depicts the former president as a sulking paranoid who suffers from the influence of a severe, unloving mother. The film was widely criticized for its historical inaccuracies—in some cases, flights of fantasy—such as Nixon's supposed responsibility for the 1960s Bay of Pigs fiasco in Cuba, which, according to Stone, shaped some of his disastrous political decisions.

Nicolas Cage won the best actor award for his role in Mike Figgis's *Leaving Las Vegas,* in which Cage plays a despairing middle-aged man who forges a relationship with a Las Vegas prostitute (Elisabeth Shue). Woody Allen explores a similar relationship in *Mighty Aphrodite,* which he wrote, directed, and starred in. Co-starring Helena Bonham Carter and Mira Sorvino, the movie played off the form, setting, and enduring themes of classical Greek tragedy as it showed the positive transformations in their lives as a middle-aged sports writer befriended the mother of his adopted child, an ignorant prostitute. Despite critical acclaim for the quality of the acting and writing—Mira Sorvino won the Academy Award as best supporting actress and Allen was nominated for best screenplay—some criticized the movie as a self-serving attempt by Allen to show himself as a good parent after Mia Farrow's accusation in 1992 that he had abused their adopted child. Feminists further criticized the aging Allen for continuing to cast much younger women as his romantic interests. *Seven,* starring Morgan Freeman and Brad Pitt, also explores the seamy sides of society as a detective on the verge of retirement tracks a serial murderer who matches his victims to the seven deadly sins.

Clint Eastwood directed himself and Meryl Streep in his adaptation of *The Bridges of Madison County,* James Robert Waller's popular 1992 novel about the love affair of a middle-aged photographer and a rural Iowa homemaker. Jane Austen's *Emma* (1816) was the inspiration for Amy Heckerling's comedy *Clueless,* which places a smart but superficial 1990s "Valley girl" at the center of Austen's story about a young woman who has an overly high opinion of herself. Directed by Ang Lee and starring Emma Thompson and Hugh Grant, *Sense and Sensibility* offered a more straightforward and beautifully filmed adaptation of another Austen novel, about striking a proper balance between passion and reason. Amanda Root and Ciaran Hinds starred in Roger Michell's *Persuasion,* an adaptation of still another Austen novel. Richard Dreyfus starred in Stephen Herek's *Mr. Holland's Opus,* the inspirational story of a high school band teacher.

Massimo Troisi, Philippe Noiret, and Maria Grazia Cucinotta starred in Michael Radford's sentimental comedy *Il Postino* (The Postman). Released in Europe in 1994, the Italian-made movie about the friendship of the exiled Chilean poet Pablo Neruda and an ignorant, inexpressive mailman attracted a popular following in the United States, where it was released in 1995. The Dis-

Alicia Silverstone (right) starred in *Clueless*, an adaptation of Jane Austen's *Emma*, played by teenagers and set in contemporary America. *(Photofest)*

ney Corporation's successful *Toy Story*, directed by John Lasseter and featuring the voices of Tom Hanks, Tim Allen, and Don Rickles, became the first fully computer-animated feature film. Disney also enjoyed success with *Pocahontas*, an animated film about the Indian princess who saved the life of the British colonist John Smith of Virginia.

The expiration of the Federal Communication Commission's (FCC's) financial interest and syndication rule for the first time enabled television networks to own the programming produced for prime-time viewing. This created financial pressure on established production studios, many of which depended on supplying programming to the networks as a steady source of revenue. Consequently, beginning with the 1995 merger of Disney with Capitol Cities/ABC, the owner of ABC-TV, several major production studios merged with television networks during the second half of the decade. In 1995, Warner Brothers, an established film production studio, formed the WB television network, and in 1996, Warner Brothers affiliated with the Turner Broadcast Network. In 1995, Paramount, another film production studio, also formed a major television network, UPN, and in 1999, CBS merged with Viacom, the parent company of Paramount, and with Blockbuster Video and the Simon & Schuster publishing house. These mergers shaped the growing 1990s trend of creating megacorporations that could control all aspects of the production and marketing of a creative idea, from its publication in book form to its adaptation as a movie to its release and distribution on video and its treatment as a made-for-television film or television series or miniseries.[11]

Although the hospital drama *ER* was the top-rated program for the 1995–96 season, overall situation comedies remained the most popular shows, led by *Seinfeld, Friends, Caroline in the City, The Single Guy, Home Improvement,* and *Boston Common. NFL Monday Night Football, 60 Minutes,* and the police drama *NYPD Blue* were also among the top 10. New programming also emphasized comedy. Notable comedy debuts included *Cybill,* starring Cybill Shepherd and Christine Baranski; *Mad About You,* with Helen Hunt and Paul Reiser; *The Single Guy,* starring Jonathan Silverman and Ernest Borgnine; *The Nanny,* featuring Fran Drescher; and *Caroline in the City,* starring Lea Thomson. Daytime television saw the continuing popularity of raucous audience-participation talk shows hosted by Ricki Lake, Jerry Springer, and others who sought to shock viewers with sensational topics, especially sexual infidelity and other forms of personal betrayal. On the *Jenny Jones* show one man was so humiliated when a male acquaintance unexpectedly confessed his secret love for him before a live television audience that he later killed his admirer. For the second year in a row, *Frasier* won the Emmy as outstanding comedy series (1994–95 season); *NYPD Blue* won as outstanding dramatic series.

The murder by a fan of the 23-year-old Mexican-American singer Selena distressed millions of fans fond of her Tejano blend of American and Hispanic influences. Also distressed were legions of followers of the rock band the Grateful Dead, who disbanded after the death of Jerry Garcia, its lead singer of 30 years. The Beastie Boys, Foo Fighters, Smashing Pumpkins, Red Hot Chili Peppers, and A Tribe Called Quest performed in the First Tibetan Freedom Concert, which Adam Yauch of the Beastie Boys organized in Los Angeles. The proceeds went to the Millareppa Foundation, committed to exposing human rights violations by the Chinese government in Tibet.

The singer Michael Jackson, who had previously been made to retract violent and arguably lewd gestures on an earlier video, publicly apologized after complaints that his newest album, *History of the Past, Present, and Future, Book I,* contained anti-Semitic lyrics. Nonetheless, the album was among the most popular of the year, along with Mariah Carey's *Daydream,* Natalie Merchant's *Tiger Lily,* Garth Brooks's *The Hits, Cracked Rear View* by Hootie & the Blowfish, and Smashing Pumpkins's *Melloncollie.* Fusion of different musical styles remained innovative and appealing, as such groups as US3 popularized acid jazz, a mixture of jazz and hip-hop styles, and vocalists such as Holly Cole and Cassandra Wilson won national audiences with jazz interpretations of popular songs. An accomplished lyricist with an appealing voice, Jewel (surnamed Kilcher) drew on both folk and pop traditions in her first album, *Pieces of You,* which sold some 10 million copies.

Trying to appeal to younger audiences, the Philadelphia Orchestra introduced "interactive concerts" in which audiences could e-mail requests at intermission for the second-half program. As did symphony orchestras, ballet groups suffered from severe financial pressures, and the world-acclaimed Joffrey Ballet Company moved from New York to Chicago to prevent bankruptcy. The innovative modern dance choreographer Twyla Tharp premiered her *Americans We,* featuring music by several 19th-century American composers, and Benjamin Britten introduced *How Near Heaven.*

All of the major professional sports except football, whose players had previously accepted a uniform salary cap across the league, contended with labor unrest in 1995. In April, professional baseball players terminated the strike that prematurely ended the 1994 season after a federal judge ordered owners to restore key elements of the expired collective bargaining agreement: free-agent bidding, salary arbitration, and an anticollusion provision. After a compressed spring training, the shortened season opened late but concluded successfully after only 144 games. Teams struggled to regain the loyalty of their fans, many of whom felt betrayed by the cancellation of the previous season and by what they perceived as unforgivably greedy behavior by both players and owners: millionaires quarreling with multimillionaires at the expense of fans who truly cared for the game. Nonetheless, fans throughout the country were enthusiastic when the Baltimore shortstop Cal Ripken, Jr., who was widely respected for his professionalism and serious work ethic, eclipsed Lou Gehrig's record of 2,130 consecutive games played. Before Ripken's achievement, the conventional wisdom had been that Gehrig's "iron man" record, set between 1925 and 1939, would never be broken.

The National League's Atlanta Braves won the World Series, defeating the Cleveland Indians in six games. Barry Larkin of the Cincinnati Reds and Mo Vaughn of the Boston Red Sox were the leagues' MVPs. The Cy Young Awards went to the Seattle Mariner Randy Johnson and Atlanta's Greg Maddux, who became the first pitcher in modern times to win consecutive earned-run-average (ERA) titles with performances below 1.80 earned runs per 9 innings pitched and the first pitcher ever to win four consecutive Cy Young Awards. Cleveland's Albert Belle led the major leagues with 50 home runs.

Two expansion teams, the Carolina Panthers and the Jacksonville Jaguars, joined the NFL in 1995; the Raiders returned to Oakland after playing in Los Angeles between 1982 and 1994; and before the season the Rams moved to Saint Louis, leaving Los Angeles without a professional football team for the first time since 1946. The Cleveland Browns outraged thousands of loyal fans when they announced their decision to move the franchise to Baltimore for the 1996 season. Dallas defeated Pittsburgh in Super Bowl XXX to claim the NFL championship (played in January 1996), and the Green Bay Packers' quarterback Bret Favre was named MVP. The Miami Dolphin quarterback Dan Marino broke Fran Tarkington's long-standing record for most career touchdowns. Marino also became the all-time leader in passes completed and yards gained. In the first season of the Bowl Alliance, which matches the two highest-ranked college teams in games that rotate among the major "bowls," the University of Nebraska won the Fiesta Bowl and recognition as the top college football team of the year. Eddie George of Ohio State won the Heisman Trophy.

Hockey's labor problems shortened the season by four months after the owners locked out the players.

The Miami Dolphin quarterback Dan Marino broke Fran Tarkenton's long-standing National Football League (NFL) record for most touchdowns thrown in a career. *(Photofest)*

The New Jersey Devils went on to win the NHL's Stanley Cup. Professional basketball ended a 79-day management lockout when the players' union agreed to a six-year contract. The lockout occurred during the off-season, but teams were prohibited from signing draft picks and making trades while it lasted. The agreement allowed the league to begin its season on time and play a full schedule of games. The Houston Rockets, led by the center Hakeem Olajuwon, became the lowest-seeded team ever to win the NBA championship when they defeated the Orlando Magics in a four-game sweep. The center David Robinson of the San Antonio Spurs was the league's MVP.

Pete Sampras and Steffi Graf won the singles events at the U.S. Tennis Open, and the United States won the international Davis Cup competition. Corey Pavin won the USGA Open in golf, and Thunder Gulch, ridden by Gary Stevens, won the Kentucky Derby. Steve Fossett, an American stockbroker, became the first person to cross the Pacific Ocean in a hot-air balloon. The downhill skier Picabo Street became an internationally known celebrity after winning five World Cup races, and the former heavyweight boxing champion Mike Tyson returned to the ring after serving two years in prison for sexual assault. He defeated the little known Peter McNeeley in just 89 seconds, provoking outcries of protest from fans who paid up to $1,500 per ticket to watch the match. Tyson received $25 million for the fight; McNeeley's purse was $700,000.

CHRONICLE OF EVENTS

January 1: A four-month cease-fire begins in Bosnia.

January 1: Austria, Sweden, and Finland are admitted to the European Union, raising the total of member states to 15.

January 3: The former defense secretary Dick Cheney announces that he will not seek the Republican nomination for president.

January 4: The Republicans Newt Gingrich of Georgia and Robert "Bob" Dole of Kansas formally assume their new positions as Speaker of the House and Senate majority leader; Henry Hyde of Illinois becomes chairman of the House Judiciary Committee, in which he will later oversee the impeachment of Clinton, and the archconservative Jesse Helms of North Carolina becomes chairman of the Senate Foreign Relations Committee. The Democrats Richard Gephardt of Missouri and Thomas Daschle of South Dakota are the House and Senate minority leaders.

January 4: Eighty-two Canadians are named to the Order of Canada, an honor bestowed on people who have made outstanding contributions to their field. Among the recipients are the former prime ministers Joe Clark and John Turner; the Nobel Prize–winning chemist Michael Smith; Ellen Fairclough, the first female Canadian cabinet member; and Arthur Gelber, a Toronto-based patron of the arts.

January 5: Clinton names Michael McCurry to replace Dee Dee Myers as White House press secretary.

January 7: Viktor Vorobyov, the commanding general of Russian troops suppressing the rebellion in Chechnya, is killed in Grozny.

January 9: Gingrich fires Christina Jeffrey, his appointee as House historian, after learning of remarks she had made eight years earlier criticizing a school history program for not including the Nazi point of view about the Holocaust or that of the Ku Klux Klan when discussing contemporary American race issues.

January 10: By a 99-0 vote, the Senate unanimously confirms Robert E. Rubin as secretary of the treasury.

January 11: The National Hockey League Players Association (NHLPA) saves the 1994–95 season by accepting the owners' final contract offer. The new agreement, reached 103 days after the owners locked out the players, makes the NHL the first major professional sports league to have unrestricted free agency without also imposing a salary cap.

January 12: Qubilah Bahiyah Shabazz, the daughter of the black nationalist leader Malcolm X, is arrested on federal charges of attempting to hire someone to kill Louis Farrakhan, a leader in the Nation of Islam.

January 12: Britain announces a partial troop withdrawal from Northern Ireland.

January 13: Eight gray wolves are reintroduced to Yellowstone National Park in Wyoming as part of a program to protect the endangered species.

January 17: An earthquake kills thousands and creates some 275,000 refuges in and around Kobe, Japan.

January 22: Suicide bombers kill 21 people and injure at least 60 more in the Israeli beach resort of Netanya.

January 24: Clinton delivers his State of the Union address, in which he promises a "new covenant" between a smaller and more efficient government and its citizens, who must assume greater civic responsibility.

January 26: Republicans in the House of Representatives fulfill the first promise of their Contract with America when they vote overwhelmingly to amend the Constitution to require a balanced federal budget every year, beginning in 2002.

January 27: The House majority leader, Dick Armey, provokes the criticism of gay-rights advocates after referring to Representative Barney Frank, one of three openly homosexual members of Congress, as "Barney Fag." Armey subsequently apologizes to Frank and maintains that he had accidentally mispronounced Frank's name.

January 30: A car bomb kills 42 people in an Algerian shopping center.

January 31: Clinton authorizes a $20 billion line of credit to help Mexico overcome its growing financial crisis.

February 1: For the first time since the Vietnam War, the United States and Vietnam establish liaison offices in their respective capitals.

February 3: NATO holds its first military exercises in the former East Germany.

February 3: Clinton proposes raising the minimum wage by 90 cents to $5.15 an hour.

February 3: The singer Barbra Streisand, an outspoken supporter of Clinton's, attacks Gingrich's efforts to cut funding for the arts in a speech at Harvard University's John F. Kennedy School of Government.

February 3: Dr. Henry Foster, an African-American physician and former medical school professor who is Clinton's nominee for surgeon general, stirs controversy when he informs reporters than he has performed abortions—fewer than 12 in 30 years of practice—primarily in cases involving rape, incest, or danger to the mother's life. His nomination is subsequently defeated.

February 6: For the first time since 1975, U.S. astronauts link up with Russian cosmonauts as the space shuttle *Discovery* docks with the *Mir* space station.

February 7: The rap artist Tupac Shakur is sentenced to a year and a half in prison for sexually abusing a woman in a New York hotel room in 1993.

February 7: Ramzi Ahmed Yousef, the alleged mastermind of the 1993 World Trade Center bombing, is arrested in Pakistan. He is extradited and flown to New York the next day. Yousef is also accused of complicity in the 1994 bombing of a Philippine Airlines flight en route to Japan and in an attempt to assassinate Pope John Paul II in January 1995.

February 8: The United Nations votes to send a force of 7,000 peacekeepers to Angola.

February 8: Clinton appoints the retired air force general Michael P. C. Carns to succeed R. James Woolsey as director of the CIA.

February 9: The former vice president Dan Quayle announces he will not seek the Republican nomination for president.

February 16: At the behest of Republican congressional leaders, Attorney General Janet Reno begins a preliminary criminal investigation into the business dealings of commerce secretary Ronald H. Brown.

February 17: Colin Ferguson, the gunman who killed eight people on a Long Island Railroad train in 1993, is sentenced to 200 years in prison.

February 17: Peru and Ecuador sign a cease-fire agreement after weeks of border skirmishes.

February 21: Mexico and the United States agree to a $20 billion aid package aimed at stabilizing Mexico's currency and enabling it to avoid defaulting on its debt.

February 22: A federal grand jury indicts the former interior secretary James Watt on charges of 25 counts of perjury and obstruction of justice related to influence peddling at the Department of Housing and Urban Development (HUD) during the 1980s, when Watt served under Reagan.

February 22: The American stockbroker Steve Fossett becomes the first person to cross the Pacific Ocean in a hot-air balloon.

February 23–24: Clinton makes his first state visit to Canada, where he meets with Prime Minister Jean Chretien and oversees the signing of an "open-skies" agreement reducing restrictions on air travel between the United States and Canada. Air Canada announces that it will introduce 20 new routes between the neighboring countries.

February 24: The Texas senator Phil Gramm declares his candidacy for the Republican presidential nomination.

February 26: China and the United States sign a pact resolving their trade dispute over copyright infringement.

February 28: The former secretary of education and governor of Tennessee Lamar Alexander announces he will run for the Republican nomination for president.

February 28: A federal grand jury indicts Neil Ainley, the former president of a small Arkansas bank, on five counts of violating federal banking law. The indictment stems from the independent prosecutor Kenneth Starr's investigation of the Whitewater affair.

March 2: The Republican attempt to pass a constitutional amendment requiring a balanced federal budget fails by one vote in the Senate.

March 8: First Lady Hillary Rodham Clinton announces that the United States will begin an international program for educating women.

March 8: The Republican senator Mark Hatfield of Oregon survives an attempt by younger, more conservative Republicans to strip him of his chairmanship of the Senate Appropriations Committee, in retaliation for his casting the deciding vote against the balanced budget amendment.

March 10: After the air force general Michael P. C. Carns withdraws from consideration for directorship of the CIA, Clinton nominates the deputy defense secretary, John Deutch. Deutch is confirmed on May 9.

March 17: Clinton meets with Gerry Adams, the leader of the political wing of the Provisional Irish Republican Army, and grants him permission to make unlimited trips to the United States for fund-raising purposes.

March 20–30: The predominantly Muslim army of the government of Bosnia violates a cease-fire that had been effect since January 1, when it launches an offensive against Bosnian Serb positions.

March 20: Eight people are killed and thousands harmed after terrorists release the deadly nerve gas Sarin in five subway trains in Tokyo, Japan.

March 21: Japanese police raid the headquarters of the religious sect Aum Shinrikyo (Supreme Truth), suspected in the gas attack on the Tokyo subway system.

March 22: The Russian cosmonaut Valeri Polyakov returns to Earth after a record-setting 438 days in outer space.

March 26: Seven of the 15 nations in the European Union eliminate their border controls; with the other states are expected to follow suit soon, except Britain, which insists on maintaining its borders.

March 27: Maryland enacts a ban on smoking in most workplaces.

March 31: The United States transfers peacekeeping responsibilities in Haiti to the United Nations.

April 2: Major league baseball's players' strike ends after 234 days.

April 7: House Republicans gather on the steps of the Capitol to celebrate the fulfillment of their Contract with America, most of whose provisions they passed within the first 100 days of the new session, as promised. Senate passage of many of the bills remains pending and, in some cases, problematic.

April 9: Alberto Fujimori is reelected president of Peru after winning 64 percent of the vote.

April 10: Dole announces his candidacy for the Republican nomination for president.

April 10: Russian soldiers destroy the Chechen farming village of Samashki and massacre scores of unarmed civilians.

April 10: A tough ban on smoking in public places takes effect in New York City.

April 13: Representative Robert Dornan of California enters the race for the Republican presidential nomination.

April 19: Senator Richard Lugar of Indiana announces his candidacy for the Republican presidential nomination.

April 19: A suspected gas attack injures 300 in Yokohama, Japan.

April 19: The United States suffers its worst act of domestic terrorism to date when the Alfred P. Murrah federal building is destroyed by a truck bomb in Oklahoma City, Oklahoma. The attack kills 149 adults, 19 children, and one unborn child; injures 500; and causes more than $600 million worth of damage.

April 20: One person dies in a bomb blast at the provincial legislature building in Charlottetown, Prince Edward Island, in Canada. Authorities wonder whether the attack was a "copycat" of the Oklahoma City bombing.

April 21: The FBI arrests Timothy McVeigh as its prime suspect in the Oklahoma City bombing and raids the home of his associates, Terry and James Nichols.

April 24: Gilbert Murray, the chief lobbyist for the California Forestry Association, is killed by a bomb attributed to the Unabomber.

April 30: Citing Iran's links to terrorist organizations and its aspirations to build nuclear weapons, Clinton imposes a total trade ban.

May 1: The four-month cease-fire ends in Bosnia at noon. Shortly thereafter, Bosnian Serb snipers kill two women walking home through the streets of Sarajevo. Croatian forces break through UN-patrolled cease-fire lines and capture a Serbian-held town 65 miles east of Zagreb, the capital of Croatia, forcing thousands of Bosnian Serb civilians to flee to Serbian-held cities in Bosnia.

May 1: Qubilah Shabazz, whose mother and others had previously accused Louis Farrakhan of complicity in Malcolm X's assassination in 1965, acknowledges her attempt to hire a hit man to assassinate Farrakhan. Her acknowledgment is part of a plea agreement in which she is placed on probation in exchange for forgoing a trial.

May 2: Bosnian Serb forces initiate a major assault on Zagreb.

May 3: In an effort to get tough on crime and defray the cost of incarceration, Alabama reinstates the practice of having prisoners perform labor while chained together in so-called chain gangs.

May 3: The former president George H. W. Bush, a lifetime member of the NRA, resigns to protest an organization fund-raising letter that compares federal agents to Nazis.

May 5: Speaking at Michigan State University commencement exercises, President Clinton criticizes militia groups who justify violence against government by maintaining that "government is a conspiracy to take your freedom away." In an article in the *Detroit Free Press* Clinton also criticizes the conservative talk-show host and convicted Watergate felon G. Gordon Liddy for advising listeners about how to shoot federal agents.

May 9: Bob Dole, the future Republican nominee for the presidency, angers many Arab Americans, wins support of some Jewish Americans, and provokes controversy in the United States and Middle East by proposing that the United States move its embassy in Israel from Tel Aviv to Jerusalem.

May 10: President Clinton arrives in Moscow to celebrate the 50th anniversary of Germany's surrender to Allied forces (VE day) and to conduct a summit meeting with President Yeltsin.

May 11: Representatives of 174 countries approve an indefinite extension of the Nuclear Nonproliferation Treaty.

May 16: Shoko Asahara, the leader of the Supreme Truth religious sect, is arrested in conjunction with the March gas attack on the Tokyo subway system.

May 16: Police in Washington, D.C., respond to a security threat by closing off traffic in front of the White House for several hours.

May 17: The Conservative Jacques Chirac is inaugurated president of France. He appoints Alain Juppe, a former foreign affairs minister, as premier.

May 17: By a vote of 96-3, the Senate approves a resolution creating a special committee to hold hearings into the president and first lady's conduct in the Whitewater affair.

May 17: The Senate Select Committee on Ethics announces that it has found "substantial credible evidence" supporting charges that Senator Bob Packwood of Oregon committed sexual harassment, obstruction of justice, and influence peddling. The committee's findings initiate a special triallike procedure to determine whether the Senate should censure or punish Packwood.

May 20: In response to a heightened terrorist alert, the two-block section of Pennsylvania Avenue in front of the White House is closed to vehicular traffic.

May 23: A Secret Service agent shoots and wounds 37-year-old Leland W. Modjeski after he leaps over a fence at the South Lawn of the White House and runs toward the presidential residence carrying an unloaded handgun. The Secret Service agent Scott Giambattista is wounded by the same bullet as he fights with Modjeski.

May 27: The actor Christopher Reeve, an accomplished horseman who is best known for his movie role as Superman, is paralyzed from the neck down after being thrown from his horse during a riding competition.

May 28–30: Bosnian Serbs seize more than 370 UN peacekeeping troops and military observers, including 34 British soldiers guarding the UN safe haven of Goražde. Borrowing a tactic employed by Saddam Hussein in 1990, the Bosnian Serbs chain 20 of the captured men to potential NATO bombing targets, where they serve as "human shields" to prevent retaliation.

May 31: Clinton offers NATO "temporary use" of U.S. ground forces in Bosnia.

May 31: Dole condemns the U.S. entertainment industry for promoting depraved music and films that distort children's values.

June 1: Austria's parliament votes to create a $50.5 million fund to compensate victims of the Nazis during World War II.

June 2: After UN condemnation and the establishment of the British–French Rapid Reaction Force, Bosnian Serb commanders release 126 of the UN hostages. While on a reconnaissance air patrol, U.S. Air Force captain Scott O'Grady is shot down over Serbian positions in northwest Bosnia.

June 7: Clinton issues the first veto of his presidency when he rejects congressional legislation to cut $16.4 billion from spending previously appropriated by Congress for the 1995 fiscal year. Congressional leaders acknowledge that they do not have sufficient votes to override the veto.

June 7: A federal grand jury indicts the Arkansas governor, Jim Guy Tucker, for conspiring to defraud the IRS and Small Business Administration in schemes involving cable-television firms. Tucker becomes the highest official yet to be indicted on charges stemming from the Whitewater investigation.

June 8: After Captain O'Grady, who had been presumed dead after being shot down over Bosnia, establishes radio contact, he is rescued by two American helicopter crews. Bosnian Serbs open fire as he is lifted to safety, but O'Grady escapes without injury and becomes a war hero back home.

June 11: Clinton and Gingrich appear together before a town meeting in Claremont, New Hampshire, during which they answer questions about Medicare, UN peacekeeping, and other matters of domestic and foreign policy.

June 14: Bosnian Serbs begin an eight-day siege of the Muslim safe haven of Zepa.

June 14: Chechen rebels take 2,000 hostages and demand that Russia withdraw its troops from Chechnya.

June 14: The Houston Rockets win the NBA championship for the second straight year.

June 15: Prosecutors in the O. J. Simpson trial are deeply embarrassed after Simpson, at their insistence, tries on one of the blood-stained gloves from the murder scene but cannot fit it on his hand.

June 20: Southern Baptists, the largest Protestant denomination in the United States, vote to repent formally the church's past support of slavery and to ask forgiveness from all blacks.

June 20: The President's Advisory Committee on Human Radiation Experiments reports that during the 1950s the federal government secretly collected tissue samples from human corpses to measure the effects of radioactive fallout from nuclear weapons tests.

June 21: The CIA accuses China of selling components for missile systems to Pakistan and Iran.

June 22: California governor Pete Wilson formally announces his candidacy for the Republican presidential nomination.

June 23: Disney's animated film *Pocahontas* opens in the United States.

June 25: Bosnian Serb artillery and sniper fire kills at least nine civilians, including four children, in Sarajevo.

June 26: President Hosni Mubarak of Egypt survives an assassination attempt in Ethiopia while en route to a summit meeting of the Organization of African Unity.

June 26: Representatives of more than 100 nations gather in San Francisco to celebrate the 50th anniversary of the UN Charter.

June 28: South Africa's president Nelson Mandela establishes the Truth and Reconciliation Commission to expose human rights violations committed during the period of apartheid.

June 29: A crowded five-story department store collapses in Seoul, South Korea, killing more than 60 and injuring more than 850. Poor construction practices and poor government oversight are blamed.

June 29: The U.S. space shuttle *Atlantis* docks with the Russian space station *Mir.*

July: Amazon.com becomes an immediate hit when it opens the first large-scale online bookstore.

July 9: Pete Sampras defeats Boris Becker in four sets to win his third consecutive Wimbledon tennis championship.

July 11: Bosnian Serbs capture Srebrenica, a Muslin enclave that had been designated as a safe haven by the United Nations. Some 20,000 refugees and 400 Dutch peacekeeping troops flee, but Bosnian Serbs seize thousands of men and boys, many of whom are later executed in the name of ethnic cleansing.

July 11: President Yeltsin of Russia is hospitalized for heart problems.

July 13: Clinton accepts the recommendations of the Defense Base Closure and Realignment Commission to close 79 military bases throughout the nation and to consolidate 26 others. The commission calculates that 43,742 military and civilian jobs will be lost, along with another 49,823 civilian jobs dependent on the bases.

July 14: The FBI deputy director, Larry Potts, is demoted because of his role in the 1992 standoff in Ruby Ridge, Idaho, where one federal agent and the wife and son of a fugitive, Randy Weaver, were killed in gunfire that resulted from AFT and FBI efforts to arrest Weaver.

July 19–August 1: The House Judiciary Committee and the House Committee on Government Reform and Oversight hold joint hearings into the 1993 federal raid on the Branch Davidian compound in Waco, Texas.

July 21: NFL owners approve the Los Angeles Raiders' proposal to move back to Oakland, where the franchise originated.

July 21: Monica Seles plays her first public tennis match since she was stabbed on the court in Hamburg, Germany, in 1993. In an exhibition matched promoted as the "Return of the Champions," Seles defeats the retired star Martina Navratilova 6-3, 6-2.

July 24: Bosnian Serbs overrun the Muslim safe haven of Zepa. After some 7,000 Muslims are permitted to evacuate under UN escort, the soldiers loot the city and burn it down.

July 27: The death toll from a heat wave in Chicago reaches 529.

July 27: Clinton dedicates the Korean War Memorial on the Mall in Washington, D.C., three years after ground was broken on the project in June 1992.

July 28: Croatia introduces a massive counteroffensive as its army crosses into Bosnia, unites with Bosnian Croats and Muslims, and drives Bosnian Serb forces from areas they had occupied.

July 28: The Senate votes 98-0 to bar senators and their staffs from accepting vacations, expensive meals, or other substantial gifts from anyone other than close friends and relatives. The ban does not extend to any other branch of government and therefore does not require approval of the House or president.

July 28: Twenty-three-year-old Susan Smith is sentenced to life in prison for drowning her two sons while she was allegedly suffering from deep depression and emotional damage caused by abuse she had suffered in the past.

July 30: Russian and Chechen leaders sign an agreement intended to end the fighting in the breakaway republic of Chechnya.

August 2: Israeli settlers, angered by Rabin's plan to transfer authority over the West Bank to the Palestinian National Authority, clash with Israeli police during protest rallies.

August 3: The British Antarctic Survey confirms the continuing depletion of the ozone layer over Antarctica, where measurements show values less than 40 percent of those recorded in the 1960s, when the observations were first made.

August 5: Combined Croatian and Bosnian Muslim forces hand Bosnian Serbian troops their first major defeat as they drive the Serbs from Knin, the capital of the Serbian-held region of Krajina in Croatia. Tens of thousands of Croatian Serbs flee as refugees; hundreds of others are killed.

August 5: In a ceremony in Hanoi, Secretary of State Warren Christopher officially restores diplomatic relations with Vietnam.

August 6: Sixty thousand people gather in Peace Park in Hiroshima, Japan, where they observe a minute of silence to commemorate the 50th anniversary of the atomic bombing of the city at the end of World War II.

August 7: Yeltsin returns to work.

August 8: Two of Saddam Hussein's daughters and their husbands, both generals in Iraq's army, flee to Jordan.

August 8: Abdullah Al-Amin, the 1960s black radical then known as H. Rap Brown, pleads not guilty to weapons possession and assault charges related to a July shooting.

August 10: Senate and House committees conclude their hearings into the Whitewater affair without finding conclusive evidence of wrongdoing.

August 10: Clinton enacts FDA regulations intended to restrict the advertising and sale of tobacco products to children.

August 11: On the 50th anniversary of the atomic bombing of Nagasaki, Clinton announces that the United States, as will Great Britain, will renounce all nuclear testing, even tests of safety procedures that had been permitted by existing treaties.

August 15: Timothy McVeigh and Terry Nichols plead not guilty of bombing the Oklahoma City federal building.

August 17: A federal grand jury indicts James McDougal and Susan McDougal, the Clintons' business partners in the Whitewater investment scheme, on charges of bank fraud and conspiracy.

August 26: Dole announces that he has returned a campaign contribution from the Log Cabin Republicans, an organization of homosexual Republicans with whose political goals Dole disagrees.

August 28: In retaliation for an attack that kills 37 civilians in Sarajevo, NATO planes bomb Bosnian Serb positions around the city, and NATO issues an ultimatum demanding the withdrawal of Bosnian Serb heavy weapons.

August 28: The fashion designer Calvin Klein cancels a controversial advertising campaign featuring young models in sexually provocative poses after critics across the country's political spectrum charge that it sexually exploits children.

September 3: The NFL opens its season with the debut of two expansion teams, the Carolina Panthers and the Jacksonville Jaguars, both of whom lose their opening game.

September 4: Clinton defends affirmative action and legal immigration, which have been attacked by some Republican candidates.

September 5: Defying international protests, France tests a nuclear bomb beneath Mururoa Atoll, a coral island southeast of Tahiti, in the Pacific Ocean.

September 6: The Baltimore Oriole shortstop Cal Ripken, Jr., appears in his 2,131st consecutive major league game, breaking the New York Yankee first

The All-Star Baltimore Oriole infielder Cal Ripken, Jr., won widespread respect for his work ethic when he broke Lou Gehrig's record for consecutive games played. *(Photofest)*

baseman Lou Gehrig's record for consecutive games played. Clinton, Gore, and the retired Yankee outfielder Joe DiMaggio attend the sellout event at Oriole Park in Camden Yards, Maryland.

September 7: Bob Packwood resigns from the Senate after the Senate Ethics Committee votes unanimously to recommend his expulsion for sexual misconduct, influence peddling, and obstruction of the committee's investigation of the charges against him.

September 8: Foreign ministers of Serbia, Croatia, and Bosnia, meeting in Geneva with the U.S. assistant secretary of state Richard Holbrooke, agree in principle to allow Bosnia to remain a sovereign independent nation but to divide it into a Serbian republic and a predominantly Muslim and Croat federation.

September 12: The French army officially pardons Captain Alfred Dreyfus, a Jewish officer wrongly convicted of high treason more than 100 years earlier.

September 19: At the behest of the attorney general and the FBI, the *Washington Post* and the *New York Times* publish a lengthy manifesto by the Unabomber condemning industrialized society, in the hope that the terrorist will honor his pledge to stop targeting people if the essay is printed.

September 20: Under pressure from Milošević and in compliance with a NATO ultimatum, Bosnian Serbs begin removing heavy weapons from around Sarajevo.

September 20: Tanzu Ciller, Turkey's first female prime minister, who was elected in June 1993, resigns.

September 22: Showgirls, a movie about Las Vegas strippers, opens nationwide. It is the first big-budget film by a major studio to be released with a restrictive NC-17 rating.

September 28: Rabin and Arafat sign an accord giving a large degree of self-determination to Palestinians on the West Bank. The agreement is condemned by militant Jewish settlers and militant Palestinians.

September 29: Pete Wilson withdraws from the race for the Republican presidential nomination.

September 29: The CIA announces that director John Deutch has fired two agents and reprimanded eight others for mishandling covert operations in Guatemala in the early 1990s.

October 1: Sheik Omar Abdel Rahman is convicted of 48 charges of conspiring to wage a "war of urban terrorism" against the United States. He is sentenced to life in prison on January 17, 1996.

October 2: The Supreme Court opens its 1995–96 term.

October 3: A jury of 10 women and two men acquits O. J. Simpson of charges that he murdered his wife, Nicole Brown Simpson, and her friend Ronald Goldman.

October 4: Pope John Paul II arrives in Newark, New Jersey, to begin a five-day visit to the eastern United States.

October 5: Secretary of State Richard Holbrooke negotiates a 60-day cease-fire in Bosnia, although fighting remains intense near some Bosnian Serb–held strongholds.

October 9: An earthquake kills more than 60 people in west-central Mexico.

October 15: Iraqi voters almost unanimously reelect Saddam Hussein to another seven-year term.

October 16: Louis Farrakhan leads some 400,000 black men on his Million Man March on Washington, D.C.

October 17: A bomb on a Paris underground train injures 26 people.

October 23: A Houston jury convicts Yolanda Saldivar, the founder and former president of Selina Quantanilla Perez's fan club, of the murder of the Mexican-American singer.

October 24: A total eclipse of the Sun is visible from India to Vietnam.

October 26: For the second time since July, Yeltsin is rushed to the hospital for severe health problems.

October 30: Voters in Quebec vote by a narrow margin to maintain their federation with the rest of Canada.

October 30: Claiming that he will not allow drug peddlers to lower the cost of doing business, Clinton signs into law a bill maintaining stiffer penalties for offenses involving crack cocaine than for those involving powdered cocaine. The law had been criticized for inflicting more severe punishment on poorer cocaine users, who were more likely to use inexpensive, highly addictive crack, than on more affluent users more likely to use the drug in its powdered form.

November 1: Talks for ending the war in Bosnia begin in Dayton, Ohio.

November 3: The professional basketball season opens.

November 4: While addressing a peace rally in Tel Aviv, Rabin is assassinated by a Jewish student opposed to concessions Rabin made to the Palestinian National Authority.

November 6: The Cleveland Browns football team announces its intention to move to Baltimore, effective beginning in the 1996 season. The team is renamed the Baltimore Ravens.

November 8: Colin Powell announces that he will not run for the presidency in 1996.

November 11: Defying international protest, the military rulers of Nigeria execute the dissident writer Ken Saro-Wiwa and eight other critics who have condemned the regime's exploitation of the nation's oil reserves and its record of environmental degradation.

November 11: The newest James Bond thriller, *Goldeneye,* starring Pierce Brosnan, opens at Radio City Music Hall in New York.

November 13: Claiming that they contain extreme proposals that would imperil the environment and funding for education and public health, Clinton vetoes two stopgap budget bills that would have enabled the federal government to pay its immediate debts and remain in operation.

November 15: According to the Starr report, Clinton begins his sexual relationship with the 23-year-old Monica Lewinsky, who had begun a White House internship in July. The affair lasts through March 1997.

November 15: Shimon Peres is sworn in as Israel's new prime minister.

November 21: The presidents of Bosnia, Croatia, and Serbia culminate 21 days of meetings at the Wright-Patterson Air Force Base in Dayton, Ohio, by initialing the Dayton peace accord.

November 24: The former Italian premier Silvio Berlusconi stands trial with four associates on charges of embezzlement and false accounting.

November 27: Gingrich announces that he will not run for president in 1996.

November 28: To combat the spread of mad cow disease to humans, Britain bans the sale of meat from the backbone of cattle.

November 28: Russia agrees to place its peacekeeping forces in Bosnia under U.S. command.

December 1: A $243.3 billion defense appropriations bill becomes law without Clinton's signature.

December 1: Twelve people, including former and current army officers, are arrested in connection with the 1994 bombing of a Jewish community center in Buenos Aires, Argentina.

December 3: South Korea's former president Chun Doo Hwan is arrested for staging the coup that put him in power in 1989.

December 6: Clinton vetoes a massive budget reconciliation bill designed to balance the federal budget by 2002 because, he maintains, it cuts programs for students, the poor, and the elderly; increases taxes for working families; and undermines various environmental regulations.

December 6: The House Ethics Committee votes unanimously to appoint a special counsel to investigate charges that Gingrich violated tax laws while teaching a college history course in Georgia.

December 7: The *Galileo* space probe enters orbit around Jupiter and sends an observation capsule into its surface. The capsule, filled with recording instruments, transmits data about the planet's chemical characteristics, temperature, and density before burning up.

December 8: Russian and Chechen leaders sign an agreement granting Chechnya greater autonomy within the Russian Federation and amnesty for rebel fighters in exchange for their agreement to stop fighting and surrender their weapons.

December 12: Israel hands over Nablus, the most important West Bank town, to the Palestinian National Authority.

December 14: All of the warring factions in Bosnia sign the Dayton peace accord, which calls for an end to the fighting and for the introduction of 60,000 UN peacekeepers, including 20,000 Americans.

December 15: The EU designates *euro* as the name of its new currency.

December 18: The Dow-Jones industrial average falls by 100 points, its greatest single-day loss in more than four years.

December 18: Delayed for three days by fog, the first contingent of American peacekeepers arrives in Bosnia.

December 20: After acrimonious public feuding between Britain's prince Charles and his wife, Princess Diana, Queen Elizabeth II issues a statement urging them to divorce.

December 21: An American Airlines plane flying from Miami to Cali, Colombia, crashes into a mountain, killing 147. Seventeen people survive.

December 23: The bodies of 16 members of the Solar Temple cult are discovered on an Alpine hillside in France. In October 1994, 53 members died under mysterious circumstances in Switzerland.

December 28: Clinton vetoes a defense authorization bill that would have required development of a missile-defense system and limited his ability to deploy U.S. troops throughout the world.

December 31: The Senate rejects a measure approved by the House that would have allowed federal workers furloughed since December 16 to return to work.

EYEWITNESS TESTIMONY

We of the Kennedy and Johnson administrations who participated in the decisions on Vietnam acted according to what we thought were the principles and traditions of this nation. We made our decisions in light of those values.

Yet we were wrong, terribly wrong. We owe it to future generations to explain why.

Former secretary of defense Robert S. McNamara admitting in 1995 to grave policy mistakes made in the 1960s concerning the Vietnam War, in the preface to his book In Retrospect: The Tragedy and Lessons of Vietnam *(1995), p. xx.*

"X" is over. Kurt Cobain's in heaven, *Slackers* is at Blockbuster, and the media refers to anyone aged 13 to 30 as Xers. Which only proves that marketers and advertisers never understood that X is not a chronological age, but a way of looking at the world.

Douglas Coupland, author of the novel Generation X *(1991), lamenting in 1995 the media coverage of Generation X, in Jon Steel,* Truth, Lies, and Advertising *(1998), p. 87.*

If you are not a philosophically committed conservative it might be difficult to understand the fear of Washington that is a key part of the conservative experience. Since 1932 conservatives have been struggling with an increasingly liberal Democratic Party. Most conservatives are driven by a distrust both of government and of ideas that undermine what they know to be American values. For most of the more than sixty years since Franklin Delano Roosevelt came to power they have felt their ideas and way of life to be under increasing pressure. . . .

Therefore, in January 1995, when we were all sworn in, to be accommodating to our political opponents was simply not a possibility. Our freshman class was a group of idealists who were really outraged by the Clinton tax increase, by Clinton's proposal for nationalized health care, and by the Democrats' whole package of liberal social policies in welfare, quotas, set-asides, and so on. As for the leadership, we were bonded together by the experience of drawing up the Contract With America and our mutual pledge to do everything in our power to see that it passed. We were riding the tide of history. How could we engage in the same kind of betrayal we had once so bitterly condemned in other Republicans?

In retrospect I still think we were right to follow the path of no compromise, but we should have realized and prepared ourselves for the consequence of doing so.

Former House speaker Newt Gingrich describing the political position of newly elected Republican members of Congress after he officially became Speaker of the House on January 4, 1995, in Gingrich, Lessons Learned the Hard Way *(1998), pp. 67–69.*

The ascension of Newt Gingrich to the position of Speaker meant that I had no legislative responsibility at all. He cared not a whit what bills I wanted to pass. There was no communication from the Speaker's office to the Democratic caucus—we were actually passing notes around to find out things like: What time are we going to start tomorrow? I don't think the Democratic leader, Dick Gephardt, was ever invited to Gingrich's office. The Republicans were on such a high, they were having nosebleeds. There was no support from the Democratic Party. Our members had not yet learned to work together, each thinking they'd all cut their own deals with the new guy. Even the moderate Republicans were playing "get along, go along"—fearful they could lose their positions in the House. They didn't fear Gingrich as much as the power of the new hard-liners that were elected in 1994.

Former Democratic congresswoman Pat Schroeder of Colorado commenting on changes in the House of Representatives after Newt Gingrich became Speaker of the House on January 4, 1995, in Schroeder, 25 Years of House Work . . . and the Place Is Still a Mess *(1998), pp. 211–213.*

God knows what [Chung] could have gotten my mother to say.

President Bill Clinton responding on January 5, 1995, to a claim made by Speaker of the House Newt Gingrich's mother, Kathleen Gingrich, during a television interview with the newscaster Connie Chung on January 4, 1995, that her son called First Lady Hillary Rodham Clinton "a bitch," in Thomas E. Hitchings, ed., Facts On File Yearbook 1995 *(1996), p. 3.*

I would like to share with you a deep concern I have about our country.

I am not concerned that a different political party now controls Congress. Voters have sent strong messages of dissatisfaction in mid-term elections for decades. What concerns me is the mean spirit in the message of the victors.

You know the types, critical of everything, impossible to please, incapable of compromise. They rule by fear and ridicule. Some come close to urging armed rebellion to "rescue" our country from the "enemy within."

Newt Gingrich, Jesse Helms, Strom Thurmond and others preach mistrust of our government. Soon they will be making policy decisions. I fear that unsophisticated and less tolerant people will see this hatred of government as a green light to cause serious trouble.

One of those angry and misguided citizens is John Trochmann, a white supremacist and founder of the new Militia of Montana. In a thinly veiled warning, he recently stated that "we don't want to go to the cartridge box [to take back our country]; but we will if we have to." . . .

What really concerns me is that these misguided extremists believe our newly elected leaders approve of their twisted views, and that these extremists will now encourage other angry citizens to take matters into their own hands.

We recently established a Militia Task Force to monitor this growing armed citizen movement.

On a broader scale, we saw an increasing number of hate crimes committed in 1994 by ordinary citizens unconnected with hate groups. Radio talk show hosts, who promoted Newt Gingrich and his friends, daily spew out intolerance of anyone or anything unlike themselves.

I believe this is motivating angry people to vent their hostilities through rudeness and even violence.

A letter dated January 9, 1995, from Morris Dees, chief trial counsel for the Southern Poverty Law Center, to the organization's supporters, in Dees, Gathering Storm: America's Militias *(1996), pp. 128–129.*

The subject of my talk is the artist as citizen. I guess I can call myself an artist. . . . But I am, first and foremost, a citizen: a tax-paying, voting, concerned American citizen who happens to have opinions—a lot of them—which seems to bother some people. . . .

When I was asked to speak here a year ago, I was much more optimistic. We had seven women in the Senate, bringing the hope of full representation for more than half the population. And, we had a President who judged our ethnic, cultural and artistic diversity as a source of strength rather than weakness.

Then came the election of 1994, and suddenly the progress of the recent past seemed threatened by those who hunger for the "good old days" when women and minorities knew their place. In this resurgent reactionary mood, artists derided as the "cultural elite" are convenient objects of scorn; and those institutions which have given Americans access to artistic works—such as the National Endowment for the Arts and the Corporation for Public Broadcasting—are in danger of being abolished. . . .

William Bennett, in calling recently for the elimination of the Arts agencies, charged that they were corrupt for supporting artists whose work undermines "mainstream American values." Well, art does not exist only to entertain—but also to challenge one to think, to provoke, even to disturb, in a constant search for the truth. To deny artists, or any of us, for that matter, free expression and free thought—or

The singer Barbra Streisand spoke out strongly for freedom of artistic expression. *(Photofest)*

worse, to force us to conform to some rigid notion of "mainstream American values"—is to weaken the very foundation of our democracy.

Actress/singer Barbra Streisand defending the arts and artists on February 3, 1995, at Harvard University's Kennedy School of Government. Available online. URL: http://www.artsusa.org/common/contenta.asp?id=433.

Madonna is usually at her best when drawing from a radical urban gay subculture that still has few allies in the mainstream. The queerness and blackness she embraces and the womanhood she embodies puts a twist on the banality of mass popularity and makes it political. . . . even her failures are more fascinating than some of her peers' successes.

Music critic Barry Walters writing about the career of the singer/performer Madonna in "The Ten That Mattered Most: 1985–1995," Spin, April 1995, p. 48.

With a deafening roar, a red-orange fireball lit the sky as the payload tore upward at more than 7,000 miles per hour, ripping a huge crater from the ground to the roof. The blast hurled people through the air, crushing them under falling walls and ceilings as the gouged north face came down in a gigantic cascade of concrete, steel, and shattered glass. . . .

Hundreds of men, women, and children were caught in the vacuum-vortex of the explosion inside the Murrah Building. In less than a second, concrete, glass, steel, dust, and gas fumes mixed with mangled bodies, burned flesh, and severed limbs. . . . Fifty people were instantly killed between the eighth and six floors. . . . twenty people were immediately killed between the fifth and fourth floors. One man, who had a desk facing the north windows, was ripped apart by the glass blizzard. A forty-year-old single mother was crushed to death beneath a huge concrete girder. . . .

The second floor took the full force of the explosion. The blast hit most of the youngsters in the face, blowing them backward, instantly killing fifteen children and their three teachers. One toddler had his brain blown out of his head. . . . The infants resting in their cribs never had a chance. Their human remains, tiny arms and legs, were found a block away.

Another eighteen workers instantly died on the first floor. Twenty-four bystanders were also killed.

They included a sixty-one-year-old milk truck driver who had gone to the Murrah Building to sign up for his retirement pension, his fifty-six-year-old wife, and their four-year-old granddaughter.

Author Mark S. Hamm describing in 1997 the carnage created by the truck bomb that destroyed the Alfred P. Murrah federal building in Oklahoma City, Oklahoma, on April 19, 1995, in James Haley, ed., Post–Cold War America: 1992–Present (2003), pp. 75–77.

The shock of what the rescuers found in the rubble had long since worn off, replaced with a loathing for the people who had planted the bombs that killed their friends, neighbors and children.

One by one they said the same thing: this does not happen here. It happens in countries so far away, so different, they might as well be on the dark side of the moon. It happens in New York. It happens in Europe.

It does not happen in a place where, debarking at the airport, passengers see a woman holding a sign that welcomes them to the Lieutenant Governor's annual turkey shoot. . . .

"We're just a little old cowtown," said Bill Finn, a grime-covered firefighter. . . . "You can't get no more Middle America than Oklahoma City."

Journalist Rick Bragg describing the reaction of Oklahoma City residents to the bombing of the Alfred P. Murrah federal building, on April 19, 1995, in Bragg, "In Shock, Loathing, Denial: This Doesn't Happen Here," New York Times, April 20, 1995, p. 1.

Why does a God of love and mercy that we read about and hear about allow such terrible things [as the recent Oklahoma City bombing] to happen?

Over 3,000 years ago, there was a man named Job who struggled with the same question. He asked why because he was a good man and yet disaster struck him suddenly and swiftly. . . . His wife and friends said: Curse God and die. And in the midst of his suffering he asked this question: Why? . . .

What are some of the lessons we can learn from what has happened? First, there's a mystery to it. I've been asked why God allows it. I don't know. I can't give a direct answer. I have to confess that I have never fully understood even for my own satisfaction. I have to accept by faith that God is a God of love and mercy and compassion even in the midst of suffering. . . .

The Bible says God is not the author of evil, and it speaks of evil in First Thessalonians as a mystery. There's something about evil we will never fully understand this side of eternity. But the Bible . . . tells us that there is a devil, that Satan is very real and he has great power. It also tells us that evil is real and that the human heart is capable of almost limitless evil when it is cut off from God and from the moral law.

> *The Reverend Billy Graham discussing the nature of evil in a sermon delivered on April 25, 1995, six days after the Oklahoma City bombing, in Robert Torricelli and Andrew Carroll, eds.,* In Our Own Words *(1999), pp. 413–415.*

Your broadside against federal agents deeply offends my own sense of decency and honor, and it offends my concept of service to this country.

> *Former president George H. W. Bush submitting his resignation from the National Rifle Association (NRA) on May 3, 1995, in a letter to the NRA president, Thomas Washington, in Thomas E. Hitchings, ed.,* Facts On File Yearbook 1995 *(1996), p. 358.*

If the feds act like thugs, we're going to call them thugs.

> *Walter La Pierre, executive vice president of the NRA, on May 21, 1995, referring to former president George H. W. Bush's public resignation after an NRA fundraising letter called federal agents "jackbooted government thugs" in "Nazi bucket helmets," in Clifton Daniel, ed.,* 20th Century Day by Day *(2000), p. 1,418.*

We apologize to all African-Americans for condoning and/or perpetuating individual and systematic racism in our lifetime. . . . We ask for forgiveness from our African-American brothers and sisters, acknowledging that our own healing is at stake.

> *Text from a resolution passed by the Southern Baptist Convention on June 20, 1995, repenting the church's past support of slavery and other racist practices, in Thomas E. Hitchings, ed.,* Facts On File Yearbook 1995 *(1996), p. 450.*

If we wished to return to the ratio of police officers to violent crimes which gave many of us peace and security in the 1960s, we would have to add not 100,000 new police officers [as proposed by President Clinton] but about *five million.* . . .

People hire police officers because they are afraid—afraid of violence. Their fear is occasionally a source of puzzlement and mild disdain in the press, which cannot understand why so many Americans say that crime is the nation's most urgent problem and their own greatest fear. . . .

Our greatest fear is of violence from a nameless, faceless stranger. Officials have always reassured citizens by stating that the great majority of murders . . . are committed by a relative or an acquaintance of the victim's; a 1993 Department of Justice report said the figure for 1988 was eight out of ten.

Unfortunately, the report described only murders in which the killer was known to prosecutors and an arrest was made. It did not mention that more and more killers remain unknown and at liberty after a full police investigation; every year the police make arrests in a smaller proportion of murder cases. In our largest cities the police now make arrests in fewer than three out of five murder cases. In other words, two out of every five killers are completely untouched by the law. . . .

The missing killers are almost certainly not family members, friends, or neighbors. Rather, they are overwhelmingly strangers to their victims, and their acts are called "stranger murders." . . .

Attacks across racial lines are a special case of crimes by strangers. Most crimes, including 80 percent of violent crimes, are committed by persons of the same race as their victims.

> *Author Adam Walinsky discussing trends in violent crimes in America in Walinsky, "The Crisis of Public Order,"* Atlantic, *July 1995, pp. 40, 46–47.*

I had only ever seen him on TV and I never thought of him as attractive. With his big red nose and coarse, wiry-looking gray hair he's an old guy. There were tons and tons of women in the White House with crushes on him and I thought, "These people are just crazy. They have really bad taste in men." I mean, girls my own age were saying that this old guy was cute, that he was sexy. I thought, "Gee, this place is weird. What's wrong with Washington?" . . .

I remember being very taken aback [the first time I saw him]. My heart skipped a beat, my breathing came a little faster and there were butterflies fluttering in my tummy. He had a glow about him that was magnetic. He exudes a sexual energy. I thought to myself: "Now I see what all the girls are talking about."

Monica Lewinsky describing the first time she saw Bill Clinton live, at a ceremony on the White House lawn in July 1995, in Andrew Morton, Monica's Story *(1999), p. 57.*

1,952 Bulldogs and one bitch.

A slogan printed on T-shirts by resentful classmates after the enrollment of Shannon Faulkner on August 14, 1995, at the previously all-male Citadel military academy in Charleston, South Carolina, in Lois Gordon and Alan Gordon, American Chronicle *(1991), p. 905.*

In short, it feels to me that his [the Unabomber's] appeal to nature is entirely utilitarian . . . rather than a heartfelt passion, of which he seems to have very few in any case. But if nature does not inspire his vision of the future, it is hard to tell what does. Presumably he would want, as a self-described anarchist, some kind of world where "people live and work as individuals and small groups," using "small scale technology . . . that can be used by small-scale communities without outside assistance." But he nowhere bothers to hint at how this future society would operate (other than to say it would burn all technical books), nor does he refer to any in the long line of anarcho-communal writers . . . who have given a great deal of thought to the configurations of just such a society.

It's true that the Unabomber offers the defense at one point that "a new kind of society cannot be designed on paper" and when revolutionaries or utopians set up a new kind of society, "it never works

Snubbed by fellow cadets, Shannon Faulkner received death threats and hate mail when she became the first woman ever to enroll at the Citadel military academy. *(AP/Wide World Photos)*

out as planned." That gives him leeway to avoid discussing what kind of world he wants . . . unfortunately, it also leaves a gaping hole in his treatise. Even those who agree that the industrial system should be torn down will want to get some idea of what is supposed to replace it before they are moved to endorse the cause, much less become the revolutionaries the Unabomber wants.

Political commentator Kirkpatrick Sale analyzing the arguments in the treatise published by the so-called Unabomber, Theodore Kaczynski, on September 19, 1995, in James Haley, ed., Post–Cold War America: 1992–Present (2003), pp. 105–106.

If you are given anything less than a complete, sensible, and satisfactory response, satisfying you beyond a reasonable doubt to these fifteen questions . . . you would have to find Mr. Simpson not guilty. . . .

One. Why . . . did the blood show up on the sock almost two months after a careful search for evidence? . . . And why . . . was the blood applied when there was no foot in it? . . .

Three. Why was the glove still moist when [Detective Mark] Fuhrman found it if Mr. Simpson had dropped it seven hours earlier? . . .

Four. If Mark Fuhrman . . . speaks so openly about his intense genocidal racism to a relative stranger . . . how many of his coworkers, the other detectives in this case, were also aware that he lied when he denied using the N-word yet failed to come forward? . . .

Seven. For what purpose was [the detective Philip] Vannatter carrying Mr. Simpson's blood in his pocket for three hours and a distance of twenty-five miles instead of booking it down the hall at Parker Center?

Eight. Why did Deputy District Attorney Hank Goldberg, in a desperate effort to cover up for the missing 1.5 millimeters of Mr. Simpson's blood, secretly go out to the home of police nurse Thano Peratis without notice to the defense and get him to contradict his previous sworn testimony at both the grand jury and the preliminary hearing? . . .

Eleven. Why, following a bitter struggle allegedly with Mr. Goldman, were there no bruises or marks on O. J. Simpson's body?

Twelve. Why do bloodstains with the most DNA not show up until weeks after the murder?

Thirteen. Why did Mark Fuhrman lie to us?

Fourteen. Why did Phil Vannatter lie to us?

And finally, fifteen. . . . How come the gloves just don't fit?

Johnny Cochran, defense attorney for O. J. Simpson, summarizing the main points in Simpson's murder defense in his closing argument on September 28, 1995, in Robert Torricelli and Andrew Carroll, eds., In Our Own Words *(1999), pp. 420–422.*

It wasn't a matter of favoritism. It was a matter of evidence.

Juror Brenda Moran explaining on October 4, 1995, why the jury acquitted O. J. Simpson on October 3, 1995, in Timothy Egan, "With Spotlight Shifted to Them, Some Simpson Jurors Talk Freely," New York Times, *October 5, 1995, p. 1.*

I am a middle-class 62 year old white woman. I found myself glued to the trial on TV. I watched almost every minute of it. I was shocked at the things being said in the media coverage. Obviously, they weren't watching the actual trial. I believe the police decided—the media decided—and so many people like sheep followed and decided that he [Simpson] must be the one who did it . . . obviously, as I said, they didn't watch the trial! The glove really didn't fit! The evidence was tainted—I believe tampered with by the police who had decided he did it and they weren't going to take a chance he would get off. Incidentally, it was proven in the next couple years that they did just that in other cases—One man was freed because of it and the LA Police were under investigation for planting evidence etc. One of the foremost Forensic men in the country testified and explained that the sock with the blood had had the blood poured on it—it wasn't as the prosecution tried to portray it. . . . I believe that the killers thought they were killing Fay Ressnik (who had been staying there until the day before) who owed some big time money for drugs, with no means to pay. I believe she was to be killed to send a message to others that you don't get by with that. Fay Ressnik had talked to Nicole on the phone that day—I think she had heard something and knew there may be some trouble and she warned Nicole . . . explaining why Nicole, in a well kept kitchen, had a large knife laying out on the counter top. Ron Goldman simply turned out to be in the wrong place at the wrong time. To me, anyone who really watched the trial would have come to the same conclusion—not guilty!

An independent contractor and Internet commentator who has the screen name yiab *describing her reactions to the acquittal of O. J. Simpson on October 3, 1995, in yiab, "O. J. Simpson Not Guilty," June 21, 2004. Available online. URL: http://boards.biography.com/ threadedout.jsp?forum=30035&thread=300004292.*

Outside the courtroom, pandemonium reigned. Blacks, dressed in African liberation colors and brandishing banners professing Simpson's innocence, were shouting for joy, raising their fists in victory, and dancing in the streets. Whites, standing symbolically on the other side of the barricades, seemed shocked and bewildered at first, then frustrated and angry, women crying and hugging each other to seek solace from their pain at this miscarriage of justice. . . .

This time, the congregants at Rev. Murray's church were celebrating the verdict, clapping their hands and singing "Hallelujah!" On Potrero Hill, O. J.'s old friends and neighbors were jumping up and down, yelling that their homeboy had been vindicated. Black law students at Howard University in Washington, D.C., were overjoyed, loudly proclaiming that the system had finally worked for a black man. . . .

Whites all over the nation initially responded . . . with shock, anger, and outrage. Scenes of whites in corporate offices, suburban shopping malls, and upscale restaurants showed expressions of dismay, disgust, and even despair. White women . . . seemed particularly upset about the verdict, protesting that O. J. had gotten away with spouse abuse and murder, sending a chilling message to battered women everywhere. . . .

In New York's Times Square . . . the large, frenetic crowd of shoppers, tourists, and bike messengers suddenly turned into two opposing camps, people of color and whites. . . . It appeared that blacks and Latinos were hugging each other and exuberantly exchanging high fives, while whites were momentarily stunned and immobilized by the news.

Author Jewelle Taylor Gibbs describing in 1996 the mixed reactions of blacks and whites to O. J. Simpson's acquittal on October 3, 1995, in James Haley, ed., Post–Cold War America: 1992–Present *(2003), pp. 69–71.*

We have a problem with the fact that the man who calls us together continues to be a racist, sexist, homophobic, anti-Christian.

Abraham Foxman of the Anti-Defamation League describing Minister Louis Farrakhan, who organized a Million Man March for black men on October 16, 1995, in Charles Bierbauer, "Million Man Messenger, Not Message, Causing Division," October 15, 1995. Available online. URL: http://www.cnn.com/ US/9510/megamarch/10-15.

But let's look at a speech delivered by a White slave holder on the banks of the James River in 1712. . . . He said, "In my bag I have a fool proof method of controlling black slaves. . . . I use fear, distrust, and envy for control purposes."

I want you to listen. What are those three things? Fear, envy, distrust. For what purpose? Control. To control who? The slave. Who is the slave? Us. . . .

And so, as a consequence, we as a people now have been fractured, divided and destroyed, filled with fear, distrust and envy. . . .

We talking about moving toward a perfect union. Well, pointing out fault, pointing out our wrongs is the first step. . . .

But, then, the hardest part is to go to the person or persons whom your faults have ill-affected and confess to them. That's hard. That's hard. But, if we want a perfect union, we have to confess the fault. Well, what happens after confession? There must be repentance. When you repent, you feel remorse or contrition or shame for the past conduct. . . .

And if you don't repent, you'll do it over and over and over again. But to stop it where it is, and Black men, we got to stop what we're doing where it is. We cannot continue the destruction of our lives and the destruction of our community. But that change can't come until we feel sorry. . . .

But, when it comes to doing something about the evil that we've done we fall short. But, atonement means satisfaction or reparation for a wrong or injury. It means to make amends. . . .

And the sixth stage is forgiveness. . . . You're not liberated until you can forgive. . . .

The seventh tone, the leading tone that leads to the perfect union with God, is reconciliation and restoration because after forgiveness, now, we are going to be restored to what? To our original position. . . . It means to resolve differences. It can mean to establish or re-establish a close relationship between previously hostile persons.

Minister Louis Farrakhan addressing the Million Man March on October 16, 1995, in Farrakhan, "Minister Farrakhan Challenges Black Men: Transcript from Minister Louis Farrakhan's Remarks at the Million Man March," October 17, 1995. Available online. URL: http://www.cnn.com/US/9510/megamarch/march.html.

State and local school leaders, teachers, parents, and citizens need to understand what they are up against [in school reform], what has to be done differently, and how much is at stake.

They can begin by recognizing, and tolerating no longer, the vast inertia of an educational establishment entrenched in many university faculties of education; in well-heeled interest associations, with their bureaucracies, journals, and conventions . . . in textbook publishing houses and the aggressive new industries of educational technology and assessment. . . .

Starting school reform by first deciding what every child should learn strikes most people as only common sense. But to many American educators, it spells revolutionary change—change far deeper than questions of school choice, methods, or managements. Means and management are not the problem. The overused business analogy breaks down: business first decides the content of its product; means follow. But educators, unwilling to focus on subject matter, have never decided what content everyone should know; the curriculum stays frozen, incoherent and unequal. For more than a decade American citizens have wanted high, common standards—the only new idea for their schools in a century. But to get them, they will have to work around the establishment and overturn the status quo.

Author Paul Gagnon discussing the need for curriculum-based school reform in Gagnon, "What Should Children Learn?" Atlantic, December 1995, pp. 65–66.

8

Clinton Prevails Again
1996

Cast as a referendum on Clinton's character, as well as on his job performance, the presidential campaign dominated the year's domestic politics. Republicans called for tax cuts and pointed to allegations of Clinton's wrongdoing in the Whitewater affair, charges of sexual harassment, and other alleged personal misconduct. Meanwhile, Clinton pointed to improvements in the economy and, backing away from the ambitious liberal agenda of his first two years, called for substantial welfare reform, more modest social reforms, and improvements in education. The beneficiary of decreasing crime rates, a booming economy, and the lowest unemployment rate in six years, Clinton won 49 percent of the popular vote to defeat the Republican challenger Robert Dole and the third-party candidate Ross Perot. Republicans, however, retained control of both chambers of Congress.

Terrorist attacks continued to mount throughout the world, including in the United States. Less than two weeks after Timothy McVeigh went on trial for the 1995 Oklahoma City bombing, the Summer Olympics were marred by a bomb that killed two people in Atlanta and injured more than 100 more. Richard Jewell, a security guard, was improperly identified as a suspect shortly after the bombing. He was later cleared but only after FBI agents had hastily identified him to the press. Jewell later won a $500,000 settlement from NBC for news coverage that impugned him in its rush to judgment. In 1998, Eric Robert Rudolph, an outspoken opponent of abortion and the federal government and with ties to white supremacist groups, was charged with the crime; he was arrested in 2003 and pled guilty in 2005.[1] The FBI arrested Theodore "Ted" Kaczynski, the elusive Unabomber, whom they tracked to a remote cabin in Montana after Kaczynski's brother recognized his writing style from the manifesto Kaczynski published in 1995. Kaczynski, who condemned modern technology and consumerism, was believed to be responsible for 16 bomb attacks over the previous 17 years. And federal agents arrested 12 members of the Viper Militia, an Arizona paramilitary organization caught with machine guns and other weapons and materials for making bombs, as well as a videotape containing instructions for gaining illegal entry, placing illegal devices, and destroying buildings. The small paramilitary group, which started as a rifle club, was suspected of planning to blow up federal buildings in Phoenix, Arizona. Americans also fell victim to terrorism overseas when 19 U.S. airmen died in an attack on their apartment building in Saudi Arabia.[2]

On the other hand, advances in medicine and science generated optimism, as the World Health Organization announced that smallpox had been eliminated and all remaining stocks of smallpox virus would be destroyed within three years. Treatment of AIDS also progressed as a powerful combination of drugs made it possible to eliminate HIV from the blood, although not from the body. The capacity to transmit vast quantities of electronic data expanded as fiber optics permitted cables to carry the equivalent of 12 million simultaneous telephone calls. And the discovery of a 4.5-billion-year-old meteorite that contained evidence of a life-form that may have originated on Mars excited the imagination of both scientists and the public at large.

INTERNATIONAL DEVELOPMENTS

U.S. relations with Cuba reintensified in February after Cuban military aircraft shot down two unarmed civilian planes piloted by members of Brothers to the Rescue, a Cuban exile group who searched for rafters and other Cubans seeking to escape Fidel Castro's Communist regime by sea. The Cuban government maintained the planes had been disseminating anti-Castro literature over Havana before the attack, which Cuba maintained took place over Cuban territorial waters. The United States, insisting that the planes had been fired upon over international seas, condemned the death of the four men aboard the planes, three of whom were U.S. citizens. The incident provoked UN condemnation of Cuba and congressional passage of the Helms-Burton Cuban Liberty and Democratic Solidarity Act of 1996, which allowed U.S. citizens to file in U.S. courts for financial compensation for the property they lost to the Cuban regime when it took power in 1959. The legislation, which Clinton signed into law, also restricted the movement of Cuban diplomats within the United States, closed off charter air routes to and from Cuba, and expanded the broadcasting range of the government-funded anti-Castro radio station Radio Marti.

After a U.S. veto of the reelection of Egypt's Boutros Boutros-Ghali as UN secretary-general, Ghana's American-educated Kofi Annan was elected to the post in November. Annan was considered more closely attuned to U.S. sensibilities than Boutros-Ghali, who had been a particular target of Republicans in Congress, who had threatened to delay U.S. dues payments to the United Nations further if he were reelected.

In September, in response to Iraqi military action against protected Kurdish areas, Clinton ordered Operation Desert Strike against targets within Iraq. The action was supported by Germany, Japan, and Britain but opposed by Russia, France, Spain, New Zealand, and China. Fears that the attack might escalate into a second Persian Gulf War did not materialize, however. The United States strengthened its military ties with Japan when Clinton and Prime Minister Ryutaro Hashimoto signed the Alliance of the 21st Century, in which the United States agreed to retain troops in Asia beyond the millennium, and Japan consented to assume a more active role in its region's defense.

Although nations and organizations throughout the world condemned France for a series of nuclear tests it conducted in 1995 and early 1996, in

September it signed the Comprehensive Nuclear Test Ban Treaty, joining the other four publicly acknowledged nuclear-armed countries—China, Russia, Great Britain, and the United States. (Israel, South Africa, and India were also widely believed to possess nuclear weapons.) In another act that restricted nuclear arms, the U.S. Senate ratified the START II treaty, which cut U.S. and Russian arsenals to about one-third of their 1993 levels.

Terrorism erupted once again in Great Britain as a series of bombings by the IRA ended a 17-month cease-fire and led to the exclusion of Sinn Féin, the political arm of the IRA, from so-called all-party negotiations on the future of Northern Ireland. Conducted with the encouragement of Clinton and chaired by the former senator George Mitchell, the talks began in June, after the election of delegates by voters in Northern Ireland. They continued throughout the year, despite additional bombings and escalating violence between the IRA and British military forces.

After months of intense fighting in which Chechen civilians and combatants on both sides experienced heavy casualties, Russia and Chechnya signed a peace treaty in May. The agreement called for Russia to withdraw its troops by the end of the year, and it did. Both sides further agreed to delay the issue of Chechen sovereignty until 2001. Altogether, some 90,000 died in the insurrection. Romanians citizens voted to replace the Communist government that had held power since the 1989 overthrow of the dictator Nicolae Ceaușescu.

As Bosnia prepared to hold its first free elections since the end of the fighting in December 1995, the United Nations opened an International War Crimes Tribunal at the Hague, and in March the tribunal began arresting Bosnian Serbs believed to be responsible for murdering thousands of Bosnian civilians while carrying out policies of ethnic cleansing. At the behest of President Nelson Mandela, South Africa established the Truth and Reconciliation Commission in April to assign accountability for the deaths and other abuses inflicted upon civilians during the nearly half-century of apartheid.

In April, tensions once again escalated between North and South Korea, after North Korea renounced the demilitarized zone (DMZ), between the two countries, which had been established as part of the 1953 armistice that ended the fighting in the Korean War but did not provide a final peace settlement. Subsequent North Korean military exercises in their section of the DMZ provoked a state of heightened alert in South Korea. Then, in September, a submarine filled with armed North Korean commandos ran aground off the coast of South Korea. One commando was captured, and the rest died fighting South Korean troops. The incident heightened further fears of war; in late December, however, North Korea, which was suffering greatly from famine, made an unprecedented apology, followed by an agreement to participate in direct peace talks with South Korea under U.S. auspices.

Hopes faded in 1996 that the 1994 and 1995 Oslo Accords would afford a peaceful solution to the Israeli-Palestinian conflict. In April, despite continuing suicide bombings inside Israel, both sides briefly shared some optimism as the Palestine Liberation Organization (PLO) eliminated from its charter language calling for the destruction of Israel, and the ruling Israeli Labor Party dropped its opposition to the formation of a Palestinian state. But Yasser Arafat, the first president of the new self-ruling Palestinian National Authority, made minimal efforts to curb the rash of terrorist attacks that were killing scores of civilians inside Israel, and Israel's prime minister Shimon Peres, who took office after the 1995 assassination of Yitzhak Rabin, instituted a policy to take military action against insurgent organizations operating within areas that had been transferred to Palestinian rule, notably Hamas and the Islamic Jihad. Nonetheless, the suicide bombings continued, and by May many Israelis felt angry and betrayed by Peres's ineffective efforts to gain peace by conceding territory and granting Palestinian autonomy. Consequently, they voted Peres out of office and replaced him with Benjamin Netanyahu, a conservative hard-liner opposed to new concessions.

Additional bombings postponed the Israeli withdrawal from the West Bank, a movement the accords called for in return for Israeli national security. Then, an Israeli effort in late September to open a historic tunnel running beneath both Jewish and Muslim holy sites ignited a new outbreak of violence in which more than 70 Palestinians and Israelis were killed, as Israeli soldiers battled with Palestinian police in the West Bank and Gaza Strip. A summit conference among Clinton, Arafat, and Netanyahu failed to resolve the tunnel crisis or achieve progress in further implementing the Oslo agreements. While Israel contended with Palestinian unrest on the West Bank, it also responded to attacks from Hezbollah fundamentalists in Lebanon, who launched a series of rocket attacks against northern Israel on the eve of the Passover holy day in late March. Israel retaliated, and fears of a new Israeli invasion provoked thousands of Lebanese to evacuate from the border. A U.S. brokered cease-fire ended the crisis in late April, but not before a number of Lebanese civilians were killed, including 97 whose bomb shelter was accidentally destroyed in the village of Qana, an act for which Peres immediately apologized and offered compensation.

A bloody civil war in Liberia spawned more than 1 million refugees and provoked a U.S. military operation to evacuate foreigners, including some 54 Americans. The army of Zaire and Zairean Tutsi forces defeated Hutu militias who had been terrorizing some 700,000 refugees inside Zaire, making possible their return to Rwanda.

Islamic extremists known as the Taliban seized control of Afghanistan's capital city, Kabul. The Taliban had been among the Afghan rebel groups, called "freedom fighters" by the then-president Reagan, whom the United States armed with sophisticated weapons in the 1980s in support of their ultimately successful rebellion against the nine-year Soviet occupation. Upon capturing Kabul, the Taliban immediately executed the former president, Mohammed Najibullah, who had been a leading figure in the Soviet-backed regime in the 1980s, and imposed strict Islamic rule that, among other policies, forbade women to receive an education and imposed numerous additional restrictions on them. However, the Taliban was compelled to retreat from positions in the mountains, which were controlled by rival rebel factions known as the Northern Alliance.

Terrorism also plagued other societies throughout the world. The most dramatic incident was the capture by leftist guerrillas of some 500 politicians and businessmen and businesswomen attending a garden party at the Japanese embassy in Lima, Peru. Among those taken prisoner in the December attack by the outlawed Tupac Amaru organization were Peru's foreign minister and Japan's ambassador. The crisis persisted through April 1997, when government troops freed 71 of the 72 remaining hostages, killing all 17 rebels and one of the hostages. In December a bomb detonated at rush hour in the Paris Metro, killing two and injuring 20. Earlier in the year, Sri Lankan separatists known as the Tamil Tigers detonated a car bomb in the nation's capital city, Colombo, killing at least 55 and injuring 1,400. Antigovernment Islamic terrorists murdered 18 Greek tourists near the Egyptian pyramids, and 127 people died when a hijacked Ethiopian airliner crashed into the sea after running out of fuel.

Widely reported acts of mass murder and attempted mass murder by individuals also shocked people throughout the world, as a former Boy Scout leader killed 16 young children and a teacher in the Scottish town of Dunblane; a 33-year-old British man attacked a group of schoolchildren with a machete at Saint Luke's Infants' School in Wolverhampton, England; and a mentally disturbed gunman killed 35 and wounded 18 in the tourist town of Port Arthur, Australia, on the island of Tasmania.

GOVERNMENT AND SOCIETY

President Clinton's reelection campaign was bolstered by a strengthening economy, his willingness to accommodate some key conservative concerns within his moderately liberal agenda, and his successes in international diplomacy, including the Israeli-Palestinian Oslo agreements, the restoration of democracy in Haiti, and the Dayton accords, which ended the fighting in the former Yugoslavia. During the campaign he promised to reduce the size of government while still insisting on its importance for providing economic and national security and protecting the environment. Although Clinton had opposed the proposal for a constitutional amendment mandating a balanced federal budget, he promised to balance the budget within seven years but to impose smaller tax cuts and smaller reductions in Medicare spending than Republicans were advocating.

Clinton, who vetoed a ban on a procedure for late-term abortions before the election, distinguished himself from his Republican challengers in that he believed women should retain the right to choose to terminate unwanted pregnancies, although he also maintained that abortion should be an option of last resort. Having tried unsuccessfully in 1993 to eliminate the ban on gays in the military, Clinton generally favored reducing restrictions on homosexuals, and most Republican candidates did not. Nonetheless, although he questioned its motives and found the bill unnecessary and divisive, Clinton signed the Defense of Marriage Act, which denied federal recognition to same-sex marriages, as he maintained marriage is the union between one man and one woman. Clinton supported a higher minimum wage, job-training vouchers for the unemployed, continuation of an earned income tax credit for the working poor, modest health insurance reform, merit scholarships for the top 5 percent of high school students, a tax deduction for college tuition, tax cuts for families, tighter gun control measures and retention of the controversial 1994 ban on certain types of assault weapons, and a renewed war on drugs and on crime that he would fortify by increasing the number of officers in local police departments by 100,000.

Clinton benefited from residual public anger about the government shutdown at the end of 1995, for which a majority of Americans blamed Republicans in Congress, and from a fissure in the Republican Party that pitted religiously oriented social conservatives on the party's far Right against fiscal conservatives who were more secular in their social orientation and tended to occupy the party's center. Moderate conservatives ultimately prevailed, as Dole won the nomination. Dole, who, if elected at age 73, would have become the oldest person in the nation's history to assume the office, ran as a centrist experienced in making government work. He advocated a $548 billion tax cut and promised to reduce the size of government, but in a gradual, phased-in process, and he favored abolishing the existing tax code and the IRS and substituting "lower and flatter" rates. Dole promoted a constitutional amendment that would require a 60 percent "supermajority" before Congress could raise income taxes, and he promised to reduce capital gains taxes to rates comparable to those in Germany and Japan. Maintaining that he would implement programs to promote family values, Dole advocated prayer in the public schools and opposed federal funding of abortions. Nonetheless, he favored language in the party platform that would express toleration for abortion-rights supporters, a position that was shared by a large majority of Republicans[3] but alienated many vocal and politically active abortion foes. He also favored repealing the 1994 federal ban on semiautomatic weapons, making English the official language of the United States, and passing a constitutional amendment to forbid desecration of the American flag.

Lamar Alexander, a former governor of Tennessee, ran somewhat to the right of Dole, promoting himself as an activist conservative intent on shifting the locus of power from the federal government back to the states and local communities. He favored deep cuts to the capital gains tax and a balanced budget amendment to the Constitution, as well as massive reform of the welfare system that would include cessation of payments to able-bodied adults after a set period and jail time for so-called deadbeat dads who failed to fulfill their child-support obligations. Opposed to legalized abortion, Alexander advocated school prayer, tort reform to address problems emanating from the existing "litigious culture" in the United States, abolition of the Department of Education, and term limits for Congress.

As did Alexander, the publisher Malcolm (Steve) Forbes positioned himself as a political outsider. Running as a fiscal conservative, the president and chief executive of *Forbes,* a well-respected business magazine, promoted Reagan era supply-side economics, replacement of the existing tax code with a 17 percent flat tax, and elimination of capital gains taxes.

Many social conservatives rallied around Patrick Buchanan, a former television commentator and talk-show host who had served in the administrations of Presidents Nixon, Ford, and Reagan and unsuccessfully opposed the incumbent George H. W. Bush for the Republican Party's nomination in 1992. Buchanan ardently opposed abortion, and he loudly denounced the feminist and gay rights movements. He also blamed lax immigration policies for many of the nation's social and economic problems and promoted an "America first" policy that would erect a fence along portions of the Mexican border to stem illegal immigration, institute a five-year moratorium on legal immigration, make English the nation's official language, and implement a largely isolationist foreign policy. Buchanan also opposed the global economy and advocated scrapping the NAFTA and GATT trade agreements and imposing tariffs on goods from Japan, China, and developing nations to protect the jobs and wages of American workers. He proposed replacing the current income tax code with a flat tax of less than 17 percent on income above $25,000.

Many critics, even prominent conservatives, spoke out against Buchanan's apparent racial, gender, and ethnic intolerance. Dole went so far as to describe his contest against Buchanan as a fight for the "heart and soul of the Republican Party,"[4] and William F. Buckley, Jr., the editor of the influential rightist magazine *National Review*, accused Buchanan of anti-Semitism. Buchanan was also criticized for alleged ties to white supremacist groups and for past remarks calling the 1960s civil rights leader Martin Luther King, Jr., an immoral, evil demagogue. Consequently, going into the primary season, many observers believed Buchanan's isolationism and other far-Right beliefs would render him too distant from the party's mainstream to be a serious contender for the nomination. But after he narrowly defeated Dole and Alexander in the New Hampshire primary, Buchanan emerged as a viable candidate, and he remained Dole's most effective and persistent challenger throughout the primary season. He ultimately endorsed Dole rather than run as a third-party candidate, as he had earlier threatened, and the official Republican platform adopted at the national convention reflected many of Buchanan's social positions, including opposition to abortion, expanded rights for homosexuals, and lax immigration policies. The platform also called for a constitutional amendment that would deny automatic citizenship to children born to illegal immigrants in the United States, for voluntary prayer in public schools, abolition of the Department of Education in order to end "federal meddling in our schools," a balanced budget with reduced government spending, an across-the-board 15 percent tax cut, and a reduction of the top tax rate on capital gains by 50 percent.

Ross Perot, who ran for president unsuccessfully in 1992, ran again in 1996 as the nominee of the Reform Party, which he founded in 1995. Campaigning primarily as a fiscal conservative, Perot opposed NAFTA, which he maintained had sent 500,000 jobs to Mexico. He also criticized the existing U.S. trade and budget deficits, endorsed tax reform, and promoted extensive tax cuts. The consumer and environmental activist Ralph Nader ran as the Green Party candidate. Nader used his campaign to challenge the two-party political system, in which, he maintained, both parties are overly influenced by corporate interests.

Clinton's reelection in November marked the first time since 1944 that a Democratic president was reelected. The Clinton/Gore ticket captured 49.2 percent of the popular vote, won in 31 states, and garnered 379 electoral votes. The Republican candidate, Senate majority leader Robert "Bob" Dole of Kansas, and his New York running mate, Jack Kemp, a former congressman and former secretary of the Department of Housing and Urban Development (HUD), gained 40.8 percent of the vote; the Reform Party candidate, Ross Perot, received 8.5 percent, down from 19 percent in 1992. Clinton fared especially well with younger and poorer voters, winning 53 percent of voters between 18 and 29, compared to 34 percent for Dole and 11 percent for Perot. Fifty-nine percent of voters who earned less than $15,000 yearly voted for Clinton, whereas 53 percent who had income above $100,000 voted for Dole.[5]

Clinton's victory was widely regarded as a remarkable political comeback after Democrats lost control of Congress in 1994 in an apparent repudiation of Clinton's policies. Clinton's popularity in 1996 failed to carry over to

Congress, however, as Republicans gained two Senate seats, increasing their majority to 55 to 45. Even though Republicans lost 10 seats in the House, they nonetheless retained a slim majority there as well, with 226 seats to 207 for the Democrats and two independents. After the elections, Republicans reelected Trent Lott, who had replaced Dole as Senate majority leader when Dole stepped down during the campaign. Democrats reelected Tom Daschle of South Dakota as Senate minority leader and Richard Gephardt of Missouri as House minority leader, and Gingrich was narrowly reelected Speaker of the House in early January 1997.

Much of Clinton's success in the 1996 election derived from his ability to steer the Democratic Party toward the country's political center during his presidency. At times he even promoted positions traditionally associated with the Republican Party—much to the chagrin, and sometimes outrage, of many Republicans, who felt outmaneuvered by him. For instance, in his State of the Union address Clinton declared an end to the "era of big government" and made balancing the federal budget, reducing crime, and strengthening the American family top priorities. He also implemented major welfare reform when he won passage of the Personal Responsibility and Work Opportunity Act of 1996. Republicans had long called for welfare reform; in fact, it was part of Gingrich's Contract with America. But in January Clinton vetoed the bill Congress passed in 1995 because he believed it failed to offer adequate employment opportunities for those leaving welfare or to provide sufficiently for impoverished children. Welfare critics had long complained that prolonged welfare ultimately created an underclass of poor who were content to live on their federal "handouts" and were disinclined to take significant steps to educate themselves better and otherwise improve their economic condition. Some critics further charged that welfare actually provided an economic incentive for unmarried poor women to have babies.

Unlike other Democrats who traditionally defended welfare as a lifeline for those unable to compete in the economy, Clinton concurred on several points with the critics, and the Personal Responsibility and Work Opportunity Act made substantial changes to the system. It required the head of most families who were receiving welfare to secure work within two years or lose benefits, and it capped the total time a person could receive welfare benefits in his or her lifetime at five years. It penalized single mothers who refused to identify their child's father, and it insisted that unmarried teenage mothers live at home and remain in school in order to retain their benefits. Although the act created no public jobs to employ those leaving welfare, it funded block grants to the states, which could then administer the funds as they deemed best—another traditionally Republican approach to public spending. By tightening eligibility requirements and reducing food stamp allocations, the act was expected to save $56 billion. Moreover, it mandated that states succeed in shifting at least 20 percent of those in their caseloads from welfare to work by the end of 1997, and 50 percent by 2002, or have their block grants reduced. In fact, by 2004, welfare rolls had dropped to approximately 2 million, less than half the number of recipients when Clinton signed the legislation. Proponents pointed to this reduction as evidence of the policy's success, particularly in job training and job retention even during the economic downturn of the early 21st century. But critics argued that the act simply rendered needy would-be recipients ineligible.[6] Clinton also signed legislation imposing tougher measures to curb illegal immigration, but only after provisions affecting children and legal immigrants were eliminated. Nonetheless, thousands of Hispanics protesting the anti-immigrant and anti-Hispanic sentiment they perceived in the legislation rallied in Washington, D.C., a month before the election.

Clinton also obtained the bipartisan support necessary to increase the minimum wage from $4.25 to $5.15 per hour. The Kennedy-Kassebaum health bill enabled workers to carry their health insurance coverage from one job to another and limited the ability of insurance companies to exclude applicants for health coverage on the basis of preexisting conditions. Clinton also signed a telecommunications bill that made the most extensive changes to communication law in 62 years. The legislation eliminated many rules limiting competition in the radio, television, and telephone-service markets; reduced restrictions on media ownership; and imposed criminal penalties for distributing pornography to minors over the Internet. However, in 1997, the Supreme Court struck down the pornography provision. Clinton also supported legislation giving the president a so-called line-item veto, enabling him or her to eliminate certain portions of a spending bill without vetoing the entire measure. Part of the Republican's Contract with America, the line-item veto promised to reduce wasteful government spending, but critics, including many Democrats, complained that it gave too much power to the executive branch, and in 1998, the Supreme Court concurred, striking down the legislation because it upset the balance of powers between the executive and legislative branches of government.

Clinton's efforts to draw attention to the growing danger of terrorist attacks and to strengthen the nation's ability to combat terrorism met with only partial success. Congress passed a $1 billion antiterrorism bill that allowed the government to deny entry to the United States to and to deport foreign members of terrorist organizations, to prosecute individuals who raise funds for terrorist groups, and to require criminals convicted of federal charges to pay restitution to their victims. However, the legislation deleted or weakened several provisions sought by Clinton, including ones that would have expanded the federal government's wiretapping powers, required manufacturers of many incendiary materials to include identifying "taggants" to enable authorities to trace their origin, and allowed the military to become involved in cases of domestic terrorism involving biological and chemical weapons. The final bill did authorize military involvement when nuclear weapons were involved.

Congress's failure to pass a budget acceptable to Clinton in 1995 led to a shutdown of inessential government services that lasted from December 16 to January 6, 1996, when Clinton signed one stopgap budget bill and two others that restored funding in some portions of the government through September. Yet, despite a series of stopgap, continuing budget resolutions that kept the government functioning, the president and Congress remained deadlocked, and by the end of January only seven of the 13 appropriations bills to fund the federal government for the 1996 fiscal year had been approved. In early February, Clinton signed a $265 defense authorization bill similar to one he vetoed in December 1995 but without earlier provisions calling for a missile-defense system, restrictions on the president's ability to deploy U.S. troops as UN peacekeepers, or a requirement that the president receive congressional authorization to fund any overseas military deployment costing more than $100 million. A provision remained, however, requiring the dismissal of all service members who tested positive for the AIDS-causing HIV, despite Clinton's criticism of it. Throughout the winter, Clinton and Congress kept the rest of the government running via a series of continuing budget resolutions and agreements to raise the federal debt ceiling. Finally, on April 25, Congress passed an omnibus spending bill for the remaining nine cabinet-level departments that had not yet been funded for fiscal 1996.

Not anxious during an election year to anger further a public already exasperated by the government's inability to conduct its business because of partisan intransigence, Congress and the president agreed upon an omnibus budget appropriation for fiscal 1997 in a timely manner. Passed in September, the bill, which funded nine cabinet departments and hundreds of programs and agencies, included many features Clinton lobbied for, including $6.5 billion for domestic projects such as counterterrorism, wildfire containment in the West, and disaster aid to hurricane victims. Clinton also won an agreement to shift $1 billion from defense spending to some of his domestic priorities. Republicans celebrated their reduction of discretionary spending by $30 billion, which kept the government on schedule in its plan to balance the budget by 2002.

In one of his first acts after his reelection in November, Clinton appointed the UN ambassador Madeleine Albright as secretary of state, replacing Warren Christopher, who resigned after completing Clinton's first term. Albright, who was born in Czechoslovakia, became the first woman to serve as secretary of state in U.S. history. Also departing after the election were White House chief of staff Leon Panetta, Defense secretary William Perry, Energy secretary Hazel O'Leary, HUD secretary Henry Cisneros, and Labor secretary Robert Reich. In an effort to build bipartisan support for his military policies, Clinton chose William Cohen, a retiring Republican senator from Maine, as the new secretary of defense, and Transportation secretary Federico Pena to replace O'Leary. Clinton replaced CIA director John Deutch with Anthony Lake, the former head of the National Security Council, who was known for his pragmatism.

There were more women in America than men in 1996, by a ratio of 134 to 128. College Board scores for graduating high school seniors showed the highest average scores in 24 years on the mathematics section and an overall improvement in average scores. The ratio of public schools to private schools was seven to one, and more than one-third (37 percent) of high school graduates went on to college. The cancer mortality rate dropped for the first time since the 1930s; the volume of e-mail exceeded that of surface mail, sometimes dubbed snail mail; and for the first time more money was spent on computers than on television sets.[7]

After winning reelection, President Bill Clinton appointed the United Nations (UN) ambassador, Madeleine Albright, the nation's first female secretary of state. *(AP/Wide World Photos)*

Transportation disasters plagued the nation when an Amtrak train collided with a commuter train in Maryland, killing 11; a low-fare Valuejet airliner crashed in the Florida Everglades, killing 109; and a TWA flight crashed shortly after takeoff from New York's JFK International Airport, killing 228. A total of 37,494 fatal auto accidents killed 42,065 people on U.S. highways.[8] Overseas, the midair collision near New Delhi, India, of a Russian cargo plane and a jumbo passenger jet carrying Indian workers to Saudi Arabia killed more than 350; a Dominican jet en route to Frankfurt, Germany, plunged into the Atlantic Ocean, killing all 189 passengers and crew members; and a Peruvian jet crashed into the Pacific shortly after takeoff, killing 70.

The Supreme Court agreed to hear Clinton's appeal that Paula Jones's civil lawsuit against him should be postponed until after he completed his presidency. Although Clinton eventually lost the appeal, the Court's willingness to hear it delayed further action on the case until 1997, well after the November elections. As the Jones and Whitewater cases continued to undermine the public perception of Clinton's personal integrity, the Republican-dominated House Ethics Committee ruled that Gingrich had violated House rules by allowing a telecommunications entrepreneur to volunteer in his office. In December 1995, the committee had ruled against the Speaker for improperly using public funds to promote his own business interests.

In separate decisions the Supreme Court upheld a federal law prohibiting "indecent programming" on daytime and prime-time television and radio and a Florida law requiring job applicants in the city of North Miami to swear that they had not used tobacco products within the previous year. In a ruling applauded by gay-rights activists, it struck down an amendment to the Colorado state constitution that forbade any government entity to pass statutes or implement policies that prohibited discrimination against homosexuals. Maintaining that racially based gerrymandering violated the Fourteenth Amendment's guarantee of equal protection, the Court struck down race-based redistricting plans that had created majority black and Hispanic congressional districts in North Carolina and Texas. It also denied a challenge that would have required the government to recalculate the 1990 census in order to correct an estimated undercount of some 4 million people, many of whom were minorities and/or illegal immigrants living primarily in cities with large immigrant populations such as New York, Los Angeles, Miami, Houston, and Chicago.

In a controversial decision that provoked strong emotions among both feminists and antifeminists, the Court terminated Virginia Military Institute's (VMI's) 157-year tradition of admitting only male students when it ruled that the state-funded institution violated women's Fourteenth Amendment right to equal protection when it banned them from attending. The Court further decided that the government could seize property used for criminal activity, even if the owner was not engaged in the illegal action; that manufacturers were not entitled to reimbursement from the government to cover costs of settling lawsuits brought against them by veterans harmed by Agent Orange, a carcinogenic defoliant used by the U.S. military during the Vietnam War; that the Republican Party of Virginia violated the Federal Voting Rights Act of 1965 when it charged attendance fees to the party's 1994 nominating convention; that workers could sue employers for age discrimination, even if they were replaced by people older than 40; and that credit card companies could charge late-payment fees, even if a cardholder lived in a state that prohibited such fines. A circuit court judge in Hawaii declared that an existing state ban on same-sex marriages was unconstitutional, an anticipated decision that prompted Congress to pass and Clinton to sign the Defense of Marriage Act. The ruling did not go into effect, pending an appeal to the Supreme Court scheduled for 1997.

BUSINESS

The economy performed well in 1996, a development that aided Clinton's reelection. On October 14, for the first time in history, the Dow–Jones industrial index closed above 6,000. It ended the year at 6,448, up 1,331 points, or 26 percent, from 1995. Its low was 5,200. The GDP grew by 4.4 percent, slightly less than in the previous year, and the unemployment rate fell to 5.4 percent, down by 0.2 percent from 1995. Top managers fared especially well in the corporate-friendly environment, as the average salary for chief executive officers (CEOs) increased by an unprecedented 54 percent from 1995 to $5.78 million, more than 200 times the average total compensation of workers, whose salary grew by 2.9 percent.[9] The robust economy produced some concerns about inflation, which rose from 2.5 percent in 1995 to 3.3 percent in 1995,[10] and about a trade deficit that increased by 8.7 percent to $114.23 billion.[11] Passage of the Telecommunications Act of 1996 promoted competition, reduced regulation, and encouraged more rapid development of new technology.

Commerce secretary Ronald Brown died in April along with 32 other Americans and two Croatians when the U.S. Air Force jet carrying them crashed in Croatia. The group of government officials and business representatives was touring Croatia and Bosnia-Herzegovina to explore business possibilities associated with rebuilding the former Yugoslavia. Brown, who at the time of his death was fending off allegations of business improprieties, had been a close friend of Clinton's and one of the nation's top African-American politicians. He was a leading spokesperson for the administration's trade and economic policies, and business leaders had praised his efforts to help U.S. companies obtain contracts in developing and industrialized countries. He was succeeded by U.S. trade representative Mickey Kantor, who stepped down from the post as commerce secretary at the end of the year.

The 1993 conviction of Charles Keating, a central figure in the savings and loan scandal of the late 1980s and early 1990s, was overturned by a federal judge who ruled that the jury who had convicted Keating were predisposed against him. Keating had served four and a half years of a 12 1/2-year sentence before his release from federal prison.

In an effort to avert a trade war with the United States, China agreed to enforce laws prohibiting copyright piracy more strictly. And in response to complaints from U.S. lumber producers that Canadian firms were "dumping" softwood in the United States at unfairly low prices, Canada agreed to restrict the amount of such lumber it would export over the next five years.

General Motors won praise from environmentalists after it announced that it would introduce its first electrically powered car, the EV1, which it planned to market in Saturn dealerships in California and Arizona. On the other hand, human rights activists condemned the singer and television personality Kathy Lee Gifford when it was revealed that clothes sold by WalMart under her label were being manufactured abroad under sweatshop conditions.

NATURE AND THE ENVIRONMENT

Reporting on the continuing effects of the 1986 meltdown of a nuclear reactor at Chernobyl, in the Ukraine, the European Union concluded that as many as 30 million Ukrainians, of a total population of 50 million, remained at risk from radioactive contamination stemming from contaminated water that washed into rivers used for drinking, fishing, and irrigation. Although the U.S. Defense Department denied the existence of a distinct Gulf War syndrome accountable for debilitating symptoms experienced by some veterans, it notified some 20,000 soldiers that they might have been exposed to harmful fallout resulting from the destruction of an Iraqi chemical weapons dump in March 1991, shortly after the cessation of hostilities.

Clinton signed the Water Resources Development Act providing $3.8 billion for federal water projects, including $75 million to restore the Florida Everglades. The need for such restoration was underscored by an unrelated study by the Nature Conservancy, a private conservation group, that concluded that approximately one-third of the 20,000 native U.S. plant and animal species it recently examined were imperiled. Degradation of habitats emerged as the greatest threat to wildlife; freshwater mussels, crayfish, amphibians, and freshwater fish were at highest risk for endangerment or extinction.

The so-called Blizzard of '96 dropped between one and a half and three feet of snow from Virginia to Massachusetts, shutting down airports throughout the East Coast, closing federal offices in Washington, D.C., and cutting mail service in New York City. Hurricane Fran struck North and South Carolina, causing millions of dollars worth of damage and killing 12 people, and a wildfire destroyed more than 40,000 acres in Alaska and caused more than 1,000 residents to evacuate. Other natural disasters included a tornado that destroyed 80 villages in Bangladesh and killed more than 500 people and a volcano in North Island, New Zealand, that covered a nearby town with ash and caused the closure of nearby airports.

SCIENCE AND TECHNOLOGY

The discoveries of two planets beyond the solar system capable of containing life-sustaining water, and a third, Jupiter-like extrasolar planet, excited the imagination of people worldwide, as they suggested the likelihood that numerous water-bearing planets exist throughout the universe and hence the possibility, and perhaps even the probability, of the existence of extraterrestrial life. Those probabilities were further enhanced by revelations based on photographs from the *Hubble Space Telescope* showing that the universe contains more galaxies than previously believed, in a wide variety of shapes, sizes, and colors. Other scientists studying a halo of previously unseen objects around the Milky Way suggested the phenomenon might account for some of the unexplained missing mass, or "dark matter," believed to compose most of the universe. But it was the discovery of a 4.5-billion-year-old meteorite of a bacterium believed to have originated on Mars that made headline news and stirred interest among the public as it shifted the search for extraterrestrial life-forms much closer to home. Many were excited by the possibility of life beyond Earth; others found the prospect frightening, especially as it coincided with such treatments in the popular culture as the alien invasion in the year's hit movie *Independence Day*. Moreover, some religious figures were dismayed because, in their view, the presence of extraterrestrial life would diminish the special role humanity plays in God's plan and would otherwise contradict the Bible.

Cooperation in outer space between former cold war foes strengthened when the U.S. space shuttle *Atlantis* linked with the Russian space station *Mir*, and for the first time an American astronaut remained aboard for an extended stay on *Mir*. Because of a delay in the *Atlantis* mission on which she was scheduled to return to Earth, 53-year-old Shannon Lucid stayed on *Mir* for 188 days, setting records for the longest stay in space by a woman and by a U.S. astronaut. *Columbia* set a record for the longest space shuttle flight when it completed a mission lasting 16 days and 22 hours. A Russian probe intended for Mars malfunctioned and crashed into the Pacific Ocean, but the U.S. *Pathfinder* probe was launched successfully and landed on Mars on July 4, 1997. NASA launched an additional spacecraft on a four-year Near Earth Asteroid Rendezvous (NEAR) mission to orbit and study asteroid 433 Eros—the first such up-close investigation of an asteroid. The mission acquired unexpected significance when the asteroid Toutatis moved to within 3 million miles of Earth, a distance considered dangerously close.

Creating hope for future treatment of AIDS, scientists at the National Institute of Allergy and Infectious Diseases identified a protein that plays a critical role in permitting the most common strain of the AIDS-producing HIV to infect human cells. Elsewhere, researchers at the University of Texas published an article identifying *BRCA-1,* the gene critical for the formation of breast cancer, which is estimated to cause 44,000 deaths each year in the United States.[12] A team of U.S. and German scientists identified a gene that influences the degree of anxiety people experience by regulating levels of serotonin, a chemical in the brain known to affect moods.

In a development that had far-reaching legal implications, a study published in *Science* revealed the first causal link between smoking of tobacco and development of lung cancer—a connection that the tobacco industry had long maintained was unproven. New federal dietary guidelines for the first time endorsed a vegetarian diet and acknowledged the potential benefits of moderate alcohol consumption. A study of 4,000 black and white adults published in the *American Journal of Public Health* found that working-class blacks who said they had experienced racial discrimination had higher blood pressure than working-class whites or professional blacks, although the results were not conclusive.

A team of researchers from Canada, Indonesia, and the United States published a study suggesting that *Homo erectus,* an evolutionary predecessor of modern humans (*Homo sapiens*), persisted more than 200,000 years longer than previously believed and may have coexisted with *Homo sapiens.* Other scientists concluded that life on Earth originated some 3.85 billion years ago, approximately 350 million years earlier than previously believed, and paleontologists working at an archaeological site in the Sahara Desert found the 93-million-year-old fossilized remains of a new dinosaur species believed to be related to *Tyrannosaurus rex*. Scientists mapping the Earth's inner core described a 1,500-mile-wide solid rock sphere surrounded by an outer core of moving liquid iron some 1,300 miles across.

LITERATURE, THE ARTS, SPORTS, AND POPULAR CULTURE

That independent filmmaking had truly come into its own became evident when four of five of the year's Academy Award nominees for best picture were made by independents: Joel Coen's *Fargo,* Mike Leigh's *Secrets and Lies,* Scott Hicks's *Shine,* and Anthony Minghella's *The English Patient. The English Patient* was named best picture and Minghella best director; *Shine's* Geoffrey Rush was voted best actor, and *Fargo's* Frances McDormand best actress. Lush adaptations of novels about 19th-century gentility also attracted viewers seeking deeper aesthetic experiences than those typically offered by Hollywood films. Jane Austen's novels, in particular, attracted receptive audiences with Douglas McGrath's adaptation of *Emma* (1816), starring Gwyneth Paltrow and Jeremy Northam, and Simon Langton's adaptation of *Pride and Prejudice* (1813), which features Colin Firth and Jennifer Ehle. Jane Campion appealed to similar high-brow tastes in her adaptation of Henry James's *The Portrait of a Lady* (1881), which stars Nicole Kidman, John Malkovich, and Barbara Hershey. Following up on his acclaimed productions of *Henry V* (1989) and *Much Ado About Nothing* (1993), Kenneth Branagh emerged as the decade's premier cinematic interpreter of William Shakespeare, as he directed and starred in a production of *Hamlet* updated to the 19th century. Branagh also spoofed himself in *A Midwinter's Tale,* a comedy about a struggling actor who is determined to direct and star in *Hamlet.*

Nicole Kidman and John Malkovich starred in *The Portrait of a Lady,* one of several 19th-century novels of manners to be adopted for film. *(Photofest)*

Cameron Crowe's *Jerry Maguire* popularized the demand "Show me the money!" in a story about a sports agent and his client, starring Tom Cruise and Cuba Gooding, Jr. Cruise also costarred with Jon Voight, Vanessa Redgrave, and Emmanuelle Béart in Brian De Palma's *Mission Impossible,* an action film based on a popular television series of the 1960s. Edward Zwick's *Courage under Fire* was one of only two films made during the 1990s by Hollywood studios about the 1991 Persian Gulf War. (The other was David Russell's *Three Kings,* 1999.) Appealing both to a growing interest in stories about strong women and contemporary controversies about combat roles for women, *Courage under Fire* starred Meg Ryan and Denzel Washington in the story of a black officer's efforts to discern the truth about the wartime actions of a female helicopter pilot who is under consideration to receive the Medal of Honor. Madonna appeared as Evita Perón in Alan Parker's adaptation of Andrew Lloyd Webber's musical *Evita*, about the lowly born, ambitious Argentine woman who went on to marry the nation's president in 1945. The casting of Madonna, a controversial rock singer known for her sexually explicit lyrics and provocative videos, sparked protests in Argentina, where much of the population had revered Evita Perón before her death in 1952. The special effects made Roland Emmerich's *Independence Day*, the year's top-grossing film ($306.1 million),[13] in which Will Smith, Jeff Goldblum, and Randy Quaid teamed up to save the world. Bette Midler, Goldie Hawn, and Diane Keaton play middle-aged divorcées seeking revenge on their former husbands in Hugh Wilson's *The First Wives Club*, which found a niche audience among divorced women and others who felt they had been misused by men. Hawn also teamed with Alan Alda, Drew Barrymore, Edward Norton, and Woody Allen in Allen's only musical comedy, *Everyone Says I Love You*, a lighthearted, energetic parody of the musical genre in which Allen also pays homage to the Marx Brothers.

The year's top box-office stars were men who played action roles. Sandra Bullock and Michelle Pfeiffer, ranked fifth and 10th, respectively, were the only women in the top 10, which was led by Cruise and Mel Gibson and included Arnold Schwarzenegger, Sean Connery, and Harrison Ford. John Travolta, Robin Williams, and Kevin Costner, known for playing more sensitive roles, were also among the 10 top draws.

Election coverage and campaign advertising permeated the airwaves, as the Republican and Democratic Parties and the campaigns of Dole and Clinton broadcast 1,397 hours of advertisements between April 1 and November 4 in the nation's top 75 media markets. Combined, they spent approximately $130 million on ads, as Democrats outspent Republicans, $70 million to $60 million.[14]

David Brinkley, a highly respected if somewhat acerbic news broadcaster who pioneered network news when he paired with Chet Huntley in 1956, sullied his imminent retirement when, unaware that he was on the air, he made disparaging remarks about Clinton shortly after Clinton's reelection. Brinkley apologized personally to the president in his final broadcast. In the year when the FCC insisted that networks air at least three hours of educational television for children each week, and the government established a television rating system so parents could monitor the content of shows their children watched, cable television claimed a 41 percent share of prime-time viewers,[15] many of whom, especially younger audiences, sought out the more visually innovative, sexually explicit, and otherwise less restrictive programming offered by cable stations. Rosie O'Donnell made her debut as a daytime talk show host and soon attracted a considerable following among viewers who appreciated her wit, her support of children's causes, and her compassionate style, which contrasted sharply with that of her rival hosts, Ricki Lake, Jerry Springer, and others, who encouraged public raunchiness and arguments among guests and live audiences. But Oprah Winfrey, another thoughtful and insightful interviewer, commanded the highest talk-show ratings in television history. The highest-paid entertainer in the world in 1995–96 ($171 million),[16] Winfrey promoted literacy and stimulated interest in provocative literature by introducing her on-air book club, in which she interviewed such authors as the Nobel Prize

The top-rated talk-show host Oprah Winfrey promoted reading and literacy when she introduced her on-air book club. *(AP/Wide World Photos)*

winner Toni Morrison and discussed works of literature that the viewing audience read in preparation for the discussions. The following year, as a result of the book club's rapid success, *Newsweek* named Oprah the most important person in books and media for 1997.

Situation comedies continued to be the most popular programs, although *ER,* a hospital drama, was the top-rated show for the second year in a row. It was followed by the comedies *Seinfeld, Suddenly Susan, Friends,* and *The Single Guy.* Much of the new programming sought to appeal to experiences common to men and women in the 1990s. *Suddenly Susan,* for example, starred the former model and child movie star Brooke Shields as a single woman trying to find her own identity and thrive on her own professionally and socially after she has left her longtime boyfriend and husband-to-be at the altar. Bill Cosby, whose *Cosby Show* had been the top-rated program from 1985 to 1990, reunited with co-star Phylicia Rashad in *Cosby,* in which he plays a suddenly unemployed 60-year-old man trying to adjust to a forced retirement caused by corporate downsizing. *Spin City* appealed to contemporary cynicism about politicians, as Michael J. Fox played a deputy mayor of New York charged with putting a favorable "spin" on the foolish antics of the handsome but insensitive and inept mayor. Starring John Lithgow and Jane Curtin, *Third Rock from the Sun* provided an absurdist view of contemporary human life, as experienced by aliens from another planet trying to pass as Earthlings. *Moesha,* an upbeat sitcom, starred the pop singer Brandy Norwood as an inner-city teenager who reflects on the events that shape her life and relationships. Hoping to tap into some of the apocalyptic anxieties associated with the coming change in millennia, *Millennium,* starring Lance Henriksen as a psychic former FBI agent, centers on efforts by a secret organization to prepare for the battle between good and evil expected at the turn of the century. For the third consecutive year *Frasier* won the Emmy Award as outstanding comedy series. *ER* won as outstanding drama.

The former secretary of defense Robert McNamara's admission in 1995 that the Vietnam War had been poorly conceived and executed provoked several literary responses in 1996, among them Paul Hendrickson's *The Living and the Dead: Robert McNamara and Five Lives of a Lost War*, which follows five people from very disparate backgrounds and circumstances united by their different kinds of connections to "McNamara's War." James Carroll's *An American Requiem: God, My Father, and the War That Came between Us* won the National Book Award in nonfiction for its exploration of the rift between a Vietnam-era air force general and his sons, who refuse for moral reasons to fight the war.

In *Hitler's Willing Executioners: Ordinary Germans and the Holocaust* Daniel Jonah Goldhagen presents evidence demonstrating the widespread complicity of ordinary German civilians—merchants, civil servants, farmers, academics, and others—in carrying out the Nazi's World War II program to exterminate European Jewry. In the aftermath of the Oklahoma City bombing, Morris Dees, chief trial counsel for the Southern Poverty Law Center, a nonprofit organization known for teaching tolerance and taking legal action against hate groups such as the Ku Klux Klan, published *Gathering Storm: America's Militia Threat*, which documents the ideologies and activities of far-Right extremists behind elements of the nation's growing militia movement. *At a Century's Ending: 1982–1995*, the speeches, editorials, book reviews, and other public appearances of the cold war architect George F. Kennan, focuses on the superpower politics of the late 1980s and early 1990s, including a rebuttal of conservatives' claim that Reagan's hard-line policies caused the collapse of the Soviet Union. Kennan also provides autobiographical sketches describing his experiences as a U.S. ambassador in Stalinist Russia and recollections from the formative days of the cold war.

Promoting greater adult sensitivity to and involvement in child rearing, First Lady Hillary Clinton's *It Takes a Village* became a nonfiction best seller. James Fallows argues in *Breaking the News: How the Media Undermine American Democracy* that public distrust of and disaffection with the news stem from the media practice of ignoring substantive issues while focusing instead on newsmakers' "spin" management and political gamesmanship. Melissa Faye Greene's *The Temple Bombing* explores the culture of racism and anti-Semitism in the South. Richard Kluger won the Pulitzer Prize in nonfiction for *Ashes to Ashes*, a history of cigarettes in America and their impact on public health and the economy. Frank McCourt's *Angela's Ashes*, the story of an impoverished Irish woman's struggle to keep her family together despite her husband's alcoholism and her own depression, won the prize for biography. Alan Parker adapted it to film in 1999.

Literary fiction included several works notable for their stylistic experimentation and intermingling of realism with surrealism. Among these was *On with the Story*, John Barth's postmodern arrangement of embedded short stories, which integrates quantum physics with the apocalyptic sensibilities accompanying the demise of the 20th century and with the author's life, which was moving toward its later stages. Another experimental work, Robert Coover's *John's Wife*, describes the literal and symbolic disappearances of a woman who had become the focus of a community's longings. Joyce Carol Oates's *We Were the Mulvaneys* depicts the implosion of a seemingly ideal American family, and William Kennedy's *The Flaming Corsage* describes Albany at the turn of the 20th century. In *Unlocking the Air and Other Stories* Ursula LeGuin has collected a variety of stories published in the *New Yorker, Harper's, Playboy,* and other mainstream magazines. Although LeGuin is best known as a renowned science fiction author, most of these stories address such challenging real-life topics as children's dealing with a retarded parent and adults' coping with a retarded infant. Steven Millhauser won the Pulitzer Prize in fiction with *Martin Dressler: The Tale of an American Dreamer,* a novel about a turn-of-the-20th-century entrepreneur whose sense of doom and failure increases even as he experiences his greatest successes. Andrea Barrett won the National Book Award for her collection *Ship Fever and Other Stories,* which combines scientific investigation with emotional development and social exploration.

The future poet laureate Robert Pinsky published *The Figured Wheel;* Campbell McGrath, a future winner of the MacArthur Award, published his third volume of poetry, *Spring Comes to Chicago;* Robert Fagles released a new, critically acclaimed verse translation of Homer's *The Odyssey;* and Lisel Mueller won the Pulitzer Prize for *Alive Together: New and Selected Poems.*

Best-selling fiction included the anonymously authored satire of the Clintons, *Primary Colors* (the *Newsweek* columnist Joe Klein later acknowledged authorship); Terry McMillan's *How Stella Got Her Groove Back,* about a professional 42-year-old divorced mother whose orderly, if hectic, life is thrown into disarray after she meets a younger man while vacationing in Jamaica; and such genre fiction as Tom Clancy's *Executive Orders,* Mary Higgins Clark's *Moonlight Becomes You,* and John Grisham's *The Runaway Jury.*

Terrence McNally, who won the 1995 Tony Award for *Love! Valor! Compassion!,* repeated in 1996 with *Master Class,* an homage to the opera diva Maria Callas, which opened in late 1995 and starred Zoe Caldwell. August Wilson premiered his play *Seven Guitars,* about a blues musician and his companions in the late 1940s. Also opening on Broadway were the British playwright David Hare's *Skylight,* about two friends, and Ronald Harwood's *Taking Sides,* an exploration of the life of the conductor Wilhelm Furtwangler, who refused to renounce Hitler and remained in Germany during World War II to conduct the Berlin Philharmonic but also refused to join the Nazi Party and aided individual Jews. The Tony-winning director Walter Bobbie revived John Kander and Fred Ebb's musical *Chicago,* a dark and cynical comedy about a murderess who became a celebrity. *Chicago* went on to receive the 1997 Tony Award as best musical revival, and its stars, James Naughton and Bebe Neuwirth, won as best leading actor and actress in a musical. Jonathan Larson won the 1996 Tony for best musical with *Rent,* an innovative rock opera about life on New York's Lower East Side, based on Giacomo Puccini's opera *La Bohème* (1896). *Rent,* which features such rock numbers as "Rent," "Out Tonight," and "What You Own," was the first play since *A Chorus Line* in 1976 to win both the Pulitzer Prize in drama and the Tony Award as best musical; Larson, however, died of an aortic aneurysm the night of the show's final preview.

The death at age 79 of the renowned blues and gospel singer Ella Fitzgerald, known as "the First Lady of Jazz," also cast a pallor over the world of music, as did the assassination in Las Vegas of the 25-year-old rap performer

Tupac Shakur, whose extremely violent lyrics had been a frequent target of criticism in the mainstream culture. Shakur's death was suspected to be related to an ongoing feud between so called East Coast and West Coast rappers. The rap artist Snoop Doggy Dog (Calvin Broadus) and his bodyguard were cleared of murder charges in the death of Philip Woldermariam.

New works of classical music were debuted by Philip Glass, John Williams, Ellen Taaffe Zwilich, and David Diamond, and the Metropolitan Opera celebrated the conductor James Levine's 25-year association with the company. The New York City Opera debuted George Whyte and Jost Meier's controversial work *The Dreyfus Affair,* which reenacts the rampant anti-Semitism of turn-of-the-20th-century France, and "The Three Tenors," Luciano Pavarotti, Plácido Domingo, and José Carreras, attracted large, enthusiastic opera audiences throughout their worldwide tour.

Popular hit songs included the Spanish-language "Macarena" by The Bayside Boys, "Because You Loved Me" by Celine Dion, "Exhale" by Whitney Houston, "Hey Lover" by LL Cool J, and Eric Clapton's Grammy-winning single "Change the World." Dion's *Falling into You* won as best album. Hillary Rodham Clinton's album *It Takes a Village,* based on her book, won as best spoken-word album.

The NAMES Project Quilt was displayed in its entirety for the last time when it was spread over the National Mall in Washington, D.C. Begun in 1987, the quilt, which contained the names of people who had died of AIDS, by 1996 consisted of some 38,000 panels that covered the entire Mall. Afterward, the quilt was too large to be viewed in full, but it continued to grow, exceeding 44,000 panels and 84,000 names.[17]

In what was celebrated as a victory of humans over machines, the Russian chess champion Garry Kasparov recovered from an initial loss to defeat Deep Blue, the world's top chess-playing computer, in a six-game tournament.

Despite the shock of the fatal bomb blast during a concert at Atlanta's Centennial Olympic Park, the Summer Olympic Games proceeded more or less as scheduled, but with heightened security. Altogether, 197 countries participated, and the United States led with 44 gold medals, followed by Russia with 26 and Germany with 20. The U.S. sprinter Michael Johnson, who broke the long-standing record for the men's 200-meter race, won gold medals in that competition and the 400-meter race, an Olympic first. The long jumper Carl Lewis won his ninth gold medal; Dan O'Brien won the decathlon; and the women's gymnastic team won its first gold medal on the final effort by the injured Kerri Strug. Amy Van Dyken became the first American woman to win four gold medals in swimming events, and beach volleyball made its debut as an Olympic sport. Unrelated to the 1996 Olympic Games, John du Pont, a member of the prominent du Pont family, killed the 36-year-old former Olympic gold medal wrestler Dave Schultz at du Pont's Olympic training center for wrestlers in Newton Square, Pennsylvania. Du Pont was later convicted of the murder but found to be mentally ill.

The entry of Tiger Woods into professional golf injected new life and interest into a sport that was generally associated with white middle- and upper-class suburbanites. After winning three consecutive national junior golf titles and then three consecutive U.S. amateur titles in a span of six years, 20-year-old Woods turned professional during the summer of 1996. In his first two months he won two tournaments and finished in the top five in five others, tying long-held records, winning almost $735,000, and garnering $60 million in endorsements, notably with Nike, and a $2.2 million book contract. A dark-skinned man of mixed racial background who looks African American, Woods energized professional golf with his commanding performances, while attracting a broader, younger, and more ethnically and culturally diverse audience to the sport. Despite the "Tigermania" phenomenon, however, Steve Jones won the prestigious USGA Open.

In baseball, 1996 was called the Year of the Homer, as 59 players hit more than 30 home runs and three teams broke the 35-year record for home run totals compiled by a single team. The sudden increase in home-run production led to widespread speculation that the baseballs or the players or both were "juiced"—that the balls were wound differently to make them more lively, and/or some players were using steroids or other performance-enhancing drugs.

The New York Yankees defeated the Atlanta Braves in six games to win their first World Series championship in 18 years. Oakland's Mark McGwire led the major leagues with 52 home runs. The Atlanta pitcher John Smoltz and the Toronto Blue Jay Pat Hentgen won the Cy Young Award, and the Houston Astro Ken Caminiti and the Texas Ranger Juan Gonzales were the National and American League MVPs. In an effort to avert the labor strife that had plagued the sport in recent years, owners and players agreed to a new five-year contract that included a luxury tax on payrolls and a revenue-sharing clause, in which the 13 clubs who had the highest revenues would partly subsidize the 13 lowest-earning teams.

Bret Favre completed a record-setting 39 touchdown passes while leading the Green Bay Packers to their first championship season since their glory days under the head coach Vince Lombardi in the 1960s. Green Bay defeated the New England Patriots 35-21 in the Super Bowl, which was played in January 1997, and Favre was the league MVP. Don Shula, the head coach who had the most wins in NFL history, was pressured into retirement by the Miami Dolphins, after 26 years with the team. His replacement was the two-time Super Bowl winner Jimmy Johnson, who had resigned from the Dallas Cowboys in 1994. The University of Florida Gators became the top-ranked college football team after they defeated the Florida State University Seminoles in the Sugar Bowl. The Gator quarterback Danny Wuerfel edged out the University of Tennessee quarterback Peyton Manning in the Heisman Trophy competition.

Magic Johnson made a brief effort to return to professional basketball after his retirement in 1991, but his comeback lasted only three and a half months. On the other hand, Michael Jordan, who had retired after the 1993 season and tried unsuccessfully to play professional baseball in 1994, ended his retirement at the end of the 1994–95 season and returned full time in 1995–96 to win the basketball MVP award. He also led the Chicago Bulls to their first championship since they won three in a row with him between 1991 and 1993. The University of Kentucky won the men's college basketball competition, and Marcus Camby of the University of Massachusetts was named player of the year. Hockey's Colorado Avalanche swept the Florida Panthers in four games to win the Stanley Cup. The U.S. team defeated Canada's to win hockey's World Cup for the first time. Pete Sampras and Steffi Graf both won the singles competitions at the U.S. Tennis Open for the second consecutive year; Evander Holyfield, an 8-1 underdog, claimed the boxing heavyweight title when he scored the technical knockout of Mike Tyson; and Grindstone, ridden by Jerry Bailey, won the Kentucky Derby.

CHRONICLE OF EVENTS

January 1: Permit holders in Texas and Oklahoma are allowed to carry concealed weapons.

January 2: In accordance with the 1995 Dayton agreement, U.S. peacekeeping troops begin to deploy in Bosnia.

January 2: The former secretary of the interior James Watt, the highest-ranking Reagan administration official to be charged in a scandal involving influence peddling in the Department of Housing and Urban Development (HUD) during the 1980s, pleads guilty to a misdemeanor charge of attempting to mislead a federal grant jury. In return, prosecutors agree to drop 18 felony charges of perjury and influence peddling.

January 5: In compliance with the Whitewater investigation, the White House releases Hillary Clinton's billing records from the Rose Law Firm.

January 5: Japan's premier Tomiichi Murayama resigns in response to a stagnant economy and a banking crisis.

January 6: Clinton signs a stopgap funding bill that ends the longest government shutdown in U.S. history. He also signs two other bills funding certain agencies and programs through September 30, 1996.

January 7–8: A massive blizzard paralyzes the East Coast.

January 8: François Mitterrand, the former president of France, dies at age 79.

January 9: Clinton vetoes a Republican-sponsored welfare reform bill because, he maintains, it does not provide incentives for finding work, and it threatens to increase the suffering of poor children.

January 9: The U.S. Eighth Circuit Court of Appeals rules 2-1 that Paula Jones may bring her civil suit against Clinton while he is serving in office. The suit charges Clinton with committing sexual harassment while he was governor of Arkansas.

January 11: The Japanese parliament elects Ryutaro Hashimoto as premier.

January 11: Britain's former prime minister, Margaret Thatcher, criticizes her successor and fellow Conservative Party member John Major for straying from conservative fiscal policies.

January 11: In his weekly radio broadcast, Clinton pledges to "break the backs" of criminal youth gangs terrorizing the inner cities.

A U.S. court of appeals ruling permitted Paula Jones to bring her sexual harassment suit against President Bill Clinton to court while he was still in office. *(AP/Wide World Photos)*

January 15: The Israeli prime minister Benjamin Netanyahu and Yasser Arafat, head of the Palestinian National Authority (PNA), sign a long-delayed agreement for an Israeli troop pullout from the West Bank city of Hebron.

January 15: Speaking at the official Martin Luther King, Jr., Day celebration at the Ebenezer Baptist Church in Atlanta, where King had preached, Clinton defends affirmative action and the peacekeeping mission to Bosnia.

January 15: Andreas Papandreou resigns as prime minister of Greece. He is succeeded by Costas Simitis.

January 17: The astronomers Geoffrey W. Marcy and R. Paul Butler report the discovery of planets beyond the solar system capable of containing life-sustaining water. One of the planets orbits the star 47 Ursa Major in the Big Dipper constellation; the other orbits 70 Virginis in the constellation Virgo.

Both are comparatively close to Earth, about 35 million light-years away. The astronomer Christopher Burrows announces the discovery of a Jupiter-like planet orbiting the star Beta Pictoris, and NASA announces that the search for extrasolar planets will be among its top priorities over the next 25 years.

January 20: Arafat is overwhelmingly elected president of the new Palestinian National Authority.

January 23: In his State of the Union address Clinton declares that the era of big government is over.

January 24: Poland's premier, Jozef Oleksy, resigns amid charges that he had passed state secrets to Soviet and Russian intelligence agents between 1990 and 1995.

January 26: The Senate votes overwhelmingly to ratify the START II treaty, which reduces U.S. and Russian arsenals to about one-third of their 1993 levels.

January 26: Clinton signs another stopgap continuing resolution to sustain government programs through March 15.

January 30: The basketball star Magic Johnson, who had retired in 1991 after testing positive for HIV, returns to play for the Los Angeles Lakers.

February 1: A new law in Texas permits relatives of murder victims to view the execution of the murderer.

February 2: The singer/dancer Gene Kelly dies.

February 3: In compliance with the Dayton peace accords, Bosnian Serbs end their siege of Sarajevo, and Serbs, Croats, and Muslims withdraw forces from other parts of Bosnia.

February 5–11: Pope John Paul II travels through Central and South America, making stops in Guatemala, Nicaragua, El Salvador, and Venezuela.

February 7: In the first peaceful transfer of power in Haiti's history from one democratically elected president to another, René Préval succeeds outgoing president Jean-Bertrand Aristide.

February 8: Clinton signs a telecommunications act that introduces the greatest changes to communications law in 62 years.

February 9: NFL owners approve a proposal by Cleveland Browns owner Art Modell to move the franchise to Baltimore.

February 10: The IRA ends a 17-month cease-fire when it explodes a bomb near a railway station in the heart of London's Docklands.

February 10: Clinton signs a $265 defense authorization bill.

February 11: Two car bombs explode in Algiers, killing 17. No one claims responsibility; the government suspects that Islamic militants are responsible.

February 12: In Gaza, Arafat officially takes office as president of the Palestinian National Authority.

February 16: An Amtrak train collides head-on with a commuter train in Silver Spring, Maryland, killing three crew members and eight passengers.

February 19: Canada introduces the two-dollar coin to replace its two-dollar bill.

February 19: The World Health Organization (WHO) confirms that at least 13 people have died in Gabon in an outbreak of the Ebola virus. Gabon is the second African nation within a year to experience a deadly Ebola outbreak, after Zaire's in 1995.

February 20: The conservative candidate Pat Buchanan wins the Republican primary in New Hampshire, edging out his rivals, Robert Dole and Lamar Alexander. The victory establishes Buchanan, who represents the far Right on the Republican political spectrum, as a viable candidate.

February 22: Prime Minister Chirac announces that France will end its draft and eliminate its land-based nuclear weapons.

February 22: The assistant secretary of state, Richard Holbrook, who brokered the Dayton Peace Accord, resigns.

February 22: Clinton renominates Alan Greenspan for a third four-year term as chairman of the Federal Reserve Board.

February 23: Two sons-in-law of Iraq's president Saddam Hussein are killed three days after returning to Baghdad. They had defected to Jordan in August 1995.

February 24: Cuban military aircraft shoot down two unarmed civilian planes piloted by members of the Cuban exile group Brothers to the Rescue. All four aboard are killed.

February 25: Dr. Haing S. Ngor is found murdered outside his home in Los Angeles. Ngor was a Cambodian refugee who survived torture and went on to win an Academy Award for his supporting role in *The Killing Fields* (1984), a film about the massacres committed by Cambodia's Khmer Rouge government in the 1970s.

February 25: Palestinian suicide bombers affiliated with Hamas explode bombs in Jerusalem and the coastal town of Ashkelon, killing 27, including two American students. Hamas announces that the attack was retaliation for the assassination of one of its leaders.

February 27: Steve Forbes wins the Arizona and Delaware presidential primaries; Dole wins in North and South Dakota. Buchanan finishes second in South Dakota and third in the other states.

February 29: The Senate confirms the Persian Gulf War hero General Barry R. McCaffrey as the new "drug czar"—director of the Office of National Drug Control Policy.

March 2: The UN ambassador Madeleine Albright addresses Miami's Cuban exile community in the Orange Bowl during a memorial service for the civilian exiles shot down by Cuban jets on February 24.

March 3–4: Suicide bombings kill 33 in Jerusalem and Tel Aviv, raising to 61 the number of Israelis killed in the past nine days and provoking Peres to declare that his government will wage war against Hamas. However, Arafat condemns the attack and Peres resists pressure to end talks with the Palestinian National Authority. Hamas maintains the bombings were a response to the killing of one of its operatives in January.

March 4: The Whitewater-related trial of Arkansas governor Jim Guy Tucker and James and Susan McDougal opens.

March 6: After losing to Dole in primaries held in 11 states on March 2 and March 5, Lamar Alexander withdraws from the race for the Republican presidential nomination.

March 6: Canada's finance minister Paul Martin presents the budget for the 1996–97 fiscal year. The plan calls for reduced spending on social programs in an effort to narrow the budget deficit.

March 12: On so-called Super Tuesday Robert Dole essentially clinches the Republican nomination with victories in all seven states holding primaries. Steve Forbes withdraws, but Pat Buchanan vows to continue his campaign.

March 12: Clinton signs a bill increasing the federal debt limit through March 29.

March 12: Clinton signs the Helms-Burton law, which strengthens the U.S. embargo against Cuba by penalizing foreign investment in the country.

March 13: With Syria absent, leaders of the Palestinian National Authority and 27 nations, including Israel, the United States, and 13 Arab nations, reaffirm the Israeli-Palestinian peace process and condemn suicide bombings and other acts of terrorism.

March 13: Thomas Hamilton massacres 16 children and one teacher in the small Scottish town of Dunblane.

March 14: Canada's Radio-Television and Telecommunications Commission orders the nation's television broadcasters, cable networks, and other programming providers to establish a rating system that indicates the levels of violence in their programs.

March 20: In the second high-profile trial of Lyle and Erik Menendez, a Los Angeles jury convicts the brothers of killing their affluent parents. They are sentenced to life imprisonment without parole on April 17.

March 24–25: Hillary Clinton visits U.S. troops serving in Bosnia.

March 25: In San Francisco 176 gay couples marry when the city grants homosexuals the right to city-sanctioned marriages.

March 25: Some 20 people, armed members of an antitax organization known as the Freemen and their wives and children, face off against approximately 100 law enforcement agents in eastern Montana, after the FBI arrests two of the group's leaders on charges of committing fraud and making death threats.

March 26: Robert Dole wins the California, Nevada, and Washington primaries and officially secures the Republican nomination for president. Pat Buchanan places a distant second in California and Washington and third, after Steve Forbes, in Nevada.

March 29: The government avoids going into default when Clinton signs another measure raising the federal debt limit.

March 29: Attorney General Janet Reno announces that the government intends to resolve the standoff with the Freemen peacefully and to avoid armed confrontation and siege tactics.

April 2: A controversial Defense Department study concludes that there is no evidence of a so-called Gulf War syndrome. Since the conclusion of the Persian Gulf War in 1991, veterans have been complaining of symptoms including chronic fatigue, rashes, memory loss, and other ailments.

April 3: FBI agents arrest Theodore Kaczynski as the Unabomber.

April 3: Commerce secretary Ronald Brown dies along with 34 others when the U.S. Air Force jet car-

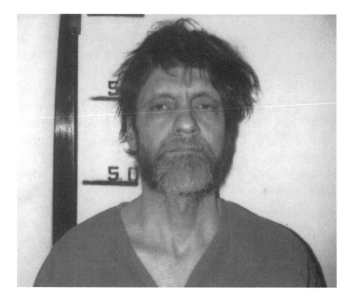

Ted Kaczynski, the so-called Unabomber, was arrested after targeting promoters of high technology for 17 years. *(AP/Wide World Photos)*

rying them crashes into a mountain in bad weather near Dubrovnik, Croatia.

April 4: North Korea announces it will no longer respect the demilitarized zone (DMZ) separating it from South Korea.

April 5–7: North Korea stages military exercises in its sector of the DMZ. In response, South Korea raises its intelligence monitoring to its highest level in 14 years and convenes an emergency national security council meeting to assess the situation.

April 5: Monica Lewinsky is transferred from the White House to the Pentagon.

April 9: Clinton signs legislation giving him and future presidents a line-item veto.

April 9: The former representative Dan Rostenkowski of Illinois pleads guilty to two counts of mail fraud as part of a plea agreement in which he will serve 17 months in prison and pay a $100,000 fine.

April 10: Clinton vetoes a bill to ban an abortion procedure used to terminate late-term pregnancies.

April 24: Clinton signs the antiterrorism bill.

April 25: Congress approves a $159.4 billion omnibus spending bill that ends its months-long budget stalemate with Clinton. Clinton signs it on April 26.

April 28: Clinton testifies for three and a half hours as a defense witness in the fraud trial of his for-

mer Whitewater associates James and Susan McDougal and Governor Jim Guy Tucker of Arkansas.

May 4: The Associated Press publicizes a recently declassified 1955 document that indicates that North Korea sent several American prisoners of war (POWs) to the Soviet Union during the Korean War.

May 8: South Africa adopts a new, democratic constitution.

May 11: A ValuJet airliner flying from Miami to Atlanta crashes in the Florida Everglades, killing 109.

May 14: After a brief comeback, Magic Johnson retires from basketball for the final time.

May 15: Robert Dole, the Senate majority leader, announces that he will quit the Senate by June 11 to devote his energies fully to his campaign.

May 16: Clinton announces a limited ban on land mines.

May 20: Iraq and the United Nations sign an agreement allowing Iraq to export a limited amount of oil in order to pay for additional food and medical supplies.

May 21: Some 400 Sicilian police surround the villa of the alleged Mafia boss Giovanni Brusca and secure his arrest.

May 27: Yeltsin and Chechen rebel leader Zelimkhan Yandarbiyev agree to end hostilities by the end of June. However, they fail to resolve the basic difference at the heart of their dispute—the Chechen demand for independence.

May 28: Jim Guy Tucker and James and Susan McDougal are convicted on several Whitewater-related charges involving illegal loans. The White House issues a statement pointing out that Clinton was in no way involved with the allegations for which the trio was convicted. Tucker, who succeeded Clinton as governor, resigns on July 15 and is sentenced to four years' probation on August 19.

May 31: LSD (lysergic acid diethylamine) advocate Timothy Leary, who popularized the "mind-expanding" hallucinogen during the 1960s, dies at age 75. On April 21, 1997, his ashes, along with those of the *Star Trek* creator Gene Roddenberry, are launched into space aboard a Pegasus rocket.

June 6: For the second time in two years the Senate narrowly defeats a constitutional amendment requiring a balanced federal budget.

June 9: King Bhumibol of Thailand, the world's longest-reigning monarch, celebrates his 50th year on the throne.

June 10: Talks on the future of Northern Ireland open, but without Sinn Féin, which is excluded as a result of renewed IRA terrorism.

June 12: Clinton denounces a recent string of 33 fires in southern black churches that have apparently been deliberately set over the past 18 months.

June 12: The Southern Baptist Convention votes to censure the Walt Disney Company for its decision to offer health insurance benefits to homosexual partners of its employees.

June 13: The federal standoff with armed members of the Freemen ends after 81 days when the last 16 members surrender peacefully.

June 15: The IRA detonates a large bomb in Manchester, England, injuring some 200 people.

July 1: Federal agents arrest 12 members of the Arizona paramilitary group known as the Viper Militia, who are suspected of planning to blow up several federal buildings.

July 1: Australia enacts the world's first law permitting voluntary euthanasia.

July 4: Despite his failing health, Boris Yeltsin is reelected president of Russia with 53.7 percent of the vote. His Communist opponent, Gennadi Zyuganov, claims 40.4 percent.

July 5: Scientists at the Roslin Institute in Scotland clone the first adult mammal, Dolly the sheep. They do not announce their achievement however, until February 23, 1997.

July 14: Timothy McVeigh goes on trial for the 1995 bombing of the Oklahoma City federal building.

July 16: Clinton delays by six months implementation of a controversial portion of the Helms-Burton law that would have permitted U.S. citizens to sue, in U.S. courts, users of their property confiscated in Cuba by the Castro regime.

July 17: TWA Flight 800 explodes shortly after takeoff from New York's JFK International Airport, killing all 228 aboard.

July 19: The Summer Olympics, featuring some 11,000 athletes of 197 nations, open in Atlanta, Georgia.

July 27: A bomb explodes during a concert in Atlanta's Centennial Olympic Park, killing two and injuring more than 100.

August 1: The Somali warlord General Mohammed Aidid dies of wounds incurred on July 24 in factional fighting in the capital city, Mogadishu.

August 3: In a special Olympic ceremony, the boxer Muhammad Ali, formerly known as Cassius Clay, receives an honorary gold medal to compensate for the one he refused during the 1960 Olympic Games in Rome.

August 4: In the final day of the 1996 Olympics, Josia Thugwane becomes the first black South African to win a gold medal, when he places first in the men's marathon.

August 6: NASA scientists announce that they believe they have discovered evidence that life once existed on Mars in fragments of a 4.5-billion-year-old meteorite found in Antarctica.

August 6: Clinton signs a bill reauthorizing the Safe Drinking Water Act of 1974.

August 9: For only the second time in the United States, a jury holds a tobacco company responsible for adverse health affects of cigarette smoking when the Brown & Williamson Tobacco Corporation is found liable and required to pay $750,000 in damages to a cancer-stricken Florida man who had smoked for 40 years.

August 15: Dole receives the Republican nomination for president.

August 18: Clinton celebrates his 50th birthday.

August 21: The former South African president F. W. de Klerk apologizes before the Truth and Reconciliation Commission for pain and suffering caused by almost a half-century of apartheid.

August 23: A truce calling for a partial Russian withdrawal and establishment of joint Russian-Chechen patrols to keep the peace begins in Chechnya.

August 28: Prince Charles and Princess Diana of England are divorced after public revelations of extramarital affairs by both partners. Diana is stripped of her title, Her Royal Highness.

August 29: Clinton accepts the Democratic nomination for president. Gore is renominated for vice president.

August 30: Louis Farrakhan, leader of the Nation of Islam in the United States, accepts a controversial human rights award from Libya, a nation sanctioned by the United States and others for sponsoring terrorism.

September 3: The United States launches 27 cruise missiles against targets in Iraq in retaliation for Iraqi attacks on ethnic Kurds in northern Iraq.

September 7: Hurricane Fran strikes the Carolinas, killing 12 and causing millions of dollars in damage.

September 7: In an apparent drive-by shooting, the rap artist Tupac Shakur is shot in Las Vegas after attending a boxing match. He dies on September 13.

September 9: Susan McDougal is imprisoned for refusing to testify before a grand jury investigating the Whitewater affair.

September 17: The former vice president Spiro T. Agnew dies.

September 18: Bosnia holds free elections for the first time since the end of the fighting.

September 18: A North Korean submarine carrying armed commandos runs aground off the coast of South Korea. Within a week, 20 of the commandos and three South Korean soldiers are killed. Ultimately, 24 North Koreans are killed and one is captured.

September 19: IBM announces that beginning January 1, 1997, it will extend health-care coverage and other benefits to same-sex partners of employees.

September 21: Clinton signs the Defense of Marriage Act, which denies federal recognition of same-sex marriages and prohibits granting of federal benefits to partners in such marriages.

September 21: In a secret ceremony on Cumberland Island off the Georgia coast, 35-year-old John F. Kennedy, Jr., son of the late president John F. Kennedy, marries 30-year-old Carolyn Bessette, a former public relations executive for the fashion designer Calvin Klein Inc.

September 24: The five publicly acknowledged nuclear-armed nations—China, France, Russia, Great Britain, and the United States—sign the Comprehensive Nuclear Test Ban Treaty.

September 25–26: Riots and pitched battles between armed Palestinian police and Israeli soldiers begin in the West Bank and Gaza Strip after Israelis in Jerusalem open a new entrance to an archaeological tunnel at a religious site revered by both Muslims and Jews. It is the most extensive rioting since 1993.

September 27: Victorious Taliban leaders capture the capital city, Kabul, and install an Islamic theocracy in Afghanistan.

September 28: Clinton signs a bill that imposes tougher new measures to fight illegal immigration.

September 30: Clinton signs an omnibus spending bill that funds nine cabinet-level departments, as well as dozens of agencies and hundreds of programs for the 1997 fiscal year.

October 6: Clinton and Dole debate about the economy, Medicare spending, foreign policy, and their respective tax-cut proposals in the first of two presidential debates. The third-party candidate Ross Perot has been excluded from the debates.

October 7: The Supreme Court opens its second term.

October 14: The Dow-Jones industrial index closes above 6,000 for the first time.

October 15: The pop star Madonna gives birth to a baby girl.

October 16: Responding to questions from audience members in a San Diego town hall–type forum, Clinton and Dole discuss health care, Social Security, military spending, affirmative action, gay rights, and Clinton's personal integrity in their second of two debates.

October 23: A civil trial opens to determine whether O. J. Simpson is responsible for the "wrongful deaths" of his former wife, Nicole Brown Simpson, and her friend Ronald Goldman.

October 26: The Justice Department announces that the security guard Richard Jewell is no longer a target in its investigation of the bombing at the Olympics.

October 30: Former South African police colonel Eugene de Kock is sentenced to life in prison for murder and other crimes committed under apartheid.

November 5: The Democrats Clinton and Gore are reelected in a landslide victory over their Republican challengers, Dole and Kemp. Republicans retain control of both houses of Congress, however.

November 5: Fifty-six percent of Californian voters elect to allow doctors to prescribe marijuana for treating gravely ill patients.

November 7: The U.S. Army announces that it will investigate rape charges against senior officers at the Aberdeen Proving Ground in Maryland.

November 10: Evander Holyfield claims boxing's WBA heavyweight title by defeating Mike Tyson.

November 14: The singer Michael Jackson, who divorced Lisa Marie Presley earlier in the year, marries a Los Angeles nurse, Debbie Rowe, who is pregnant with their child.

November 19: Thirty-six people are rescued when a fire breaks out in the Channel Tunnel between France and England.

November 29: The UN War Crimes Tribunal issues its first sentence when it condemns a Bosnian Serb corporal for taking part in the 1995 massacre of Muslims at Srebrenica, where some 1,200 unarmed civilians had been killed.

November 29: The asteroid Toutatis passes dangerously close when it approaches within 3 million miles of Earth.

December 17: The UN General Assembly elects Kofi Annan of Ghana to replace Egypt's Boutros Boutros-Ghali as secretary-general.

December 17: Leftist guerrillas take 500 hostages at a garden party in the Japanese embassy in Lima, Peru.

December 17: The Red Cross removes all its foreign staff from Chechnya after five of its nurses are shot to death in their sleep by masked gunmen.

December 29: North Korea apologizes for the September incident in which a submarine filled with its commandos went aground off South Korea.

December 30: After passage in November of referendums in California and Nevada legalizing use of marijuana for medicinal purposes, federal officials announce they will prosecute physicians who prescribe marijuana and other illegal drugs.

December 30: Accepting the North's apology, South Korea returns the remains of the 24 North Korean commandos its forces killed after the grounding of the submarine. The United States announces that North Korea has agreed to direct peace talks with South Korea.

December 30: The last Russian troops withdraw from Chechnya, effectively leaving the republic in rebel control.

EYEWITNESS TESTIMONY

As we wind up our century and our millennium . . . it is no surprise that the "terminary malady" afflicts us. Of the End of Art we have been hearing ever since this century's beginning, when Modernism arrived on the stage of Western Civ. Picasso, Pound, Stravinsky—all felt themselves to be as much terminators as pioneers . . . groundbreakers, yes, but gravediggers as well, for the artistic tradition that preceded and produced them. By midcentury we were hearing not only of the Death of the Novel—that magnificent old genre that was born a–dying, like all of us; that has gone on vigorously dying since . . . but likewise of the Death of Print Culture and the End of Modernism, supplanted by the electronic visual media and by so-called Postmodernism. And not long ago, believe it or not, there was an international symposium on "The End of *Post*modernism"—just when we thought we might be beginning to understand what that term describes. In other jurisdictions, we have Professor Whatsisname on the End of History, and Professor So-and-So on the End of Physics (indeed, the End of Nature), and Professor Everybody-and-Her-Brother on the End of the Old World Order with the collapse of the Soviet Union and of international Communism.

In short and in sum, endings, endings everywhere; apocalypses large and small. Good-bye to the tropical rainforests, good-bye to the whales, good-bye to mountain gorillas and the giant pandas and the rhinoceri. . . . Good-bye to the oldest continuous culture on the planet: the Marsh Arabs of Southern Iraq, in process of extermination by Saddam Hussein even as I speak. Good-bye to once-so-cosmopolitan Beirut and once-so-hospitable Sarajevo. . . . The end of this,

Rent updated and revived the rock opera genre. *(Photofest)*

the end of that; little wonder we grow weary of "endism," as I have heard it called.

The narrator discussing the sense of impending conclusion associated with the termination of the millennium in John Barth, On with the Story *(1996), pp. 14–15.*

The subject of the work is death at an early age. And in one of the dark dramatic coincidences theater occasionally springs on us, its 35-year-old author died only weeks before its opening. Yet no one who attends Jonathan Larson's *Rent,* the exhilarating landmark rock opera at the New York Theater Workshop, is likely to mistake it for a wake.

Indeed, this vigorous tale of a marginal band of artists in Manhattan's East Village, a contemporary answer to *La Bohème,* rushes forward on an electric current of emotion that is anything but morbid. Sparked by a young, intensely vibrant cast . . . and sustained by a glittering, inventive score, the work finds a transfixing brightness in characters living in the shadow of AIDS. Puccini's ravishingly melancholy work seemed, like many operas of its time, to romance death; Mr. Larson's spirited score and lyrics defy it.

Theater critic Ben Brantley reviewing the award-winning rock opera Rent, *in Brantley, "Rent," New York* Times, *February 14, 1996, p. C11.*

I was struck by the joy of these pilots in committing cold-blooded murder. Frankly, this is not *cojones* [testicles]. This is cowardice.

UN ambassador Madeline Albright on February 25, 1996, seeking UN condemnation of Cuba for shooting down two unarmed planes piloted by anti-Castro Cuban exiles on February 24, 1996, in Albright, Madam Secretary *(2003), p. 205.*

Señora Cojones! Madam Cojones!

Epithets of approval shouted to the UN ambassador Madeleine Albright by members of the Cuban exile community in a memorial service at Miami's Orange Bowl on March 2, 1996, in Albright, Madam Secretary *(2003), p. 206.*

If there is any lesson to be learned from this book, it surely must be that pious rhetoric and the evocation of values mean nothing when not forthrightly tied to strategies and policies that might help us to realize them in the lives of ordinary American families. The appalling evidence of children's distress and alienation leaves no doubt that a village cannot raise a child. It takes a family—ideally a mother and a father—to raise a child, and the village's first responsibility is not to hamper them in doing so. But then, rhetoric notwithstanding, Mrs. Clinton does not ultimately attribute much importance to mere parents, since, as she affirms in conclusion, "Children, after all, are citizens too."

The reviewer Elizabeth Fox-Genovese taking issue with Hillary Rodham Clinton's book It Takes a Village *(1996), in Fox-Genovese, "It Takes a Village: and Other Lessons Children Teach Us," National Review, March 11, 1996, p. 62.*

Liberalism, once the dominant ideology in American politics . . . is today beset on all sides. Since 1988, when George [Herbert Walker] Bush made "liberal" an epithet akin to "communist," few political leaders have claimed that label. Republican politicos and pundits, and not a few Democrats as well, now blame every fault, real and imagined, of American life on the "failures" of liberalism. Political theorists, meanwhile, assail liberalism for an obsession with individual rights that undermines a sense of community and the collective good. A source of confusion is that liberalism is used in different senses: Modern liberalism means activist government, while "classical liberalism" suggests protecting individual liberty against the state. . . .

In *Democracy's Discontent,* Sandel builds upon his earlier critique to offer a full historical account of the evolution of liberalism within the United States. . . . Embedded in Sandel's account is a salutary reminder that the meaning of freedom has changed markedly over time. Today, "freedom" is invoked mainly by proponents of lower taxes, the right to bear arms and a "free market." . . . For much of our history, however, political leaders assumed that freedom depended on egalitarian economic institutions.

Professor Eric Foner reviewing Michael J. Sandel's book Democracy's Discontent: America in Search of a Public Philosophy, *in Foner, "Liberalism's Discontents," Nation, May 6, 1996, p. 34.*

Are women's rights human rights? During the cold war the United States granted political refugee status to virtually any escapee from the Soviet Union and its satellites. . . . Yet even by the narrowest definition of political rights, millions of women around the globe are as deprived as were the inhabitants of the evil empire—unable to vote, travel freely, own property, speak their minds. By any more expansive definition of liberty, even more millions of women qualify as human rights victims. For all its faults, Communism did not permit the legal murder of women by male relatives for supposed crimes against the family "honor," use rape as a weapon of terror, deny widows custody of their children or permit young girls to be sold into polygamous marriages.

That's not the way our government sees it of course: Can you imagine Jimmy Carter inviting, say, Pakistan to release to the U.S. its rape victims jailed for the crime of fornication in the same buoyant spirit he dared Castro to let loose the Marielitos? If one took seriously the government's fine words on human rights, one could not begin to understand how George Bush declared the one-child policy of China a human rights violation justifying American asylum . . . while ignoring the four-child policy of Ceauşescu's Romania, which featured many of the same totalitarian measures—mandatory gynecological inspections, coercive monitoring of pregnancies, economic sanctions for reproductive noncooperators. Still less could one understand how we came to defend Kuwait, of all places, as a bastion of democracy, producing the truly weird paradox of U.S. women soldiers flexing their newly won military muscles to reinstate a barely constitutional monarchy that denied most men and all women the vote.

Political commentator Katha Pollitt arguing that abuses of women's rights are abuses of human rights in Pollitt, "Women's Rights, Human Rights," Nation, May 13, 1996, p. 9.

August Wilson is the best American historical playwright ever. The plays of our other leading playwrights—O'Neill, Odets, Miller, Williams, Albee—are usually set in contemporary times, or, like Miller's *The Crucible,* are allegories about contemporary issues. . . .

Wilson, by contrast, has an interest in American history for its own sake. A high school dropout, he describes himself as a graduate of the free Carnegie Library in Pittsburgh, where he grew up. . . .

Wilson's latest play, *Seven Guitars,* is set in 1948. The postwar period was one of new opportunities for blacks in America, especially in music. Innovative jazz stars like Charlie Parker, and blues stars like Muddy Waters, achieved fortune and fame beyond the black community. The hero of *Seven Guitars,* Floyd Barton, is a blues guitarist who has had one hit record, but made no money on it. . . . Floyd is talented and charming, but dogged by bad luck and wrong choices. . . .

The undercurrent of violence that runs throughout the play becomes overt. As in Wilson's *Ma Rainey's Black Bottom,* the focus is on the violence blacks do to other blacks. There is white racism in the background of the play. . . . But, as always, Wilson does not depict his characters as mere passive victims, but as free agents.

Theater critic Richard Hornby reviewing August Wilson's Seven Guitars *in Hornby, "Forty-Second Street,"* Hudson Review, *Summer 1996, pp. 284–285.*

Boasting a cast of some 50 major characters, with dizzying shifts of perspective and narration, the book circles endlessly around common events seen from different vantage points. It is the achievement of this difficult and demanding work that the impact on the reader is ultimately illumination rather than exhaustion. Coover's disturbing probings into the psyches of his characters and his ability to commingle private fantasies with public events so merge individual and group perspectives that the reader loses the ability to separate individual dialogues from collective consciousness. This fusion of the personal and the public gives the book an unsettling and almost nightmarish quality. . . . This is a profoundly original work of fiction. Ranging from farce to sadomasochism, alternating social criticism with Borgesian "magic realism," *John's Wife* is an altogether singular and memorable achievement by one of this country's most powerful voices.

Reviewer Steve Brzezinski discussing Robert Coover's novel John's Wife *(1996) in Brzezinski, "John's Wife,"* Antioch Review, *Summer 1996, p. 364.*

Women seeking and fit for a V.M.I.-quality education cannot be offered anything less under the state's obligation to afford genuinely equal protection.

Supreme Court justice Ruth Bader Ginsburg justifying the Court's 7-1 vote on June 26, 1996, requiring that Virginia Military Institute [V.M.I.] admit female students, in Linda Greenhouse, "Military College Can't Bar Women, High Court Rules," New York Times, *June 27, 1996, p. 1.*

It was very clear to me now that she [Linda Tripp] wanted to be a player. She secretly had a crush on him [Clinton], and, while she enjoyed living through me, there was another part of her that was jealous of my relationship with the President.

Monica Lewinsky describing the response of her confidant, Linda Tripp, after Lewinsky's meeting alone with President Bill Clinton on the morning of July 4, 1996, in Andrew Morton, Monica's Story *(1999), p. 123.*

Our nation, though wounded and scathed, has outlasted revolutions, civil war, world war, racial oppression and economic catastrophe. . . . And what enabled us to accomplish this has little to do with the values of the present. After decades of assault upon what made America great, upon supposedly obsolete values, what have we reaped? What have we created? What do we have?

What we have in the opinions of millions of Americans is crime and drugs, illegitimacy, abortion, the abdication of duty, and the abandonment of children. And after the virtual devastation of the American family, the rock upon which this country was founded, we are told that it takes a village, that is the collective, and thus the state, to raise a child.

The state is now more involved than it ever has been in the raising of children. And children are now more neglected, more abused and more mistreated than they have been in our time. This is not a coincidence. This is not a coincidence. And with all due respect, I am here to tell you it does not take a village to raise a child. It takes a family to raise a child. . . .

No one can deny the importance of material well-being. And in this regard, it is time to recognize we have surrendered too much of our economic liberty. I do not appreciate the value of economic liberty nearly as much for what it has done in keeping us fed, as to what it's done in keeping us free. The freedom of the marketplace is not merely the best guarantor of our prosperity. It is the chief guarantor of our rights, and a government that seizes control of the economy for the good of the people ends up seizing control of the people for the good of the economy.

And our opponents portray the right to enjoy the fruits of one's own time and labor as a kind of selfishness against which they must fight for the good of the nation. But they are deeply mistaken, for when they gather to themselves the authority to take the earnings and direct the activities of the people, they are fighting not for our sake but for the power to tell us what to do.

Senator Robert Dole of Kansas accepting the Republican presidential nomination on August 15, 1996, in Dole, "Nomination Acceptance Speech" (1996). Available online. URL: http://www.4president.org/speeches/dolekemp1996convention.htm.

Fifteen years ago, Jim was White House press secretary. . . . All our dreams had come true. But then one rainy afternoon in March, our dreams were shattered by an assassination attempt on President Reagan. President Reagan was shot. And so was Jim. . . .

Every year in this country, nearly 40,000 Americans are killed with a firearm. More than 100,000 more are wounded. Every two hours another child is killed with a gun. And with each death and each wound, another American dream, another American family, is shattered.

This must stop. Jim and I decided that we should do something about it. Not as Republicans, but as Americans. . . . That's why we supported legislation that would require a waiting period for the purchase of a handgun. The idea was simple: Establish a "cooling off" period and give police the time they need to conduct a background check on the buyer.

Introduced in 1987, the Brady bill was an overnight success. Every major national law enforcement group endorsed it. So did former Presidents Reagan, Carter, Ford and Nixon. In fact, nine out of 10 Americans supported a waiting period. It just made sense.

But year after year, the gun lobby defeated the Brady bill. The National Rifle Association said that seven days, or even seven hours, was just too long to wait to buy a handgun: It was an inconvenience.

Well, listen, our family can tell the gun lobby a little bit about inconvenience. . . . And about the despair and the pain that can result from a gunshot wound. But don't take our word for it. Ask anyone whose life has been touched by gun violence. . . .

Since the Brady law went into effect on February 28, 1994, the Brady law has stopped more than 100,000 convicted felons and other prohibited purchasers from buying a handgun. . . . Today, and every day, the Brady law is stopping an estimated 85 felons from buying a handgun.

Sarah Brady, wife of Ronald Reagan's press secretary, Jim Brady, on August 26, 1996, addressing the Democratic National Convention about gun control, in Brady, Speech before the 1996 Democratic National Convention. Available online. URL: http://www.pbs.org/newshour/convention96/floor_speeches.

Look at the facts, just look at the facts: 4.4 million Americans now living in a home of their own for the first time; hundreds of thousands of women have started their own new businesses. More minorities own businesses than ever before. Record numbers of new small businesses and exports.

Look at what's happened. We have the lowest combined rates of unemployment, inflation, and home mortgages in 28 years. Look at what happened—10 million new jobs, over half of them high-wage jobs. . . . We have increased our investments in research and technology. We have increased investments in breast cancer research dramatically. We are developing a supercomputer—a supercomputer that will do more calculating in a second than a person with a hand-held calculator can do in 30,000 years. More rapid development of drugs to deal with HIV and AIDS and moving them to the market quicker have almost doubled life expectancy in only four years. . . .

On crime—we're putting 100,000 police on the streets. . . . We stopped 60,000 felons, fugitives, and stalkers from getting handguns under the Brady Bill. We banned assault rifles. We supported tougher punishment and prevention programs to keep our children from drugs and gangs and violence. Four years now—for four years now the crime rate in America has gone down. . . .

On welfare, we worked with states to launch a quiet revolution. Today there are 1.8 million fewer people on welfare than there were the day I took the oath of office. We are moving people from welfare to work. . . .

This must be a campaign of ideas, not a campaign of insults. The American people deserve it. . . .

I want to build a bridge to the 21st century, where our children are not killing other children anymore. . . . I want to build a bridge to the 21st century with a clean and safe environment. . . .

The real choice is whether we will build a bridge to the future or a bridge to the past; about whether we believe our best days are still out there or our best days are behind us; about whether we want a country of people all working together or one where you're on your own.

President Bill Clinton accepting the Democratic nomination for president on August 29, 1996, in Clinton, Acceptance Speech for the 1996 Presidential Nomination (1996). Available online. URL: http://www.pbs.org/newshour/convention96/floor_speeches.

The problem, as all experienced lawyers know, is that the truth is not always black and white. It often comes in muted shades of gray, especially in cases like Whitewater, where slight enhancements of recollection about subjective states of mind could change an innocent transaction into a culpable one. Contrast the inducements that are now almost certainly being offered James McDougal by Whitewater prosecutors with the "promise" [to pay legal bills] made by Clinton. McDougal is facing years of imprisonment after his recent Arkansas conviction. His former wife, Susan, who was more peripheral to the scheme, received a sentence of two years. Jim McDougal can expect an even harsher sentence, unless he now changes what he has already said publicly—namely, that he knows nothing incriminating about the President or First Lady. Prosecutors have postponed his sentencing explicitly "to influence" his testimony. They are holding the sword of Damocles over his head with one hand and promising him a carrot—in the form of years lopped off his sentence—with the other. Of course, they only want him to tell "the truth," but they want him to tell the prosecution's "truth" rather than President Clinton's "truth."

President Clinton also wants the subpoenaed witnesses "to tell the truth," but he does not want that "truth" to be influenced by threats of prosecution that cannot be defended against because of lack of resources. In that respect, the Clinton promise can be viewed as an inadequate effort at trying to level a playing field that will always be tilted heavily in favor of prosecutors, since a prosecutor can generally deliver far more than a defendant can ever promise.

Law professor Alan M. Dershowitz responding in September 1996 to charges made by the conservative organization Judicial Watch, accusing President Bill Clinton of witness tampering and bribery because he offered to pay legal fees for witnesses subpoenaed in the investigation of the Whitewater affair, in Dershowitz, Sexual McCarthyism (1998), p. 62.

Aesthetically, it's a joy to watch a pro like Ms. Oates take apart this proud, happy and likable family step by inexorable step . . . while making you hope all along that she'll spare them. And the modest measure of recompense and reconciliation she eventually hands the survivors doesn't outrage our sense of probability, however our sense of justice may suffer. . . . [The novel] works not simply because of its meticulous details and gestures, or because "family" is a hot-button issue these days, or because Ms. Oates has borrowed the primal narrative of Western culture to give her story subliminal oomph. Mere hard work and canny calculation could get a writer that far. What keeps us coming back to Oates Country is something stronger and spookier: her uncanny gift of making the page a window, with something happening on the other side that we'd swear was life itself.

Reviewer David Gates celebrating Joyce Carol Oates's novel We Were the Mulvaneys *(1996) in Gates,* "American Gothic," New York Times Book Review, *September 15, 1996, p. 11.*

Ethnicity plus stage spectacle equals a smash hit formula on Euro-American stages. It has for a couple of centuries now. Producers of both highbrow and lowbrow entertainments have understood the thrill of the exotic, especially when it's posed against the familiar. These fusions seem more plentiful than ever in recent years. As funding cutbacks reduce performance activity among indigenous music and dancemakers, as the costs of high-art performing institutions continue to

Adaptations of traditional folk dances such as the Irish *Riverdance* (above) were popular during the 1990s. *(Photofest)*

rise, spectacle becomes an increasingly viable staging ground for collaborations and even experiment. Unlike the perilous nonprofit arts, spectacle rests on the edge of commercial enterprise; its high costs can yield high revenues. . . .

While still recovering from *Riverdance,* I realized that I'd seen half a dozen similar shows in the past few months. They all focused on a national or ethnic style, but they all reinvented the tradition in some way to suit modern agendas. The Balé Folclórico da Bahia fused European contemporary dance ideas about design and body shaping with traditional Brazilian dance and martial arts. Conjunto Folklorico Nacional de Cuba reconstructed folk and social dances in handsome period costumes emphasizing a strife-free Afro-Hispanic cultural duality. The National Ballet of Spain's programming was devoted to stagy versions of folk and flamenco dancing. . . .

Although ethnic shows may want us to believe we're seeing some "pure" essence of a people, we know that culture and cultural forms don't remain static. Tribal groups migrate and mix; their dances get suppressed or exploited; technology adds its enhancements. Politics often pays the piper and calls the tune. . . .

Dance critic Marcia B. Siegal discussing the growing interest in folk dancing during the first part of the 1990s in "Multicult—the Show," Hudson Review, *Autumn 1996, p. 463.*

To understand what golf is now, don't watch Tiger Woods. Watch who watches Tiger Woods. Young black women in tight jeans and heels. Tour caddies, back out on the course after hauling a bag 18 holes. White arbitrageurs with cell phones. Giant groups of fourth-graders, mimicking their first golf swings. Pasty golf writers who haven't left the press tent since the days of Fat Jack [Nicklaus]. Hispanic teens in Dallas Cowboys jerseys trying to find their way around a golf course for the first time in their lives. Bus drivers and CEOs and mothers with strollers catching the wheels in the bunkers as they go. . . .

Whoo-boy. Maybe those Nike ads had it right. Is golf ready for this? Golf used to be four white guys sitting around a pinochle table talking about their shaft flexes and deciding whether to have the wilted lettuce soup. Now golf is [the fashion model] Cindy Crawford sending Woods a letter. A youngster who'd been promised a round of golf with Woods was

The spectacular success of Tiger Woods in his debut year reinvigorated professional golf. *(AP/Wide World Photos)*

bouncing all around his Orlando home two weeks ago, going, "When is Tiger coming? When is Tiger coming?" The kid's name? [the baseball star] Ken Griffey, Jr. . . .

When was the last time a 20-year-old showed up and grabbed an entire sport by the throat?

Sportswriter Rick Reilly, on October 28, 1996, describing the impact of Tiger Woods's recent entry into professional golf, in James Haley, ed., Post–Cold War America: 1992–Present *(2003), pp. 116–117.*

You're really seeing the culmination of one of the great political comebacks in American history. Bill Clinton two years ago was considered, rightfully so, politically dead. He is anything but tonight. I think one thing, Jim, we've got a little piece of evidence tonight, second-term Presidents, as we've discussed on this program, have a little bit of a problem of over-reach. It happened with FDR, with Ronald Reagan, also Richard Nixon—Bill Clinton too, after winning the governorship in '79, after winning the presidency in 1992, went a little bit far. . . . One question I think we will have to watch for with Bill Clinton the next year or two is, is this someone who remains the disciplined politician of 1996, or is this someone who was so delighted to be re-elected that there is that kind of overreach that we've seen in history?

Presidential historian Michael Beschloss on election night analyzing President Bill Clinton's reelection on November 5, 1996, in "The Meaning of the Election, 1996," on The Newshour with Jim Lehrer, *November 5, 1996. Available online. URL: http://www.pbs.org/newshour/bb/election/november96/final_11-5.html.*

Well, I'm struck by the thought that between now and four years from now, Bill Clinton's place in history will be determined. There's such a mystery to that moment. Think about FDR when he was elected in '32. Could he ever have imagined that he would have four terms and eventually preside over the greatest war in human history? . . . Could Reagan have imagined when he was elected after a hard-fought contest with Carter that he would be re-elected by an even greater majority and probably could have run for a third or fourth term? So it's so interesting to just contemplate where Clinton stands now, and that really his place in history all lays before him. It all depends on what he does in these months ahead.

Presidential historian Doris Kearns Goodwin on election night analyzing President Bill Clinton's reelection on November 5, 1996, in "The Meaning of the Election— November 5, 1996." Available online. URL: http://www.pbs.org/newshour/bb/election/november96/final_11-5.html.

Each side has something to crow about tonight, and neither side has bragging rights. You know, usually when a President runs and wins re-election, he does it by a big margin. . . . Yes, he's got a comeback—yes, the first man since FDR on the Democratic side. Even so, at 50 percent, it's not this big send-off that he

needed for his presidency. The Republicans can crow about keeping the House, keeping the Senate probably . . . but even so, they don't have the big send-off they had two years ago. So I think tonight we're in a situation where nobody quite knows whether these folks can govern together. . . . And so I think the real issue for Bill Clinton now—the next eleven weeks to me are more important than the past eleven weeks—whether he can manage this transition, put his team together, put his agenda together, and deal with these underlying questions of these scandals as Bob Woodward talked about tonight.

David Gergen of U.S. News & World Report *analyzing President Bill Clinton's reelection on November 5, 1996, in "The Meaning of the Election," on* The Newshour with Jim Lehrer, *November 5, 1996. Available online. URL: http://www.pbs.org/newshour/bb/election/november96/final_11-5.html.*

In the current political climate, it is the view of a growing number of Cuban-Americans that such complacency regarding domestic policy can no longer be afforded. Having been content with the domestic policy status quo, it has only been in the mid-1990's that Cuban-Americans have been alerted to the extent to which they too have vested interests in domestic policy decisions. "Cuban exceptionalism" with regard to both immigration and domestic policy is increasingly a vestige of the past. Cuban-Americans now have more substantive policy interests in common with other Latino populations than has ever previously been evident. The 1996 election results are the most obvious indication of this in that it reversed the overwhelming support Cubans have shown for the Republican party and its candidates in past elections, and was at the least more proximate to the electoral outcomes evident among Latinos at large.

Professor Dario Moreno writing on January 29, 1998, about the significance of the presidential election of November 5, 1996, for Cuban exiles, in Dario Moreno, "Cuba's in the 1996 Presidential Election" (1998). Available online. URL: http://www.fiu.edu/~morenod/scholar/1996.htm.

9 Let the Good Times Roll

1997

In the year that saw the announcement of the birth of Dolly the sheep, the first mammal ever to be born as the result of genetic cloning, the U.S. economy enjoyed its strongest year of the decade. The stock market smashed the new records it set in 1996, as the Dow–Jones industrial average gained almost 2,000 points—nearly 27 percent—to close above 8,000 for the first time. Fortunes were made literally overnight when start-up Internet companies made initial public offerings (IPOs) that were snapped up by investors eager to capitalize on the World Wide Web, which promised to revolutionize the way business was conducted. In other sectors, corporate mergers created companies of unprecedented size, while inflation and unemployment rates remained low, and the GDP grew at its highest rate since 1989.

International efforts to address broadly shared human problems included the Kyoto Protocol, created to reduce levels of smog-causing greenhouse gas emissions, and a multinational pact to expand financial services available in the global economy. The United States ratified the 1993 Chemical Weapons Convention, which banned developing, trafficking, and using chemical weapons; provided strict provisions for verification of compliance; and called for destruction of all chemical weapons stocks by 2007. But, although the United States unilaterally banned the export of land mines, neither it nor Russia nor China joined the 120 nations that signed the Ottawa Treaty calling for their abolition. Clinton rejected the treaty because he believed it would undermine the security of South Korea and compromise the safety of American soldiers on the Korean DMZ, where mines were employed to protect against an invasion from North Korea, with whom South Korea remained technically at war.

Before the Ottawa convention, Britain's Princess Diana led an international effort to ban land mines, indicating the large number of civilian casualties they caused each year,[1] and the International Campaign to Ban Landmines won the year's Nobel Peace Prize. Millions of people throughout the world grieved when, shortly before the Ottawa Treaty was signed, Diana was killed in a car crash in Paris while being pursued aggressively by media paparazzi. The pop singer Elton John's tribute to the late princess Diana, "Candle in the Wind," became the best-selling single recording in history, selling 31.8 million copies

People throughout the world grieved the death of Britain's Princess Diana. *(Photofest)*

in just over a month. John donated all of the proceeds from sales to Diana's favorite charities.

Although the rate of violent crime dropped throughout the nation, it remained in the public eye as the jury in a civil suit found O. J. Simpson responsible for the death of Nicole Brown Simpson and Ronald Goldman and awarded the families of the two victims $33.5 million in compensatory and punitive damages. Timothy McVeigh was convicted and sentenced to death for the 1995 Oklahoma City bombing. Terry Nichols, McVeigh's coconspirator, was convicted for his role in the mass murder and, in 1998, was sentenced to life in prison. Bombings of abortion clinics resumed in 1997 throughout various parts of the nation; 39 members of the Heaven's Gate cult committed suicide outside San Diego, California, apparently in the hope of being transported to an unidentified flying object (UFO) concealed behind the newly discovered Hale-Bopp comet; a former Palestinian English teacher intent on killing as many "Zionists" as possible in their "den" in New York City, opened fire on the observation deck of the Empire State Building, killing a Danish tourist and wounding six others; and a serial killer gunned down the fashion designer Gianni Versace and murdered several others before committing suicide in Miami Beach. The public also reacted with widespread shock and sympathy to the murder of Ennis Cosby, the son of television personality Bill Cosby, who was shot while changing a flat tire on a freeway ramp in Los Angeles. Police later arrested an 18-year-old Ukrainian immigrant believed to be part of a Russian car-theft gang. The killings in Pearl, Mississippi, and West Paducah, Kentucky, of several high school girls by high school boys armed with guns further shocked the nation and led to renewed calls for stricter gun control, along with vocal defenses of the constitutional right to bear arms. Crime was also the topic of Don DeLillo's best-selling novel *Underworld,* as well as of such popular genre fiction as Carl Hiaasen's *Lucky You,* Les Standiford's *Deal on Ice,* and James W. Hall's *Red Sky at Night.*

INTERNATIONAL DEVELOPMENTS

For the first time since the late 1970s, liberal governments held power simultaneously in the United States, Britain, and Canada, after a landslide Labour Party victory in Britain removed the Conservative Party from power and installed Labour leader Tony Blair as the new prime minister; and Canada's ruling Liberal Party, led by Prime Minister Jean Chretien, retained power in parliamentary elections, despite losing some seats. Two months after Blair's election, the IRA announced a new cease-fire, and Sinn Féin, its political organization, was subsequently invited to join multiparty peace talks concerning the fate of Northern Ireland.

The former cold war enemies Russia and NATO signed a treaty in May calling for mutual security and cooperation and permitting former Soviet allies from the Warsaw Pact to join NATO, but in April UN peacekeepers were required to go to Albania in the wake of violence centering around the nation's economic collapse and ethnic strife. Russia and China signed an agreement settling their border in central Asia.

The death in February of China's most powerful leader, 92-year-old Deng Xiaoping, marked a significant change in that nation's power structure. Deng, who had held power since 1978, had implemented important free-market reforms that opened China to greater trade with the West, but he steadfastly resisted political reforms and expansion of civil rights for Chinese citizens. The 70-year-old Communist Party general secretary, President Jiang Zemin, succeeded Deng as the country's most powerful figure and took Deng's plans for economic reform even further by introducing a privatization plan that reduced the state's ownership of and control over some of China's 300,000 industries. But Jiang too resisted calls for enhanced political freedoms, despite efforts by growing underground, dissident movements who used e-mail and the Internet to bypass the government's suppression of their viewpoint. Jiang was in power on midnight, June 30, when Britain peacefully transferred ownership of Hong Kong to China after its 99-year lease on the colony expired. The transfer was conducted under terms of an Anglo-Chinese Joint Declaration that required the existing social and legal systems to remain fundamentally unchanged. Even so, the transfer contributed to a devastating autumn crash in the Hong Kong stock market. Jiang met in October with Clinton during a U.S.-Chinese summit on nuclear, environmental, and trade issues, the first visit to the United States by a Chinese head of state since 1989. Jiang received cordial receptions from U.S. business leaders anxious for access to the large and largely untapped Chinese market, and from Clinton, who nonetheless insisted that Jiang had been "on the wrong side of history" during the 1989 massacre of prodemocracy protesters in Tiananmen Square, which Jiang oversaw. Denunciation of Jiang by the public at large was more severe, and throughout his visit he was beset by protesters and condemned by members of Congress, who denounced China's human rights abuses.

These abuses and sweatshop labor conditions in China and Indonesia were also targets of protest at the Asia-Pacific Economic Cooperation trade conference in Vancouver, Canada. Scandal and economic collapse provoked voters in South Korea to end five years of single-party rule and elect opposition leader Kim Dae Jung as president. Shortly before the December election, North and South Korea opened their first formal talks for a peace treaty to end the Korean War, which had been fought between 1950 and 1953.

Saddam Hussein provoked an international crisis in October when he expelled American weapons inspectors from the UN inspection team in Iraq who were verifying compliance with the peace treaty that ended the 1991 Persian Gulf War. The crisis defused soon afterward, when Saddam Hussein relented and readmitted the inspectors, whom he had accused of spying for the United States. But at the year's end the situation remained tense, as the UN Security Council denounced the restrictions and impediments that Iraq was creating in the search for weapons of mass destruction, especially its refusal to permit inspectors' entry to some 50 presidential palaces throughout the country.

Elsewhere in the Middle East, the United States defended Turkey's right of self-defense after Turkish troops launched an offensive in northern Iraq against Kurdish guerrillas seeking autonomy for Turkey's Kurdish population. Meanwhile, voters in Iran demonstrated their desire for a less rigid theocracy when they overwhelmingly elected as president the comparatively moderate Ayatollah Khatami. The nation's fundamentalist clergy, however, who still exercised considerable power, undermined Khatami's ability to initiate substantial reform. Arab-Israeli relations further deteriorated as bombings continued to kill civilians throughout Israel. Moreover, Netanyahu's decision to build new Jewish settlements in Arab sections of Jerusalem angered many Palestinians and prompted an economic boycott of Israel by the Arab League, and suspension of multinational talks on such regional issues as arms control and tourism. Islamic militants in Algeria killed hundreds of civilians in their ongoing campaign to topple that nation's secular government. Tutsi rebels seized control in Zaire, where they dissolved that nation and founded the new Democratic Republic of Congo.

A dramatic raid in April on the Japanese ambassador's residence in Lima, Peru, resulted in the liberation of 71 of the 72 hostages taken at a party for diplomats and business representatives in December 1996 by members of the leftist Tupac Amaru Revolutionary Movement (MRTA). All 14 rebel captors, two government soldiers, and one hostage, a Peruvian Supreme Court justice, were killed in the attack that ended the crisis. The daring raid was widely viewed as a political success for Peru's president, Alberto Fujimori, who, since suspending the constitution and disbanding Congress in 1992, had been waging an aggressive campaign against the MRTA and the even more potent Shining Path, a Maoist revolutionary group who had been fighting against the government since 1980. In response to intensifying cries of a growing economic crisis, the legislature in Ecuador removed the flamboyant president, Abdala Bucaram Ortiz, on grounds of mental incapacity. Ortiz, who often referred to himself as "El Loco," or "the Madman," had been accused of widespread corruption. Fabian Alarcon, the president of the Congress, was named interim president.

GOVERNMENT AND SOCIETY

Clinton began his second term confronted by ongoing allegations of sexual harassment and improprieties in the Whitewater affair and by a Republican Congress led by his outspoken critic, House Speaker Newt Gingrich. Despite the divisive and sometimes vindictive partisanship that characterized most of Clinton's presidency, however, the president called for and finally achieved bipartisan cooperation on legislation to balance the federal budget by 2002, increase spending for education, provide health insurance for children, and expand health care for those unable to afford medical insurance. He was unable, however, to gain "fast-track" authority to negotiate trade agreements without submitting them to possible amendment by Congress. As did the United States, Canada also appropriated modest increases for social programs while continuing its practice of deficit reduction, begun in 1994, with the goal of balancing the budget by 2000.

A significant part of Clinton's domestic agenda was directed toward creating a truly integrated society characterized by harmonious race relations and mutual acceptance among ethnic groups. To this end Clinton created significant minority representation in his new cabinet and other positions of power within the administration, and he publicly defended affirmative action programs, although he sought to improve them. He also called for government action against hate crimes and initiated a yearlong public dialogue about race, intended to elevate the level of understanding and appreciation that Americans had for one another and draw attention to the divisive, destructive, and self-destructive nature of prejudicial attitudes. Clinton publicly honored the nine black students who led the effort in 1957 to desegregate the public schools in his home state, Arkansas, and he acknowledged past racially motivated abuses for which the U.S. government had been partly or fully responsible. He awarded seven Medals of Honor—six of them posthumously—to black soldiers who had shown exceptional valor during World War II. None of the previous 433 Medals of Honor for World War II heroism had been awarded to a black soldier. Clinton also drew attention to the past practice of racially driven scientific abuse when he apologized to the survivors and family members of 399 black men whose syphilis was untreated by federally funded researchers at Tuskegee University who were studying the long-term effects of the disease. The men, of whom approximately 100 died of syphilis-related ailments between 1932 and 1972, had been told they were being treated for "bad blood."

In June politics mixed with natural disaster after floods devastated the Red River valley, where the border cities of Grand Forks, North Dakota, and East Grand Forks, Minnesota, experienced what was called a 500-year flood—one so severe it was statistically expected to occur only once in 500 years. Counting on Clinton to back down from a veto threat, lest he seem to be denying essential aid to disaster victims, Congress attached several unrelated amendments that Clinton opposed to the disaster-relief bill. However, claiming that Republicans were "playing politics with the lives of Americans in need,"[2] Clinton vetoed the legislation. Four days later, after polls showed that the majority of Americans blamed Republicans for the standoff, Congress resubmitted an acceptable emergency spending bill that provided $5.6 billion for disaster relief to 35 states, including those in the Upper Midwest. The outcome was regarded as a major political victory for Clinton, and it revealed growing divisions between moderates and more partisan conservatives within the Republican Party.

Despite his legislative successes, Clinton remained the target of Republican-led charges that he had acted improperly in the Whitewater affair, in which his former business partners had been convicted. Independent Counsel Kenneth Starr reversed his decision to resign and instead intensified his investigation of charges that Clinton had committed sexual harassment while governor of Arkansas. In addition, revelations that Clinton had been inviting people to socialize with him, and even stay as overnight guests in the White House, in return for making large donations to the Democratic Party provoked his critics to charge that he was essentially selling access to the president and demeaning the publicly owned presidential residence. Both Congress and the Justice Department opened investigations of the practice, and Vice President Al Gore was investigated for violating fund-raising regulations. But Republicans complained of political partisanship when Attorney General Janet Reno declined to name an independent counsel for either case. Although the Justice

Department and House of Representatives continued their investigations of these matters throughout the year, the Senate dropped its investigation in the fall, citing absence of strong evidence of illegal activity. A grand jury, however, indicted the former agriculture secretary, Mike Espy, who served during Clinton's first term, on charges that he accepted more than $35,000 worth of gifts from companies subject to regulation by his department and that he later tried to mislead investigators about his activities. Espy was acquitted in 1998. Former secretary of housing and urban development Henry Cisneros, who also served during Clinton's first term, was indicted for lying during his 1993 confirmation hearing about payments he made to a former mistress. Cisneros, who in 1999 pleaded guilty to a misdemeanor charge, was among those Clinton pardoned before leaving office in January 2001.

The Republican leadership also suffered from accusations of wrongdoing. Gingrich began the year by receiving a $300,000 fine and a formal reprimand by the House for using tax-exempt donations for political purposes and submitting false information to the House Ethics Committee. Although the scandal did not drive him from his position, it fueled later unsuccessful efforts by members of his own party to remove him from the post.

Between 300,000 and 500,000 black women held a Million Woman March in Philadelphia in October; there participants endorsed a 12-point platform calling for assistance to women who had been imprisoned, support for independent black schools, solutions to homelessness, establishment of health centers that would employ so-called traditional remedies, release of so-called political prisoners, and renewed investigation of allegations that the CIA was responsible for spreading the use of crack cocaine in inner-city black communities.

As has occurred at other landmark moments in history, the approaching new millennium elicited in some people a sense of optimism and hope for a fresh new beginning for them and for humanity as a whole. Such individuals believed the human race was on the cusp of a spiritual awakening that could enable people to transcend their self-destructive attitudes and behavior and attain deeper understanding that could lead to peace, harmony, and personal growth. But for others the year 2000 loomed more ominously, spawning premonitions of an upcoming apocalypse. The latter appears to have motivated the suicides between 1994 and 1997 of some 74 members of the Solar Temple sect, including five who died in Quebec, Canada, in March 1997. These deaths occurred just four days before the ritual suicides in the exclusive Rancho Santa Fe suburb of San Diego, California, of 39 members of the Heaven's Gate cult. Led by the 66-year-old Marshall Herff Applewhite, a former opera singer who was among the suicides, the cult had been financed by earnings from Higher Source, an Internet-related business that designed Web pages for clients. Applewhite's teaching combined the apocalyptic Revelations of the New Testament with astrology, New Age spirituality, and the belief that, after their death, members of the cult would be transported to heaven by a UFO concealed in the tail of the approaching Hale-Bopp comet.

Although his death was probably unrelated to any doomsday scenarios, the 50-year-old Italian fashion designer Gianni Versace was shot down in front of his Miami Beach mansion by Andrew Cunanan, a 27-year-old serial killer who committed suicide eight days later on a nearby houseboat during an extensive manhunt.

In one of its most far-reaching decisions, the Supreme Court unanimously rejected Clinton's request to delay proceedings in the civil lawsuit filed against him by Paula Jones alleging Clinton had sexually harassed her while he was governor of Arkansas. Asserting that the civil case would not significantly impede the president's ability to perform his official duties, the Court for the first time permitted that a president be sued while in office for actions outside the realm of his or her official duties, and it made possible the further developments in the Jones case that ultimately caused Clinton to be impeached in December 1998.

The Supreme Court upheld a court order requiring that antiabortion protesters maintain a 15-foot buffer zone outside clinic entrances and struck down a provision in the 1996 Telecommunications Act that outlawed the display or distribution of "indecent" or "patently offensive" material to minors over the Internet. The Court overturned a Georgia law requiring candidates for political office to undergo drug testing before being allowed to appear on ballots, and, citing First Amendment protections, it overturned a key provision of the 1993 Brady handgun bill that required law-enforcement officials to conduct background checks on potential gun purchasers. The Court also invalidated the 1993 Religious Freedom Restoration Act on the ground that Congress exceeded its authority when it attempted to define the level of protection for religious expression given by the Constitution.

The Court upheld states' rights to ban doctor-assisted suicide and enact laws requiring convicted sex offenders to notify communities of their residence. It ruled that former employees are covered by the same law that protects current employees from retaliation against claims of discrimination; that employers cannot fire employees and then contract out their jobs in order to reduce costs of health insurance and other employee benefits; and that the Constitution's prohibition of double jeopardy does not prohibit the government from levying both civil and criminal fines for the same offense.

BUSINESS

The United States prospered during the year, despite turmoil abroad, the serious decline in the once-promising Asian economy, and the sudden collapse of the Hong Kong stock market after China assumed control over the former British colony. The U.S. economy grew at a robust 6.2 percent, and the unemployment rate dropped to 5.0 percent. Moreover, some 10,700 mergers and acquisitions among U.S. firms were reported, accounting for $919 billion worth of transactions, a record 47 percent increase from the previous year. The telecommunications field underwent the greatest number of mergers, totaling more than $90 billion. Banking, financial services, hotels, casinos, and utilities also experienced heavy activity. Worldwide, mergers increased by a record 48 percent, accounting for $1.1 trillion.[3]

But the growing interdependence of the global economy became apparent on October 27, when the crash of the Hong Kong stock market provoked the worst single-day loss on record on the New York Stock Exchange, and the Dow-Jones industrial average, which had crossed the 8,000 barrier for the first time in July, fell 554 points to 7,161. The market quickly recouped the loss, however, as the Dow posted a record-setting 337-point gain the next day. It closed the year at 7,908.25, up 1,459.98 points, or 22.6 percent, from its 1996 closing. After experiencing healthy growth rates of around 4.5 percent for the previous three years, the GDP grew in 1997 by 6.2 percent, while the inflation rate dropped by about one-quarter, to 2.5 percent, despite conventional wisdom that a robust economy would produce inflation. The booming economy also produced jobs, causing the unemployment rate to drop from 5.4 percent in 1996 to 5.0 percent.[4]

As personal computers continued to become more affordable—the cost for a desktop unit dropped below $1,000—Andrew Steven Grove, the chairman and CEO of the Intel Corporation, was named *Time* magazine's Man of the Year for his role in making smaller and exponentially more powerful microchips. Meanwhile, the long-desired compatibility between Microsoft's Windows operating system and the operating system on Apple computers moved closer to realization after Microsoft announced it would invest $150 million in the financially debilitated Apple corporation. The dominance of computers in contemporary society was further highlighted when IBM's Deep Blue prevailed over the reigning chess champion Garry Kasparov in a widely viewed rematch of the 1996 contest, which Kasparov had won.

Citing the potential damage to the nation's economy, Clinton invoked emergency powers granted under the Railway Labor Act of 1926 to block a planned strike by American Airlines pilots. It was the first time since 1966 that a president intervened to prevent an airline strike. The Teamster's union won key concessions on wages, pension issues, and the creation of additional full-time positions after waging a 15-day strike against United Parcel Service (UPS), which nearly shut down the world's largest package delivery service. The walkout by 185,000 workers was the largest in the United States in more than a decade.

The tobacco industry suffered major blows when it agreed to settlements with state and federal governments. First the Liggett Group, Inc., the smallest of the five major U.S. tobacco companies, agreed in March to settle lawsuits brought by 22 states seeking to recover the costs of treating patients suffering from smoking-related illnesses. As part of the settlement, Liggett acknowledged that cigarette smoking was addictive and caused cancer, a conclusion that the tobacco industry had steadfastly rejected for decades. In addition to paying 25 percent of its pretax profits for the next 25 years into a fund to compensate the states and class-action plaintiffs, Liggett agreed to print warning labels on its cigarettes stating that smoking is addictive. Later, the industry agreed to a $368 billion settlement with the federal government in which it would make annual payments starting at $8.5 billion and eventually rising to $15 billion. In return, the industry would be immune from future state and class-action lawsuits. The industry also agreed to pay $60 billion in punitive damages for past deceptions about the dangers of smoking; to pay for antismoking campaigns throughout the nation; to eliminate advertising from billboards, storefronts, the Internet, and sporting events; and to place stronger warnings on cigarette packages.

Canada's Hibernia oil platform went into production in November, furnishing 40,000 barrels of oil per day. Jointly owned by the Canadian government and a consortium of oil companies and located in the so-called Iceberg Alley southeast of Newfoundland, the billion-dollar platform was designed to withstand the impact of a 1-million-ton iceberg.

Under the auspices of the World Trade Organization (WTO), the United States and 101 other countries signed the Global Financial Services Agreement, intended to facilitate international trade further by dismantling barriers in the banking, insurance, and investment sectors. The United States, which pressured Asian and Latin American countries to permit greater foreign ownership and operation of their financial services, was among the greatest beneficiaries of the pact.

In addition to causing severe hardships that threatened the stability of President Suharto's 31-year rule, Indonesia's financial crisis had a ripple effect that undermined other Asian economies and finally prompted the International Monetary Fund (IMF) to agree in principle to grant a $43 billion loan, in return for economic reforms and Indonesia's promise to curb rampant official corruption. The pact was concluded in January 1998. The Asian financial crisis also led South Korea, which had recently enjoyed a flourishing economy, to seek a bailout from the IMF.

NATURE AND THE ENVIRONMENT

In addition to the catastrophic 500-year flood in the Upper Midwest, California suffered from heavy winter rains and melting snow from the Sierra Nevada mountains that flooded the central and northern portions of the state, killing at least 29 and causing more than 70 percent of the state's counties to be declared disaster areas. Twenty-seven people died and dozens more were left homeless on May 27, when the worst tornado to strike Texas in a decade devastated the town of Jarrell. In October, Hurricane Pauline struck Mexico's Pacific coast with winds of 115 mph, causing extensive flooding that killed at least 230 people and rendered some 20,000 homeless. Effects of the El Niño weather phenomenon involving warming ocean currents in the Pacific Ocean off the coast of South America intensified Pacific hurricanes such as Pauline but contributed to a mild hurricane season in the Atlantic, where no hurricane landfalls occurred.

Internationally, in September two earthquakes struck central Italy, killing 11, including four people in Assisi who died inside the 13th-century Basilica of Saint Francis when it collapsed in an aftershock, also destroying greatly prized frescoes and other works of art. An earthquake in northern Iran killed some 2,400 people and injured 6,000 more, and a volcano killed several people on the Caribbean island of Montserrat, where villages were engulfed by boiling lava and clouds of hot ash. Wildfires that spread during the summer through Borneo and Sumatra created one of the most severe ecological disasters in modern times, and out-of-control forest fires in Indonesia left a thick haze over much of Southeast Asia in September and October, causing tens of thousands of Indonesians and Malaysians to be treated for smoke inhalation and other respiratory ailments and leading to a lethal collision between an Indian cargo ship and a supertanker.

The National Cancer Institute declared that between 10,000 and 75,000 people in 23 counties in Colorado, Montana, Idaho, South Dakota, and Utah were at increased risk for contracting thyroid cancer as a result of nuclear bomb tests conducted by the U.S. government between 1951 and 1962.

Clinton approved new air quality standards that further restricted the amounts of soot and ground-level ozone permissible in factory emissions, and he gave critical support to the Kyoto Protocol, the pact that emerged from a UN-sponsored summit meeting among leaders of 150 nations. The Kyoto Protocol for the first time established binding limits on nations' emissions of carbon dioxide and five other so-called greenhouse gases. The treaty called for 38 industrialized nations to reduce their combined greenhouse-gas emissions between 2008 and 2012 to levels approximately 5 percent below their 1990 levels.

SCIENCE AND TECHNOLOGY

The specter of Mary Shelley's fictional Dr. Frankenstein's creating human life in his laboratory suddenly loomed as a real possibility after genetic researchers in Scotland announced in February that they had successfully cloned the first adult mammal, Dolly the sheep, in July 1996. The process, which many had hitherto considered impossible, involved substituting an adult sheep's cell nucleus for an egg cell nucleus and then implanting it in a ewe, whose offspring had deoxyribonucleic acid (DNA) identical to that of the adult whose nucleus was used. Although Dr. Ian Wilmut and his team of scientists in the government-financed Roslin Institute in Edinburgh denied having any intention to extend their research to human subjects, news of their success caused many observers to speculate that someone eventually would attempt to replicate the process with people, and that the creation of human clones was now almost inevitable, regardless of whatever moral and religious objections or legal barriers might be introduced. Public reaction to the cloning of Dolly was mixed. On the one hand, many experienced a sense of awe at the magnitude of the accomplishment. But others decried what seemed to them as a blasphemous assumption of godlike powers over the creation of life, and governments throughout the world, including the United States, rushed to ban human cloning.

The year saw the first significant decline of deaths caused by AIDS in the United States in the epidemic's 16-year history, as new protease inhibitors demonstrated their efficacy. In Africa and other parts of the world where such drugs were typically unaffordable, however, AIDS death rates soared to horrific proportions.

NASA's land rover *Sojourner* became the first autonomous human-made vehicle to travel on another planet when *Pathfinder* landed on Mars on the fourth of July and launched *Sojourner,* which ran until September 27 before running out of power, more than two months longer than predicted. The additional eight weeks provided a wealth of data for scientists and revealed indications that water once existed on the surface of the planet. *Pathfinder*'s landing stirred interest throughout the world, perhaps more than any other space event since *Apollo 11* landed on the Moon, and NASA's *Pathfinder* Web sites broke all known records on the Internet.

The *Galileo* space probe sent back pictures suggesting that liquid water, whose presence is a precondition for life, probably exists beneath the surface of Mars's moon Europa, and astronauts of the space shuttle *Discovery* upgraded the *Hubble Space Telescope,* which subsequently showed in unprecedented detail images of the dying phases of stars. Despite vocal protests that its plutonium fuel could create a health and environmental disaster in Florida if the craft were to explode on takeoff, NASA also launched the *Cassini* orbiter to study Saturn, where, after "slingshotting" around Venus and the Earth in 1998 and 1999, it was scheduled to arrive in December 2000. Disaster nearly struck the Russian *Mir* space station when it collided with a supply ship, leaving its three-man crew in darkness, with a diminishing level of oxygen. About three weeks later, however, the U.S. space shuttle *Atlantis* docked successfully, delivered supplies and equipment, and picked up the U.S. astronaut Jerry Linenger, who had been aboard *Mir* six months.

Earth-based scientists reported finding the first direct evidence of an "event horizon," a defining characteristic of the black hole phenomenon, which had been theoretically predicted but not empirically verified. In what some observers considered the most complete analysis of the fate of the universe ever conducted, the astrophysicists Fred Adams and Greg Laughlin concluded that the end of the universe will result not from gravitational implosion, as previously theorized, but from a progression of energy loss that will occur in a four-stage evolutionary process. According to their model, the first stage of the universe is the Stelliferous Era, in which vast numbers of high-energy stars and galaxies are formed. We are still in this stage, which will be followed by a 1,000-trillion-year Degenerate Era, during which the bright stars will die out and only dormant stars and other objects will illuminate the universe. Next, the Black Hole Era will see the collapse of the dead stars into black holes that will trap all light. The end of the universe will occur thousands of trillions of years in the future, after the Dark Era, during which the black holes will dissolve into a "soup" of photons, electrons, neutrinos, and other subatomic particles.

Using Rolls-Royce engines from a Phantom fighter jet, the Thrust Super Sonic Car became the first vehicle to break the sound barrier on land when it shattered the world's land-speed record, reaching 714 mph in Nevada's Black Rock Desert.

Archaeologists in Athens claimed to have discovered ruins of the Lyceum, the fourth-century B.C. school where Aristotle taught philosophy; scientists in Watson Brake, Louisiana, found a ring of 11 earthen mounds created approximately 5,400 years ago, making them the oldest such complex in the Americas. Their purpose, however, remained unknown.

LITERATURE, THE ARTS, SPORTS, AND POPULAR CULTURE

Interest in the past and our ability to comprehend it featured prominently in the year's literature, fine arts, and popular culture. Philip Roth won the Pulitzer Prize for *American Pastoral,* his fictional treatment of American history from the early cold war and Vietnam War eras; in *Mason & Dixon,* the reclusive novelist Thomas Pynchon imagines colonial America even as he questions our ability ever to reconstruct the past, accurately, while asserting the necessity of trying. Early American history is also the subject of a widely viewed television documentary produced by the popular historian Ken Burns, who chronicles Meriwether Lewis and William Clark's exploration of the Louisiana Territory, which the United States purchased from France in 1803. History also played well in movies, as James Cameron's *Titanic,* which was celebrated for its accurate reproduction of the "unsinkable" ocean liner that sank on its maiden voyage, won Academy Awards for best director and best picture. In *Amistad* Stephen Spielberg reconstructs the story of early 19th-century African slaves who win freedom in a U.S. court after they seize control of the slave ship on which they have been imprisoned. Wynton Marsalis's *Blood on the Fields,* a three-hour musical meditation on slavery, won the first Pulitzer Prize awarded for jazz.

Contemporary social and political issues were the subject of several successful movies. Spielberg's *The Lost World,* a digitally modeled sequel to his *Jurassic Park* (1993), is about genetic engineering run amok. Paul Thomas Anderson's *Boogie Nights* centers on the pornographic film industry, and Dustin Hoffman and Robert De Niro co-starred in Barry Levinson's cinematic satire *Wag the Dog,* which highlights the cynical way politicians manipulate the media for political purposes. Harrison Ford portrays a more traditionally patriotic picture of the American presidency in Wolfgang Petersen's *Air Force One,* and in Ridley Scott's *G.I. Jane* the star, Demi Moore, is a strong-willed woman who endures physical hardship, gender discrimination, and political and gender betrayal to become a member of the elite, and hitherto exclusively male, U.S. Navy Seals.

The television comedian Ellen DeGeneres reflected the social debate over homosexuality in network television when her character on her show *Ellen* revealed that she is a lesbian. Cable television demonstrated that it had come into its own when HBO won more Emmy nominations than any other network, and the liberal agenda of *Murphy Brown* continued to foment controversy when the title character used marijuana to lessen her pain after chemotherapy treatment for breast cancer.

Charles Frazier won the National Book Award for his first novel, *Cold Mountain,* a narrative loosely based on Homer's *Odyssey* about a wounded southern Civil War deserter who is trying to return home to the woman he loves. Cynthia Ozick published *The Puttermesser Papers,* which draws on Jewish folklore as it renders the surreal existence of a brilliant female Jewish lawyer struggling with an ancient golem figure in contemporary New York City. Robert Stone's *Bear and His Daughter* offers a collection of stories covering contemporary topics ranging from abortion to drug dealing, and John Dufresne's *Love Warps the Mind a Little* is a tragic-comic story of a would-be writer who wrecks his marriage, begins life anew with his mistress, and then discovers new qualities in himself when he is compelled to serve as her primary caregiver after she has a severe illness. The popular genre writers Danielle Steel (*The Ghost, Special Delivery,* and *The Ranch*), John Grisham (*The Partner*), Sidney Sheldon (*The Best Laid Plans*), and Mary Higgins Clark (*Pretend You Don't See Her* and *A Stranger Is Watching*) all published best-sellers.

Jared Diamond's *Guns, Germs, and Steel: The Fates of Human Societies* won the Pulitzer Prize in nonfiction for its analyses of the rise and fall of human societies throughout history. Sebastian Junger found a surprisingly large readership for *The Perfect Storm,* about the sinking of a fishing boat in the North Atlantic in October 1991, during the confluence of three tumultuous weather systems. Charles Wright's *Black Zodiac* won the Pulitzer Prize in poetry. Other notable volumes of poetry included William Meredith's *Effort at Speech,* Frank Bidart's *Desire,* Sarah Linday's *Primate Behavior,* and Sonia Sanchez's *Does Your House Have Lions?* The poet Allen Ginsberg, one of the founders of the 1950s Beat movement, died at age 70.

Two Henry James novels were adapted for cinema, Agniezka Holland's *Washington Square,* starring Jennifer Jason Leigh, Maggie Smith, and Albert Finney, and Iain Softley's *Wings of the Dove,* starring Helena Bonham Carter, Linus Roache, and Charlotte Rampling. Although *Titanic*'s love story about romance between the social classes aboard the supposedly unsinkable ocean liner enjoyed the greatest publicity and box-office success, its young stars, Leonardo DiCaprio and Kate Winslet, lost out for best actor and best actress to their older competitors Helen Hunt and Jack Nicholson, who starred in James Brooks's love comedy, *As Good As It Gets.* The comedian Will Smith teamed with Tommy Lee Jones in Barry Sonnefield's campy movie about federal agents assigned to fight space aliens, *Men in Black,* and Kim Basinger, Russell Crowe, and Kevin Spacey revived the film noir tradition of seamy and steamy detective work in Curtis Hanson's *L.A. Confidential.* Robin Williams starred in Gus Van Sant's *Good Will Hunting,* about a professor and therapist who help a young emotionally troubled janitor at the Massachusetts Institute of Technology realize his potential as a natural mathematical genius. Robert Duvall directed and starred as a charismatic Pentecostal preacher who has a criminal past in *The Apostle,* and Woody Allen starred and directed in his most postmodern, self-referential movie, *Deconstructing Harry,* in which he plays a narcissistic author who embodies, to an extreme, all of the worst characteristics attributed to Allen since his breakup with Mia Farrow. Harrison Ford (*Air Force One*) and Julia Roberts (*My Best Friend's Wedding*) were the first and second top box office draws, respectively. The next eight were all men: Leonardo DiCaprio, Will Smith, Tom Cruise, Jack Nicholson, Jim Carrey, John Travolta, Robin Williams, and Tommy Lee Jones.

Although no Pulitzer Prize was awarded for drama in 1997, *The Last Night at the Ballyhoo,* Alfred Uhry's romantic comedy about racial prejudice among Jews in Atlanta, won the Tony Award as best play, and Peter Stone's *Titanic* won as best musical. In *Barrymore,* Christopher Plummer impressed audiences with his portrayal of John Barrymore, the self-destructive Hollywood actor of a famous acting family in the earlier days of cinema. Lynne Thigpen won acclaim for her role as a feminist nominated for U.S. surgeon general in Wendy Wasserstein's political study *An American Daughter.* Pam Gems's *Stanley* presents the life of the modern British painter Stanley Spencer; Stephen Churchett's *Tom and Clem* imagines a fictitious encounter between the former British prime minister Clement Atlee and the homosexual politician Tom Driberg; Jonathan Reynolds's *Stonewall Jackson's House* presents a play within a play as a theater company debates whether to stage a play written by a white man about a black woman who sold herself into slavery; and in *The Young Man from Atlanta* a 63-year-old man is compelled to review his life after losing the job he has held for 40 years.

Situation comedies remained popular on network television, although they yielded some to dramas. *Seinfeld,* a comedy, overtook the hospital drama *ER* as the top-rated show of the 1997–98 season. *ER* was number two, followed by a new sitcom, *Veronica's Closet,* starring Kirstie Alley, formerly of *Cheers,* who plays a successful but demanding businesswoman with a miserable love life. *Friends; Union Square,* a new show with a *Friends*-like premise and a trendy Manhattan setting; *Home Improvement,* a sitcom starring Tim Allen; and *Frasier* were also among the top-10 shows, as were *Monday Night Football, 60 Minutes,* and *Touched by an Angel,* a fantasy about a young angel who inspires people to make positive changes in life. Although it did not make the top 10, *The Practice,* a new drama about a Boston law firm that handles low-income criminal clients, received critical acclaim. *Frasier* and *Law and Order* won the Emmy Award as best comedy and drama, respectively. The comparatively new Fox Network, which started in 1986, targeted a younger audience with innovative programming, including a new off-the-wall comedy, *Ally McBeal,* which starred Calista Flockhart as a neurotic lawyer in a law firm staffed by eccentric attorneys. The even-newer Warner Brothers network scored an unexpected hit with *Buffy the Vampire Slayer,* a campy spinoff of the also campy 1992 movie of the same title. *Buffy's* treatment of witchcraft upset some religious viewers but appealed to many teenagers and young adults. Although they were eccentric and not to be taken seriously, both *Buffy* and *Ally McBeal* appealed to a new generation of viewers eager to see empowered women in professional roles or other positions of competence and authority. *Ally McBeal* also regularly featured African Americans, Asians, and characters of other ethnic backgrounds as competent professionals readily accepted as friends, sometimes lovers, of the main characters.

Cable television could afford to be even more daring, and it captured large audiences of teenagers and young adults with the debut of such shows as *South Park,* a social satire on the Comedy Central channel that many middle Americans found sacrilegious, disrespectful, twisted, gruesome, and/or offensive but many younger people considered clever and funny and an accurate, if iconoclastic, representation of contemporary American society. The animated show centers on a group of third graders who regularly use profanity and sometimes victimize and sometimes are victims of other children or of one another. Their

Ally McBeal was an off-the-wall comedy that revolved around an intelligent but socially awkward professional woman. *(Photofest)*

parents, teachers, and leading social figures display a range of neuroses, as well as characteristics of knee-jerk liberalism and right-wing paranoia.

Singers of a wide range of ages and styles found success in 1997. Bob Dylan, who became prominent as a folk singer in the 1960s, won a Grammy Award for his new album, *Time Out of Mind;* Barbra Streisand, who also established herself in the 1960s, had a best-selling album, *Higher Ground.* Meanwhile, the young new British all-woman band the Spice Girls, promoted "Girl Power," attracting a vast international audience, most of them teenagers and young adults, by projecting strength, individuality, and sexiness. Hit singles of the year included the Spice Girls' "Wannabe," LeAnn Rimes's "How Do I Live?," Aerosmith's "Falling in Love (Is Hard on the Knees)," and George Strait's "One Night at a Time." Shawn Colvin's *Sunny Came Home* won the Grammy as best song and best record. Best-selling albums included No Doubt's *Tragic Kingdom,* Celine Dion's *Falling into You,* Mariah Carey's *Butterfly,* and the prophetically titled *Life after Death* by the rapper Notorious B.I.G., who was murdered in March. The singer John Denver, best known for his acoustic guitar–based ballads of the 1960s and 1970s, died at age 53, when the single-passenger plane he was piloting crashed into Monterey Bay, California. More happily, the singer Paul McCartney of the rock bands the Beatles and Wings was knighted by Queen Elizabeth.

The British pop group the Spice Girls promoted "Girl Power." *(Photofest)*

In Major League Baseball's first year of interleague play, the Florida Marlins, formed in 1993, became the youngest expansion team to win the World Series when it defeated the Cleveland Indians in the 11th inning of the deciding seventh game. Florida, which entered the playoffs as a wild card, was the first team to win a championship that did not also finish first in its division. Larry Walker, the right fielder for the Colorado Rockies, and the Seattle Mariner center fielder Ken Griffey, Jr., were the National and American League MVPs. The pitchers Pedro Martinez of the Montreal Expos and Roger Clemens of the Toronto Blue Jays won the Cy Young Award, and Mark McGwire, who began the season in the American League with the Oakland As and finished it on the National League's Saint Louis Cardinals, led the major leagues with 58 home runs. The Cuban baseball star Orlando Hernandez, the half brother of the World Series MVP Livan Hernandez of the Marlins, defected along with his girlfriend and six others by making a dangerous late December raft voyage from Cuba to the Bahamas. Hernandez, known as El Duque, signed in 1998 as a pitcher for the New York Yankees.

The quarterback John Elway and running back Terrell Davis led the Denver Broncos to the NFL championship, as the Broncos defeated the Green Bay Packers in Super Bowl XXXII, played in January 1998. Green Bay's quarterback, Bret Favre, and the Detroit Lion running back Barry Sanders shared the MVP honor. Sanders, who led the league in rushing with 2,053 yards, became only the third player in NFL history to run for more than 2,000 yards. The University of Michigan and the University of Nebraska were each named the top college team by competing polls. Michigan's Charles Woodson became the first defensive player to win the Heisman Trophy. Bill Parcells, the greatly respected head coach of the New England Patriots, resigned because of disagreements with the owner, Robert Craft, and signed a new six-year contract with a division rival, the New York Jets. In his four years with the Patriots, Parcells had engineered the team's transformation from one of the poorest in the league to conference champion.

Led by their star center Michael Jordan, who was named the playoffs' MVP for the second consecutive year after returning from retirement, the Chicago Bulls defended their NBA basketball title by defeating in six games the surprisingly resilient Utah Jazz, in Utah's first championship series. Utah's Karl Malone was the league MVP. The University of Arizona was the nation's top college basketball team, and Tim Duncan of Wake Forest was the college player of the year. The growing popularity of women's sports was evident in the 1996 founding of the Women's National Basketball Association (WNBA), which began its first season in 1997.

For the first time since 1955, the Detroit Red Wings won hockey's Stanley Cup when it swept the Philadelphia Flyers in a four-game series. The Australian Patrick Rafter and 16-year-old Martina Hingis of the Czech Republic won the singles events in the U.S. Tennis Open, played for the first time in the newly completed Arthur Ashe Stadium. The stadium was named in memory of the first African American to win the men's singles championship (1968). The 1997 tournament was also notable for the first U.S. Open appearance of Venus Williams, who lost to Hingis in the championship match. Williams, who, with her younger sister, Serena, went on to dominate women's tennis, was the first black woman to reach the finals since Althea Gibson won the tournament in 1957; she was also the first unseeded women to appear in the finals since Darlene Hard in 1958.

Ernie Els won golf's USGA Open, but Tiger Woods became the youngest player ever to win the prestigious U.S. Masters Tournament. The 14-year-old figure skater Tara Lipinski became the youngest person to win the U.S. national figure-skating championship when she defeated the defending champion, 15-year-old Michelle Kwan. Todd Eldredge won his fourth men's skating title. The former heavyweight champion Mike Tyson was banned from boxing after he bit off part of the ear of his opponent, Evander Holyfield, in a championship fight. And Silver Charm, ridden by the jockey Gary Stevens, won the Kentucky Derby.

CHRONICLE OF EVENTS

January 3: President Clinton again suspends for six months a controversial provision of the Helms-Burton law that would allow U.S. citizens to sue foreign, non-Cuban companies operating in Cuba that use the confiscated properties of exiles.

January 7: Gingrich is narrowly reelected Speaker of the House.

January 13: Clinton awards the Medal of Honor, the nation's highest award for bravery in combat, to seven African-American soldiers who served in World War II.

January 15: Accompanied by a Red Cross official and wearing an armored vest, Princess Diana of England walks through a minefield in Angola to publicize the dangers posed by land mines buried throughout the world.

January 16: Ennis Cosby, the 28-year-old son of the television star Bill Cosby, is murdered during a suspected armed robbery.

January 20: Clinton and Gore are sworn in for a second term.

January 21: For the first time in its 208-year history, the House of Representatives imposes sanctions on its Speaker when it formally reprimands and fines Gingrich for committing financial improprieties and submitting false information to the House Ethics Committee.

January 22: Madeleine Albright and William Cohen are unanimously confirmed as secretary of state and secretary of defense, respectively, by votes of 99-0. Cohen is the only Republican member of Clinton's cabinet.

January 26: The Green Bay Packers win Super Bowl XXXI, defeating the New England Patriots 35-21.

January 30: The remaining ashes of Mahatma Gandhi, whose program of nonviolent civil disobedience led to India and Pakistan's independence from Britain in 1947, are scattered in the Ganges River, after lying unclaimed in a bank vault since his assassination in 1948.

January 31: Violent demonstrations occur in Albania, and the country falls into economic and political chaos, after the collapse of a number of so-called pyramids in which millions of Albanians have invested their earnings.

February 4: Clinton delivers his State of the Union address.

February 4: A jury in the civil trial of O. J. Simpson finds him responsible and financially liable for the "wrongful death" of his former wife, Nicole Brown Simpson, and her friend Ronald Goldman. He is ordered to pay $8.5 million in compensatory damages to the two families. On February 10, the jury orders him to pay an additional $25 million in punitive damages.

February 11–21: In a series of five space walks, astronauts of the space shuttle *Discovery* upgrade the *Hubble Space Telescope* with new observation equipment to enhance its accuracy and efficiency.

February 13: The Dow-Jones industrial average closes above 7,000 for the first time.

February 13: Debbie Rowe, wife of the pop star Michael Jackson, gives birth to their son.

February 19: China's longtime leader, Deng Xiaoping, dies at age 92.

February 21: Reversing his decision earlier in the week to step down from the post and accept a position as dean of the law school at Pepperdine University, Kenneth Starr announces that he will remain as independent counsel for the Whitewater investigation.

February 23: The British newspaper *Observer* reports that on July 5, 1996, scientists, for the first time, cloned an adult mammal, a sheep named Dolly. The researchers at the Roslin Institute in Scotland publish the full results of their experiments in the February 27 issue of the scientific journal *Nature.*

February 23: Ali Abu Kamal, a 69-year-old Palestinian schoolteacher intent on killing "Zionists," opens fire on the observation deck of the Empire State Building, killing one person and injuring six before killing himself.

February 25: A Pennsylvania jury finds John du Pont guilty of murdering the Olympic wrestler Dave Schultz, but it also determines that he was mentally ill. Du Pont faces possible confinement in a mental institution or a maximum of 20 to 40 years in prison and a fine of up to $50,000.

March 1: Miners in Germany go on strike, as a record 4.6 million German workers are unemployed.

March 3: Toronto initiates a ban on tobacco smoking in restaurants, bars, and doughnut shops. The city council eases some provisions on April 14, in response to public protests.

March 4: Senate Republicans fall one vote short of the required two-thirds majority in their bid to pass a balanced budget amendment to the Constitution.

March 9: The rapper Notorious B.I.G. is shot to death while sitting in a car after a Soul Train Awards party.

March 13: At Buckingham Palace, Queen Elizabeth of Britain knights the musician Paul McCartney, formerly of the 1960s rock band the Beatles and more recently with the band Wings.

March 13: A Jordanian soldier acting alone fires on a group of Israeli schoolgirls at a border site in the northern Jordan Valley, killing seven and wounding six other members of the group. Jordan's King Hussein immediately issues an apology and travels to Israel on March 16 to offer personal condolences to the families.

March 17: Complaining that the confirmation process has become "a political circus," Anthony Lake, Clinton's choice to head the CIA, withdraws his name from nomination. Clinton then nominates the deputy director, George Tenet, whose nomination is later confirmed.

March 19–April 2: Ten members of the Viper Militia are sentenced to prison after pleading guilty in December 1996 to conspiring to make bombs and possessing machine guns. The group is suspected of planning to blow up federal buildings in Phoenix, Arizona, although prosecutors are unable to provide evidence of specific plans.

March 19: The World Health Organization (WHO) announces a program to halt a global tuberculosis epidemic by preventing at least 10 million deaths in the next 10 years.

March 20: Conceding that cigarette smoking is addictive and causes cancer, the Liggett Group, Inc., agrees to settle lawsuits brought by 22 states.

March 22: In an apparent group suicide, five members of the apocalyptic Order of the Solar Temple sect die in a fire in Quebec, Canada.

March 22: Canadian immigration officials arrest a Saudi man suspected of being involved in the 1996 bombing of a U.S. military housing complex in Saudi Arabia. He is deported to the United States on June 17.

March 25: Treasure hunters discover the wreck of a Spanish galleon that sank off the coast of Ecuador in 1654, carrying a cargo of gold and silver now valued at approximately $4 billion.

March 26: Under the leadership of the former teacher Marshall Herf Applewhite, 39 members of the Heaven's Gate religious cult commit suicide, anticipating that they will be transported to heaven by a UFO secreted in the tail of the Hale-Bopp comet.

March 29: According to the Starr report, Clinton and Monica Lewinsky have their last sexual encounter.

March 31: In response to Israel's decision to construct new Jewish settlements in historically Arab East Jerusalem, the Arab League votes to freeze relations with Israel, impose an economic boycott, and suspend multilateral talks on regional issues, including arms control and tourism.

April 3: The government of Zaire collapses after victories by rebel forces.

April 6: An Italian-led multinational peacekeeping force is deployed to Albania.

April 12: Authorities in Bosnia thwart a plot to assassinate Pope John Paul II hours before his arrival in Sarajevo.

April 13: At age 21, the golfer Tiger Woods becomes the youngest player ever to win the prestigious U.S. Masters Tournament at the all-male National Golf Club in Augusta, Georgia.

April 14: James McDougal, Clinton's former business partner, is sentenced to three years imprisonment for fraud and conspiracy.

April 15: More than 200 Muslim pilgrims are killed in Saudi Arabia when fire breaks out in their camp outside the holy city of Mecca.

April 17: Gingrich states that he will accept personal responsibility for the $300,000 fine imposed on him by the House by paying it with private funds, instead of using campaign donations or establishing a defense fund to raise contributions. But, fearing that the threat of crippling personal fines might intimidate lawmakers, he encourages the House to declare that his use of private funds is a voluntary decision and not a precedent. He further announces that he will borrow the money from the Republican presidential nominee Robert Dole.

April 18–19: Grand Forks, North Dakota, and East Grand Forks, Minnesota, suffer devastation when the Red River floods.

April 22: Starr gains a six-month extension of the grand jury investigation into the Whitewater affair.

April 22: Peruvian soldiers storm the Japanese embassy in Lima, where left-wing Tupac Amaru guerrillas have been holding 72 diplomats and Japanese business representatives hostage since December 1996. All 14 captors, two government soldiers, and one hostage are killed. The remaining hostages are released unharmed or with minor injuries.

April 26: Iraqi president Saddam Hussein defies the UN-mandated no-fly zone when he orders Iraqi helicopters to fly a group of elderly pilgrims through the zone en route to the holy city of Mecca, Saudi Arabia.

April 26: The newly discovered Hale-Bopp comet makes its closest approach to Earth at a distance of 125 million miles, rendering it readily visible to the naked eye.

April 30: The television character Ellen Morgan, played by the comedian Ellen DeGeneres, reveals that she is lesbian. Oprah Winfrey plays her therapist.

May 1: Neo-Nazis and left-wing groups clash in violent May Day demonstrations across Germany.

May 2: Britain's Labour Party wins a landslide victory over the incumbent Conservative Party. Labour leader Tony Blair becomes the new prime minister.

May 27: The Supreme Court rejects Clinton's request to delay proceedings in the Paula Jones sexual harassment lawsuit.

May 27: Russia and NATO agree to consider one another adversaries no longer and to establish mutual relations, cooperation, and security.

Ellen DeGeneres's television character, Ellen, instigated new arguments over the acceptability of homosexuality when she revealed that she was a lesbian. *(Photofest)*

May 29: The African nation of Zaire expires, and the Democratic Republic of Congo is formed in its place. The former rebel leader Laurent Kabila, a Tutsi, is sworn in as president of the new nation.

May 29: The Clintons travel to Britain to congratulate Blair.

May 31: Canada opens the 12.9-kilometer Confederation Bridge joining Prince Edward Island to New Brunswick. With pilings designed to serve as ice-breakers, this is the longest bridge in the world to traverse ice-covered waters.

June 2: Canada's ruling Liberal Party retains power after parliamentary elections, despite losing 19 seats in the House of Commons.

June 2: A jury in Denver, Colorado, convicts Timothy McVeigh of committing the 1995 Oklahoma City bombing that killed 169 people.

June 4: Chinese dissidents commemorate the eighth anniversary of the Tiananmen Square massacre by inaugurating *Tunnel,* a prodemocracy electronic magazine written by intellectuals within China and distributed by computers in the United States to e-mail addresses in China.

June 8: Clinton vetoes a Republican-crafted package for emergency disaster relief to the Upper Midwest, scene of recent devastating floods, because it contains a number of unrelated amendments he opposes.

June 11: The Swiss Bank Association announces that up to $4 billion resides in unclaimed accounts opened during World War II by Jewish victims of the Holocaust.

June 11: Britain enacts the toughest gun control regulations in the world when, in the aftermath of the 1996 Dunblane massacre, Parliament votes overwhelmingly to impose a total ban on handguns.

June 12: Clinton approves a revised disaster-relief package that omits the objectionable amendments and provides $5.6 billion in emergency aid for 35 states.

June 13: Timothy McVeigh is sentenced to death for the Oklahoma City bombing.

June 14: In a speech delivered in San Diego, California, Clinton initiates a one-year "campaign against racism."

June 19: After a record-setting civil trial in Britain that lasted more than 300 days, two environmentalists are found to have libeled the McDonalds Corporation.

June 20: Major tobacco companies agree to pay almost $370 billion to defray state Medicaid costs for the treatment of smoking-related diseases.

June 21: The WNBA opens its first basketball season.

June 23: Betty Shabazz, the widow of the assassinated black nationalist leader Malcolm X, dies three weeks after her 12-year-old grandson sets fire to her apartment in Yonkers, New York.

June 23: Cambodian guerrillas announce the capture of the former Khmer Rouge leader Pol Pot, who was responsible for millions of deaths in Cambodia during the 1970s.

June 25: The 11-year-old *Mir* space station is crippled after colliding with a supply ship.

June 30: As its 99-year lease expires at midnight, Britain transfers authority of Hong Kong to China, ending 156 years of colonial rule.

July 4: Pathfinder lands on Mars, completing a seven-month journey from Earth.

July 10: Efforts by some House Republicans fail to dislodge Gingrich as House Speaker.

July 15: The Italian fashion designer Gianni Versace is murdered outside his oceanfront villa on Miami Beach.

July 16: The Dow-Jones industrial average exceeds 8,000 for the first time.

July 17: In the aftermath of his unsuccessful effort to remove Gingrich as Speaker of the House, Congressman Bill Paxon resigns as chairman of the House Leadership.

July 19: The IRA announces it will reinitiate a cease-fire in Britain and Northern Ireland.

July 30: The Dow-Jones industrial average peaks for the year at 8,245.89.

August 5: Clinton signs two bills to enact a bipartisan plan to balance the federal budget by 2002.

August 11: Clinton becomes the first president to exercise a line-item veto when he strikes down three special-interest provisions from a budget Congress passed in July.

August 26: The final network broadcast of *Roseanne* airs on ABC.

August 27: A grand jury indicts the former agriculture secretary Mike Espy for accepting illegal gifts from companies his department regulates.

August 29: After the IRA cease-fire, Sinn Féin is invited to join multiparty talks about Northern Ireland.

Roseanne, a situation comedy starring Roseanne Barr and John Goodman as working-class Americans trying to get by, ended after nine years. *(Photofest)*

August 29: Hundreds of Algerian civilians are killed by Islamic militants in a predawn attack on a village 15 miles from the capital city, Algiers.

August 30: UN secretary-general Kofi Annan states that the increasing violence in Algeria now requires some kind of international effort to effect peace.

August 31: Leaders of the Algerian rebel group Islamic Salvation Front (FIS) declare they are willing to initiate an immediate cease-fire and open negotiations with the government, but the foreign ministry rejects UN secretary-general Kofi Annan's suggestion as unacceptable meddling in its internal affairs.

August 31: England's princess Diana; her Egyptian companion, Dodi Fayed; and their driver die in a Paris car crash while being pursued by paparazzi on motorcycles.

September 5: Mother Teresa, a nun of the Missionaries of Charity order who won the Nobel Prize in Peace for her work with poor people in India, dies at age 87.

September 5: Sir Georg Solti, the former music director and principal conductor of the Chicago Symphony Orchestra who won more Grammy Awards than any performer, classical or popular, dies at age 84.

September 6: Princess Diana is buried in Westminster Abbey.

September 8: At least 200 die when a ferry sinks offshore in Haiti.

September 13: Mother Teresa receives a state funeral in India. She is the first person in a nongovernmental position since Gandhi in 1948 to receive the honor, usually reserved for heads of state.

September 15: Sinn Féin delegates enter the peace talks about Northern Ireland.

September 23–25: The Senate Finance Committee holds hearings that detail abuses of taxpayers by the Internal Revenue Service (IRS).

September 25: Clinton honors the so-called Little Rock Nine, who, as high school students in 1957, disregarded death threats by an angry mob to desegregate Central High School in Little Rock, Arkansas.

September 26: A Canadian judge pardons two women convicted of manslaughter and shortens the sentences of other women convicted of violent crimes because they had a history of being battered or sexually abused. In some cases, the victims of the women's crimes were not the people who had abused the perpetrators.

September 26: An Indonesian airliner crashes in northern Sumatra, killing 234.

September 26: Two earthquakes strike central Italy, killing 11 and causing the 13th-century basilica of Saint Francis in Assisi to collapse.

fall: Linda Tripp begins secretly taping her conversations with Monica Lewinsky.

early October: The conservative Rutherford Institute, which is helping defray Paula Jones's legal expenses in her lawsuit against Clinton, receives the first of three anonymous tips claiming that Clinton is having a sexual affair with Lewinsky.

October 1: Police in Pearl, Mississippi, arrest 16-year-old Luke Woodham for killing his mother at home with a knife and then going to Pearl High School and shooting nine girls, two of whom die, including his former girlfriend. On October 7, six more teenagers are charged with conspiracy in connection with the murders.

October 8: Federal Reserve Board chairman Alan Greenspan warns of inflation that could potentially undermine the robust economy if the domestic demand for labor continues to grow faster than the supply.

October 10: Starr issues a report concluding that the death of the White House deputy counsel Vincent Foster in July 1993 was a suicide. Starr's report, regarded as the most definitive to date, ends a three-year investigation that reaffirms conclusions reached by four previous inquiries.

October 22: The Hong Kong stock market loses more than 10 percent of its value, producing instability in the Asian market and economies.

October 25: Between 300,000 and 500,000 black women hold a Million Woman March in Philadelphia.

October 26: The Florida Marlins win baseball's World Series.

October 27: In response to the Hong Kong market crash, the U.S. stock market suffers its most severe single-day decline, as the Dow-Jones industrial average falls by 554 points.

October 28: The stock market rebounds, as the Dow Jones average climbs 337 points to set a new single-session record for point gain.

October 29: Clinton meets with China's president, Jiang Zemin, in Washington, D.C., where they discuss nuclear, trade, and environmental issues.

October 29: Iraq orders all U.S. members of a UN arms inspection team to leave the country within seven days.

October 31: Unable to find any "smoking guns," the Senate Government Affairs Committee suspends its hearings into allegations that President Clinton, Vice President Gore, and/or White House staff had committed serious campaign finance abuses during the 1996 election.

October 31: Acknowledging that Christians' "misinterpretation of the Gospels" had encouraged discrimination against Jews, Pope John Paul II condemns the failure of many Christians to oppose the Nazi genocide of World War II.

November 8: Clinton announces that he will appropriate $13.2 million and appoint an independent counsel to oversee government investigations into the causes of the so-called Gulf War syndrome suffered by veterans of the Persian Gulf War.

November 10: Clinton opens a daylong conference on hate crimes at George Washington University.

November 17: Islamic extremists in Egypt kill 70 people, including 60 foreign tourists, at Hatshepsut's tomb in Luxor's Valley of the Kings.

November 18: A self-proclaimed racist skinhead kills an African immigrant in Denver, Colorado.

November 22: South Korea seeks a $90 billion bailout from the IMF.

November 24–25: Some 2,000 protesters in Vancouver denounce labor conditions and human rights abuses in China and Indonesia as Canada hosts a conference of the 18-member Asia-Pacific Economic Cooperation trade organization.

December 1–11: Representatives of more than 150 nations, including the United States, participate in a UN summit on global warming in Kyoto, Japan, that produces the first treaty to establish limits on nations' emissions of greenhouse gases.

December 1: Fourteen-year-old Michael Carneal opens fire with a .22-caliber handgun at Heath High School in West Paducah, Kentucky, killing three girls and injuring five other students. Upon his arrest, Carneal is found to have three additional clips of ammunition and four more guns.

December 2–4: Delegates of 41 nations meet in the first international conference to discuss efforts to recover gold stolen from World War II–era victims of the Nazi Holocaust and to establish a new fund to compensate surviving Holocaust victims. The United States pledges to contribute $4 million to help set up the fund and up to $25 million in the future.

December 3: Clinton hosts a town-hall meeting in Akron, Ohio, to promulgate the ongoing national dialogue on race relations that he had called for in June.

December 4: In Ottawa, Canada, 120 nations, excluding Russia, China, and the United States, sign a treaty to ban land mines worldwide.

December 4: The European Union votes to ban most tobacco advertising by 1999.

December 5: Monica Lewinsky appears on the witness list for the Paula Jones sexual harassment suit against Clinton.

December–January 1998: The Washington, D.C., attorney Vernon Jordan, a close friend of Clinton's, assists Monica Lewinsky in securing a lawyer for her testimony in the Paula Jones case and arranges for her to obtain job interviews in New York City.

December 9–10: Accompanied by representatives of China and the United States, diplomats for North and South Korea hold talks in Geneva, Switzerland, directed toward formally concluding the Korean War.

December 15: The Defense Department announces that it will vaccinate all U.S. military personnel against anthrax, one of the most lethal biological agents extant.

December 16: Nelson Mandela resigns after five years as South Africa's first black president.

December 18: Five decades of single-party rule end in South Korea with the election as president of opposition leader Kim Dae Jung.

December 18: Clinton announces that U.S. troops will remain in Bosnia after the withdrawal of the current NATO-led Stabilization Force.

December 19: Monica Lewinsky is subpoenaed to be deposed in the Paula Jones case and produce gifts from Clinton.

December 21: Silvio Berlusconi, the former premier of Italy, is charged with trying to bribe judges in Rome.

December 22: The government of Mexico is blamed for its passivity and accused by some of complicity in the massacre of 45 Indian men, women, and children in the southern state of Chiapas.

December 22: Clinton visits Sarajevo, the capital of Bosnia-Herzegovina.

December 24: Lewinsky quits her job at the Pentagon.

December 25: The popular undersea explorer Jacques Cousteau dies at age 87.

December 28: Lewinsky meets with Clinton and receives gifts from him.

December 29: Ninety-seven civilians are killed in fighting between the government of Algeria and Islamic extremists.

December 31: Warning that failure to appoint judges will erode the quality of justice in the United States, Chief Justice William Rehnquist criticizes Congress for not filling federal court vacancies.

December 31: Michael Kennedy, the 39-year-old son of the late senator Robert F. Kennedy, is killed in a skiing accident in Aspen, Colorado.

EYEWITNESS TESTIMONY

At this last presidential inauguration of the 20th century, let us lift our eyes toward the challenges that await us in the next century. . . .

As times change, so government must change. We need a new government for a new century—humble enough not to try to solve all our problems for us, but strong enough to give us the tools to solve our problems for ourselves; a government that is smaller, lives within its means, and does more with less. Yet where it can stand up for our values and interests in the world, and where it can give Americans the power to make a real difference in their everyday lives, government should do more, not less. The preeminent mission of our new government is to give all Americans an opportunity—not a guarantee, but a real opportunity—to build better lives. . . .

The challenge of our past remains the challenge of our future—will we be one nation, one people, with one common destiny, or not? Will we all come together, or come apart?

The divide of race has been America's constant curse. And each new wave of immigrants gives new targets to old prejudices. Prejudice and contempt, cloaked in the pretense of religious or political conviction, are no different. These forces have nearly destroyed our nation in the past. They plague us still. They fuel the fanaticism of terror. And they torment the lives of millions in fractured nations all around the world. . . .

As this new era approaches we can already see its broad outlines. Ten years ago, the Internet was the mystical province of physicists; today, it is a commonplace encyclopedia for millions of schoolchildren. Scientists now are decoding the blueprint of human life. Cures for our most feared illnesses seem close at hand.

The world is no longer divided into two hostile camps. Instead, now we are building bonds with nations that once were our adversaries. Growing connections of commerce and culture give us a chance to lift the fortunes and spirits of people the world over. And for the very first time in all of history, more people on this planet live under democracy than dictatorship. . . .

With a new vision of government, a new sense of responsibility, a new spirit of community, we will sustain America's journey. . . . In this new land, education will be every citizen's most prized possession. . . . The knowledge and power of the Information Age will be within reach not just of the few, but of every classroom, every library, every child. . . . Our streets will echo again with the laughter of our children, because no one will try to shoot them or sell them drugs anymore. Everyone who can work, will work, with today's permanent under class part of tomorrow's growing middle class. New miracles of medicine at last will reach not only those who can claim care now, but the children and hardworking families too long denied.

We will stand mighty for peace and freedom, and maintain a strong defense against terror and destruction. Our children will sleep free from the threat of nuclear, chemical or biological weapons. Ports and airports, farms and factories will thrive with trade and innovation and ideas. And the world's greatest democracy will lead a whole world of democracies.

President Bill Clinton presenting his vision for the future in his second inaugural speech on January 20, 1997. Available online. URL: http://www.bartleby.com/124.

I do think that there are some issues on which the country wants to see progress that we can have bipartisan agreement. They want to see progress toward a balanced budget and responsible reform of entitlement programs. I think that's possible. They want to see us do something about the inner cities and maybe particularly about our capital city where both the President and Speaker Gingrich have spoken eloquently. I think that's possible. The drug problem I think is another area, and if we see positive movement on some of those key areas, which is definitely possible, in my judgment, that would be good bipartisanship.

Former Republican Minnesota congressman Vin Weber considering the possibilities for bipartisan cooperation in President Bill Clinton's second term, in "Civil Discourse," The Newshour with Jim Lehrer, *January 22, 1997. Available online. URL: http://www.pbs.org/newshour/bb/ congress/january97/civil_1-22.html.*

"It's unbelievable," said Dr. Lee Silver, a biology professor at Princeton University, who said the announcement [of the cloning of Dolly] had come just in time for him to revise his forthcoming book so the first chapter will no longer state that such cloning is impossible.

"It basically means that there are no limits," Dr. Silver said. "It means all of science fiction is true. They

The cloning of Dolly the sheep opened a new range of desirable and undesirable possibilities for genetic engineering. *(AP/Wide World Photos)*

said it could never be done and now here it is, done before the year 2000."...

For Dr. Wilmut [who led the research team that performed the cloning], the main interest of the experiment is to advance animal research. PPL [Therapeutics Company], for example, wants to clone animals that can produce pharmacologically useful proteins, like the clotting factor needed by hemophiliacs.... The cloned animals would produce immense amounts of the proteins in their milk, making the animals into living drug factories....

Researchers could use the same method to make animals with human diseases, like cystic fibrosis, and then test therapies on the cloned animals. Or they could use cloning to alter the proteins on the surfaces of pig organs, like the liver or heart, making the organs more like human organs. Then they could transplant those organs into humans....

"The genie is out of the bottle," said Dr. Ronald Munson, a medical ethicist at the University of Missouri in St. Louis. "This technology is not, in principle, policeable....

"I had an idea for a story once," Dr. Munson said, in which a scientist obtains a spot of blood from the cross on which Jesus was crucified. He then uses it to clone a man who is Jesus Christ—or perhaps cannot be....

"There's something ironic" about the study [Munson] said. "Here we have this incredible technical accomplishment, and what motivated it? The desire for more sheep milk of a certain type." It is, he said, "the theater of the absurd acted out by scientists."

New York Times science reporter Gina Kolata presenting scientists' responses to news released on February 23, 1997, that a team of geneticists in Scotland had, in July 1996, performed the first successful cloning of a mammal, Dolly the sheep, in James Haley, ed., Post–Cold War America: 1992–Present *(2003), pp. 124–127.*

We've had a history in this country of the tobacco industry—you may recall the image of all of the CEOs standing before Congress, swearing to tell the truth, and then proceeding to say that there were no health side effects and that the product wasn't addictive. Today for the first time in the history of this industry we have a CEO of one of the five largest tobacco companies in our country admitting that it predicted, admitting that it causes the kinds of health care problems we have thought all the way along, and admitting that they're targeting minors in their advertising. . . .

One by one every one of the major companies is saying, well, they might consider settlement [of the lawsuit filed by 22 states against them]. I think they too are beginning to see the writing on the wall, but we as attorneys general will settle for nothing less in any settlement than they stop preying on kids; they have got to be regulated by the FDA regs and others; they have got to tell the American consumers the truth; and they've got to pay and reimburse consumers for the Medicaid costs incurred because of the health-care related issues that they've created.

Christine Gregoire, attorney general of Washington State, reacting to the March 20, 1997, admission by the Liggett Group that cigarette smoking is addictive and causes cancer in "Smoking Gun," The Newshour with Jim Lehrer, *March 20, 1997. Available online. URL: http://www.pbs.org/newshour/bb/health/march97/tobacoo_3-20.html.*

[The activities of the rifle club] kind of got out of hand, way out of hand.

Thirty-three-year-old Randy Nelson, a member of the Viper Militia, after being sentenced to prison on March 20, 1997, for conspiring to make bombs that authorities alleged were intended for destroying federal buildings in Phoenix, Arizona, in Thomas E. Hitchings, Facts On File Yearbook 1997 *(1998), p. 229.*

The [U.S. militia] movement is different now than it was two years ago. Many of the active militias have gone underground, become somewhat secretive in their activities, and have combined with or become common-law court units. . . . It's not the media or the Anti-Defamation League that has accused some militias and common-law courts of being anti-Semitic or racist. The materials that they produce . . . do that. No one has to do it for them. . . .

Today we believe that there is a strong anti-government movement in the country but that it's not just militia-oriented. The militias continue to get together, to stockpile armaments, to train in a paramilitary fashion, and to gather survivalist gear. But on the surface many of them have taken a more normal route. They've wended their way into the common-law court movement. They're still practicing anti-government activities but in the form of paper terrorism, as opposed to terrorism with guns and hand grenades. We believe it's a strong movement. We believe that it's a movement that should cause all decent Americans to be concerned, not fearful but concerned. Certainly law enforcement is concerned and has shown it. . . . The FBI has added 250 more people to their domestic terrorism squad, and they have set up a new Center for Domestic Terrorism in Washington, D.C. . . .

Gail Gans, director of fact finding at the Anti-Defamation League, discussing the activities of U.S. militias in "Hanging Tough," The Newshour with Jim Lehrer, *April 3, 1997. Available online. URL: http://www.pbs.org/newshour/bb/law/april97/militia_4-3.html.*

I believe the greatest challenge we face . . . is also our greatest opportunity. Of all the questions of discrimination and prejudice that still exist in our society, the most perplexing one is the oldest, and in some ways today, the newest: the problem of race. Can we fulfill the promise of America by embracing all our citizens of all races . . .?

What is it that we must do?. . . . First, we must continue to expand opportunity. Full participation in our strong and growing economy is the best antidote to envy, despair and racism. And most important of all, we simply must give our young people the finest education in the world. . . .

Over the coming year I want to lead the American people in a great and unprecedented conversation about race. . . . Honest dialogue will not be easy at first. We'll all have to get past defensiveness and fear and political correctness and other barriers to honesty. Emotions may be rubbed raw, but we must begin. . . .

We have torn down the barriers in our laws. Now we must break down the barriers in our lives, our minds and our hearts. More than 30 years ago, at the high tide of the civil rights movement, the Kerner Commission said we were becoming two Americas, one white, one black, separate and unequal. Today, we face a different choice: will we become not two, but many Americas, separate, unequal and isolated? Or will we draw strength from all our people and our ancient faith in the quality of human dignity, to become the world's first truly multiracial democracy? That is the unfinished business of our time—to lift the burden of race and redeem the promise of America.

President Bill Clinton on June 14, 1997, calling for a yearlong national dialogue on race, in Thomas E. Hitchings, Facts On File Yearbook 1997 *(1998), p. 428.*

I've never seen anything like it in my life. People go to the kiosk and say: "Do you have any new cigarettes for me to try?."

Andre Calantzopoulos, managing director for the Philip Morris Company's operation in Poland, describing on June 22, 1997, the opening of new post–cold war markets for American tobacco products in Eastern Europe, Asia, and the Middle East, in Jane Perlez, "Fenced In at Home, Marlboro Man Looks Abroad," New York Times, *June 24, 1997, p. 1.*

We believe that homosexuality is a choice. We believe it's a very bad choice, with serious consequences. You know, if you lived next door to me and I lived next door to you, you would be free to put what you want in your front yard. You're perfectly welcome to do that. But if what you put in your front yard begins to cause the property value of my home to be devalued, I'd have every right to speak up.

What we're saying to Disney is this: You've got a great front yard. You've got some wonderful landscape, some beautiful flowers. But there's a part of your front yard in which you have begun to dump some moral trash. And this is disappointing to us.

The Reverend Tom Elliff of the Southern Baptist Convention explaining the Baptists' decision to boycott the Disney Corporation for its toleration of homosexuality, in "Not Going to Disneyworld," The Newshour with Jim Lehrer, *June 18, 1997. Available online. URL: http://www.pbs. org/newshour/bb/religion/disney_6-18.html.*

The question of sex, somehow when churches talk about morality, it always seems to come around to sex somehow. The deep issue is, is whether sex is being expressed with love and with caring and with commitment.

And those are very high and very biblical standards. To affirm those standards would be in the best

traditions of all of our churches. The blunt instrument of an economic boycott I think is just too heavy.

The Reverend Philip Wogaman of the Foundry United Methodist Church responding to the Southern Baptist Convention boycott of the Disney Corporation in "Not Going to Disneyworld," The Newshour with Jim Lehrer, *June 13, 1997. Available online. URL: http://www.pbs.org/newshour/bb/religion/disney_6-18.html.*

I think this is a significant moment in the course of these culture wars and has to be understood in light of seven or eight years of American reaction to the growing incivility with which companies like Disney treat . . . traditional values or traditional family values . . . [by] promoting sitcoms like *Ellen.* . . . [and] their own internal policies of drawing an equality between gay couples and married couples. . . .

And there were two possible responses, one of which is for the moral absolutists to say in the name of tolerance and niceness and smiley face and being part of the happiest place on earth like Disneyland, we are going to change the way we look at things, and try for a nicer approach. The other is to say we are going to draw a line in the sand and see what happens.

John Podhoretz of The Weekly Standard *discussing why the Southern Baptist Convention chose to boycott the Disney Corporation in* "Not Going to Disneyworld," The Newshour with Jim Lehrer, *June 13, 1997. Available online. URL: http://www.pbs.org/newshour/bb/religion/disney_6-18.html.*

We no longer presume that public employees will inculcate religion simply because they happen to be in a sectarian environment.

From Supreme Court justice Sandra Day O'Connor's majority opinion on the Court's 5-4 decision on June 23, 1997, to permit public school systems to send teachers into parochial schools to offer remedial assistance to needy children, in Linda Greenhouse, "Court Eases Curb on Aid to Schools with Church Ties," New York Times, *June 24, 1997, p. 1.*

They do an inadequate job of opening the doors to college. They direct far too little relief to the middle class. They include time-bomb tax cuts that threaten to explode the deficit.

President Bill Clinton on June 30, 1997, criticizing tax cuts proposed by Congress, in James Bennet, "Clinton Outlines Tax Cut Plan," New York Times, *July 1, 1997, p. 1.*

The images that you see . . . show a perfectly deployed rover that has driven down a perfectly deployed ramp, making its first track in the soil of this planet, opening a new era of exploration.

NASA project manager Jacob Matijevic celebrating the successful landing on Mars of the Pathfinder *spaceship on July 4, 1997, and its deployment of the land rover* Sojourner, *in "Pathfinder and the Little Rover That Could," September 4, 1997. Available online. URL: http://www.cnn.com/TECH/9706/pathfinder.*

G.I. Jane reps [repeats] a recurrence in [the director Ridley] Scott's work of his strong sympathy for resourceful, ballsy women, first witnessed in *Alien* and most recently seen in *Thelma & Louise.* [Demi] Moore's tendency to take herself too seriously has been a problem in the past, but her fierce determination and humorless dedication she brings to her role are big pluses here, and she makes the extension of O'Neill's will, and body, entirely believable. Physically, she looks as hard as any of the guys, and only the musicvideo-style shots of her feverishly doing one-armed push-ups smack of star ego and trendy body fetishizing.

Film critic Todd McCarthy reviewing G.I. Jane *in* Variety, *August 11–17, 1997; reprinted in Paul M. Sammon,* Ridley Scott *(1999), p. 151.*

[Is the public] being insidiously conditioned to accept the idea of drafting women should the U.S. become involved in another really big war?

Film critic Bill Delaney questioning the political agenda of Ridley Scott's G.I. Jane, *which was released in mid-August 1997, in Delaney, "G.I. Jane,"* Magill's Cinema Annual *(1998), pp. 218–220.*

South Park is not a sign of impending apocalypse, although regular viewers do occasionally watch an animated Jesus and animated Satan square off in a kung-fu match. But it is another sign of yet another turn of the page in the ongoing saga of American humor. . . .

And whether humor will be used to combat that nihilism [implicit in postmodern society] or contribute to it remains to be seen, but postmodern is definitely the flavor of choice for cutting-edge comedy as the millennium approaches. *Seinfeld,* "the show about nothing," . . . drew an estimated 70 million viewers [to its final show]. At the same time, much of the TV humor that merges cult status with mainstream success has been animated. *The Simpsons,* cartoonist Matt Groening's brilliant takeoff on the television culture that spawned it, now is the longest-running sitcom on television. After *Beavis and Butthead* [a show featuring two animated teenage heavy-metal fans] finished its MTV run, creator Mike Judge found new success with Fox's *King of the Hill. Daria,* on MTV, and the Comedy Channel's controversial *South Park* have achieved critical—and with *South Park,* popular—success in their first year on the air.

Daria, MTV's animated take on a highly intelligent, socially isolated adolescent girl's sometimes-strained relationships . . . may be typical of the best appeal of this new comedy . . . but it's not nihilist. It is, like much else emerging from generation X, a very shrewd critique of the baby boomers. That's really what it's about—all these kids moving and living in postmodern culture, and they don't seem terribly impressed with it, either.

Humor scholar Michael Rust commenting in 1998 on South Park, *which debuted on August 13, 1997, and other new trends in postmodern television comedy, in James Haley, ed.,* Post–Cold War America: 1992–Present *(2003), pp. 109–110.*

Today I want to talk to you about guns: Why we have them, why the Bill of Rights guarantees that we can have them, and why my right to have a gun is more important than your right to rail against it in the press.

I believe every good journalist needs to know why the Second Amendment must be considered more essential than the First Amendment. This may be a bitter pill to swallow, but the right to keep and bear arms is not archaic. . . . These words may not play well at the Press Club, but it's still the gospel down at the corner bar and grill.

And your efforts to undermine the Second Amendment, to deride it and degrade it, to readily accept diluting it and eagerly promote redefining it, threaten not only the physical well-being of millions of Americans but also the core concept of individual liberty our founding fathers struggled to perfect and protect....

I say that the Second Amendment is, in order of importance, the first amendment. It is America's First Freedom, the one right that protects all the others.... The right to keep and bear arms is the one right that allows "rights" to exist at all.

Either you believe that, or you don't, and you must decide.

Because there is no such thing as a free nation where police and military are allowed the force of arms but individual citizens are not. That's a "big brother knows best" theater of the absurd that has never boded well for the peasant class, the working class, or even for reporters....

Please, go forth and tell the truth. There can be no free speech, no freedom of the press, no freedom to protest, no freedom to worship your god, no free-dom to speak your mind, no freedom from fear, no freedom for your children and for theirs, for anybody, anywhere, without the Second Amendment freedom to fight for it.

If you don't believe me, just turn on the news tonight. Civilization's veneer is wearing thinner all the time.

National Rifle Association president Charlton Heston addressing the National Press Club on September 11, 1997. Available online. URL: http://www. whyonearth.com/heston/heston.html.

Given our current movie culture, it is easy to forget that *"film noir"* used to mean something more than a vaguely malevolent atmosphere, a criminal misadventure and a lethal woman. Today, even one of those elements is enough to summon the epithet *"noir."* . . . Fortunately, Curtis Hanson's *L.A. Confidential,* adapted from James Ellroy's massive *policier,* is dead serious about its historical backdrop, its relation to the generic lineage of *noir* storytelling but also to the social–political climate in which the series flourished and expired. Instead of feeding off the usual suspects, *L.A. Confidential* circles back to the early Fifties to revisit two intertwined but often overlooked branches of the *noir* family tree: the rogue cop saga and the exposé of municipal corruption. Although it engages in the requisite glut of senseless mayhem, there is for a change an insistence on self-recognition, on the grim reciprocity between personal and institutional practices of violence. Equally important . . . Los Angeles is presented as not just a setting but a state of mind, an urban mythology stamped with the false promise of endless opportunity and filtered by the projections of Hollywood's dream factory.

Film critic Paul Arthur reviewing L.A. Confidential, *which premiered in mid-September 1997, in Arthur, "L.A. Confidential," Cineaste, vol. 23, no. 3 (1988), p. 41.*

The actor Charlton Heston is a staunch defender of the constitutional right to bear arms. *(Photofest)*

As DeLillo zooms in on each sphere of action, and each psyche, he achieves an unsurpassed intensity of sensory and psychological detail, which is rendered with exquisite tenderness. He never once loses this quality, this warmth and sorrow, as the narrative sways back and forth in time, and as more and more compelling characters and situations are introduced. There's Nick Shay, a waste-management expert burdened by a violent past; Klara Sax, an artist creating a monumental work in the middle of the desert out of decommissioned B-52s; and incendiary genius Lenny Bruce. Like novelists E. L. Doctorow and Thomas Pynchon, DeLillo uses historical figures to great effect, but DeLillo is a far more emotive and spiritual writer, and *Underworld* is a ravishingly beautiful symphony of a novel.

Reviewer Donna Seaman extolling Don DeLillo's Underworld *in Seaman, "Underworld," Booklist, August 1997, p. 1847.*

As black women, we must take our rightful place in this society. For many years we have been overlooked and treated as second class citizens in this world. The black woman is and always will be the very core of who we are as a people in any society. I especially enjoyed the message that Sister Soldier gave, telling the sisters to stop claiming sisterhood if you are out here mistreating another sister in any way. You have one sister trying to take another sister's man, while smiling in that same sister's face. Don't call that your sister because a real sister is not going to do that. Another thing you have is this pettiness of one sister talking about another sister behind her back about how she may be dressed or how much she weighs. . . .

The other point brought out was how we as women have been entrusted with the ability to give life to the male and female. It is in our power to raise and cultivate those children to become great people in this world. . . .

There were many messages given but what I walked away feeling and knowing is that we are a power to be reckoned with. The black woman has the power to give birth to her babies, love and take care of her family, hold down a full time job, run a household, love and support her man and everything else she has to do. It is high time that we sisters demand to be treated like the true African queens that we are. In all, the march was, to say the least, a true life changing experience that I hope will make us strive even harder to become the people we were meant to be.

Participant Anisa Maat describing her experience of the Million Woman March held October 25, 1997, in Maat, "The Million Woman March." Available online. URL: http://www.angelfire.com/ga/ dalaniaamon/index43.html.

I think Asia will come out of this crisis wiser about economic policies, somewhat more cautious, less likely to engage in the kinds of investments that produce a real estate bubble, and maybe, most importantly, I think Asian countries will learn to attach greater importance to regulation and supervision of their financial institutions because that's been a critical element in each of the places where a crisis has erupted. Over-extended banks—they get to a point they can't make any more loans and can't cover the financing that they've incurred, themselves.

Robert Denham of the Salomon Brothers investment firm analyzing the Asian financial crisis that was the topic of the Asia Pacific Economic Cooperation (APEC) meeting in Vancouver, Canada, on November 24–25, 1997, in "Asia's Economic Woes," The Newshour with Jim Lehrer, *November 25, 1997. Available online. URL: http://www.pbs.org/newshour/bb/asia/ july-dec97/apec_11-25.html.*

10

Monica and Impeachment
1998

Although Clinton presided over a strong economy and enjoyed popular approval of his handling of the presidency, as attested by Democratic gains in the 1998 midterm election, the Republican-dominated House of Representatives impeached the president on December 19 for allegedly committing perjury in the Paula Jones lawsuit and obstructing justice in the related investigation of his affair with the former White House intern Monica Lewinsky. Despite Clinton's public denial that he had had a sexual relationship with Lewinsky, many, if not most, Americans believed he was lying about the affair, though most did not consider that appropriate or sufficient ground for his removal from office. Moreover, many believed that Clinton's partisan enemies, the independent counsel Kenneth Starr among them, had deliberately forced the president into a no-win situation in which he must either lie or humiliate himself publicly by commenting on personal conduct unrelated to his performance in office.

The tobacco industry admitted lying about its past claims and practices, as it acknowledged targeting teenage smokers. It also agreed to pay a $206 billion settlement to many states in response to lawsuits filed to recover funds spent on treating patients for smoking-related diseases. The industry suffered an additional setback when a Florida jury for the first time awarded punitive damages against a tobacco company for its role in the death of a smoker who died of lung cancer.

Although the rate of violent crime dropped for the sixth consecutive year nationwide, highly publicized murders of children by other children shocked the nation and renewed arguments over gun control, child rearing, and the culture of violence in America. Terrorism also reemerged as a national concern after operatives suspected to be aligned with the Islamic terrorist Osama bin Laden killed more than 250 people in Kenya and Tanzania when they simultaneously exploded bombs outside U.S. embassies in those nations. Fighting began again in the Balkans, this time in Kosovo, and India and Pakistan raised fears of nuclear war after both nations tested nuclear devices. But Britain and Ireland concluded a peace agreement, and voters in Puerto Rico again rejected both independence and statehood.

In movies, Warren Beatty's *Bulworth* satirized the corruption of American politics, Steven Spielberg depicted the heroism of ordinary American soldiers during the World War II D-day invasion in *Saving Private Ryan,* and Roberto Benigni celebrated the triumph of the human spirit under the most oppressive of circumstances in *Life Is Beautiful.* An exciting home-run race between the Saint Louis Cardinal Mark McGwire and the Chicago Cub Sammy Sosa distracted the nation somewhat from the Lewinsky scandal, as McGwire hit his 62nd home run, breaking Roger Maris's single-season record, and then, after being overtaken temporarily by Sosa, went on to lead the league with 70.

INTERNATIONAL DEVELOPMENTS

Although the Dayton peace agreement concluded the war in Bosnia in late 1995, civil strife reerupted in the former Yugoslavia as Serbia's premier, Slobodan Milošević, tried to suppress a militant separatist movement that in February and March seized control of much of Serbia's Kosovo region. Kosovo had belonged to Albania before World War I, and approximately 90 percent of the population were ethnic Albanians, who became the targets of the Serbian army. Atrocities were also committed by rebels of the Kosovo Liberation Army (KLA), who killed close to 200 ethnic Serbs in the region. But widely reported acts of rape, looting, murder of ethnic Albanian civilians, and leveling of entire villages by the Serbian army provoked the United Nations to condemn Serbia. The fighting, which was most intense between April and October, produced some 40,000 refugees before threats on October 12 of NATO air strikes pressured Milošević to agree to a cease-fire with the KLA and to withdraw Serbian forces from the region.

The agreement, brokered by the U.S. special envoy, Richard Holbrooke, called for establishment of an international "verification force" of some 2,000

Serbian atrocities in Kosovo stopped temporarily after the North Atlantic Treaty Organization (NATO) threatened retaliatory air strikes. *(AP/Wide World Photos)*

soldiers, who assumed positions in November to monitor the truce. In Bosnia, the NATO peacekeeping forces arrested General Radislav Krstić, a Bosnian Serb wanted for overseeing war crimes committed in Srebrenica in 1995. Krstić was then arraigned to stand trial at the Hague Tribunal for war crimes. The tribunal imprisoned a Bosnian Croat paramilitary commander found guilty of allowing one of his soldiers to torture and rape a civilian detainee.

Suffering from a failing economy, Russia again experienced institutional change as Yeltsin fired Prime Minister Viktor Chernomyrdin and revamped his cabinet in order to enact his economic reforms during the last two years of his presidency. Meanwhile, the NATO alliance reached the Russian border, as the U.S. Senate ratified the "NATO-enlargement" treaty to include, by 1999, the former Soviet allies Poland, Hungary, and the Czech Republic. Organized crime and nascent neofascism, especially among the younger population, continued to threaten Russia from within, and the viability of the truce in Chechnya came into question after Islamic rebels decapitated four Western engineers who had been sent there to repair the republic's telephone system, which had been destroyed in the fighting.

Personal efforts by Clinton and his appointed representative, former senator George Mitchell, Britain's prime minister Tony Blair, Ireland's prime minister Bertie Ahern, and leaders of Ulster political parties culminated in the signing of a historic peace agreement to resolve the ongoing crisis in Northern Ireland. Known as the Good Friday Accord because its was signed on Good Friday, April 10, the pact called for greater cross-border interaction between Ireland and Northern Ireland; an understanding that Catholics in Northern Ireland would participate equally in the region's constitutional, political, and economic processes; and a countrywide referendum to create a new assembly in Ulster. The agreement further stipulated that Northern Ireland, which had a majority Protestant population, would not unite with predominantly Catholic Ireland without the consent of a majority of Northern Ireland's citizens. The agreement, which voters in Northern Ireland approved in May, was jeopardized in August, but not undermined, by a massive bomb attack by an IRA splinter group that killed 29 Catholics and Protestants, most of them women and children, in the worst atrocity committed in almost 30 years. The local leaders of Northern Ireland's opposing Catholic and Protestant factions, John Hume and David Trimble, received the year's Nobel Peace Prize for securing the agreement.

In his first official trip to China, Clinton gained unprecedented access to the Chinese citizenry as he appeared on national television with Premier Jiang Zemin. Clinton expressed his differences with Jiang about China's record on human rights, Chinese rule in Tibet, and the 1989 Tiananmen Square massacre. Clinton later spoke to students at Beijing University about the importance of human rights to political and economic stability. Although his appearances excited and inspired many Chinese citizens, especially younger ones, the government maintained its practice of political repression, and in December the United States protested the arrests of human rights dissidents, including those who were using e-mail and the Internet to disseminate antigovernment views.

Human rights abuses in Burma also attracted international attention as the opposition leader, Aung San Suu Kyi, went on a hunger strike to protest her party's exclusion from Burmese politics. After demonstrations on her behalf, Suu Kyi ended her strike but continued efforts to gain political freedom, but without immediate results. Widespread poverty in Indonesia, resulting from the nation's ongoing economic crisis and systemic government corruption, culminated in weeks of violence that left thousands dead in the capital city, Jakarta, and finally forced the resignation of the long-serving president, Suharto. Suharto's handpicked successor, Jusuf Habibie, who immediately ordered a military crackdown on protesting dissidents, failed to satisfy demands for serious democratic reforms.

Religious and politically based antipathies raised the long-standing enmity between India and Pakistan to dangerous levels. In March, India elected as its prime minister Atal Behari Vajpayee, the head of the hard-line anti-Islamic Hindu Nationalist Party. Pakistan, a majority Muslim state, voted in October to establish Islamic law. Although India had been long known to have a nuclear military capacity, a series of Indian underground tests in May, the first in 24 years, provoked Pakistan to test its own nuclear devices for the first time, creating what some Western newspapers called "the first Islamic bomb." Tensions between the nations became especially heated in the contested region of Kashmir, where border skirmishes between Indian and Pakistani troops erupted. The situation created worldwide concern that a nuclear war between the two nations, who had already fought three wars in the past 50 years, might result. The international community imposed sanctions on both countries, although Clinton later lifted some of the most severe economic restrictions on Pakistan, whose economy was particularly hard hit by them, and the IMF gave Pakistan a $3.3 billion financial aid package.

Terrorism, which had been declining worldwide over the past few years, resurfaced in August, when two U.S. embassies became the targets of coordinated car bomb attacks in East Africa. Some 250 Africans and 12 Americans died in the bombings, mostly in Nairobi, Kenya. Two weeks later, Clinton ordered air strikes against the Afghani headquarters of Osama bin Laden, a Saudi-born renegade prince and leader of the anti-Western Islamic al-Qaeda terrorist organization. In November, a federal grand jury indicted bin Laden and five members of al-Qaeda for the bombings in Nairobi and Dar es Salaam, Tanzania. The U.S. retaliatory attacks, involving more than 50 cruise missiles, killed 23 people at bin Laden's base in southern Afghanistan and stirred anti-U.S. sentiment in Afghanistan, where Western aid workers had to be evacuated. But bin Laden escaped and went on to engineer the air attacks on the Pentagon and New York's World Trade Center in 2001. Afghanistan's ruling Taliban regime, which supported bin Laden, continued to impose strict Islamic law: banning ownership of television sets, satellite dishes, and video recorders; forbidding women to attend school; forbidding men to trim their beard; and requiring all residential downstairs windows to be blackened, so women inside could not be viewed from the street. The Taliban saw military gains in its efforts to win control over the remaining 15 percent of the country not under its power.

Some 1.5 million Afghan refugees fled to camps in northeastern Iran, where the more moderate popularly elected president, Khatami, also faced stiff opposition from Islamic extremists who began executing supporters of free speech. Among those to die were the writer Mohammed Jafar Pouyandeh and the poet Mohammed Mokhtari, both outspoken opponents of censorship. An Islamic insurrection also continued in Algeria, where roughly 1,000 civilians died each month in terrorist acts committed by Muslims opposed to the ruling secular regime. Since 1992, at least 65,000 Algerians had died at the hands of Islamic fundamentalists[1]—more than the total of U.S. soldiers killed in 10 years of fighting in Vietnam. Ethiopia and Eritrea went to war over Badme, a barren 150-square-mile piece of land at the border of the two nations that had been incorporated into a federation in 1952. But the Islamic government of Sudan and the rebel Sudanese People's Liberation Army negotiated a cease-fire, ending 15 years of civil war but failing to alleviate its devastating effect on the civilian population.

Throughout the year Iraq vacillated in its willingness to permit inspections of its suspected weapons sites as required by the peace treaty that concluded the 1991 Persian Gulf War. In January, Clinton appeared before the nation to warn that he was preparing to authorize air strikes to ensure compliance, but the situation eased several days later, after Saddam Hussein signed an accord with the United Nations permitting unconditional access. However, throughout the year, Saddam Hussein periodically challenged the inspectors' authority, and on December 16, at the height of the impeachment hearings, Clinton ordered Operation Desert Fox, a series of air attacks intended to ensure compliance. Britain also participated in the attacks, which much of the international community, including China, France, Russia, and many Arab nations, condemned. Although he declared that the four-day operation succeeded in significantly damaging Iraq's capacity to produce weapons of mass destruction, Clinton, who terminated the bombings just hours after the House voted to impeach him on December 19, later maintained that he might have taken even stronger measures against what he perceived as a growing Iraqi threat but felt vulnerable to accusations that he was trying to distract the nation from the impeachment charges at a crucial time in the proceedings.

Elsewhere in the Middle East, Clinton and Jordan's ailing King Hussein personally brokered the Wye Agreement between Israel and the Palestinian National Authority, so called for its meeting place at the Wye Plantation near Washington, D.C. The pact, signed in late October, called for further Israeli withdrawal from the West Bank in return for Arafat's commitment to condemn bombings inside Israel and curtail the terrorist groups responsible for them. The agreement further reaffirmed the commitment on both sides to proceed with "final status" talks over such controversial issues as the future of Jerusalem and the right of those Arabs who had been displaced during the 1948 war for independence to return to live in Israeli. These matters had been deferred in the 1994 Oslo agreement. Shortly after concluding the Wye Agreement, the Palestinian National Authority opened its first international airport in the Gaza Strip, as well as a gambling casino in the West Bank city of Jericho, built with Austrian and Palestinian funds and frequented by hundreds of Israelis eager to partake in the entertainment.

In Rwanda, a war crimes tribunal condemned people found guilty of committing genocide, including a radio announcer who had urged Hutu to cleanse their communities of Tutsi "cockroaches." Despite complaints by Amnesty International that the defendants had not received sufficient opportunities to prepare their defense and an appeal for amnesty from Pope John Paul II, the first four executions for genocide since the end of World War II took place on April 24 before tens of thousands of cheering witnesses gathered at a football field in Kigali. During a tour of Africa, Clinton publicly acknowledged that the international community had failed to live up to its responsibilities when it did not intervene sooner to stop the genocide.

Many Chilean victims of atrocities committed by forces loyal to the former president, General Pinochet, cheered his arrest in London, after Spain requested his extradition for allegedly encouraging the torture of Spanish citizens in Chile during his rule. Britain's highest court, the Law Lords, however, overturned a High Court decision to extradite the former dictator. Nonetheless, the incident energized human rights groups, who, during the proceedings, received access to previously classified documents from the United States and elsewhere. The decision not to extradite was reversed in 1999, but in 2000 Pinochet won an appeal on medical grounds and returned home, where he continued to face investigations by Chilean authorities.

Concurrently with the profusion of recent and ongoing atrocities, a number of governments and institutions issued apologies for past abuses. Although Japan declined to compensate surviving World War II POWs, Prime Minister Ryutaro Hashimoto apologized to Britain's prime minister Tony Blair for the slave labor and harsh treatment British citizens endured, and he agreed to increase Japan's contribution to a joint fund intended to reconcile the nations. Japan also apologized to China for atrocities committed during its 1937 invasion and the occupation that followed; however, many Chinese found Japan's gesture inadequate. Standing before the remains of Emperor Nicholas II in Saint Petersburg, Russian president Boris Yeltsin apologized for the massacre of the royal family during the Bolshevik revolution of 1918. New Zealand apologized to the native Maori people of the South Island and allocated almost $100 million to compensate for historic acts in which their lands and treasures were taken, in violation of an 1840 treaty. Australia returned to the original Aborigine owners land that Britain had used for atomic testing in the 1950s and 1960s, after spending tens of millions of dollars to make the property inhabitable again for the indigenous Tjarutja people. Canada signed a treaty with an indigenous Indian nation in British Columbia, giving members of the Nisga'a people rights to self-government in a 745-square-mile area and access to natural resources from which they had been barred for more than 100 years. Fifty other Indian groups in British Columbia pursued similar claims. Cambodia apologized to its citizens for the 1970s reign of terror promulgated by the Khmer Rouge, whose leader during the period, Pol Pot, died in April.

Germany apologized for massacring thousands of Herero in 1904 in Namibia (then the German colony of Southwest Africa). The Swiss banking industry, responding to threats of sanctions by U.S. states and municipalities, agreed to pay $1.25 billion to Jewish survivor groups in compensation for unreturned assets collected during the Holocaust, and Germany's Deutsche Bank acknowledged "its moral and ethical responsibilities for the darkest chapter in history" when it admitted accepting almost 10,000 pounds of gold taken from Jewish victims during World War II, including melted-down gold fillings from teeth, wedding rings, and other jewelry. Although Germany offered no financial restitution in 1998, in 1999, its largest banks and companies agreed to contribute a total of $60 billion to surviving slave laborers who had been forced to work, often under inhumane conditions, for such private companies as Krupp and Volkswagen. In 1998, Germany also returned to the chief rabbi in

Rome sacks of jewels and other treasures stolen from Jews in Trieste in 1943. Italy's largest insurance company agreed to pay $100 million to Holocaust victims and their heirs who had purchased policies before and during the war.

The AIDS epidemic ravaging Africa invited comparisons to previous deadly plagues, including the Black Death that devastated 14th-century Europe and the worldwide influenza epidemics of 1918 and 1919 that each killed up to 20 million people. AIDS was the third leading cause of death in the world, after malaria and tuberculosis. It was followed by automobile-related fatalities, which accounted for more than 3 million deaths in the United States between 1899, when 26 people were killed, and 1998. Since 1961, an average of more than 45,000 Americans had died each year as a result of traffic accidents.[2] The World Health Organization found worldwide increases in debilitating mental disorders, including depression, alcoholism, drug abuse, and suicide.

GOVERNMENT AND SOCIETY

Clinton's sexual liaison with Lewinsky, which lasted between November 1995 and March 1997, surfaced in early January 1998, when Kenneth Starr received credible evidence that Clinton may have lied under oath when he denied in his deposition in the Paula Jones sexual harassment case that he and Lewinsky had had a sexual relationship. A panel of judges granted Starr authority to broaden his existing Whitewater investigation to include the new charges, and in June, Linda Tripp, a confidant of Lewinsky's, told the grand jury that she had secretly recorded 20 hours of telephone conversations in which Lewinsky spoke of her sexual experiences with the president. Tripp also revealed that Lewinsky had a dress stained with Clinton's semen, which Lewinsky turned over to Starr. FBI analysis of the DNA indicated that the semen was Clinton's, and in his final report Starr used this evidence to demonstrate that Clinton had, in fact, had sexual intercourse with Lewinsky. After Starr granted Lewinsky immunity from prosecution, she testified in August that she and Clinton had engaged in sexual activity in the Oval Office, but she denied that he pressured her to lie to protect him. Soon afterward, Clinton admitted in closed-circuit testimony televised to the grand jury that he and Lewinsky had, indeed, been sexually involved, although he was careful in his choice of words to avoid admitting that he had lied in his deposition in the Jones case. In September, Starr reported to the House that Clinton had lied under oath about his sexual connection with Lewinsky and had tampered with witnesses during the investigation, and he recommended that Clinton be impeached for perjury and obstruction of justice. (Ironically, in April a federal judge dismissed Jones's lawsuit as being "without merit." Jones appealed the decision, however, and Clinton agreed in November to settle the claim for $850,000, stating that he did not want to draw out the case further.) The Whitewater grand jury, for which Starr was first appointed independent counsel, concluded in May without issuing indictments against either Bill Clinton or Hillary Rodham Clinton.

The House released the Starr report and Clinton's videotaped testimony to the public in October, but if the intention was to gain public support for impeachment, the strategy failed. Overall, viewers were impressed by Clinton's humility and composure. Moreover, much of the public believed it was inappropriate for Congress to investigate information about a president's personal life, which Clinton had been made to reveal in intimate and embarrassing detail. A large part of the electorate also believed that the push for impeachment was politically motivated by the Republican independent counsel and Republican House of Representatives. In October, the House voted to have the House Judiciary Committee determine whether the Starr report contained sufficient grounds for impeachment. That committee recommended four articles of impeachment on December 11–12, and on December 19, the full House voted along party lines to impeach Clinton, making him only the second president, after Andrew Johnson in 1868, to stand trial before the Senate for "high crimes and misdemeanors." As was Johnson, Clinton was subsequently acquitted by the Senate.

The midterm congressional elections took place in November, between the release of the Starr report and the decision to impeach. Contrary to expectations that the president's problems would undermine his party, Democrats made significant gains throughout the nation. They gained five seats in the House, reducing the Republican majority to 12, and won the governorship of California. The election results were generally interpreted as approval of the strong economy and low unemployment rate and as the public's repudiation of the perceived partisan motivation for the impeachment effort. Two days after the election, Gingrich, assuming responsibility for the Republican losses, shocked his colleagues and surprised the country when he announced that he would not run for reelection as Speaker for the new Congress, which would begin in January 1999, and that he probably would resign from Congress.

Although such Republicans as Henry Hyde of Illinois, the chairman of the House Judiciary Committee, berated Clinton for immoral behavior, others maintained that the central issues in the impeachment were the charges that Clinton had lied under oath and tried to thwart Starr's investigation. Nonetheless, much of the public perceived that the impeachment concerned Clinton's adultery. Consequently, when new information surfaced that Hyde and other outspoken Republican critics also had committed adultery, many accused them of hypocrisy.

Indeed, "playing the sex card" boomeranged on several of Clinton's accusers and helped turn public sentiment in his favor. In September, Representative Helen Chenoweth of Idaho, who had been among the first to call for Clinton's resignation over the Lewinsky scandal, confessed to having had a long-term affair with a married man more than a decade earlier. Representative Dan Burton of Indiana, a ranking Republican, who was conducting a fund-raising investigation of the Clinton campaign, admitted that he had fathered a child in an extramarital affair. And on September 16, less than a week before the House released Clinton's televised testimony, *Salon,* an Internet magazine, revealed that Hyde had cheated on his wife in the 1960s, when he was in his mid-40s. Calling it a "youthful indiscretion," Hyde immediately acknowledged the affair but insisted that it was irrelevant to the impeachment question. Bob Livingston of Louisiana, whom Republicans elected in November to succeed Gingrich as Speaker, during the impeachment debate dramatically confessed to several adulterous affairs. In a speech delivered on the House floor, Livingston resigned his post, which he had yet to assume, and stated he would leave Congress in six months. Gingrich, too, who had pilloried Clinton for his sexual conduct, later admitted to having a long-term sexual affair outside his marriage, even while he was publicly condemning Clinton.

Though Clinton had been put on the defensive over the Lewinsky affair, he stood his ground on his political agenda and surprised many observers by scoring significant political victories, even during the height of the impeachment process. Notably, in the fall, he threatened to veto the omnibus spending bill and potentially shut down the federal government unless Congress released $17.9 billion in new credits to help the IMF address the global financial crisis and funded his education initiatives calling for the hiring of 100,000 additional elementary school teachers over seven years. Cognizant of the political defeat they suffered in 1996 after shutting down the government in late 1995, the Republican Congress acceded to Clinton's demands. They also funded numerous self-serving "pork barrel" items that Clinton condemned and that Senator John McCain, an Arizona Republican who regularly monitored such practices, criticized as the most wasteful legislation he had seen in his 16 years in Congress.

But Clinton's behavior in regard to the Lewinsky sex scandal further divided an already divided nation. Many liberals, while regarding Clinton's sexual infidelity in the White House as inappropriate, even repugnant and personally reprehensible, were nonetheless inclined to view the affair primarily as a personal matter between consenting adults. Therefore, they regarded the liaison as largely irrelevant to their assessment of the president's performance as chief executive, in which capacity he had promoted equal opportunities for women, homosexuals, and members of minorities, as well as introducing initiatives for education, environmental protection, and other traditionally liberal causes. But for many conservatives the Lewinsky affair, itemized in seamy detail in public testimony, provided stark evidence that the moral degeneracy fomented by liberal tolerance had spread to the highest office in the land.

Violent crime among children continued to alarm the nation. The young age of the perpetrators was especially disturbing when two boys in Arkansas, ages 11 and 13, engineered a hoax fire drill and then opened fire on their teachers and classmates, killing four girls and a teacher and injuring 12 others in the third school killing in the country in five months. A month later, a 14-year-old boy shot and killed a teacher and wounded three other people at a school dance in Pennsylvania; and a month after that, a 15-year-old boy in Oregon killed his parents before reporting to school, where he killed two students and wounded 22 others with a semiautomatic rifle. Two boys, aged seven and eight, were charged in juvenile court with the murder of an 11-year-old girl, whom they knocked unconscious with a rock, dragged into a wooded area, sexually molested, and suffocated. Increases in on-the-job violence were a less publicized development among adults, as murder surpassed machine-related accidents as the second largest cause of job-related deaths, after automobile accidents.

The Supreme Court made several important decisions that affected the functions of state and federal government. It declared the Line Item Veto Act of 1996 unconstitutional because it upsets the balance between the legislative and executive branches of government. It ruled that the attorney-client confidentiality privilege persists even after a client dies; that police cannot conduct a full search of automobiles after ticketing motorists for minor violations; that the federal government can consider standards of decency when awarding federal arts grants; and that public television stations can exclude lesser-known political candidates from participating in televised debates.

The Court also decided that the Professional Golfer's Association (PGA) cannot prohibit disabled golfers from using golf carts in tournaments, though other competitors have to walk the courses; that people infected with the AIDS-causing HIV are entitled to protections provided by the 1990 Americans with Disabilities Act; that same-sex harassment in the workplace violates federal civil rights law; that employees who reject sexual advances by a supervisor can pursue sexual harassment suits, even if they suffer no retaliation; and that employers are liable for acts of sexual harassment by their supervisory staff, even when they are unaware of the supervisors' misconduct.

The Supreme Court of Canada ruled that Quebec could not declare its independence from the federation without the consent of the federal government and Canada's other nine provinces. Nonetheless, voters in Quebec province elected the separatist Parti Québécois into power. That Court also ruled that provinces must extend laws banning discrimination to protect homosexuals and that school authorities can search students without first obtaining a warrant.

BUSINESS

Although financial crises continued to plague much of the rest of the world, the U.S. economy remained robust. Despite a 512-point drop on August 31, in response to the financial crisis in Russia and its anticipated worldwide impact, the Dow-Jones industrial average closed at 9,181, up 1,273 points from 1997, a gain of 16.1 percent. It reached a high of 9,374, and 1998 was the fourth consecutive year of double-digit percentage gains, a new record. The inflation rate dropped by one-third to 1.6 percent, and the unemployment rate dropped to 4.5 percent, compared to 5.0 percent in 1997, to the lowest rate since 1970. However, the GDP grew by only 4.3 percent, about the same as experienced between 1994 and 1996, but significantly less than the 6.2 percent the economy enjoyed in 1997.[3] The 1998 fiscal year also saw the first federal budget surplus since 1969, a $70 billion surplus that was attributed to increased tax revenues from the strong economy and reduced spending on government programs.

Although the Clinton administration generally acceded to large corporate mergers, the Justice Department and 20 states filed two antitrust suits against Microsoft, accusing the corporation of illegal marketing and trade practices. Filed after settlement talks failed, the suits maintained that Microsoft, which manufactures the widely used Windows computer operating system, tried to use its near-monopoly to dominate other segments of the software market unfairly.

The administration raised no objections to the planned merger of Exxon and Mobil, the world's largest and second-largest oil companies. When completed, Exxon's $75.3 billion purchase of Mobil became the largest in history, and it created the world's largest corporation in terms of annual revenue. The merger of automakers Daimler-Benz and Chrysler was also among the 11,652 mergers and acquisitions in 1998, a record-setting number of transactions worth $1.61 trillion—78 percent more than the $919 billion in 1997. Most of the mergers and acquisitions occurred within the banking industry, followed by telecommunications and then petroleum.

Congress extended copyrights on songs and books from 50 to 70 years after the author's death. Copyrights held by companies were increased to 95 years. Entertainment companies lobbied hard for this legislation, especially the Walt Disney Company, whose exclusive rights on the Mickey Mouse cartoon character would otherwise have expired in 2003.

Ford, Chrysler, and General Motors introduced new car models with advanced technology for achieving greater fuel efficiency. These included electric cars and hybrid vehicles that switched between battery and gasoline power and could travel up to 80 miles on a gallon of gas, while emitting only one-third the pollutants of conventional internal combustion engines. The hybrids were considerably more costly than conventional automobiles, however. Meanwhile, Volkswagen introduced its New Beetle to the U.S. market. Evoking the original Beetle, the most popular car in history, the New Beetle was safer than its predecessor, and it was manufactured in Mexico for both European and U.S. markets.

Leaders of 34 nations in the Western Hemisphere meeting in Santiago, Chile, at the second Summit of the Americas agreed to initiate formal talks for forming a Free Trade Area of the Americas, which, if approved, would by 2005 create a free-trade zone containing some 800 million people and stretch throughout the entire hemisphere.

Although the economies of the United States, Italy, Spain, and France prospered, other nations throughout the world endured difficult economic times. South Korea's economy also enjoyed a sharp turnaround, as its Composite Stock Index gained 49.5 percent. But the financial crisis in Asia continued to have widespread economic and political ramifications. In addition to causing the resignation in Indonesia of Suharto, who stepped down in May after more than three decades of rule, the economic crisis led to the resignation of Japan's prime minister Hashimoto, who resigned in July after his government announced that the nation was officially experiencing a recession. That revelation reduced the value of stocks in markets across the world. Although Russia joined the so-called G-7, the group of the world's seven richest nations—making the organization the G-8—its faltering economy compelled Yeltsin to restructure his cabinet in August, just five months after installing it, and, in November, to obtain $625 million worth of grain, beef, and pork from the United States and $500 million in aid from the EU. Brazil's once-encouraging economy also fell into disarray as a result of the Asian crisis and a nearly 50 percent increase in domestic interest rates. In October, Clinton personally implored the International Monetary Fund (IMF) to take measures to assist Brazil, and, in November, it provided a $41.5 billion loan package, in return for Brazil's pledge to install major economic reforms. Overall, Brazil's market index fell by 33.4 percent; Mexico's declined by nearly 40 percent.[4]

NATURE AND THE ENVIRONMENT

The El Niño Pacific Ocean phenomenon that had occurred in 1997 also affected weather events in 1998. A spate of tornadoes that killed 40 people in Florida in February was attributed to El Niño. Unlike in 1996, however, the phenomenon failed to suppress hurricane activity in the Atlantic Ocean, where

Hurricane Georges ravaged the Caribbean before striking Alabama and Florida, and as many as 10,000 people died in El Salvador, Nicaragua, and Honduras as a result of flooding and landslides when Hurricane Mitch, a category 5 storm with winds in excess of 155 mph, made landfall in Central America. Wildfires in central Florida forced 120,000 people to evacuate homes, and smoke from the fires caused lethal traffic accidents. A January ice storm in eastern Canada, the most expensive natural disaster in the nation's history, killed at least 25, caused an estimated $1.4 billion in damage, and left some 3 million Canadians without power. The same weather system caused freezing rain in the northeastern United States, also causing several deaths and widespread power loss.

Flooding from heavy rains in England caused thousands of people to evacuate their home and produced more than $25 million in damage. Flooding along the Yangtze River killed some 3,000 people in China; floods left much of Bangladesh and parts of Vietnam under water; mud slides from Mount Sarno outside Naples killed more than 80 people, left hundreds more homeless, and devastated six towns in Italy; a strong earthquake killed between 3,000 and 5,000 in Afghanistan; another earthquake killed more than 100 in eastern Turkey.

Several environmental groups decried deteriorating conditions worldwide. Wild Atlantic salmon are on the verge of extinction—the victims of industrial waste, polluted runoff from farms, and the construction of dams on the rivers in which they spawn. The World Wide Fund for Nature warned that industrial pollution threatens to kill the most exotic sea animals off the coasts of Britain, and the World Conservation Union, working in conjunction with more than 600 scientists around the world, concluded that 25 percent of all mammal and amphibian species are at risk of extinction, as are 31 percent of all fish species, 20 percent of all reptiles, and 11 percent of all birds. The organization cited destruction of forests, wetlands, grasslands, chaparral, and other natural habitats as the leading cause. It also concluded that 30 percent of the world's coral reefs are in critical condition.[5] In addition, wildfires in Indonesia threatened to exterminate orangutans. Scientists who believed in the politically controversial theory that Earth is undergoing global warming pointed to the fact that July temperatures throughout the world were the highest ever recorded.

SCIENCE AND TECHNOLOGY

In the same year that saw the death of Alan Shepard, the first U.S. astronaut to fly into outer space, Senator John Glenn, who, in 1962 became the first American to orbit the Earth, returned to outer space at age 77. Although some dismissed the voyage as a publicity stunt for NASA, the space agency maintained that Glenn's flight would enable them to perform scientific tests on the effects of space travel on aging. Russia launched the first section of an international space station to be assembled in outer space. Two teams of astronomers for the first time viewed the formation of a group of planets around a young star, while another team reported viewing a complete "Einstein ring," a phenomenon predicted by Albert Einstein in which the light from a distant star is bent by another massive body between the Earth and that star. Neutrinos, the most common subatomic particles, which had long been believed to have no mass, were shown to have mass, a discovery that some believed may account for much of the undetected "dark matter" that constitutes most of the mass of the universe. The announcement of a very small possibility that an asteroid might collide with Earth on October 26 caused consternation among some people, especially those who feared an end-of-the-millennium cataclysm. Most scientists, however, dismissed the likelihood as so small as to be essentially nonexistent.

By 1998, some 102 million people throughout the world had access to the Internet, which linked approximately 1.8 million Web sites.[6]

After a Chicago scientist announced plans to clone a human being by using the methods developed to create Dolly the sheep, the first cloned mammal, Clinton called for a law banning human cloning, and the Food and Drug Administration asserted its authority to regulate cloning. Elsewhere, researchers of the Geron Corporation and the University of Texas succeeded in genetically altering adult human cells to extend their life span, possibly even "immortalizing" them. Although the scientists pointed out that this technique did not promise a general cure for aging, because it did not prevent disease, it had potential uses for the treatment of diseases associated with the aging of cells, including some conditions of the eyes and skin. Two teams of scientists, one from Britain and the other from the United States, completed the first map of the entire genome, or genetic code, of a multicellular animal, a microscopic worm. A fertility clinic in Virginia developed a method to increase the probability that a couple could have a child of designated gender through artificial insemination. Genetic testing was used to identify the serviceman from the Vietnam War who was buried in the Tomb of the Unknowns in Arlington National Cemetery, and the procedure was predicted to eliminate the unknown soldier phenomenon in future wars.

Dr. Arpad Pusztai, a renowned researcher of food safety, was fired from the Rowett Institute, Britain's prestigious research lab, after he stated on television that he would not eat genetically engineered foods because they had not had sufficient testing procedures. His position was challenged by the food industry, which helped fund the institute, and, for many, Pusztai's controversial dismissal demonstrated a troubling ability of industry to influence scientific research and scientific discourse. In 1999, 20 scientists in other countries announced their support for Pusztai.

The public enthusiastically greeted the FDA's approval of Viagra, a prescription medication for treating male impotence. News that moderate alcohol consumption each day reduces the risk of heart attack and strokes also attracted public interest, especially as use of alcohol is opposed by certain religious beliefs. Studies also showed that folic acid, vitamin B_6 supplements, and potassium in bananas and other foods reduce the risk of heart disease. Doctors in France performed the first human limb transplantation, in which a man received a new hand. Scientists working for Abbott Laboratories reported that they had isolated a painkilling chemical, ABT-594, from the toxic poison secreted by a South American frog. Believed to be substantially more powerful than morphine, ABT-594 began human trials in Europe. Radon, a gas sometimes found inside homes, especially older homes, was shown to contribute to lung cancer, especially among tobacco smokers. Herceptin was proved effective against some forms of breast cancer. Medical researchers defied conventional wisdom when they demonstrated that new brain cells can grow after birth and that human embryonic stem cells may be able to grow tissues to replace cells and organs lost to disease. This last development provoked public controversy, as antiabortion activists feared the discovery might encourage the practice of abortion to provide embryos as a stem-cell source.

Anthropologists discovered what they believed was the so-called missing link in human evolution between people and apes, when they unearthed a 3-million-year-old skeleton that suggested that early humans were similar to apes and inhabited trees. Czech archaeologists working in Egypt opened the first ancient tomb to be discovered since that of the pharaoh Tutankhamen in 1923. The tomb, which was the burial site of a pharaonic priest who died around 525 B.C., contains inscriptions that provide information about the influence of Persia in Egypt at that time. Israeli archaeologists found the oldest ruins of a Jewish temple yet discovered. The synagogue, which dated to approximately 60 B.C., was uncovered in the West Bank, outside Jericho, among the ruins of a Maccabean palace.

LITERATURE, THE ARTS, SPORTS, AND POPULAR CULTURE

Although social conservatives exerted considerable political influence, they were less successful in the realm of popular culture. Their diminishing ability to incorporate their visions of acceptable social and sexual behavior into entertainment programming concerned them greatly, because they recognized the power of popular culture to shape the attitudes, values, and views of reality held by the public in general and young people in particular. Therefore, conservative activists worked to curb the most extreme expressions of what they regarded as deviant or degenerate behavior. But although they succeeded in restricting government funding for the arts, especially those supported by the National Endowment for the Arts, First Amendment protections of free speech greatly limited the government's ability to censor the media. In addition, the Internet offered an ever-increasing range of largely unregulated sexual and social behavior for computer users to explore online.

Moreover, sexually liberated, personally empowered women routinely appeared in commercial advertising and in virtually every popular medium, except perhaps certain genres of religious music and gangsta rap, which is often misogynistic. Appealing especially to younger audiences, images of strong, independent women were projected in music by such groups as the popular all-woman rock band the Spice Girls; by highly rated established television shows featuring intelligent, sexually active single women, such as *Friends* and *Seinfeld;* by new programs, such as *Felicity, Jesse,* and HBO's popular comedy *Sex and the City,* which centers on the quest for love and good times by four unmarried professional New York women in their 30s; and by such diverse movie releases as John Madden's *Shakespeare in Love,* Jonathan Demme's *Beloved,* Shekhar Kapur's *Elizabeth,* and Peter Farrelly and Bobby Farrelly's *There's Something about Mary.* In addition to showcasing liberated and assertive women, a growing portion of popular culture also showed Americans of different races and ethnic backgrounds relating easily with one another as professional equals, and sometimes as close friends, romantic interests, and/or sexual partners.

Even homosexuality, which had been taboo throughout the history of American culture, found new acceptance in the late 1990s. Although the television comedy *Ellen* ended in July, barely a year after Ellen DeGeneres's title character "came out" and revealed that she is a lesbian during the show's third season, *Will & Grace* debuted in September. Apart from *Ellen*, whose character was not apparently gay at its inception, *Will & Grace*, about the non-sexual friendship of a sexually active gay man and a sexually active straight woman, was the first network show to feature a homosexual as a central character. Moreover, Will's homosexuality and Grace's promiscuity are matter-of-factly accepted, without negative judgment.

Although independent filmmakers had established themselves in 1996, when the winner and three of the runners-up for the Academy Award were produced by independents, not until *Shakespeare in Love* beat out the patriotic and critically acclaimed *Saving Private Ryan* was the impact of independent film production on the contemporary film industry fully recognized. The independent Italian director and actor Roberto Benigni won the Academy Award as best actor in *Life Is Beautiful,* an uplifting story about a man's effort to sustain his son's spirits during the Holocaust. The movie also won as best foreign film. François Girard won an Academy Award for directing *The Red Violin,* a series of vignettes spanning 300 years and three continents and unified by the presence in the life of the characters of a finely crafted violin. Akira Kurosawa, the celebrated Japanese filmmaker who attained worldwide prominence in 1950 with *Rashomon,* died at age 88.

The year's most financially successful movies were Michael Bay's *Armageddon* ($201.6 million), *Saving Private Ryan* ($190.4 million), and *There's Something about Mary* ($173.7 million).[7] Other notable films included Gary Ross's *Pleasantville,* which offers a critical view of 1950s conformity, homogeneity, and sexual and emotional repression; *Beloved,* based on Toni Morrison's 1987 novel about a runaway slave who kills her child rather than allow her return to bondage; Terrence Malick's World War II film *The Thin Red Line,* starring Sean Penn and Nick Nolte as soldiers fighting at Guadalcanal; and Peter Weir's *The*

Steven Spielberg's highly realistic *Saving Private Ryan* was one of many efforts by baby boomers to pay homage to their parents' generation, who fought World War II. *(Photofest)*

Truman Show, which stars Jim Carrey as a young man who, unknown to him, grows up on a totally manipulated television set in which his life is broadcast live as an ongoing soap opera. The top box office stars were Harrison Ford, John Travolta, Tom Hanks, Robin Williams, Leonardo DiCaprio, Sandra Bullock, Julia Roberts, Tom Cruise, Will Smith, and Brad Pitt.

As the new millennium approached, the American Film Institute released its list of the top movies of the century. Heading the list, which clearly favored established classics, were *Citizen Kane* (Orson Welles, 1941), *Casablanca* (Michael Curtis, 1942), *The Godfather* (Francis Ford Coppola, 1972), *Gone with the Wind* (Victor Fleming, 1939), *Lawrence of Arabia* (David Lean,1962), *The Wizard of Oz* (Victor Fleming, 1939), and *The Graduate* (Mike Nichols, 1967).

The Modern Library published its list of 100 best novels of the 20th century, which also favored earlier-written works. The ranking was headed by James Joyce's *Ulysses* (1922), F. Scott Fitzgerald's *The Great Gatsby* (1925), Joyce's *A Portrait of the Artist as a Young Man* (1916), Vladimir Nabokov's *Lolita* (1955), Aldous Huxley's *Brave New World* (1932), William Faulkner's *The Sound and the Fury* (1929), and Joseph Heller's *Catch-22* (1961). An art historian discovered the manuscript of *The Royal House of Savoy,* published 150 years after it was written by the popular French novelist Alexandre Dumas.

Michael Cunningham's Pulitzer Prize–winning novel *The Hours,* a fantasy about three women living at different times during the 20th century, plays off Virginia Woolf's *Mrs. Dalloway* (1925). Other works of new fiction included Philip Roth's *I Married a Communist,* about long-term repercussions of the 1950s red scare; Toni Morrison's *Paradise,* about the complex relationships among the inhabitants of the all-black town of Ruby, Oklahoma, and the violence directed against women there; Alice McDermott's *Charming Billy,* a reminiscence about the sad life of an alcoholic Irish American; Robert Coover's *Ghost Town,* which turns the stereotypes of the Old West into a semisurreal fantasy; Tom Wolfe's *A Man in Full,* about racial strife and high society in contemporary Atlanta; Russell Banks's *Cloudsplitter,* a fictional account of the life of the abolitionist and religious zealot John Brown; and Dan Wakefield's *Under the Apple Tree: A Novel of the Home Front,* about a young boy's experiences at home in Illinois while his brother is overseas fighting in World War II. Robert MacNeil, the former cohost of the prestigious MacNeil-Lehrer news show on public television, published *Breaking News,* a novel about an aging news broadcaster filled with doubts about himself and about the sleazy industry in which he works. Writers of genre fiction continued to attract wide audiences, notably John Grisham (*The Street Lawyer*), Tom Clancy (*Rainbow Six*), Stephen King (*Bag of Bones*), Mary Higgins Clark (*All Through the Night*), and Danielle Steel (*The Klone and I: A High-Tech Love Story* and *Long Road Home*). Steel, a romance novelist, also published *His Bright Light: The Story of Nick Traina,* a nonfiction, autobiographical story about the suicide of her son, who suffered from severe depression. The British author J. K. Rowling enjoyed immense success with her children's fantasy *Harry Potter and the Sorcerer's Stone* (titled *Harry Potter and the Philosopher's Stone* in Britain, where it was first released).

As the baby boomers entered their forties and fifties, many who during the 1960s had vowed never to trust anyone older than 30, gained new appreciation for their parents' generation, who had emerged from the hardships of the Great Depression and World War II to build a vibrant and prosperous postwar

America. The new admiration found expression in movies such as *Saving Private Ryan* and *The Thin Red Line,* which celebrate the routine heroism of ordinary citizen soldiers, and in such books as *The Greatest Generation* by the television journalist Tom Brokaw. Other nonfiction included Harold Bloom's *Shakespeare: The Invention of the Human,* Alan Dershowitz's *Sexual McCarthyism,* and William Bennett's *The Death of Outrage: Bill Clinton and the Assault on American Ideals.* John McPhee won the Pulitzer Prize for *Annals of the Former World,* a geological history of North America. The poet Mark Strand won the prize for *Blizzard of One.* In *Without: Poems* Donald Hall describes the process of watching his wife undergo a painful bone marrow procedure but nevertheless die of leukemia. The *New Yorker* editor Deborah Garrison also issued a volume of poetry, *A Working Girl Can't Win: And Other Poems,* which was praised for its accessibility to general readers and which speaks in the voice of an intelligent young career woman preoccupied with sex, men, office politics, domesticity, and clothes. Jewel Kilcher, a popular singer known simply as Jewel, also published a volume of poetry, *A Night without Armor.*

The playwright Paula Vogel won the Pulitzer Prize for *How I Learned To Drive,* a drama about a prepubescent girl's incestuous relationship with her uncle. The French writer Yasmina Reza won the 1998 Tony Award for best play for *Art,* about friends arguing over a work of minimalist art. *The Lion King,* based on the 1994 Disney movie, won as best musical. Notable Broadway revivals included William Shakespeare's comedy *Twelfth Night;* Samuel Beckett's absurdist drama *Waiting for Godot;* and Arthur Miller's story of an immigrant dock worker, *A View from the Bridge,* which won the Tony as best revival. Popular revivals of musicals included *The Sound of Music* and *Cabaret,* which won a Tony as best revival of a musical. New musicals included Lynn Ahrens and Stephen Flaherty's *Ragtime,* which is based on the 1975 novel by E. L. Doctorow about life in the early 20th century, and Jason Robert Brown's *Parade.* The British playwright David Hare had two new Broadway openings: *The Blue Room* starred Nicole Kidman in a contemporary reworking of Arthur Schnitzler's *La Ronde,* a 19th-century play about sex among the social classes, and *The Judas Kiss,* which starred Liam Neeson in the story of the witty homosexual Irish playwright Oscar Wilde.

The Lewinsky scandal attracted large audiences to cable television, which aired extensive coverage of the unfolding impeachment process. Viewers were also attracted to a special feature of *60 Minutes* in which Dr. Jack Kevorkian, an advocate of doctor-assisted suicide for the terminally ill, played a videotape showing an assisted suicide he had performed. Kevorkian was then arrested on charges of first-degree murder and was convicted of second-degree murder in 1999. A Texas jury decided against cattle ranchers who claimed that the television talk-show host Oprah Winfrey had slandered the U.S. cattle industry in 1996, when she and one of her guests had warned against consuming the meat of cattle raised in the United States because U.S. producers routinely fed cows ground-up animal parts, a practice blamed for the spread of mad cow disease. The ranchers had argued for $12 million in damages because the price of cattle futures dropped by more than 10 percent the day after the show aired.

The top-rated shows of the 1998–99 season showed more balance between drama and comedy than previous seasons, although comedy still prevailed. The most widely viewed shows were *ER, Frasier, Friends, Veronica's Closet, Jesse—*

a new sitcom about a single mother in Buffalo—*60 Minutes, Touched by an Angel,* and *Home Improvement. Seinfeld* enjoyed the fourth-highest ratings of any final show when the series aired its last episode in May, but fans of *NYPD Blue* were disappointed when the sensitive police detective Bobby Simone suffered a fatal heart attack in November, a development written into the script when the actor Jimmy Smits decided to leave the show. *The Practice* won the Emmy Award as outstanding dramatic series, and *Frasier* won its fifth consecutive award as best comedy series. David Kelley produced both shows, the first person to produce both the best comedy and the best drama. Helen Hunt, star of the comedy *Mad about You,* won the Emmy as best actress in a comedy series for her fourth consecutive year. John Lithgow, who had trained as a Shakespearean actor, won as best actor in a comedy series, *Third Rock from the Sun.* Although it did not win, *The Sopranos,* HBO's new series about a New Jersey Mafia family, was the first cable show to be nominated for best drama, and the *Sopranos* star Edie Falco won as best actress in a dramatic series. Dennis Franz of *NYPD Blue* won as best dramatic actor. The popular game show *The Price Is Right,* which began in 1957, had its 5,000th televised episode.

Celine Dion, whose album *Talk about Love* was a best seller, won the Grammy Award for best record for *My Heart Will Go On.* Lauryn Hill won for best album for *The Miseducation of Lauryn Hill.* Other hit albums included the soundtrack from *Titanic, Backstreet Boys* by the Backstreet Boys, *Sevens* by Garth Brooks, *Yourself or Someone Like You* by matchbox 20, and *Spiceworld* by the Spice Girls. The 17-year-old Britney Spears enjoyed her breakthrough success at the end of the year with her album *. . . Baby One More Time.* As did the Spice Girls, Spears appealed primarily to teenagers and young adults, a powerful consumer group, who bought more than 10 million copies of her album in the first year of its release. Spears's sexually provocative attire caused many parents to object that she was too young to be promoting herself as a sex icon and was sending a harmful

The success of HBO's humanistic crime drama *The Sopranos* helped establish the credibility of cable television's programming. *(Photofest)*

message to young girls. Spears, however, maintained that her revealing outfits simply mirrored contemporary fashions already popular among teenagers. Even as big swing bands enjoyed a revival, Frank Sinatra, who began his career singing in the bands of the 1930s and 1940s, died at age 82.

When Mark McGwire of the Saint Louis Cardinals broke Roger Maris's single-season home run record on September 8, he eradicated a record that had endured for 37 years, longer than Babe Ruth held it before Maris hit his 61st homer. Sammy Sosa also broke Maris's record, completing the year with 66 home runs and winning praise from First Lady Hillary Clinton, a Chicago native and a Cub fan. An immigrant from the Dominican Republic, Sosa also became an instant hero in his homeland and in portions of New York City and other urban centers with large Dominican populations. McGuire finished the season with 70 home runs, to lead the major leagues. The New York Yankees, who won 114 regular-season games, a record in the American League, swept the San Diego Padres in four games to win their 24th major league championship. Sosa won the National League's MVP award; Juan Gonzalez of the Texas Rangers won in the American League. Atlanta's Tom Glavine and Toronto's Roger Clemens won the Cy Young Award for pitching; it was a record-setting fifth award for Clemens.

The Denver Broncos repeated as Super Bowl champions when they defeated the Atlanta Falcons, who were playing in their first Super Bowl. Denver's running back Terrell Davis was named the league's MVP, and the Miami Dolphins quarterback, Dan Marino, became the first player to throw more than 400 touchdowns. The undefeated University of Tennessee defeated Florida State University to win the college national championship—its first since 1951—and running back Ricky Williams of the University of Texas won the Heisman Trophy.

Led once again by Michael Jordan, who repeated as MVP of the playoffs for the third straight year, the Chicago Bulls won their third consecutive NBA championship in 1997–98. Jordan was also named MVP for the regular season. The University of Kentucky won the men's college basketball title by defeating the University of Utah, and Antawn Jamison of the University of North Carolina was selected player of the year. Labor disputes led the NBA owners to declare a lockout at the beginning of the 1998–99 season; however, play resumed in 1999.

The Detroit Red Wings won hockey's Stanley Cup. Pete Sampras's victory at Wimbledon made him only the second man to win five championships at the prestigious tennis tournament. But Australian Patrick Rafter won the U.S. Tennis Open, and Lindsay Davenport prevailed in the women's single's competition. Golfer Lee Janzen won the USGA open. Real Quiet, ridden by Kent Desormeaux, ran first in the Kentucky Derby.

Fifteen-year-old ice skater Tara Lipinski became the youngest person to win a gold medal in the history of the Winter Olympics. Other winners included skiers Jonny Moseley and Picabo Street and the U.S. women's hockey team. Charismatic runner Florence Griffith-Joyner died of a sudden epileptic episode; known affectionately as Flo-Jo, she had won three gold medals in the 1988 Summer Olympics.

CHRONICLE OF EVENTS

January 5–9: An ice storm causes severe damage in Canada along a corridor stretching from Ottawa to Montreal. Some 3 million people in Quebec are left without electricity, heat, and water for up to a month. Portions of New York, Maine, New Hampshire, and Vermont are also rendered disaster areas by freezing rain from the same system.

January 5: Republican congressman Sonny Bono, the former husband, musical partner, and 1960s television cohost of singer Cher, dies in a skiing accident at age 62.

January 6: Vandals sever the head of the bronze statue of the Little Mermaid, which overlooks the harbor in Copenhagen, Denmark. The statue depicts a popular character in one of the beloved fairy tales of Hans Christian Andersen.

January 7: Monica Lewinsky signs an affidavit in the Paula Jones lawsuit denying that she had a sexual relationship with Clinton.

January 7: The government of Canada makes an unprecedented apology for acts of racism committed in the past against its Native American population.

January 8: The United Nations initiates a campaign to raise funds for aid to the starving population of North Korea.

January 11: The British foreign secretary Robin Cook announces that he is having an affair with his former secretary, whom he intends to marry after divorcing his wife.

January 12: Japan apologizes to Britain for atrocities committed against British citizens in Japanese-occupied territories during World War II.

January 12: Linda Tripp contacts independent counsel Kenneth Starr and gives him more than 20 hours of recorded telephone conversations of President Clinton and Monica Lewinsky.

January 13: Tripp, wearing a hidden recording device, meets Lewinsky in Arlington, Virginia. Starr's investigators tape the conversation about Lewinsky's relationship with Clinton.

January 15: The International Monetary Fund (IMF) agrees to bail out Indonesia with a $43 billion loan.

January 16: A panel of federal judges approves Starr's request to expand his investigation to include Clinton's alleged obstruction of justice in the Paula Jones case.

January 16: When Lewinsky appears for another meeting with Tripp, Starr's investigators confront her and take her to a room for prolonged questioning.

January 17: Clinton denies having a sexual relationship with Lewinsky in a sealed deposition given for the Jones case.

January 21: Clinton's relationship with Lewinsky is reported in the press. Clinton, appearing on PBS's *Newshour with Jim Lehrer,* denies that he had an improper sexual relationship or any other kind of improper relationship with Lewinsky.

January 22: Theodore Kaczynski, the so-called Unabomber, pleads guilty to a series of bombings that occurred over almost 20 years, killing three and injuring more than 20.

January 22: Pope John Paul II begins a five-day tour of Cuba, during which he meets with Fidel Castro, whose suppression of personal and political freedoms the pope condemns. The pope also calls for the release of Cuba's political prisoners and the end of the U.S. economic embargo.

January 26: In a press conference Clinton asserts, "I did not have sexual relations with that woman." He also denies encouraging Lewinsky to lie about their relationship.

January 27: Clinton urges shoring up the Social Security system, expresses support for the global economy, and introduces a 10-point plan for improving education in his State of the Union address.

February 2: Clinton proposes the first balanced budget in 30 years.

February 2: The Centers for Disease Control and Prevention (CDC) announces that U.S. deaths from AIDS decreased in the first half of 1997 by 44 percent compared to the number of deaths in the first half of 1996.

February 3: Texas executes the first woman prisoner in 135 years. She has been convicted of murder.

February 3: A low-flying U.S. jet on a training mission in the Italian Alps kills 20 skiers when it severs the wires supporting a gondola ski lift. Marine captain Richard Ashby, the pilot, and Marine captain Joseph Schweitzer, the navigator, are subsequently charged with involuntary manslaughter. The incident outrages many Italians and provokes demands for banning of U.S. military flights in the region.

February 4: An earthquake in Afghanistan kills some 5,000 and leaves 30,000 homeless.

February 5: The House Judiciary Committee releases internal corporate documents describing tobacco industry marketing strategies directed at teenagers and members of minority groups.

February 7–20: The Winter Olympics are played in Nagano, Japan.

February 10: Voters in Maine repeal a 1997 gay rights law, making Maine the first state to repudiate such a statute.

February 12: A federal judge declares that the presidential authority to exercise a line-item veto, approved by Congress in 1996 and exercised for the first time in 1997, is unconstitutional. The decision sets the stage for a future definitive Supreme Court ruling.

February 17: In a television address to the nation, Clinton warns that he is prepared to launch a campaign of air strikes against Iraq if it does not "seriously diminish" its capacity to produce forbidden weapons.

February 19: NATO announces that it will send a new, smaller peacekeeping force to Bosnia.

February 20: In the aftermath of two recent bombings, Sinn Féin, the political arm of the IRA, is expelled from ongoing peace talks between the governments of Britain and Ireland. If no further bombing ensues, however, Sinn Féin can rejoin the negotiations.

February 22: Tensions in the Middle East subside when Iraq and the United Nations sign an agreement brokered by UN secretary-general Kofi Annan in which Iraq agrees to immediate and unconditional access to suspected Iraqi weapons sites.

February 28: Serbian police kill at least 24 ethnic Albanian civilians in retaliation for an attack by the KLA.

March 1: The Milton S. Eisenhower Foundation reports that a prediction in 1968 by the National Advisory Commission on Civil Disorders, known as the Kerner Commission, that the United States was "moving toward two societies, one black, one white—separate and unequal," has largely come true.

March 5: The *Washington Post* reports that Clinton admitted in a deposition in the Jones lawsuit that he had given gifts to Lewinsky.

March 6: The U.S. Army honors three Vietnam veterans who risked their life to halt the 1968 massacre of hundreds of unarmed Vietnamese civilians by U.S. soldiers.

March 8: James McDougal, Clinton's former business partner, who was convicted and jailed in 1996 for his role in the Whitewater affair, dies in prison of a sudden heart attack.

March 10: Indonesia's president Suharto is reelected for a seventh term despite his country's ongoing economic crisis and reports of rampant corruption.

March 16: Pope John Paul II apologizes to Jews for the failure of the Roman Catholic Church to take stronger action to oppose the Nazi genocide.

March 17: Zhu Rongji becomes China's prime minister.

March 22: Sinn Féin rejoins talks over the fate of Northern Ireland.

March 23: Clinton begins a tour of Africa to encourage formation of businesses between the United States and the nations of that continent.

March 23: Yeltsin fires Russia's prime minister and its entire cabinet.

March 24: Two boys, ages 11 and 13, kill four schoolgirls and their teacher and injure 12 more when they open fire on their classmates at Westside Middle School in Jonesboro, Arkansas.

March 25: The EU announces that 11 countries will adopt the euro as their common currency in 1999.

March 25: A UN panel approves an arms embargo against the Federal Republic of Yugoslavia in response to government atrocities against ethnic Albanians in Kosovo.

April 1: A federal judge in Little Rock, Arkansas, dismisses the sexual harassment civil suit filed by Paula Jones against Clinton.

April 10: On Good Friday, parties in the peace talks chaired by the former senator George Mitchell sign a peace agreement for Northern Ireland.

April 13: Dolly the sheep, the world's first cloned mammal, who was born in 1996, gives birth to a female lamb named Bonnie.

April 14: As part of his yearlong dialogue on race, Clinton holds a televised town-hall-style meeting on the role of race in American sports.

April 16: Jones says she will appeal the dismissal of her sexual harassment lawsuit against Clinton.

April 20: Linda McCartney, wife of the British musician Paul McCartney, dies of breast cancer at age 56.

April 24: A 14-year-old middle-school student opens fire at a school dance near Edinboro, Pennsylvania, killing one teacher and wounding another teacher and two students.

April 30: The State Department announces a general decline in terrorism throughout the world.

May 1: Eldridge Cleaver, spokesman for the 1960s militant Black Panther organization, dies at age 63.

May 4: Kaczynski, the so-called Unabomber, is sentenced to four life sentences with no possibility of parole.

May 4: A federal judge rules that Clinton cannot invoke executive privilege or attorney-client privilege to prevent his aides from testifying in Starr's investigation of obstruction of justice.

May 6: Astronomers throughout the world announce they recently witnessed an enormous explosion from a far edge of the universe that occurred some 12 billion years ago and that probably outshone the rest of the universe for a matter of seconds. They publish the discovery in *Nature* on May 7.

May 7: The grand jury investigating the Whitewater affair expires without issuing charges against President Clinton or Hillary Rodham Clinton.

May 10: Sinn Féin, the political wing of the Irish Republican Army, endorses the Northern Ireland peace accord.

May 11: India provokes international protest when it conducts its first nuclear tests in 24 years.

May 13: India conducts a second nuclear test.

May 14: The popular entertainer Frank Sinatra dies at age 82.

May 14: Millions tune in to the final episode of *Seinfeld,* in which the self-absorbed main characters are tried and convicted for their egregious failure to obey a good samaritan law.

May 15: The *New York Times* reports that Johnny Chung, a former fund-raiser for the Democratic Party, channeled money from the Chinese government to the party during the 1996 election campaigns. Within days, the House and Senate initiate investigations.

May 18: The Justice Department and attorneys general of 20 states file two separate antitrust suits against the Microsoft Corporation.

May 21: Suharto resigns amid rioting in Jakarta that has left thousands dead.

May 21: A 15-year-old boy kills his parents and then goes on a shooting spree at his high school in Springfield, Oregon, killing two students and wounding 22.

May 23: Voters in Northern Ireland overwhelmingly approve the Good Friday peace agreement.

May 28: Pakistan explodes its first nuclear device.

May 29: Barry Goldwater, a former U.S. senator and the unsuccessful Republican presidential candidate in 1964, dies at age 89.

June 4: Terry Nichols is sentenced to life in prison for his role in the 1995 Oklahoma City bombing, which killed 169.

June 4: The House votes 224-203 in favor of a constitutional amendment to allow prayer in schools and religious symbols in federal buildings—61 votes short of the two-thirds majority requisite for a constitutional amendment.

June 5: War between Ethiopia and Eritrea begins.

June 6: Sex and the City, starring Sarah Jessica Parker, Kim Cattrall, Cynthia Nixon, and Kristin Davis, debuts on HBO.

June 7: In Jasper, Texas, three men associated with the Ku Klux Klan beat a disabled black man, then drag him behind a pickup truck until he dies.

June 8: The National Rifle Association elects the actor Charlton Heston president.

Sex and the City pioneered new territory on American television by openly centering on women's sex lives. *(Photofest)*

June 10: A jury in Jacksonville, Florida, awards the first punitive damages ever awarded in a tobacco-related lawsuit when it holds the Brown & Williamson Tobacco Corporation liable for the lung cancer death of a smoker. The award totals $500,000 in compensatory damages and $450,000 in punitive damages.

June 12: In Belleville, Illinois, three white youths drag a 17-year-old black youth alongside their sport utility vehicle, causing major injuries.

June 12: Japan sends shock waves throughout the world economy when it announces that it is officially in a recession.

June 14: The Chicago Bulls win the NBA championship for the third consecutive year when they defeat the Utah Jazz in six games.

June 16: The Detroit Red Wings defeat the Washington Capitals to win hockey's Stanley Cup.

June 18: The *Boston Globe* fires the columnist Patricia Smith, a Pulitzer Prize finalist, after she admits fabricating sources and quotations to "slam home a salient point."

June 25: Clinton arrives for a nine-day official visit to China.

June 25: Pakistan's former prime minister Benazir Bhutto and her husband are indicted for allegedly laundering money, which is held in their Swiss bank accounts.

June 28: Clinton astounds Chinese viewers when he appears on Chinese television and criticizes actions and policies of the Chinese government.

June 29: Clinton tells students at Beijing University that no country can achieve political stability or economic prosperity without embracing human rights and promoting individual freedoms.

June 30: Linda Tripp, confidant of Monica Lewinsky, testifies before the Washington, D.C., grand jury investigating Clinton.

July 1: The Protestant leader David Trimble is elected the first minister of Northern Ireland's new assembly.

July 2: Jiang opens the world's largest airport in an expansive ceremony in Hong Kong. Designed by the British architect Sir Norman Foster, the facility cost $20 billion to build and can handle up to 87 million passengers yearly.

July 6: The actor/singer Roy Rogers, the "King of the Cowboys," dies at age 86.

July 7: The media mogul and former prime minister of Italy, Silvio Berlusconi, is sentenced to two years and nine months in prison for bribing tax executives.

July 13: In response to Japan's failing economy, Hashimoto resigns as prime minister. He is succeeded on July 30 by Obuchi Keizo.

July 17: Clinton is served with a grand jury subpoena, which is later withdrawn in return for his agreement to testify.

July 22: Alan Shepard, the first American to enter outer space, dies at age 74.

July 24: The 41-year-old Russell E. Weston, Jr., kills two police officers at the U.S. Capitol in the deadliest attack at the building since Congress first met there in 1800 and the first shooting there since 1954, when Puerto Rican nationalists opened fire on House members, wounding five.

July 29: Jerome Robbins, who choreographed such Broadway hits as *West Side Story* (1957) and *Fiddler on the Roof* (1964), dies at age 79.

August 5: Iraq suspends its cooperation with UN weapons inspectors.

August 6: Lewinsky testifies before a grand jury about her relationship with Clinton.

August 7: Coordinated car bomb attacks outside U.S. embassies in Nairobi, Kenya, and Dar es Salaam, Tanzania, kill more than 250 people, including 12 Americans.

August 10: Salvagers working in the North Atlantic recover a section of the *Titanic's* hull, a year after the success of James Cameron's movie about the sinking of the supposedly unsinkable ship on its maiden voyage, on April 14, 1912.

August 15: A bomb planted by an IRA splinter group known as the Real IRA kills 29 Catholics and Protestants in Omagh, Northern Ireland.

August 17: Testifying before a grant jury via video link, Clinton admits that he had a sexual relationship with Lewinsky. On a television interview afterward, he admits that he misled the public about the affair but denies that he lied under oath or persuaded Lewinsky to lie.

August 17: Russia devalues the ruble in response to its economic crisis.

August 19: The Real IRA, a splinter group that had renounced the Good Friday Accord, announces a suspension of violence.

August 21: In response to the embassy bombings in Kenya and Tanzania, Clinton orders air strikes against the headquarters of the Saudi-born terrorist leader Osama bin Laden, whose al-Qaeda organization is believed to be responsible.

August 21: A Mississippi jury convicts the former Ku Klux Klan leader Samuel Bowers of murder for ordering and planning the 1966 killing of the civil rights activist Vernon Dahmer, Sr., whose business had been used as a voter-registration venue for blacks.

August 25: A bombing of the Planet Hollywood restaurant in Cape Town, South Africa, is believed to be retaliation for the missile attacks against bin Laden's headquarters in Afghanistan.

August 31: Relations between Japan and North Korea deteriorate after North Korea tests a medium-range ballistic missile over the Sea of Japan.

September 1: Clinton visits Russia to offer a show of support for Yeltsin during a time of economic crisis.

September 3: All 229 people aboard a Swissair flight from New York to Geneva die when their jet crashes into Saint Margaret's Bay near Nova Scotia, Canada.

September 3: Senator Joseph Lieberman of Connecticut, a political ally of the president's, calls Clinton's conduct in the Lewinsky affair "disgraceful" and "immoral."

September 4–5: Clinton visits the Irish Republic and Northern Ireland in support of the peace process.

September 8: Mark McGuire hits his 62nd home run, breaking Roger Maris's single-season home-run record.

September 9: Kenneth Starr presents the final report on his investigations of Clinton to the House of Representatives.

September 11: The House releases the 445-page Starr report to the public. The report, which contains graphic accounts of Clinton and Lewinsky's sexual conduct, becomes a best seller.

The chairman of the House Judiciary Committee, Henry Hyde, was one among several critics of President Bill Clinton who admitted that they had extramarital affairs. *(AP/Wide World Photos)*

September 11: Speaking before an assembly of religious leaders, Clinton admits that he "sinned" in his conduct with Lewinsky.

September 16: Salon, an online magazine, publishes an article documenting an adulterous love affair Congressman Henry Hyde, chairman of the House Judiciary Committee, had had while he was in his mid-40s.

September 21: The House releases the videotape of Clinton's August 17th grand jury testimony. Televison networks then broadcast the video.

September 21: The sprinter Florence Griffith-Joyner dies of a sudden epileptic episode.

September 27: Germany ends 16 years of rule by the conservative Christian Democrat Party when the left-wing Social Democrats prevail in elections.

October 1: The UN Security Council condemns Serb massacres of ethnic Albanians, and NATO announces it is preparing air strikes against the Serbian forces.

October 2: Gene Autry, the "Singing Cowboy" and owner of the California Angels baseball team, dies at age 91. He had appeared in almost 100 movies in the 1930s, 1940s, and 1950s; starred in a weekly television show during the 1950s; and recorded nearly 600 songs, including "Back in the Saddle Again."

October 7: Congress approves legislation extending existing copyright laws for 20 years.

October 8: Talks between the IMF and World Bank concerning ways to deal with the economic crisis in Asia conclude. Clinton warns that measures must be taken to restore these economies, which are crucial to the global economy.

October 8: The House votes 258-176 to investigate whether it has sufficient grounds for impeaching Clinton.

October 9: The Pakistani national assembly votes to establish Islamic law.

October 9: The government of Italy collapses when Premier Romano Prodi loses a vote of confidence.

October 12: NATO authorizes air strikes against Serbia if it does not end its actions against ethnic Albanians in Kosovo.

October 13: Milošević agrees to withdraw Serbian forces from Kosovo.

October 14: The fugitive Eric Rudolph is charged with the bombing at the 1996 Olympic Games in Atlanta.

October 17: When General Augusto Pinochet visits London, British authorities arrest him for crimes against humanity dating back to the period when he was dictator in Chile.

October 21: The New York Yankees clinch their 24th World Series championship when they defeat the San Diego Padres.

October 21: Despite the Lewinsky scandal, Clinton gains a political victory when he signs an omnibus spending bill that includes funding for several of his education initiatives and the IMF.

October 23: Israel and the Palestinian Authority sign the Wye Agreement.

October 26–27: Most Serbian troops withdraw from Kosovo.

October 26–31: Hurricane Mitch, a category 5 on a five-point scale, kills more than 9,000 people in Central America.

October 27: Finding Serbia in "substantial compliance," NATO lifts its threat of immediate air strikes.

October 28: Clinton announces that the federal government has had a budget surplus of $70 billion for fiscal 1998.

October 29: U.S. senator John Glenn returns to outer space for the first time since 1962.

November 2: Delegates of more than 160 nations begin a two-week-long meeting to work out plans for implementing the 1997 Kyoto Protocol to curb global warming.

November 3: In the midterm elections, Democrats gain 12 seats in the House and the governorship of California, but Republicans retain control of both chambers of Congress. Voters in Oregon, Washington, Nevada, Arizona, and Alaska support initiatives to legalize marijuana use for medicinal purposes.

November 4: A federal grand jury in New York City indicts the fugitive Saudi millionaire Osama bin Laden for ordering the bombings of U.S. embassies in Kenya and Tanzania. Five members of bin Laden's al-Qaeda terrorist group are also charged.

November 6: After Republican failures in the midterm elections, Gingrich shocks his colleagues when he resigns as Speaker of the House and indicates that he will probably vacate his seat in Congress in January.

November 11: Clinton warns that the United States will attack Iraq without further notice unless it permits immediate and unconditional resumption of UN weapons inspections.

November 13: Although the case was dismissed in April, Clinton avoids an appeal by settling the Paula Jones lawsuit, agreeing to pay her $850,000.

November 13: The IMF agrees to loan Brazil $41.5 billion over three years to help it through its financial crisis. In return, Brazil agrees to institute major economic reforms.

November 14: Delegates of 170 nations at a UN conference on climate change vote to adopt a compliance system to ensure that greenhouse gas emissions are reduced by 2000.

November 15: Iraq averts air strikes by the United States and Britain when it agrees to cooperate with UN weapons inspections.

November 17: Linda Tripp's secret recordings of her conversations with Lewinsky are released by the House Judiciary Committee, which had released transcripts in October.

November 18: The House elects Bob Livingston of Louisiana as Speaker to succeed Gingrich in January 1999.

November 20: The tobacco industry agrees to pay $206 billion to 46 states in settlement of a lawsuit seeking compensation for money spent by the states for treating patients for smoking-related diseases. (Florida, Minnesota, Mississippi, and Texas had previously concluded separate settlements with tobacco manufacturers.) Part of the settlement calls for creation of a $250 million campaign to reduce smoking by minors and a $1.45 million national antismoking campaign.

November 23: The Georgia Supreme Court strikes down an 1833 antisodomy law forbidding oral and anal sex between either heterosexuals or homosexuals.

November 24: The Palestinian National Authority opens its first international airport in the Gaza Strip.

November 25: The government of Turkey collapses after a vote of no confidence.

December 1: Exxon announces plans to purchase Mobil for $75.3 billion.

December 2: A federal jury acquits the former agriculture secretary Mike Espy on 30 charges of corruption.

December 8: A 27-year-old Texas woman who had had fertility treatments gives birth to the first of eight babies. The other seven are delivered on December 20.

December 11–12: The House Judiciary Committee approves four articles of impeachment.

December 13: Citizens of Puerto Rico vote to retain the status quo, rejecting proposals either to become the 51st U.S. state or to seek independence.

December 14: Clinton meets an enthusiastic welcome when he visits the Gaza Strip.

December 16: Clinton authorizes massive U.S. and British air strikes against Iraq in response to its failure to cooperate with UN weapons inspections.

December 17: Congressman Bob Livingston acknowledges he has had several adulterous affairs.

December 19: Livingston resigns as House Speaker before ever assuming the post. He promises to resign from Congress in six months and urges Clinton to follow his example.

December 19: The House of Representatives votes to impeach Clinton on two counts of perjury, one count of obstruction of justice, and one count of abuse of power.

December 19: Clinton and Britain's prime minister Tony Blair conclude the bombing campaign against Iraq, which they declare has been successful.

December 21: The Israeli parliament votes overwhelmingly to hold early elections after Netanyahu fails to gain support for his peace policies.

EYEWITNESS TESTIMONY

African Americans continue to suffer disproportionately from chronic and preventable disease compared with white Americans. Of the three leading causes of death in African Americans—heart disease, cancer, and stroke—smoking and other tobacco use are major contributors. . . .

Approximately 2 million American Indians and Alaska Natives live in the United States. Although many tribes consider tobacco a sacred gift and use it during religious ceremonies and as traditional medicine, the tobacco-related health problems they suffer are caused by chronic cigarette smoking and spit tobacco use. . . . Nationally, lung cancer is the leading cause of cancer death among American Indians and Alaska Natives. . . .

Smoking is responsible for 87% of the lung cancer deaths in the United States. In 1993, lung cancer was the leading cause of cancer death (22.3%) among Asian Americans and Pacific Islanders. . . . Asian Americans and Pacific Islanders had the lowest rates of death from coronary heart disease among the primary racial/ethnic groups in the United States. . . .

Overall, lung cancer is the leading cause of cancer deaths among Hispanics. Lung cancer deaths are about three times higher for Hispanic men (23.1 per 100,000) than for Hispanic women (7.7 per 100,000). The rates of lung cancer deaths per 100,000 were higher among Cuban American men (33.7) than among Puerto Rican (28.3) and Mexican American (21.9) men. Coronary heart disease is the leading cause of death for Hispanics living in the United States.

From David Satcher, "Tobacco Use among U.S. Racial/Ethnic Minority Groups: A Report of the Surgeon General," 1998. Available online. URL: http://www.cdc.gov/tobacco/research_data/ international/wntd598.htm.

I still have nightmares about it . . . the sense of being trapped and drowning.

Monica Lewinsky describing her experience being interrogated on January 16, 1998, by FBI agents working with the independent counsel Kenneth Starr, in Andrew Morton, Monica's Story *(1999), p. 180.*

The crisis in Asia has occurred after several decades of outstanding economic performance. Annual GDP growth in the ASEAN-5 (Indonesia, Malaysia, the

President Bill Clinton's failure to admit that he had had an affair with Monica Lewinsky led to his impeachment. *(Photofest)*

Philippines, Singapore, and Thailand) averaged close to 8 percent over the last decade. Indeed, during the 30 years preceding the crisis per capita income levels had increased tenfold in Korea, fivefold in Thailand, and fourfold in Malaysia. . . .

So what went wrong? Let me start with the common underlying factors. The key domestic factors that led to the present difficulties appear to have been: first, the failure to dampen overheating pressures that had become increasingly evident in Thailand and many other countries in the region and were manifested in large external deficits and property and stock market bubbles; second, the maintenance of pegged exchange rate regimes for too long, which encouraged external borrowing and led to excessive exposure to foreign exchange risk in both the financial and corporate sectors; and third, lax prudential rules and financial oversight, which led to a sharp deterioration in the quality of banks' loan portfolios. . . . Reluctance to tighten monetary conditions and to close insolvent financial institutions has clearly added to the turbulence in financial markets.

Although the problems in these countries were mostly homegrown, developments in the advanced economies and global financial markets contributed significantly to the buildup of the imbalances that eventually led to the crises. Specifically, with Japan and Europe experiencing weak growth since the beginning of the 1990s, attractive domestic investment opportunities have fallen short of available saving; meanwhile, monetary policy has remained appropriately accommodative, and interest rates have been low. Large private capital flows to emerging markets, including the so-called "carry trade," were driven, to an important degree, by these phenomena and by an imprudent search for high yields by international investors without due regard to potential risks. Also contributing to the buildup to the crisis were the wide swings of the yen/dollar exchange rate over the past three years.

The crisis erupted in Thailand in the summer.

Stanley Fischer, first deputy managing director of the International Monetary Fund, discussing the Asian economic crisis at the Midwinter Conference of the Bankers' Association for Foreign Trade, Washington, D.C., on January 22, 1998, in Fischer, "The Asian Crisis: A View from the IMF." Available online. URL: http://www.imf.org/external/np/speeches/1998/012298.htm.

During late January, 1998, Americans were riveted to their TV sets. The days surrounding Sunday, January 25, presented the strange, exciting confluence of three radically disparate events—all brought home into the living room with live footage and endless commentary.

For the media frenzy surrounding two of the occasions we were duly prepared: Super Bowl XXXII, one of the world's most-watched television programs, and the historic visit of His Holiness Pope John Paul II to communist Cuba. The latter represented the first time a pope had ever set foot on the island nation and, for citizens, a rare opportunity for sanctioned religious expression under the dictator Fidel Castro.

A Midwest-raised Catholic living in Miami, I had months before considered joining the local diocese-sponsored group headed to see the pontiff. Truth be told, I was less interested in catching a glimpse of John Paul II than in earning the right to brag to my northern family and friends that I had spent a long weekend in that forbidden, beautifully ramshackle country. It was an opportunity to travel to Havana legally under cover of religiosity. Meanwhile, Cuban Miami, which is to say most of Miami, was in an uproar; many of the exiled faithful were predicting the beginning of a new era, even another revolution, in their homeland.

All thoughts of my making the trip to Cuba ended on Christmas when my father presented me with a ticket to the Super Bowl as a gift. Several weeks later, I flew to San Diego to attend my first professional football game, a meeting between the Denver Broncos and the Green Bay Packers. My husband, not invited, ate his heart out.

For the next few days, I periodically tuned in to CNN in my motel room, wanting and expecting to see news of the pope in Cuba. Instead, all the networks were running, continuously it seemed, previously recorded video of a female White House intern and President Bill Clinton exuberantly embracing at some crowded street gathering. News had just broken that Clinton was being investigated for reportedly encouraging the young woman, with whom it was rumored he had had an affair, to lie to lawyers in an unrelated sexual harassment suit against him. As lurid details about their alleged Oval Office dalliance came to light, calls for Clinton's impeachment grew louder. I remember thinking the scandal was probably some politically motivated doing of a few Clinton foes.

On Sunday, January 25, with 90 million television viewers watching, Denver beat defending champion Green Bay, 31-24, in a rare Super Bowl that thrilled to the very last moment. Earlier that day, as many as 1 million Cubanos turned out in Havana's Revolution Square to see a frail, inspiring spiritual leader extol the importance of religious freedom, while the powerful image traveled around the world. The next day the President of the United States sternly proclaimed before rolling cameras, his index finger pointing in emphasis, "I did not have sexual relations with that woman"—a statement he would publicly recant seven months later.

University administrator Alexandra Pecharich describing the confluence on January 25, 1998, of Super Bowl XXXII, Pope John Paul II's historic visit to Cuba, and the breaking news about President Clinton's sexual liaison with Monica Lewinsky, in private correspondence with the author on June 7, 2004.

I do believe that this is a battle. I mean, look at the very people who are involved in this, they have popped up in other settings. This is the great story here, for anybody who is willing to find it and write about it and explain it, this vast right-wing conspiracy that has been conspiring against my husband since the day he announced for president. A few journalists have kind of caught on to it and explained it, but it has not yet been fully revealed to the American public. And, actually, you know, in a bizarre sort of way, this [the Monica Lewinsky scandal] may do it.

First Lady Hillary Rodham Clinton declaring on
NBC's Today Show *on January 27, 1998, that a*
conspiracy of right-wing antagonists is trying to
undermine her husband, in Sidney Blumenthal,
The Clinton Wars *(2003), p . 374.*

For 209 years, it has been the President's duty to report to you on the state of the union. Because of the hard work and high purpose of the American people, these are good times for America. We have had more than 14 million new jobs, the lowest unemployment in twenty-four years, the lowest core inflation in thirty years, incomes are rising, and we have the highest home ownership in history. Crime has dropped for a record five years in a row, and welfare rolls are at their lowest levels in twenty-seven years. Our leadership in the world is unrivaled. Ladies and gentlemen, the state of our union is strong. . . .

We have moved past the sterile debate between those who say government is the enemy and those who say government is the answer. My fellow Americans, we have found a third way. We have the smallest government in thirty-five years, but a more progressive one. We have a smaller government but a stronger nation. . . .

For three decades, six presidents have come before you to warn of the damage deficits pose to our nation. Tonight, I come before you to announce that the federal deficit, once so incomprehensibly large that it had eleven zeros, will be simply zero.

Now, if we balance the budget for next year, it is projected that we'll then have a sizable surplus in the years that immediately follow. What should we do with this projected surplus? I have a simple four-word answer: Save Social Security first.

From President Bill Clinton's State of the Union speech
on January 27, 1998, in Sidney Blumenthal,
The Clinton Wars *(2003), pp. 376–377.*

We looked at what has happened in the 30 years since the original Kerner Commission report came out, and what we found is there's been good progress in many areas, for example, the African-American middle class has increased, and high school graduation rates for African-Americans have

improved. We also found at the same time, though, that there have been a lot of negatives. For example, employment in inner cities is at Depression levels at the same time that we celebrate a supposedly robust economy. The rich have been getting richer at the same time the poor have been getting poorer. The working class has been getting poor. The middle class has also lost ground to the rich. You mentioned the increase in child poverty.

Today, our child poverty rate is four times higher than in western Europe and today, for example, the rate of incarceration of African-American men is four times higher than in pre-Mandela apartheid South Africa. And so when you look at income, when you look at wealth, when you look at wages, when you look at employment, when you look at education, when you look at the bias of the criminal justice system, you see a growing breach, and that's why we have said, on balance, things are getting worse.

Lynn Curtis of the Milton S. Eisenhower Foundation
describing findings of the foundation's update of the so-
called Kerner Report that, in 1968, warned that the
United States was becoming "two societies, one black, one
white, separate and unequal," in "A Nation Divided,"
The Newshour with Jim Lehrer, *March 2, 1998.*
Available online. URL: http://www.pbs.org/
newshour/bb/race_relations/jan-june98/
commission_3-2.html.

Well, I think it's *deja vu* all over again that the Kerner Commission report, itself, was a quite unbalanced and simplistic analysis of the social trends of the 50's and 60's, quite mistaken in many ways. But it, unfortunately, created a tradition of doom and gloom and simplistic analysis which, after the fifth anniversary, the tenth anniversary, the twentieth anniversary all provoked much comment unfailingly to stress that nothing has gotten better. Indeed, things have gotten worse.

Now, the Eisenhower Commission report isn't quite as simplistic as that, but it does seem to me rather lurid and misleading in fundamental ways. For example, it stresses wealth disparities with some figures I find impossible to verify. It claims one percent hold 90 percent of the wealth. The latest Census Bureau study of this shows that the top 20 percent own only 43 percent.

More important, in terms of the stress on continued black child poverty, that is, indeed, true and very alarming. The question is: What is causing it? We know, in fact, that it is very closely linked to the fact that 70 percent of all black children today are born out of wedlock. And there is an enormously close correlation between being born out of wedlock, growing up without a father in the household, and being poor. Indeed, 85 percent of all poor black children today are living with their mother and no father. And this is a problem—I would strongly stress—that obviously would not be ameliorated one wit if every white racist dropped dead tomorrow.

Professor Stephan Thernstrom of Harvard University disagreeing with the findings of the updated Kerner Report in "A Nation Divided," The Newshour with Jim Lehrer, March 2, 1998. Available online. URL: http://www.pbs.org/newshour/bb/race_relations/ jan-june98/commission_3-2.html.

Sometime in April [of 1999] me and V [Vodka—nickname of Dylan Klebold] will get revenge and will kick natural selection up a few notches. Armed with the following; a terroist bag full of noisey crickets, noisey crickets strapped to WD40 cans, pipe bombs with a shit load of shrapnel, fire bombs, chlorine gas bombs, and smoke bombs [spellings are Harris's].

From the April 26, 1998, diary entry of the future Columbine High School killer Eric Harris, in "Columbine Killer Envisioned Crashing Plane in NYC," December 6, 2001. Available online. URL: http://www.cnn.com/2001/US/12/05/ columbine.diary.

Mr. Clinton seems exhilarated—and horrified—by the visual evidence of China's transformation: the cybercafés packed with espresso-drinking, Internet-addicted students, just yards away from one-room huts with open fires, all bathed in air so polluted that the other side of the street is hazy.

Journalist Bronwen Maddox describing Clinton's response to his nine-day visit to China, which began on June 25, 1998, in Martin Gilbert, A History of the Twentieth Century, vol. 3 (2000), p. 861.

Bill woke me up just as he had done months earlier. This time he didn't sit by the bed, but paced back and forth. He told me for the first time that the situation [with Monica Lewinsky] was much more serious than he had previously acknowledged. He now realized he would have to testify that there had been an inappro-

priate intimacy. He told me what happened between them had been brief and sporadic. He couldn't tell me seven months ago, he said, because he was too ashamed to admit it and he knew how angry and hurt I would be.

I could hardly breathe. Gulping for air, I started crying and yelling at him. "What do you mean? What are you saying? Why did you lie to me?"

I was furious and getting more so by the second. He just stood there saying over and over again, "I'm sorry. I'm so sorry. I was trying to protect you and Chelsea." . . . Up until now I only thought that he'd been foolish for paying attention to the young woman and was convinced that he was being railroaded. I couldn't believe he would do anything to endanger our marriage and our family. I was dumbfounded, heartbroken and outraged that I'd believed him at all.

Former first lady Hillary Rodham Clinton describing her reaction when her husband, President Bill Clinton, revealed on August 15, 1998, that he had, in fact, been intimate with Monica Lewinsky, in Hillary Rodham Clinton, Living History (2004), pp. 465–466.

The missiles missed him [Osama bin Laden], apparently just by a matter of hours. In the annals of damned-if-you-do-or-damned-if-you-don't situations, this was a classic. In spite of clear evidence that bin Laden was responsible for the embassy bombings [in Kenya and Tanzania], Bill was criticized for ordering the attack . . . to divert attention from his own troubles and the growing talk of impeachment by both Republicans and commentators, who still didn't understand the dangers presented by terrorism in general and bin Laden and al Qaeda in particular.

Former first lady Hillary Rodham Clinton describing President Bill Clinton's decision to order air strikes on August 21, 1998, against al-Qaeda training camps in Afghanistan, four days after publicly acknowledging he had had intimate relations with Monica Lewinsky, in Hillary Rodham Clinton, Living History (2004), p. 469.

The bombings in East Africa are yet another reminder that, even in the modern world, there is still such a thing as radical evil. There are certain people who kill Americans just because they believe it is the right thing to do—indeed, a blessed thing to do. . . .

The president and his foreign policy advisers often speak as if they appreciate the meaning of what national security advisor Sandy Berger last week duly labeled "unadulterated evil," but their policies and actions are not truly commensurate with their words. The threat of indictment does not strike fear in the hearts of those who plan attacks like those in East Africa—much less does it deter them. The only language international terrorists, and the nations that sponsor them, understand is the language of effective and appropriate force; yet force is precisely the instrument of national power with which the Clintonites are most uncomfortable. Meanwhile, out there, in the shadows, the plausible conviction spreads that you can attack American embassies with murderous results and pay no serious price.

Excerpt from "Blasted," an August 31, 1998, editorial in New Republic *magazine criticizing Clinton's failure to use appropriate force against terrorists, written in the aftermath of the embassy bombings in Nairobi, Kenya, and Dar es Salaam, Tanzania, on August 7, 1998, in James Haley, ed.,* Post–Cold War America: 1992–Present *(2003), p. 131.*

Though there was little fighting, the zone nevertheless presented a glimpse of the apocalypse. Dense smoke poured into the sky, minarets emerging like rare blooms. Columns of tanks, armored personnel carriers and vehicle-mounted anti-aircraft guns swept out of the shattered ruins eastward.

Behind them, scarcely a single Albanian remained. Dead dogs and livestock littered the fields; smashed cars and tractors lay overturned on the verges of empty roads; bandanna-clad police looted and burnt whatever the shelling and shooting had left behind.

Journalist Anthony Loyd describing the damage inflicted by Serbian troops on a rural town in Kosovo in early September 1998, in Martin Gilbert, A History of the Twentieth Century, *vol. 3 (2000), p. 853.*

The next day I . . . [experienced] the most peculiar White House meeting I ever attended. Chief of Staff Erskine Bowles had told me that the session's purpose was to allow President Clinton to apologize to the cabinet for not being truthful about Lewinsky. The press had a special interest in what the President would say to [the Health and Human Services secretary] Donna Shalala and me. We were the two women from the cabinet who had defended him in front of television cameras . . . back in January. As a result, some women's groups were outraged that we hadn't resigned. . . .

[Clinton] began by saying that he owed us an explanation. He said he was really sorry for what he had done. . . . Then he said that the reason he had done it was that he had been in a rage for the past four and a half years. He had been a good actor and had put on a smile but had been angry throughout. He talked in that vein for some time, without making eye contact with me or anyone else—then stopped.

As he spoke, I felt lost. The President had started out in a way I had expected, but the rest was surprising and did not make much sense. I wasn't sure he

The bombings of the U.S. embassies in Nairobi, Kenya (above), and Dar es Salaam, Tanzania, were attributed to Osama bin Laden's al-Qaeda network. *(AP/Wide World Photos)*

had really apologized. . . . I also didn't understand the rage. . . . In any case, what kind of excuse was that? . . .

[Shalala] said bluntly that the President had behaved inexcusably and that it was more important for a leader to have the right morals than the right policies. The President didn't quarrel with Donna's characterization . . . but he added a little testily that, if her logic prevailed, the nation would have been better off if Richard Nixon had been elected in 1960 instead of John Kennedy.

Secretary of State Madeleine Albright describing a meeting on September 10, 1998, in which President Bill Clinton apologized to the cabinet for the Lewinsky scandal, in Albright, Madam Secretary *(2003), pp. 355–356.*

I want to grab some weak little freshman and just tear them apart like a . . . wolf. Show them who is god. Strangle them, squish their head, bite their temples into the skull, rip off their jaw.

From the November 17, 1998, diary entry of the future Columbine High School killer Eric Harris, in "Columbine Killer Envisioned Crashing Plane in NYC," December 6, 2001. Available online. URL: http://www.cnn.com/2001/US/ 12/05/columbine.diary/.

The only thing certain now is uncertainty. The smart money shouts that President Clinton will never resign, and he vows to serve "until the last hour of the last day" of his second term. The smart money argues that the Senate will never muster the 67 votes needed to remove the wounded President from office. . . . The smart money insists that someone will cut a deal soon to end all this.

Maybe so. But the smarter money whispers, "Remember."

Remembering that everyone in Washington, including Representative Henry J. Hyde, the chairman of the Judiciary Committee, said the House would never, ever vote impeachment along partisan lines. Wrong. Remember that all the pundits predicted Democratic losses in the midterm elections, and when the opposite happened, they said impeachment was dead. Twice wrong. . . .

In the toxic politics of the century's end in Washington, the inconceivable has finally become the commonplace.

The wholly unanticipated announcement by Representative Robert L. Livingston, Republican of

Louisiana, that he would not serve as Speaker . . . after his equally unanticipated disclosure . . . of several extramarital affairs, only deepened the capital's prolonged sense of insecurity.

The deadly sweep of the scythe of neo-Puritanism appears unstoppable, at least for the moment. . . .

Political analyst R. W. Apple describing the sense of uncertainty that followed the impeachment of President Bill Clinton on December 19, 1998, in Apple, "What Next? Don't Guess," New York Times, *December 20, 1998, p. 1.*

I am confident we have achieved our mission. We have inflicted significant damage on Saddam's weapons of mass destruction programs on the command structures that direct and protect that capability and on his military and security infrastructure.

President Bill Clinton announcing on December 19, 1998, the cessation of a four-day bombing campaign against Iraq, in Steven Lee Myers, "U.S. and Britain End Raids on Iraq, Calling Mission a Success," New York Times, *December 20, 1998, p. 1.*

There have been so many bombshells. We have bombshells in Baghdad and we have bombshells in the House of Representatives. You can't turn your back for 10 seconds.

Representative Michael Castle of Delaware commenting on the unexpected announcement on December 19, 1998, by Representative Bob Livingston of Louisiana, that, after revelations of his adulterous affairs, he would not serve as Speaker of the House, in Katharine Q. Seelye, "Livingston Urges Clinton to Follow Suit," New York Times, *December 20, 1998, p. 1.*

The most significant political story of 1998 is not that the President had oral sex with a 22-year-old White House intern. . . [but] that most citizens don't seem to think it's significant. . . . Rarely has such an unexpected popular consensus been so clear. And rarely has such a clear consensus been so unexpected. . . .

In 1998, we all learned something surprising about ourselves. That's what makes the public reaction, not the events themselves, the political story of the year. . . .

Americans don't necessarily think adultery and perjury are perfectly O.K. What they may think—what they certainly know, from personal experience—is that life is complicated and people often make a mess of it. . . .

Is there anybody with no secrets he or she would be tempted to commit perjury for? That's not a blanket excuse for perjury. But when the perjury was a your-secrets-or-your-life stickup staged by a prosecutor who couldn't nail his target on anything else, anyone with an ounce of imagination is tempted to excuse it. . . .

One thing people could be saying in their opposition to impeachment is that we all have the right to our flaws—even the President. Or at least that we don't want the government wringing them out of us. In that sense the new tolerance is not a rejection of conservative values but an application of the lessons conservatives have been teaching. If you can't trust government to raise taxes or educate children, why on earth would you trust it to discipline people for sexual misbehavior and the inevitable complications that follow. . . . Maybe what America decided in 1998 was not to abandon morality. Maybe we just decided to privatize it.

Political commentator Michael Kinsley analyzing on December 28, 1998, why most Americans opposed the impeachment of President Bill Clinton on December 19, 1998, in Stephen Ambrose and Douglas Brinkley, eds., Witness to America (1999), pp. 585–587.

11 Fin de Siècle and Y2K
1999

The resolution of the Clinton impeachment, the robust economy, and the promise of ever-increasing advances in technology, the Internet, genetics, medicine, space exploration, and other realms created optimism in the final year of the millennium. On the other hand, at least since the Middle Ages, the conclusions of centuries have elicited fears of apocalypse, and 1999 was no exception. In the secular West, these concerns centered mostly, but not exclusively, on technological catastrophes rather than divine retribution. In particular, many feared that computers everywhere would crash at the new year because many software applications would not be able to distinguish the year 2000 from the year 1900. The so-called Y2K[1] problem attracted considerable media coverage, and governments, businesses, and private users made costly efforts to protect themselves against this eventuality, which, in the final result, proved to be only a minor problem. The expenditures to address the possibility, estimated as high as $600 billion worldwide, were not made entirely in vain, as they permitted extensive computer upgrades, enhanced networking capabilities, improved compatibility, and updated contingency plans for system failures. Y2K budget allocations also enabled businesses and communities to upgrade their emergency equipment and improve crisis planning.[2]

Warfare and terrorism also introduced an element of fear about the approaching new millennium. NATO waged a successful air war that ended Serbia's ethnic cleansing in its province of Kosovo. The United States and the United Nations both imposed economic sanctions on Afghanistan for harboring Osama bin Laden, whose al-Qaeda organization had been implicated in the 1998 embassy bombings in Africa and had apparently sponsored an Algerian-born man who was intercepted at the Canadian border with bomb-making material about two weeks before gala New Year celebrations were scheduled to begin. Authorities in the Middle East also arrested 12 operatives linked to Osama bin Laden accused of planning New Year's Eve attacks. But no terrorist plots succeeded on New Year's Eve, and people throughout the world gathered in massive crowds to experience extravagant celebrations of the passing of the 20th century into the 21st.[3]

357

INTERNATIONAL DEVELOPMENTS

NATO, which officially admitted former the Warsaw Pact members Hungary, Poland, and the Czech Republic at the beginning of the year, successfully prosecuted an air war against Serbia during the spring in order to halt atrocities Serbian forces were committing against ethnic Albanians in Kosovo. The major fighting in Kosovo had ceased in October 1998, after NATO's threats of air attacks convinced Serbia's president, Milošević, to withdraw his forces from the province. But the conflict erupted again in January 1999, when Serbian troops reentered and massacred ethnic Albanians in the region. The Security Council immediately condemned Serbia, and NATO, acting on behalf of the United Nations, again threatened to attack Serbian targets if its government failed to conclude a peaceful settlement to the conflict. Talks in February and early March failed to yield results when Milošević refused to allow a substantial peacekeeping contingent into the province. After the talks broke down, Serbia launched a new offensive, and NATO responded by initiating a 78-day air campaign that targeted both Serbian ground troops and military-related centers in downtown Belgrade, Serbia's capital. The air war did not hinder the Serbs from driving hundreds of thousands of ethnic Albanians from their home. But the air strikes devastated Belgrade and other parts of Serbia, and in June Milošević agreed to withdraw all army and police units from the region, permit the repatriation of some 700,000 refugees, and allow the United Nations to establish a peacekeeping force. Clinton hailed the resolution as a "victory for a safer world." Before the victory was achieved, however, NATO's accidental bombing of the Chinese embassy in Belgrade killed three Chinese citizens and threatened to disrupt the closer ties that Clinton had been trying to forge with China. The United States subsequently agreed to pay $4.5 million in compensation. After the air war, a sizable UN peacekeeping force entered Kosovo, and an initial conflict with Russia over its role in the peacekeeping operation was quickly resolved. A Serbian ally, Russia had opposed the war and sought unsuccessfully to halt the air campaign after it began in favor of renewing diplomatic efforts.

A separatist movement also plagued Russia, which fell victim to a terrorist campaign by Chechen rebels who attacked civilian targets in Moscow and elsewhere. Consequently, the Russian military resumed its military action against Chechnya, which it had suspended in compliance with a 1996 peace agreement. The Russian economy continued to falter as President Yeltsin replaced two premiers in an effort to overcome opposition to his economic reforms in the Communist-dominated Russian assembly. Although Yeltsin readily survived an impeachment effort in May, poor health and political and economic turmoil prompted him to step down as the nation's first democratically elected president on December 31. Yeltsin named as acting president Vladimir Putin, the premier as of 2005 and a former official in the KGB, the Soviet espionage agency.

Although the leaders of India and Pakistan met in February to resolve their disputes and reduce the threat of nuclear war, each nation tested ballistic missiles capable of striking the other with nuclear payloads. The situation was exacerbated by border skirmishes in the spring and early summer over the contested Kashmir region, involving both Pakistani military forces and Kashmiri separatists affiliated with Pakistan. The tensions diminished after Clinton met with Pakistani prime minister Nawaz Sharif in early July. Afterward, Sharif reaffirmed the 1972 cease-fire line that divided Kashmir into Indian- and Pakistani-controlled sectors. He also agreed to take steps to remove the militant separatists from the Indian sector. In October, however, less than a week after India's ruling Hindu National-ist Party easily prevailed in popular elections, military leaders displeased with Sharif's concessions overthrew him in a bloodless coup. Sharif was subsequently charged with treason although his trial was postponed until 2000, when he was convicted and sentenced to life in prison but later allowed to go into exile in Saudi Arabia. Later in the year, U.S. and UN offices in Pakistan fell under rocket attacks believed to be in response to anticipated UN sanctions against the Taliban regime in Afghanistan, which refused to surrender Osama bin Laden to the United States. The situation in the region was further exacerbated in late December when five men demanding the release of Kashmiri separatists hijacked an Indian passenger plane to Afghanistan and threatened to kill more than 150 passengers and crew members. The situation was resolved when India released three jailed Pakistani militants on December 31. One passenger was killed, and the hijackers were allowed to escape. One of the freed militants, Omar Sayeed Sheikh, went on to execute the American journalist Daniel Pearl in 2002. He also provided money to the hijackers who conducted the attacks on the Pen-tagon and World Trade Center on September 11, 2001. Some intelligence agents believe the 1999 hijacking was a practice run for the 2001 hijackings.

Indonesia's general assembly chose Abdurrahman Wahid, a Muslim cleric, as the country's first democratically elected president. Wahid then formed a so-called national unity cabinet with representatives of all parties in the legislature. He also appointed a civilian defense minister, a move intended to reduce the political influence of the military. A popular vote for independence in East Timor ended Indonesia's 24-year occupation, but the United Nations had to deploy peacekeepers in response to atrocities by pro-Indonesian militias. China, which officially sanctioned only five religions, initiated a crackdown on the growing Falun Gong spiritual movement, which endorsed *qigong* and other Buddhism-inspired practices for more fully actuating mental, physical, and spir-itual potential by cultivating connection to the fundamental energy of the uni-verse. Practitioners maintained that Falun Gong is not a religion and that its mostly middle-aged and elderly practitioners are law-abiding, but the govern-ment outlawed it in July, despite days of protest rallies throughout the country.

Revelations that the United States was using the UN weapons-inspection program to spy on the Iraqi regime vindicated long-standing Iraqi accusations and complicated the ongoing conflict between the nations. Richard Butler, head of the UN Special Commission (UNSCOM) in charge of the inspec-tions, denied that UNSCOM knew about or cooperated with the U.S. espi-onage, but aides to the UN secretary-general Kofi Annan asserted the existence of "convincing evidence" that UNSCOM had worked with the United States to collect information that might help depose Saddam Hussein. Subsequently, Iraqi violations of the no-fly zones increased, followed by U.S. retaliatory air strikes. At the end of the year, Iraq rejected a plan by the United Nations that would have allowed the resumption of weapons inspections.

The death of King Hussein, who had ruled Jordan for 45 years and helped mediate peace agreements in the Middle East, raised anxieties for the future, as

Hussein had been widely viewed as a force of stability in the region. Shortly before his death, Hussein unexpectedly altered the line of royal succession, displacing his younger brother and naming his oldest son, Prince Abdullah, as his successor.

Israel's election in May of Ehud Barak as prime minister was generally interpreted as an expression of Israel's greater willingness to seek peace and a repudiation of the hard-line policies of the incumbent prime minister, Benjamin Netanyahu. Palestinians greeted the change of Israeli leadership with cautious optimism, and Arafat personally congratulated Barak on his victory. One of Barak's first acts was to outline to Clinton a self-imposed 15-month deadline for achieving a full peace settlement with the Palestinian National Authority, and in September, Barak and Arafat agreed to set a timetable for talks on a permanent peace agreement and to provide for the withdrawal of Israeli troops from the West Bank, as called for in the 1998 Wye Agreement, in return for cessation of bombing attacks and other acts of violence against Israeli civilians by Palestinians. Subsequently, Barak reached an agreement with Israeli settlers to close 10 of the 42 settlements that Israel had established since the signing of the 1998 Wye Agreement, with the approval of Netanyahu. Barak also took steps to resume peace negotiations with Syria that had been suspended for nearly four years.

Relations between Turkey and Greece improved as each nation sent rescue workers to assist the other in the aftermath of devastating earthquakes that struck Turkey in August and Greece in September.

As outlined in an earlier treaty, ownership of the Panama Canal transferred from the United States to Panama on December 14. The newly created Inuit territory of Nunavut officially joined the Canadian federation in February. Many islands in the eastern Caribbean, including Cuba, Jamaica, the Cayman Islands, Puerto Rico, and the U.S. and British Virgin Islands, were severely damaged by Hurricane Lenny, a powerful late-season storm with winds that reached 150 mph.

In response to disturbing reports of children's working in sweatshop conditions and estimates that some 300,000 children throughout the world had been forced into military service, 174 member states of the International Labor Organization, including the United States and Western Europe, signed a treaty banning the harshest forms of child labor, including slavery, debt bondage, drug production and trafficking, prostitution, pornography, work likely to harm the "health, safety or morals" of children, and forced recruitment of children into the military. The treaty's original language had banned service by everyone younger than age 18, and human rights activists were disappointed by a change that permitted voluntary enlistment in the armed services. The new provision allowed the United States, Britain, the Netherlands, and Germany to continue to recruit 17-year-old volunteers. Defenders of the provision argued that the treaty's purpose had never been to address this practice but to stop the forced service of much younger children in militias and paramilitary organizations. One report had estimated that approximately 120,000 children were fighting in conflicts in Africa, some as young as seven years old.[4] A provision banning labor that deprived children of an education was voted down after representatives of developing nations argued that it would not be enforceable.

GOVERNMENT AND SOCIETY

On February 12, the Senate acquitted Clinton of the charges of impeachment that the House of Representatives had sent forward in December 1998. Although a two-thirds majority was required, Clinton's opponents were unable to muster even a simple majority, as all 45 Democrats supported the president, along with some Republicans, who crossed party lines to acquit him. Their failure to gain more than half the votes in the Republican-dominated Senate was widely regarded as a humiliating defeat for the House managers who prosecuted the case against the president. But many senators in both parties took pains to point out that the vote to acquit was not an endorsement of Clinton's behavior, which they condemned as "shameful" and "disgraceful." Despite Clinton's subsequent apology to the nation for his inappropriate actions and a call for national unity, the nation remained deeply divided by partisan politics, and Clinton's reputation was significantly tarnished and his effectiveness diminished by scandal.

Scandal also plagued other once-trusted elements of the society, as the International Olympic Committee (IOC) revealed that some of its ranking members had been bribed by business leaders who convinced the IOC to hold the 2002 Winter Olympics in Salt Lake City, Utah. Moreover, a Miami jury concluded that the tobacco industry had been adding addictive properties to cigarettes and then concealing the practice; a congressional report found that the Pentagon had illegally spent hundreds of millions of dollars on projects that lawmakers had never approved; and a federal judge ruled that the Microsoft Corporation was guilty of unfair, monopolistic labor practices.

Clinton and the Republican-controlled Congress remained at odds over many domestic issues, and the 1999 session concluded with much of the proposed legislation unfinished, stalled, or vetoed by Clinton. In September, the president vetoed legislation that would have depleted the budget surplus by granting a $792 billion tax cut over 10 years. Clinton opposed the size of the cuts, which he maintained would jeopardize efforts to protect Social Security and Medicare and to pay off some of the national debt. On the other hand, the Senate refused to ratify the Comprehensive Test Ban Treaty, an accord endorsed by Clinton that would have prohibited nuclear testing. It was the first time since the Senate defeated the 1920 Treaty of Versailles, which established the League of Nations, that the Senate did not approve a major international security agreement supported by the president.

Congress also failed to approve an omnibus budget appropriation bill until nearly six weeks past the October 1 deadline, although it averted a government shutdown by passing stopgap continuing resolutions that were acceptable to Clinton. The final bill offered few major changes in spending policy, but it allocated $1.3 billion for Clinton's initiative to hire 100,000 additional classroom teachers, as well as $1.8 billion for implementing the 1998 Arab-Israeli peace agreement. Congress passed, and Clinton signed, a $268 billion defense appropriation and $21.3 billion for energy, water, and nuclear weapons programs.

Although reports showed that violent crime had diminished to the lowest level in 26 years, the nation was horrified by yet another spate of shootings in public schools. The worst occurred outside Denver, at Columbine High School in Littleton, Colorado, where, on April 20, two disaffected teenage students celebrated Adolf Hitler's birthday by firing rifles and throwing bombs at their classmates and teachers, killing 13 and wounding 23 before killing themselves. The Columbine shootings caused parents throughout the country to fear for their children's safety at school, and they intensified ongoing arguments over the desirability and efficacy of gun control. But they did not deter the NRA from holding its annual convention in Denver less than two weeks later, despite massive protests. Exactly one month after the Columbine killings, a 15-year-old student injured six fellow students at a high school in Georgia. These and other school shootings prompted tougher laws for juvenile offenders throughout the country. In Michigan, a jury convicted 13-year-old Nathaniel Abraham of second-degree murder. Abraham, who had shot and killed a stranger when he was 11 years old, was believed to be the youngest person in the United States ever to be tried as an adult for first-degree murder. Seven teenagers and young adults died in September, when Larry Ashbrook, an unemployed 47-year-old man known for his angry outbursts and violent temper, broke into a religious rally they were attending at a Baptist church in Fort Worth, Texas, and opened fire with two handguns.

Violence in the workplace also occurred again, as a worker killed seven coworkers at Xerox Corporation in Honolulu, Hawaii, and an Atlanta-based securities day trader killed nine coworkers and wounded 13 more before committing suicide. Earlier in the same month, another Atlanta man murdered his girlfriend and four of her five children before killing himself in what, to that point, had been the deadliest mass shooting in Atlanta in the 20th century.

On the same day as the Georgia school shootings, the Senate overwhelmingly approved a juvenile crime bill that strengthened gun-control laws, but the House defeated a weaker version of the measure. Clinton introduced a separate

The massacre of students and faculty at Columbine High School was the worst of a spate of murders of children by other children. *(AP/Wide World Photos)*

initiative providing $15 million in federal grants for gun buy-back programs, enough to purchase and destroy up to 300,000 privately owned guns.

Clinton's offer to commute the prison sentences of 16 members of the Armed Forces of National Liberation (FALN) proved controversial. A Puerto Rican independence group, the FALN had been responsible for numerous bombings in the United States between 1974 and 1983. Clinton insisted that the prisoners, none of whom had been directly involved in attacks that killed or injured people, renounce violence and comply with normal parole requirements. Law enforcement officials criticized the offer because they feared it would encourage other terrorists. And Republicans complained that the gesture was intended to help Hillary Rodham Clinton win the votes of New York's Puerto Rican population in her planned run for the U.S. Senate in 2000. However, Hillary Clinton criticized the offer after the FALN members failed immediately to renounce violence—although they did later. Human rights activists throughout the world praised the release of the prisoners because they maintained that the initial sentences had been excessively severe.

Tragedy continued to befall the family of assassinated president John F. Kennedy, as Kennedy's son, John F. Kennedy, Jr.; his son's wife, Carolyn Bessette Kennedy; and her sister, Lauren Bessette, died when an airplane that Kennedy, Jr., was piloting crashed into the ocean off Massachusetts. Founder of the political magazine *George,* Kennedy, Jr., had long been considered one of the nation's most desirable bachelors until his marriage in 1996 to Bessette, a fashion industry executive. The search for the missing bodies, which were recovered four days later, received extensive media coverage, and the deaths were widely mourned.

Striking down a Colorado law, the Supreme Court limited states' ability to regulate the process by which initiatives are placed on ballots. The Court also voided a local antiloitering ordinance intended to prevent gang members from gathering on public streets, and it reinstated fishing rights granted to Chippewa Indians by an 1837 treaty. It restricted citizens' rights to sue states for failing to comply with federal laws and decided that government authorities cannot release information from police records to private companies seeking to use the data for commercial purposes. It ruled that police can search the belongings of automobile passengers, even if only the driver is suspected of illegal behavior. It further ruled that police could not allow "ride along" journalists and photographers to accompany them into private residences as they conduct searches and make arrests; that execution by electrocution does not constitute cruel and unusual punishment; that the Census Bureau cannot use statistical sampling to compile the national census; that states cannot pay lower welfare benefits to new state residents than to long-established ones; that health insurers are not immune from prosecution under federal law; that the FCC, and not the states, has the authority to set policy on opening the $100 billion local telephone market to competition; that Congress has the authority to outlaw obscene e-mail messages and faxes; and that school boards can be sued for damages if they fail to stop students from sexually harassing other students. In a ruling believed to pave the way for same-sex marriages, the Vermont Supreme Court ruled that the state government must offer homosexual couples the same benefits and legal rights that it offers heterosexual married couples.

Business

The economy continued to improve, as the Dow–Jones industrial average passed the 10,000 mark for the first time in history, creating expectations for long-term prosperity. It closed at 11,497, up 2,315 points, or 25 percent, from its 1998 closing—the fifth straight year it registered double-digit percentage gains. Computer and technology stocks were among the strongest performers, and initial public offerings (IPOs), which were dominated by computer companies, raised a record $69.2 billion, up from the previous high of $49.9 billion in 1996.[5] The success of technology stocks also created record highs on the NASDAQ exchange, which specializes in smaller stocks and new technologies. Although the year ended with strong economic growth, marked by an increase of 5.8 percent in the GDP in the final quarter, overall the GDP rose by only 4.0 percent, compared to 4.3 percent the previous year, and the unemployment rate was at 4.2 percent, down from 4.5 percent in 1998.[6]

Despite a congressional report charging that since the 1950s spies had been giving U.S. nuclear secrets to China and despite the arrest for espionage of a Chinese-born nuclear scientist working at a U.S. facility, Clinton supported China's admission to the World Trade Organization (WTO) in November after China agreed to reduce obstacles to foreign investment and imported goods. But riots disrupted the organization's December meeting and incurred millions of dollars worth of damage in Seattle as protesters violently maintained that multinational corporations were curtailing workers' rights and weakening environmental protections as the global economy spread throughout the world.

A trade war between Canada and the United States was averted when the nations agreed to allow U.S. magazines that publish "split-run" editions in Canada to sell a limited amount of advertising space to Canadian advertisers.

The movement toward full economic integration of the European Union (EU) took a major step forward with the introduction of the euro as the common currency of 11 of the participating nations. Britain, Denmark, and Sweden chose not to participate, and Greece failed to meet the qualifications to do so.

Nature and the Environment

Natural disasters contributed to the apocalyptic spirit at the century's end. In early May a single storm system spawned 76 large, destructive tornadoes in Oklahoma and the Midwest and high winds and thunderstorms in Tennessee, Kentucky, and Arkansas. These storms collectively killed more than 50 people. The winds in one of the tornadoes outside Oklahoma City had winds between 260 and 318 miles per hour, the strongest ever recorded; it was also the most destructive tornado ever recorded. A record-breaking heat wave in late July and early August spread from the Midwest to the East Coast, contributing to severe drought and causing at least 200 deaths.

Described by some as the "big brother" of Hurricane Andrew, the category 5 storm that devastated much of south Florida in 1992, Hurricane Floyd caused extensive damage from Florida to New England when, after passing over the Bahamas as a strong category 4 storm, it veered north, away from south Florida, which was preparing for a direct hit. Finally, Floyd made landfall near Wilmington, North Carolina, before passing over Cape Hatteras and moving back out to sea and then striking Rhode Island, Connecticut, and Massachusetts. The huge storm, which at one point measured some 300 miles in diameter—almost the full length of Florida—caused extensive flooding in North Carolina and Virginia, which only weeks before had been pounded by heavy rains from Hurricane Dennis, which had stalled for several days just off the Outer Banks before finally moving ashore as a wet tropical storm. Then Hurricane Irene, a late-season storm, first struck south Florida and the Florida Keys, causing millions of dollars in damage and killing eight people, and then turned north toward the Carolinas. Although it did not make landfall, Irene dumped an additional four to six inches of rain on the already-flooded region. Hurricane Lenny was another powerful late-season storm that inflected heavy damage on the islands of the eastern Caribbean.

A year-end four-day storm with hurricane-force winds killed 74 people in France, flooded the River Seine in Paris, and left millions without electricity as they prepared for their millennium celebrations. Floods in China left more than 5 million people homeless. A powerful earthquake measuring 7.4 on the Richter scale struck northwest Turkey, killing tens of thousands near the Sea of Marmara and setting the nation's largest oil refinery on fire for days. Hundreds more died in Istanbul, where several buildings collapsed. A second tremor almost as strong as the first hit western Turkey three months later, also killing hundreds. Athens suffered scores of deaths when it was struck by a tremor measuring 5.9 on the Richter scale, the strongest earthquake in Greece in 80 years. Colombia and Taiwan also suffered devastating earthquakes, and mudslides in Venezuela took between 20,000 and 50,000 lives.

The Consumer's Union, a consumer advocacy group, reported that most U.S. produce contained higher levels of pesticide residue than found on imported fruits and vegetables, and the Environmental Protection Agency (EPA) for the first time invoked the 1996 Food Quality Protection Act to restrict the use of methyl parathion and azinphos methyl, commonly used pesticides, which are believed to pose special risks to children.

Japan suffered its worst nuclear event since World War II when an accident at a nuclear fuel processing plant initiated an uncontrolled nuclear chain reaction that elevated radiation levels in the plant to lethal levels and released radioactive gas into the atmosphere. At least 55 workers were exposed to dangerous levels of radiation, and two were hospitalized in critical condition.

Arguments that global warming is, in fact, occurring were strengthened by data issued by the World Meteorological Organization showing that the 1990s was the warmest decade on record, and that the 20th century was the warmest century in 1,000 years. However, news from the National Oceanic and Atmospheric Administration (NOAA) was more encouraging. Its studies indicated that the hole in the ozone layer appeared to be narrowing in the aftermath of the 1987 ban on chlorofluorocarbons. Overpopulation remained an environmental and political concern, however, as the UN World Population Fund predicted that the world's population would reach 6 billion in October and 8.9 billion by 2050.

SCIENCE AND TECHNOLOGY

Astronomers used data gathered from the *Hubble Space Telescope* to recalculate the age of the universe, which they concluded is between 12 and 15 billion years old. Another team of scientists discovered the first system of multiple planets orbiting a single star, apart from the Sun. On the other hand, researchers were disappointed first, when programming errors caused the *Mars Climate Orbiter* to crash into the planet and then, when they unexpectedly lost radio contact with the *Mars Polar Lander* as it entered the planet's atmosphere. Its mission had been to seek evidence of frozen water. Nonetheless, scientists using data from the unmanned *Mars Global Surveyor* orbiting the planet concluded that a large ocean had existed in Mars's northern regions some 2 billion years ago. Russia decommissioned its *Mir* space station after 13 years, eight years later than originally anticipated. A total solar eclipse occurred across parts of Europe, the Middle East, and the Indian subcontinent on August 11.

A panel appointed by the National Academy of Sciences' Institute of Medicine concluded that marijuana contains about 30 active substances moderately helpful in alleviating pain, nausea, and loss of appetite associated with AIDS and with muscle spasms associated with multiple sclerosis. The panel rejected claims that marijuana is beneficial for treating glaucoma. The report, which was heralded by proponents of legalizing marijuana for medicinal purposes, pointed to dangers of marijuana smoking, but not of other forms of ingestion. Scientists of the United States and Uganda discovered that giving infected mothers and their newborn babies a single dose of the drug nevirapine is an inexpensive and effective way to reduce the transmission of the AIDS-causing HIV from mothers to their children. This and other new treatments for AIDS during the 1990s continued to yield effects in the United States, where the National Center for Health Statistics announced that AIDS was no longer among the top 15 causes of death. The disease continued to spread in epidemic proportions in developing nations, however, especially in Africa, where most of the population do not have access to costly medications.

In a breakthrough development that occurred years ahead of schedule, an international group of geneticists working on the Human Genome Project mapped the sequence of genes in a single human chromosome. The importance of the sequence to genetic understanding and genetic engineering is considered to be akin to that of the groundbreaking discovery of DNA's double-helix structure in the 1950s. A separate genetic study, based on observations of mutations of a specific gene found in living people, concluded that lineages of African and non-African humans separated 189,000 years ago, approximately 70,000 years earlier than previously believed.

Federal investigators determined that two 1997 studies showing that electromagnetic fields from power lines contribute to cancer formation had been based on falsified data. The controversy over the safety of electromagnetic radiation (EMR) remained, as critics maintained it could cause leukemia or brain tumors.

Dinosaur fossils discovered in Madagascar dating from the middle to late Triassic period, 225 million to 230 million years ago, were believed to be the oldest ever found. Scientists in Siberia found the intact frozen carcass of a woolly mammoth that had lived some 20,000 years ago.

LITERATURE, THE ARTS, SPORTS, AND POPULAR CULTURE

Although multiculturalism remained a controversial matter, America's growing openness to other cultures was evident in the Asian origins of the year's National Book Award and Pulitzer Prize winners in fiction and poetry. British-born and of Indian descent, Jhumpa Lahiri won the Pulitzer Prize for *Interpreter of Maladies,* a story collection about Indians displaced by political events and transplanted to the United States. The Chinese-born author Ha Jin won the National Book Award for his novel *Waiting,* about a Chinese doctor torn between the expectations of his traditional culture and new values asserted by the Communist revolution. Ai, a professor at Oklahoma State University who describes herself as a mixture of Japanese, Choctaw-Chickasaw, black, Irish, Southern Cheyenne, and Comanche, won the National Book Award for *Vice: New & Selected Poems.* In that work Ai imagines the voices of major and minor figures from past and present American cultures interacting with one another. In *The Secret Names of Women* Lynne Barrett, a professor at Florida International University, also assumes an array of voices, mostly those of women in unusual circumstances, ranging from singers in an all-girl rock band to a California woman whose voice Marilyn Monroe imitated to a homicidal Elvis impersonator. Barrett's colleague and MacArthur Award winner, poet Campbell McGrath, published a new volume of poetry, *Road Atlas and Other Poems.*

The best-selling horror writer Stephen King was severely injured when he was struck by a minivan near his home in rural Maine. Nonetheless, King published three novels during the year: *The Girl Who Loved Tom Gordon, Hearts in Atlantis,* and *Storm of the Century.* Other best-selling fiction included Thomas Harris's *Hannibal,* the sequel to *Silence of the Lambs* (1988), about a cannibalistic, but highly cultured and well-spoken psychopath; Danielle Steel's romance novels *Bittersweet, Irresistible Forces,* and *Granny Dan;* Anne Rice's *Vittorio the Vampire;* Nora Roberts's *River's End,* about the lurid murder of a Hollywood star; John le Carré's *Single & Single;* and John Grisham's *The Testament.* The British children's author J. K. Rowling published two new volumes in her immensely popular Harry Potter fantasy series: *Harry Potter and the Chamber of Secrets* and *Harry Potter and the Prisoner of Azkaban.* By the end of the decade, all three Harry Potter books occupied positions on the top-10 lists, prompting the *New York Times* to establish a separate list for children's literature in order to create openings on its best-seller list for adult fiction. The Nobel Prize winner Toni Morrison and her son, Slade Morrison, published a children's book, *The Big Box.*

Nonfiction included *All Too Human: A Political Education* by George Stephanopoulos, who served in the White House during Clinton's first term, and Andrew Morton's *Monica's Story,* about Monica Lewinsky. Mark Bowden published *Black Hawk Down,* an account of a failed U.S. attempt to arrest the Somali warlord General Mohammed Farah Aidid, in 1993 (later the basis of Ridley Scott's 2001 film). In his best-selling *Business @ the Speed of Thought: Using a Digital Nervous System* (later resubtitled *Succeeding in the Digital Economy*)

Microsoft chairman Bill Gates suggests fundamental new ways for using computer technology to solve business problems. John Dower's *Embracing Defeat: Japan in the Wake of World War II* won both the Pulitzer Prize and the National Book Award in nonfiction.

Broadway openings in the 1998–99 season included David Hare's *Amy's View*, about an actress and her daughter; Hare's one-man play *Via Dolorosa* about the Middle East; Harold Pinter's *Ashes to Ashes*, in which a professor probing into his wife's past comes to realize how poorly he knew her; William Foeller's *Nixon's Nixon*, which presents an imaginary dialogue between the former president Richard Nixon and the former secretary of state Henry Kissinger on the eve of Nixon's resignation; Patrick Marber's *Closer*, which follows the erotic relationships among two men and two women over several years; David Marshall Grant's comedy *Snakebit*, about a homosexual social worker who hosts two married friends; Lisa Kron's *2.5 Minute Ride*, the reminiscences of a Jewish lesbian; and Thulaini Davis's *Everybody's Ruby*, based on an actual killing of a white man by his black lover in Florida during the 1950s and a subsequent investigation of the murder trial by the novelist Zora Neale Hurston. Margaret Edson won the Pulitzer Prize for *Wit*, a drama about a dying literary scholar who uses her academic skills to interpret her situation, the people attending her, and her own life. Warren Leight's *Side Man*, an all-male version of Peter Ilyich Tchaikovsky's *Swan Lake*, won the Tony Award as best play, and *Fosse*, a dance revue celebrating the work of the director/choreographer Bob Fosse, won as best musical. Other musicals included Frank Wildhorn, Gregory Boyd, and Jack Murphy's *The Civil War*, which offers perspectives of slaves, as well as those of soldiers on both sides of the conflict, and *It Ain't Nothin' but the Blues*, a revue that traces the history of the blues.

Charles Schulz, creator of the long-running cartoon *Peanuts*, announced his retirement and the cessation of the popular comic strip, effective January 4, 2000. Schulz who died in February 2000, had also adapted the strip into popular animated television shows.

The acclaimed independent film director Stanley Kubrick died shortly after completing his enigmatic but psychologically and sexually provocative *Eyes Wide Shut*, which starred Tom Cruise and Nicole Kidman in a cinematic adaptation of Arthur Schnitzler's dreamlike novel *Traumnovelle* (1926). Although the release of *Star Wars I—The Phantom Menace*, the long-awaited "prequel" to George Lucas's popular *Star Wars* trilogy, was a major media event, Andy Wachowski and Larry Wachowski's *The Matrix* proved to be more enduring. It starred Keanu Reeves, Laurence Fishburne, and Carrie-Anne Moss in the story of a computer hacker who discovers that his entire environment is a computer-generated illusion created by machines that feed on human energy. Russell Crowe, Al Pacino, and Christopher Plummer starred in Michael Mann's *The Insider*, based on the suppression by network executives of a *60 Minutes* story about a former tobacco company executive's evidence of industry deception. *American Beauty*, Sam Mendes's exposé of suburban life starring Kevin Spacey, Annette Bening, and Mena Suvari, won Academy Awards as best film, director, and actor (Spacey). The academy's decision to confer a lifetime achievement award on the director Elia Kazan provoked an outpouring of protest from people who objected to Kazan's cooperation during the 1950s with the establish-

Kevin Spacey starred in *American Beauty,* an exposé of suburban America. *(Photofest)*

ment of an industry blacklist that denied employment to actors, writers, and directors alleged to have Communist Party affiliation.

M. Night Shyamalan's *The Sixth Sense* was a popular thriller about a boy who communicates with the dead. In Spike Jonze's imaginative comedy *Being John Malkovich* unscrupulous entrepreneurs discover how to enter the mind of the actor John Malkovich and experience reality through his eyes. They then sell 15-minute admissions into Malkovich's mind to willing tourists for huge sums. Lasse Hallstrom's adaptation of John Irving's 1985 novel *Cider House Rules* was a critically acclaimed coming-of-age story; James Mangold's *Girl, Interrupted* adapts Susanna Kaysen's 1993 memoir about the experiences of a suicidal teenage girl in a mental institution. Although Winona Ryder had the starring role, Angelina Jolie established herself as a major actress in her role as a compelling sociopath. Patricia Rozema's *Mansfield Park,* starring Embeth Davidtz, gives a feminist spin to Jane Austen's 1814 novel of the same title.

Bronwen Hughes's *Forces of Nature* is a screwball comedy that stars Ben Affleck as a groom who is trying to travel to his wedding, despite the distractions of his free-spirited road companion, played by Sandra Bullock. Harold Ramis's *Analyze This* stars Robert De Niro, Billy Crystal, and Lisa Kudrow in a comedy about a psychiatrist and soon-to-be groom whose life is turned upside down when he takes on a Mafia boss as a patient. Will Smith and Kevin Kline starred in Barry Sonnenfeld's *The Wild Wild West,* one of several 1990s films to tap into baby boomers' nostalgia for the television shows of their childhood. The top box office hits were *The Phantom Menace* ($430.5 million); *The Sixth Sense* ($276.4 million); John Lasseter, Lee Unkrich, and Ash Bannon's animated *Toy Story 2* ($208.6 million); Jay Roach's *Austin Powers: The Spy Who Shagged Me* ($205.5 million); and *The Matrix* ($171.4 million).[7]

During the 1999–2000 season, reality shows asserted themselves for the first time as a major force in television programming. Although it did not debut until January 2000, ABC's *Who Wants to Be a Millionaire?,* hosted by

Regis Philbin, dominated the ratings, as its three different weekly segments finished as the first, second, and third top-ranked programs of the season. It was followed by established programs: *ER, Friends, Frasier, Monday Night Football, The Practice, 60 Minutes,* and *Touched by an Angel.*

The Practice, a television drama about a Boston law firm that represents society's underclass, received the 1999 Emmy Award as outstanding drama series, and *The West Wing,* a new fast-paced political drama, quickly gained a devoted following. Notable for its strong writing and the comparative depth of its presentation of the political maneuvering involved in presidential politics and executive action, *The West Wing* received the 2000 Emmy Award as outstanding dramatic series for the 1999–2000 season. It was written and conceived by Aaron Sorkin and starred Martin Sheen as a liberal U.S. president loosely patterned on Clinton. The show, which draws on current political events, features the White House staff as they try to balance policy and political expedience.

In winning the 1999 award as outstanding comedy series, Fox's off-beat *Ally McBeal* ended *Frasier's* five-year run, from 1994 to 1998. The growing level of acceptance of homosexuals in the culture was evident in the fact that in 2000 *Will & Grace* won the award as best comedy series of the 1999–2000 season. Also in 1999, the popular talk-show host Oprah Winfrey cofounded Oxygen Media, a company dedicated to producing cable and Internet programming for women.

Readers of *Rolling Stone* magazine, a publication about contemporary music, voted the Backstreet Boys as Artists of the Year. As did their rivals 'N Sync, the Backstreet Boys came across as playful, fun-loving, but not aggressive or sexually threatening. In this respect they contrasted with top female singers, such as Britney Spears and the Spice Girls, who made the most of their sex appeal. Among the year's hit singles were "Believe" by Cher, Whitney Houston's "Heartbreak Hotel," "Smooth" by Santana, and "Kiss Me" by Sixpence None the Richer. Ricky Martin's "Livin' la Vida Loca" became the most successful single ever issued by a Latin recording artist, and his album *Ricky Martin* was also a best seller. Other top-selling albums included *Fly* by the Dixie Chicks, a sexy all-female country band, and *Supernatural* by Santana, which won the Grammy Award as best album.

The groups R.E.M., Texas, and Ladysmith Black Mambazo from South Africa and the performers Puff Daddy and Sheryl Crow were among those who participated in a worldwide Internet fund-raiser to alleviate global poverty. An estimated 125 million listeners logged on to the NetAid Web site in the largest "Webcast" to date. The event was organized by Cisco Systems, an Internet company, and by the UN Development Fund. Woodstock '99, which celebrated the 30th anniversary of the original Woodstock rock concert, attracted a live crowd of some 200,000, as well as a large television audience who watched the

The success of *Will & Grace* suggested a new level of acceptance of homosexuality in American culture. *(Photofest)*

The Dixie Chicks projected female sexuality, strength, and independence. *(Photofest)*

performances as a pay-per-view cable event. Among the groups and performers to appear were Jewel, Sheryl Crow, Creed, Metallica, Limp Bizkit, Collective Soul, Rage against the Machine, DMX, Offspring, and the Red Hot Chili Peppers, whose *Californication* was a hit. The concert, which took place in the summer heat on an open field in Rome, New York, was marketed more extensively than the original event, and it was marred by random violence, sexual assaults and other attacks against women, and a pervasive undertone of anger that contrasted sharply with the spirit of "peace and love" attributed to the first Woodstock concert, which took place during the Vietnam War in 1969.

The singers Bruce Springsteen, Paul McCartney, Dusty Springfield, Curtis Mayfield, Billy Joel, Del Shannon, and the Staple Singers were inducted into the Rock and Roll Hall of Fame, and Billy Joel received the Special Award of Merit for his "inspired songwriting skills" and "exciting showmanship." Joel later announced his plans to devote his future efforts to classical music. The performer Mel Tormé died at age 73, and Seiji Ozawa, the longtime music director and principal conductor of the Boston Symphony Orchestra, resigned to become music director of the Vienna State Opera in Austria. The former Beatle George Harrison was stabbed several times in the chest at his home by an unknown assailant, who apparently believed that Harrison was the devil. Harrison's wife wrestled the knife from the hand of the would-be murderer, who escaped before police arrived.

A controversial exhibition at the Brooklyn Museum of Art provoked New York's mayor Rudolph Giuliani to attempt to withhold $7.2 million in city funding for the museum. "Sensation: Young British Artists from the Saatchi Collection," which first opened in London in 1997, featured images calculated to shock and disgust viewers, including a bisected pig, a 14-foot shark floating in formaldehyde, and a work by Chris Ofili entitled *The Holy Virgin,* a stylized painting of the Virgin Mary adorned with numerous cutouts of buttocks featured in pornographic magazines and a clump of elephant excrement. The exhibition provoked considerable commentary throughout the country, both by those anxious to defend artists' rights to self-expression and by those opposed to using public funds for promoting such objectionable forms of expression. *The Holy Virgin,* in particular, engendered charges of blasphemy and deteriorating moral values.

Baseball's New York Yankees passed hockey's Montreal Canadiens as the most successful professional sports franchise in the 20th century when they defeated the Atlanta Braves to win their 25th World Series. The Braves third baseman Chipper Jones and the Texas Rangers catcher Ivan "Pudge" Rodriguez were the National and American Leagues' MVPs. The pitchers Randy Johnson of the Arizona Diamondbacks and Pedro Martinez of the Boston Red Sox were the Cy Young recipients. The Saint Louis Cardinal Mark McGwire, who set a new single-season home-run record in 1998, again edged out the Chicago Cub Sammy Sosa to lead the Major Leagues with 65 home runs. The retired major league players Orlando Cepeda, Nolan Ryan, George Brett, and Robin Yount, and "Smokey" Joe Williams of the Negro Leagues were inducted into the Hall of Fame. The year also saw an unsuccessful labor action by more than 50 umpires, who submitted their resignation in order to hasten contract negotiations. When the strategy failed and the umpires withdrew the resignations, 22 were not reinstated and lost their job. They were replaced by umpires from the Minor Leagues. The owners also voted to eliminate the position of league president and to assign those duties to the commissioner's office.

The Rams defeated the expansion Tennessee Titans in Super Bowl XXXIV to win their first NFL championship since moving to Saint Louis from Los Angeles. The Rams quarterback Kurt Warner, who joined the Miami Dolphin Dan Marino as the only person to throw 40 touchdowns in a single season, was named league MVP. The Rams running back Marshall Faulk's 2,429 total yards from scrimmage surpassed the previous record set by the Detroit Lion Barry Sanders. Professional football returned to Cleveland when the Browns opened their first season as a new expansion team. The Florida State University Seminoles defeated the Virginia Tech Hokies to claim the college championship. The University of Wisconsin running back Ron Dayne won the Heisman Trophy.

The NBA season, whose opening was delayed for months during a player-lockout initiated in 1998 by the owners, finally began in early February, after the conclusion of a six-year collective bargaining agreement. The San Antonio Spurs went on to win the championship in the shortened season that was played without the Chicago Bulls star Michael Jordan, who retired before the season began, as did the Bulls' coach, Phil Jackson. Jackson returned to the NBA a year later as head coach of the Los Angeles Lakers. The Spurs forward Tim Duncan was the playoff MVP, and Karl Malone of the Utah Jazz (nicknamed the Mailman because he "delivered") was the season MVP. The University of Connecticut won its first men's national basketball championship, and Purdue University won the women's title. The Dallas Stars won hockey's Stanley Cup.

In tennis, the Americans Pete Sampras and Lindsay Davenport won the men's and women's singles events at Wimbledon. Serena Williams won her first Grand Slam singles title when she defeated the top-seeded Martina Hingis in the finals of the U.S. Open, and Andre Agassi, who lost in the Wimbledon final to Sampras, won the French Open and the U.S. Open. The French Open victory made Agassi only the fifth man ever to win all four Grand Slam tennis championships, and the first since Rod Laver in 1969. Agassi was also the first man to win Grand Slam championships on all three tennis surfaces: grass, clay, and hard court. Although he and Sampras had dominated the sport in the early 1990s, by 1997 Agassi dropped to number 141 in the world rankings, and his career appeared to be in irreparable decline. After his divorce from the model/actress Brooke Shields in early 1999, however, Agassi began to win tournaments again, and at the end of the year, he was ranked first in the world. His achievements in 1999 were considered the most impressive comeback in the history of men's tennis. Steffi Graf, who won 22 Grand Slam events during her career, including all four championships in 1988 and an Olympic gold medal, retired after 17 years on the women's tour. (Graf, regarded by many as the best female tennis player in the history of the sport, married Agassi in 2001.)

Juli Inkster became the second woman in modern times to win all four major tournaments sponsored by the Ladies Professional Golf Association. At age 23, Tiger Woods became the youngest player to win two major tournaments when he defeated the Spaniard Sergio Garcia by one stroke to capture the men's Professional Golfers Association (PGA) championship. Woods also won the World Golf Championship in Sotogrande, Spain, giving him the most successful season of any PGA player in 25 years. The U.S. cyclist Lance Armstrong overcame life-threatening testicular cancer to win the Tour de France bicycle race, and the U.S. women's team won the World Cup in soccer.

Andre Agassi became the first man since Rod Laver in 1969 to win all four Grand Slam tennis events. *(Photofest)*

CHRONICLE OF EVENTS

January 1: The European Union (EU) introduces the euro as its currency in 11 participating nations.

January 1: Vice President Al Gore announces that he will run for the Democratic presidential nomination in 2000.

January 4: A federal jury awards $10 million in damages to a woman who claims she has been injured by silicone breast implants.

January 6: The United States confirms media reports and Iraqi accusations that the United States has used the UN weapons inspection program to spy on Iraq. According to U.S. and UN officials, U.S. agents have worked with UN Special Commission (UNSCOM) inspectors for almost three years on "Operation Shake the Tree," monitoring radio transmissions from the military and intelligence forces that guard Saddam Hussein. British and Israeli personnel reportedly have helped interpret the data.

January 6: The House elects Dennis Hastert, an Illinois Republican, to replace Newt Gingrich as Speaker.

January 7: Chief Justice William Rehnquist opens President Clinton's impeachment trial before the U.S. Senate.

January 11–25: The United States and Iraq clash over the no-fly zones in the southern and northern parts of the country. On January 25, a U.S. missile strikes civilian sites near Basra in southeastern Iraq.

January 11: The State Department reports that, according to sources from the Iraqi opposition, Saddam Hussein's regime has executed approximately 500 military officers suspected of disloyalty.

January 12: Clinton pays Paula Jones $850,000 as the final settlement of her lawsuit for sexual harassment.

January 13: The Chicago Bulls basketball star Michael Jordan, considered by many the best player in NBA history, announces his retirement.

January 14–21: The Senate hears opening presentations of both sides in Clinton's impeachment trial. Acting as prosecuting attorneys, the House managers, led by the Republican Henry Hyde of Illinois, argue that Clinton should be removed from office because he lied under oath and obstructed justice in the Paula Jones lawsuit. Clinton's lawyers maintain that these charges are untrue and are based on a one-sided interpretation of unsubstantiated testimony and circumstantial evidence. They further maintain that, even if true, the claims do not merit impeachment because they do not threaten the U.S. system of democracy or render him unfit for office.

January 15: Serbian troops kill 45 ethnic Albanian civilians in Kosovo. The Security Council condemns the killings the next day.

January 19: Clinton delivers his State of the Union address, calling for stronger programs for retirees and for investment of the budget surplus to "save" Social Security, whose funds are projected to be depleted by 2032.

January 22: The Defense Department announces that the number of military personnel discharged as homosexuals rose in 1998 to 1,145—nearly double the number in 1993, the year before the "Don't ask; don't tell" policy went into effect.

January 22: Pope John Paul II visits Mexico and the United States.

January 26: King Hussein of Jordan changes the line of succession, replacing his brother as heir apparent with his oldest son, Prince Abdullah. Hussein then flies to the Mayo Clinic in Rochester, Minnesota, for treatment of a recurrence of cancer.

January 29: Stating that the claim had been filed in the wrong county, a Florida state appeals court vacates a 1998 verdict in which a jury awarded $1 million in punitive damages against the Brown & Williamson Tobacco Corporation.

January 30: NATO authorizes air strikes against Serbia if it does not attend peace talks or arrive at a peaceful settlement to the conflict in Kosovo.

February 1: House manager Ed Bryant of Tennessee deposes Lewinsky for the impeachment trial.

February 2: House manager Asa Hutchinson of Arkansas deposes Clinton's friend and adviser Vernon Jordan, Jr., for the impeachment trial.

February 2: A civil jury in Portland, Oregon, finds against the creators of an antiabortion Web site that has "wanted" posters that include the names of abortion providers. The jury agrees that the posters amount to a hit list that threatens potentially lethal violence, and it awards $107 million in damages to the Planned Parenthood Foundation of America and a group of doctors.

February 3: House managers James Rogan of California and Lindsey Graham of South Carolina depose the White House aide Sidney Blumenthal for the impeachment trial.

February 3: The former vice president Dan Quayle announces his candidacy for the Republican nomination for president.

February 3: House minority leader Dick Gephardt of Missouri announces that he will not seek the Democratic nomination for president.

February 4: Germany's largest bank, Deutsche Bank AG, admits that it helped finance the Nazi regime's construction of the World War II death camp at Auschwitz, Poland.

February 4: The Senate votes against calling witnesses to testify in the impeachment trial but allows the House managers to present videotaped depositions by Monica Lewinsky, Vernon Jordan, and Sidney Blumenthal.

February 4: Quebec declines to sign the "Framework to Improve the Social Union for Canadians," which the other nine Canadian provinces endorse.

February 5: The NBA opens its 53rd season, after a 204-day player lockout by management.

February 6: The Senate views excerpts from the videotaped depositions of Lewinsky, Jordan, and Blumenthal.

February 7: King Hussein of Jordan dies. He is succeeded by his 37-year-old son, Abdullah.

February 10: A California jury awards a former smoker who has inoperable lung cancer $50 million in damages in a suit filed against the Philip Morris Company, the nation's largest tobacco company.

February 10: Vice President Al Gore announces that reading scores for elementary and secondary school children have improved since 1994.

February 11: The Arkansas Supreme Court rules that David Hale is not protected against state charges related to the Whitewater affair. Hale, who has accused Clinton of being a party to a fraudulent loan, has received immunity from prosecution in the federal Whitewater investigation headed by Starr.

February 12: The Senate acquits Clinton of the impeachment charges. It votes 55-45 against the charge of perjury and 50-50 on the charge that Clinton has obstructed justice during the investigation.

February 12: Germany creates a fund to compensate Nazi-era prisoners who were used as slave laborers in German companies before and during World War II.

February 18: Senator Robert Smith of New Hampshire announces his candidacy for the Republican presidential nomination.

February 26: Henry J. Lyons, president of the National Baptist Convention USA, is convicted in Largo, Florida, on charges that he stole money that had been donated to the organization, one of the leading black denominations in the United States.

March 4: A military court-martial jury acquits the marine captain Richard Ashby of involuntary manslaughter in the 1998 accident in which Ashby's jet severed the cables on a ski lift in the Italian Alps, killing 20 people. Italians are outraged by the acquittal.

March 6: The *New York Times* reports that during the 1980s, China obtained secret information from the Los Alamos National Laboratory that enabled it to develop nuclear warheads. On March 8, the department of energy fires the scientist Wen Ho Lee, who is suspected of complicity.

March 8: Baseball star Joe DiMaggio, who led the New York Yankees to nine World Series between 1936 and 1951, dies at age 84.

March 9: Former Tennessee governor Lamar Alexander announces his candidacy for the Republican presidential nomination in 2000.

March 10: Former secretary of labor and secretary of transportation Elizabeth Dole, wife of the Republican presidential nominee in 1996, establishes an exploratory committee to consider her candidacy for the 2000 Republican nomination.

March 11: Kenneth Starr announces that he has asked the Justice Department to assume responsibility for an investigation of improper leaks from his office during his investigation of the Lewinsky scandal.

March 16: The businessman Malcolm (Steve) Forbes announces his candidacy for the Republican presidential nomination.

March 16: All 20 members of the EU's executive branch, known as the European Commission, resign a day after an independent panel reports allegations of widespread corruption and financial mismanagement.

March 17: A day after resigning as president of the National Baptist Convention USA, Lyons pleads guilty to federal fraud and tax evasion charges.

March 17: The NATO general Wesley Clark tells the House Armed Services Committee that Serbia is "prepared to resume the conflict on a very large scale" if peace talks with the Kosovo Liberation Army (KLA) fail. Other diplomats warn that Serbia appears to be preparing a major offensive against the KLA in southern Kosovo.

March 18: A federal judge rules that payments owed by U.S. telephone companies to Cuba can be paid to the families of four Cuban Americans shot down by Cuban jets in 1996. The families had been awarded $187 million in damages in 1997.

March 18: Ethnic Albanians sign a peace agreement intended to end the yearlong conflict between Serbia and the KLA. But Serbia rejects the agreement because it calls for stationing of 28,000 peacekeepers in Kosovo.

March 20: International observers who are monitoring the cease-fire in Kosovo leave the region because intensified violence prevents them from doing their job. Serbia launches a new offensive in the Drenica region of Kosovo, driving 40,000 to 50,000 ethnic Albanians from their home.

March 24: Led by the United States, NATO initiates an air campaign against Serbia in response to continuing violence against ethnic Albanians in Kosovo.

March 26: The Security Council rejects a Russian-sponsored resolution to end the air campaign against Serbia and seek a diplomatic solution.

March 26: A Michigan jury convicts Dr. Jack Kevorkian of second-degree murder for the 1998 killing of Thomas Youk, a terminally ill man suffering from Lou Gehrig's disease. Youk had signed a form consenting to the killing, which Kevorkian videotaped and broadcast in 1998 on the news show *60 Minutes.*

March 26: A state jury in Arkansas convicts the Whitewater figure and Clinton accuser David Hale of lying to state regulators.

March 28: Fidel Castro and some 50,000 fans attend the first game played in Cuba by a U.S. professional baseball team since March 1959. The Baltimore Orioles defeat the All-Star Cuban team in extra innings by a score of 3-2.

March 29–30: The United States and North Korea make no significant progress during talks concerning North Korea's missile program.

March 29: The Dow-Jones industrial average closes above 10,000 for the first time when it ends the day at 10,006.78.

March 30: NATO expands the scope of its air campaign against Serbia to include targeting government ministries and military facilities in downtown Belgrade, Serbia's capital.

March 30: An Oregon jury holds the Philip Morris Tobacco Company liable for the death of a long-time cigarette smoker and awards $79.5 million in punitive damages to the deceased man's family, the largest award ever ordered for a smoking-related lawsuit.

April 2: U.S. and British jets resume bombing targets in Iraq, ending a suspension of air raids that began on March 17.

April 4–6: Christians and Muslims clash in the West Bank city of Nazareth on Easter Sunday as a result of Christian fears that a planned mosque will overshadow the Church of the Annunciation.

April 8: Iraq rejects UN recommendations for ending the stalemate over weapons inspections. Iraq further demands that economic sanctions be removed.

April 8: Secret Serbian documents indicating that Serbia had begun planning in November 1998 to initiate a program of ethnic cleansing in Kosovo are leaked to the German government.

April 11: India tests an intermediate-range ballistic missile capable of carrying a nuclear warhead.

April 12: A federal judge in Arkansas holds Clinton in contempt of court for giving "intentionally false" testimony in the Paula Jones sexual harassment lawsuit.

April 13: NATO initiates what Clinton calls "a more intense version of the current phase" of its air campaign against Serbia. NATO, which has been criticized for restricting information, releases to the public its most detailed assessment of the air campaign to date. The assessment concludes that although all branches of the Serbian military have been damaged, Miloševič does not appear any closer to surrendering.

April 14–15: Pakistan tests two missiles capable of carrying nuclear warheads.

April 14: NATO planes attack oil production facilities, air defenses, Serbian troops, command and control centers, and supply routes in Belgrade.

April 14: The independent counsel Kenneth Starr confounds many when he testifies that he opposes renewal of the 1978 law that allows for the appointment of independent counsels.

April 20: Two students at Columbine High School in Littleton, Colorado, use rifles and homemade bombs to kill 13 students and teachers and wound more than 30 during a half-hour killing spree. The attack ends when the students, the 18-year-old Eric Harris and the 17-year-old Dylan Klebold, commit suicide.

April 22: Russell Weston, Jr., who killed two Capitol Police officers during an attack on the U.S. Capitol building in July 1998, is ruled mentally incompetent to stand trial.

April 26: Set to strike on the 13th anniversary of the meltdown of the Soviet nuclear reactor at Chernobyl, the so-called Chernobyl virus corrupts more than 1 million computers worldwide. A recent college graduate in Taiwan is believed to be responsible.

April 27: Robyn Anderson, the 18-year-old girlfriend of Dylan Klebold, admits she provided two shotguns and a rifle used in the Columbine attack.

May 1: At the urging of the U.S. civil rights leader the Reverend Jesse Jackson, Milošević releases three captured U.S. soldiers.

May 1: Some 8,000 demonstrators protest the NRA convention in Denver.

May 3: Police arrest a recent graduate of Columbine High School on charges that he provided one of the guns used in the deadly attack on April 20.

May 3: Approximately 76 tornadoes kill at least 47 people, injure 700, and damage 2,000 homes when they strike Oklahoma, Kansas, Nebraska, Texas, and South Dakota. Eleven counties in Oklahoma and one in Kansas are declared disaster areas. Outside Oklahoma City, the largest tornado, estimated to be a mile wide, is the most powerful and most destructive on record.

May 5–6: The same storm system that spawned the devastating Midwest tornadoes two days earlier produces thunderstorms and high winds that kill four people in Tennessee.

May 7: Working from outdated maps of Belgrade, NATO planes mistakenly bomb the Chinese embassy, killing three Chinese citizens and sparking massive protests throughout China. Protesting before the Security Council, China calls the attack a "barbaric" violation of the UN Charter.

May 8: Clinton and NATO secretary-general Javier Solana apologize for the unintentional bombing of the Chinese embassy.

May 12: Treasury secretary Robert Rubin, widely credited as the architect of Clinton's economic policy, announces he will resign effective July 4.

May 12: One day before the Communist Party–dominated parliament is scheduled to debate a motion to impeach President Boris Yeltsin, he fires Premier Yevgeny Primakov, the third premier he has fired in 14 months. In response, the parliament votes

243-20 in favor of a nonbinding resolution calling for the ailing Yeltsin's resignation.

May 17: Israeli voters elect Labor Party leader Ehud Barak as prime minister.

May 24: The World Health Organization votes to delay destroying the last known samples of the smallpox virus until 2002 to give researchers time to develop vaccinations and treatments in the event of a new outbreak.

May 25: Sergei Khrushchev announces his plan to become a U.S. citizen. His father, Nikita Khrushchev, headed the Soviet Union during the height of the cold war.

May 26–June 10: India initiates a series of air strikes on Islamic militants in the disputed region of Kashmir.

May 27: The Senate Web site is shut down after a computer hacker breaks into the system and publishes an obscene message.

June 1: Nine people die when an American Airlines airplane crashes in heavy weather on the airport runway in Little Rock, Arkansas.

June 2: Twenty American Indian tribes file suit against the four largest U.S. tobacco companies, claiming that they have been unfairly excluded from a November 1998 settlement between the companies and 46 states.

June 2: South Africa's ruling African National Congress (ANC) overwhelmingly wins the nation's second multiracial democratic election.

June 3: Milošević and the Serbian parliament accept a peace agreement that will end NATO's 10-week bombing campaign.

June 4: First Lady Hillary Rodham Clinton announces she will form a committee to consider whether she should run for the New York Senate seat being vacated by the Democratic senator Daniel Patrick Moynihan.

June 9: Serbia agrees to a NATO plan calling for it to withdraw all of its forces from Kosovo.

June 9: Clinton orders federal law enforcement agencies to collect data relevant to the practice of racial profiling.

June 12: Russian troops unexpectedly occupy the airport in Priština, the capital of Kosovo, hours before NATO peacekeepers arrive. The move complicates ongoing talks about Russia's role in the peacekeeping operation.

June 12: Texas governor George W. Bush initiates his campaign to secure the Republican nomination for president.

June 19: The popular horror-fiction author Stephen King suffers a broken hip, punctured lung, broken leg, and multiple broken ribs when a minivan strikes him as he is walking along a rural road near his home in Lovell, Maine.

June 20: NATO's air campaign against Serbia formally concludes after it verifies that Serbia has withdrawn all of its forces from Kosovo.

June 20: The Dallas Stars defeat the Buffalo Sabres to win hockey's Stanley Cup.

June 22: Senator Orrin Hatch of Utah announces his candidacy for the Republican presidential nomination.

June 25: The San Antonio Spurs defeat the New York Knicks to claim the NBA basketball championship.

June 30: Webster Hubbell, a longtime friend of President Clinton's, pleads guilty to making false statements to federal regulators and to tax evasion in the Whitewater case. Hubbell's pleas conclude the Whitewater proceedings.

June 30: The independent counsel law that authorized Starr's investigation of Clinton expires and is not renewed.

July 4–6: A heat wave envelops the East Coast, raising temperatures above 100 degrees Fahrenheit in New York and Washington, D.C. Power blackouts also occur throughout the region, and at least 31 New Yorkers die of heat-related causes.

July 5: NATO and Russia agree on Russia's role in the peacekeeping force in Kosovo.

July 6: The United States imposes economic sanctions on the Taliban regime in Afghanistan in response to the Taliban's harboring of Osama bin Laden, whom a U.S. jury has indicted for ordering the 1998 embassy bombings in Kenya and Tanzania.

July 16: John F. Kennedy, Jr.; his wife, Carolyn Bessette Kennedy; and her sister, Lauren Bessette, die when the small plane Kennedy is piloting crashes into the Atlantic Ocean near the Massachusetts island of Martha's Vineyard. Their bodies are recovered in the ocean on July 20 and early July 21, and they are buried at sea on July 22.

July 17: After the New York congressman Michael Forbes switches his affiliation from the Republican Party to the Democratic Party, the Republican major-

John F. Kennedy, Jr.; his wife, Carolyn Bessette Kennedy; and her sister, Lauren Bessette, perished when their small plane crashed into the Atlantic Ocean. *(Photofest)*

ity in the House drops to 222 Republicans, 211 Democrats, and one independent, who typically votes along with the Democrats.

July 20: The European Parliament, the legislative branch of the European Union, elects French delegate Nicole Fontaine as its president.

July 22: The Chinese government bans the Falun Gong spiritual movement after three days of protests of government harassment by Falun Gong members.

July 23: Fourteen Serbian farmers are massacred in Kosovo in the worst ethnic violence since the arrival of UN peacekeepers six weeks earlier.

July 23–25: Some 200,000 attend the Woodstock '99 concert in Rome, New York. The concert is marred by excessive heat and violence.

July 26: After driving Pakistani-backed rebels from the Indian sector of Kashmir, Indian military officials announce they are restoring the 1972 Line of Control, which divides the contested region.

July 29: A federal judge in Arkansas orders Clinton to pay approximately $89,000 in legal fees stemming from his "intentionally false testimony" in the Paula Jones civil lawsuit.

July 29: Mark Barton, a securities trader, kills nine coworkers and wounds 13 more before shooting himself in Atlanta. Barton killed his wife and two children earlier in the week.

July 30: A Maryland jury indicts Linda Tripp on wiretapping charges for her secret recordings of conversations with Monica Lewinsky.

August 9: Yeltsin fires Premier Sergei Stepashin less than three months after appointing him.

August 17: A powerful earthquake in northwestern Turkey kills up to 40,000 in cities near the Sea of Marmara and hundreds more as far west as Istanbul.

September 5: Barak and Arafat sign a pact aimed at reviving the stalled peace process. Egypt's president Hosni Mubarak, Jordan's king Abdullah II; and the U.S. secretary of state Madeleine Albright witness the signing.

September 6: An assailant is shot and killed in Port Said, Egypt, after attacking and slightly wounding Mubarak.

September 7: The strongest earthquake in 80 years strikes in and around Athens, Greece, killing scores of people and destroying or severely damaging more than 100 buildings.

September 7: The former secretary of housing and urban development Henry Cisneros concludes a four-year investigation by pleading guilty to one misdemeanor count of lying to the FBI about payments made to his mistress.

September 9: Multiple bombings kill almost 300 in Russia, including victims in apartment buildings and a shopping mall in Moscow. Chechen separatists are believed to be responsible.

September 14–17: Massive Hurricane Floyd passes over the Bahamas as a strong category 4 storm, and then, after threatening south Florida, turns north and makes landfall near Wilmington, North Carolina, before passing over Cape Hatteras, moving back out to sea, and then striking Rhode Island, Connecticut, and Massachusetts.

September 15: The 47-year-old Larry Ashbrook opens fire in a Baptist church in Fort Worth, Texas, killing seven and wounding seven, one of them fatally, before taking his own life. Ashbrook, who pauses in the midst of his assault to reload, uses a 9-mm semiautomatic handgun and a .380-caliber handgun. He fires three clips of ammunition inside the church.

September 22: The pilot episode of *West Wing* debuts on NBC.

September 23: Clinton vetoes legislation calling for massive tax cuts.

September 23: A Texas jury confers the death penalty on one of the men found guilty of chaining a black man to a pickup truck and dragging him to his death in 1998.

September 27: Quayle drops out of contention for the Republican presidential nomination.

September 27: Senator John McCain of Arizona announces his candidacy for the Republican presidential nomination.

September 28: Unable to meet its budget deadline, Congress passes a stopgap spending measure to keep the government running after 2000. Clinton signs the bill on September 30.

September 28: Clinton vetoes a spending bill for the District of Columbia because, he maintains, it contains unacceptable riders that would prevent local residents from deciding local matters.

September 29: Clinton signs legislation providing $21.3 billion for energy, water, and nuclear weapons programs. The bill omits a requested appropriation for $35 million to enhance computer security at Energy Department facilities.

September 30: A day after the release of a report in which a dozen U.S. Army veterans describe killing civilians at No Gun Ri, South Korea, during the

Martin Sheen starred as the president of the United States in *West Wing,* a fast-paced drama based on contemporary politics. *(Photofest)*

Korean War, Secretary of Defense William Cohen orders a new investigation of the incident, in which 100 to 200 South Korean civilians allegedly were killed over a three-day period in late July 1950.

October 2: Clinton, Arafat, and Barak meet in Oslo, Norway, to discuss the Middle East peace process.

October 4: The Supreme Court opens its 1999–2000 session with 44 cases on its docket.

October 7: In India Prime Minister Vajpayee easily retains power as Hindu Nationalists prevail in national elections.

October 8: A London court approves the extradition to Spain of the former Chilean military ruler General Augusto Pinochet.

October 11: The world's human population reaches 6 billion, according to projections by the UN's World Population Fund.

October 12: Military leaders depose Pakistan's prime minister Sharif in a bloodless coup.

October 13: By a vote of 48-51, the Senate refuses to ratify the Comprehensive Test Ban Treaty.

October 14: The Philip Morris Company, the largest U.S. tobacco producer, concedes for the first time that research has shown cigarette smoking is addictive and causes lung cancer and other potentially fatal diseases.

October 18: Starr resigns as independent counsel.

October 20: Elizabeth Dole drops out of the race for the 2000 Republican presidential nomination.

October 20: The city council of Charleston, South Carolina, becomes the first municipal body to designate the Ku Klux Klan as a terrorist organization.

October 20: An article in the November/December issue of *The Bulletin of the Atomic Scientists,* based on partially declassified Defense Department documents, reports that the United States secretly deployed approximately 12,000 nuclear weapons to 18 countries and nine territories during the height of the cold war. The article maintains that in 1954 Morocco became the first foreign country to house U.S. nuclear weapons.

October 21: Russian forces advance within six miles of Grozny, the capital of Chechnya.

October 21: Clinton signs a second continuing resolution to keep the federal government running in the absence of a budget appropriation bill.

October 25: Overcoming reservations about budget gimmicks and unnecessary spending, Clinton signs a $268 billion defense bill.

October 27: The New York Yankees sweep the Atlanta Braves in four games to win their 25th World Series.

October 31: All 217 people aboard an EgyptAir flight die when the plane crashes into the Atlantic Ocean shortly after departing from New York's John F. Kennedy International Airport. The FBI finds no evidence of sabotage.

November 2: A court in Cuba orders the U.S. government to pay Cuba $181 billion in compensatory and punitive damages resulting from effects of U.S. policies. The judgment is not enforceable, however.

November 14: The United Nations imposes economic sanctions on Afghanistan for its refusal to surrender Osama bin Laden to the United States.

November 17: A Michigan jury convicts the 13-year-old Nathaniel Abraham of second-degree murder for a crime he committed when he was 11. Abraham is the first person to be tried under the state's new juvenile justice law, which permits children of any age to be tried as adults.

November 17: The United Methodist Church defrocks a pastor for performing a wedding that violated the church's 1998 ban on homosexual marriages.

November 23: Hillary Clinton announces her candidacy for the Democratic nomination for the open U.S. Senate seat in New York.

November 25: Six-year-old Elián Gonzalez is rescued at sea on Thanksgiving Day, after his mother drowns while trying to escape from Cuba with him on a raft. Elián is taken to live with cousins in Miami, but in 2000 he becomes the central figure in an international incident after the fiercely anti-Castro cousins refuse to honor his father's demand that Elián be returned to Cuba to live with him. The situation climaxes on April 22, 2000, when armed federal agents forcibly seize Elián from his cousins' house and unite him with his father, who then returns to Cuba with his son.

November 30–December 3: The WTO meets in Seattle amid violent and destructive street protests by groups opposed to the corporate domination, repressive labor practices, and environmental degradation that they believe characterize the global economy.

December 1: A federal immigration court releases the 39-year-old Nasser Ahmed, an associate of the convicted terrorist Sheik Omar Abdel Rahman, after he has been held for three years in federal prison on secret evidence.

December 11: Pope John Paul II celebrates the conclusion of 20 years of restoration work on the Vatican's Sistine Chapel, which features famous frescoes by Michelangelo.

December 11: Huge demonstrations take place in Havana, Cuba, calling for the return of Elián Gonzalez.

December 12: The writer Joseph Heller, known as the author of *Catch-22* (1961) and other novels, dies at age 76 of heart failure.

December 14: In a ceremony headed by the former president Jimmy Carter, who signed the Panama Canal treaties in 1977, the United States formally passes control of the canal to Panama, which assumes operational control on December 31.

December 14: Customs officials arrest an Algerian-born man who is trying to smuggle more than 130 pounds of bomb-making material into the United States from Canada, presumably with the intention of using it for a terrorist attack against Americans celebrating the arrival of the new millennium. Ahmed Ressam is believed to have ties to al-Qaeda and to have attended Osama bin Laden's training facility in Afghanistan.

December 14: The State Department announces the arrest of 12 people in the Middle East suspected of planning attacks on U.S. targets on New Year's Eve. The suspects are alleged to have connections to bin Laden.

December 14: The German government and several major German corporations agree to establish a $5.1 billion fund to compensate people forced into slave labor by the Nazi regime during World War II.

December 15–16: Israel and Syria resume direct peace talks after a four-year hiatus.

December 16: A report issued by a UN panel faults the United Nations and major world powers, especially the United States, for failing to act to prevent the 1994 genocide in Rwanda.

December 17: The Security Council approves a new arms-monitoring system for Iraq, regarded as a first step for sending weapons inspectors back into the nation.

December 18: Iraq rejects the weapons-monitoring regime because the United Nations has retained its economic embargo and the no-fly zones over portions of Iraq.

December 19–27: A crew from the space shuttle *Discovery* repairs and replaces equipment aboard the *Hubble Space Telescope.*

December 24: Five men hijack an Indian passenger jet to Afghanistan and demand the release of imprisoned Kashmiri separatists. The hijacking crisis is resolved on December 31, when India frees three Pakistani militants.

December 31: Beset by economic and political woes, an ailing Yeltsin resigns as president of Russia. He names Premier Vladimir Putin acting president.

December 31: In its final issue of the millennium *Time* magazine names the atomic physicist Albert Einstein the "Person of the Century."

December 31: Extravagant fireworks displays and other gala celebrations greet the arrival of the new millennium at midnight, local time, throughout the world. Feared acts of terrorism and computer crashes at midnight caused by the so-called Y2K bug do not occur.

EYEWITNESS TESTIMONY

There are numerous incidents where the negotiation of a national past intersects with the challenge of multiculturalism. Curatorial debates at the Smithsonian over exhibitions such as the "West as America" (1991) and the Enola Gay (1995) both raised anger and protest at revisionist histories daring to present, respectively, the frontier experience as a question of capitalist exploitation, sexism, and genocide, and the Hiroshima bombing as one of several possible actions on the part of the U.S. government. As the self-appointed guardian of American memory, Steven Spielberg turned *Schindler's List* (1993), *Amistad* (1997), and *Saving Private Ryan* (1998) into cultural master memories, humanist dramas infused with themes of redemption and collective (national) remembrance. . . . In different ways, these indicate the negotiation, representation, and battles of ownership fought over common national memory.

> *Film scholar Paul Grainge commenting on the politicization of American history throughout the 1990s, in Grainge,* Monochrome Memories: Nostalgia and Style in Retro America *(2002), p. 9.*

We have got to stop acting like partisan senators and act like jurors.

> *Republican senator Ted Stevens complaining on January 7, 1999, about the partisan nature of Clinton's impeachment proceedings, in Marion Farrier, editor in chief,* Facts On File Yearbook 1999 *(2000), p. 3.*

We knew a hell of a lot of information about presidential security. . . . Saddam's personal security apparatus and the apparatus that conceals weapons of mass destruction are one and the same.

> *Weapons inspector Scott Ritter on January 7, 1999, admitting in the* Boston Globe *that UN weapons inspectors in Iraq gathered military intelligence for the United States, in Martin McLaughlin, "UN Inspectors in Iraq Helped Spy for the CIA," January 7, 1999. Available Online. URL: http:// www.wsws.org/articles/1999/ jan1999/iraq-j07.shtml.*

The secretary-general [of the United Nations] has become aware of the fact that UNSCOM directly facilitated the creation of an intelligence collection system for the United States in violation of its mandate. The United Nations cannot be party to an operation to overthrow one of its member states. In the most fundamental way, that is what's wrong with the UNSCOM operation.

> *An anonymous source close to UN secretary-general Kofi Annan describing in the* Washington Post *on January 7, 1999, Annan's response to revelations that UN weapons inspectors in Iraq (UNSCOM) were giving military intelligence to the United States, in Martin McLaughlin, "UN Inspectors in Iraq Helped Spy for the CIA," January 7, 1999. Available Online. URL: http://www.wsws.org/articles/1999/jan1999/iraq-j07.shtml.*

The President's tenure of office would have been less secure [if the Senate had convicted President Andrew Johnson]. . . . I don't think there would have been a lot more impeachments. But the congressional authority to impeach would have acted more like a Sword of Damocles designed not to fall, but to hang, and to threaten the president.

And I think that any time that a president of one party confronted a congress, controlled by large majorities of the opposite party, it wouldn't be just the usual weapons with which Congress and the president fence with one another—you know, vetoes, and overrides, and insertions and appropriation bills, and withholding of appropriated funds.

You know, the president and Congress have been fencing with one another for a long time with those various weapons. But Congress would then have an additional weapon in its arsenal, which would be the threat of impeachment.

> *Chief Justice William Rehnquist discussing on January 13, 1999, the possible long-term consequences that might have ensued had the Senate convicted President Andrew Johnson on articles of impeachment in 1868, in "Mr. Chief Justice,"* The Newshour with Jim Lehrer, *January 22, 1997. Available online. URL: http://www.pbs.org/newshour/bb/congress/jan-june99/rehnquist_1-13.html.*

I want to say again to the American people how profoundly sorry I am for what I said and did to trigger these events and the great burden they have imposed on the Congress and on the American people. . . . This

Chief Justice William Rehnquist presided over the Senate trial that acquitted President Bill Clinton on all four articles of impeachment. *(AP/Wide World Photos)*

can be and this must be a time of reconciliation and renewal for America.

President Bill Clinton addressing the nation on February 12, 1999, after his acquittal by the Senate of all charges of impeachment, in James Bennet and John M. Broder, "President Says He Is Sorry and Seeks Reconciliation," New York Times, February 13, 1999, p. 1.

I don't think indicting and criminally trying him [Clinton], after what we have all been through, is going to be helpful to the country. I think we should try to find areas we can agree on and get some legislation passed....

We felt if the story were told coherently, chronologically, that maybe the public would focus on it and move from its total indifference to concern. That hope was unrequited.

Representative Henry Hyde, chairman of the House Judiciary Committee, commenting on the Senate votes of February 12, 1999, to acquit President Clinton of the charges of impeachment, in Lizette Alvarez, "A Dispirited Hyde Opposes Indicting Clinton," New York Times, February 13, 1999, p. 1.

I underwent the sort of culture shock that naturally occurs when one moves from the very structured environment of the Supreme Court to what I shall call, for want of a better phrase, the more free-form environment of the Senate....

I leave you now a wiser, but not a sadder man. I have been impressed by the manner in which the majority leader and the minority leader have agreed on procedural rules in spite of the differences that separate their two parties on matters of substance. I have been impressed by the quality of debate in closed session on the entire question of impeachment as provided for in the Constitution.

Chief Justice William Rehnquist describing his experience presiding over the Senate impeachment trial of President Bill Clinton, in "The President's Acquittal: The Chief Justice: Rehnquist Goes with the Senate Flow: 'Wiser, but Not a Sadder Man,'" New York Times, February 13, 1999, p. 12A.

We act to prevent a wider war, to defuse a powder keg at the heart of Europe that has exploded twice before in this century with catastrophic results. . . .

President Milošević, who over the past decade started the terrible wars against Croatia and Bosnia, has again chosen aggression over peace. He has violated the commitments that he himself made last fall to stop the brutal repression in Kosovo.

President Bill Clinton announcing on March 24, 1999, that U.S.-led NATO forces had begun an air campaign against Serbia, in Francis X. Clines, "Missiles Rock Kosovo Capital, Belgrade and Other Sites," New York Times, March 25, 1999, p. 1.

Forty years, we've been waiting for this. It is a big moment. I wish it happened a long time ago, but who am I?

A Cuban baseball fan describing his enthusiasm for an exhibition game played in Havana on March 28, 1999, between the Cuban All-Stars and the Baltimore Orioles in "Cubans Came Close, but No Cigar in Revolutionary Game in Cuba," March 28, 1999. Available online. URL: http://www. latinosportslegends.com/ Cuba_vs_Orioles-game1.htm.

They had this all laid down to times, 11.15 am, 11.20 am or whatever, that they were going to go in and then it's rock 'n' roll time. . . . They were monitoring the lunchroom. It was very intentional, the timing of this. They wanted to do as much damage as they could possibly do and destroy as many children as they could, to go out in flames. They expected to die. . . . They were going for a big kill. . . .

The diary goes back one year. The timeline stretches to the day this all happened. It was very intentional, the timing of this thing. They've been building bombs for a considerable period of time. . . .

It was Hitler's birthday. That appears to be [the reason for conducting the massacre on April 20]. . . .

A barrel that they cut off one of the sawed-off shotguns was clearly visible lying on the dresser in one of the rooms. A lot of this was clearly visible. The parents should have been aware of it. I think I would be a little concerned about my son's room if I went in there and I found sawed-off shotgun barrels. . . .

There are other people involved in this. I have been concerned all along there was too much weaponry, too many bombs, placed in there for it being physically possible for two people to carry in that morning.

The Jefferson County, Colorado, sheriff, John Stone, commenting on April 23, 1999, about diary entries describing preparations made by Eric Harris and Dylan Klebold for massacring fellow students at Columbine High School on April 20, 1999, in "Killer's Diary Surfaces Entries Detail a Full Year of Planning." Available online. URL: http://massmurder.zyns.com/ eric_harris_dylan_klebold_04.html.

I'm full of hate and I love it. I HATE PEOPLE, and they better fucking fear me if they know what's good for 'em. . . .

Who can I trick into my room first? I can sweep someone off their feet, tell them what they want to hear, be all nice and sweet, and then "f__k 'em like an animal, feel them from the inside," as Reznor said [referring to Trent Reznor of the band Nine Inch Nails]. . . .

Today, along with Vodka [nickname of Dylan Klebold] and someone else who I won't name, we went downtown [to a gun show] and purchased the following; a double barrel 12 ga. shotgun, a pump action 12 ga. shotgun, a 9 mm carbine, 250 9 mm rounds, 15 12-ga. slugs, 40 shotgun shells, 2 switch blade knives, and a total of 4 10-round clips for the carbine . . . we . . . have. . . . GUNS! We f__ing got em you sons of bitches! HA!! HAHAHA! . . .

[If they eluded police after attacking the high school, they would set bombs] around houses, roads, bridges, buildings and gas stations, anything that will cause damage and chaos. . . . It'll be like the LA riots, the oklahoma bombing, WWII, vietnam, duke and doom all mixed together. . . . I want to leave a lasting impression on the world. . . .

If by some weird as shitt luck my and V survive and escape we will move to some island somewhere or maybe mexico, new zelend or some exotic place where americans cant get us. if there isnt such a place, then we will hijack a hell of a lot of bombs and crash a plane into NYC with us inside iring away as we go down. [spellings are Harris's]

Excerpts from Eric Harris's diary entries leading up to the April 20, 1999, Columbine High School massacre, released April 23, 1999, in "Columbine Killer Envisioned Crashing Plane in NYC," December 6, 2001. Available online. URL: http://www.cnn.com/ 2001/US/12/05/columbine.diary.

The community is in shock. Families and neighbors huddle together and, in my neighborhood at least, avoid the media events as much as possible. Everyone has some connection with at least one victim. . . . The more we learn, the more incredulous we become. This is a neighborhood of conservatives, staunch supporters of law enforcement, but everyone I talk to is stunned by the indifference or incompetence of our supposed protectors. . . .

Everyone I talk to also finds the media hype contemptible. There are constant interviews with Wellington Webb, the mayor of Denver, and with the mayor of Littleton. What do they have to do with anything? The attempts by some reporters to wheedle the kids and the victims' parents into calling for more gun control are particularly despicable. . . .

The cultural elite is using our own tragedy to thrash us soundly. Televisions and newspapers echo with the causes of the carnage all failures of us Coloradans: Lack of gun control, insufficient number of mental health workers, meanness of jocks. The cultural elite sense this is a golden opportunity, much like the Oklahoma City bombing. . . . And if all kids had to periodically see government mental health workers, think what influence they would have. Not to mention that the elites, or at least many of their friends, would have a lot more well-paying government jobs.

And so the choruses of trendy ideas ring out: Gun rights are indefensible in the wake of slaughter. Promoting athletics in schools is archaic; it increases testosterone, adrenaline, and self-confidence, making jocks more independent and less likely to submit to community goals. . . . (The shooters are said to be targeting athletes and minorities, but the media utterly separate those groups: The minorities are the lambs, the athletes goats.)

Dale Anema, father of a boy who was present at the massacre at Columbine High School in Littleton, Colorado, on April 20, 1999, railing against liberal responses to the tragedy, in James Haley, ed., Post–Cold War America: 1992–Present *(2003), pp. 143–144.*

On the way down to the storm, pessimism ran rampant that we could possibly see no tornadoes. Little did we know the show was barely starting . . . and that the most destruction ever visited upon the state of Oklahoma was about to occur. Scientific analysis and observation would give way to amazement, then awe,

then the sobering realization of human carnage, frustration . . . then finally, numb exhaustion.

Between Blanchard and Ninnekah, we made a few bad road decisions, but still managed to get within view of the storm's updraft by the time we were [east] of Ninnekah. . . . It was a large, circular, visibly rotating updraft area with very wide separation between the main updraft region and the precipitation of the vault and forward flank regions. Physical concepts of storm-type evolution were being slam-dunked by this rare, spectacular exception! Storm-relative "anvil-level" flow obviously wasn't representing the tremendous downshear precipitation, separation and venting which we were observing under the equilibrium level. The seeding influence from other anvils wasn't mattering either, despite our storm's entrapment in the anvil of the one farther [west]. . . .

By the time we could see under the base . . . there was already a furiously whirling wall cloud; and wispy tendrils of cloud material were beginning to dance along the ground beneath. Tornado! And the first of many to come.

The next few hours would give us, by far, the most productive storm intercept ever in our 13 concurrent years of it: the most tornadoes, the greatest variety of tornado shapes and sizes, the most violent and destructive (Bridge Creek, F5 damage, $750 million and counting), and perhaps the biggest (Abell/Mulhall, up to 1.5 miles wide, rivaling Rich's Allison tornado on 8 June 1995). The tally: 11 tornadoes, 2 after dark, 2 violent wedges, at least 4 multiple-vortex tornadoes, and 3 separate times when two tornadoes were observed simultaneously.

Storm chaser Roger Edwards's description of the tornado system that devastated parts of Oklahoma on May 3, 1999, in Edwards, "Central Oklahoma Tornado Intercept: 3 May 1999." Available online. URL: http://webserv.chatsystems.com/~tornado/3may99.

On a hot summer afternoon in August 1998, 37-year-old U.S. Army Sergeant First Class Rossano V. Gerald and his young son Gregory drove across the Oklahoma border into a nightmare. A career soldier and a highly decorated veteran of Desert Storm and Operation United Shield in Somalia, SFC Gerald, a black man of Panamanian descent, found that he could not travel more than 30 minutes through the state without being stopped twice: first by the Roland City Police Department, and then by the Oklahoma Highway Patrol.

During the second stop, which lasted two-and-half hours, the troopers terrorized SFC Gerald's 12-year-old son with a police dog, placed both father and son in a closed car with the air conditioning off and fans blowing hot air, and warned that the dog would attack if they attempted to escape. Halfway through the episode—perhaps realizing the extent of their lawlessness—the troopers shut off the patrol car's video evidence camera. . . .

How did it come to be, then, that . . . SFC Gerald found himself standing on the side of a dusty road next to a barking police dog, listening to his son weep while officers rummaged through his belongings simply because he was black? . . .

Significant blame for this rampant abuse of power also can be laid at the feet of the government's "war on drugs," a fundamentally misguided crusade enthusiastically embraced by lawmakers and administrations of both parties at every level of government. From the outset, the war on drugs has in fact been a war on people and their constitutional rights, with African Americans, Latinos and other minorities bearing the brunt of the damage.

Law professor David A. Harris writing in June 1999 about racial profiling in the United States in a special report for the American Civil Liberties Union, in Harris, "Driving While Black: Racial Profiling on Our Nation's Highways" (1999). Available online. URL: http://www.klas-tv.com/Global/story.asp?S=1113071&nav=168bDlBn.

The other canard about [Tennessee] Williams and [Arthur] Miller is that where the former is supposedly an apolitical writer, concerned only with poetic dialogue and psychologically deep characters, the latter is . . . about social problems. The *Nightingales* production revealed the depth of Williams' social conscience, but social commentary is not absent in his later plays. Consider Tom's bitter remarks in *Glass Menagerie* on the Depression, the rise of Fascism, Guernica. . . . Conversely, a fiftieth-anniversary production of Miller's *Death of a Salesman*, running on Broadway concurrently with the Williams piece, was a stimulus to rethink Miller's reputation as a left-wing propagandist.

Death of a Salesman bears no resemblance to left-wing literature of the thirties. Willy is no proletarian hero; not only is he not in the working class, but he lacks the naive idealism, the burning sense of injustice

combined with the longing for a better world. . . . Willy loves the capitalist system. . . . No one in the play, least of all Willy himself, suggests that his problems would be swept away by a revolution.

The capitalist system, then, is not the problem in *Salesman*, but rather Willy's understanding of it.

Theater critic Richard Hornby reviewing the revivals of Tennessee Williams's Nightingales *and Arthur Miller's* Death of a Salesman, *in Hornby, "Forty-Second Street,"* Hudson Review, *Summer 1999, p. 285.*

I don't know if these kids haven't been raised to have pride in themselves, but I've just never seen that kind of anger [in an audience]. I think the implications of it are more than it just being about kids coming together for the weekend for a rock show. I think it's how they feel about their situation, and my question is, "What made them so mad?" I just thought it was very demoralizing. I would absolutely not play Woodstock again. . . .

The pay-per-view cameras were on the naked women three-fourths of the time and only showing music one-fourth of the time. I've never watched TV and saw so many women completely nude and dancing in front of the camera. . . . [The four charges of sexual assault] seems like a low number. There were topless girls on guys' shoulders who were constantly being groped. These kids were out of control. . . .

I also had a sense of conflicting feelings. You had these women who were being groped, and they were doing nothing to stop it. And you had women, porn-shaven, dancing for the camera. . . . The message that was coming across in the music was self-loathing, and that's what the kids were there to hear. . . . From watching on TV, I kept thinking there had to be deaths and rapes, and if there were only four [rapes], that's incredible.

Singer Sheryl Crow describing the anger of the crowd at Woodstock '99, July 23–25, 1999, in Larry Flick, Carla Hay, Melinda Newman, and Chris Morris, "In Woodstock's Wake, Hard Questions" (1999); in James Haley, ed., Post–Cold War America: 1992–Present *(2003), p. 154.*

The contents of this exhibition may cause shock, vomiting, confusion, panic, euphoria, and anxiety. If you suffer from high blood pressure, a nervous disor-

Anger and violence abounded at the Woodstock '99 rock festival in Rome, New York. *(AP/Wide World Photos)*

der, or palpitations, you should consult your doctor before viewing this exhibition.

> *From a poster warning potential viewers of "Sensation: Young British Artists from the Saatchi Collection," which opened at the Brooklyn Museum of Art on September 27, 1999, in Marc Oxoby,* The 1990s *(2003), pp. 234–235.*

Most harmful of all is the message that Microsoft's actions have conveyed to every enterprise with the potential to innovate in the computer industry. . . . Through its conduct Microsoft has demonstrated that it will use its prodigious market power to harm any firm that insists on pursuing initiatives that could intensify competition against one of Microsoft's core products.

> *The federal district court Judge Thomas Penfield Jackson ruling on November 5, 1999, that Microsoft exercised a monopoly in the computer industry, in Joel Brinkley, "U.S. Judge Declares That Microsoft Is a Market-Stifling Monopoly: Gates Retains Defiant Stance,"* New York Times, *November 6, 1999, p. 1.*

If we commit ourselves to this [rehabilitation], we can ensure our safety now and in the future. The safety net of a delayed sentence removes too much of the urgency. We can't continue to see incarceration in adult prison as a long-term solution. The danger is that we won't take rehabilitation seriously if we know we can utilize prison in the future. To sentence juveniles to adult prison is ignoring the possibility that we are creating a more dangerous criminal by housing juveniles with hardened adults.

> *Judge Eugene Moore announcing his decision on January 13, 2000, to sentence the 13-year-old Nathaniel Abraham to the custody of the juvenile system and placement at boys' training school, upon his conviction on November 17, 1999, of second-degree murder, in "Kids and Crime,"* The Newshour with Jim Lehrer, *January 14, 2000. Available online. URL: http://www.pbs.org/ newshour/bb/youth/jan-june00/ kids_crime_1-14.html.*

Well, I think the judge missed a prime opportunity to do some good. He had an opportunity to transform this young man from a bad situation into a better situation. And he's actually giving some trust to a system that's been derelict in its duties for so very long to improve itself within eight years. I don't have that kind of confidence. And I think that he should have given him a blended sentence. . . .

Our criminal justice system has really been derelict in its duties for setting up a system where young men have to answer and be accountable. I think that the judge could have transformed him by putting him into a blended sentence, giving us the opportunity—and I agree with Mr. [James] Fox, that the system right now as it is situated, the old system, the adult system, would not be able to rehabilitate this

young man. And I'm not calling for that. But I am calling for something better, something different. Even a boot camp situation would have been better than what the judge has given him in detention.

Law professor Linda Collier discussing the sentencing on January 13, 2000, of the 13-year-old Nathaniel Abraham, who, on November 17, 1999, became the youngest American to be tried and convicted as an adult for a murder, in "Kids and Crime," The Newshour with Jim Lehrer, January 14, 2000. Available online. URL: http://www.pbs.org/newshour/bb/youth/ jan-june00/kids_crime_1-14.html.

Professor Solanka made the mistake of flipping briefly to CNN, where it was all Elián, all the time. . . . A little boy had been rescued from a rubber ring in the

Celebrants in New York City joined millions around the world who welcomed the 21st century. *(AP/Wide World Photos)*

sea, his mother drowned, and at once the religious hysteria had begun. The dead mother became almost a Marian figure and there were posters reading ELIÁN, SAVE US. The cult, born of Miami's necessary demonology—according to which Castro the devil, Hannibal-the-Cannibal Castro, would eat the boy alive, would tear out his immortal soul and munch it down with a few fava beans and a glass of red wine—instantly developed a priesthood as well. The dreadful media-fixated uncle was anointed pope of Eliánismo, and his daughter, poor Marisleysis, with her "nervous exhaustion," was exactly the type who would, any day now, start witnessing the seven-year-old's first miracles. . . . Meanwhile in Cuba, the little boy was being transformed into quite another totem. A dying revolution, a revolution of the old and straggle-bearded, held the child up as proof of its renewed youth. In this version, Elián rising from the waters became an image of the revolution's immortality: a lie.

Fictional character Professor Malik Solanka's ruminations on public response to the rescue on November 25, 1999, of the six-year-old Cuban refugee Elián Gonzalez, in Salman Rushdie's novel Fury *(2001), p. 137.*

Early in December 1999, the head of CIA's Counterterrorism Center, Cofer Black, called. "We have to go to battle stations. . . . This is the real deal. . . . Jordan infiltrated a cell, planning lots of bang-bang for New Year's. The Radisson Hotel, Christian tourist sites, lots of dead Americans. Deal is, Dick, I don't think this is it. You know bin Laden, he likes attacks in multiple locations. They're like cockroaches. You see one, but you know that means there's a nest of them." . . .

The break came in an unlikely location. A pleasant boat ride from British Columbia to Washington state ended with a routine screening by U.S. Customs officers. One passenger in line fidgeted, would not make eye contact. When the Customs officer . . . went to pull him out of line, he bolted. . . . A few minutes later Ahmed Ressam was in custody. His car held explosives, and a map of Los Angeles International Airport.

If that fact were not enough to send us spinning, CIA had learned further details about the al-Qaeda plot in Jordan. The head of the cell, who had helped assemble the bombs, had recently quit his job—as a cab driver in Boston.

The counterterrorism "czar" of the United States, Richard A. Clarke, describing a foiled terrorist attack in early December 1999, in Clarke, Against All Enemies *(2003), pp. 203, 211.*

Happy New Year!

Spoken by millions of people throughout the world on New Year's Eve, December 31, 1999, as the 20th century and second millennium drew to their conclusions.

EPILOGUE

Final Thoughts on the Decade

This book was written between the summers of 2003 and 2004—only a few years after the conclusion of the 1990s. Yet in many ways the final decade of the 20th century already seems distant. Certainly the presidential election of 2000, which replaced eight years of moderately liberal Democratic governance with a neoconservative administration, and the terrorist attacks that damaged the Pentagon and destroyed New York's World Trade Center on September 11, 2001, did much to change the tenor of the times, as did the economic downturn that reversed the general prosperity that characterized most of the 1990s.

When asked about their recollections of the decade, many people initially had difficulty seizing on specific memories, although, when they were pressed, certain major events stood out: the Persian Gulf War; the genocides in Bosnia, Rwanda, and Kosovo; NATO's air war against Serbia; the cycle of raised and dashed hopes for peace between Israel and the Palestinians; the federal raid on the Branch Davidian compound in Waco, Texas; the Oklahoma City bombing; the bombings of the World Trade Center and Atlanta's Centennial Olympic Park; the videotaped Rodney King beating and the Los Angeles riots that followed acquittal of the police officers who beat him; the O. J. Simpson "Trial of the Century"; the Columbine High School massacre; and revelations about President Clinton's affair with Monica Lewinsky and his subsequent impeachment and acquittal.

Younger respondents pointed to the emergence of rap, grunge, and other forms of alternative, youth-oriented music; television fans spoke of a golden era of situation comedies that included *Cheers, Murphy Brown, Frasier, Seinfeld,* and *Friends,* and of innovative, sexually provocative, iconoclastic programming on the newly emerging Fox and cable networks, including such animated social satires as *The Simpsons* and *South Park* and such unlikely dramas as *The X-Files, Sex and the City,* and *The Sopranos.*

Film aficionados noted the growing impact of computer-generated effects on the medium and the emergence of such independent filmmakers as Spike Lee, the Coen brothers, Anthony Minghella, and Quentin Tarantino. They also pointed to the growing number of African-American stars and the increased prominence of black, Hispanic, and Asian characters, who had traditionally been relegated to secondary status in American films. Others spoke of increasingly sympathetic and more fully developed depictions of homosexuals and physically and emotionally strong, competent, independent, sexually liberated women. Similarly, theatergoers discussed the proliferation of high-quality plays by and about women and homosexuals, and they lamented the extent to which theater and the other arts had been decimated by the AIDS epidemic, which seemed to take an especially high toll on artists, actors, and other creative people.

Residents of south Florida cringed at their recollections of Hurricane Andrew, the most expensive natural disaster ever to strike the United States, and Bahamians and Carolinians recalled the devastation wrought by Hurricane Floyd, a storm so large and powerful it was called Andrew's big brother. Catastrophic floods, wildfires, earthquakes, and tornadoes featured prominently in the memories of people in other parts of the nation.

On the other hand, sports enthusiasts celebrated the achievements by baseball stars Cal Ripken, Jr.; Mark McGwire; and Sammy Sosa; football quarterbacks Dan Marino and John Elway; golfer Tiger Woods; basketball standouts Magic Johnson and Michael Jordan; ice skater Nancy Kerrigan; bicyclist Lance Armstrong; downhill skier Picabo Street; and tennis champions Pete Sampras, Andre Agassi, and Steffi Graf, among many others. They noted the growing popularity of women's sports and bemoaned seasons of professional competition shortened by labor disputes.

More business-oriented respondents recalled the soaring stock market, the rise and fall of the so-called dotcoms and other high-tech companies, the record-setting corporate mergers, a balanced federal budget, and the rare phenomenon of strong economic growth coupled with low inflation.

Biologists spoke in awe about the cloning of Dolly the sheep, completion of the humane genome map, and other achievements in genetic engineering, and astronomers gushed about the *Hubble Space Telescope,* the *Cosmic Background Explorer,* and the possibilities of extraterrestrial life implicit in the discoveries of new planets outside the solar system and a bacterium believed to have originated on Mars.

E-mail and the World Wide Web had, by 2003, become so ingrained in their way of life that several individuals had difficulty recalling that throughout much of the 1990s these were new and developing technologies. But once they recollected a time before the Internet, virtually everyone spoke of its profound impact and that of cell phones, hand-held computer organizers, and other modes of telecommunication that not only facilitate personal communication and the transfer of data but also change the way people conduct their life and relate to one another.

For many people, the 1990s now seems a blur. This may be attributable in part to the aging process or to the way humans store memories in their brain. But, although many people enjoyed significant gains in their income and standard of living during the period, they also experienced an accelerated pace of living that was a by-product of the proliferation of high-tech gadgetry. During the 1990s it became especially difficult for professionals, and others, to leave their work behind them at the end of the day or over weekends. Whereas people in earlier times were unable to conduct business while commuting in their car or on public transportation or while traveling on trains and airplanes between cities, cell phones and laptop computers took away even those periods of comparative quietude. Moreover, wider opportunities for travel and entertainment in the 1990s and expanded activities for children enriched lives in many ways, but they also diminished time available for simple relaxation, creative imagination, and personal introspection. Indeed, *stress management* became one of the catchwords of the decade.

In his poem "For the Time Being" (1944), W. H. Auden wrote, "Nothing like It has happened before," referring, presumably, to 20th-century industrialization, urbanization, mass media, high-speed transportation, worldwide warfare, and other experiences and capabilities unknown in any previous era in human history. The poet's observation has become ever more true with each passing generation, and, arguably, developments in the 1990s set that decade as far apart from the rest of the 20th century as the 20th century was from the 19th century. At no other time in history had the entire world been so dominated militarily by a single nation capable of striking with overwhelming force within hours against almost any place on the map. At no other time had scientists possessed the ability to clone mammals or perform other acts of bioengineering so sophisticated that the researchers acquired almost godlike powers to create new life-forms and blur the lines of what it means to be human. Nor could astronomers in earlier decades observe deep space with such clarity that they could look back almost to the very origin of the universe to see the formation of now-ancient galaxies or discover new solar systems. At no other time had ordinary citizens throughout the globe enjoyed nearly instant worldwide access to enormous stockpiles of information or to one another's personal perspectives, thoughts, and opinions. Rarely before the advent of the World Wide Web could private citizens share with an international audience their literary writings, musical compositions, and works of visual art, all at minimal expense.

Never before had the risk of global catastrophe caused by widespread environmental degradation been so great, the fusion of consumerism with everyday experience been so extensive, or the economic and cultural influence of large corporations been so overwhelming. Even as genetic engineering and other advances in medical research promised to increase life spans, cure hitherto incurable diseases, and reverse aging, nuclear, chemical, and biological threats from proliferating terrorist organizations threatened to wipe out entire urban centers. Even as the economy flourished and standards of living rose as the global economy matured, global warming, diminution of the world's rain forests, and the torn ozone layer in the Earth's atmosphere—necessary for filtering out deadly ultraviolet radiation from the Sun—loomed as catastrophes in the making.

The 1990s was a decade characterized by deeply partisan political and cultural divisions that were not easily reconciled because they were centered on fundamental differences about strongly held beliefs concerning the nature of morality, patriotism, proper action, acceptable sexual practices, and appropriate gender roles. Even people who otherwise shared a common preoccupation with spiritual well-being were often pulled apart by contradictions that pitted traditional religious practices against new interpretations of sacred texts and alternative, nonreligious approaches to spirituality.

Since the 1950s, and arguably even since the Civil War, traditional practices and social arrangements have increasingly lost their legal standing in the United States. Throughout the 20th century rulings by what conservatives denounced as "activist judges" struck down traditional practices, and these rulings, along with local, state, and federal legislation, gave legal bases to an ongoing evolution that has broadened America's view of acceptable social values, attitudes, and practices.

These changes were welcomed by many in the 1990s, especially but not exclusively in the center and Left of the political spectrum, who embraced new opportunities for them and others to discover and realize their greatest potential by following unconventional paths. Pointing to the achievements and contributions made by individuals whose group had been historically excluded from full participation in society, they argued that expanded opportunities and legal rights for women, homosexuals, and racial and ethnic minorities more completely realized the principles of individual freedom and equality on which the nation had been founded.

But others, more typically from the center or Right of the political spectrum, bitterly opposed the changes, which they felt degraded the nation's social and moral fabric. Their opposition to expanded rights for women and homosexuals fueled partisan passions throughout the 1990s. To these critics, America's basic sense of morality was being undermined by new gender roles they considered unnatural, by sexual practices they regarded as deviant, and by legalized abortion, which they considered murder. Some argued that by abandoning the Christian virtues they believed had been and should remain at the heart of American society, the United States was even endangering its ability to survive as a nation. Others objected to the outspoken, political nature of the feminist movement and its role in creating a culture of political correctness. Among these were fans of conservative radio talk show hosts such as Rush Limbaugh, a popular, aggressively antiliberal radio personality known for labeling feminists as "feminazis."

Although it was rarely discussed in these terms, many of the points of conflict stemmed from inherent discrepancies between capitalism and Christianity. In particular, the 1990s was marked by a fundamental clash in values between consumer capitalism and the Protestant ethic. This conflict provoked tension and confusion, especially among young people who were most attuned to the disparities and unsure what to believe or how to behave. If, on the one hand, the Protestant ethic encouraged thrift, restraint, prudence, self-control, self-sacrifice, self-improvement through hard work, piety, humility, and extensive preparations for the future, consumer capitalism bombarded Americans with advertisements telling them to spend freely, find happiness in ownership and sensual gratification, indulge their passions and their impulses, be proud and boastful, find easy paths to success, and live for the moment.

The messages were especially mixed when the subject was sex. On the one hand, sex has long been used as a successful marketing ploy, and advertisers, publishers, entertainers, and movie and film producers have earned large profits by showing the public what it clearly wanted to see—more nudity, more overtly sexual behavior, more sexually aggressive women, and a wider range of modes of sexual activity. On the other hand, in Christian theology lasciviousness is a sin, and Christians were encouraged to be modest in their sex appeal, to remain virgins until marriage, and to be monogamous within their marriage. Thus, throughout the decade Americans were pulled in powerful but opposite directions in these matters of fundamental values and primal impulses.

Indeed, establishing the parameters of permissible sexual behavior was an especially divisive issue, as it interjected a powerful, visceral dimension that shaped and intensified responses on both sides. Proponents of homosexual rights and nontraditional heterosexual sexual arrangements outside marriage maintained that sexual behavior in a free society should be a personal choice between or among consenting individuals. Apart from the need to prevent and assume responsibility for sexually transmitted diseases and unwanted pregnancies, sexual intercourse itself was not inherently a moral issue to them.

But for many of their opponents, sex was an intensely moral matter treated explicitly in the Bible and other sacred texts. In their mind, institutionalized tolerance of religiously prohibited sexual practices, including homosexual intercourse, was tantamount to ongoing blasphemy conducted at a national scale. Consequently, along with legalized abortion, it placed the entire country at risk for catastrophic divine retribution.

Thus, as the decade drew to a close, the United States was far from being at peace with itself, even as it enjoyed unrivaled power, cultural influence, and wealth. In a world that was fracturing primarily along ethnic lines in places such as Bosnia and Rwanda, the United States splintered in deep conflicts about what was moral and immoral, which outcomes of public policy were desirable and undesirable, and which actions were right and wrong. These differences became most evident during Clinton's impeachment, and they persisted into and even intensified during the opening years of the new millennium. Consequently, for the United States the greatest legacy of the 1990s may prove to be the challenges of reconciling these diametrically opposite conceptions of what the nation stands for, tolerates, and aspires to become. Perhaps the greatest of these challenges will be for partisan opponents to find the will and the way to suspend moral judgments about one another and seek common ground with fellow citizens whose practices and beliefs they find personally offensive and morally indefensible.

APPENDIX A
Documents

1. United Nations Resolutions Concerning Iraq and Kuwait, August 2, 1990–April 3, 1991
2. Charter of Paris for a New Europe: A New Era of Democracy, Peace and Unity, November 21, 1990
3. President George H. W. Bush's announcement of the commencement of Operation Desert Storm, January 16, 1991
4. Anita Hill's testimony at the Senate confirmation hearing for Clarence Thomas, October 11, 1991
5. Clarence Thomas's Senate confirmation testimony, October 11, 1991
6. The Twenty-seventh Amendment to the U.S. Constitution, May 7, 1992
7. Republican Contract with America, September 27, 1994
8. Welfare Reform: An Analysis of the Issues by Isabel V. Sawhill, issued by the nonpartisan Urban Institute, May 1, 1995
9. Introduction to the Unabomber's manifesto: "Industrial Society and Its Future" by Theodore Kaczynski, September 19, 1995
10. Supreme Court decision in *Clinton v. Jones,* allowing Paula Jones's civil lawsuit against President William Jefferson Clinton to proceed, May 27, 1997
11. Conclusions from the report by Independent counsel Kenneth Starr recommending impeachment of President William Jefferson Clinton, submitted to Congress on September 9, 1998
12. President William Jefferson Clinton's response to Referral of Office of Independent Counsel, September 12, 1998
13. Articles of Impeachment of President William Jefferson Clinton passed by the U.S. House of Representatives, December 19, 1998

1. UNITED NATIONS RESOLUTIONS CONCERNING IRAQ AND KUWAIT, AUGUST 2, 1990–APRIL 3, 1991

Resolution 660, August 2, 1990

The Security Council, Alarmed by the invasion of Kuwait on 2 August 1990 by the military forces of Iraq . . .

1. Condemns the Iraqi invasion of Kuwait;

2. Demands that Iraq withdraw immediately and unconditionally all its forces to the positions in which they were located on 1 August 1990;

3. Calls upon Iraq and Kuwait to begin immediately intensive negotiations for the resolution of their differences and supports all efforts in this regard, and especially those of the League of Arab States. . . .

Resolution 661, August 6, 1990

The Security Council, Reaffirming its resolution 660 (1990) of 2 August 1990 . . .

Determined to bring the invasion and occupation of Kuwait by Iraq to an end and to restore the sovereignty, independence and territorial integrity of Kuwait . . .

1. Determines that Iraq so far has failed to comply with paragraph 2 of resolution 660 (1990) and has usurped the authority of the legitimate Government of Kuwait;

2. Decides, as a consequence, to take the following measures to secure compliance of Iraq . . . and to restore the authority of the legitimate Government of Kuwait;

3. Decides that all States shall prevent:

(a) The import into their territories of all commodities and products originating in Iraq or Kuwait exported there from after the date of the present resolution . . .

(c) The sale or supply by their nationals or from their territories or using their flag vessels of any commodities or products, including weapons or any other military equipment . . . but not including supplies intended strictly for medical purposes, and, in humanitarian circumstances, foodstuffs, to any person or body in Iraq or Kuwait.

4. Decides that all States shall not make available to the Government of Iraq or to any commercial, industrial or public utility undertaking in Iraq or Kuwait . . .

Resolution 662, August 9, 1990

The Security Council . . .

Gravely alarmed by the declaration by Iraq of a "comprehensive and eternal merger" with Kuwait . . .

1. Decides that annexation of Kuwait by Iraq under any form and whatever pretext has no legal validity, and is considered null and void. . . .

Resolution 664, August 18, 1990

The Security Council . . .

1. Demands that Iraq permit and facilitate the immediate departure from Kuwait and Iraq of the nationals of third countries and grant immediate and continuing access of consular officials to such nationals;

2. Further demands that Iraq take no action to jeopardize the safety, security or health of such nationals;

3. Reaffirms its decision in resolution 662 (1990) that annexation of Kuwait by Iraq is null and void, and therefore demands that the Government of Iraq rescind its orders for the closure of diplomatic and consular missions in Kuwait and the withdrawal of the immunity of their personnel, and refrain from any such actions in the future. . . .

Resolution 665, August 25, 1990

The Security Council . . .

Gravely alarmed that Iraq continues to refuse to comply with [previous] resolutions . . . and in particular at the conduct of the Government of Iraq in using Iraqi flag vessels to export oil,

1. Calls upon those Member States co-operating with the Government of Kuwait which are deploying maritime forces to the area to use such measures commensurate to the specific circumstances as may be necessary . . . to halt all inward and outward maritime shipping in order to inspect and verify their cargoes and destinations and to ensure strict implementation of the provisions related to such shipping laid down in resolution 661 (1990). . . .

Resolution 666, September 13, 1990

The Security Council,

Recognizing that circumstances may arise in which it will be necessary for foodstuffs to be supplied to the civilian population in Iraq or Kuwait in order to relieve human suffering . . .

1. Decides that . . . the Committee shall keep the situation regarding foodstuffs in Iraq and Kuwait under constant review. . . .

4. Requests further that in seeking and supplying such information particular attention will be paid to such categories of persons who might suffer specially, such as children under 15 years of age, expectant mothers, maternity cases, the sick and the elderly. . . .

Resolution 667, September 16, 1990

The Security Council . . .

Recalling the Vienna Conventions of 18 April 1961 on diplomatic relations and of 24 April 1963 on consular relations, to both of which Iraq is a party,

Considering that the decision of Iraq to order the closure of diplomatic and consular missions in Kuwait and to withdraw the immunity and privileges of these missions and their personnel is contrary to the decisions of the Security Council, the international Conventions mentioned above and international law,

Deeply concerned that Iraq . . . has committed acts of violence against diplomatic missions and their personnel in Kuwait,

Outraged at recent violations by Iraq of diplomatic premises in Kuwait and at the abduction of personnel enjoying diplomatic immunity and foreign nationals who were present in these premises,

Considering that the above actions by Iraq constitute aggressive acts and a flagrant violation of its international obligations which strike at the root of the conduct of international relations in accordance with the Charter of the United Nations . . .

1. Strongly condemns aggressive acts perpetrated by Iraq against diplomatic premises and personnel in Kuwait, including the abduction of foreign nationals who were present in those premises;

2. Demands the immediate release of those foreign nationals as well as all nationals mentioned in resolution 664 (1990) . . .

4. Further demands that Iraq immediately protect the safety and well-being of diplomatic and consular personnel and premises in Kuwait and in Iraq and take no action to hinder the diplomatic and consular missions in the performance of their functions. . . .

Resolution 670, September 25, 1990

The Security Council . . .

1. Calls upon all States to carry out their obligations to ensure strict and complete compliance with resolution 661 (1990). . . .

2. Confirms that resolution 661 (1990) applies to all means of transport, including aircraft;

3. Decides that all States . . . shall deny permission to any aircraft to take off from their territory if the aircraft would carry any cargo to or from Iraq or Kuwait other than food in humanitarian circumstances. . . .

Resolution 674, October 29, 1990

The Security Council . . .

1. Demands that the Iraqi authorities and occupying forces immediately cease and desist from taking third State nationals hostage, and mistreating and oppressing Kuwaiti and third State nationals . . .

2. Invites States to collate substantiated information in their possession or submitted to them on the grave breaches by Iraq . . .

5. Demands that Iraq ensure the immediate access to food, water and basic services necessary to the protection and well-being of Kuwaiti nationals and of nationals of third States in Kuwait and Iraq. . . .

Resolution 677, November 28, 1990

The Security Council . . .

1. Condemns the attempts by Iraq to alter the demographic composition of the population of Kuwait and to destroy the civil records maintained by the legitimate Government of Kuwait;

2. Mandates the Secretary-General to take custody of a copy of the population register of Kuwait, the authenticity of which has been certified by the legitimate Government of Kuwait and which covers the registration of the population up to 1 August 1990;

3. Requests the Secretary-General to establish, in co-operation with the legitimate Government of Kuwait, an Order of Rules and Regulations governing access to and use of the said copy of the population register. . . .

Resolution 678, November 29, 1990

The Security Council . . .

1. Demands that Iraq comply fully with resolution 660 (1990) and all subsequent relevant resolutions, and decides, while maintaining all its decisions, to allow Iraq one final opportunity, as a pause of goodwill, to do so;

2. Authorizes Member States co-operating with the Government of Kuwait, unless Iraq on or before 15 January 1991 fully implements . . . the foregoing resolutions, to use all necessary means to uphold and

implement resolution 660 (1990) and all subsequent relevant resolutions and to restore international peace and security in the area....

Resolution 686, March 2, 1991

The Security Council . . .

Taking note of the suspension of offensive combat operations by the forces of Kuwait and the Member States cooperating with Kuwait . . .

Bearing in mind the need to be assured of Iraq's peaceful intentions, and the objective . . . of restoring international peace and security in the region,

Underlining the importance of Iraq taking the necessary measures which would permit a definitive end to the hostilities,

Affirming the commitment of all Member States to the independence, sovereignty and territorial integrity of Iraq and Kuwait . . .

1. Affirms that all twelve resolutions noted above continue to have full force and effect;

2. Demands that Iraq implement its acceptance of all twelve resolutions noted above and in particular that Iraq:

(a) Rescind immediately its actions purporting to annex Kuwait;

(b) Accept in principle its liability for any loss, damage, or injury arising in regard to Kuwait and third States, and their nationals and corporations . . .

(d) Provide all information and assistance in identifying Iraqi mines, booby traps and other explosives as well as any chemical and biological weapons and material in Kuwait, in areas of Iraq where forces of Member States cooperating with Kuwait . . . are present temporarily, and in adjacent waters. . . .

Resolution 687, April 3, 1991

The Security Council . . .

8. Decides that Iraq shall unconditionally accept the destruction, removal, or rendering harmless, under international supervision, of:

(a) All chemical and biological weapons and all stocks of agents and all related subsystems and components and all research, development, support and manufacturing facilities;

(b) All ballistic missiles with a range greater than 150 kilometers . . .

9. Decides, for the implementation of paragraph 8 above, the following: (a) Iraq shall submit to the Secretary-General, within fifteen days of the adoption of the present resolution, a declaration of the locations, amounts and types of all items specified in paragraph 8 and agree to urgent, on-site inspection . . .

The yielding by Iraq . . . for destruction, removal or rendering harmless . . . of all items specified under paragraph 8 (a) above . . .

12. Decides that Iraq shall unconditionally agree not to acquire or develop nuclear weapons or nuclear-weapons-usable material or any subsystems or components or any research, development, support or manufacturing facilities related to the above . . . and to accept the plan discussed . . . below for the future ongoing monitoring and verification of its compliance with these undertakings. . . .

2. CHARTER OF PARIS FOR A NEW EUROPE: A NEW ERA OF DEMOCRACY, PEACE AND UNITY, NOVEMBER 21, 1990

We, the Heads of State or Government of the States participating in the Conference on Security and Cooperation in Europe [CSCE], have assembled in Paris at a time of profound change and historic expectations. The era of confrontation and division of Europe has ended. We declare that henceforth our relations will be founded on respect and co-operation.

Europe is liberating itself from the legacy of the past. The courage of men and women, the strength of the will of the peoples and the power of the ideas of the Helsinki Final Act have opened a new era of democracy, peace and unity in Europe.

Ours is a time for fulfilling the hopes and expectations our peoples have cherished for decades: steadfast commitment to democracy based on human rights and fundamental freedoms; prosperity through economic liberty and social justice; and equal security for all our countries.

The Ten Principles of the Final Act will guide us towards this ambitious future, just as they have lighted our way towards better relations for the past fifteen years. Full implementation of all CSCE commitments must form the basis for the initiatives we are now taking to enable our nations to live in accordance with their aspirations.

Human Rights, Democracy and Rule of Law

We undertake to build, consolidate and strengthen democracy as the only system of government of our nations. In this endeavor, we will abide by the following:

Human rights and fundamental freedoms are the birthright of all human beings, are inalienable and are guaranteed by law. Their protection and promotion is the first responsibility of government. Respect for them is an essential safeguard against an over-mighty State. Their observance and full exercise are the foundation of freedom, justice and peace.

Democratic government is based on the will of the people, expressed regularly through free and fair elections. Democracy has as its foundation respect for the human person and the rule of law. Democracy is the best safeguard of freedom of expression, tolerance of all groups of society, and equality of opportunity for each person.

Democracy, with its representative and pluralist character, entails accountability to the electorate, the obligation of public authorities to comply with the law and justice administered impartially. No one will be above the law.

We affirm that, without discrimination, every individual has the right to: freedom of thought, conscience and religion or belief, freedom of expression, freedom of association and peaceful assembly, freedom of movement;

No one will be: subject to arbitrary arrest or detention, subject to torture or other cruel, inhuman or degrading treatment or punishment; everyone also has the right: to know and act upon his rights, to participate in free and fair elections, to fair and public trial if charged with an offense, to own property alone or in association and to exercise individual enterprise, to enjoy his economic, social and cultural rights.

We affirm that the ethnic, cultural, linguistic and religious identity of national minorities will be protected and that persons belonging to national minorities have the right freely to express, preserve, and develop that identity without any discrimination and in full equality before the law.

We will ensure that everyone will enjoy recourse to effective remedies, national or international, against any violation of his rights. Full respect for these precepts is the bedrock on which we will seek to construct the new Europe. Our States will cooperate and support each other with the aim of making democratic gains irreversible.

Economic Liberty and Responsibility

Economic liberty, social justice and environmental responsibility are indispensable for prosperity. The free will of the individual, exercised in democracy and protected by the rule of law, forms the necessary basis for successful economic and social development. We will promote economic activity which respects and upholds human dignity....

Friendly Relations Among Participating States

.... to uphold and promote democracy, peace and unity in Europe, we solemnly pledge our full commitment to the Ten Principles of the Helsinki Final Act. We affirm the continuing validity of the Ten Principles and our determination to put them into practice.... We renew our pledge to refrain from the threat or use of force against the territorial integrity or political independence of any State.... We reaffirm our commitment to settle disputes by peaceful means. We decide to develop mechanisms for the prevention and resolution of conflicts among the participating States....

Security

Friendly relations among us will benefit from the consolidation of democracy and improved security. We welcome the signature of the Treaty on Conventional Armed Forces in Europe by twenty-two participating States, which will lead to lower levels of armed forces. We endorse the adoption of a substantial new set of Confidence- and Security-building Measures which will lead to increased transparency and confidence among all participating States....

Unity

Europe whole and free is calling for a new beginning. We invite our peoples to join in this great endeavor. We note with great satisfaction the Treaty on the Final Settlement with respect to Germany signed in Moscow on 12 September 1990. . . . The establishment of the national unity of Germany is an important contribution to a just and lasting order of peace for a united, democratic Europe aware of its responsibility for stability, peace and cooperation....

The CSCE and the World

The destiny of our nations is linked to that of all other nations. We support fully the United Nations and the enhancement of its role in promoting international peace, security and justice. We reaffirm our commitment to the principles and purposes of the United Nations as enshrined in the Charter and condemn all violations of these principles. We recognize with satisfaction the growing role of the United Nations in world affairs and its increasing effectiveness, fostered by the improvement in relations among our States. . . .

3. President George H. W. Bush's Announcement of the Commencement of Operation Desert Storm, January 16, 1991

Just two hours ago, allied air forces began an attack on military targets in Iraq and Kuwait. These attacks continue as I speak. Ground forces are not engaged.

This conflict started August second when the dictator of Iraq invaded a small and helpless neighbor. Kuwait—a member of the Arab League and a member of the United Nations—was crushed, its people brutalized. Five months ago, Saddam Hussein started this cruel war against Kuwait. Tonight, the battle has been joined. . . .

As I report to you, air attacks are under way against military targets in Iraq. We are determined to knock out Saddam Hussein's nuclear bomb potential. We will also destroy his chemical weapons facilities. Much of Saddam's artillery and tanks will be destroyed. . . .

Our objectives are clear: Saddam Hussein's forces will leave Kuwait. The legitimate government of Kuwait will be restored to its rightful place, and Kuwait will once again be free. Iraq will eventually: comply with all relevant United Nations resolutions, and then, when peace is restored, it is our hope that Iraq will live as a peaceful and cooperative member of the family of nations, thus enhancing the security and stability of the Gulf.

Some may ask, Why act now? Why not wait? The answer is clear: The world could wait no longer. Sanctions, though having some effect, showed no signs of accomplishing their objective. Sanctions were tried for well over five months, and we and our allies concluded that sanctions alone would not force Saddam from Kuwait.

While the world waited, Saddam Hussein systematically raped, pillaged, and plundered a tiny nation, no threat to his own. He subjected the people of Kuwait to unspeakable atrocities—and among those maimed and murdered innocent children.

While the world waited, Saddam sought to add to the chemical arsenal he now possesses an infinitely more dangerous weapon of mass destruction: a nuclear weapon. And while the world waited, while the world talked peace and withdrawal, Saddam Hussein dug in and moved massive forces into Kuwait. . . .

While the world waited, Saddam Hussein met every overture of peace with open contempt. While the world prayed for peace, Saddam prepared for war. . . .

Saddam was warned over and over again to comply with the will of the United Nations: Leave Kuwait, or be driven out. Saddam has arrogantly rejected all warnings. Instead, he tried to make this a dispute between Iraq and the United States of America.

Well, he failed. Tonight, twenty-eight nations—countries from five continents, Europe and Asia and Africa and the Arab League—have forces in the Gulf area standing shoulder to shoulder against Saddam Hussein. These countries had hoped the use of force could be avoided. Regrettably, we now believe that only force will make him leave. . . .

I've told the American people before that this will not be another Vietnam, and I repeat this here tonight. Our troops will have the best possible support in the entire world, and they will not be asked to fight with one hand tied behind their back. . . .

Thomas Paine wrote many years ago, "These are the times that try men's souls." Those well-known words are so very true today. But even as planes of the multinational forces attack Iraq, I prefer to think of peace, not war. I am convinced not only that we will prevail but that out of the horror of combat will come the recognition that no nation can stand against a world united, no nation will be permitted to brutally assault its neighbor. . . .

Tonight, as our forces fight, they and their families are in our prayers. May God bless each and every one of them and the coalition forces at our side in the Gulf, and may He continue to bless our nation, the United States of America.

4. Anita Hill's Testimony at the Senate Confirmation Hearing for Clarence Thomas, October 11, 1991

Mr. Chairman, Senator Thurmond, members of the committee, my name is Anita F. Hill, and I am a professor of law at the University of Oklahoma. . . . In 1981, I was introduced to now Judge Thomas by a mutual friend. Judge Thomas . . . was anticipating a political appointment and asked if I would be interested in working with him. He was, in fact, appointed as assistant secretary of education for civil rights. After he had taken that post, he asked if I would become his assistant, and I accepted that position. . . .

During this period at the Department of Education, my working relationship with Judge Thomas was positive. I had a good deal of responsibility and independence. I thought he respected my work and that he trusted my judgment.

After approximately three months of working there, he asked me to go out socially with him. What happened next and telling the world about it are the two most difficult things, experiences of my life. . . .

I declined the invitation to go out socially with him, and explained to him that I thought it would jeopardize what at the time I considered to be a very good working relationship. I had a normal social life with other men outside the office. I believed then, as now, that having a social relationship with a person who was supervising my work would be ill advised. I was very uncomfortable with the idea and told him so.

I thought that by saying "no" and explaining my reasons, my employer would abandon his social suggestions. However, to my regret, in the following few weeks he continued to ask me out on several occasions. . . .

My working relationship became even more strained when Judge Thomas began to use work situations to discuss sex. On these occasions, he would call me into his office for reports on education issues and projects, or he might suggest that because of the time pressures of his schedule we go to a government cafeteria. After a brief discussion of work, he would turn the conversation to a discussion of sexual matters. His conversations were very vivid.

He spoke about acts that he had seen in pornographic films involving such matters as women having sex with animals, and films showing group sex or rape scenes. He talked about pornographic materials depicting individuals with large penises or large breasts involved in various sex acts. . . .

He began to show displeasure in his tone and voice and his demeanor in continued pressure for an explanation. He commented on what I was wearing in terms of whether it made me more or less sexually attractive. . . .

One of the oddest episodes I remember was an occasion in which Thomas was drinking a Coke in his office. He got up from the table at which we were working, went over to his desk to get the Coke, looked at the can and asked, "Who has put pubic hair in my Coke?"

On other occasions he referred to the size of his own penis as being larger than normal, and he also spoke on some occasions of the pleasures he had given to women with oral sex. . . .

I declined any comment to newspapers, but later when Senate staff asked me about these matters, I felt that I had a duty to report. I have no personal vendetta against Clarence Thomas. I seek only to provide the committee with information which it may regard as relevant.

It would have been more comfortable to remain silent. I took no initiative to inform anyone. But when I was asked by a representative of this committee to report my experience, I felt that I had to tell the truth. I could not keep silent.

5. CLARENCE THOMAS'S SENATE CONFIRMATION TESTIMONY, OCTOBER 11, 1991

Mr. Chairman, Senator Thurmond, members of the committee: as excruciatingly difficult as the last two weeks have been, I welcome the opportunity to clear my name today. . . .

The first I learned of the allegations by Professor Anita Hill was on September 25, 1991, when the FBI came to my home to investigate her allegations. . . . I was shocked, surprised, hurt, and enormously saddened.

I have not been the same since that day. For almost a decade my responsibilities included enforcing the rights of victims of sexual harassment. As a boss, as a friend, and as a human being I was proud that I have never had such an allegation leveled against me, even as I sought to promote women, and minorities into nontraditional jobs. . . .

I have been wracking my brains, and eating my insides out trying to think of what I could have said or done to Anita Hill to lead her to allege that I was interested in her in more than a professional way, and that I talked with her about pornographic or x-rated films.

Contrary to some press reports, I categorically denied all of the allegations and denied that I ever attempted to date Anita Hill, when first interviewed by the FBI. I strongly reaffirm that denial. Let me describe my relationship with Anita Hill. . . .

Throughout the time that Anita Hill worked with me I treated her as I treated my other special assistants. I tried to treat them all cordially, professionally, and respectfully. And I tried to support them in their endeavors, and be interested in and supportive of their success.

I had no reason or basis to believe my relationship with Anita Hill was anything but this way until the FBI visited me a little more than 2 weeks ago. I find it particularly troubling that she never raised any hint that she was uncomfortable with me. She did not raise or mention it when considering moving with me to EEOC from the Department of Education. And she never raised it with me when she left EEOC and was moving on in her life. . . .

This is a person I have helped at every turn in the road, since we met. She seemed to appreciate the continued cordial relationship we had since day one. She sought my advice and counsel, as did virtually all of the members of my personal staff. . . .

The fact that I feel so very strongly about sex harassment and spoke loudly about it at EEOC has made these allegations doubly hard on me. I cannot imagine anything that I said or did to Anita Hill that could have been mistaken for sexual harassment. . . .

When I stood next to the President in Kennebunkport, being nominated to the Supreme Court of the United States, that was a high honor. But as I sit here, before you, 103 days later, that honor has been crushed. From the very beginning charges were leveled against me from the shadows—charges of drug abuse, anti-Semitism, wife-beating, drug use by family members, that I was a quota appointment, confirmation conversion, and much, much more. And now, this.

I have complied with the rules. I responded to a document request that produced over 30,000 pages of documents. And I have testified for 5 full days under oath. I have endured this ordeal for 103 days. Reporters sneaking into my garage to examine books I read. Reporters and interest groups swarming over divorce papers, looking for dirt. Unnamed people starting preposterous and damaging rumors. Calls all over the country specifically requesting dirt. This is not American. This is Kafka-esque. It has got to stop. It must stop for the benefit of future nominees, and

our country. Enough is enough. . . . This is not what America is all about. . . .

Mr. Chairman, I am proud of my life, proud of what I have done, and what I have accomplished, proud of my family, and this process, this process is trying to destroy it all. . . .

Mr. Chairman, I am a victim of this process and my name has been harmed, my integrity has been harmed, my character has been harmed, my family has been harmed, my friends have been harmed. There is nothing this committee, this body or this country can do to give me my good name back, nothing.

I will not provide the rope for my own lynching or for further humiliation. I am not going to engage in discussions, nor will I submit to roving questions of what goes on in the most intimate parts of my private life or the sanctity of my bedroom. These are the most intimate parts of my privacy, and they will remain just that, private. . . .

I think that this today is a travesty. I think that it is disgusting. I think that this hearing should never occur in America. This is a case in which this sleaze, this dirt was searched for by staffers of members of this committee, was then leaked to the media, and this committee and this body validated it and displayed it in prime time over our entire Nation. . . .

This is a circus. It is a national disgrace. And from my standpoint, as a black American, as far as I am concerned, it is a high-tech lynching for uppity-blacks who in any way deign to think for themselves, to do for themselves, to have different ideas, and it is a message that, unless you kow-tow to an old order this is what will happen to you: You will be lynched, destroyed, caricatured by a committee of the U.S. Senate, rather than hung from a tree.

6. THE TWENTY-SEVENTH AMENDMENT TO THE U.S. CONSTITUTION, MAY 7, 1992

No law, varying the compensation for the services of the senators and representatives, shall take effect, until an election of representatives shall have intervened.

7. REPUBLICAN CONTRACT WITH AMERICA, SEPTEMBER 27, 1994

As Republican Members of the House of Representatives and as citizens seeking to join that body we propose not just to change its policies, but even more important, to restore the bonds of trust between the people and their elected representatives.

That is why, in this era of official evasion and posturing, we offer instead a detailed agenda for national renewal, a written commitment with no fine print.

This year's election offers the chance, after four decades of one-party control, to bring to the House a new majority that will transform the way Congress works. That historic change would be the end of government that is too big, too intrusive, and too easy with the public's money. It can be the beginning of a Congress that respects the values and shares the faith of the American family.

Like Lincoln, our first Republican president, we intend to act "with firmness in the right, as God gives us to see the right." To restore accountability to Congress. To end its cycle of scandal and disgrace. To make us all proud again of the way free people govern themselves.

On the first day of the 104th Congress, the new Republican majority will immediately pass the following major reforms, aimed at restoring the faith and trust of the American people in their government:

FIRST, require all laws that apply to the rest of the country also apply equally to the Congress;

SECOND, select a major, independent auditing firm to conduct a comprehensive audit of Congress for waste, fraud or abuse;

THIRD, cut the number of House committees, and cut committee staff by one-third;

FOURTH, limit the terms of all committee chairs;

FIFTH, ban the casting of proxy votes in committee;

SIXTH, require committee meetings to be open to the public;

SEVENTH, require a three-fifths majority vote to pass a tax increase;

EIGHTH, guarantee an honest accounting of our Federal Budget by implementing zero base-line budgeting.

Thereafter, within the first 100 days of the 104th Congress, we shall bring to the House Floor the following bills, each to be given full and open debate, each to be given a clear and fair vote and each to be immediately available this day for public inspection and scrutiny.

1. THE FISCAL RESPONSIBILITY ACT: A balanced budget/tax limitation amendment and a legislative line-item veto to restore fiscal responsibility to an out-of-control Congress, requiring them to live under the same budget constraints as families and businesses.

2. THE TAKING BACK OUR STREETS ACT: An anti-crime package including stronger truth-in-sentencing, "good faith" exclusionary rule exemptions, effective death penalty provisions, and cuts in social spending from this summer's "crime" bill to fund prison construction and additional law enforcement to keep people secure in their neighborhoods and kids safe in their schools.

3. THE PERSONAL RESPONSIBILITY ACT: Discourage illegitimacy and teen pregnancy by prohibiting welfare to minor mothers and denying increased [Aid to Families with Dependent Children] AFDC for additional children while on welfare, cut spending for welfare programs, and enact a tough two-years-and-out provision with work requirements to promote individual responsibility.

4. THE FAMILY REINFORCEMENT ACT: Child support enforcement, tax incentives for adoption, strengthening rights of parents in their children's education, stronger child pornography laws, and an elderly dependent care tax credit to reinforce the central role of families in American society.

5. THE AMERICAN DREAM RESTORATION ACT: A $500 per child tax credit, begin repeal of the marriage tax penalty, and creation of American Dream Savings Accounts to provide middle class tax relief.

6. THE NATIONAL SECURITY RESTORATION ACT: No U.S. troops under U.N. command and restoration of the essential parts of our national security funding to strengthen our national defense and maintain our credibility around the world.

7. THE SENIOR CITIZENS FAIRNESS ACT: Raise the Social Security earnings limit which currently forces seniors out of the work force, repeal the 1993 tax hikes on Social Security benefits and provide tax incentives for private long-term care insurance to let older Americans keep more of what they have earned over the years

8. THE JOB CREATION AND WAGE ENHANCEMENT ACT: Small business incentives, capital gains cut and indexation, neutral cost recovery, risk assessment/cost-benefit analysis, strengthening the

Regulatory Flexibility Act and unfunded mandate reform to create jobs and raise worker wages.

9. THE COMMON SENSE LEGAL REFORM ACT: "Loser pays" laws, reasonable limits on punitive damages and reform of product liability laws to stem the endless tide of litigation.

10. THE CITIZEN LEGISLATURE ACT: A first-ever vote on term limits to replace career politicians with citizen legislators.

Further, we will instruct the House Budget Committee to report to the floor and we will work to enact additional budget savings, beyond the budget cuts specifically included in the legislation described above, to ensure that the Federal budget deficit will be less than it would have been without the enactment of these bills.

Respecting the judgment of our fellow citizens as we seek their mandate for reform, we hereby pledge our names to this Contract with America.

8. Welfare Reform: An Analysis of the Issues by Isabel V. Sawhill, Issued by the Nonpartisan Urban Institute, May 1, 1995

No one likes the current welfare system. Governors complain that federal law is overly prescriptive and are willing to take less federal money in return for more flexibility. The public believes that welfare is anti-work and anti-family although polls show that the public wants welfare reformed in ways that do not penalize children. Welfare recipients find dealing with the system degrading and demoralizing; most would prefer to work. Experts note that welfare has done little to stem the growth of poverty among children. In all but two states, welfare benefits (including food stamps) are insufficient to move a family above the poverty line.

In short, the current indictment against the welfare system has four particulars:

- It does not provide sufficient state flexibility.
- It does not encourage work.
- It is responsible for the breakdown of the family, especially for a rising tide of out-of-wedlock births.
- It has done little to reduce poverty, especially among children.

The chapters in this volume address how much truth there is in these propositions and assess the ability of current proposals to deal with the complaints. . . .

PROVIDING STATE FLEXIBILITY: States already have substantial flexibility; they could be provided more without eliminating the current federal role in securing a safety net for the poor. Block grants will lead to new inequities and to insufficient public accountability.

ENCOURAGING WORK: Encouraging work among welfare recipients necessitates that funds be provided for this purpose. But, according to several authors, what is required is not so much major new investments in education and training as resources devoted to helping people find jobs in the private sector. . . .

REDUCING OUT-OF-WEDLOCK BIRTHS: The majority of women on welfare had their first child as a teenager. Most of these births now occur outside of marriage and are unintended. However, there is little support in the research literature for the proposition that denying benefits to this group will prevent such pregnancies from occurring. Modest impacts on marriage and abortion are more likely.

REDUCING CHILD POVERTY: Moving more children out of poverty requires that income from a low-wage job be combined with child care, health insurance, the Earned Income Tax Credit, and support from both parents. Child support reform in particular could reduce poverty and welfare costs as much as anything else that recently has been proposed. . . .

In sum, measured against the objectives of providing adequate flexibility to the states, encouraging work, strengthening the family, and reducing poverty, most current proposals are found wanting.

9. Introduction to the Unabomber's Manifesto: "Industrial Society and Its Future" by Theodore Kaczynski, September 19, 1995

Introduction

1. The Industrial Revolution and its consequences have been a disaster for the human race. They have greatly increased the life-expectancy of those of us who live in "advanced" countries, but they have destabilized society, have made life unfulfilling, have subjected human beings to indignities, have led to widespread psychological suffering (in the Third World to physical suffering as well) and have inflicted severe damage on the natural world. The contin-

ued development of technology will worsen the situation. It will certainly subject human beings to greater indignities and inflict greater damage on the natural world, it will probably lead to greater social disruption and psychological suffering, and it may lead to increased physical suffering even in "advanced" countries.

2. The industrial-technological system may survive or it may break down. If it survives, it MAY eventually achieve a low level of physical and psychological suffering, but only after passing through a long and very painful period of adjustment and only at the cost of permanently reducing human beings and many other living organisms to engineered products and mere cogs in the social machine. Furthermore, if the system survives, the consequences will be inevitable: There is no way of reforming or modifying the system so as to prevent it from depriving people of dignity and autonomy.

3. If the system breaks down the consequences will still be very painful. But the bigger the system grows the more disastrous the results of its breakdown will be, so if it is to break down it had best break down sooner rather than later.

4. We therefore advocate a revolution against the industrial system. This revolution may or may not make use of violence: it may be sudden or it may be a relatively gradual process spanning a few decades. We can't predict any of that. But we do outline in a very general way the measures that those who hate the industrial system should take in order to prepare the way for a revolution against that form of society. This is not to be a POLITICAL revolution. Its object will be to overthrow not governments but the economic and technological basis of the present society.

5. In this article we give attention to only some of the negative developments that have grown out of the industrial-technological system. Other such developments we mention only briefly or ignore altogether. This does not mean that we regard these other developments as unimportant. For practical reasons we have to confine our discussion to areas that have received insufficient public attention or in which we have something new to say. For example, since there are well-developed environmental and wilderness movements, we have written very little about environmental degradation or the destruction of wild nature, even though we consider these to be highly important.

10. SUPREME COURT DECISION IN *CLINTON V. JONES,* ALLOWING PAULA JONES'S CIVIL LAWSUIT AGAINST PRESIDENT WILLIAM JEFFERSON CLINTON TO PROCEED, MAY 27, 1997

This case raises a constitutional and a prudential question concerning the Office of the President of the United States. Respondent, a private citizen, seeks to recover damages from the current occupant of that office based on actions allegedly taken before his term began. The President submits that in all but the most exceptional cases the Constitution requires federal courts to defer such litigation until his term ends and that, in any event, respect for the office warrants such a stay. Despite the force of the arguments supporting the President's submissions, we conclude that they must be rejected. . . .

[Bill Clinton] does not contend that the occupant of the Office of the President is "above the law," in the sense that his conduct is entirely immune from judicial scrutiny. The President argues merely for a postponement of the judicial proceedings that will determine whether he violated any law. . . .

Rather than arguing that the decision of the case will produce either an aggrandizement of judicial power or a narrowing of executive power, petitioner [Clinton] contends that—as a by-product of an otherwise traditional exercise of judicial power—burdens will be placed on the President that will hamper the performance of his official duties. . . .

Petitioner's predictive judgment finds little support in either history or the relatively narrow compass of the issues raised in this particular case. As we have already noted, in the more than 200-year history of the Republic, only three sitting Presidents have been subjected to suits for their private actions. If the past is any indicator, it seems unlikely that a deluge of such litigation will ever engulf the Presidency.

11. CONCLUSIONS FROM THE REPORT BY INDEPENDENT COUNSEL KENNETH STARR RECOMMENDING IMPEACHMENT OF PRESIDENT WILLIAM JEFFERSON CLINTON, SUBMITTED TO CONGRESS ON SEPTEMBER 9, 1998

There is Substantial and Credible Information that President Clinton Committed Acts that May Constitute Grounds for an Impeachment

Introduction

Pursuant to Section 595(c) of Title 28, the Office of Independent Counsel (OIC) hereby submits substantial and credible information that President Clinton obstructed justice during the *Jones v. Clinton* sexual harassment lawsuit by lying under oath and concealing evidence of his relationship with a young White House intern and federal employee, Monica Lewinsky. After a federal criminal investigation of the President's actions began in January 1998, the President lied under oath to the grand jury and obstructed justice during the grand jury investigation. There also is substantial and credible information that the President's actions with respect to Monica Lewinsky constitute an abuse of authority inconsistent with the President's constitutional duty to faithfully execute the laws.

There is substantial and credible information supporting the following eleven possible grounds for impeachment:

1. President Clinton lied under oath in his civil case when he denied a sexual affair, a sexual relationship, or sexual relations with Monica Lewinsky.

2. President Clinton lied under oath to the grand jury about his sexual relationship with Ms. Lewinsky.

3. In his civil deposition, to support his false statement about the sexual relationship, President Clinton also lied under oath about being alone with Ms. Lewinsky and about the many gifts exchanged between Ms. Lewinsky and him.

4. President Clinton lied under oath in his civil deposition about his discussions with Ms. Lewinsky concerning her involvement in the *Jones* case.

5. During the *Jones* case, the President obstructed justice and had an understanding with Ms. Lewinsky to jointly conceal the truth about their relationship by concealing gifts subpoenaed by Ms. Jones's attorneys.

6. During the *Jones* case, the President obstructed justice and had an understanding with Ms. Lewinsky to jointly conceal the truth of their relationship from the judicial process by a scheme that included the following means: (i) Both the President and Ms. Lewinsky understood that they would lie under oath in the *Jones* case about their sexual relationship; (ii) the President suggested to Ms. Lewinsky that she prepare an affidavit that, for the President's purposes, would memorialize her testimony under oath and could be used to prevent questioning of both of them about their relationship; (iii) Ms. Lewinsky signed and filed the false affidavit; (iv) the President used Ms. Lewinsky's false affidavit at his deposition in an attempt to head off questions about Ms. Lewinsky; and (v) when that failed, the President lied under oath at his civil deposition about the relationship with Ms. Lewinsky.

7. President Clinton endeavored to obstruct justice by helping Ms. Lewinsky obtain a job in New York at a time when she would have been a witness harmful to him were she to tell the truth in the *Jones* case.

8. President Clinton lied under oath in his civil deposition about his discussions with Vernon Jordan concerning Ms. Lewinsky's involvement in the *Jones* case.

9. The President improperly tampered with a potential witness by attempting to corruptly influence the testimony of his personal secretary, Betty Currie, in the days after his civil deposition.

10. President Clinton endeavored to obstruct justice during the grand jury investigation by refusing to testify for seven months and lying to senior White House aides with knowledge that they would relay the President's false statements to the grand jury—and did thereby deceive, obstruct, and impede the grand jury.

11. President Clinton abused his constitutional authority by (i) lying to the public and the Congress in January 1998 about his relationship with Ms. Lewinsky; (ii) promising at that time to cooperate fully with the grand jury investigation; (iii) later refusing six invitations to testify voluntarily to the grand jury; (iv) invoking Executive Privilege; (v) lying to the grand jury in August 1998; and (vi) lying again to the public and Congress on August 17, 1998—all as part of an effort to hinder, impede, and deflect possible inquiry by the Congress of the United States.

The first two possible grounds for impeachment concern the President's lying under oath about the nature of his relationship with Ms. Lewinsky. The details associated with those grounds are, by their nature, explicit. The President's testimony unfortunately has rendered the details essential with respect to those two grounds, as will be explained in those grounds.

12. PRESIDENT WILLIAM JEFFERSON CLINTON'S RESPONSE TO REFERRAL OF OFFICE OF INDEPENDENT COUNSEL, SEPTEMBER 12, 1998

Note: This official statement was made through President Clinton's lawyer.

On May 31, 1998, the spokesman for Independent Counsel Kenneth W. Starr declared that the Office's Monica Lewinsky investigation "is not about sex. This case is about perjury, subornation of perjury, witness tampering, obstruction of justice. That is what this case is about." (i) Now that the 450-page Referral to the United States House of Representatives . . . (the "Referral") is public, it is plain that "sex" is precisely what this four-and-a-half year investigation has boiled down to. The Referral is so loaded with irrelevant and unnecessary graphic and salacious allegations that only one conclusion is possible: its principal purpose is to damage the President.

The President has acknowledged and apologized for an inappropriate sexual relationship with Ms. Lewinsky, so there is no need to describe that relationship in ugly detail. No one denies that the relationship was wrong or that the President was responsible. The Referral's pious defense of its pornographic specificity is that, in the Independent Counsel's view: "the details are crucial to an informed evaluation of the testimony, the credibility of witnesses, and the reliability of other evidence. Many of the details reveal highly personal information; many are sexually explicit. This is unfortunate, but it is essential."

Narrative at 20. This statement is patently false. Any fair reader of the Referral will easily discern that many of the lurid allegations, which need not be recounted here, have no justification at all, even in terms of any OIC [Office of Independent Counsel] legal theory. They plainly do not relate, even arguably, to activities which may be within the definition of "sexual relations" in the President's *Jones* deposition, which is the excuse advanced by the OIC. They are simply part of a hit-and-run smear campaign, and their inclusion says volumes about the OIC's tactics and objectives. . . .

Spectacularly absent from the Referral is any discussion of contradictory or exculpatory evidence or any evidence that would cast doubt on the credibility of the testimony the OIC cites (but does not explicitly quote). This is a failure of fundamental fairness which is highly prejudicial to the President and it is reason alone to withhold judgment on the Referral's allegations until all the prosecutors' evidence can be scrutinized—and then challenged, as necessary, by evidence from the President.

The real critique can occur only with access to the materials on which the prosecutors have ostensibly relied. Only at that time can contradictory evidence be identified and the context and consistency (or lack thereof) of the cited evidence be ascertained. Since we have not been given access to the transcripts and other materials compiled by the OIC, our inquiry is therefore necessarily limited. But even with this limited access, our preliminary review reaffirms how little this highly intrusive and disruptive investigation has in fact yielded. In instance after instance, the OIC's allegations fail to withstand scrutiny either as a factual matter, or a legal matter, or both. The Referral quickly emerges as a portrait of biased recounting, skewed analysis, and unconscionable overreaching.

In our Preliminary Memorandum, filed yesterday, at pages 3–12; we set forth at some length the various ways in which impeachable "high Crimes and Misdemeanors" have been defined. Nothing in the Referral even approximates such conduct. In the English practice from which the Framers borrowed the phrase, "High Crimes and Misdemeanors" denoted political offenses, the critical element of which was *injury to the state.* Impeachment was intended to redress public offenses committed by public officials in violation of the public trust and duties. Because presidential impeachment invalidates the will of the American people, it was designed to be justified for the gravest wrongs—offenses against the Constitution itself. In short, only "serious assaults on the integrity of the processes of government," (2) and "such crimes as would so stain a president as to make his continuance in office dangerous to the public order," (3) constitute impeachable offenses. The eleven supposed "grounds for impeachment" set forth in the section of the Referral called "Acts That May Constitute Grounds for an Impeachment" ("Acts") fall far short of that high standard, and their very allegation demeans the constitutional process. The document is at bottom overreaching in an extravagant effort to find a case where there is none.

Allegation I—Perjury in January 17, 1998, Deposition

We begin our response to the OIC's charge that the President committed perjury in his January 17 deposition in the *Jones* case with these simple facts: the President's relationship with Ms. Lewinsky was wrong; he admitted it was wrong; and he has asked for the forgiveness of his family and the American people. The perjury charges in the Referral in reality serve one principal purpose for the OIC—to provide an opportunity to lay out in a public forum as much salacious, gratuitous detail as possible with the goal of damaging the President and the presidency.

The OIC begins its catalogue of "acts that may constitute grounds for impeachment" with the allegation that "[t]here is substantial and credible information that President Clinton lied under oath as a defendant in *Jones v. Clinton* regarding his sexual relationship with Monica Lewinsky." Acts at 5. The OIC contends that, for legal reasons, it must discuss its allegations of sexual activity in detail and then goes out of its way to supply lurid detail after lurid detail that are completely irrelevant to any legal claim, obviously hoping that the shock value of its footnotes will overcome the absence of legal foundation for the perjury allegation.

In reaching any fair judgment as to the merits of the OIC's claim that the President's testimony establishes a basis for impeachment, it is important to understand a few additional points. First, the OIC barely acknowledges the elements of perjury, including, in particular, the substantial burden that must be met to show that the alleged false statements were made "knowingly," Preliminary Memorandum at 52, or that they were material to the *Jones* proceeding.

Second, the OIC ignores the careful standards that the courts have mandated to prevent the misuse of perjury allegations. As was set out in detail in our Preliminary Memorandum, pages 51–64, literally true statements cannot be the basis for a perjury prosecution, even if a witness intends to mislead the questioner. Likewise, answers to inherently ambiguous questions cannot constitute perjury. And, normally, a perjury prosecution may not rest on the testimony of a single witness. . . .

Instead of acknowledging the well-settled legal limits on perjury cases, or grappling with the important limitations on perjury prosecutions, the OIC has chosen to fill its report with unnecessary and salacious sex—details that cause pain and damage for absolutely no legitimate reason.

13. Articles of Impeachment of President William Jefferson Clinton Passed by the U.S. House of Representatives, December 19, 1998

House Resolution 611: Resolved, that William Jefferson Clinton, President of the United States, is impeached for high crimes and misdemeanors, and that the following Articles of Impeachment be exhibited to the United States Senate. . . .

Article I

In his conduct while president of the United States, William Jefferson Clinton, in violation of his constitutional oath faithfully to execute the office of president of the United States and, to the best of his ability, preserve, protect and defend the Constitution of the United States, and in violation of his constitutional duty to take care that the laws be faithfully executed, has willfully corrupted and manipulated the judicial process of the United States for his personal gain and exoneration, impeding the administration of justice, in that on August 17th, 1998, William Jefferson Clinton swore to tell the truth, the whole truth and nothing but the truth before a federal grand jury of the United States. Contrary to that oath, William Jefferson Clinton willfully provided perjurious, false and misleading testimony to the grand jury concerning one or more of the following:

One, the nature and details of his relationship with a subordinate government employee;

Two, prior perjurious, false and misleading testimony he gave in a federal civil rights action brought against him;

Three, prior false and misleading statements he allowed his attorney to make to a federal judge in that civil-rights action;

And four, his corrupt efforts to influence the testimony of witnesses and to impede the discovery of evidence in that civil-rights action. . . .

Article II

In his conduct, while president of the United States, William Jefferson Clinton . . . has prevented, obstructed and impeded the administration of justice and has to that end engaged personally and through his subordinates and agents in a course of conduct or scheme designed to delay, impede, cover up and conceal the existence of evidence and testimony related to a federal civil rights action brought against him in a duly instituted judicial proceeding. The means used to implement this course of conduct or scheme included one or more of the following acts:

One, on or about December 17, 1997, William Jefferson Clinton corruptly encouraged a witness in a federal civil rights action brought against him to execute a sworn affidavit in that proceeding that he knew to be perjurious, false and misleading.

Two, on or about December 17, 1997, William Jefferson Clinton corruptly encouraged a witness in a federal civil rights action brought against him to give perjurious, false and misleading testimony if and when called to testify personally in that proceeding.

Three, on or about December 28, 1997, William Jefferson Clinton corruptly engaged in, encouraged or supported a scheme to conceal evidence that had been subpoenaed in a federal civil rights action brought against him.

Four, beginning on or about December 7, 1997, and continuing through and including January 14, 1998, William Jefferson Clinton intensified and succeeded in an effort to secure job assistance to a witness in a federal civil rights action brought against him, in order to corruptly prevent the truthful testimony of that witness in that proceeding at a time when the truthful testimony of that witness would have been harmful to him.

Five, on January 17, 1998, at his deposition in a federal civil rights action brought against him, William Jefferson Clinton corruptly allowed his attorney to make false and misleading statements to a federal judge characterizing an affidavit in order to prevent questioning deemed relevant by the judge. Such false and misleading statements were subsequently acknowledged by his attorney in a communication to that judge.

On or about January 18 and January 20, 21, 1998, William Jefferson Clinton related a false and misleading account of events relevant to a federal civil rights action brought against him, to a potential witness in that proceeding in order to corruptly influence the testimony of that witness.

On or about January 21, 23 and 26th, 1998, William Jefferson Clinton made false and misleading statements to potential witnesses in a federal grand jury proceeding in order to corruptly influence the testimony of those witnesses. The false and misleading statements made by William Jefferson Clinton were repeated by the witnesses to the grand jury, causing the grand jury to receive false and misleading information.

In all of this, William Jefferson Clinton has undermined the integrity of his office, has brought disrepute on the presidency, has betrayed his trust as president, and has acted in a manner subversive of the rule of law and justice, to the manifest injury of the people of the United States. Wherefore, William Jefferson Clinton, by such conduct, warrants impeachment and trial and removal from office and disqualification to hold and enjoy any office of honor, trust or profit under the United States.

APPENDIX B

Biographies of Major Personalities

Albright, Madeleine (Marie Jana Korbel)

(1937–) *ambassador to the United Nations (1993–1996), secretary of state (1997–2001)*

Born in Prague, Czechoslovakia, as Marie Jana Korbel, Albright was the daughter of a Czech diplomat and his wife. In 1939, the family fled to England after the Nazis occupied Czechoslovakia. Throughout most of her life she believed her parents had exiled for political reasons, but in 1997, as a result of the vetting for her appointment as secretary of state, she learned that her parents were Jewish and that three of her grandparents had died in the Holocaust. After the war, the family returned to Czechoslovakia but fled again after the Communist takeover in 1948. They immigrated to the United States the same year.

In 1959, Albright graduated from Wellesley College in Massachusetts, where she majored in political science. That year she also took the name Albright when she married the newspaper journalist Joseph Albright, with whom she had three daughters. They divorced in 1982. Albright received her master's degree (1968) and Ph.D. (1976) from Columbia University. She then worked for Zbigniew Brzezinski, President Jimmy Carter's National Security Advisor. From 1978 to 1981, Albright was on the staff of both the National Security Council and the White House, where she was responsible for foreign policy legislation. During the Reagan and Bush administrations she studied developments and trends in the Soviet Union and Eastern Europe as a senior fellow in Soviet and Eastern European affairs at the Center for Strategic and International Studies; she cofounded and became president of the Center for National Policy; and she joined the faculty of Georgetown University's School of Foreign Service, where she taught courses in international affairs, U.S. foreign policy, Russian foreign policy, and Central and Eastern European politics.

President Bill Clinton appointed Albright ambassador to the United Nations, where she had a difficult relationship with Secretary-General Boutros Boutros-Ghali. A staunch anticommunist, she won considerable respect for her impassioned condemnation of Fidel Castro in 1996, after Cuban jets shot down a civilian plane carrying Miami-based Cuban exiles. Clinton nominated her as secretary of state in December 1996, and when she was unanimously confirmed in January 1997, she became the first woman to hold that office in American history.

As secretary of state, Albright took an active role in shaping and implementing U.S. foreign policy. Her belief that the international community at large, and the United States in particular, should protect human rights made her a proponent of military intervention in the former Yugoslavia and elsewhere, and it placed her at odds with Secretary of Defense William Cohen and others within the Clinton administration who advocated using military force with greater restraint. Among the issues Albright dealt with while in office were the Balkan conflicts, the ongoing Middle East peace efforts, North Korea's efforts to develop nuclear weapons, and the expansion of NATO to include Eastern European nations formerly affiliated with the Soviet Union. Albright published her autobiography, *Madam Secretary,* in 2003.

Allen, Woody (Allan Stewart Konigsberg)

(1935–) *film actor, writer, director*

Born Allan Stewart Konigsberg in the Bronx, New York, to first-generation Jewish Americans of Austrian and Russian descent, Allen disliked school, which he found boring and demeaning, and his academic performance was indifferent. As a teenager he enjoyed sports; studied the clarinet, which became a lifelong passion; and began performing magic tricks. After graduating from high school he wrote jokes and enrolled at New York University and New York's City College but dropped out.

In 1955 Allen began working as part of NBC's Writers Development Program and moved to Hollywood to write for the *Colgate Comedy Hour.* He soon became one of television's most successful comedy writers, working for such stars as Sid Caesar and Art Carney. He did not respect the television medium or find the work satisfying, however, and in 1959 he quit to start a new career as a stand-up comedian. That same year Allen entered psychoanalysis, which he continued through 1998, when he quit after declaring he no longer needed it after his marriage to his third wife, Soon-Yi Previn. Allen's experience in therapy informs much of his work, either as the target of his humor or as the basis for his exploration of character and human interaction, or as both.

After initially working free at coffeehouses, where he could hone his comic skills, Allen became one of the most successful stand-up comedians in the country, attracting large audiences in Las Vegas venues and appearing first as a frequent guest and later as a guest host on *The Tonight Show.*

Allen's transition to film occurred in 1964, when Charles K. Feldman approached him to write the script for and act in the comic farce *What's New, Pussycat?* In 1966, he published his first story in *The New Yorker,* wrote his first full-length Broadway play, and had his debut as film director with *What's Up, Tiger Lily?*

Allen's early comic films won him a following. *Play It Again, Sam* (1972), was his first major success as a film director, and it began his cinematic collaboration with the actress Diane Keaton. (Their romantic relationship ended about 1970.) Between 1972 and 1977, Allen and Keaton costarred in three additional comedies, including *Annie Hall* (1977), which is based loosely on their relationship and marks Allen's development from a director of comedy and farce to a director of funny films that seek to explore human relationships and behavior in a serious, artistic fashion. His subsequent films often employ experimental narrative techniques and are usually informed by an absurdist, sometimes nihilistic worldview.

Allen met Mia Farrow in late 1979, and in 1980 they became a couple, although they never married and maintained separate residences. Farrow starred in 13 of Allen's films between 1982 and 1992, including some of his finest and most enjoyed movies, such as *Hannah and Her Sisters* (1986), *Radio Days* (1987), and

Crimes and Misdemeanors (1989). Their romantic and cinematic relationship ended in 1992, after Farrow discovered Allen was having an affair with her adopted daughter, Soon-Yi Previn. (The conductor/composer André Previn is Soon-Yi's adopted father). Farrow subsequently accused Allen of sexually molesting their adopted daughter Dylan. The resulting scandal became a media event that pushed the normally private Allen into the headlines and made his personal life the topic of conversation throughout the world. An investigation found insufficient grounds for filing criminal charges against Allen, but the judge presiding over the later custody trial was highly critical and denied him custody of or visitation rights with the children. Allen and Previn married in 1998 and went on to adopt children of their own.

Although his productive collaboration with Farrow ended in 1992, Allen directed some of his finest and most innovative movies during the remainder of the decade, including *Bullets over Broadway* (1994), which equates the morality of mobsters with that of artists who take themselves too seriously and for which Dianne Wiest received the Academy Award as best supporting actress and Allen received a nomination as best director; *Mighty Aphrodite* (1995), for which Mira Sorvino won the Academy Award as best supporting actress; *Deconstructing Harry* (1997), which uses a postmodern narrative structure to exaggerate grotesquely all of the worst things people said about Allen after his breakup with Farrow; and *Celebrity* (1998), which critiques America's obsession with celebrities. A gifted writer as well as director, Allen received Academy Award nominations during the 1990s for best original screenplay for *Alice* (1990), *Husbands and Wives* (1992), *Bullets over Broadway* (with Doug McGrath), *Mighty Aphrodite,* and *Deconstructing Harry.* His play *Central Park West* enjoyed 343 performances on Broadway in 1995, as part of *Death Defying Acts,* a trilogy of one-act plays by Allen, Elaine May, and David Mamet.

Berners-Lee, Tim (1955–   ) *computer software developer*
Born in London and educated at Queen's College at Oxford University, Berners-Lee is credited with developing the World Wide Web. As a student in the mid-1970s, he built his first computer by using a soldering iron, TTL gates, an M6800 processor, and an old television. After graduation, he developed transaction systems, message relays, and bar code technology

for the British-based Plessey Telecommunications Ltd. In 1980, Berners-Lee served as consultant software engineer at CERN, the European Particle Physics Laboratory in Geneva, Switzerland. During that time he developed *Enquire,* his first program for storing information by using random associations.

Between 1981 and 1984, Berners-Lee developed and distributed real-time control firmware, graphics and communications software, and a generic macro language while working for John Poole's Image Computer Systems Ltd. In 1984, he accepted a fellowship at CERN to work on distributed real-time systems for scientific data acquisition and system control.

In 1989, Berners-Lee proposed the creation of the World Wide Web, a global hypertext project. Based on the earlier *Enquire* work, it was designed to enable people to share information via a network of hypertext documents. He created the first World Wide Web server, httpd, and the first client, WorldWideWeb. In April 1992, CERN released the Web to the public, thereby inaugurating the era of the Internet.

Between 1991 and 1993, Berners-Lee continued to upgrade the design of the Web, incorporating responses he received from users. He founded the World Wide Web Consortium at the Laboratory for Computer Science (LCS) at Massachusetts Institute of Technology (MIT) and since has served as director of the World Wide Web Consortium, which coordinates Web development worldwide. In 1999, he became the first holder of the 3Com Founders chair at LCS. His publications include *Weaving the Web: The Original Design and Ultimate Destiny of the World Wide Web by Its Inventor* (1999), which discusses the past, present, and future of the Internet.

Bush, George Herbert Walker (1924–)
congressman (1967–1971), CIA director (1975–1977), U.S. vice president (1981–1989), U.S. president (1989–1993)

Son of the Republican senator Prescott Bush, George Herbert Walker Bush was born in Milton, Massachusetts, and attended the prestigious Phillips Academy. He joined the U.S. Naval Reserve upon graduating in 1941 and served with distinction during World War II. In 1943, he became the youngest pilot in the navy. After the war, Bush attended Yale University and graduated in 1948. He went to work in the oil industry and, in 1954, founded the successful Zapata Off-Shore Company, which made him a million-

aire. While supporting Barry Goldwater for president, Bush won the Texas Republican Senate nomination but lost the general election in 1964. In 1966, he won election to the U.S. House of Representatives and in 1968 he was reelected. In 1970, after losing a Senate bid to the conservative Democrat Lloyd Bentsen, Bush was appointed ambassador to the United Nations by President Richard Nixon. In that capacity he supported the Middle East peace proposals initiated by Secretary of State William Rogers and urged concerted world action against the narcotics trade.

After the 1972 elections, Nixon named Bush chairman of the Republican National Committee, but he was largely ineffective as a result of the Watergate scandal. After Nixon's resignation Bush accepted an appointment by President Gerald Ford to lead the U.S. liaison office in the People's Republic of China. In November 1975, Ford appointed Bush director of the CIA, a post he held through the remainder of Ford's presidency. Bush contended for the Republican vice-presidential nomination in 1976, but Ford chose Senator Robert Dole instead. After Ford's defeat in the general election, Bush returned to private life, serving as chairman of the First National Bank of Houston. In 1980, he challenged the front-runner Ronald Reagan for the presidential nomination but lost in a surprisingly close contest. Reagan named him as his running mate, and Bush served as vice president during both of Reagan's terms, during which he cultivated ties to right-wing Republicans. Many social conservatives remained suspicious of his commitment to their agenda, however, and he did not enjoy the same level of support from them that Reagan did.

The extent of Bush's role in the Iran-contra affair was not established in 1988, when he defeated Michael Dukakis for the presidency. But a 1992 independent counsel's report concluded that despite his claims that he had been "out of the loop," Bush had been significantly involved in the Reagan era scheme that sold U.S. arms to Iran in return for promises to free American hostages in Lebanon. The profits from the arms sales were then illegally diverted to pay a number of intermediaries and support the anticommunist contras in Nicaragua, in direct violation of congressional prohibitions. Bush and his defenders maintained that the report, which was released just before the presidential election, was biased and politically motivated.

In December 1989—the end of his first year in office—Bush ordered an invasion of Panama, which concluded in the arrest of Panama's dictator and former CIA informant President Manuel Noriega, whom Bush accused of complicity in drug smuggling. Bush maintained Reagan's policy of supporting the right-wing military dictatorship in El Salvador in its civil war against pro-Communist populists, a war that finally concluded in 1991, with a negotiated peace settlement. Bush also retained Reagan's hard line against Fidel Castro's Communist regime in Cuba.

Bush initially took a hard line against Soviet leader Mikhail Gorbachev, of whom he was suspicious. But the rapidly spreading collapse of communism in Eastern Europe and the Soviet Union compelled him to reconsider and offer greater support to Gorbachev. During the summer of 1989, Gorbachev and Bush engaged in secret dialogues to arrange a summit meeting, and the Soviets assured the Americans that they would not intervene militarily in Eastern Europe to support the Communist regimes there. After Gorbachev made this position public, the Communist empire quickly collapsed.

In September 1990, Great Britain, France, the United States, and the Soviet Union signed a peace treaty with East and West Germany officially concluding World War II and establishing the withdrawal of the Soviet army from Eastern Europe. And on November 17 to 19, leaders of all the European states, the United States, Canada, and the Soviet Union met in Paris, where they signed a new charter regulating relations among all the participants, a nonaggression agreement between members of NATO and the defunct Warsaw Pact, and the Treaty on Conventional Forces in Europe (CFE), which reduced the number of troops and tanks opposing each other in Europe. Upon signing the Charter of Paris on November 21, 1990, Bush declared that the cold war was officially over.

In the aftermath of the cold war Bush and Gorbachev worked together to promote world stability and establish "a new world order." In July 1991, the Warsaw Pact dissolved, and shortly thereafter Bush traveled to Moscow, where he and Gorbachev signed the Strategic Arms Reduction Treaty (START). This was the first treaty to reduce long-range nuclear stockpiles instead of merely limiting their growth. Afterward Bush flew to Kiev in support of Gorbachev's efforts to hold the Soviet Union together. Bush however, declined to grant Gorbachev the massive amounts of economic aid the Soviet leader insisted he needed to maintain stability, which he had expected in return for concessions on arms control and for withdrawal of Soviet troops from Afghanistan.

Bush also worked to improve relations with China, offering most-favored-nation trade status, offering to sell military planes, and largely ignoring the 1989 uprising in Tiananmen Square in which the Chinese army routed students who were demanding democratic freedoms.

In 1990, Bush formed the first major post–cold war military alliance when he assembled a large international coalition to oppose Iraq's annexation of oil-rich Kuwait. And in January and February 1991, the U.S.-led alliance won a quick and stunning victory in the Persian Gulf War. Bush ordered an end to the fighting before the Iraqi forces were completely destroyed, however, and Iraqi president Saddam Hussein's subsequent refusal to cooperate with UN weapons inspections and his ruthless military persecution of Iraqi Kurds diminished the substantial political gain Bush initially achieved from the war.

During Bush's presidency, the unemployment rate rose and the economy faltered, falling into recession in 1991 for the first time since 1982. He appointed two conservative justices to the Supreme Court, David Souter and Clarence Thomas, and negotiated the North American Free Trade Agreement (NAFTA), whose passage through Congress Bill Clinton later secured. Although he opposed abortion and made other concessions to the Moral Majority and religious Right, many of the latter were frustrated because he did not take stronger action to repeal legalized abortion or otherwise accommodate their social agenda. On the other hand, Bush's probusiness fiscal policies appealed to fiscal conservatives, if not to environmentalists, who deplored administration policies that appeared to sacrifice environmental interests for economic gains. Nor was Bush widely supported by organized labor, which maintained that his policies valued corporate profits more than the well-being of workers.

Despite the high approval ratings that followed the success of the Panama invasion and the Persian Gulf War, the failing economy and revelations of Bush's actual role in the Iran-contra affair left him politically vulnerable, and Bush lost his reelection bid to Clinton in 1992.

Bush's speeches and statements are collected in *Public Papers of the Presidents of the United States, George H. W. Bush (1989–1993).*

Clinton, Hillary Rodham (1947–) *first lady of the United States (1993–2001), U.S. senator (2001–)*
Born in Chicago, Clinton grew up in Park Ridge, a Chicago suburb. Her father owned a textile business that afforded the family a comfortable living. As a teenager she identified with the Republican Party, the party of her parents, and in 1964 she campaigned for the conservative presidential candidate Barry Goldwater. In 1965 she enrolled in Wellesley College, where she became a Democrat, and in 1968 she was a volunteer in the presidential campaign of the antiwar candidate Eugene McCarthy. Clinton graduated Wellesley in 1969 and then enrolled at Yale Law School, where she was influenced by the Yale alumna Marian Wright Edelman, a lawyer and children's rights advocate. In 1974 she joined the faculty at the University of Arkansas School of Law, where she renewed her acquaintance with her fellow professor and Yale Law School graduate Bill Clinton, whom she married in 1975. Subsequently, she joined the prominent Rose Law Firm in Little Rock, Arkansas, where she later became a partner. While also promoting her husband's political aspirations, Clinton built her own legal career, serving on the boards of several high-profile corporations and being twice named (1988, 1991) by the *National Law Journal* as one of the nation's 100 most influential lawyers. She also worked on programs that aided children and the disadvantaged during this time.

Hillary Clinton was credited with saving her husband's 1992 presidential campaign when, in response to accusations that he had committed adultery, the couple appeared on the television news show *60 Minutes* and spoke forthrightly about their rocky marriage. After his election, Bill Clinton appointed her to lead a task force charged with formulating legislation for providing universal health care coverage, but the effort failed to win passage in Congress. She was implicated in alleged wrongdoings in the Whitewater affair and the so-called Travelgate matter, in which staff of the White House travel office were fired and then reinstated. No findings were made against her in either matter.

As a forceful, outspoken, successful professional woman, Hillary Clinton was championed by feminists and vilified by religious fundamentalists and other conservatives who believed that women should remain subservient to men. As the 1996 election approached, Hillary Clinton assumed a more traditional role as first lady. In 1998, she defended her husband against charges that he had had an adulterous affair with Monica Lewinsky, claiming that he was the target of a "vast, right-wing conspiracy." Although emotionally distraught by his subsequent admission that the charges about the affair were accurate, she agreed to remain married. The couple subsequently entered marriage counseling, from which both maintain they benefited. In 1999, Hillary Clinton established residency in New York, so she could run for the Senate seat vacated by Daniel Patrick Moynihan, and, as the Democratic nominee, she was elected in 2000.

Her publications include *It Takes a Village* (1996), which describes her views about child rearing, and her autobiography, *Living History* (2003).

Clinton, William Jefferson (Bill Clinton)
(1946–) *Arkansas attorney general (1976–1978), Arkansas governor (1978–1980, 1982–1992), U.S. president (1993–2001)*
Born in Hope, Arkansas, Clinton never knew his biological father, a traveling salesman who died in a car accident shortly before his birth. His mother, Virginia Dell Blythe, subsequently married Roger Clinton, and Bill eventually took his stepfather's name. Clinton's interest in public service was inspired when, as a teenager in 1963, he met President John F. Kennedy, who was assassinated about four months later.

In 1964, Clinton attended Georgetown University in Washington, D.C., where he majored in international affairs. He was elected student president during his freshman and sophomore years, and during his junior and senior years he was an intern for Senator J. William Fulbright, the Arkansas Democrat who chaired the U.S. Senate Committee on Foreign Relations. Clinton graduated in 1968, at the height of the Vietnam War, which he, as did Fulbright, opposed. He received a draft deferment to continue his studies as a prestigious Rhodes scholar at Oxford University in England. He later tried to extend the deferment by applying to the Reserve Officers' Training Corps (ROTC) program at the University of Arkansas School of Law but soon changed his plans and returned to Oxford, thereby making himself eligible for the draft. He was not chosen, however. His opposition to the war and his efforts to avoid service later became political liabilities. After completing his studies at Oxford, Clinton enrolled in the Yale University Law School in 1973. After graduation he joined the faculty of the University of Arkansas School of Law, where he taught until 1976.

In 1974, Clinton ran unsuccessfully for a seat in the U.S. House of Representatives, and in 1975, he married the attorney Hillary Rodham, a fellow Yale Law graduate, who promoted his political career. In 1976, he won election as attorney general of Arkansas, and in 1978 he became governor at the age of 32, the youngest governor in the country. His practice of raising taxes to fund public works projects was unpopular, however, and he failed to be reelected in 1980, the year Ronald Reagan was voted in as president. Clinton regained the governorship in 1982 and was reelected by large margins. A pragmatic centrist, Clinton appealed to Arkansas conservatives by imposing mandatory competency testing for teachers and students and stimulating investment in the state by granting tax breaks to industries.

Clinton's campaign for the 1992 Democratic presidential nomination was nearly undermined by Gennifer Flowers, an Arkansas woman who charged that he had had a 12-year extramarital affair with her, a charge that Clinton denied. After he and Hillary Rodham Clinton spoke frankly about their marital difficulties on *60 Minutes,* the widely viewed news show, he regained popular favor and went on to win the nomination over California governor Jerry Brown, Senator Tom Harkin of Iowa, Senator Bob Kerrey of Nebraska, Senator Paul Tsongas of Massachusetts, and Senator Al Gore of Tennessee, whom Clinton selected as his vice-presidential candidate. Emphasizing the weak economy and the failure of the incumbent president, George Herbert Walker Bush, to create sufficient jobs or otherwise address the needs of working Americans, Clinton and Gore prevailed in the general election and were inaugurated in January 1993.

Clinton suffered several setbacks in the first years of his presidency. His efforts to integrate homosexuals fully into the military met steep resistance, and in the end he settled for an indecisive "Don't ask; don't tell" policy on homosexuality, which retained the ban on gays in the armed services but protected servicemen and servicewomen from being questioned about their sexual preferences. Likewise, Clinton's ambitious plan for a national health-care system, formulated under the leadership of Hillary Rodham Clinton, failed, and his continued support of Bush's peacekeeping effort in Somalia led to a humiliating withdrawal at the end of 1993. Moreover, barely a month after Clinton took office, Islamic terrorists exploded a car bomb in the parking garage of New York's World Trade Center,

and shortly after that a federal raid on armed followers of David Koresh in Waco, Texas, ended in the death of some 75 of Koresh's followers, including at least 17 children who were inside the compound.

On the other hand, despite opposition from his own party, Clinton secured passage of the North American Free Trade Agreement (NAFTA), which Bush had negotiated and which created a free-trade zone for the United States, Canada, and Mexico. And during his first term, Congress enacted a deficit-reduction package, along with several major bills related to education, crime prevention, the environment, and women's and family issues. These included the Violence against Women Act and the Family and Medical Leave Act, which Bush had previously vetoed. After vetoing a Republican-sponsored bill mandating welfare reform in 1995, because he believed it failed to provide adequate safeguards for children, in 1996 Clinton and Congress agreed to a compromise bill that instituted the first significant welfare reform in decades.

In an effort to make his administration "look more like America," Clinton appointed a historic number of women and minorities to the cabinet and other influential positions. Janet Reno became the highest-ranking woman in the history of the executive branch when Clinton named her the nation's first female attorney general. Two other women also received cabinet appointments during his first term, as did blacks and Hispanics. In August, Clinton appointed Ruth Bader Ginsberg to fill the Supreme Court vacancy created by the retiring justice Byron R. White. Ginsberg became the second female Supreme Court justice in American history, after the Reagan appointee Sandra Day O'Connor. In his second term Clinton named Madeleine Albright the first female secretary of state.

Despite the domestic setbacks during his first term, Clinton achieved success in international diplomacy, securing an agreement from North Korea not to develop its nuclear capabilities, reaching an accord with Cuba to halt the mass exodus of refugees to the United States, and, with assistance from the former president Jimmy Carter, effecting the resignation of the military junta in Haiti and a late-year cease-fire in Bosnia. Clinton also mediated the historic Oslo Agreement between Israel and the Palestine Liberation Organization, in which the longtime enemies agreed to work toward peace and the ultimate creation of a Palestinian homeland. Clinton stimulated international trade by ending an embargo on Vietnam and dropping the linkage between China's human rights abuses and its ability to conduct business with the United States.

In 1994, the nation enjoyed an increase in the GDP of more than 50 percent and a decrease in the rate of unemployment. Nonetheless, the Democrats lost both chambers of Congress that year in the midterm elections, giving Republicans total control of the legislature for the first time in 40 years. Clinton interpreted the Republican victory as the public's repudiation of his more liberal policies, and he subsequently moved toward the political center. The Georgia congressman Newt Gingrich, an outspoken critic of Clinton's, was elected Speaker of the House, setting the stage for years of bitter partisanship that dominated the rest of Clinton's presidency. A budget showdown between Clinton and Congress in late 1995 and early 1996 resulted in the longest shutdown of nonessential government services in the nation's history. Clinton was generally perceived to have prevailed, and the majority of the public blamed the Republicans more than Clinton for the government's inability to perform its duties. This, along with the strong economy and Clinton's more centrist policies, enabled Clinton easily to defeat the Republican challenger, Robert Dole, in the 1996 presidential election.

Clinton's second term was characterized by an exceptionally robust economy; during it he fulfilled his promise of balancing the federal budget for the first time since 1969. The vibrant economy also produced historically high levels of home ownership, the lowest unemployment rate in nearly 30 years, and sizable gains in the stock markets, including an increase in the Dow-Jones average of some 4,500 points between 1996 and 1999.

Clinton also directed considerable attention to the deep racial divisions remaining within the nation, which he considered both inherently pernicious and dangerous to the overall well-being of the United States. Consequently, he gave significant power within his new administration to individuals of diverse racial and ethnic background, and he publicly defended affirmative action programs, although he sought to improve them. He also called for government action against hate crimes and initiated a year-long public dialogue about race, intended to elevate the level of understanding and appreciation of Americans for one another.

Overall, however, Clinton's ability to implement his domestic agenda was restricted by his ideological differences with Congress, which resulted in a series of political stalemates, or gridlock, and by his sex scandal with Monica Lewinsky, which culminated in his impeachment by the House of Representatives in December 1998 and his subsequent acquittal by the Senate in February 1999. The Lewinsky scandal was an outgrowth of the so-called Whitewater affair and a civil lawsuit claiming sexual harassment filed against Clinton by Paula Jones. Ironically, none of the charges against Clinton in either of those matters was sustained by the legal processes through which they proceeded.

In 1994, Attorney General Janet Reno appointed Robert E. Fiske, a former federal prosecutor, as special counsel to investigate charges that Bill Clinton and Hillary Rodham Clinton had improperly used political influence in their transactions with their business partner James B. McDougal in an investment deal involving the Whitewater Development Corporation, which later became bankrupt. Although McDougal was eventually convicted on charges of making illegal loans, and 10 others were convicted of related crimes, the four-year investigation did not find the Clintons culpable. But in late 1994, after Congress reenacted the independent counsel legislation that had expired in 1992, a panel of federal judges replaced Fiske and named as independent counsel Judge Kenneth Starr, a conservative Republican loosely affiliated with some of Clinton's political enemies. As independent counsel Starr enjoyed far-ranging powers of investigation that exceeded those of Special Prosecutor Fiske, and, unlike Fiske, he was not answerable to the attorney general. Other charges that Starr investigated during his four-year inquiry, but for which he found insufficient grounds for prosecution, were the suicide under questionable circumstances of Vincent Foster, a longtime friend of the Clintons'; the so-called Travelgate allegations involving the firing of established White House workers; and the so-called Filegate, in which the FBI files of some Republicans were found in the White House.

Also in 1994, Paula Jones filed a civil suit against Clinton alleging he had sexually harassed her while he was governor. Clinton lost a series of legal appeals requesting that the suit be deferred until after he was out of office, and after a Supreme Court ruling in 1997, the case moved forward (see Appendix A). Jones's attorneys received anonymous tips in October 1997, claiming that Clinton and Lewinsky, a former

White House intern in her early 20s, had been having a sexual affair, which, according to Starr's investigation, they conducted between November 1995 and March 1997. Claiming that Clinton's sexual conduct with Lewinsky was relevant to Jones's claim of harassment, Jones's attorneys deposed Clinton and Lewinsky in January 1998, and, while under oath, both denied having a sexual relationship. Clinton then reiterated his denial publicly. A federal judge in Arkansas dismissed Jones's suit in April 1998, characterizing it as "without merit," but revelations that Clinton may have lied in his deposition provided probable grounds for an appeal, and, to forestall that eventuality, Clinton settled the case in November 1998, agreeing to pay Jones $850,000.

When Starr received credible evidence that Clinton may have lied under oath, he broadened his existing Whitewater investigation to include the new charges. After conducting an extensive investigation in which Clinton and Lewinsky were compelled to reveal intimate details about their relationship before a grand jury in testimony later released to the public, Starr recommended in September 1998 that Clinton be impeached for committing perjury and for allegedly trying to influence Lewinsky's testimony. According to polls, the majority of the public appeared to believe that the charges were politically motivated and/or that they did not constitute an impeachable offense, as they did not pertain to Clinton's performance as president. Nonetheless, the Republican-dominated House voted to approve four articles of impeachment on December 11 and 12, making Clinton only the second U.S. president to be impeached. The Constitution requires a two-thirds majority vote by the Senate to convict a president, but the House managers who prosecuted the case failed to win even a simple majority, despite Republican control of the Senate, and Clinton was acquitted on February 12, 1999.

Throughout the impeachment process Clinton's public approval ratings actually increased, and Republicans suffered defeats in the November 1998 midterm elections, provoking Gingrich to resign as Speaker and subsequently give up his seat in Congress. Moreover, Clinton largely prevailed in setting the budget that fall, gaining $17.9 billion for credits to alleviate the global financial crisis and funding for his education initiatives, which called for hiring 100,000 additional elementary school teachers over seven years.

At the height of the impeachment process Clinton also ordered air strikes against Iraq in response to that nation's refusal to permit inspectors to monitor Iraq for weapons of mass destruction, as required by the treaty that ended the 1991 Persian Gulf War. Clinton took other aggressive steps in 1999 as well. He authorized a successful air war against Serbia, which compelled Serbia to end its practice of ethnic cleansing in its province of Kosovo, and he ordered missile attacks against terrorist training camps run by Osama bin Laden in Afghanistan in retaliation for al-Qaeda bombings of U.S. embassies in Africa. These failed, however, apparently by minutes, to kill bin Laden. Clinton also oversaw the expansion of NATO, which officially admitted the former Warsaw Pact members Hungary, Poland, and the Czech Republic in 1999.

In 2000, Clinton supported Gore's candidacy for president but maintained a relatively low profile during the campaign, as Gore chose to distance himself from the scandals that marred Clinton's presidency.

Clinton's speeches and statements are collected in *Public Papers of the Presidents of the United States, William J. Clinton (1994–2001)*. In 2004, he published his autobiography, *My Life*.

Cobain, Kurt (1967–1994) *lead singer of the rock band Nirvana*
Born in Aberdeen, Washington, Cobain and his Seattle-based rock group Nirvana were considered by some to be a voice for the so-called Generation X, Americans born in the 1960s, immediately after the post–World War II baby boom generation (born roughly 1946–1964). Combining elements of punk, heavy metal, and contemporary alternative music that became known as grunge rock, or Seattle grunge, Cobain assailed what he considered the hypocritical, materialistic corporate values of middle America. His expressions of despair and self-loathing attracted large audiences among Generation X and successor generations. Nirvana's 1991 album *Nevermind*, featuring the hit single "Smells Like Teen Spirit," sold 10 million copies. Other albums included *Bleach* (1990) and *In Utero* (1993). Shortly after recording the song "I Hate Myself and Want to Die," Cobain apparently committed suicide, distressing millions of fans throughout the world. He was survived by his wife, fellow rock performer Courtney Love.

Gates, Bill (1955–) *software designer and president of the Microsoft Corporation*
Born and raised in Seattle, Washington, Gates and his two sisters were children of an attorney and a teacher known for her work in philanthropic causes. Gates developed both his technological and his entrepreneurial skills at an early age. He attended public elementary school before transferring to the private Lakeside School, where he began programming computers at age 13. In high school he and a group of other students computerized their school's payroll system. He also formed Traf-O-Data, a company that sold traffic-counting systems to local governments.

In 1973, Gates enrolled in Harvard University, where he met Steve Ballmer, now Microsoft's chief executive officer, and developed a version of the BASIC programming language for the first microcomputers, which were then being developed for personal use. The success of that project led Gates to drop out of Harvard during his junior year and, along with his childhood friend Paul Allen, form the Microsoft company in 1975. Microsoft emerged as a major force in the industry in 1980 after it licenced its MS-DOS operating system to IBM for use on its first microcomputer, the IBM PC (personal computer), which first appeared on the market in 1981. As the IBM PC became the industry standard for personal computers, MS-DOS became the standard for operating systems in personal computers, and by the early 1990s, Microsoft had sold more than 100 million copies of its MS-DOS system.

One of the most important developments in the technological revolution of the late 20th century was the introduction in 1990 of the third version of Microsoft's Windows©, a computer operating system that was both comprehensible and affordable to middle-class and working-class users. As did the operating system used by Microsoft's less successful competitor Apple, Windows© replaced the more cumbersome and difficult-to-understand MS-DOS with a comparatively easy-to-use point-and-click system that was more visually oriented than word oriented, and hence more user friendly. Windows© thus made it feasible for average citizens to purchase computers for home use and to use them for a growing range of personal interests and needs. At the same time, Windows© facilitated the almost universal use of computers for both routine and specialized business practices. By 1993, Windows 3.0© and its later versions were selling at a rate of 1 million copies per month, and nearly 90 percent of the world's

personal companies employed a Microsoft operating system. The Windows 95© operating system, released in 1995, represented another significant step forward in personal computing, as it, for the first time, fully integrated MS-DOS with Windows©.

In addition to developing operating systems, Microsoft produced business-oriented software that was compatible with Windows©, such as word-processing and spreadsheet programs. Moreover, as the Internet developed, Microsoft entered the field. In 1994, Microsoft and McCaw Cellular Communications agreed to spend $9 billion to send 840 satellites into orbit to relay information around the world. That year, Microsoft also introduced its popular Internet Explorer© to compete with a web browser developed by Netscape. Both companies made their browsers free to users, a marketing strategy that stimulated the explosive growth in Internet use during the 1990s.

In 1996 Microsoft began bundling Internet Explorer© with Windows© and had begun the process of integrating Explorer© directly into Windows©. In response, Netscape accused Microsoft of violating a 1995 consent decree and sued. This suit, in turn, provoked the U.S. Department of Justice to reopen a broad investigation of Microsoft, and in 1998, it and 20 states filed two antitrust suits, accusing it of illegal marketing and trade practices. In 1999, a federal judge ruled that the Microsoft Corporation was guilty of unfair, monopolistic labor practices. The suit remained in litigation as of 2004.

Gates's book, *The Road Ahead* (1995) and *Business @ the Speed of Thought: Using a Digital Nervous System* (1999), which describes fundamentally new approaches to ways that computer technology can be used to solve business problems, were best sellers. (*Business @ the Speed of Thought* was later resubtitled *Succeeding in the Digital Economy*.) He donated the proceeds of both to nonprofit organizations that support the use of technology in education and skills development. He has also donated extensively to other philanthropic causes, included programs related to global health and learning. Gates also founded Corbis, which is developing a comprehensive digital archive of art and photography from public and private collections around the world.

Gingrich, Newton (Newt Gingrich) (1943–) *Republican congressman (1979–1998) and House Speaker (1995–1998)*
Born in Pennsylvania, Gingrich attended various military academies before enrolling in Atlanta's Emory

University. He graduated in 1965 and then went on to Tulane University in New Orleans, where he received his master's degree (1968) and doctorate (1971) in modern European history. He accepted a teaching position at West Georgia College in 1970.

A political conservative who favored a balanced federal budget, lower taxes, smaller government, and greater power for the states, Gingrich ran unsuccessfully for Congress in 1974 and 1976; in 1978 he was elected to represent a district outside Atlanta. Gingrich quickly established a reputation as being combative. In the 1980s he and other conservatives took advantage of television coverage by the new C-SPAN cable network to read inflammatory material into the *Congressional Record* during the "special orders" period that follows House sessions. His aggressive pursuit of charges that the Democratic House Speaker, Jim Wright, had engaged in improper financial dealings forced Wright to resign in 1989.

That same year, Gingrich was elected House minority whip by a narrow margin, and in 1994 he spearheaded the national strategy that enabled Republicans to gain control of both chambers of Congress for the first time since 1954. The centerpiece of the campaign was Gingrich's Contract with America, which promised that Republicans would enact specific legislation within the first 100 days of the 104th Congress, if they became the majority party. (see Appendix A) After the election, Gingrich was elected Speaker, and, with the sole exception of the bill calling for term limits, the House succeeded in passing all of the provisions within the first 100 days. Some provisions of the contract coincided with Clinton's agenda, especially in such areas as middle-class tax cuts and increased military spending, and these became law. But the balanced budget amendment failed by one vote to gain the necessary two-thirds majority in the Senate, and only five of the measures called for in the contract were enacted by the end of the year.

The political atmosphere during Gingrich's tenure as Speaker was especially partisan, and his first year concluded in a dramatic budget showdown with Clinton that resulted in the longest shutdown of nonessential government operations in the nation's history. Overall, 280,000 workers were furloughed throughout most of December 1995 and early January 1996 and another 480,000 deemed essential to government operations worked without pay. The majority of the public blamed Gingrich and the Republicans for the closings, and his

perceived willingness to stop the government from functioning in order to gain his political objectives played a significant role in the Republican defeats of 1996. On the other hand, after the budget showdown, Clinton's approval ratings passed 50 percent for the first time in his presidency.

In 1997, for the first time in its 208-year history, the House imposed economic sanctions on its Speaker when it fined Gingrich $300,000 and formally reprimanded him for using tax-exempt donations for political purposes and submitting false information to the House Ethics Committee. Although the scandal did not drive him from his position, it fueled later unsuccessful efforts by members of his own party to unseat him as Speaker, and it compromised his moral authority for criticizing Clinton's ethics—though Gingrich nonetheless continued to do so. (It was later revealed that Gingrich had been conducting an extramarital affair while condemning Clinton for the same behavior.)

In November 1998, after Republicans suffered additional defeats in the midterm congressional elections, Gingrich announced that he would resign as Speaker and give up his House seat in January 1999.

Among the books Gingrich has authored are *Contract with America* (1994); *To Renew America* (1995), a best seller; and *Lessons Learned the Hard Way: A Personal Report* (1998).

Greenspan, Alan (1925–   ) *chairman of the Board of Governors of the U.S. Federal Reserve System (1987–   )*
Born in New York City, Greenspan received his bachelor's degree (1948), master's degree (1950), and Ph.D. (1977) in economics from New York University, where he developed an enthusiasm for the laissez-faire form of capitalism advocated by the writer Ayn Rand. After heading his own consulting firm for 10 years, Greenspan served as an adviser to President Richard Nixon between 1969 and 1974 and then as chairman of the Council of Economic Advisers from 1974 to 1977 and chairman of the National Commission on Social Security Reform from 1981 to 1983. In 1987, President Ronald Reagan nominated him to succeed Paul A. Volcker as chairman of the Federal Reserve Board. President Bill Clinton reappointed him three times, and, as of 2005, he was serving his fourth consecutive four-year term in that post.

Greenspan's anti-inflationary monetary policies have been credited for much of the economic expansion that began in March 1991 and that, on February

1, 2000, officially became the longest period of sustained economic growth in U.S. history. He also advocated a balanced federal budget, which was achieved during Clinton's second term. In 1998, in response to the Asian economic crisis that began in 1997, Greenspan lowered U.S. interest rates to cushion the economy. With the Asian financial recovery, however, he initiated a series of interest-rate hikes in June 1999 that continued into 2000 in order to curb inflationary pressures from the lowest unemployment rates in three decades, from so-called overextended stocks, particularly within the technology sector, and from what he regarded as "unsustainable" rates of growth. Although some criticized these policies as unnecessary, overly cautious, and perhaps even counterproductive, by mid-2000 the economy slowed, the stock market became less speculative, and inflation rates remained comparatively low.

Kushner, Tony (1956–) *playwright*

Born in New York City to the classically trained musicians William and Sylvia Deutscher Kushner, Tony Kushner grew up in Lake Charles, Louisiana, where his family moved after inheriting a lumber business. He received his bachelor's degree from Columbia University, where he majored in English literature (1978) and his master's degree in directing from New York University (1984). In the early 1980s, Kushner founded a theater group and began writing and producing plays. He gained national prominence in 1992 and 1993 with the success of *Angels in America: A Gay Fantasia on National Themes,* a two-part play about homosexuals' living through the AIDS epidemic in the 1980s. The first part, *Millennium Approaches,* won the 1993 Pulitzer Prize and the 1993 Tony Award; the second part, *Perestroika,* won the 1994 Tony Award. The plays' success highlighted the persistence of the AIDS epidemic and expressed the unique experiences encountered by homosexuals in the United States.

Kushner's other plays include *A Bright Room Called Day* (1985); *Slavs! Thinking About the Longstanding Problems of Virtue and Happiness* (1995), an exploration of the collapse of the Soviet Union and its philosophical and environmental consequences; *Henry Box Brown, or the Mirror of Slavery* (1998); *Terminating, or Lass Meine Schmerzen Nicht Verloren Sein, or Ambivalence, in Love's Fire* (1998); and *Homebody/Kabul* (2001), which, written before the September 11, 2001, terrorist attacks, linked aspects of the modern Western world to the fanatical politics of Afghanistan's Taliban. Kushner has also adapted works by other writers, including Ariel Dorfman and Bertolt Brecht.

Kushner was playwright-in-residence at the Juilliard School of Drama from 1990 to 1992 and served on the faculty of New York University's Dramatic Writing program. He has received a 1990 Whiting Foundation Writers Award, along with fellowships from the New York Foundation for the Arts, the New York State Council on the Arts, and the National Endowment for the Arts.

Lewinsky, Monica (1974–) *White House intern involved in a sex scandal with President Bill Clinton*

Lewinsky grew up in an affluent household in Beverly Hills, California. Her parents divorced in 1987 after a turbulent marriage. As a student at Beverly Hills High School, Lewinsky had a five-year sexual relationship with her married drama teacher, who later admitted the affair. She attended junior college in Santa Monica, California, before transferring to Lewis and Clark College in Portland, Oregon. While still in college, Lewinsky was one of 1,000 interns accepted by the White House each year. Her first assignment, which began in June 1995, was in the office of Chief of Staff Leon Panetta, in which capacity she met Clinton. According to the Starr report, their sexual relationship began on November 15, 1995, and lasted through March 29, 1997. In December 1995, she received a paid job in the Office of Legislative Affairs. She was transferred in April 1996 to a job with the Defense Department in the Pentagon. There she befriended Linda Tripp, to whom she confided details about her relationship with Clinton. She also gave Tripp for safekeeping a dress stained with Clinton's semen, which Tripp convinced her not to clean. The dress was later introduced as proof of the affair.

Lewinsky was subpoenaed as a witness in the Paula Jones sexual harassment case against Clinton in December 1997, two months after the conservative Rutherford Institute, which was defraying Jones's legal expenses, received anonymous tips about Lewinsky's relationship with the president. On January 7, 1998, Lewinsky signed, under oath, an affidavit swearing that she had no information relevant to the Jones case and that she had never had a sexual relationship with Clinton. Five days later, Tripp contacted the independent counsel, Kenneth Starr, and gave him tapes of phone conversations she had secretly recorded in which Lewinsky discussed her relationship with Clinton. Tripp also secretly recorded a face-to-face conversation with Lewinsky on January 13, which presumably helped convince a panel of federal judges on January 16 to authorize Starr to widen his Whitewater investigation to include the possibility that Clinton obstructed justice in the Jones case. That same day, investigators from Starr's office confronted Lewinsky and took her to a room for questioning. After receiving immunity from prosecution, Lewinsky testified before a grand jury on August 6, 1998, about her relationship with Clinton. Her testimony constituted part of the evidence that the House of Representatives considered when it voted in December 1998 to impeach Clinton for perjury and obstruction of justice. Although she did not testify in person, her videotaped deposition was introduced as evidence in the 1999 Senate trial in which Clinton was acquitted.

Limbaugh, Rush (1951–) *conservative radio talk show host*

Born in Cape Girardeau, Missouri, the son of a wealthy, influential conservative judge, Limbaugh grew up in southeastern Missouri. After dropping out of college, he pursued his dream of a career in radio. He was fired from some of his first on-air jobs for being too inflammatory, and after several years in music radio, Limbaugh accepted a position as director of promotions with the Kansas City Royals baseball team. In 1984, he achieved success when station KFBK in Sacramento, California, hired him to replace Morton Downey, Jr., a radio personality known for his inflammatory and, to many, offensive style. Limbaugh soon became the most popular host in Sacramento. He gained a substantially larger audience in 1988, when he signed a two-year contract with EFM Media Management and moved to New York City. By 1993, Limbaugh's nationally syndicated show was the most popular in the country. In 2001, he became the highest-paid personality in the history of radio, when he agreed to an eight-year $250 million contract with Premiere Radio Networks.

Known for his aggressive, morally superior style and for his ridicule and demeaning of liberals—Hillary Rodham Clinton and feminists ("feminazis") were favorite targets—Limbaugh was the dominant figure in the profusion in the 1990s of hard-edged radio talk shows dedicated to promoting conservative agendas. After the 1995 Oklahoma City bombing,

President Bill Clinton accused Limbaugh and his cohorts of fostering a "climate of hate," casting people with opposing experiences and values as malicious enemies. But Limbaugh retained his combative manner, as he provided a forum for a right-wing perspective that received less attention in other media but found a large and receptive audience across the country. His show and others like it contributed significantly to political gains achieved by Republicans during the decade. Between 1992 and 1996, he also hosted *Rush Limbaugh,* a syndicated television talk show, which he promoted as "America, the way it ought to be." His publications include *The Way Things Ought to Be* (1992) and *See, I Told You So* (1993).

Morrison, Toni (Chloe Anthony Wofford)

(1931–) *Nobel Prize–winning novelist*

Originally named Chloe Anthony Wofford, Morrison was born in Lorain, Ohio, the daughter of a midwestern African-American family who celebrated many forms of black American culture, including the stories, songs, and folk tales that have since informed her fiction. She received her bachelor's degree from Howard University in 1953 and her master's degree from Cornell University in 1955. Between 1955 and 1964 Morrison taught at Texas Southern and Howard Universities, after which she became a fiction editor, while also writing her own novels. She later taught writing at the State University of New York at Albany before joining the faculty at Princeton University in 1989.

Morrison's novels deal with black Americans, especially the experience of slavery and the unique problems and situations faced by black women, who, in her fiction, often suffer at the hands of other blacks, as well as of whites. Her first novel, *The Bluest Eye* (1970), centers on an adolescent black girl obsessed by white standards of beauty; *Sula* (1973) also addresses the pressures for conformity. Morrison achieved national prominence in 1977 with the publication of *Song of Solomon,* and she received the Pulitzer Prize for *Beloved* (1987), which tells the story of a runaway slave woman who kills her daughter rather than allow her to be taken back into slavery. In 1992, Morrison published *Jazz,* a story of blacks who move to Manhattan during the 1920s told from multiple viewpoints and patterned after the improvisational structure of jazz musical compositions. That year she also published *Playing in the Dark: Whiteness and the Literary Imagination,* a work of criticism. She also edited and wrote the introduction to *Race-ing Justice, En-gendering Power: Essays on Anita Hill, Clarence Thomas, and the Construction of Social Reality* (1992). She returned to fiction in *Paradise* (1998), about the complex relationships among and the violence directed against women by the inhabitants of an all-black utopian community in Ruby, Oklahoma. In 1999, with her son, Slade, and the illustrator Giselle Pottershe, Morrison published her first children's book, *The Big Box,* a picture book whose story line was conceived by Slade at age nine. The narrative follows three children who have been imprisoned because their imagination threatens the adult world. Morrison was awarded the Nobel Prize in literature in 1993.

Powell, Colin (1937–) *major general in the U.S. Army, National Security Advisor (1987–1989), chairman of the Joint Chiefs of Staff (1989–1993), secretary of state (2001–2005)*

An African-American son of immigrants from Jamaica, Powell grew up in a multiethnic neighborhood in Harlem, where, among other things, he learned the smattering of Yiddish that later served him well on his diplomatic assignments to Israel. He attended the City College of New York, where he majored in geology and joined the Reserve Officers' Training Corps (ROTC). Upon graduating in 1958, he joined the army as a lieutenant and had Ranger and paratrooper training at Fort Benning, Georgia.

Powell rose through the ranks over the next 30 years, serving two tours of duty in Vietnam, where he was decorated for valor and twice wounded; taking the advanced Pathfinders course of airborne Ranger training, in which he graduated first in his class; attending the Army Command and General Staff College; earning a master's degree in business administration at George Washington University; and attending the National War College, the training school for generals. There Powell was influenced by the writings of the 19th-century Prussian military philosopher Karl von Clausewitz, who believed that no one should start a war without first being clear what the goals are and how they will be achieved, that political leaders must set the war's objectives and armed forces achieve them, and that wars must retain popular support. Powell concluded that America's failure to adhere to these principles led to the debacle of Vietnam, and throughout his career he has remained very cognizant of them.

After a series of commands, Powell was promoted to major general in 1983, shortly before returning to Washington, D.C., as senior military assistant to Defense Secretary Caspar Weinberger. Powell served in that capacity until 1986, when he was promoted to lieutenant general and named commander of the Army's V Corps, then stationed in Germany. At the personal behest of President Reagan, however, he returned to Washington in late 1986 to assume the post of Deputy National Security Advisor after the Iran-contra scandal. Powell and Frank Carlucci, the new National Security Advisor, helped devise U.S. policy during the later stages of the Iran-Iraq Gulf War, in which the U.S. Navy escorted Kuwaiti oil tankers carrying Iraqi oil through the Persian Gulf.

In November 1987, Reagan appointed Powell National Security Advisor. Carlucci replaced Weinberger as secretary of defense. Powell helped negotiate the INF treaty with the Soviet Union, which reduced the number of intermediate-range nuclear missiles in Europe, and he participated in the Washington, D.C., and Moscow summit meetings of Reagan and Gorbachev. Powell also played an indirect role in selecting General Norman Schwarzkopf as commander in chief of the military's Central Command.

After the election of George H. W. Bush in 1988, Powell declined opportunities to head the CIA or serve as deputy secretary of state. Instead, he returned to the army, in which he was promoted to four-star general, the highest military rank. In August 1989, Bush appointed him chairman of the Joint Chiefs of Staff in preference to 14 more senior four-star generals.

Four months later, after a U.S. Marine was killed and civilians were threatened, Powell recommended that the United States invade Panama, remove Manuel Noriega from power, destroy his military power base, and restore the elected Endara government. He then oversaw Operation Just Cause, the 1989 invasion of Panama, which achieved those objectives.

Immediately after Iraq's conquest of Kuwait on August 2, 1990, Powell briefed Bush on his military options. In the months leading up to the war, he performed both diplomatic and military functions as he helped make arrangements with the Saudis and prepared a battle plan with Schwarzkopf and Secretary of Defense Richard Cheney. He also helped convince Bush of the need to call up the reserves and otherwise amass a large force that could win a swift and overwhelming victory.

Powell's initial preference had been to give economic sanctions against Iraq time to work—according to some sources he was willing to wait up to two years—but he complied with Bush's plan to pursue a military solution. During the war Powell oversaw the fighting, and on February 13, after U.S. jets bombed a Baghdad bunker and killed more than 200 civilians, he assumed personal responsibility for approving targets within Baghdad. He supported Bush's decision to end the war without deposing Saddam Hussein.

Bush reappointed Powell to a second term as chairman of the Joint Chiefs of Staff on May 22, four months before his first term was due to expire. In Powell's second term he oversaw the reduction of the U.S. military force in the post–cold war era. He tried unsuccessfully to eliminate battlefield artillery-fired nuclear shells, which he believed were prone to malfunction, expensive to modernize, and largely irrelevant in an era of highly accurate conventional weapons. When, in late 1991, Bush requested new proposals for nuclear disarmament, Powell helped formulate policies that eliminated short-range nuclear weapons from the U.S. arsenal, grounded the nuclear-armed bombers from the Strategic Air Command, removed nuclear weapons from all ships except Trident submarines, eliminated multiple independently targetable reentry vehicles (MIRVs), and closed many Minuteman missile silos.

Powell was approached by both the Democratic and the Republican Parties to run for vice president in 1992, but he declined. He oversaw the U.S. expedition to Somalia that Bush initiated and Clinton concluded, and he advised the new president on the intensifying situation in Bosnia and on the issue of permitting gays to serve in the military. Powell opposed allowing homosexuals to serve, as he believed doing so would cause many disruptions within the military and create problems when heterosexuals and homosexuals shared barracks. As a compromise position, he suggested the "Don't ask; don't tell" solution that eventually became the policy of the Clinton administration.

Powell retired in September 1993, after completing his second term as chairman of the Joint Chiefs. In 1994, he accompanied the former president Jimmy Carter to Haiti, where, at the last minute, they convinced the military dictator Raoul Cedras to surrender power and leave the country before an imminent American invasion aimed at restoring the elected government of Jean-Bertrand Aristide. In 2000, President-elect George W. Bush selected Powell as secre-

tary of state, and in January 2001, Powell became the first African American to assume the post, a position he held until 2005. Citing a later-discredited imminent threat from Iraq's alleged stockpile of weapons of mass destruction, he presented the administration's justification for invading Iraq and overthrowing Saddam Hussein's regime in 2003. Powell published his memoirs, *My American Journey,* in 1995.

Reno, Janet (1938–   ) *U.S. attorney general (1993–2001)*
Born in Miami, Florida, the daughter of a police reporter and an investigative journalist, Reno received her bachelor's degree from Cornell University and her law degree (LL.B) from Harvard University. She worked in private practice for eight years before serving as staff director for the Florida House Judiciary Committee in 1971–72. Reno subsequently joined the state attorney's office in what is now Miami-Dade County, where she specialized in juvenile cases. She was appointed Florida's first female state attorney in 1978, and then was elected to the post five times, in it she developed a reputation for vigorously prosecuting child-abuse and drug-related crimes. In early 1993, Clinton appointed her attorney general after his first two choices had to withdraw their nominations after revelations that they had hired illegal aliens as domestic workers. When Reno was sworn in as the first female U.S. attorney general in March 1993, she became the highest-ranking woman ever to serve in the executive branch to that date.

Barely a month after assuming office Reno authorized a deadly and controversial raid on a heavily fortified compound outside Waco, Texas, that federal agents had besieged in February after followers of the Branch Davidian leader, David Koresh, killed four members of the Bureau of Alcohol, Firearms, and Tobacco (AFT). Reno assumed responsibility for the April 19 raid in which a fire, believed to have been set by the Davidians themselves, killed some 100 Davidians, including at least 17 children. Justifying her decision before Congress, Reno testified that she was convinced the Davidians, who had enough supplies to last a year, would not surrender and that the ongoing siege placed the children inside the compound and the agents surrounding it in continuous danger. Her forthright assumption of responsibility earned her the admiration of many Americans. But the raid provoked the enmity of others, who regarded the government action as an egregious assault on its own citizens. Among those outraged by the Waco incident was Timothy McVeigh, who, in 1995, bombed the federal building in Oklahoma City in retaliation.

Reno ordered another controversial assault against private citizens in April 2000, when, after her negotiations with the Miami relatives of the seven-year-old Elián González broke down, agents broke into the Cuban refugees' home and seized the boy, who, on Thanksgiving Day 1999, had been rescued and taken to the United States after the raft he and his mother were using to flee Cuba sank, and his mother drowned. After the raid, Elián was reunited with his father, who continued to reside in Cuba and was demanding the return of his son. To the family and much of the Miami exile community, Reno's action was outrageous because it took the boy back to the Communist-ruled island his mother had died trying to escape. On the other hand, Reno maintained that she was enforcing federal and international law by taking Elián from his cousins, after they refused to give him up and dared her to take him by force. A photograph of Elián's cringing in fear as a heavily armed officer approached him sparked outrage throughout the world. A later picture, however, showed him standing happily with his father, and many Americans supported Reno's decision to do whatever was necessary to reunite the father and son.

While in office Reno also worked to broaden laws against child pornography and regulate violence on television. Despite pressure from Republicans, she refused to appoint a special prosecutor or to bring charges against Vice President Al Gore for alleged violations of campaign law. But she did appoint Robert Fiske as special prosecutor to investigate charges against Clinton in the Whitewater affair in 1994. Her effort to appoint Fiske to the more powerful independent counsel position after Congress reenacted the independent counsel legislation later that year failed, however, and a panel of federal judges named the conservative judge Kenneth Starr instead. Starr went on to investigate Clinton's affair with Monica Lewinsky and recommend that Clinton be impeached.

Schwarzkopf, General H. Norman (1934–   )
commander in chief of the U.S. Central Command (1988–1991), supreme commander of allied forces in the Persian Gulf War (1990–1991)

Schwarzkopf was born in Trenton, New Jersey, on August 22, 1934, the son of a German-American father and a West Virginian mother who was distantly related to Thomas Jefferson. His father, General Herbert Norman Schwarzkopf, was a West Point graduate, who organized the first New Jersey state police force and led the investigation of the kidnapping of Charles Lindbergh's baby. As a boy, Schwarzkopf spent a year in Iran, where his father had been assigned during World War II to train and reorganize the Iranian national police force, and there he developed an appreciation of Islamic culture. He attended the U.S. Military Academy at West Point from 1952 to 1956 and graduated in the top 10 percent of his class (42nd of 485).

Upon graduating from West Point and receiving the rank of lieutenant, Schwarzkopf joined the infantry and attended the Airborne School at Fort Benning, Georgia. He earned his paratrooper badge in 1957, and, over the next 31 years, he rose through the ranks by serving in Berlin during the cold war crisis there in 1960–61; completing two tours of duty in Vietnam, where he was wounded in action and received numerous promotions and medals for valor; attending the War College, where he studied international defense and national security issues, with a special emphasis on China and the Soviet Union; and serving with distinction during the Grenada invasion of 1983. In 1988, Schwarzkopf was promoted to four-star general, the highest rank in the army, and in November he assumed the position of commander in chief (CINC) of the U.S. Central Command, whose responsibilities included portions of the Middle East and Southwest Asia, including Saudi Arabia and Kuwait.

Schwarzkopf's familiarity with Islamic customs and Arabic culture helped him establish smooth relationships with Arab military and political leaders, but in 1989 he began to perceive Saddam Hussein as a threat to the region. On February 8, 1990, Schwarzkopf reported his concerns to the Senate Armed Services Committee. Nonetheless, although wary of Saddam Hussein, Schwarzkopf supported the administration's position that Iraq offered a counterbalance to the regional threat posed by Iran.

At the same time, Schwarzkopf began to prepare for the possibility of Iraqi aggression, and on July 23, 1990, as the Iraqis were massing troops on the Kuwaiti border, Schwarzkopf initiated a five-day exercise in Florida that anticipated a rapid U.S. response to an Iraqi invasion of Kuwait. On August 1, the day before the invasion, Schwarzkopf briefed Defense secretary Richard Cheney and the Joint Chiefs of Staff, giving his opinion that Iraq would probably attack but limit its objectives to seizing the Kuwaiti portion of the Rumalia oil field and Warbah and Bubiyan islands in the Persian Gulf. Dick Kerr, the deputy director of the CIA, expressed a similar assessment.

Immediately after the invasion, Schwarzkopf flew back to Washington, D.C., to brief Bush and the National Security Council. He believed Iraq's greatest strengths were the size of its army and its arsenal of chemical weapons and that its vulnerabilities were its highly centralized command and control, dependence on foreign nations for spare parts, and inexperience in defending against deep operations far behind the main battle front. These were the same weaknesses Schwarzkopf later exploited in his battle plan.

In late August Schwarzkopf moved from his Florida headquarters to the Saudi capital of Riyadh, where his first job was to prepare for a seemingly imminent Iraqi invasion. He also began to coordinate planning with the other coalition forces under his command and with Saudi military and political leaders.

Between the end of October, when Bush committed to an offensive action to force the Iraqis from Kuwait, and January 17, 1991, when the air campaign began, Schwarzkopf worked on preparations for the offensive. He initiated Operation Hail Mary, the secret westward shift of U.S., French, and British armored divisions that enabled the allies to strike a devastating "left-hook" into the Republican Guard's vulnerable western flank. During the air campaign, Schwarzkopf objected to the diversion of his bombers to target Iraqi Scud missiles, whose military value was comparatively low, but whose political value was quite high as a result of their potential to draw Israel into the war and thereby disrupt the coalition. His objections were overruled, however, and Scud hunting remained a priority throughout the air campaign.

After several delays, Schwarzkopf launched the allied ground offensive at 4:00 A.M. Sunday, February 24, local time. Operation Desert Storm exceeded expectations: Within three days the coalition forces had decimated the Republican Guard armored divisions and were prepared to enter Kuwait City. Schwarzkopf told Bush he was prepared to annihilate the remaining Iraqi forces, but he acceded without objection to Bush's controversial decision to call a cease-fire.

On April 20, the day he departed the Middle East to return to the United States, Schwarzkopf became the first foreigner to receive the Saudi's Order of King Abdul Aziz First Class decoration. He returned home to a hero's welcome, and, after his retirement from the army shortly thereafter after 35 years of service, he was mentioned as a possible Republican candidate for vice president. Schwarzkopf, however, declined to run for that or any other office. He published his memoirs, *It Doesn't Take a Hero,* in 1992.

Seinfeld, Jerome (Jerry Seinfeld) (1954–)
television comedian
Born in Brooklyn, New York, to a sign maker and his wife, Seinfeld was the second of two children. He grew up on Long Island and attended college at the State University of New York at Oswego and Queens College of the City University of New York, where he majored in communications and theater and received his bachelor's degree in 1976. He then began working in New York comedy clubs, often without pay, while supporting himself with odd jobs.

After Rodney Dangerfield included him on a special for HBO, Seinfeld obtained a recurring role on the situation comedy *Benson* in 1980, but he was fired after only four episodes over artistic differences. His first appearance on *The Tonight Show,* however, then hosted by Johnny Carson, was well received, and subsequent visits on that program and *Letterman* attracted a growing national following. After starring in a number of cable television specials, Seinfeld was approached by NBC to star in a situation comedy. He and his friend Larry David then began working on *The Seinfeld Chronicles,* which appeared as a pilot on July 5, 1989. Renamed *Seinfeld,* the sitcom premiered in 1990 as a show about the often trivial situations faced by a comedian and his friends in New York—a "show about nothing," as one of the characters calls it. The program received little fanfare at first but gained popularity in its second season. By the 1993–94 season it was the third most popular show on television, and in 1994–95 *Seinfeld* was the top-rated program. In 1995–96 and 1996–97, *Seinfeld* ranked second, after *ER,* but it regained its number-one ranking in 1997–98. Its final episode, broadcast on May 14, 1998, enjoyed the fourth-highest ratings of any final show in American television history.

Simpson, Orenthal James (O. J. Simpson)
(1947–) *football player, television commentator, actor, accused murderer*
Simpson was born in San Francisco, where he grew up and played high school football, initially as a tackle and

then as a fullback. He attended San Francisco City College from 1965 to 1966 and then transferred to the University of Southern California, where he was a two-time All American before winning the Heisman Trophy in 1968, the year he joined the National Football League (NFL). As a member of the Buffalo Bills he set numerous rushing records, and he was inducted into the NFL's Hall of Fame after he retired in 1979.

Simpson remained in the public eye as a sports commentator and actor, and he became a popular and widely respected celebrity. In the black community he was especially admired as a black man who had risen to the top of white-dominated American society. He was known for his Hertz rental car television commercials, in which he ran through airports, swerving around passengers and leaping over suitcases to catch his plane. He also played a dim-witted assistant detective in the three popular *Naked Gun* comedy films that appeared between 1988 and 1994.

Simpson divorced his first wife, and in 1979, a year after their separation, their first child drowned. While still married to his first wife, Simpson met the 17-year-old Nicole Brown, a white waitress, whom he married in 1985. Their first child was born seven months later. Brown Simpson often complained to friends and family that Simpson beat her because she liked to flirt with other men. Simpson denied ever beating his wife, however, and said her injuries resulted from friendly play. She filed for divorce in 1992.

On June 13, 1994, Nicole Brown Simpson and her friend Ronald Goldman were stabbed to death at her townhouse in the wealthy Los Angeles community of Brentwood, and four days later O. J. Simpson was arrested for the crime, after a nationally televised low-speed police chase during which crowds gathered along the freeway to cheer him and chant his nickname, Juice. At Simpson's high-profile trial, for which he hired a so-called dream team of attorneys headed by Johnny Cochran, the prosecution maintained that DNA evidence proved Simpson's guilt. The defense, on the other hand, claimed that he was a victim of police evidence tampering, and during his trial evidence of racism among the arresting officers surfaced. Simpson's acquittal in 1995 highlighted the racial divisions within the United States. It was met with great skepticism, even outrage, by many white Americans, who trusted the almost-complete reliability of DNA evidence, whereas many black Americans found credible Simpson's claim that he had been framed by racially moti-

vated police officers. A jury in a subsequent civil trial, which required a lower standard of proof, later found Simpson responsible for the death of Goldman and Brown Simpson. The criminal trial also sparked a national debate over whether the judicial system treated wealthy Americans differently than it treated citizens unable to afford a dream team of attorneys.

Stewart, Martha (Martha Kostyra) (1941–   )
author and television personality

Born Martha Kostyra in Jersey City, New Jersey, Stewart grew up in a Polish-American home in which she learned to cook, sew, garden, and manage a household. As a child she planned birthday parties for neighbors, and she worked her way through Barnard College by modeling. While still a student, she married a law student, Andrew Stewart, and in 1965 they had a daughter, Alexis. Although she prospered working as a stockbroker for a Wall Street firm, in 1973 the family moved to Westport, Connecticut, where they restored and redecorated a Federal-style farmhouse. This experience and the restoration of later homes in the Hamptons and Manhattan left Stewart with the skills and sensibilities she presented in her popular books, magazines, and television show.

A successful catering business Stewart began in 1976 with a partner, Norma Collier, called her to the attention of numerous prestigious clients. Her first book, *Entertaining* (1982), gave her national exposure, and in 1993, she began hosting *Martha Stewart Living,* a syndicated daytime television show that became immensely popular. She published *The Martha Stewart Cookbook* in 1995.

During the 1990s Stewart emerged as an icon of the successful woman, who not only exhibited good taste and impeccable homemaking skills but also proved to be a savvy businesswoman capable of building a financial empire. Although some feminists objected that her focus on homemaking represented a step backward for women still trying to be accepted as equals in the workplace, and others complained that she set an unreasonable standard for most women, who had neither the time nor the resources to emulate her, throughout the decade millions of American women, and a growing number of men, were inspired by her creativity and resourcefulness in creating uplifting environments and appetizing menus. However Stewart's reputation was tarnished in 2003, when a federal grand jury indicted her on nine criminal counts from the Securities and

Exchange Commission (SEC). The presiding judge threw out the charge of securities fraud, the most serious accusation against her, but on March 5, 2004, a jury convicted Stewart and her former stock broker Peter Bacanovic of lying about a stock sale, conspiracy, and obstruction of justice. They were each sentenced to five months in prison, five months of home confinement, and two years probation; Stewart was also fined $30,000. She served her jail sentence at Alderson Federal Prison, a minimum security facility, between October 8, 2004, and March 4, 2005. Although under house arrest through summer 2005, Stewart has resumed an active role in her many enterprises.

Winfrey, Oprah (1954–) *television talk-show host*
Winfrey was born in Kosciusko, Mississippi, to an African-American family. Growing up in a small farming community, she was sexually abused by a number of male relatives and friends of her mother's. When she was about 12 years old she moved to Nashville, Tennessee, to stay with her father, a barber and businessman, and her life improved.

Television interested Winfrey when she was a young woman, and after graduating high school she became a news anchor for the local CBS television station. She attended Tennessee State University, from which she graduated in 1976, and then became a reporter and coanchor for the ABC news affiliate in Baltimore. In 1977, Winfrey began cohosting a Baltimore morning show entitled *People Are Talking,* which enabled her to demonstrate her mastery of the personal talk-show format. Known for her friendly and inviting demeanor, Winfrey in 1984 accepted an offer to take over *A.M. Chicago,* a talk show suffering from poor ratings. Her major competitor was Phil Donahue, a host known for his more aggressive style. Despite Donahue's popularity, Winfrey soon elevated her show from last to first place in the ratings, and in 1985 her program was renamed *The Oprah Winfrey Show.* After national syndication in 1986, it went on to become the top-rated talk show on television, a position it retained through the 1990s, and it won several Emmy Awards. By 1995, Winfrey was the world's highest-paid entertainer, earning $171 million per year.

In 1985, in her first acting role, Winfrey received a nomination as best supporting actress in Steven Spiel-

berg's adaptation of Alice Walker's novel *The Color Purple* (1982). This success led to additional roles, and Winfrey soon formed her own production company, Harpo Productions, which began to buy film rights to literary works. These included Connie May Fowler's *Before Women Had Wings,* an adaptation of which Winfrey both starred in and produced in 1997. She also starred in the 1989 television miniseries adaptation of Gloria Naylor's *The Women of Brewster Place* (1982) and Jonathan Demme's 1998 adaptation of Toni Morrison's novel *Beloved* (1987).

In 1996, in order to promote literacy and stimulate greater interest in provocative and insightful literature, Winfrey began her popular on-air book club, in which she announced selections two to four weeks in advance and then discussed them with a select group of people. Among her first guests was Morrison, the 1993 Nobel Prize winner, whose novel *The Song of Solomon* (1977) was a selection. The book club quickly became a huge success, and Winfrey's selections routinely became best sellers. In 1997, *Newsweek* named her the most important person in books and media.

Winfrey was also active in numerous philanthropic causes, and she used her show to raise public consciousness about the prevalence of child abuse. She also testified before a U.S. Senate Judiciary Committee on behalf of the National Child Protection Act to create a nationwide database of convicted child abusers. In 1993, President Bill Clinton signed the so-called Oprah Bill into law. Using herself as an example, Winfrey also publicized the dangers of obesity, and her efforts at weight loss attracted international attention. She lost an estimated 90 pounds and competed in the Marine Corps Marathon in Washington, D.C., in 1995 but later experienced difficulty in maintaining her ideal weight. In 1986, the National Organization for Women awarded her the Woman of Achievement Award, and between 1989 and 1992 the National Association for the Advancement of Colored People conferred on Winfrey its Image Award four times. *TV Guide* chose her as the Television Performer of the Year for 1997. In 1998, *Time* designated her as one of the 100 most influential people of the 20th century, and in 1999, she cofounded Oxygen Media, a company dedicated to producing cable and Internet programming for women.

APPENDIX C
Tables, Graphs, and Maps

CHANGE IN U.S. POPULATION, 1990–2000

Rank	Area	CENSUS POPULATION		CHANGE, 1990 TO 2000	
		April 1, 2000	April 1, 1990	Numeric	Percent
1	California	33,871,648	29,760,021	4,111,627	13.8
2	Texas	20,851,820	16,986,510	3,865,310	22.8
3	New York	18,976,457	17,990,455	986,002	5.5
4	Florida	15,982,378	12,937,926	3,044,452	23.5
5	Illinois	12,419,293	11,430,602	988,691	8.6
6	Pennsylvania	12,281,054	11,881,643	399,411	3.4
7	Ohio	11,353,140	10,847,115	506,025	4.7
8	Michigan	9,938,444	9,295,297	643,147	6.9
9	New Jersey	8,414,350	7,730,188	684,162	8.9
10	Georgia	8,186,453	6,478,216	1,708,237	26.4
11	North Carolina	8,049,313	6,628,637	1,420,676	21.4
12	Virginia	7,078,515	6,187,358	891,157	14.4
13	Massachusetts	6,349,097	6,016,425	332,672	5.5
14	Indiana	6,080,485	5,544,159	536,326	9.7
15	Washington	5,894,121	4,866,692	1,027,429	21.1
16	Tennessee	5,689,283	4,877,185	812,098	16.7
17	Missouri	5,595,211	5,117,073	478,138	9.3
18	Wisconsin	5,363,675	4,891,769	471,906	9.6
19	Maryland	5,296,486	4,781,468	515,018	10.8
20	Arizona	5,130,632	3,665,228	1,465,404	40.0
21	Minnesota	4,919,479	4,375,099	544,380	12.4
22	Louisiana	4,468,976	4,219,973	249,003	5.9
23	Alabama	4,447,100	4,040,587	406,513	10.1
24	Colorado	4,301,261	3,294,394	1,006,867	30.6
25	Kentucky	4,041,769	3,685,296	356,473	9.7
26	South Carolina	4,012,012	3,486,703	525,309	15.1
27	Oklahoma	3,450,654	3,145,585	305,069	9.7
28	Oregon	3,421,399	2,842,321	579,078	20.4
29	Connecticut	3,405,565	3,287,116	118,449	3.6
30	Iowa	2,926,324	2,776,755	149,569	5.4
31	Mississippi	2,844,658	2,573,216	271,442	10.5
32	Kansas	2,688,418	2,477,574	210,844	8.5
33	Arkansas	2,673,400	2,350,725	322,675	13.7
34	Utah	2,233,169	1,722,850	510,319	29.6
35	Nevada	1,998,257	1,201,833	796,424	66.3
36	New Mexico	1,819,046	1,515,069	303,977	20.1
37	West Virginia	1,808,344	1,793,477	14,867	0.8
38	Nebraska	1,711,263	1,578,385	132,878	8.4
39	Idaho	1,293,953	1,006,749	287,204	28.5
40	Maine	1,274,923	1,227,928	46,995	3.8
41	New Hampshire	1,235,786	1,109,252	126,534	11.4
42	Hawaii	1,211,537	1,108,229	103,308	9.3
43	Rhode Island	1,048,319	1,003,464	44,855	4.5
44	Montana	902,195	799,065	103,130	12.9
45	Delaware	783,600	666,168	117,432	17.6
46	South Dakota	754,844	696,004	58,840	8.5
47	North Dakota	642,200	638,800	3,400	0.5
48	Alaska	626,932	550,043	76,889	14.0
49	Vermont	608,827	562,758	46,069	8.2
(NA)	District of Columbia	572,059	606,900	−34,841	−5.7
50	Wyoming	493,782	453,588	40,194	8.9
(NA)	United States	281,421,906	248,709,873	32,712,033	13.2

Source: U.S. Census Bureau.

General Demographic Characteristics for the United States, 1990 and 2000

SUBJECT	1990		2000	
	Number	Percent	Number	Percent
Total Population	248,709,873	100.0	281,421,906	100.0
SEX AND AGE				
Male	121,239,418	48.7	138,053,563	49.1
Female	127,470,455	51.3	143,368,343	50.9
Under 5 years	18,354,443	7.4	19,175,798	6.8
5 to 9 years	18,099,179	7.3	20,549,505	7.3
10 to 14 years	17,114,249	6.9	20,528,072	7.3
15 to 19 years	17,754,015	7.1	20,219,890	7.2
20 to 24 years	19,020,312	7.6	18,964,001	6.7
25 to 34 years	43,175,932	17.4	39,891,724	14.2
35 to 44 years	37,578,903	15.1	45,148,527	16.0
45 to 54 years	25,223,086	10.1	37,677,952	13.4
55 to 59 years	10,531,756	4.2	13,469,237	4.8
60 to 64 years	10,616,167	4.3	10,805,447	3.8
65 to 74 years	18,106,558	7.3	18,390,986	6.5
75 to 84 years	10,055,108	4.0	12,361,180	4.4
85 years and over	3,080,165	1.2	4,239,587	1.5
Median age (years)	32.9	(X)	35.3	(X)
18 years and over	185,105,441	74.4	209,128,094	74.3
Male	88,655,140	35.6	100,994,367	35.9
Female	96,450,301	38.8	108,133,727	38.4
21 years and over	173,378,573	69.7	196,899,193	70.0
62 years and over	37,629,695	15.1	41,256,029	14.7
65 years and over	31,241,831	12.6	34,991,753	12.4
Male	12,565,173	5.1	14,409,625	5.1
Female	18,676,658	7.5	20,582,128	7.3
RACE[1]				
One race[1]	248,709,873	100.0	274,595,678	97.6
White	199,686,070	80.3	211,460,626	75.1
Black or African American	29,986,060	12.1	34,658,190	12.3
American Indian and Alaska Native	1,959,234	0.8	2,475,956	0.9
Asian	6,908,638	2.8	10,242,998	3.6
Asian Indian	815,447	0.3	1,678,765	0.6
Chinese	1,645,472	0.7	2,432,585	0.9
Filipino	1,406,770	0.6	1,850,314	0.7
Japanese	847,562	0.3	796,700	0.3
Korean	798,849	0.3	1,076,872	0.4
Vietnamese	614,547	0.2	1,122,528	0.4
Other Asian[2]	779,991	0.3	1,285,234	0.5
Native Hawaiian and Other Pacific Islander	365,024	0.1	398,835	0.1
Native Hawaiian	211,014	0.1	140,652	—
Guamanian or Chamorro	49,345	—	58,240	—
Samoan	62,964	—	91,029	—
Other Pacific Islander[3]	41,701	—	108,914	—
Some other race	9,804,847	3.9	15,359,073	5.5
Two or more races[1](NA)	(NA)	(NA)	6,826,228	2.4
Race alone or in combination with one or more other races:[1, 4]				
White	(NA)	(NA)	216,930,975	77.1
Black or African American	(NA)	(NA)	36,419,434	12.9
American Indian and Alaska Native	(NA)	(NA)	4,119,301	1.5
Asian	(NA)	(NA)	11,898,828	4.2
Native Hawaiian and Other Pacific Islander	(NA)	(NA)	874,414	0.3
Some other race	(NA)	(NA)	18,521,486	6.6
HISPANIC OR LATINO AND RACE[5]				
Total population	248,709,873	100.0	281,421,906	100.0
Hispanic or Latino (of any race)	22,354,059	9.0	35,305,818	12.5
Mexican	13,495,938	5.4	20,640,711	7.3
Puerto Rican	2,727,754	1.1	3,406,178	1.2
Cuban	1,043,932	0.4	1,241,685	0.4
Other Hispanic or Latino	5,086,435	2.0	10,017,244	3.6
Not Hispanic or Latino	226,355,814	91.0	246,116,088	87.5
White	188,128,296	75.6	194,552,774	69.1

SUBJECT	1990		2000	
	Number	**Percent**	**Number**	**Percent**
RELATIONSHIP				
Total population	248,709,873	100.0	281,421,906	100.0
In households	242,012,129	97.3	273,643,273	97.2
Householder	91,947,410	37.0	105,480,101	37.5
Spouse	50,708,322	20.4	54,493,232	19.4
Child	76,728,438	30.9	83,393,392	29.6
Own child under 18 years	57,461,020	23.1	64,494,637	22.9
Other relatives	11,950,582	4.8	15,684,318	5.6
Under 18 years	4,666,052	1.9	6,042,435	2.1
Nonrelatives	10,677,377	4.3	14,592,230	5.2
Unmarried partner[6]	3,187,772	1.3	5,475,768	1.9
In group quarters	6,697,744	2.7	7,778,633	2.8
Institutionalized population	3,334,018	1.3	4,059,039	1.4
Noninstitutionalized population	3,363,726	1.4	3,719,594	1.3
HOUSEHOLDS BY TYPE				
Total households	91,947,410	100.0	105,480,101	100.0
Family households (families)	64,517,947	70.2	71,787,347	68.1
With own children under 18 years	30,877,675	33.6	34,588,368	32.8
Married-couple family	50,708,322	55.1	54,493,232	51.7
With own children under 18 years	23,494,726	25.6	24,835,505	23.5
Female householder, no husband present	10,666,043	11.6	12,900,103	12.2
With own children under 18 years	6,028,409	6.6	7,561,874	7.2
Nonfamily households	27,429,463	29.8	33,692,754	31.9
Householder living alone	22,580,420	24.6	27,230,075	25.8
Householder 65 years and over	8,824,845	9.6	9,722,857	9.2
Households with individuals under 18 years	33,587,134	36.5	38,022,115	36.0
Households with individuals 65 years and over	22,154,422	24.1	24,672,708	23.4
Average household size	2.63	(X)	2.59	(X)
Average family size	3.16	(X)	3.14	(X)
HOUSING OCCUPANCY				
Total housing units	102,263,678	100.0	115,904,641	100.0
Occupied housing units	91,947,410	89.9	105,480,101	91.0
Vacant housing units	10,316,268	10.1	10,424,540	9.0
For seasonal, recreational, or occasional use	3,081,923	3.0	3,578,718	3.1
Homeowner vacancy rate (percent)	2.1	(X)	1.7	(X)
Rental vacancy rate (percent)	8.5	(X)	6.8	(X)
HOUSING TENURE				
Occupied housing units	91,947,410	100.0	105,480,101	100.0
Owner-occupied housing units	59,024,811	64.2	69,815,753	66.2
Renter-occupied housing units	32,922,599	35.8	35,664,348	33.8
Average household size of owner-occupied units	2.75	(X)	2.69	(X)
Average household size of renter-occupied units	2.42	(X)	2.40	(X)

Represents zero or rounds to zero. (X) Not applicable. (NA) Not available.

[1] Census 2000 terminology and categories are used for data on race. Because individuals could report only one race in the 1990 census and could report one or more races in Census 2000, data on race for 1990 and 2000 are not comparable. See "Population by Race and Hispanic or Latino Origin for the United States: 1990 to 2000," (PHC-T-1). At www.census.gov, select Population Tables/Reports, then select List of Tables.

[2] Other Asian alone, or two or more Asian categories.

[3] Other Pacific Islander alone, or two or more Native Hawaiian and Other Pacific Islander categories.

[4] In combination with one or more of the other races listed. The following six numbers may add to more than the total population and the six percentages may add to more than 100 percent because individuals may report more than one race.

[5] Census 2000 terminology is used for ethnic categories. The corresponding term for "Hispanic or Latino" in the 1990 census was "Hispanic origin."

[6] Sample data on unmarried-partner households, as shown in U.S. Bureau of the Census, 1990 Census of Population, *Social and Economic Characteristics* (1990 CP-2), report series published 1993–1994.

Source: U.S. Bureau of the Census, 1990 Census of Population, *General Population Characteristics* (1990 CP-1), and 1990 Census of Housing, *General Housing Characteristics* (1990 CH-1), report series published 1992–1993; and Summary Tape File (STF) 1A, series released 1991, and Census 2000.

CHANGE IN POPULATION OF 25 LARGEST CITIES, 1990–2000

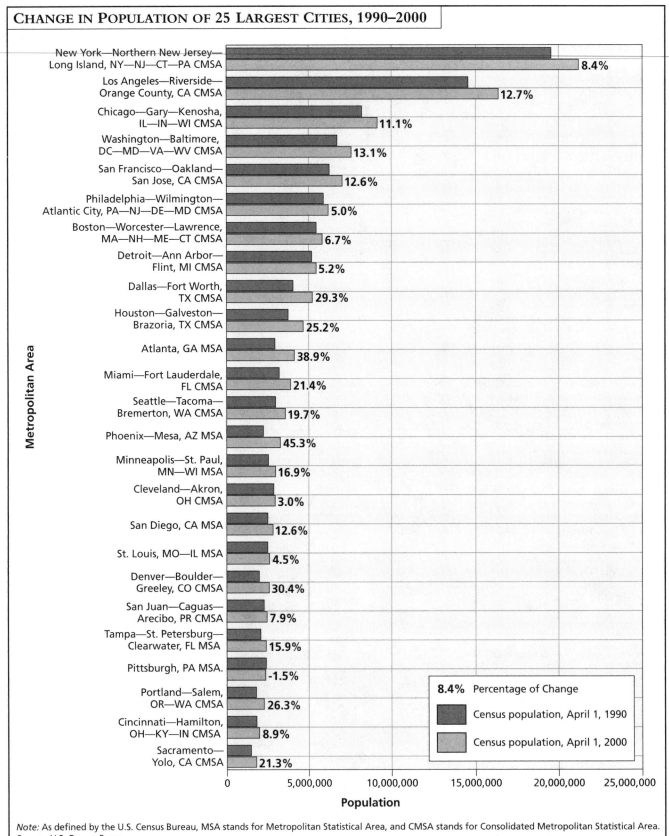

New York—Northern New Jersey—Long Island, NY—NJ—CT—PA CMSA **8.4%**

Los Angeles—Riverside—Orange County, CA CMSA **12.7%**

Chicago—Gary—Kenosha, IL—IN—WI CMSA **11.1%**

Washington—Baltimore, DC—MD—VA—WV CMSA **13.1%**

San Francisco—Oakland—San Jose, CA CMSA **12.6%**

Philadelphia—Wilmington—Atlantic City, PA—NJ—DE—MD CMSA **5.0%**

Boston—Worcester—Lawrence, MA—NH—ME—CT CMSA **6.7%**

Detroit—Ann Arbor—Flint, MI CMSA **5.2%**

Dallas—Fort Worth, TX CMSA **29.3%**

Houston—Galveston—Brazoria, TX CMSA **25.2%**

Atlanta, GA MSA **38.9%**

Miami—Fort Lauderdale, FL CMSA **21.4%**

Seattle—Tacoma—Bremerton, WA CMSA **19.7%**

Phoenix—Mesa, AZ MSA **45.3%**

Minneapolis—St. Paul, MN—WI MSA **16.9%**

Cleveland—Akron, OH CMSA **3.0%**

San Diego, CA MSA **12.6%**

St. Louis, MO—IL MSA **4.5%**

Denver—Boulder—Greeley, CO CMSA **30.4%**

San Juan—Caguas—Arecibo, PR CMSA **7.9%**

Tampa—St. Petersburg—Clearwater, FL MSA **15.9%**

Pittsburgh, PA MSA. **-1.5%**

Portland—Salem, OR—WA CMSA **26.3%**

Cincinnati—Hamilton, OH—KY—IN CMSA **8.9%**

Sacramento—Yolo, CA CMSA **21.3%**

Metropolitan Area

0   5,000,000   10,000,000   15,000,000   20,000,000   25,000,000

Population

8.4%   Percentage of Change

Census population, April 1, 1990

Census population, April 1, 2000

Note: As defined by the U.S. Census Bureau, MSA stands for Metropolitan Statistical Area, and CMSA stands for Consolidated Metropolitan Statistical Area.
Source: U.S. Census Bureau

DOW JONES INDUSTRIAL AVERAGE, 1990–1999

THE WORLD'S 10 BIGGEST MERGERS, 1998–2000

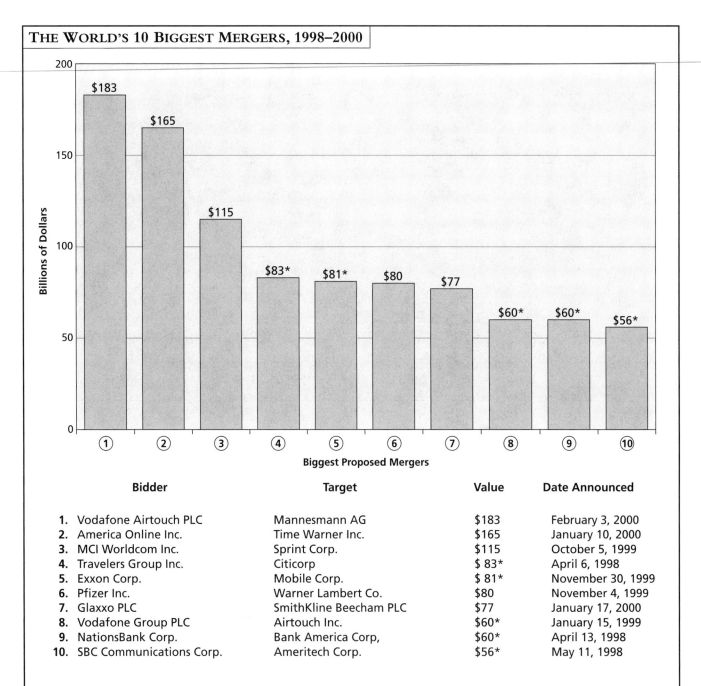

	Bidder	Target	Value	Date Announced
1.	Vodafone Airtouch PLC	Mannesmann AG	$183	February 3, 2000
2.	America Online Inc.	Time Warner Inc.	$165	January 10, 2000
3.	MCI Worldcom Inc.	Sprint Corp.	$115	October 5, 1999
4.	Travelers Group Inc.	Citicorp	$ 83*	April 6, 1998
5.	Exxon Corp.	Mobile Corp.	$ 81*	November 30, 1999
6.	Pfizer Inc.	Warner Lambert Co.	$80	November 4, 1999
7.	Glaxxo PLC	SmithKline Beecham PLC	$77	January 17, 2000
8.	Vodafone Group PLC	Airtouch Inc.	$60*	January 15, 1999
9.	NationsBank Corp.	Bank America Corp,	$60*	April 13, 1998
10.	SBC Communications Corp.	Ameritech Corp.	$56*	May 11, 1998

Note: These were the 10 biggest proposed mergers and takeovers through February 3, 2000, ranked by the value of the transactions upon announcement of the deal. Figures are in billions of dollars and do not include assumption of debt.

* Deal has since been completed, and its value may have changed due to market fluctuations or changes in the deal's final terms.

U.S. PRESIDENTIAL ELECTION, 1992: ELECTORAL VOTE

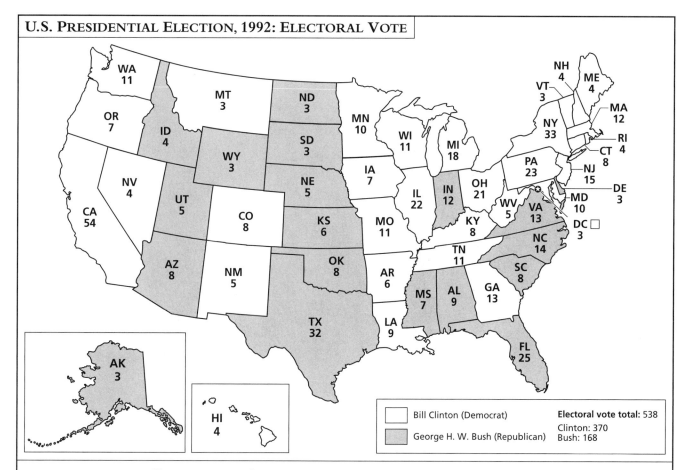

Bill Clinton (Democrat)

George H. W. Bush (Republican)

Electoral vote total: 538
Clinton: 370
Bush: 168

State	Clinton Votes	Pct.	Bush Votes	Pct.	Perot* Votes	Pct.
Alabama	686,571	41	798,439	48	180,514	11
Alaska	63,498	32	81,875	41	55,085	27
Arizona	525,031	37	548,148	39	341,148	24
Arkansas	498,548	54	333,909	36	98,215	11
California	4,815,039	47	3,341,726	32	2,147,409	21
Colorado	626,207	40	557,706	36	362,813	23
Connecticut	680,276	42	575,778	36	347,638	22
Delaware	125,997	44	102,436	36	59,061	21
D.C.	186,301	86	19,813	9	9,284	4
Florida	2,051,845	39	2,137,752	41	1,041,607	20
Georgia	1,005,889	44	989,804	43	307,857	13
Hawaii	178,893	49	136,430	37	52,863	14
Idaho	136,249	29	201,787	43	129,897	28
Illinois	2,379,510	48	1,718,190	35	832,484	17
Indiana	829,176	37	970,457	43	448,431	20
Iowa	583,669	44	503,077	38	251,795	19
Kansas	386,832	34	444,599	39	310,458	27
Kentucky	664,246	45	616,517	42	203,682	14
Louisiana	815,305	46	729,880	42	210,604	12
Maine	261,859	39	207,122	31	205,076	30
Maryland	941,979	50	671,609	36	271,198	14
Massachusetts	1,315,016	48	804,534	29	630,440	23
Michigan	1,858,275	44	1,587,105	37	820,855	19
Minnesota	998,552	42	737,649	32	552,795	24
Mississippi	392,929	41	481,583	50	84,496	9

State	Clinton Votes	Pct.	Bush Votes	Pct.	Perot* Votes	Pct.
Missouri	1,053,040	44	811,057	34	518,250	22
Montana	153,899	38	143,702	36	106,869	26
Nebraska	214,064	30	339,108	47	172,043	24
Nevada	185,401	38	171,378	35	129,532	26
New Hampshire	207,264	39	199,623	38	120,029	23
New Jersey	1,366,609	43	1,309,724	41	505,698	16
New Mexico	259,500	46	212,393	38	91,539	16
New York	3,246,787	50	2,241,283	34	1,029,038	16
North Carolina	1,103,716	43	1,122,608	44	353,845	14
North Dakota	98,927	32	135,498	44	70,806	23
Ohio	1,965,204	40	1,876,445	39	1,024,598	21
Oklahoma	473,066	34	592,929	43	319,978	23
Oregon	525,123	43	394,356	32	307,860	25
Pennsylvania	2,224,897	45	1,778,221	36	896,177	18
Rhode Island	198,924	48	121,916	29	94,757	23
South Carolina	476,626	40	573,231	48	138,140	12
South Dakota	124,861	37	136,671	41	73,297	22
Tennessee	933,620	47	840,899	43	199,787	10
Texas	2,279,269	37	2,460,334	40	1,349,947	22
Utah	182,850	26	320,559	45	202,605	29
Vermont	125,803	46	85,512	31	61,510	23
Virginia	1,034,781	41	1,147,226	45	344,852	14
Washington	855,710	44	609,912	32	470,239	24
West Virginia	326,936	49	239,103	36	106,367	16
Wisconsin	1,035,943	41	926,245	37	542,660	22
Wyoming	67,863	34	79,558	40	51,209	26

*Perot did not earn any electoral votes.

U.S. PRESIDENTIAL ELECTION, 1996: ELECTORAL VOTE

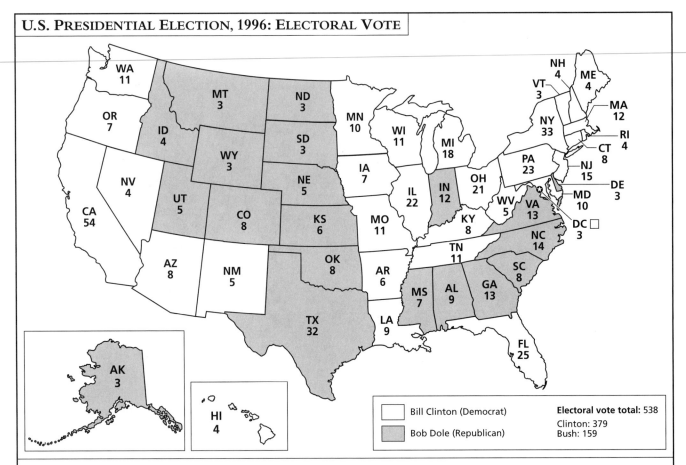

State	Clinton Votes	Pct.	Dole Votes	Pct.	Perot* Votes	Pct.
Alabama	664,503	43	782,029	51	92,010	6
Alaska	66,508	33	101,234	51	21,536	11
Arizona	612,412	47	576,126	44	104,712	8
Arkansas	469,164	54	322,349	37	66,997	8
California	4,639,935	51	3,412,563	38	667,702	7
Colorado	670,854	44	691,291	46	99,509	7
Connecticut	712,603	52	481,047	35	137,784	10
Delaware	140,209	52	98,906	37	28,693	11
D.C.	152,031	85	16,637	9	3,479	2
Florida	2,533,502	48	2,226,117	42	482,237	9
Georgia	1,047,214	46	1,078,972	47	146,031	6
Hawaii	205,012	57	113,943	32	27,358	8
Idaho	165,545	34	256,406	52	62,506	13
Illinois	2,299,476	54	1,577,930	37	344,311	8
Indiana	874,668	42	995,082	47	218,739	10
Iowa	615,732	50	490,949	40	104,462	9
Kansas	384,399	36	578,572	54	92,093	9
Kentucky	635,804	46	622,339	45	118,768	9
Louisiana	928,983	52	710,240	40	122,981	7
Maine	311,092	52	185,133	31	85,290	14
Maryland	924,284	54	651,682	38	113,684	7
Massachusetts	1,567,223	62	717,622	28	225,594	9
Michigan	1,941,126	52	1,440,977	38	326,751	9
Minnesota	1,096,355	51	751,971	35	252,986	12
Mississippi	385,005	44	434,547	49	51,500	6
Missouri	1,024,817	48	889,689	41	217,103	10
Montana	167,169	41	178,957	44	55,017	14
Nebraska	231,906	35	355,665	53	76,103	11
Nevada	203,388	44	198,775	43	43,855	9
New Hampshire	245,260	50	196,740	40	48,140	10
New Jersey	1,599,932	53	1,080,041	36	257,979	9
New Mexico	252,215	49	210,791	41	30,978	6
New York	3,513,191	59	1,861,198	31	485,547	8
North Carolina	1,099,132	44	1,214,399	49	165,301	7
North Dakota	106,405	40	124,597	47	32,594	12
Ohio	2,100,690	47	1,823,859	41	470,680	11
Oklahoma	488,102	40	582,310	48	130,788	11
Oregon	326,099	47	256,105	37	73,265	11
Pennsylvania	2,206,241	49	1,793,568	40	430,082	10
Rhode Island	220,592	60	98,325	27	39,965	11
South Carolina	495,878	44	564,856	50	63,324	6
South Dakota	139,295	43	150,508	46	31,248	10
Tennessee	905,599	48	860,809	46	105,577	6
Texas	2,455,735	44	2,731,998	49	377,530	7
Utah	220,197	33	359,394	54	66,100	10
Vermont	138,400	54	80,043	31	30,912	12
Virginia	1,070,990	45	1,119,974	47	158,707	7
Washington	899,645	51	639,743	36	161,642	9
West Virginia	324,394	51	231,908	37	70,853	11
Wisconsin	1,071,859	49	845,172	39	227,426	10
Wyoming	77,897	37	105,347	50	25,854	12

*Perot did not earn any electoral votes.

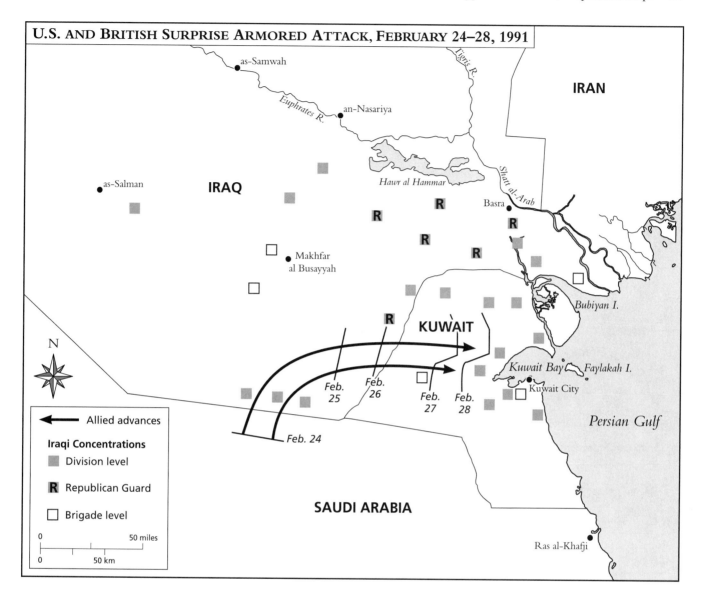

U.S. AND BRITISH SURPRISE ARMORED ATTACK, FEBRUARY 24–28, 1991

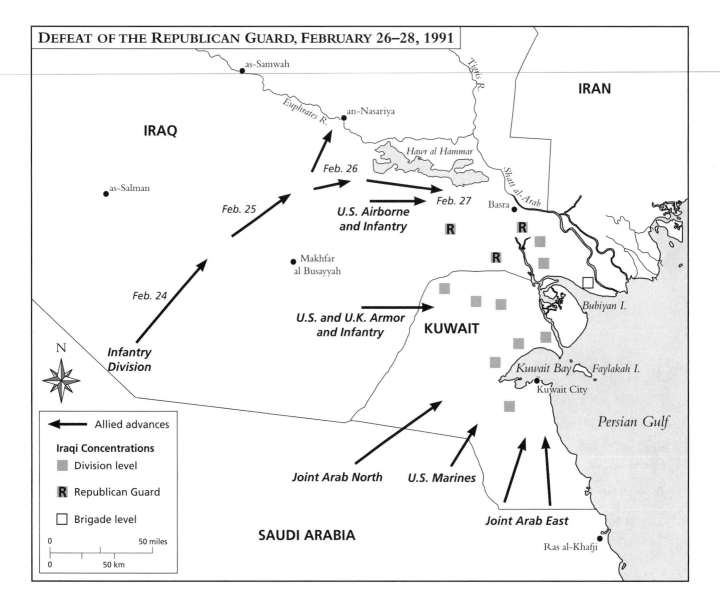

DEFEAT OF THE REPUBLICAN GUARD, FEBRUARY 26–28, 1991

IRAN

as-Samwah

Euphrates R.

Tigris R.

an-Nasariya

IRAQ

Hawr al Hammar

Feb. 26

Shatt al-Arab

as-Salman

Feb. 25

Feb. 27

Basra

U.S. Airborne and Infantry

R

R

Makhfar al Busayyah

R

Feb. 24

Bubiyan I.

U.S. and U.K. Armor and Infantry

KUWAIT

N

Kuwait Bay   *Faylakah I.*

Infantry Division

Kuwait City

Persian Gulf

Joint Arab North

U.S. Marines

Joint Arab East

SAUDI ARABIA

Ras al-Khafji

Legend

→ Allied advances

Iraqi Concentrations

▦ Division level

R Republican Guard

▢ Brigade level

0 ——— 50 miles
0 ——— 50 km

FORMER YUGOSLAVIA, 1993

N

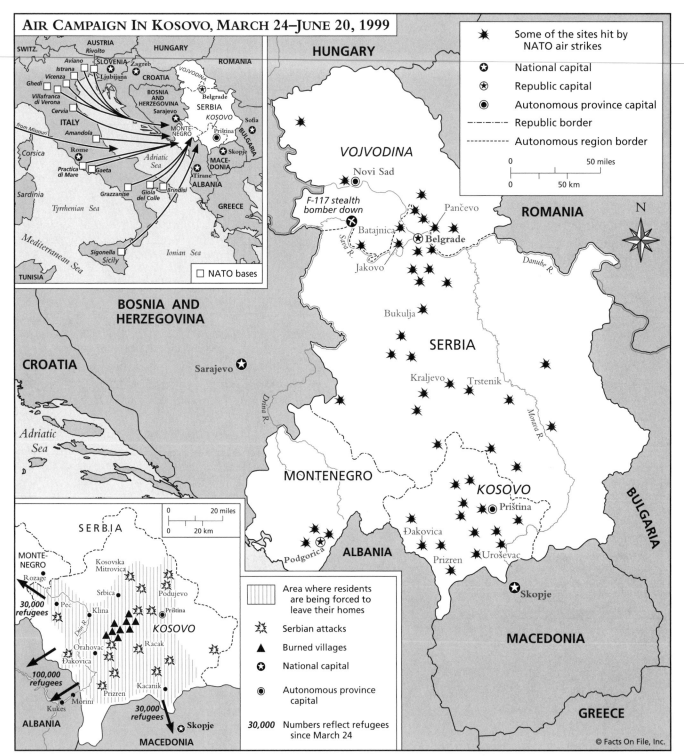

Air Campaign in Kosovo, March 24–June 20, 1999

Legend (upper right):
- Some of the sites hit by NATO air strikes
- National capital
- Republic capital
- Autonomous province capital
- Republic border
- Autonomous region border

0   50 miles
0   50 km

Inset (upper left): NATO bases

SWITZ. AUSTRIA
Rivolto
Aviano   SLOVENIA   Zagreb
Istrana   Ljubljana
Vicenza   CROATIA
Ghedi
Villafranca   BOSNIA AND
di Verona   HERZEGOVINA
Cervia   Sarajevo
ITALY   SERBIA
from Missouri   Amandola   MONTE-   KOSOVO
NEGRO   Priština   Sofia
Corsica   Rome   Adriatic   BULGARIA
Practica   Sea   Skopje
di Mare   Gaeta   MACE-
Sardinia   DONIA
Grazzanise   Tirane
Giola   Brindisi   ALBANIA
del Colle   GREECE
Tyrrhenian Sea
Sigonella   Ionian Sea
Sicily
Mediterranean Sea
TUNISIA

HUNGARY
ROMANIA
VOJVODINA
Belgrade

Main map labels:
HUNGARY
VOJVODINA
Novi Sad
F-117 stealth bomber down
Batajnica   Pančevo
Jakovo   Belgrade
Sava R.   ROMANIA
Bukulja   Danube R.
SERBIA
Kraljevo   Trstenik
Morava R.
MONTENEGRO
KOSOVO
Ðakovica   Priština
Podgorica   Uroševac
ALBANIA   Prizren
Skopje
BULGARIA
MACEDONIA
GREECE

HUNGARY

BOSNIA AND HERZEGOVINA

CROATIA

Sarajevo

Adriatic Sea

N

© Facts On File, Inc.

Lower-left inset:
SERBIA
MONTE-NEGRO
Rozage
30,000 refugees
Pec   Klina   Kosovska Mitrovica
Srbica   Podujevo
Dim R.   Priština
KOSOVO
Orahovac   Racak
Ðakovica
100,000 refugees
Prizren   Kacanik
Kukes   Morini
ALBANIA
30,000 refugees
Skopje
MACEDONIA

Inset legend:
- Area where residents are being forced to leave their homes
- Serbian attacks
- Burned villages
- National capital
- Autonomous province capital
- **30,000** Numbers reflect refugees since March 24

0   20 miles
0   20 km

NOTES

INTRODUCTION

1. Kim Phuc, "Shield Children, Women from War Horrors," *Miami Herald,* January 2, 2004, p. 23A.
2. Jonathan Taylor, ed., *Facts On File Yearbook 2001* (New York: Facts On File, 2002), pp. 347–351.
3. Leonard Quart and Albert Auster, *American Film and Society Since 1945,* 3d ed. (Westport, Conn.: Praeger, 2002), p. 196.
4. Ed Wasserman, "Why Do the Media Report Little on Foundations?" *Miami Herald,* October 20, 2003, p. 25A.
5. Rosabeth Moss Kanter, "Flabby Morals, Oversized Egos," *Miami Herald,* March 29, 2004, p. 17A.
6. David Cay Johnston, "Very Richest's Share of Income Grew Even Bigger, Data Shows," *New York Times,* June 26, 2003, p. 1A. Available online. URL: http://www.nytimes.com/2003/06/26/business/26TAX.html?th. Downloaded June 26, 2003.
7. Editors of Time-Life Books, *The Digital Decade: The '90s* (Alexandria, Va.: Time-Life Books, 2000), p. 101.
8. Quart and Auster, *American Film,* p. 168.
9. See David R. Brock, *Blinded by the Right* (New York: Crown, 2002), p. 148. Formerly associated with such conservative organizations and publications as the Heritage Foundation and the *American Spectator,* Brock played a significant role in orchestrating right-wing attacks on Clinton's reputation.

CHAPTER 1—PRELUDE TO THE 1990S: THE 1980S

1. Robert Scheer, *With Enough Shovels: Reagan, Bush and Nuclear War* (New York: Random House, 1982), pp. 3, 22–25.
2. Martin Walker, *The Cold War: A History* (New York: Henry Holt, 1993), p. 276.
3. Ibid., pp. 276–277.
4. Lois Gordon and Alan Gordon, *American Chronicle* (New Haven, Conn.: Yale University Press, 1999), pp. 758–839.
5. Tim Brooks and Earl Marsh, *The Complete Directory to Prime Time Network and Cable TV Shows: 1946–Present* (New York: Ballantine Books, 1999), p. 332.

CHAPTER 2—THE COLD WAR ENDS: 1990

1. On March 20–21, 1991, in testimony before the Senate Foreign Relations Committee, Glaspie called the transcript a distorted fabrication that contained much that was accurate but also contained errors and had been maliciously edited. She insisted that she informed Saddam Hussein that the United States would defend its vital interests and the sovereignty and integrity of its friends in the Persian Gulf.
2. U.S. Department of Defense, *Conduct of the Persian Gulf War: Final Report to Congress* (Washington, D.C.: U.S. Government Printing Office, 1992), pp. 85–86.
3. Thomas E. Hitchings, editor in chief, *Facts On File Yearbook 1991* (New York: Facts On File, 1992), pp. 237–240, 989.
4. Hitchings, *Facts On File Yearbook 1990,* 200–201.
5. Lois Gordon and Alan Gordon, *American Chronicle* (New Haven, Conn.: Yale University Press, 1999), p. 860.
6. Eloise Salholz, "Women under Assault," *Newsweek* (July 16, 1990), p. 23.
7. "A First Family Argument," *Newsweek* (January 29, 1990), p. 12.
8. Gordon and Gordon, *Chronicle,* pp. 839, 852.
9. Hitchings, *Facts On File Yearbook 1991,* p. 7.

10. *The Digital Decade: The '90s* (Alexandria, Va.: Time-Life Books, 2000), p. 97.
11. Hitchings, *Facts On File Yearbook 1990*, p. 124.
12. Gordon and Gordon, *Chronicle*, p. 860.

CHAPTER 3—DESERT STORM AND THE NEW WORLD ORDER: 1991

1. Lois Gordon and Alan Gordon, *American Chronicle* (New Haven, Conn.: Yale University Press, 1999), p. 869.
2. Thomas E. Hitchings, editor in chief, *Facts On File Yearbook 1991* (New York: Facts On File, 1992), p. 780.
3. Inspectors after the war determined that, as of January 1991, Iraq was probably six months to a year from developing a nuclear weapon—less time than anticipated for the embargo to show results.
4. U.S. Department of Defense, *Conduct of the Persian Gulf War: Final Report to Congress* (Washington, D.C.: U.S. Government Printing Office, 1992), p. 245.
5. Ibid., pp. 293–294.
6. Hitchings, *Facts On File Yearbook 1991*, pp. 16–17.
7. Ibid., p. 18.
8. Gordon and Gordon, *Chronicle*, p. 869.
9. Hitchings, *Facts On File Yearbook 1991*, pp. 401–402.
10. Gordon and Gordon, *Chronicle*, p. 869.
11. Thomas E. Hitchings, editor in chief, *Facts On File Yearbook 1992* (New York: Facts On File, 1993), p. 3.
12. Ibid., p. 21.
13. Clifton Daniel, ed., *20th Century Day by Day* (London: Dorling-Kindersley, 2000), pp. 1376–1377.
14. Gordon and Gordon, *Chronicle*, pp. 852, 861.
15. According to the historian Douglas Brinkley, the term *Generation X* originated in 1965 as the title of a self-improvement manual by the British educators Charles Hamblett and Jane Deverson, defenders of the then-current Mod culture. The rock star Billy Idol, a baby boomer, popularized the term when he used it to name his band. It subsequently evolved into a popular shorthand for the generation who followed the baby boomers, and by 1991 it generally applied to those born between about 1960 and 1980. See Brinkley, "Educating the Generation Called 'X,'" in Stephen Ambrose and David Brinkley, eds., *Wit-ness to America* (New York: HarperCollins, 1999), pp. 574–577.
16. Hitchings, *Facts On File Yearbook 1991*, p. 767.

CHAPTER 4—"IT'S THE ECONOMY, STUPID": 1992

1. Martin Gilbert, *A History of the Twentieth Century*, vol. 3 (New York: Perennial Press, 2000), p. 732.
2. Lois Gordon and Alan Gordon, *American Chronicle* (New Haven, Conn.: Yale University Press, 1999), p. 871.
3. James Haley, ed., *Post–Cold War America: 1992–Present* (San Diego, Calif.: Greenhaven Press, 2003), p. 31.
4. Gilbert, *History*, p. 743.
5. Haley, *Post–Cold War*, p. 38.
6. The full report of the Justice Department's investigation is available online. URL: http://www.byington.org/Carl/ruby/ruby1.htm.
7. Gordon and Gordon, *Chronicle*, p. 878.
8. Ibid, pp. 861, 870, 878.
9. Clifton Daniel, ed., *20th Century Day by Day* (London: Dorling-Kindersley, 2000), p. 1391.
10. National Atmospheric and Oceanographic Agency, "Hurricane Andrew." Available online. URL: http://www.nhc.noaa.gov/HAW2/english/history.shtml#andrew. Downloaded December 17, 2003.
11. Daniel, *20th Century*, p. 1380.
12. Ibid., p. 1383.

CHAPTER 5—DON'T ASK; DON'T TELL: 1993

1. David Brock, *Blinded by the Right* (New York: Crown, 2002), p. 154. For Brock's full account of the so-called Troopergate accusations, see pp. 138–159.
2. Lois Gordon and Alan Gordon, *American Chronicle* (New Haven, Conn.: Yale University Press, 1999), pp. 870, 879.
3. Clifton Daniel, ed., *20th Century Day by Day* (London: Dorling-Kindersley, 2000), p. 1392.
4. Gordon and Gordon, *Chronicle*, pp. 879, 887.
5. Thomas E. Hitchings, editor in chief, *Facts On File Yearbook 1994* (New York: Facts On File, 1995), p. 228.
6. Ibid., p. 212.

7. Thomas E. Hitchings, editor in chief, *Facts On File Yearbook 1993* (New York: Facts On File, 1994), p. 849.

CHAPTER 6—THE CONTRACT WITH AMERICA AND THE CRIME OF THE CENTURY: 1994

1. Martin Gilbert, *A History of the Twentieth Century,* vol. 3 (New York: Perennial Press, 2000), p. 781.
2. Thomas E. Hitchings, editor in chief, *Facts On File Yearbook 1994* (New York: Facts On File, 1995), p. 706.
3. Lois Gordon and Alan Gordon, *American Chronicle* (New Haven, Conn.: Yale University Press, 1999), pp. 879, 888.
4. Ibid., p. 890.
5. Thomas E. Hitchings, editor in chief, *Facts On File Yearbook 1995* (New York: Facts On File, 1996), p. 304.
6. Hitchings, *Facts On File Yearbook 1994,* p. 233.
7. Gordon and Gordon, *Chronicle,* p. 896.
8. Geril Marcus, "Kurt Cobain: Artist of the Decade," *Rolling Stone* (May 13, 1999), pp. 46–48.

CHAPTER 7—TERROR IN THE HEARTLAND: 1995

1. Thomas E. Hitchings, editor in chief, *Facts On File Yearbook 1996* (New York: Facts On File, 1997), p. 390. These figures do not include acts of domestic terrorism such as the Oklahoma City bombing.
2. Martin Gilbert, *A History of the Twentieth Century* (New York: HarperCollins, 2000), p. 813.
3. According to one poll taken immediately after Simpson was acquitted, 85 percent of black Americans concurred with the verdict, compared to only 32 percent of whites. See Jewelle Taylor Gibbs, "The Simpson Trial: Fame, Race, and Murder," in *Post–Cold War America: 1992–Present,* ed. James Haley (San Diego, Calif.: Greenhaven Press, 2003), pp. 65–72.
4. None of the final 12 jurors in the O. J. Simpson trial regularly read a newspaper, but eight regularly watched tabloid TV shows. Five indicated that they believed using force on a family member is sometimes appropriate. Five answered that they or another family member had had negative experiences with the police, and nine thought that Simp-

son was less likely to be a murderer because he was a professional athlete. The racial composition of the initial jury pool differed considerably from that of the final jury: 40 percent white, 28 percent black, 17 percent Hispanic, and 15 percent Asian.

See Jack Walraven, "The Simpson Trial Jury," Available online. URL: www.law.umkc.edupercent2Ffacultypercent2Fprojectspercent2Fftrialspercent2FSimpsonpercent2 FJurypage.html.
5. Lois Gordon and Alan Gordon, *American Chronicle* (New Haven, Conn.: Yale University Press, 1999), p. 905.
6. See Jane D. Brown, Jeanne R. Steele, and Kim Walsh-Childers, eds., *Sexual Teens, Sexual Media* (Mahwah, N.J.: Lawrence Erlbaum Associates, 2002), pp. 5–6.
7. Gordon and Gordon, *Chronicle,* pp. 888, 897.
8. Hitchings, *Facts On File Yearbook 1996,* p. 980.
9. Ibid., p. 182.
10. Thomas E. Hitchings, editor in chief, *Facts On File Yearbook 1995* (New York: Facts On File, 1996), p. 643.
11. See Leonard Quart and Albert Auster, *American Film and Society since 1945,* 3d ed. (Westport, Conn.: Praeger, 2002), p. 169.

CHAPTER 8—CLINTON PREVAILS AGAIN: 1996

1. Rudolph was also charged with the 1997 bombings of an Atlanta abortion clinic and a nightclub frequented by homosexuals and the 1998 bombing of an abortion clinic in Birmingham, Alabama. After years of hiding in the wilderness, Rudolph was apprehended in 2003, and he pleaded guilty to these charges in 2005.
2. On June 21, 2001, a federal grand jury in Alabama indicted 13 Saudis and one Lebanese man for the attack on the Khobar Towers complex in Saudi Arabia, although none of the accused was in custody. Documents released in April 2004, including a circular from the Federal Aviation Administration (FAA) issued the day after the indictment, June 22, 2001, suggested that the subsequent terrorist attack against the Pentagon and World Trade Center on September 11, 2001, may have been related to this indictment.
3. Thomas E. Hitchings, editor in chief, *Facts On File Yearbook 1996* (New York: Facts On File, 1997), p. 433. A *New York Times*/CBS News poll conducted

May 31–June 3, 1996, and reported June 8, showed that only 27 percent of Republicans favored retaining a plank in the party platform calling for a constitutional amendment banning abortion. Overall, voters preferred Clinton's stand on abortion to Dole's by 46 to 24 percent.

4. Ibid., p. 95.
5. Ibid., p. 810.
6. Robert Pear, "Despite the Sluggish Economy, Welfare Rolls Actually Shrank," *New York Times,* March 22, 2004. Available online. URL: http://www.nytimes.com/2004/03/22/national/22WELF.html. Downloaded March 22, 2004.
7. Lois Gordon and Alan Gordon, *American Chronicle* (New Haven, Conn.: Yale University Press, 1999), pp. 906, 914.
8. U.S. Department of Transportation, "Fatality Analysis Reporting System (FARS) Web-Based Encyclopedia. Available online. URL: http://www-fars.nhtsa.dot.gov/
9. Thomas E. Hitchings, publisher, *Facts On File Yearbook 1997* (New York: Facts On File, 1998), p. 258.
10. Gordon and Gordon, *Chronicle,* pp. 897, 906.
11. Hitchings, *Facts On File Yearbook 1997,* p. 121.
12. Hitchings, *Facts On File Yearbook 1996,* p. 52.
13. Ibid., p. 1015.
14. Ibid., p. 835.
15. Gordon and Gordon, *Chronicle,* p. 908.
16. Hitchings, *Facts On File Yearbook 1996,* p. 727.
17. See http://www.aidsquilt.org.

CHAPTER 9—LET THE GOOD TIMES ROLL: 1997

1. According to the International Red Cross, approximately 110 million landmines were already in place throughout the world, and a person was being killed or injured by one every 20 minutes. Altogether, landmines were estimated to kill approximately 9,600 civilians yearly and injure an additional 14,000. See Clifton Daniel, *20th Century Day by Day* (London: Dorling-Kindersley, 2000), p. 1451, and Thomas E. Hitchings, publisher, *Facts On File Yearbook 1997* (New York: Facts On File, 1998), p. 778.
2. Hitchings, *Facts On File Yearbook 1997,* p. 411.
3. Thomas E. Hitchings, publisher, *Facts On File Yearbook 1998* (New York: Facts On File, 1999), p. 3.

4. Hitchings, *Facts On File Yearbook 1997,* p. 981. See also Lois Gordon and Alan Gordon, *American Chronicle* (New Haven, Conn.: Yale University Press, 1999), pp. 906, 915.

CHAPTER 10—MONICA AND IMPEACHMENT: 1998

1. Martin Gilbert, *A History of the Twentieth Century,* vol. 3. (New York: Perennial Press, 2000), p. 866.
2. Ibid., p. 884.
3. Lois Gordon and Alan Gordon, *American Chronicle* (New Haven, Conn.: Yale University Press, 1999), pp. 915, 924. Revised GDP rate cited in Ken Park, publisher, *Facts On File Yearbook 2000* (New York: Facts On File, 2001), p. 60.
4. Thomas E. Hitchings, publisher, *Facts On File Yearbook 1998* (New York: Facts On File, 1999), p. 962.
5. Gilbert, *History,* p. 893.
6. *The Digital Decade: The '90s* (Alexandria, Va.: Time-Life Books, 2000), p. 103.
7. Hitchings, *1998,* p. 1002.

CHAPTER 11—FIN DE SIÈCLE AND Y2K: 1999

1. In computer jargon, where *K* means 1,000, *Y2K* stands for year 2000.
2. See Leslie Mizell, "A Look Back at Y2K and the Millennium Bug," in *Post–Cold War America: 1992–Present* (2003), ed. James Haley (San Diego, Calif.: Greenhaven Press, 2003), pp. 168–173.
3. Even the definition of the 21st century became a matter of debate in this contentious decade, as purists maintained that if the first year in the calendar was numbered 1 instead of 0, then 2000 was technically the final year of the 20th century, and 2001 was the first year of the 21st. But in most people's mind, and in most official celebrations, the new century began when the 1900s ended and the 2000s began. Russia, however, conducted its millennium celebration on New Year's Eve 2000.
4. Marion Farrier, editor in chief, *Facts On File Yearbook 1999* (New York: Facts On File, 2000), p. 544.
5. Ibid., p. 958.
6. Ken Parks, publisher, *Facts On File Yearbook 2000* (New York: Facts On File, 2001), pp. 21, 60.
7. Farrier, *1999,* p. 998.

BIBLIOGRAPHY

Ai. *Fate: New Poems.* Boston: Houghton Mifflin, 1991.

———. *Greed.* New York: Norton, 1993.

———. *Sin: Poems.* Boston: Houghton Mifflin, 1986.

———. *Vice: New and Selected Poems.* New York: W. W. Norton, 1999.

Albright, Madeleine. *Madam Secretary.* New York: Miramax Books, 2003.

Allen, Thomas B., et al. *CNN: War in the Gulf from the Invasion of Kuwait to the Day of Victory and Beyond.* Atlanta: Turner, 1991.

Alvarez, Lizette. "A Dispirited Hyde Opposes Indicting Clinton." *New York Times,* February 13, 1999, p. 1.

Ambrose, Stephen, and Douglas Brinkley, eds. *Witness to America: An Illustrated Documentary History of the United States from the Revolution to Today.* New York: HarperCollins, 1999.

Anderson, Craig, and Lary C. Rampp, eds. *Vocational Education in the 1990s. vol. 2, A Sourcebook for Strategies, Methods, and Materials.* Ann Arbor, Mich.: Prakken, 1993.

Anema, Dale. "A Father at Columbine High." In *Post–Cold War America: 1992–Present.* Edited by James Haley, 140–146. San Diego, Calif.: Greenhaven Press, 2003.

Angelou, Maya. *All God's Children Need Traveling Shoes.* New York: Random House, 1986.

———. *The Heart of a Woman.* New York: Random House, 1981.

———. *I Shall Not Be Moved.* New York: Random House, 1990.

Anonymous. *Primary Colors: A Novel of Politics.* New York: Random House, 1996.

Apple, R. W., Jr. "A Tempered Optimism." *New York Times,* December 9, 1987, p. 1.

———. "A Vote against Clinton." *New York Times,* November 9, 1994, p. 1.

———. "What Next? Don't Guess." *New York Times,* December 20, 1998, p. 1.

Arthur, Paul. "*L.A. Confidential.*" *Cineaste* 23, no. 3 (1998): 41.

"Asia's Economic Woes," *The Newshour with Jim Lehrer,* November 25, 1997. Available online. URL: http://www.pbs.org/newshour/bb/asia/july-dec97/apec_11-25.html. Downloaded August 4, 2004.

Atkinson, Rick. *Crusade: The Untold Story of the Persian Gulf War.* Boston: Houghton Mifflin, 1993.

Atwood, Margaret. *The Handmaid's Tale.* Boston: Houghton Mifflin, 1986.

Auden, W. H. *For the Time Being.* New York: Random House, 1944.

Austen, Jane. *Emma.* New York: St. Martin's Press, 1992.

———. *Mansfield Park.* New York: Oxford University Press, 1970.

———. *Persuasion.* New York: W. W. Norton, 1995.

———. *Pride and Prejudice.* New York: Oxford University Press, 1970.

———. *Sense and Sensibility.* New York: Oxford University Press, 1970.

Baker, James N. "Writers and Agents: The Rush to Cash In." *Newsweek,* January 22, 1990, p. 20.

Banks, Russell. *Cloudsplitter.* New York: HarperFlamingo, 1998.

———. *Rule of the Bone.* New York: HarperCollins, 1995.

Barcun, Michael. *Religion and the Racist Right: The Origins of the Christian Identity Movement.* Chapel Hill: University of North Carolina Press, 1994.

Barrett, Andrea. *Ship Fever and Other Stories.* New York: W. W. Norton, 1996.

Barrett, Lynn. *The Secret Names of Women: Stories.* Pittsburgh: Carnegie Mellon University Press, 1999.

Barth, John. *Further Fridays: Essays, Lectures, and Other Nonfiction, 1984–94.* Boston: Little, Brown, 1995.

———. *The Last Voyage of Somebody the Sailor.* Boston: Little, Brown, 1991.

———. *On with the Story: Stories.* Boston: Little, Brown, 1996.

———. *Once upon a Time: A Floating Opera.* Boston: Little, Brown, 1994.

Barthelme, Frederick. *Natural Selection.* New York: Viking, 1990.

———. *Painted Desert: A Novel.* New York: Penguin Books, 1995.

BBC World Services. *Gulf Crisis Chronology: Day-to-Day Coverage of Events in the Gulf Conflict.* Essex, England: Longman Group, 1991.

Bennet, James "Clinton Outlines Tax Cut Plan." *New York Times,* July 1, 1997, p. 1.

Bennet, James, and John M. Broder, "President Says He Is Sorry and Seeks Reconciliation." *New York Times,* February 13, 1999, p. 1.

Bennett, David. *The Party of Fear: The American Far Right from Nativism to the Militia Movement.* New York: Random House, 1995.

Bennett, William J., ed. *The Book of Virtues: A Treasury of Great Moral Stories.* New York: Simon & Schuster, 1993.

———., ed. *The Children's Book of America.* New York: Simon & Schuster, 1998.

———. *The Death of Outrage: Bill Clinton and the Assault on American Ideals.* New York: Free Press, 1998.

———. *The De-Valuing of America: The Fight for Our Culture and Our Children.* New York: Summit Books, 1992.

———. *The Moral Compass.* New York: Simon & Schuster, 1995.

Berke, Richard L. "Senate Confirms Souter, 90 to 9, as Supreme Court's 105th Justice." *New York Times,* October 3, 1990, p. 1.

Berlant, Lauren, and Lisa Duggan, eds. *Our Monica Ourselves.* New York: New York University Press, 2001.

Berman, Paul. *Debating P. C.: The Controversy over Political Correctness on College Campuses.* New York: Dell, 1992.

Bernard-Donals, Michael, and Richard R. Glejzer, eds. *Rhetoric in an Antifoundational World: Language, Culture, and Pedagogy.* New Haven, Conn.: Yale University Press, 1998, pp. 147–169.

Berners-Lee, Tim, with Mark Fischetti. *Weaving the Web: The Original Design and Ultimate Destiny of the World Wide Web by Its Inventor.* San Francisco: Harper, 1999.

Berry, Gregory. "Speaking Truth to Power: Anita Hill v. Clarence Thomas," June 9, 2004. Available online. URL: http://users.erols.com/gberry/politics/anitahil.htm. Downloaded June 14, 2004.

Bidart, Frank. *Desire.* New York: Farrar, Straus & Giroux, 1997.

Bierbauer, Charles. "Million Man Messenger, Not Message, Causing Division," October 15, 1995. Available online. URL: http://www.cnn.com/US/9510/megamarch/10-15. Downloaded August 6, 2004.

Billiere, General Sir Peter de la. *Storm Command: A Personal Account of the Gulf War.* London: HarperCollins, 1992.

"Blasted." *New Republic,* August 31, 1998. In *Post–Cold War America: 1992–Present.* Edited by James Haley, 128–131. San Diego, Calif.: Greenhaven Press, 2003.

Bloom, Harold. *Shakespeare: The Invention of the Human.* New York: Riverhead, 1998.

Blumberg, Herbert H., and Christopher C. French, ed. *The Persian Gulf War.* Lanham, Md.: University Press of America, 1994.

Blumenthal, Sidney. *The Clinton Wars.* New York: Farrar, Straus & Giroux, 2003.

Bolton, Richard, ed. *Culture Wars: Documents from the Recent Controversies in the Arts.* New York: New Press, 1992.

Bowden, Mark. *Black Hawk Down.* New York: Atlantic Monthly Press, 1999.

Brady, Sarah. Speech before the 1996 Democratic National Convention, August 26, 1996. Available online. URL: http://www.pbs.org/newshour/convention96/ floor_speeches. Downloaded June 11, 2004.

Bragg, Rick. "In Shock, Loathing, Denial: This Doesn't Happen Here." *New York Times,* April 20, 1995, p. 1.

Brantley, Ben. "Rent." *New York Times,* February 14, 1996, p. C11.

Brinkley, Douglas. "Educating the Generation Called X." In *Witness to America: An Illustrated Documentary History of the United States from the Revolution to Today.* Edited by Stephen Ambrose and Douglas Brinkley, 574–577. New York: HarperCollins, 1999.

Brinkley, Joel. "U.S. Judge Declares That Microsoft Is a Market-Stifling Monopoly: Gates Retains Defiant Stance." *New York Times,* November 6, 1999, p.1.

Broad, William J. "Experts Say U.S. Fails to Account for Its Plutonium." *New York Times,* May 20, 1994, p. 1.

Brock, David. *Blinded by the Right: The Conscience of an Ex-Conservative.* New York: Crown Publishers, 2002.

Brokaw, Tom. *The Greatest Generation.* New York: Random House, 1998.

Brooks, Tim, and Earl Marsh. *The Complete Directory to Prime Time Network and Cable TV Shows: 1946–Present.* New York: Ballantine Books, 1999.

Brown, Jane D., Jeanne R. Steele, and Kim Walsh-Childers, eds., *Sexual Teens, Sexual Media.* Mahwah, N.J.: Lawrence Erlbaum Associates, 2002.

Brzezinski, Steve. "John's Wife." *Antioch Review,* summer 1996, p. 364.

Buchanan, Edna. *Contents under Pressure.* New York: Hyperion, 1992.

———. *The Corpse Had a Familiar Face: Covering Miami, America's Hottest Beat.* New York: Random House, 1987.

———. *Miami, It's Murder.* New York: Hyperion, 1994.

———. *Never Let Them See You Cry: More from Miami, America's Hottest Beat.* New York: Random House, 1992.

———. *Nobody Lives Forever.* New York: Random House, 1990.

———. *Pulse: A Novel.* New York: Avon, 1998.

———. *Suitable for Framing.* New York: Hyperion, 1995.

Bulloch, John, and Harvey Morris. *Saddam's War.* London and Boston: Faber & Faber, 1991.

Burrough, Bryan, and John Helyar. *Barbarians at the Gate: The Fall of R.J.R. Nabisco.* New York: Harper & Row, 1990.

Bush, Barbara. Commencement Address at Wellesley College, Wellesley, Massachusetts, June 1, 1990. Available online. URL: http://www.americanrhetoric. com/speeches/barbarabush.html. Downloaded June 18, 2004.

———. *Millie's Book.* New York: Harper, 1992.

Bush, George Herbert Walker. Inauguration speech, January 20, 1989. Available online. URL: http://www.bartleby.com/124. Downloaded June 21, 2004.

———. "President George Bush Announces the Allied Air Attack on Saddam Hussein's Forces in Iraq and Kuwait." In *In Our Own Words: Extraordinary Speeches of the American Century.* Edited by Robert Torricelli and Andrew Carroll. New York: Washington Square Press, 1999.

———. *Public Papers of the Presidents of the United States, George H. W. Bush (1989–1993).* Washington, D.C.: Federal Register Division, National Archives and Records Service, General Services Administration, 1993. Available online. URL: http://www.gpoaccess. gov/pubpapers.

Bush, George H. W., and Brent Scowcroft. *A World Transformed.* New York: Knopf, 1998.

Butler, Robert Olen. *A Good Scent from a Strange Mountain.* New York: Henry Holt, 1992.

Camus, Albert. *The First Man.* New York: Knopf, 1995.

Carroll, James. *An American Requiem: God, My Father, and the War That Came between Us.* Boston: Houghton Mifflin, 1996.

Carter, Stephen L. *The Culture of Disbelief: How American Law and Politics Trivialize Religious Devotion.* New York: Basic Books, 1993.

Carver, Raymond. *Cathedral: Stories.* New York: Knopf, 1983.

———. *What We Talk about When We Talk about Love: Stories.* New York: Knopf, 1981.

"Challenger: Ride, Sally Ride." *Newsweek,* June 27, 1983, p. 34.

Charter of Paris for a New Europe, November 21, 1990. Available online. URL: http://www.osce.org/docs/english/1990-1999/summits/paris90e.htm. Downloaded August 31, 2004.

Cisneros, Sandra. *The House on Mango Street.* Houston, Tex.: Arte Público Press, 1985.

"Civil Discourse," *The Newshour with Jim Lehrer,* January 22, 1997. Available online. URL: http://www.pbs.org/newshour/bb/congress/january97/civil_1-22.html. Downloaded August 4, 2004.

Clancy, Tom. *Executive Orders.* New York: Putnam, 1996.

———. *Rainbow Six.* New York: Putnam, 1998.

Clark, Mary Higgins. *All Around the Town.* New York: Simon & Schuster, 1992.

———. *All through the Night.* New York: Simon & Schuster, 1998.

———. *I'll Be Seeing You.* New York: Simon & Schuster, 1993.

———. *Let Me Call You Sweetheart.* New York: Simon & Schuster, 1995.

———. *The Lottery Winner: Alvirah and Willie Stories.* New York: Simon & Schuster, 1994.

———. *Loves Music, Loves to Dance.* New York: Simon & Schuster, 1991.

———. *Moonlight Becomes You.* New York: Simon & Schuster, 1996.

———. *My Gal Sunday.* New York: Simon & Schuster, 1996.

———. *Pretend You Don't See Her.* New York: Simon & Schuster, 1997.

———. *Remember Me.* New York: Simon & Schuster, 1994.

———. *Silent Night.* New York: Simon & Schuster, 1995.

———. *A Stranger Is Watching.* New York: Simon & Schuster, 1997.

———. *We'll Meet Again.* New York: Simon & Schuster, 1999.

———. *You Belong to Me.* New York: Simon & Schuster, 1998.

Clark, Ramsey, et al. *War Crimes: A Report on United States War Crimes against Iraq.* Washington, D.C.: Maisonneuve Press, 1992.

Clarke, Richard A. *Against All Enemies: Inside America's War on Terror.* New York: Free Press, 2004.

Clifton, Tony. "Going into Battle with the Tiger Brigade." *Newsweek,* March 4, 1991, p. 24.

Clines, Francis X. "Missiles Rock Kosovo Capital, Belgrade and Other Sites," *New York Times,* March 25, 1999, p. 1.

Clinton, Hillary Rodham. *It Takes a Village.* New York: Simon & Schuster, 1996.

———. *Living History.* New York: Simon & Schuster, 2003.

Clinton, William Jefferson. Acceptance Speech for the 1996 Presidential Nomination, August 29, 1996. Available online. URL: http://www.pbs.org/newshour/ convention96/floor_speeches. Downloaded August 26, 2004.

———. First Inaugural Speech, January 20, 1993. Available online. URL: http://www.bartleby.com/124. Downloaded June 21, 2004.

———. *My Life.* New York: Knopf, 2004.

———. *Public Papers of the Presidents of the United States, William J. Clinton (1993–1999).* Washington, D.C.: Federal Register Division, National Archives and Records Service, General Services Administration, 2000. Available online. URL: http://www.gpoaccess.gov/pubpapers.

———. *Public Papers of the Presidents of the United States, William J. Clinton (2000–2001).* Washington, D.C.: Federal Register Division, National Archives and Records Service, General Services Administration, 2001. Available online. URL: http://www.gpoaccess.gov/pubpapers.

———. Response to Referral of Office of Independent Counsel, September 12, 1998. Available online. URL: http://icreport.access.gpo.gov/report/clinton. htm. Downloaded September 1, 2004.

———. Second Inaugural Speech, January 20, 1997. Available online. URL: http://www.bartleby.com/124. Downloaded June 21, 2004.

Coates, James. *Armed and Dangerous: The Rise of the Survivalist Right.* New York: Hill & Wang, 1987.

Cocks, Jay. "Two Scoops of Vanilli." *Time,* March 5, 1990, p. 69.

Cohen, Roger, and Claudio Gatti. *In the Eye of the Storm: The Life of General Norman Schwarzkopf.* New York: Farrar, Straus & Giroux, 1991.

"Columbine Killer Envisioned Crashing Plane in NYC," December 6, 2001. Available online. URL: http://www.cnn.com/2001/US/12/05/columbine.diary. Downloaded August 5, 2002.

Conventional Forces in Europe Treaty, November 17, 1990. Available online. URL: http://www.osce.org/docs/english/1990– 1999/cfe/cfetreate.htm. Downloaded June 18, 2004.

Coon, Carleton S. *Culture Wars and the Global Village: A Diplomat's Perspective.* Amherst, N.Y.: Prometheus Books, 2000.

Coover, Robert. *Ghost Town.* New York: Henry Holt, 1998.

————. *John's Wife.* New York: Simon & Schuster, 1996.

Cornish, Edward, ed. *The 1990s and Beyond.* Bethesda, Md.: World Future Society, 1990.

Coughlin, Con. *Saddam: King of Terror.* New York: HarperCollins, 2002.

Coupland, Douglas. *Generation X: Tales for an Accelerated Culture.* New York: St. Martin's Press, 1991.

Crichton, Michael. *Jurassic Park.* New York: Knopf, 1990.

————. *The Lost World.* New York: Knopf, 1993.

————. *Rising Sun.* New York: Knopf, 1992.

"Cubans Came Close, but No Cigar in Revolutionary Game in Cuba," March 28, 1999. Available online. URL: http://www.latinosportslegends.com/ Cuba_vs_Orioles-game1.htm. Downloaded August 5, 2004.

Cunningham, Michael. *The Hours.* New York: Farrar, Straus & Giroux, 1998.

Daniel, Clifton, ed. *20th Century Day by Day.* London: Dorling-Kindersley, 2000.

Dees, Morris, with James Corcoran. *Gathering Storm: America's Militia Threat.* New York: HarperCollins, 1996.

Delaney, Bill. "G.I. Jane." In *Magill's Cinema Annual.* Detroit: Gale Research, 1998, pp. 218–220.

DeLillo, Don. *Libra.* New York: Viking Penguin, 1988.

————. *White Noise.* New York: Viking Penguin, 1985.

Denton, Robert E., Jr., and Rachel L. Holloway, eds. *The Clinton Presidency: Images, Issues, and Communication Strategies.* Westport, Conn.: Praeger Press, 1996.

Dershowitz, Alan. *Sexual McCarthyism: Clinton, Starr, and the Emerging Constitutional Crisis.* New York: Basic Books, 1998.

Diamond, Jared. *Guns, Germs, and Steel: The Fates of Human Societies.* New York: W. W. Norton, 1997.

Dick, Philip K. *Do Androids Dream of Electric Sheep?* Garden City, N.Y.: Doubleday, 1968.

————. "We Can Remember It for You Wholesale." Available online. URL: http://web.nwe.ufl.edu/~sfenty/Wholesale.html. Downloaded August 18, 2004.

The Digital Decade—the '90s. Alexandria, Va.: Time-Life Books, 2000.

Dizdarević, Slatko. *Sarajevo: A War Journal.* New York: Fromm International, 1993.

Doctorow, E. L. *Ragtime.* New York: Random House, 1975.

Dole, Robert. Nomination acceptance speech, August 15, 1996. Available online. URL: http://www.4president.org/speeches/dolekemp1996convention.htm. Downloaded August 26, 2004.

Dower, John. *Embracing Defeat: Japan in the Wake of World War II.* New York: W. W. Norton, 1999.

Dufresne, John. *Louisiana Power and Light.* New York: W. W. Norton, 1994.

———. *Love Warps the Mind a Little.* New York: W. W. Norton, 1997.

———. *The Way That Water Enters Stone: Stories.* New York: W. W. Norton, 1991.

Editorials On File, January 1–15, 1980. New York: Facts On File, 1980.

Editorials On File, January 16–31, 1980. New York: Facts On File, 1980.

Editorials On File, April 16–30, 1980. New York: Facts On File, 1980.

Editorials On File, April 1–15, 1982. New York: Facts On File, 1982.

Editorials On File, August 16–31, 1982. New York: Facts On File, 1982.

Editorials On File, November 16–30, 1982. New York: Facts On File, 1982.

Editorials On File, April 16–30, 1984. New York: Facts On File, 1984.

Editorials On File, March 1–15, 1993. New York: Facts On File, 1993.

Editorials On File, May 1–15, 1993. New York: Facts On File, 1993.

Editorials On File, August 1–15, 1993. New York: Facts On File, 1993.

Edson, Margaret. *Wit.* New York: Dramatists Play Service, 1999.

Edwards, Roger. "Central Oklahoma Tornado Intercept," May 3, 1999. Available online. URL: http://webserv.chatsystems.com/~tornado/3may99. Downloaded August 5, 2004.

Egan, Timothy. "With Spotlight Shifted to Them, Some Simpson Jurors Talk Freely." *New York Times,* October 5, 1995, p. 1.

Eisenberg, John. *The Longest Shot: Lili E. Tee and the Kentucky Derby.* Lexington: University Press of Kentucky, 1996.

Eliot, Thomas Stearns. *Old Possum's Book of Practical Cats.* New York: Harcourt, Brace, 1939.

Elkind, David, *Parenting Your Teenager in the 1990's: Practical Information and Advice about Adolescent Development and Contemporary Issues.* Rosemont, N.J.: Modern Learning Press, 1993.

Englehardt, Colonel Joseph P. *Desert Shield and Desert Storm: A Chronology and Troop List for the 1990–1991 Persian Gulf Crisis.* Carlisle Barracks, Pa.: U.S. Army War College, Strategic Studies Institute, 1991.

Esquivel, Laura. *Like Water for Chocolate.* New York: Doubleday, 1992.

Estés, Clarissa Pinkola. *Women Who Run with the Wolves.* New York: Ballantine, 1992.

Fallows, James. *Breaking the News: How the Media Undermine American Democracy.* New York: Pantheon, 1996.

Faludi, Susan. *Backlash: The Undeclared War against American Women.* New York: Crown, 1991.

Farrakhan, Louis. "Minister Farrakhan Challenges Black Men: Transcript from Minister Louis Farrakhan's Remarks at the Million Man March," October 17, 1995. Available online. URL: http://www.cnn.com/US/9510/megamarch/ march.html. Downloaded August 5, 2004.

Farrier, Marion, editor in chief. *Facts On File Yearbook 1999.* New York: Facts On File, 2000.

Farrow, Mia. *What Falls Away: A Memoir.* New York: Bantam, 1998.

Faulkner, William. *The Sound and the Fury.* New York: Random House, 1929.

Ferro, Robert. *The Family of Max Desir.* New York: Dutton, 1983.

"First Family Argument." *Newsweek,* January 29, 1990, p. 12.

Fischer, Stanley. "The Asian Crisis: A View from the IMF," January 22, 1998. Available online. URL: http://www.imf.org/external/np/speeches/1998/ 012298.htm. Downloaded August 5, 2004.

Fitzgerald, F. Scott. *The Great Gatsby.* 1925. Reprint, New York: Chelsea House, 1986.

Fitzsimmons, Richard, and Joan P. Diana. *Pro-Choice/Pro-Life Issues in the 1990s: An Annotated, Selected Bibliography.* Westport, Conn.: Praeger, 1996.

Fleitz, Frederick, H., Jr. *Peacekeeping Fiascoes of the 1990s.* Westport, Conn: Praeger, 2002.

Flick, Larry, Carla Hay, Melinda Newman, and Chris Morris. "In Woodstock's Wake, Hard Questions." In *Post–Cold War America: 1992–Present.* Edited by James Haley, 153–162. San Diego, Calif.: Greenhaven Press, 2003.

Foner, Eric. "Liberalism's Discontents." *Nation,* May 6, 1996, pp. 34–38.

Ford, Richard. *Independence Day.* New York: Knopf, 1995.

———. *The Sportswriter.* New York: Vintage Books, 1986.

Forster, E. M. *Howard's End.* New York: Vintage Books, 1954.

———. *Passage to India.* New York: Harcourt, Brace, 1924.

———. *A Room with a View.* New York: Knopf, 1974.

Fox-Genovese, Elizabeth. "It Takes a Village and Other Lessons Children Teach Us." *National Review,* March 11, 1996, p. 62.

Frazier, Charles. *Cold Mountain.* New York: Atlantic Monthly Press, 1997.

Friedman, Thomas L. "Rabin and Arafat Seal Their Accord as Clinton Applauds 'Brave Gamble.' " *New York Times,* September 14, 1993, p. 1.

———. "Truck Loaded with TNT Wrecks Headquarters of a Marine Unit." *New York Times,* October 24, 1983, p. 1.

Frost, Linda. "The Decentered Subject of Feminism: Postfeminism and *Thelma and Louise.*" In *Rhetoric in an Antifoundational World: Language, Culture, and Pedagogy.* Edited by Michael Bernard-Donals and Richard R. Glejzer, 147–169. New Haven, Conn.: Yale University Press, 1998.

Fukuyama, Frances. *The End of History and the Last Man.* New York: Avon Books, 1993.

Gabler, Neale. "The People's Prince: What JFK Jr. Meant to America." In *Post–Cold War America: 1992–Present.* Edited by James Haley, 147–152. San Diego, Calif.: Greenhaven Press, 2003.

Gaddis, William. *A Frolic of His Own.* New York: Poseidon Press, 1994.

Gagnon, Paul. "What Should Children Learn?" *Atlantic,* December 1995, pp. 65–78.

Garrison, Deborah. *A Working Girl Can't Win: And Other Poems.* New York: Random House, 1998.

Gates, Bill. *Bill Gates Speaks: Insight from the World's Greatest Entrepreneur.* Compiled by Janet Lowe. New York: John Wiley, 1998.

———, with Collins Hemingway. *Business © the Speed of Thought: Using a Digital Nervous System.* New York: Warner, 1999.

———. *The Road Ahead.* New York: Viking, 1995.

Gates, David. "American Gothic." *New York Times Book Review,* September 15, 1996, p. 11.

Gates, Henry Louis. *Colored People: A Memoir.* New York: Knopf, 1994.

Gay, Peter. *The Cultivation of Hatred.* New York: W. W. Norton, 1993.

Geist, Charles R. *Wall Street: A History.* New York: Oxford University Press, 1997.

Gibbs, Jewelle Taylor. "The Simpson Trial: Fame, Race, and Murder." In *Post–Cold War America: 1992–Present.* Edited by James Haley, 65–72. San Diego, Calif.: Greenhaven Press, 2003.

Gilbert, Martin. *A History of the Twentieth Century,* vol. 3. New York: Perennial Press, 2000.

Gingrich, Newt. *Contract with America.* New York: Times Books, 1994.

———. *Lessons Learned the Hard Way: A Personal Report.* New York: HarperCollins, 1998.

———. *Quotations from Speaker Newt: The Little Red, White, and Blue Book of the Republican Revolution.* Edited by Amy D. Bernstein and Peter W. Bernstein. New York: Workman, 1995.

———. *To Renew America.* New York: HarperCollins, 1995.

Gleick, James. *Genius: The Life and Science of Richard Feynman.* New York: Pantheon, 1992.

Goldhagen, Daniel Jonah. *Hitler's Willing Executioners: Ordinary Germans and the Holocaust.* New York: Knopf, 1996.

Goleman, Daniel. *Emotional Intelligence: Why It Can Matter More than I.Q.* New York: Bantam, 1995.

Gonzalez, Juan. "The Rodney King Verdict and the Los Angeles Riots." In *Post–Cold War America: 1992–Present.* Edited by James Haley, 30–39. San Diego, Calif.: Greenhaven Press, 2003.

Goodman, Ellen. "Foreign Policy for Fun and Profit." *Miami Herald,* May 30, 1987, p. 19A.

Gopnik, Adam. "Cyclops." *New Yorker,* October 3, 1988, pp. 95–101.

Gorbachev, Mikhail. *Memoirs.* New York: Doubleday, 1996.

Gordon, Jeff. "There You Go Again." Available online. URL: http://www.freerepublic.com/focus/f-news/1148991/posts. Downloaded July 1, 2004.

Gordon, Lois, and Alan Gordon. *American Chronicle: Year by Year through the Twentieth Century.* New Haven, Conn.: Yale University Press, 1999.

Gore, Al, Jr. *The Earth in the Balance: Healing the Global Environment.* Boston: Houghton Mifflin, 1992.

Grainge, Paul. *Monochrome Memories: Nostalgia and Style in Retro America.* Westport, Conn.: Praeger, 2002.

Gray, John. *Men Are from Mars, Women Are from Venus.* New York: HarperCollins, 1992.

Greene, Melissa Faye. *The Temple Bombing.* Reading, Mass.: Addison-Wesley, 1996.

Greenhouse, Linda. "Court Eases Curb on Aid to Schools with Church Ties. *New York Times,* June 24, 1997, p. 1.

———. "Military College Can't Bar Women, High Court Rules." *New York Times,* June 27, 1996, p. 1.

Greve, Frank. "The B1 Bomber." *Miami Herald,* February 12, 1984, p. 1E.

Grisham, John. *The Chamber.* New York: Doubleday, 1994.

———. *The Client.* New York: Doubleday, 1993.

———. *The Firm.* New York: Doubleday, 1991.

———. *The Partner.* New York: Doubleday, 1997.

———. *The Pelican Brief.* New York: Doubleday, 1992.

———. *The Rainmaker.* New York: Doubleday, 1995.

———. *The Runaway Jury.* New York: Doubleday, 1996.

———. *The Street Lawyer.* New York: Doubleday, 1998.

———. *The Testament.* New York: Doubleday, 1999.

———. *A Time to Kill.* New York: Island Books, 1992.

Guterson, David. *Snow Falling on Cedars.* New York: Harcourt Brace, 1994.

Hackett, George. "No Justice, No Peace." *Newsweek,* May 28, 1990, pp. 18–19.

Haley, James, ed. *Post–Cold War America, 1992–Present.* San Diego, Calif.: Greenhaven Press, 2003.

Hall, Donald. *Without: Poems.* Boston: Houghton Mifflin, 1998.

Hall, James W. *Body Language.* New York: St. Martin's Press, 1998.

———. *Bones of Coral.* New York: Knopf, 1991.

———. *Buzz Cut.* New York: Delacorte Press, 1996.

———. *Gone Wild.* New York: Delacorte Press, 1995.

———. *Hard Aground.* New York: Delacorte Press, 1993.

———. *Mean High Tide.* New York: Delacorte Press, 1994.

————. *Paper Products.* New York: W. W. Norton, 1990.

————. *Red Sky at Night.* New York: Delacorte Press, 1997.

————. *Under Cover of Daylight.* New York: W. W. Norton, 1987.

Hamm, Mark S. "Terror in the Heartland: The Oklahoma City Bombing." In *Post–Cold War America, 1992–Present.* Edited by James Haley, 30–39. San Diego, Calif.: Greenhaven Press, 2003.

"Hanging Tough," *The Newshour with Jim Lehrer,* April 3, 1997. Available online. URL: http://www.pbs.org/newshour/bb/law/april97/militia_4-3.html. Downloaded on September 13, 2005.

Harris, David A. "Driving While Black: Racial Profiling on Our Nation's Highways," June 1999. Available online. URL: http://www.klas-tv.com/Global/story.asp?S=1113071&nav=168bDlBn. Downloaded August 5, 2004.

Harris, Thomas. *Hannibal.* New York: Delacorte Press, 1999.

————. *Silence of the Lambs.* New York: St. Martin's Press, 1988.

Havel, Václav. *Summer Meditations.* New York: Knopf, 1992.

Hawley, T. M. *Against the Fires of Hell: The Environmental Disaster of the Gulf War.* New York: Harcourt Brace Jovanovich, 1992.

Hayden, Joseph. *Covering Clinton: The President and the Press in the 1990s.* Westport, Conn.: Praeger, 2001.

Heller, Joseph. *Catch-22.* New York: Simon & Schuster, 1961.

Hendrickson, Paul. *The Living and the Dead: Robert McNamara and Five Lives of a Lost War.* New York: Knopf, 1996.

Herrnstein, Richard J., and Charles Murray. *The Bell Curve: Intelligence and Class Structure in American Life.* New York: Free Press, 1994.

Heston, Charlton. "The Second Amendment: America's First Freedom," September 11, 1997. Available online. URL: http://www.whyonearth.com/heston/heston.html. Downloaded June 11, 2004.

Hiaasen, Carl. *Kick Ass: Selected Columns of Carl Hiaasen.* Edited by Diane Stevenson. Gainesville: University Press of Florida, 1999.

————. *Lucky You: A Novel.* New York: Knopf, 1997.

————. *Native Tongue: A Novel.* New York: Knopf, 1991.

————. *Stormy Weather: A Novel.* New York: Knopf, 1995.

————. *Strip Tease: A Novel.* New York: Knopf, 1993.

————. *Team Rodent: How Disney Devours the World.* New York: Ballantine, 1998.

"High-Tech Workers," *The Newshour with Jim Lehrer,* April 3, 1998. Available online. URL: http://psyche.uthct.edu/nes/wwwboard/messages/102.html. Downloaded August 28, 2004.

Hijuelos, Oscar. *The Mambo Kings Play Songs of Love.* New York: Farrar, Straus & Giroux, 1989.

Hill, Anita. Testimony at the Senate Confirmation Hearing for Clarence Thomas, October 11, 1991. Available online. URL: www.mith2.umd.edu/WomensStudies/ GenderIssues/SexualHarassment/hill-thomas-testimony. Downloaded August 31, 2004.

Himmelfarb, Gertrude. *The De-Moralization of Society: From Victorian Virtues to Modern Values.* New York: Vintage Books, 1996.

Hinojosa, Rolando. *Rites and Witnesses: A Comedy.* Houston, Tex.: Arte Público Press, 1982.

Hitchings, Thomas E., editor in chief. *Facts On File Yearbook 1990.* New York: Facts On File, 1991.

———, editor in chief. *Facts On File Yearbook 1991.* New York: Facts On File, 1992.

———, editor in chief. *Facts On File Yearbook 1992.* New York: Facts On File, 1993.

———, editor in chief. *Facts On File Yearbook 1993.* New York: Facts On File, 1994.

———, editor in chief. *Facts On File Yearbook 1994.* New York: Facts On File, 1995.

———, editor in chief. *Facts On File Yearbook 1995.* New York: Facts On File, 1996.

———, publisher. *Facts On File Yearbook 1996.* New York: Facts On File, 1997.

———, publisher. *Facts On File Yearbook 1997.* New York: Facts On File, 1998.

———, publisher. *Facts On File Yearbook 1998.* New York: Facts On File, 1999.

Hohenberg, John. *Reelecting Bill Clinton: Why America Chose a "New" Democrat.* Syracuse, N.Y.: Syracuse University Press, 1997.

Holden, Stephen. "Pastiche of Columbus, Politics and Puppets, Tinged with Pathos." *New York Times,* September 9, 1992, p. C15.

Holm, Major General Jeanne. *Women in the Military: An Unfinished Revolution.* Rev. ed. Novato, Calif.: Presidio Press, 1992.

Holmes, Steven A. *Ron Brown: An Uncommon Life.* New York: John Wiley & Sons, 2000.

Homer. *The Odyssey.* Translated by Robert Fagles. New York: Viking, 1996.

Hornby, Richard. "Forty-Second Street." *Hudson Review,* summer 1996, pp. 279–285.

———. "Forty-Second Street." *Hudson Review,* summer 1999, pp. 282–288.

Howard, Philip K. *The Death of Common Sense: How Law Is Suffocating America.* New York: Random House, 1994.

Hughes, Robert. *Culture of Complaint: The Fraying of America.* New York: Oxford University Press, 1993.

Hunter, James Davison. *Before the Shooting Begins: Searching for Democracy in America's Culture War.* New York: Free Press, 1994.

———. *Culture Wars: The Struggle to Define America.* New York: Basic Books, 1991.

———. *The Death of Character: Moral Education in an Age without Good or Evil.* New York: Basic Books, 2000.

Hutchinson, Kevin Don. *Operation Desert Shield/Desert Storm: Chronology and Fact Book.* Westport, Conn.: Greenwood Press, 1995.

Huxley, Aldous. *Brave New World.* 1932. Reprint, New York: Harper & Brothers, 1946.

Ing, Dean. *Pulling Through.* New York: Ace Science Fiction Books, 1983.

Irving, John. *The Cider House Rules: A Novel.* New York: Morrow, 1985.

Ishiguro, Kazuo. *Remains of the Day.* 1989. Reprint, New York: Vintage Books, 1990.

James, Henry. *The Portrait of a Lady.* 1881. Reprint, New York: New American Library, 1964.

———. *Turn of the Screw.* 1898. Reprint, New York: W. W. Norton, 1966.

———. *Washington Square.* 1881. Reprint, New York: Modern Library, 1950.

———. *Wings of the Dove.* 1902. Reprint, New York: New American Library, 1964.

Jin, Ha. *Between Silences: A Voice from China.* Chicago: University of Chicago Press, 1990.

———. *In the Pond.* Cambridge, Mass.: Zoland Books, 1998.

———. *Under the Red Flag: Stories.* Athens: University of Georgia Press, 1997.

———. *Waiting.* New York: Pantheon, 1999.

"John Paul II Criticizes Capitalism." *Miami Herald,* May 10, 1990, p. 12A.

Johnston, David Kay. "Very Richest's Share of Income Grew Even Bigger, Data Shows." *New York Times,* June 26, 2003. Available online. URL: http://www.nytimes.com/2003/06/26/business/26TAX.html?th. Downloaded June 26, 2003.

Joyce, James. *A Portrait of the Artist as a Young Man.* New York: Chelsea House, 1988.

———. *Ulysses.* Paris: Shakespeare and Co., 1922.

Judge, Edward H., and John W. Langdon, eds. *The Cold War: A History through Documents.* Upper Saddle River, N.J.: Prentice Hall, 1999.

Junger, Sebastian. *The Perfect Storm.* New York: W. W. Norton, 1997.

Kaczynski, Theodore. "Industrial Society and Its Future," September 19, 1995. Available online. URL: http://www.panix.com/~clays/Una. Downloaded September 1, 2004.

Kallen, Stuart A., ed. *The 1990s.* San Diego, Calif.: Greenhaven Press, 2000.

Kaminer, Wendy. "Crashing the Locker Room." *Atlantic,* July 1992, pp. 59–67.

Kanter, Rosabeth Moss. "Flabby Morals, Oversized Egos." *Miami Herald,* March 29, 2004, p. 7A.

Karl, Jonathan. *The Right to Bear Arms: The Rise of America's New Militias.* New York: HarperCollins, 1995.

Karsh, Efraim, and Inari Rautsi. *Saddam Hussein: A Political Biography.* New York: Free Press, 1991.

Kaysen, Susanna. *Girl, Interrupted.* New York: Turtle Bay Books, 1993.

Kazantzakis, Nikos. *The Last Temptation of Christ.* New York: Simon & Schuster, 1960.

Keillor, Garrison. *Lake Wobegon Days.* New York: Viking, 1985.

Kelley, Kitty. *Nancy Reagan: The Unauthorized Biography.* New York: Simon & Schuster, 1991.

Kennan, George. *At a Century's Ending: 1982–1995.* New York: W. W. Norton, 1996.

Kennedy, William. *The Flaming Corsage.* New York: Viking, 1996.

———. *Ironweed.* New York: Viking, 1983.

"Kids and Crime," *The Newshour with Jim Lehrer,* January 14, 2000. Available online. URL: http://www.pbs.org/newshour/bb/youth/jan-june00/kids_crime_1-14.html. Downloaded August 6, 2004.

Kilcher, Jewel. *A Night without Armor.* New York: HarperCollins, 1998.

"Killer's Diary Surfaces: Entries Detail a Full Year of Planning," 1999. Available online. URL: http://www.massmurder.zyns.com/eric_harris_dylan_klebold_04.html. Downloaded August 6, 2004.

King, Stephen. *Bag of Bones.* New York: Scribner, 1998.

———. *Feast of Fear: Conversations with Stephen King.* Edited by Tim Underwood and Chuck Miller. New York: Carroll & Graf, 1992.

———. *Four Past Midnight.* New York: Viking, 1990.

———. *Gerald's Game.* New York: Viking, 1992.

———. *The Girl Who Loved Tom Gordon.* New York: Scribner, 1999.

———. *Hearts in Atlantis.* New York: Scribner, 1999.

———. *Insomnia.* New York: Viking, 1994.

———. *Needful Things.* New York: Viking, 1991.

———. *Nightmares and Dreamscapes.* New York: Viking, 1993.

———. *Rose Madder.* New York: Viking, 1995.

———. *Salem's Plot.* New York: Plume, 1991.

———. *Storm of the Century.* New York: Pocket Books, 1999.

Kingston, Maxine Hong. *China Men.* New York: Knopf, 1989.

———. *Tripmaster Monkey: His Fake Book.* New York: Knopf, 1989.

Klehr, Harvey, John Earl Haynes, and Fridrikh Firsov. *The Secret World of American Communism.* New Haven, Conn.: Yale University Press, 1995.

Kleinfield, N. R. "First, Darkness, Then Came the Smoke." *New York Times,* February 27, 1993, p. 1.

Kluger, Richard. *Ashes to Ashes: America's Hundred-Year Cigarette War, the Public Health, and the Unabashed Triumph of Philip Morris.* New York: Knopf, 1996.

Kolata, Gina. "Scientists Report First Cloning Ever of Adult Mammal." In *Post–Cold War America, 1992–Present.* Edited by James Haley, 122–127. San Diego, Calif.: Greenhaven Press, 2003.

Kopit, Arthur. *End of the World.* New York: Hill & Wang, 1984.

Kramer, Martin. "Islam and the West (including Manhattan)." In *Post–Cold War America, 1992–Present.* Edited by James Haley, 44–56. San Diego, Calif.: Greenhaven Press, 2003.

Kushner, Tony. *Tony Kushner in Conversation.* Ann Arbor: University of Michigan Press, 1998.

Labaton, Stephen. "Reno Sees Error in Move on Cult." *New York Times,* April 20, 1993, p. 1.

Lahiri, Jhumpa. *Interpreter of Maladies.* Boston: Houghton Mifflin, 1999.

Leavitt, David. *The Lost Language of Cranes.* New York: Knopf, 1986.

Le Carré, John. *Single and Single.* New York: Scribner, 1999.

LeGuin, Ursula. *Unlocking the Air and Other Stories.* New York: HarperCollins, 1996.

Levine, Linda. *Job Growth in the 1990s by State and Industry.* Washington, D.C.: Congressional Research Service, Library of Congress, 1996.

Lewis, Michael. *Liar's Poker: Rising through the Wreckage on Wall Street.* New York: W. W. Norton, 1989.

Lightman, Alan. *Einstein's Dream.* New York: Pantheon, 1993.

Limbaugh, Rush. *See, I Told You So.* New York: Pocket Books, 1993.

———. *The Way Things Ought to Be.* New York: Pocket Books, 1992.

Lind, Michael. "Rev. Robertson's Grand International Conspiracy Theory." *New York Review of Books,* February 2, 1995, pp. 21–25.

Linday, Sarah. *Primate Behavior.* New York: Grove Press, 1997.

Loftus, John, and Mark Aarons. *The Secret War against the Jews.* New York: St. Martin's Press, 1994.

London, Herbert. *Decade of Denial: A Snapshot of America in the 1990s.* Lanham, Md.: Lexington Books, 2001.

Ludlam, Robert. *The Scorpio Illusion.* New York: Bantam, 1993.

Lurie, Alison. *Foreign Affairs.* New York: Random House, 1984.

Maat, Anisa. "The Million Women's March," October 1997. Available online. URL: http://www.angelfire.com/ga/dalaniaamon/index43.html. Downloaded August 4, 2004.

Maclean, Norman. *Young Men and Fire.* Chicago: University of Chicago Press, 1992.

MacNeil, Robert. *Breaking News: A Novel.* New York: Nan A. Talese, 1998.

Madonna. *Sex.* New York: Warner, 1992.

Mailer, Norman. "How the Wimp Won the War." *Vanity Fair,* May 1991, p. 138.

Malcolm, Noel. *Bosnia: A Short History.* New York: New York University Press, 1996.

Mandela, Nelson. *Long Walk to Freedom.* New York: Little, Brown, 1995.

Marcus, Greil. "Kurt Cobain: Artist of the Decade." *Rolling Stone,* May 13, 1999, pp. 46–48.

Mason, Bobbie Ann. *Feather Crowns.* New York: HarperCollins, 1993.

———. *In Country.* New York: Harper & Row, 1985.

Mason, Nicholas. *Following Your Treasure Map.* Philadelphia: Xlibris, 2001.

Maugham, Somerset. *The Razor's Edge.* Philadelphia: Blakiston, 1944.

Mayer, Jane, and Jill Abramson. *Strange Justice: The Selling of Clarence Thomas.* Boston: Houghton Mifflin, 1994.

McCarthy, Cormac. *The Crossing.* New York: Knopf, 1994.

McCarthy, Todd. "G.I. Jane." In *Ridley Scott.* Edited by Paul M. Sammon. New York: Thunder's Mouth Press, 1999.

McCartney, James. "Americans 'Protected' from Bad News." *Miami Herald,* January 28, 1991, p. 17A.

McCourt, Frank. *Angela's Ashes: A Memoir.* New York: Scribner, 1996.

McDermott, Alice. *Charming Billy.* New York: Farrar, Straus & Giroux, 1998.

McGrath, Campbell. *American Noise.* Hopewell, N.J.: Ecco Press, 1993.

———. *Capitalism.* Hanover, N.H.: Wesleyan University Press, 1990.

———. *Road Atlas and Other Poems.* Hopewell, N.J.: Ecco Press, 1999.

———. *Spring Comes to Chicago.* Hopewell, N.J.: Ecco Press, 1996.

McKenzie, Richard B. *Rethinking Orphanages for the 21st Century.* Thousand Oaks, Calif.: Sage Publications, 1999. Chapter 6, by Ross D. London, "The 1994 Orphanage Debate: A Study in the Politics of Annihilation," is available online. URL: http://www.gsm.uci.edu/~mckenzie/rethink/mck97-ch6.htm. Downloaded July 8, 2004.

McLaughlin, Martin. "UN Inspectors in Iraq Helped Spy for the CIA," January 7, 1999. Available online. URL: http://www.wsws.org/articles/1999/jan1999/iraq-j07.shtml. Downloaded August 5, 2004.

McMillan, Terry. *How Stella Got Her Groove Back.* New York: Viking, 1996.

———. *Waiting to Exhale.* New York: Viking, 1992.

McMurtry, Larry. *Lonesome Dove.* New York: Simon & Schuster, 1985.

McNamara, Robert S., with Brian VanDeMark. *In Retrospect: The Tragedy and Lessons of Vietnam.* New York: Times Books, 1995.

McPhee, John. *Annals of the Former World.* New York: Farrar, Straus & Giroux, 1998.

"Meaning of the Election," *The Newshour with Jim Lehrer,* November 5, 1996. Available online. URL: http://www.pbs.org/newshour/bb/election/november96/final_11-5.html. Downloaded August 4, 2004.

Meredith, William. *Effort at Speech: New and Selected Poems.* Evanston, Ill.: TriQuarterly Books/Northwestern University Press, 1997.

Middle East Watch/Human Rights Watch. *Needless Deaths in the Gulf War: Civilian Casualties during the Air Campaign and Violations of the Laws of War.* New York: Middle East Watch/Human Rights Watch, 1991.

Milbauer, Asher Z., and Donald G. Watson, eds. *Reading Philip Roth.* New York: St. Martin's Press, 1988.

Millhauser, Steven. *Martin Dressler: The Tale of an American Dreamer.* New York: Crown, 1996.

"Mr. Chief Justice," *The Newshour with Jim Lehrer,* January 22, 1997. Available online. URL: http://www.pbs.org/newshour/bb/congress/jan-june99/rehnquist_1-13.html. Downloaded August 5, 2004.

Mizell, Leslie E. "A Look Back at Y2K and the Millennium Bug." In *Post–Cold War America, 1992–Present.* Edited by James Haley, 168–173. San Diego, Calif.: Greenhaven Press, 2003.

Monette, Paul. *Borrowed Time: An AIDS Memoir.* San Diego, Calif.: Harcourt Brace Jovanovich, 1988.

Moody, Rick. *Garden State.* Boston: Little, Brown, 1992.

———. *The Ice Storm.* Boston: Little, Brown, 1994.

———. *Purple America.* Boston: Little, Brown, 1997.

Moore, Molly. *A Woman at War: Storming Kuwait with the U.S. Marines.* New York: Scribner, 1993.

Moreland, Laurence W., and Robert P. Steed. *The 1996 Presidential Election in the South: Southern Party Systems in the 1990s.* Westport, Conn.: Praeger, 1997.

Moreno, Dario. "Cuba's in the 1996 Presidential Election," January 29, 1998. Available online. URL: http://www.fiu.edu/~morenod/scholar/1996.htm. Downloaded March 23, 2004.

Morris, Dick, with Eileen McGann. *Rewriting History.* New York: Regan Books, 2004.

Morrison, Toni. *Beloved.* New York: Knopf, 1987.

———. *The Bluest Eye.* New York: Holt, Rinehart & Winston, 1970.

———. *Jazz.* New York: Knopf, 1992.

———. *Paradise.* New York: Knopf, 1998.

———. *Playing in the Dark: Whiteness and the Literary Imagination.* Cambridge, Mass.: Harvard University Press, 1992.

————. ed. *Race-ing Justice, En-gendering Power: Essays on Anita Hill, Clarence Thomas, and the Construction of Social Reality.* New York: Pantheon Books, 1992.

————. *Song of Solomon.* New York: Knopf, 1997.

————. *Sula.* New York: Knopf, 1974.

————. *Tar Baby.* New York: Knopf, 1981.

Morrison, Toni, and Slade Morrison. *The Big Box.* New York: Hyperion Press, 1999.

Morrow, Lance, and Martha Smilgis. "Plunging into the Labyrinth." *Time,* December 23, 1991, pp. 74–76.

Morton, Andrew. *Monica's Story.* New York: St. Martin's Press, 1999.

Mydans, Seth. "Severe Earthquake Hits Los Angeles: At Least 30 Killed: Freeways Collapse." *New York Times,* January 18, 1994, p. 1.

Myers, Steven Lee. "U.S. and Britain End Raids on Iraq, Calling Mission a Success." *New York Times,* December 20, 1998, p. 1.

Naisbitt, John, and Patricia Aburdene. *Megatrends 2000: Ten New Directions for the 1990's.* New York: Morrow, 1990.

"Nation Divided?" *The Newshour with Jim Lehrer,* March 2, 1988. Available online. URL: http://www.pbs.org/newshour/bb/race_relations/jan-june98/commission_3-2.html. Downloaded August 5, 2004.

National Atmospheric and Oceanographic Agency. "Hurricane Andrew." Available online. URL: http://www.nhc.noaa.gov/HAW2/english/history.shtml#andrew. Downloaded December 17, 2003.

Naylor, Gloria. *The Women of Brewster Place.* 1982. Reprint, New York: Penguin, 1983.

Neely, Mark E., Jr. *The Fate of Liberty: Abraham Lincoln and Civil Liberties.* New York: Oxford University Press, 1991.

New York Times Theater Reviews: 1993–1994. New York: Times Books, 1996.

Nichols, Lynn H. *The Rape of Europa: The Fate of Europe's Treasures in the Third Reich and the Second World War.* New York: Knopf, 1994.

"1990 in Music." Available online. URL: http://www.wordiq.com/definition/1990_in_music. Downloaded August 24, 2004.

"90 Greatest Albums of the '90s." *Spin,* September 1999, pp. 113–164.

North, Oliver. *Under Fire: An American Story.* 1991. Reprint, New York: Harper Paperbacks, 1992.

"*Not* Going to Disneyworld," *The Newshour with Jim Lehrer,* June 18, 1997. Available online. URL: http://www.pbs.org/newshour/bb/religion/disney_6-18.html. Downloaded August 28, 2004.

Oates, Joyce Carol. *Because It Is Bitter, and Because It Is My Heart.* New York: Dutton, 1990.

———. *We Were the Mulvaneys.* New York: Dutton, 1996.

Ondaatje, Michael. *The English Patient: A Novel.* New York: Knopf, 1992.

Overbye, Dennis. "As Clock Ticks for Hubble, Some Plead for a Reprieve," *New York Times,* July 27, 2003, p. 1A. Available online. URL: http://www.nytimes.com/2003/07/27/science/27HUBB.html. Downloaded July 27, 2003.

"Overheard." *Newsweek,* January 15, 1990, p. 13.

Oxoby, Mark. *The 1990s.* Westport, Conn.: Praeger, 2003.

Ozick, Cynthia. *The Puttermesser Papers.* New York: Knopf, 1997.

Paglia, Camille. *Sex, Art, and American Culture.* New York: Vintage Books, 1992. Available online. URL: http://www.uiowa.ed/~030116/153/articles/paglia.htm. Downloaded March 23, 2004.

Parks, Ken, publisher. *Facts On File Yearbook 2000.* New York: Facts On File, 2001.

Pater, Alan F., and Jason R. Pater, eds. *What They Said in 1988.* Palm Springs, Calif.: Monitor, 1989.

———. *What They Said in 1990.* Palm Springs, Calif.: Monitor, 1991.

———. *What They Said in 1991.* Palm Springs, Calif.: Monitor, 1992.

———. *What They Said in 1992.* Palm Springs, Calif.: Monitor, 1993.

———. *What They Said in 1993.* Palm Springs, Calif.: Monitor, 1994.

———. *What They Said in 1994.* Palm Springs, Calif.: Monitor, 1995.

———. *What They Said in 1995.* Palm Springs, Calif.: Monitor, 1996.

"Pathfinder and the Little Rover That Could," September 4, 1997. Available online. URL: http://www.cnn.com/TECH/9706/pathfinder. Downloaded August 5, 2004.

Pear, Robert. "Despite the Sluggish Economy, Welfare Rolls Actually Shrank." *New York Times,* March 22, 2004, p. 21A. Available online. URL: http://www.nytimes.com/2004/03/22/national/22WELF.html. Downloaded March 22, 2004.

Penman, Ian. *Vital Signs: Music, Movies and Other Manias.* London: Serpent's Tail, 1998.

Perlez, Jane. "Fenced in at Home, Marlboro Man Looks Abroad." *New York Times,* June 24, 1997, p. 1.

Perot, H. Ross. *United We Stand.* New York: Hyperion Books, 1992.

Phillips, Jayne Anne. *Shelter.* Boston: Houghton Mifflin/Seymore Lawrence, 1994.

Phuc, Kim. "Shield Children, Women from War Horrors." *Miami Herald,* January 2, 2004, p. 23A.

Pinsky, Robert. *The Figured Wheel.* New York: Farrar, Straus & Giroux, 1996.

Pitts, Leonard, Jr. "Simpson Case Exposed Raw Feelings on Race." *Miami Herald,* June 14, 2004, p. 1B.

Pollitt, Katha. "Women's Rights, Human Rights." *Nation,* May 13, 1996, p. 9.

Powell, General Colin, with Joseph E. Persico. *My American Journey.* New York: Random House, 1995.

Price, Richard. *Clockers.* Boston: Houghton Mifflin, 1992.

Proulx, Annie. *The Shipping News.* New York: Scribner, 1993.

Putnam, Robert. *Bowling Alone: The Collapse and Revival of American Community.* New York: Simon & Schuster, 2000.

Pyle, Richard. *Schwarzkopf in His Own Words: The Man, the Mission, the Triumph.* New York: Signet, 1991.

Pynchon, Thomas. *Mason and Dixon.* New York: Henry Holt, 1997.

———. *Vineland.* Boston: Little, Brown, 1990.

Quart, Leonard, and Albert Auster. *American Film and Society since 1945.* 3d ed. Westport, Conn.: Praeger, 2002.

Quinn, Jane Bryant. "Laying Bets on the '90s." *Newsweek,* January 15, 1990, p. 53.

Randall, Thaddeus S. "Long Range Patrol: Exploring the Warrior Mystique." Master's thesis, Florida International University, 2002.

Reagan, Ronald. "Announcement of Alzheimer's Disease," November 5, 1994. Available online. URL: http://www.reagan.com/ronald/speeches/rrspeech05.shtml. Downloaded June 1, 2004.

———. First Inaugural Speech, January 20, 1981. Available online. URL: http://www.geocities.com/sentryusa2000/HOREV_FirstInaugural.htm. Downloaded June 10, 2004.

———. Second Debate with President Jimmy Carter, October 28, 1980. Available online. URL: http://www.pbs.org/newshour/debatingourdestiny/80debates/cart1.html. Downloaded July 1, 2004.

———. Second Inaugural Speech, January 21, 1985. Available online. URL: http://www.reagan.com/ronald/speeches/rrspeech0e.shtml. Downloaded June 10, 2004.

———. "Evil Empire" Speech, March 8, 1993. Available online. URL: http://www.awesome80s.com/Awesome80s/News/1983/March/8-Reagan_Evil_Empire_Speech.asp. Downloaded June 10, 2004.

Redfeld, James. *The Celestine Prophecy: An Experiential Guide.* New York: Warner, 1995.

Reich, Robert B. *Locked in the Cabinet.* New York: Knopf, 1997.

Reilly, Rick. "Tiger Woods Makes Golf History." In *Post–Cold War America, 1992–Present.* Edited by James Haley, 116–117. San Diego, Calif.: Greenhaven Press, 2003.

Relman, Arnold S. "What Market Values Are Doing to Medicine." *Atlantic,* March 1992, pp. 99–106.

Remnick, David. *Lenin's Tomb: The Last Days of the Soviet Empire.* New York: Random House, 1993.

Reno, Janet. Testimony before the Committee on the Judiciary, House of Representatives, April 28, 1993. In *Post–Cold War America, 1992–Present.* Edited by James Haley, 357–364. San Diego, Calif.: Greenhaven Press, 2003.

Report of the Congressional Committees Investigating the Iran-Contra Affair. Washington, D.C.: U.S. Government Printing Office, 1987.

Republican Contract with America. Signed by congressional candidates from the Republican National Party, September 27, 1994. Available online. URL: http://www.house.gov/house/Contract/CONTRACT.html. Downloaded June 20, 2003.

Rhodes, Richard. *Dark Sun: The Making of the Hydrogen Bomb.* New York: Simon & Schuster, 1995.

Rice, Anne. *Lasher.* New York: Knopf, 1993.

———. *Vittorio the Vampire.* New York: Knopf, 1999.

Rich, Frank. *"Angels in America: Millennium Approaches."* In *New York Times Theater Reviews 1993–1994.* New York: Times Books, 1996, p. 75.

———. *"Angels in America: Perestroika."* In *New York Times Theater Reviews 1993–1994.* New York: Times Books, 1996, p. 192.

———. *"Kiss of the Spider Woman."* In *New York Times Theater Reviews 1993–1994.* New York: Times Books, 1996, p. 74.

Ridgeway, James. *Blood in the Face: The Ku Klux Klan, Aryan Nations, Nazi Skinheads, and the Rise of a New White Culture.* 2d ed. New York: Thunder's Mouth Press, 1995.

Riegle, Donald, Jr. "U.S. Chemical and Biological Warfare–Related Dual Use Exports to Iraq and Their Possible Impact on the Health Consequences of the Gulf War," May 25, 1994. Available online. URL: http://www.gulfweb.org/bigdoc/report/riegle1.html. Downloaded June 28, 2004. [Report of the U.S. Senate's Committee on Banking, Housing and Urban Affairs with Respect to Export Administration]

Roberts, Nora. *River's End.* New York: Putnam, 1999.

Robertson, Pat. *The New World Order.* Dallas, Tex.: Word Publishing, 1991.

Rohter, Larry. "As Word Spreads in Panama, Thousands Turn out to Cheer." *New York Times,* January 4, 1990, p. 1.

Rosenbaum, David E. "Iran-Contra Report Says President Bears Ultimate Responsibility for Wrongdoing." *New York Times,* November 19, 1987, p. 1.

Rosenberg, Tina. *The Haunted Land: Facing Europe's Ghosts after Communism.* New York: Random House, 1995.

Roth, Philip. *American Pastoral.* Boston: Houghton Mifflin, 1997.

———. *I Married a Communist.* Boston: Houghton Mifflin, 1998.

———. *Operation Shylock: A Confession.* New York: Simon & Schuster, 1993.

———. *Sabbath's Theater.* Boston: Houghton Mifflin, 1995.

Rothschild, Matthew. "Allen Ginsberg." *The Progressive,* August 1994. Available online. URL: http://www.progressive.org/ginzroth9408.htm. Downloaded August 24, 2004.

Rowland, J. K. *Harry Potter and the Chamber of Secrets.* New York: Arthur A. Levine Books, 1999.

———. *Harry Potter and the Prisoner of Azkaban.* New York: Arthur A. Levine Books, 1999.

———. *Harry Potter and the Sorcerer's Stone.* New York: Arthur A. Levine Books, 1999.

Rubin, Barry, et. al *Gulfwatch Anthology: The Day-to-Day Analysis of the Gulf Crisis, August 30, 1990 to March 28, 1991.* Washington, D.C.: Washington Institute for Near East Policy, 1991.

Rushdie, Salman. *Fury.* 2001. New York: Modern Library, 2002.

———. *The Moor's Last Sigh.* New York: Pantheon Books, 1995.

———. *Satanic Verses.* New York: Viking, 1989.

Rust, Michael. "Laughs, Culture, Yadda, Yadda." In *Post–Cold War America, 1992–Present.* Edited by James Haley. San Diego, Calif.: Greenhaven Press, 2003.

Sale, Kirkpatrick. "Is There a Method in His Madness?" In *Post–Cold War America, 1992–Present.* Edited by James Haley, 96–107. San Diego, Calif.: Greenhaven Press, 2003.

Salholz, Eloise. "Women under Assault." *Newsweek,* July 16, 1990, 23.

Sammon, Paul M. *Ridley Scott.* New York: Thunder's Mouth Press, 1999.

Sanchez, Sonia. *Does Your House Have Lions?* Boston: Beacon Press, 1997.

Sandel, Michael J. *Democracy's Discontent: America in Search of a Public Philosophy.* Cambridge, Mass.: Harvard University Press, 1996.

Sasson, Jean P. *The Rape of Kuwait: The True Story of Iraqi Atrocities against a Civilian Population.* New York: Knightsbridge, 1991.

Satcher, David. "Tobacco Use among U.S. Racial/Ethnic Minority Groups: A Report of the Surgeon General," National Center for Chronic Disease Prevention and Health Promotion, 1998. Available online. URL: http://www.cdc.gov/tobacco/research_data/international/wntd598.htm. Downloaded August 5, 2004.

Sawhill, Isabel V. "Welfare Reform: An Analysis of the Issues," May 1, 1995. Available online. URL: http://www.urban.org/welfare/overview.htm. Downloaded March 22, 2004.

Scheele, Nick. "Comments Presented at the Dedication of the Graduate and Executive Education Center of Indiana University's Kelley School of Business," November 2002. Available online. URL: http://broadcast.iu.edu/ceremon/scheele/schelle.doc. Downloaded August 15, 2003.

Scheer, Robert. *With Enough Shovels: Reagan, Bush and Nuclear War.* New York: Random House, 1982.

Schell, Jonathan. *The Abolition.* 1984. Stanford, Calif.: Stanford University Press, 2000.

———. *The Fate of the Earth.* 1982. Stanford, Calif.: Stanford University Press, 2000.

Schmemann, Serge. "Two Germanys United after 45 Years with Jubilation and a Vow of Peace." *New York Times,* October 3, 1990, p. 1.

Schlosser, Eric. "Marijuana and the Law." *Atlantic,* September 1994, pp. 84–94.

Schnitzler, Arthur. *Traumnovelle.* 1926. Frankfurt, Germany: S. Fischer, 2001.

Schroeder, Pat. *24 Years of House Work . . . and the Place Is Still a Mess.* Kansas City, Mo.: Andrews McMeel, 1998.

Schwartz, Richard. *Cold War Culture.* 1998. Rev. ed. New York: Facts On File, 2000.

———. *Cold War Reference Guide.* Jefferson, N.C.: McFarland, 1997.

———. *Encyclopedia of the Persian Gulf War.* Jefferson, N.C.: McFarland, 1998.

———. *The Films of Ridley Scott.* Westport, Conn.: Praeger, 2001.

———. *Woody: From* Antz *to* Zelig: *A Reference Guide to Woody Allen's Creative Work: 1964–1998.* Westport, Conn.: Greenwood, 2000.

Schwarzkopf, H. Norman. *How We Won the War: The Press Briefings of General H. Norman Schwarzkopf.* New York: Simon & Schuster Audioworks, 1991. [sound recording]

Schwarzkopf, H. Norman, with Peter Petre. *It Doesn't Take a Hero.* New York: Bantam Books, 1992.

Seaman, Donna. "Underworld." *Booklist,* August 1997, 1847.

See, Carolyn. *Golden Days.* Berkeley: University of California Press, 1987.

Seelye, Katharine Q. "Livingston Urges Clinton to Follow Suit." *New York Times,* December 20, 1998, p. 1.

Seidlitz, Lauri. *Canada through the Decades: The 1990s.* Calgary, Canada: Weigi, 2000.

Sharp, Elaine B., ed. *Culture Wars and Local Politics.* Lawrence: University Press of Kansas, 1999.

Sheldon, Sidney. *The Best Laid Plans.* New York: Morrow, 1997.

Shields, Carol. *The Stone Diaries.* New York: Viking, 1994.

Siddiqui, Rukhsana A. *Subsaharan Africa in the 1990s.* Westport, Conn.: Praeger, 1997.

Siegel, Marcia B. "Multicult—the Show." *Hudson Review,* autumn 1998, pp. 463–467.

Simon, Bob. *Forty Days.* New York: Putnam, 1992.

Smily, Jane. *Moo.* New York: Knopf, 1995.

———. *A Thousand Acres.* New York: Knopf, 1991.

Smith, Dave. *Cuba Night.* New York: Morrow, 1990.

"Smoking Gun," *The Newshour with Jim Lehrer,* March 20, 1997. Available online. URL: http://www.pbs.org/newshour/bb/health/march97/tobacco_3-20.html. Downloaded August 4, 2004.

Smoot, George, and Keay Davidson. *Wrinkles in Time.* New York: Morrow, 1993.

Sontag, Susan. *The Volcano Lover: A Romance.* New York: Farrar, Straus & Giroux, 1992.

Standiford, Les. *Deal on Ice: A Novel.* New York: HarperCollins, 1997.

———. *Done Deal: A Novel.* New York: HarperCollins, 1993.

———. *Raw Deal: A Novel.* New York: HarperCollins, 1994.

———. *Presidential Deal: A Novel.* New York: HarperCollins, 1998.

———. *Spill.* New York: Atlantic Monthly Press, 1991.

Starr, Kenneth. "Report by Independent Counsel Kenneth Starr Recommending Impeachment of President William Jefferson Clinton," September 9, 1998. Available online. URL: http://credport.loc.gov/icreport. Downloaded September 1, 2004.

Steaman, Ian. "Gangsta Rap Captivates the Mainstream." In *Post–Cold War America, 1992–Present.* Edited by James Haley, 40–43. San Diego, Calif.: Greenhaven Press, 2003.

Steel, Danielle. *Accident.* New York: Delacorte Press, 1994.

———. *Bittersweet.* New York: Delacorte Press, 1999.

———. *Daddy.* New York: Delacorte Press, 1990.

———. *Five Days in Paris.* New York: Delacorte Press, 1995.

———. *The Ghost.* New York: Delacorte Press, 1997.

———. *The Gift.* New York: Delacorte Press, 1994.

———. *Granny Dan.* New York: Delacorte Press, 1999.

———. *Heartbeat.* New York: Delacorte Press, 1991.

———. *His Bright Light: The Story of Nick Traina.* New York: Delacorte Press, 1998.

———. *Irresistible Forces.* New York: Delacorte Press, 1999.

———. *Jewels.* New York: Delacorte Press, 1992.

———. *The Klone and I: A High-Tech Love Story.* New York: Delacorte Press, 1998.

———. *Lightning.* New York: Delacorte Press, 1995.

———. *The Long Road Home.* New York: Delacorte Press, 1998.

———. *Malice.* New York: Delacorte Press, 1996.

———. *Message from Nam.* New York: Delacorte Press, 1990.

———. *Mirror Image.* New York: Delacorte Press, 1998.

———. *Mixed Blessings.* New York: Delacorte Press, 1992.

————. *No Greater Love*. New York: Delacorte Press, 1991.

————. *The Ranch*. New York: Delacorte Press, 1997.

————. *Silent Honor*. New York: Delacorte Press, 1996.

————. *Special Delivery*. New York: Delacorte Press, 1997.

————. *Vanished*. New York: Delacorte Press, 1993.

————. *Wings*. New York: Delacorte Press, 1994.

Steel, Jon. *Truth, Lies, and Advertising*. New York: Wiley & Sons, 1998.

Steinbeck, John. *The Grapes of Wrath*. New York: Viking, 1939.

Stephanopoulos, George. *All Too Human*. Boston, Little, Brown, 1999.

Stern, Kenneth. *A Force upon the Plain: The American Militia Movement and the Politics of Hate*. New York: Simon & Schuster, 1996.

Stevenson, Richard W. "The President's Acquittal: The Chief Justice: Rehnquist Goes with Senate Flow: 'Wiser, but Not a Sadder Man.' " *New York Times,* February 13, 1999, p. 12A.

Stewart, James B. *Den of Thieves*. New York: Simon & Schuster, 1991.

Stewart, Martha, with Elizabeth Hawes. *Entertaining*. New York: Clarkson N. Potter, 1982.

————. *The Martha Stewart Cookbook*. New York: Clarkson Potter, 1995.

Stone, Robert. *Bear and His Daughter*. Boston: Houghton Mifflin, 1997.

Strand, Mark. *Blizzard of One*. New York: Knopf, 1998.

Streisand, Barbra. "The Artist as Citizen," February 3, 1995. Available online. URL: http://www.artsusa.org/common/contenta.asp?id=433. Downloaded June 11, 2004 [Speech delivered at Harvard University's John F. Kennedy School of Government]

Strickland, Ora L., and Dorothy J. Fishman, eds. *Nursing Issues in the 1990s*. Albany, N.Y.: Delmar, 1994.

Styron, William. *Sophie's Choice*. New York: Random House, 1979.

Sullivan, Walter. "Goal: 2nd Trip in 6 Months and 100 in Ship's Lifetime." *New York Times,* April 15, 1981, p. 1.

Szabo, Grant. *The Gulf War Veterans Resource Pages*. Available online. URL: http://www.gulfweb.org/. Downloaded December 4, 2003.

Tan, Amy. *The Joy Luck Club*. New York: Putnam's, 1989.

Tartt, Donna. *The Secret History.* New York: Knopf, 1992.

Taylor, Jonathan, ed. *Facts On File Yearbook 2001.* New York: Facts On File, 2002.

Taylor, Peter. *A Summons to Memphis.* New York: Knopf, 1986.

"Thelma & Louise." *Variety,* May 13, 1991. In *Ridley Scott.* Edited by Paul M. Sammon, 143–144. New York: Thunder's Mouth Press, 1999.

Thomas, Clarence. Senate Confirmation Testimony, October 11, 1991. Available online. URL: http://www.annoy.com/sectionless/doc.html?DocumentID=100506. Downloaded August 31, 2004.

Thomas, Rich. "Harvest of Red Ink." *Newsweek,* September 18, 1989, p. 38.

Thompson, Mark. "Congress Asked to Deny Funds for Failed Missile." *Miami Herald,* May 10, 1990, p. 11A.

———. "NASA Rejected Three U.S. Studies Warning of Booster Rocket Blast." *Miami Herald,* June 1, 1986, p. 1A.

Toole, John Kennedy. *A Confederacy of Dunces.* Baton Rouge: Louisiana State University Press, 1980.

Torricelli, Robert, and Andrew Carroll, eds. *In Our Own Words: Extraordinary Speeches of the American Century.* New York: Washington Square Press, 1999.

Tuch, Steven, and Jack K. Martin. *Racial Attitudes in the 1990s: Continuity and Change.* Westport, Conn.: Praeger, 1997.

Twenty-Seventh Amendment to the U.S. Constitution, May 7, 1992. Available online. URL: http://www.gpoaccess.gov/constitution/pdf/con038.pdf. Downloaded September 1, 2004.

Tyler, Anne. *The Accidental Tourist.* New York: Knopf, 1985.

———. *Breathing Lessons.* New York: Knopf, 1988.

———. *Dinner at the Homesick Restaurant.* New York: Knopf, 1982.

United Nations Resolutions Concerning Iraq, August 2, 1990–April 3, 1991. Reprinted in U.S. Department of Defense. *Conduct of the Persian Gulf War: Final Report to Congress.* Washington, D.C.: U.S. Government Printing Office, 1982, 319–331.

Updike, John. *Brazil.* New York: Knopf, 1994.

———. *Rabbit at Rest.* New York: Knopf, 1990.

———. *Rabbit Is Rich.* New York: Knopf, 1981.

"U.S. Chemical and Biological Warfare–Related Dual Use Exports to Iraq and Their Possible Impact on the Health Consequences of the Gulf War." Report by the U.S. Senate Committee on Banking, Housing and Urban Affairs with Respect to Export Administration, May 25, 1994. Available online. URL: http://www.gulfweb.org/bigdoc/report/r_2_3.html. Downloaded March 23, 2004.

U.S. Department of Defense. *Conduct of the Persian Gulf War: Final Report to Congress.* Washington, D.C.: U.S. Government Printing Office, 1992.

U.S. Department of Justice. *Department of Justice Report Regarding Internal Investigation of Shootings at Ruby Ridge, Idaho during Arrest of Randy Weaver,* 1995. Available online. URL: http://www.byington.org/Carl/ruby/ruby1.htm. Downloaded February 25, 2004.

U.S. General Accounting Office. *Women in the Military: Deployment in the Persian Gulf War.* Washington, D.C.: U.S. Government Printing Office, July 1993.

U.S. House of Representatives. Articles of Impeachment of President William Jefferson Clinton, December 19, 1998. Available online. URL: http://www.cnn.com/ALLPOLITICS/resources/1998/lewinsky/articles.of.impeachment/. Downloaded September 1, 2004.

U.S. Supreme Court. Decision in *Clinton v. Jones,* May 27, 1997. Available online. URL: http://supct.law.cornell.edu/supct/cases/name.htm. Downloaded September 1, 2004.

Value Retailing in the 1990s: Off-Pricers, Factory Outlets and Closeout Stores. Compiled by Editors of Packaged Facts, Inc. New York: Wiley, 1995.

Wakefield, Dan. *New York in the Fifties.* Boston: Houghton Mifflin/Seymour Lawrence, 1992.

———. *Returning: A Spiritual Journey.* New York: Doubleday, 1988.

———. *Under the Apple Tree: A Novel of the Home Front.* Bloomington: Indiana University Press, 1998.

Walinsky, Adam. "The Crisis of Public Order." *Atlantic,* July 1995, p. 39–54.

Walker, Alice. *The Color Purple.* New York: Washington Square Press, 1982.

Walker, Martin. *The Cold War: A History.* New York: Henry Holt & Company, 1993.

Wallace, James. "Thomas Escapes the Fury of Liberal Persecution." *The Carolinian,* October 24, 1991, p. 7. Available online. URL: http://www.compleatheretic.com/pubs/columns/thomas.html. Downloaded June 8, 2004.

Waller, James Robert. *The Bridges of Madison County.* New York: Warner Books, 1992.

Walraven, Jack. "The Simpson Trial Jury," 1995. Available online. URL: http://www.law.umkc.edu%2Ffaculty%2Fprojects%2FSimpson%2FJurypage.html. Downloaded February 20, 2004.

Walters, Barry, et al. "The Ten That Mattered Most: 1985–1995." *Spin,* April 1995, pp. 41–65.

Wasserman, Ed. "Why Do the Media Report Little on Foundations?" *Miami Herald,* October 20, 2003, p. 25A.

Weiner, John. *The Beak of the Finch: A Story of Evolution in Our Time.* New York: Random House, 1994.

Weisman, Mary Lou. "When Parents Are Not in the Best Interests of the Child." *Atlantic,* July 1994, pp. 43–63.

Weisman, Steven. "President Demands Explanation for 'Horrifying Act of Violence.'" *New York Times,* September 2, 1983, p. 1.

Weller, M., ed. *Iraq and Kuwait: The Hostilities and Their Aftermath.* Cambridge International Documents Series, vol. 3. Cambridge, England: Grotius, 1993.

West, Dorothy. *The Wedding.* New York: Doubleday, 1995.

Wharton, Edith. *The Age of Innocence.* 1920. New York: Scribner, 1968.

White, Edmund. *A Boy's Own Story.* New York: Dutton, 1982.

Whitehead, Barbara Doe. "The Failure of Sex Education." *Atlantic,* October 1994, pp. 55–80.

Wideman, John Edgar. *Philadelphia Fire.* New York: Holt, 1990.

Wilford, John Noble. "Crippen Says That Nation Is 'Back in the Space Business to Stay.'" *New York Times,* April 15, 1981, p. 1.

Will, George F. "No One Is Safe from GOP Attack Dogs," *Miami Herald,* September 1, 1992, p. 39A.

Williams, Stephen J., and Sandra J. Guerra. *Health Care Services in the 1990s.* Westport, Conn.: Praeger, 2001.

Willing, Richard. "Courts Asked to Consider Culture." *USA Today,* June 12, 1993. Available online. URL: http://www.usatoday.com/news/washington/judicial/2004-05-24-courts-culture_x.htm. Downloaded June 1, 2004.

Wills, Garry. *Lincoln at Gettysburg: The Words That Remade America.* New York: Simon & Schuster, 1992.

Wilson, Edward O. *The Diversity of Life.* Cambridge, Mass.: Harvard University Press, 1992.

Wilson, Edward O., and Bert Hölldobler. *The Ants.* Cambridge, Mass.: Harvard University Press, 1990.

Wilson, James Q. *The Moral Sense*. New York: Free Press, 1993.

Winter, Kari J. "On Being an Outlaw: A Conversation with Callie Khouri." *Hurricane Alice,* spring 1992, pp. 6–8.

Wolfe, Tom. *The Bonfire of the Vanities.* New York: Farrar, Straus & Giroux, 1987.

———. *A Man in Full.* New York: Farrar, Straus & Giroux, 1998.

———. *The Right Stuff.* New York: Farrar, Straus & Giroux, 1979.

Woodward, Bob. *The Agenda: Inside the Clinton White House.* New York: Simon & Schuster, 1994.

———. *The Choice.* New York: Simon & Schuster, 1996.

———. *The Commanders.* New York: Simon & Schuster, 1991.

Woolf, Virginia. *Mrs. Dalloway.* New York: Harcourt, Brace and World, 1925.

Wren, Christopher A. "Mandela Freed, Urges Step-Up in Pressure to End White Rule." *New York Times,* February 12, 1990, p. 1.

Wright, Charles. *Black Zodiac.* New York: Farrar, Straus & Giroux, 1997.

Yeltsin, Boris. *The View from the Kremlin.* New York: HarperCollins, 1994.

Yergin, Daniel. *The Prize: The Epic Quest for Oil, Money, and Power.* New York: Simon & Schuster, 1993.

yiab. "O.J. Simpson Not Guilty," June 21, 2004. Available online. URL: http://boards.biography.com/threadedout.jsp?forum=30035&thread=300004292. Downloaded August 9, 2004. [yiab is an Internet screen name.]

Zimmerman, Michael. "But Some Administration Appointees Reveal Their Flat-Earth View of Nature." *Miami Herald,* October 6, 1991, p. 3C.

INDEX

Locators in *italic* indicate illustrations. Locators in **boldface** indicate main entries.
Locators followed by *m* indicate maps. Locators followed by *g* indicate graphs.
Locators followed by *t* indicate tables.